This modern text is designed to prepare you for your future professional career. While theories, ideas, techniques, and data are dynamic, the information contained in this volume will provide you a quick and useful reference as well as a guide for future learning for many years to come. Your familiarity with the contents of this book will make it an important volume in your professional library.

EX LIBRIS

Money and Capital Markets
The Financial System in the Economy

Money and Capital Markets
The Financial System in the Economy

Second Edition

Peter S. Rose

Texas A & M University

1986

BUSINESS PUBLICATIONS, INC.
Plano, Texas   75075

To My Family

© BUSINESS PUBLICATIONS, INC., 1983, 1986

ISBN 0–256–03434–6

Library of Congress Catalog Card No. 85–72821

Printed in the United States of America

2 3 4 5 6 7 8 9 0 K 3 2 1 0 9 8 7 6

PREFACE

As in the first edition, this book is an attempt at a comprehensive analysis of the American financial system and of the major financial markets that make up that system. The financial system of the United States is certainly one of the world's great wonders—the envy of many less well-endowed nations. But it is also a very complex institution—fully understood by few, yet vital to all. As the first chapter of this new edition sets out, the system of financial markets performs several indispensable functions (roles) in a modern market-oriented economy. It provides a profitable and relatively low-risk outlet for the public's savings. Equally important, the financial system generates a continuing supply of credit for businesses, consumers, and governments to fuel both consumption and investment spending. It offers a means to store purchasing power for the future as well as means to raise immediately spendable funds by liquidating stocks, bonds, and other financial assets. The system of financial markets offers services that protect people and property against risk and provides a means to make payments for desired purchases of goods and services. Finally, the financial system offers a channel for the pursuit of government policies designed to move the nation closer to its broad economic goals of full employment, the avoidance of severe inflation, sustainable economic growth, and stability in the nation's international payments position.

Neither the roles of the financial system nor the nation's broad economic goals are easy to accomplish. Indeed, both the American and the global financial systems have many problems today, especially in their efforts to handle huge volumes of government debt, increasingly intense competition for financial services that readily cuts across national boundaries, deregulation of the financial sector with accompanying increases in uncertainty and risk, and a recent dramatic increase in failures among major financial institutions (particularly among banks, thrift institutions, and securities dealers). Perhaps the greatest challenge faced by modern financial systems is whether they can continue to perform their essential functions effectively even if there is a gradual erosion of public confidence in the viability and stability of important financial institutions. For without a strong consensus of public confidence and active participation from businesses, households, and governments at all levels, the financial system will begin to contract on itself, eroding its efficiency until it can no longer perform effectively its vital roles in the economy. Indeed, public confidence *is* the foundation stone upon which all financial systems are built and, without which, they cannot long survive—a truism that we will return to again and again in the pages of this book.

It is always incumbent upon an author to explain how this new edition differs from the one that preceded it. There is one *new* chapter in this edition—Chapter 11, which deals with the forecasting and hedging of interest rates in today's volatile and risk-laden economy. In addition, the sequence of chapters and of material within selected chapters has been altered in order to improve the logical flow of the book. For example, the reader familiar with the first edition will note that the original Chapter 10, Sources of Information for Financial Decision Making, has been moved forward into Part One of this new edition. This was done so that readers of the book will become aware at an early stage about where much of the data about the financial system (such as the vital Flow of Funds Accounts) comes from and how that data is assembled and used.

Changes in content and format appear in all 29 chapters of this new edition. For example, each chapter now contains an introductory information section, explaining to the reader the purpose of that chapter and giving a list of key terms and concepts to watch for in digesting the material. Homework problems now appear at the end of many of the chapters, along with the familiar study questions, to help the reader review the most relevant material. In the narrative portion of all the chapters, figures and charts have been updated to the latest available information as this new edition went to press.

New topics and concepts of special importance in today's financial system have been added throughout the text. For example, new material addresses the wider use of options and hedging strategies by major institutional investors in the money and capital markets. There is a more complete treatment of the characteristics of money market funds and of their potent impact on the sources and uses of funds by deposit-type financial institutions. Discussion of the role of important financial institutions considered in the first edition has been expanded here—especially the discussions of security dealers, investment banks, mortgage banks, real estate investment trusts, leasing companies, and financial conglomerates (symbiotics), such as Sears, Roebuck & Company and Prudential-Bache. The unfolding theory of rational expectations is an important new addition to the review of interest-rate theories in Chapter 7. An expanded discussion of the theory and concepts dealing with the inflation/interest-rate linkage and the yield curve have been added to Chapter 9. This chapter also contains a new section on duration and its uses.

There are more numerical examples throughout the book, such as explicit calculation of after-tax yields to maturity, yields on callable securities, real interest rates, and the mathematics of compound interest. New developments in each major financial market, including the appearance of new financial instruments, have been added where relevant to the flow and development of ideas. A good example is Chapter 18 where several important consumer-oriented financial services—Super NOWs, money market deposit accounts (MMDAs), universal life insurance policies, IRAs and Keoghs, and cash-management services—have been added to that chapter's discussion of the latest developments in the consumer market. Other new topics and concepts include consumer bankruptcy laws, inflation-hedged bonds, leveraged buyouts, currency futures, tax reform proposals, contemporaneous reserve accounting, shelf registrations, IS-LM analysis, new money-supply definitions, and the recent "irrelevance" controversy over the effects of government debt and government borrowing.

The new Chapter 11, dealing with interest-rate patterns, forecasting, and hedging, begins by exploring well-established patterns in market interest rates over time—patterns that any student of the financial system needs to know well. The analysis focuses initially on the importance of business-cycle fluctuations and seasonal factors in shaping movements in interest rates and security prices. Then the key benefits and problems in interest-rate forecasting are noted, followed by a step-by-step review of several widely used rate forecasting approaches (e.g., analysis of money-supply changes, econometric models, the Flow-of-Funds approach, and implied market forecasts). Due to the inherent difficulties of interest-rate forecasting many economists and financial analysts have turned to *hedging* strategies in order to insulate financial transactions from interest-rate fluctuations. The new chapter discusses four major rate-hedging devices—duration, GAP management (interest-sensitivity analysis), financial futures contracts, and interest-rate SWAPs—and how they might be used to deal with the dynamic and often treacherous character of modern financial trading.

As with the first edition, a book of the scope and size of this one has benefited from the criticisms, ideas, and information provided by many financial experts and institutions. The author is indebted especially to James C. Baker of Kent State University, Ivan T. Call of Brigham Young University, Eugene F. Drzycimski of the University of Wisconsin, Mona J. Gardner of Illinois State University, Timothy Koch of Texas Tech, David J. Leahigh of Lehigh University, Paul Leonard of Union College, Dixie Mills of Illinois State University, John P. Olienyk of Colorado State University, Coleen C. Pantalone of Northeastern University, and Richard Rivard of the University of South Florida for their review of the entire manuscript and for numerous suggestions to improve it. Organizations graciously providing reprint material or data for the book included the *Canadian Banker,* official publication of the Canadian Bankers' Association, the American Council of Life Insurance, the Chicago Board of Trade, the Insurance Information Institute, the Credit Union National Association, Dun & Bradstreet, Inc., Moody's Investor Service, the United States League of Savings Associations, the First Boston Corporation, Dow Jones Reprints, and Standard & Poor's Corporation. The author also is grateful to his family, especially to his wife Kandy Beth, for their patience and encouragement in completing this second edition. As always, however, the errors and deficiencies that remain, along with the personal opinions that appear from time to time in the pages of this book, are the responsibility of the author alone.

Peter S. Rose

CONTENTS

Different Purposes. Growth of Finance Companies. Methods of Industry Financing. Recent Changes in the Character of the Finance Company Industry. Investment Companies, 169 *The Background of Investment Companies. Regulation of Investment Companies. Tax Status of the Industry. Open-End and Closed-End Investment Companies. Goals and Earnings of Investment Companies.* Other Financial Institutions, 174 Trends Affecting All Financial Institutions Today, 177 Study Questions, 178 Problems, 179 Selected References, 180

Part Three
Interest Rates and Security Prices 181

7 Interest Rates in the Financial System 183

Functions of the Rate of Interest in the Economy, 184 The Classical Theory of Interest Rates, 185 *Saving by Households. Saving by Business Firms. Saving by Government. The Demand for Investment Funds. The Equilibrium Rate of Interest in the Classical Theory of Interest. Limitations of the Classical Theory of Interest.* The Liquidity Preference Theory, 195 *The Demand for Liquidity. The Supply of Money. The Equilibrium Rate of Interest in Liquidity Preference Theory. Limitations of the Liquidity Preference Theory.* The Loanable Funds Theory, 201 *Consumer Demand for Loanable Funds. Business Demand for Loanable Funds. Government Demand for Loanable Funds. Total Demand for Loanable Funds. The Supply of Loanable Funds. The Equilibrium Rate of Interest in the Loanable Funds Theory.* The Rational Expectations Theory, 207 Conclusions, 211 Study Questions, 212 Problems, 213 Selected References, 214

8 Relationships between Interest Rates and Security Prices 216

Units of Measurement for Interest Rates and Security Prices, 217 *Definition of Interest Rates. Basis Points. Security Prices.* Measures of the Rate of Return, or Yield, on a Loan or Security, 219 *Coupon Rate. Current Yield. Yield to Maturity. Holding-Period Yield. Calculating Yields to Maturity and Holding-Period Yields.* Yield-Price Relationships, 227 Interest Rates Charged by Institutional Lenders, 230 *The Simple-Interest Method. Add-On Rate of Interest. Discount Method. Annual Percentage Rate (APR). Compound Interest.* Conclusions, 235 Study Questions, 235 Problems, 236 Selected References, 237

9 Inflation and Yield Curves 238

Inflation and Interest Rates, 239 *The Correlation between Inflation and Interest Rates. The Nominal and Real Interest Rate. The Fisher Effect. Alternative Views on Inflation and Interest Rates.* The Maturity of a Loan, 247 *The Yield Curve and the Term Structure of Interest Rates. Types of Yield Curves. The Expectations Hypothesis. The Role of Expectations in Shaping the Yield Curve. Relative Changes in Long-Term Interest Rates. Policy Impli-*

Part Seven
Government in the Financial Markets   587

Part One

The Financial System in Perspective

1

The Role of the Financial System in the Economy

PURPOSE OF THIS CHAPTER

To explain the essential functions or roles performed by the nation's financial system within the economy. These functions are carried out through the operation of financial markets, whose basic method of operation and outstanding features are discussed in this chapter.

KEY TERMS AND CONCEPTS IN THE CHAPTER

capital market	investment	primary market
credit function	liquidity function	risk function
economic system	money market	savings
efficient market	negotiated market	savings function
financial markets	open market	secondary market
financial system	payments function	spot market
forward market	perfect market	wealth function
futures market	policy function	

This book is devoted to a study of the *financial system*—the collection of markets, individuals and institutions, laws, regulations, and techniques through which bonds, stocks, and other securities are traded and interest rates determined. The financial system is one of the most important inventions of modern society. Its primary task is to move scarce loanable funds from those who save to those who borrow for consumption and investment. By making funds available for lending and borrowing (credit) the financial system provides the means whereby modern economies grow and increase the standard of living enjoyed by their citizens. Much of the credit thus obtained goes to purchase machinery and equipment, to construct new bridges, highways, factories, and schools, and to stock the shelves of businesses with inventories of goods. Without the financial system and the credit it supplies, each of us would lead a very different and probably less enjoyable existence.

The financial system determines both the cost of credit and how much credit will be available to pay for the thousands of different goods and services we purchase daily. Equally important, what happens in this system has a powerful impact upon the health of the nation's economy. When credit becomes more costly and less available, total spending for goods and services generally falls. As a result, unemployment rises and the economy's growth slows down as businesses cut back production and reduce inventories. In contrast, when the cost of credit declines and loanable funds become more readily available, total spending in the economy usually increases, more jobs are created, and the economy's rate of growth accelerates. In truth, the financial system is an integral part of the economic system and cannot be viewed in isolation from it.

THE ECONOMY AND THE FINANCIAL SYSTEM

Flows within the Economic System

In order to better understand the role played by the financial system in our daily lives we begin by examining its position within the nation's economic system.

The basic function of any economy is to allocate scarce material resources in order to produce the goods and services needed by society. The high standard of living most of us enjoy today depends fundamentally upon the ability of the nation's economy to turn out each day the enormous volume of clothing, food, fuel, shelter, transportation services, and other essentials of modern living. This is an exceedingly complex task because scarce resources must first be procured in just the right amounts to provide the raw materials of production and combined at just the right time with labor and capital to generate the products and services demanded by consumers. In short, any economic system must combine inputs—land and other natural resources, labor and managerial skills, and capital equipment—in order to produce outputs in the form of goods and services. The economy generates a flow of production (goods and services) in return for a flow of payments, usually in the form of money (see Figure 1–1).

FIGURE 1–1

The Economic System

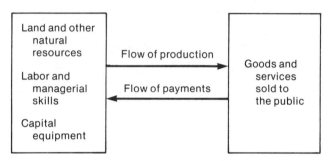

We may also depict the flows of payments and production within the economic system as a circular flow between producing units (mainly businesses and governments) and consuming units (principally households). (See Figure 1–2). In modern economies households provide labor, managerial skills, and natural resources to business firms and governments in return for income in the form of salaries, wages, rents, royalties, dividends, and so on. Most of the income received by households is spent to purchase goods and services. In 1984, for example, about 88 percent of the $3 trillion in total personal income received by individuals and families in the United States was spent for consumption of goods and services or paid out in taxes.[1] The result of this spending is a flow of funds back to producing units as income, which stimulates them to produce more goods and services in future periods. The circular flow of production and income is, thus, interdependent and never ending.

The Role of Markets in the Economic System

In most economies of the Western world, including the United States, *markets* are used to carry out this complex task of allocating resources

---

[1] In percentage terms, U.S. households in 1984 allocated about 80 percent of their total personal income for consumption expenditures; about 14 percent went for federal, state, and local taxes and fees; and the remainder—about 6 percent—was set aside as personal savings.

FIGURE 1–2

Circular Flows of Income, Payments, and Production in the
Economic System

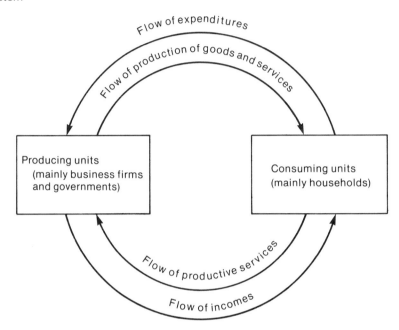

and producing needed goods and services. What is a *market?* It is an
institution set up by society to allocate resources which are scarce relative
to the demand for them. Markets are the channel through which buyers
and sellers meet to exchange goods, services, and resources.[2]

The marketplace determines what goods and services will be produced
and in what quantity. This is accomplished essentially through changes
in prices of commodities and services offered in the market. If the price
of a commodity rises, for example, this stimulates business firms to produce
and supply more of it to consumers. In the long run new firms may
enter the market (in the absence of government restrictions) to produce

---

[2] Of course, scarce resources may be allocated by government order and central
planning as well as by the marketplace. In the Soviet Union, for example, resources
flow to those uses predetermined by a central government plan. While most industrialized economies in the Western world use markets to allocate the majority of their
scarce resources today, these economies are really mixed economies, with market
mechanisms and government-directed planning operating side by side.

those goods or services experiencing increased demand and rising prices. A decline in price, on the other hand, usually leads to reduced production of a good or service, and in the long run some firms will leave the marketplace. Markets also distribute income. In a pure market system the income of an individual or business firm is determined solely by the contributions each makes to production. Markets reward superior productivity, innovation, and sensitivity to customer needs with increased profits, higher wages and salaries, and other economic benefits.

Types of Markets

There are essentially three types of markets at work within the economic system: (1) factor markets, (2) product markets, and (3) financial markets (see Figure 1–3). In factor markets consuming units sell their labor, managerial skill, and other resources to those producing units offering the highest prices. The factor markets allocate the so-called factors of production (land, labor, and capital) and distribute incomes in the form of salaries, wages, rental income, and so on to the owners of productive resources. As Figure 1–3 shows, consuming units use most of their income from the factor markets to purchase goods and services

FIGURE 1–3

Types of Markets in the Economic System

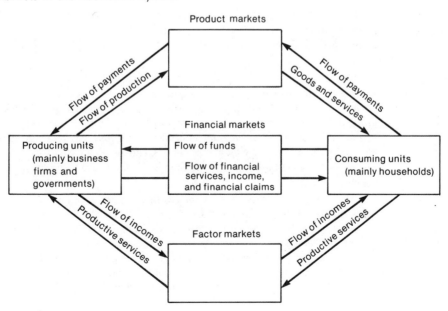

in product markets. Food, shelter, clothing, medical care, automobiles, books, theater tickets, gasoline, and swimming pools are among the many goods and services sold in product markets.

The Financial Markets and the Financial System

Of course, not all factor income is consumed. A substantial proportion of after-tax income received by household each year—$115 billion in 1983—is earmarked for personal saving. In addition, business firms save billions of dollars each year to build up equity reserves for future contingencies and to support long-term capital investment. For example, in 1984, U.S. corporations earned $287 billion in after-tax profits, of which $67 billion was set aside (undistributed) for possible future needs. It is here that the third kind of market—the *financial market*—performs a vital function within the economic system. The financial markets channel *savings*—which come mainly from households—to those individuals and institutions who need more funds for spending than are provided by current income.[3] The financial markets are the heart of the financial system, determining the volume of credit available, attracting savings, and setting interest rates and security prices.

Most of the funds set aside as savings flow through the financial markets to support *investment* by business firms and governments. Investment generally refers to the acquisition of capital goods, such as buildings, machinery, and equipment, and the purchase of inventories of raw materials, semifinished goods, and finished products.[4] Modern economies require enormous amounts of capital equipment—ships, drill presses, warehouses, housing, trucks, schools, bridges, airports, and thousands of similar items and facilities—in order to produce goods and services. Investment

---

[3] As we will see in Chapter 7, the definition of *savings* differs depending upon what type of unit in the economy is doing the saving. For households, savings is what is left over out of current income after current consumption expenditures are made. In the business sector, savings include current net earnings retained in the business after payment of taxes, stockholder dividends, and all other cash expenses. Government saving—a rare event—arises when the current budget runs a surplus of revenues over expenditures.

[4] The makeup of *investment* varies with the particular unit doing the investing. For a business firm, expenditures on fixed assets, such as buildings, machinery, and equipment, and inventories are investment expenditures. Households invest when they acquire residential housing. However, household purchases of furniture, appliances, automobiles, and other durable consumer goods are generally classified as consumption spending (i.e., expenditures on current account) and not an investment (i.e., expenditures on capital account). Government spending for buildings and other public facilities is another form of investment.

in new equipment increases the productivity of labor and ultimately leads to a higher standard of living. However, investment generally requires large amounts of funds, often far beyond the resources available to a single firm or governmental unit. By selling financial claims (i.e., stocks, bonds, etc.) in the financial markets, though, large amounts of funds can be raised quickly, and the loan repaid out of future income. Indeed, the financial markets operating within the nation's financial system make possible the *exchange of current income for future income.* Those markets determine the prices of stocks, bonds, and other financial assets, regulate interest rates, and determine the expected future income of lenders.

Those who supply funds in the financial markets receive only *promises* in return for the loan of their money. These promises are packaged in the form of attractive financial claims and financial services, such as stocks, bonds, checking accounts, savings deposits, and insurance policies (see Figure 1–4). Financial claims promise the supplier of funds a future flow of money income, which may consist of dividends, interest payments, capital gains, or other returns. Of course there is no guarantee that the expected flow of future income will ever materialize. However, suppliers of funds to the financial system expect not only to recover their original commitment of funds but also to earn additional income as a reward for waiting and for the assumption of risk.

The role of the financial markets in channeling savings into investment is absolutely essential to the health and vitality of the economic system. For example, if households were to set aside savings and those funds were not returned to the spending stream through investment by businesses and governments, the economy would begin to contract. The amount of income paid out by business firms and governments would not be matched by funds paid back to those same sectors. As a result, future payments of wages, salaries, rents, and other forms of income would begin to decline, leading to reduced consumption spending. The

FIGURE 1–4

The Financial System

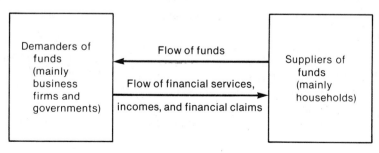

nation's standard of living would fall. Moreover, with less total spending going on, the need for labor and management skills would be curtailed, resulting in rising unemployment.

FUNCTIONS PERFORMED BY THE FINANCIAL SYSTEM AND THE FINANCIAL MARKETS

The great importance of the financial system in our daily lives can be illustrated by reviewing its different functions or roles. There are seven basic functions of the financial system in a modern economy. (See Exhibit 1–1.)

Savings Function

As we noted earlier, the system of financial markets and institutions provides a *conduit for the public's savings.* Bonds, stocks, bank deposits, and other financial claims sold in the money and capital markets provide

EXHIBIT 1–1

Functions of the Financial System

Savings Function—
  providing a potentially profitable and relatively low-risk outlet for the public's savings.

Liquidity Function—
  providing a means of raising funds by converting securities and other financial assets into cash balances.

Payments Function—
  providing a mechanism for making payments to purchase goods and services.

Policy Function—
  providing a channel for government policy to achieve the nation's goals of high employment, low inflation, sustainable economic growth, and stability in the nation's international payments position.

Wealth Function—
  providing a means to store purchasing power until needed at a future date for spending on goods and services.

Credit Function—
  providing a continuing supply of credit for businesses, consumers, and governments to support both consumption and investment spending in the economy.

Risk Function—
  providing a means to protect businesses, consumers, and governments against risks to people, property, and income.

a potentially profitable, relatively low-risk outlet for the public's savings. Those savings flow through the financial markets into investment so that more goods and services can be produced in the future, increasing society's standard of living.

Wealth Function

For those businesses and individuals choosing to save, the financial instruments sold in the money and capital markets provide an excellent way to *store wealth* (i.e., to preserve value or hold purchasing power) until funds are needed for spending in future periods. While we might choose to store our wealth in "things" (e.g., automobiles, books, clothes), such items are subject to depreciation and often carry great risk of loss. However, bonds, stocks, bank deposits, and other financial instruments do not wear out over time, usually generate current income, and normally, their risk of loss is much less than would be true of other forms of stored wealth. In 1983 well over $13 trillion in securities, deposits, and so on were held by businesses, households, and governments in the U.S. economy. Individuals and families alone held more than $6 trillion in stocks, bonds, and other financial instruments. These holdings represent stored purchasing power which will be used in future periods to finance purchases of goods and services and to increase society's standard of living.

Liquidity Function

For wealth that is stored in securities and other financial instruments, the financial marketplace provides a means of converting those instruments into ready cash with little risk of loss. Thus, the financial system provides *liquidity* for savers holding financial instruments but in need of money. In modern societies money consists mainly of deposits held at commerical banks, savings and loan associations, savings banks, and credit unions. Money is the only financial instrument possessing perfect liquidity; it can be spent as it is without the necessity of converting it into some other form. However, money generally earns the lowest rate of return of all assets traded in the financial system, and its purchasing power is seriously eroded by inflation. That is why savers generally minimize their holdings of money and hold stocks, bonds, and other financial assets until spendable funds really are needed.

Credit Function

In addition to facilitating the flow of savings into investment and providing liquidity for stored wealth, the financial markets furnish *credit* in thousands of different forms to finance both consumption and investment spending. Credit consists of a loan of funds in return for a promise of future payment. Consumers frequently need credit to purchase a home or automobile, buy groceries and fuel, repair home appliances and family automobiles, enjoy vacations, and retire outstanding debt. Businesses draw upon their lines of credit to stock their shelves with inventory, construct buildings, purchase new equipment, meet payrolls, pay taxes, make repairs, pay interest to bondholders and other creditors, take over other businesses, and grant dividends to their stockholders. State, local, and federal governments frequently borrow to construct buildings and other public facilities, meet payrolls, and cover daily cash expenses until tax revenues flow in.

The volume of credit extended by the money and capital markets today is huge and growing rapidly. As shown in Exhibit 1–2, total net credit funds raised in U.S. financial markets in 1984 (including issues of corporate stock) exceeded $800 billion, compared to just over $400 billion

EXHIBIT 1–2

Net Funds Raised in U.S. Financial Markets by Major Sectors of the U.S. Economy, 1984

Sector and Funding Source		Amount of Funds Raised ($ billions)	Percentage of Total Net Funds Raised* (percent)
Net borrowing by sector:			
Households		$241.6	29.7%
Nonfinancial Business firms:			
Farms	$ 2.2		
Nonfinancial corporations	163.5		
Other businesses	76.3		
Total for all business firms		241.9	29.7
Private financial institutions		52.3	6.4
Governments:			
U.S. government	$198.8		
Federally sponsored agencies	74.2		
State and local governments	33.0		
Total for all governments in the United States		306.0	37.6
Foreign borrowers in the United States, net		1.7	0.2
Total Net Borrowing		$843.5	103.7
Net funds raised by issuing new corporate stock (equities)		−29.8	−3.7
Total net borrowed and equity funds raised in U.S. financial markets		$813.7	100.0%

* Column does not add to exactly 100 percent due to rounding.
SOURCE: Board of Governors of the Federal System, *Flow of Funds Accounts,* 1984.

as recently as 1982. In fact, both the growth rate of total personal, business, and government debt and the ratio of total debt to total annual income in the United States in 1984 achieved their highest levels since World War II. Growth of the economy, inflation, deregulation of the financial sector, and the tax deductibility of interest payments all appear to have fueled this rapid growth in credit usage by American households and institutions.

Payments Function

The financial system also provides a *a mechanism for making payments for goods and services.* Certain financial assets, mainly checking accounts and NOW (negotiable order of withdrawal) accounts, serve as a medium of exchange in the making of payments. Commercial banks—the principal institutions within the financial system—create checkbook money for public use by making loans. In recent years, mutual savings banks and savings and loan associations along with commerical banks have offered NOW accounts and credit unions have offered "share drafts" that bear interest, as a savings account does, and permit the customer to draft the account to pay for goods and services, just like a checking account. Plastic credit cards issued by many commercial and savings banks, credit unions, oil companies, and retail stores give the customer instant access to short-term credit but also are widely accepted as a convenient means of payment.

Another type of plastic card—the debit card—is used today to charge a buyer's deposit account for purchases of goods and services and transfer the proceeds instantly by wire to the seller's account. Debit cards and other electronic means of payment, including telephone transfers, cable hookups through in-home TV sets, and computer terminals in retail stores, are likely to displace checks, currency, and other pieces of paper as the principal means of payment in the years ahead.

Risk Function

The financial markets offer businesses, consumers, and governments *protection against life, health, property, and income risks.* This is accomplished, first of all, by the sale of life and property-casualty insurance policies. Policies marketed by life insurance companies indemnify a family against possible loss of property and income following the death of a loved one. Property-casualty insurers protect their policyholders against an incredibly wide array of personal and property risks ranging from ill health, crime and vandalism, and storm damage to personal negligence and reckless driving on the nation's highways. In addition to making possible the selling of insurance policies, which are financial instruments evidencing a potential financial claim held by the policyholder, the money and capital markets have been used increasingly by businesses and consumers to "self insure" against risk. This simply means building up one's holding of securities, bank deposits, and so on as a precaution against future losses. The liquidity of most financial instruments makes it easy to raise spendable cash quickly to cover an emergency.

Policy Function

Finally, in recent decades the finanical markets have been the principal channel through which the federal government has carried out its policy of attempting to stabilize the economy and avoid excessive inflation. By manipulating interest rates, the nation's money supply, and the availability of credit, government can affect the borrowing and spending plans of the public which, in turn, influence the growth of jobs, production and the prices of goods and services. As we will see in subsequent chapters, this task of economic stabilization in the United States has been given largely to the Federal Reserve System as the nation's central bank.

TYPES OF FINANCIAL MARKETS WITHIN THE FINANCIAL SYSTEM

Charged with many different functions, the financial system fulfills its various roles through *markets* where financial claims and financial services are traded. These markets may be viewed as *channels* through which moves a vast flow of funds, continually being drawn upon by demanders of funds and continually being replenished by suppliers of funds. When the flow of funds supplied to the financial markets by households, businesses, and governments exceeds the funds flow demanded by other individuals and institutions at current interest rates, an ample supply of credit is currently available and the cost of credit—the rate of interest—will fall. On the other hand, when the flow of funds through the financial markets is small relative to the total demand for funds, there is a relatively scarce supply of credit available which eventually leads to higher interest rates. Thus, the price mechanism at work in the financial system (i.e., the rate of interest) serves to adjust the demand for and supply of available funds until all those seeking credit and willing to pay its cost are satisfied.

The Money Market versus the Capital Market

The flow of funds through the financial markets may be divided into different segments, depending upon the characteristics of financial claims being traded and the needs of different groups. One of the most important divisions in the financial system is between the money market and the capital market.

The *money market* is designed for the making of short-term loans. It is the institution through which individuals and institutions with temporary surpluses of funds meet borrowers who have temporary funds shortages. Thus, the money market enables economic units (principally business firms and governments) to manage liquidity. By convention, a security or loan maturing *within one year or less* is considered to be a money market instrument. One of the principal functions of the money market is to finance the working-capital needs of corporations and to provide governments with short-term funds in lieu of tax collections. The money market also supplies funds for speculative buying of securities and commodities. Because most loans and securities traded in the money market are large—typically in million dollar units—it is often called a *wholesale market,* catering to the largest borrowers.

In contrast, the *capital market* is designed to finance long-term investments by businesses, governments, and households. Trading of funds in the capital market makes possible the construction of factories, office buildings, highways, bridges, schools, homes, and apartments. Financial instruments in the capital market have original maturities of *more than one year* and range in size from small loans to very large, multi-million dollar credits. Thus, the capital market trades in both *wholesale* (large) loans and securities and *retail* (small) loans and securities.

Who are the principal suppliers and demanders of funds in the money market and capital market? In the money market commercial banks are the most important institutional lender to both business firms and governments. Nonfinancial business corporations with temporary cash surpluses also provide substantial short-term funds to commercial banks, securities dealers, and other corporations in the money market. Finance companies supply large amounts of working capital to major corporate borrowers, as do money market mutual funds which specialize in short-term, high-grade government and corporate securities (see Exhibit 1–3).

On the demand-for-funds side the largest borrower in the American money market is the U.S. Treasury, which borrows several billion dollars weekly. The largest and best-known U.S. corporations are also active borrowers in the money market through their offerings of short-term notes. Major securities dealers require huge amounts of borrowed funds daily to carry billions of dollars in securities held in their trading portfolios to meet customer demand. Finally, the Federal Reserve System, which is charged by Congress with responsibility for regulating the flow of money and credit in the U.S. financial system, operates on both sides of the money market.[5] Due to the large size and strong financial standing of these well-known money market borrowers and lenders, money market

---

[5] Chapters 22, 23, and 24 examine in detail the role of the Federal Reserve System in U.S. money and capital markets.

EXHIBIT 1–3

The Money Market and the Capital Market

Money Market*		Capital Market†	
Principal Suppliers of Funds	**Principal Demanders of Funds**	**Principal Suppliers of Funds**	**Principal Demanders of Funds**
Commercial banks	U.S. Treasury	Pension funds	Businesses
Nonfinancial corporations	Commercial banks	Insurance companies	Households
	Nonfinancial	Households	Governments
Finance companies	corporations	Savings and loan	
Money market mutual	Finance companies	associations	
funds	Security dealers	Commercial banks	
State and local	Federal Reserve		
governments	System		
Federal Reserve			
System			

* Securities one year and under to maturity.
† Securities more than one year to maturity.

credit instruments are considered to be high-quality, "near money" IOUs.

The principal suppliers and demanders of funds in the capital market are more varied than in the money market. An institution must be large and well known with an excellent credit rating to gain access to the money market. The capital market for long-term funds, in contrast, encompasses both well-established and lesser known individuals and institutions. Families and individuals, for example, tap the capital market when they borrow to finance a new home or automobile. State and local governments rely upon the capital market for funds to build schools, highways, and public buildings and to provide essential services to the public. The U.S. Treasury draws upon the capital market in issuing new notes and bonds to pay for federal government programs. The most important borrowers in the nation's capital market are businesses of all sizes, which issue bonds, notes, and other long-term IOUs to cover the purchase of equipment and the construction of new plants and other facilities. Ranged against these many borrowers in the capital market are financial institutions which supply the bulk of long-term funds. Prominent here are life and property-casualty insurance companies, pension funds, savings and loan associations, mutual savings banks, finance companies, and commercial banks. Each of these institutions tends to specialize in a few different kinds of loans consistent with its own cash flow needs and regulatory restrictions.

Divisions of the Money and Capital Markets

The money market and the capital market may be further subdivided into smaller markets, each important to selected groups of demanders and suppliers of funds. Within the money market, for example, is the huge U.S. Treasury bill market. Treasury bills—a short-term IOU of the U.S. government—are a safe, stable, and popular investment medium for financial institutions and nonfinancial corporations of all sizes.

Nearly as large in total dollar volume is the market for $100,000+ negotiable certificates of deposit (CDs) issued by the largest, best-known commercial banks. Banks use the funds raised from CDs and other sources to extend loans to corporations and other borrowers. Two other important money market instruments evidencing loans to corporations are bankers acceptances and commercial paper. Acceptances are promises issued by a bank to pay a fixed sum of money on a specified date in the future and usually arise from the creation of loans to finance exports and imports of goods. Commercial paper is a short-term IOU issued by a large, well-established corporation, usually to finance purchases of inventory or meet other near-term obligations.

Still another portion of the money market is devoted to trading in federal funds, which are essentially reserve balances of commercial banks held at the Federal Reserve and with other commercial banks. Federal funds are unique in being immediately available money, easily and instantly transferable from one bank to another by wire. Another segment of the money market reaches around the globe to encompass suppliers and demanders of short-term funds in Europe, Asia, and the Middle East. This is the vast and largely unregulated Eurocurrency market, where the world's major trading currencies—the dollar, the franc, the pound, the yen, and the mark—are loaned to multinational corporations and governments.

The capital market, too, is divided into several major sectors, each having special characteristics and its own collection of suppliers and demanders of funds. For example, the largest segment of the capital market is devoted to mortgage loans on both commercial and residential properties. A mortgage is a certificate evidencing a loan in which real property—land, buildings, or equipment—serves as security for repayment of the loan. State and local governments sell their tax-exempt (municipal) bonds in another sector of the capital market. Consumers borrow well over $100 billion each year in yet another segment of the capital market for purchases ranging from automobiles to home appliances. There is also an international capital market closely linked to trading in Eurodollars and other major Eurocurrencies, represented by Eurobonds.

Probably the best-known segment of the capital market is the market

EXHIBIT 1–4

Principal Financial Instruments Traded in the U.S. Money and Capital
Markets, 1984 ($ billions; end of period)

	Amount
Principal money market instruments:	
U.S. Treasury bills	$ 374.4
Bank certificates of deposit ($100,000+)	325.8
Securities issued by federal and federally sponsored agencies*	260.0
Federal funds sold and repurchase agreements	140.5
Eurodollar deposits†	365.6
Commercial paper	238.5
Bankers' dollar acceptances	75.5
Principal capital market instruments:	
Mortgages	$2,030.9
Common Stocks	1,693.3
Corporate and foreign bonds	639.5
U.S. Treasury notes and bonds‡	873.0
State and local government bonds and notes	539.2
Consumer installment loans	477.0

* Data as of November 1984.
† Liabilities owed by foreign branches of U.S. banks, payable in U.S.
dollars.
‡ Marketable issues only.
SOURCE: Board of Governors of the Federal Reserve System, *Flow
of Funds Accounts* and *Federal Reserve Bulletin,* selected issues; U.S.
Department of Commerce, *Survey of Current Business,* selected issues;
and U.S. Treasury Department, *Treasury Bulletin,* selected issues.

for corporate stock represented by the major exchanges, such as the
New York Stock Exchange (NYSE) and the American Stock Exchange
(AMEX), and a vast over-the-counter (OTC) market for individual stocks.
No matter where it is sold, however, each share of stock (equity) represents a certificate of ownership in a corporation, entitling the holder to
receive any dividends which may be paid out of current company earnings. Corporations also sell a huge quantity of notes and bonds in the
capital market each year to raise long-term funds. These securities, unlike
shares of stock, are pure IOUs, evidencing a debt owed plus an obligation
to pay interest to the holder. A list of the principal financial instruments
traded in the U.S. money and capital markets today is shown in Exhibit
1–4.

Open versus Negotiated Markets

Another distinction between markets in the financial system which
is sometimes useful is that between *open markets* and *negotiated markets*.

For example, some corporate bonds are sold in the open market to the highest bidder and bought and sold any number of times before they mature. In contrast, in the negotiated market for corporate bonds, securities generally are sold to one or a few buyers under private contract and held to maturity.

An individual who goes to his or her local banker to secure a loan for a new car enters the negotiated market for auto loans. However, a broker instructed to buy a few shares of GM stock will attempt to fill the order by contacting a seller in the open market. Most state and local government securities are sold in the open market, but a growing number are sold under a privately negotiated "treaty" with one or a few buyers. In the market for corporate stocks there are over-the-counter sales and the major stock exchanges, which represent the open market. Operating at the same time, however, is the negotiated market for stock, in which a corporation may sell its entire equity issue to a large insurance company or pension fund.

Primary versus Secondary Markets

The financial markets may also be divided into *primary markets* and *secondary markets*. The primary market is for the trading of new securities never before issued. Its principal function is the raising of financial capital to support *new* investment in buildings, equipment, and inventories. You engage in a primary-market transaction when you purchase shares of stock just issued by a company, borrow money through a new mortgage to purchase a home, negotiate a loan at the bank to restock the shelves of your business, or purchase bonds just issued by the local school district to construct new classrooms.

In contrast, the secondary market deals in securities previously issued. Its chief function is to provide liquidity to security investors—that is, provide an avenue for converting existing stocks, bonds, and other securities into ready cash. If you sell shares of stock or bonds you have been holding for some time to a relative or friend or call a broker and place an order for shares currently being traded on the American Stock Exchange, you are participating in a secondary-market transaction.

The volume of trading in the secondary market is far larger than trading in the primary market. However, the secondary market does *not* support new investment. Nevertheless, the primary and secondary markets are closely intertwined. For example, a rise in interest rates or security prices in the secondary market usually leads to a similar rise in the prices or rates on primary-market securities and vice versa. This happens because investors frequently switch from one market to another in response to differences in price and yield. Many financial institutions are active in both primary and secondary markets.

Spot versus Futures and Forward Markets

We may also distinguish between *spot markets* and *futures* or *forward markets*. A spot market is one where securities or financial services are traded for *immediate delivery* (usually within one or two business days). If you pick up the telephone and instruct your broker to purchase Telecom Corporation shares at today's going price, this is a spot market transaction. You expect to acquire ownership of Telecom shares within a matter of hours.

A futures or forward market, on the other hand, is designed to trade contracts calling for the *future delivery* of financial instruments. For example, you may call your broker and ask to purchase a contract from another investor calling for delivery to you of $1 million in U.S. Treasury bills six months from today. The purpose of such a contract would be to reduce investor risk by agreeing on a price today rather than waiting six months when Treasury bill prices might have risen. Similarly, you may be planning a business trip to London in three months and, knowing there is an active forward market for British pounds, you call your bank and ask them to find someone willing to sell pounds today at a guaranteed price for delivery three months hence. We will see more clearly how and why such transactions take place when we explore the financial futures markets in Chapter 17 and the forward markets for foreign currencies in Chapter 28.

Factors Tying All Financial Markets Together

Each corner of the financial system represents, to some extent, a distinct market with its own special characteristics. Each segment is insulated from the others to some degree by investor preferences and by rules and regulations. Yet when interest rates and security prices change in one corner of the financial system, all of the financial markets will be affected eventually. For example, a rise in money market interest rates, sometimes with a lag, leads to a rise in capital market rates and usually affects prices in the stock market as well. This implies that, even though law, regulation, tradition, and investor preferences tend to split up the financial system into many different markets, there must be forces at work to tie all the financial markets together.

Credit, the Common Commodity.
One unifying factor is the fact that the basic commodity being traded in all financial markets is credit. The money market, as we have seen, provides short-term credit, while the capital market provides long-term credit. Borrowers can switch from one market to another, seeking the most favorable credit terms. It is not uncommon, for example, for an oil company to finance the con-

struction of a drilling rig through short-term money market loans because interest rates in the capital market today are unusually high, only to seek long-term funding of the project later on when capital market conditions are more favorable. The shifting of borrowers between markets helps to weld the parts of the financial system closer together and to bring interest rates in different markets into balance with one another.

Arbitrage.   Another unifying element is profit seeking by suppliers of funds. *Speculators* in securities are continually on the lookout for small differences in prices or interest rates attached to different securities. A temporary rise in interest yields in one corner of the market, for example, quickly sends funds flowing toward that point. Speculators perform an important function in the financial markets by leveling out the prices of securities, buying those they believe are underpriced and selling those securities thought to be overpriced. Still another unifying force in the financial markets is the investors who watch for profitable opportunities by transferring funds from one market to another whenever the prices of securities in different markets appear to be out of line. *Arbitrageurs* help to maintain consistent prices between markets, aiding other security buyers in finding the best prices with minimal information cost.

Perfect and Efficient Markets.   There is considerable research evidence today suggesting that all financial markets are closely tied to one another because of their perfection and efficiency. What is a *perfect* market? It is one in which all available information affecting the value of financial instruments is freely available to everyone, the cost of carrying out transactions is zero or nearly so, and all market participants are price takers (rather than being able to dictate prices to the market). Thus, perfect competition prevails in such a market without significant government restrictions on trading and the movement of funds.

A perfect market has a very desirable characteristic: *the prices of financial instruments accurately reflect their inherent value and fully reflect all available information.* Moreover, any *new* information supplied to the market will instantly be impounded in a new set of prices. A market in which prices fully reflect all the latest available information is known as an *efficient* market. Numerous empirical tests of the financial markets, spanning two decades, suggests that they very closely approach the ideal of the perfect, efficient market's model.

THE PLAN OF THIS BOOK

This text is divided into eight major sections, each devoted to a particular segment of the financial system.

Part One of the book provides an overview of the financial system—

its role in the economy, major sectors, and basic characteristics. The emphasis here is on providing the reader with a broad-brush picture of the fundamental nature and purpose of transactions in the financial marketplace. The vital processes of saving and investment, lending and borrowing, and the creation and destruction of financial assets are described, and their critical importance to economic growth, employment, and the nation's standard of living is stressed. This section concludes with a discussion of the major sources of data available today to students and researchers interested in following movements in interest rates, security prices, and the volume of borrowing and lending going on in the financial system. A major part of this chapter is devoted to the Flow of Funds Accounts compiled by the Federal Reserve System.

Part Two is devoted to the study of financial institutions. Commercial banks, credit unions, savings and loan associations, savings banks, money market funds, insurance companies, pension funds, mutual funds, finance companies—these and other financial firms dominate our financial system today. Moreover, each plays a leading role in different markets within the financial system. For example, commercial banks are the key financial institutions active in the short-term money market on both the borrowing and lending side of that market. Savings and loan associations and savings banks are the principal sources of funds in the market for home mortgages, while insurance companies, pension funds, and mutual funds dominate activity in the corporate bond and stock markets. We will encounter each of these institutions, not only in Part Two of the book, but also later on as we discuss the particular money and capital markets where they are most active.

Part Three examines in detail the forces that shape and influence interest rates and the prices of financial instruments. The rate of interest is the key price in the financial system, channeling savings toward their most profitable uses and continually bringing the demand and supply for credit into balance. For this reason Part Three of the text devotes considerable space to developing analytical tools that aid our understanding of what sets the levels of interest rates and security prices at any given time. The section begins in Chapter 7 with a review of major theories of interest-rate determination. The "real-world" measurement and behavior of interest rates and security prices are then addressed in Chapter 8. The next two chapters in Part Three are devoted to the factors that cause the interest rate and price of one security to differ from those of another, while Chapter 11 focuses on problems and methods for forecasting interest rates and for hedging against interest-rate changes.

Part Four is aimed at the money market, beginning with an overview of the principal institutions and instruments which dominate money market activity in the United States. Subsequent chapters in this section examine the characteristics of major money market instruments, such as U.S. Treasury bills, federal funds, repurchase agreements, bank certificates of deposit, commercial paper, federal agency securities, bankers' acceptances, and Eurodollars. Principal buyers and sellers of each financial instrument, its maturity ranges, methods of calculating yields, volume of trading, and recent innovations in the market are discussed. The section concludes with a chapter on one of the newest of all short-term financial instruments—financial futures.

The borrowing habits and financial characteristics of consumers—families and individuals—are considered in Part Five. Chapter 18 presents an overview of consumer financial affairs, examining the major categories of consumer debt outstanding today and recent changes in laws and regulations affecting the consumer. Chapter 19 is devoted to the largest of all consumer debt markets—residential mortgages—where innovative new financial instruments are being developed today to make home ownership more affordable for individuals and families.

Part Six focuses on the activities of nonfinancial business firms in the money and capital markets. Chapter 20 covers business borrowing, principally the marketing, pricing, and trading activity surrounding the issuance of new corporate bonds and notes. Chapter 21 is concerned with the market for common and preferred stock. This chapter opens with a discussion of the basic characteristics of corporate stock—the rights, responsibilities, and risks attached to stock ownership—and then proceeds to examine the structure of today's equities market.

The often dominating role of governments—federal, state, and local—within the financial system is taken up in Part Seven of the text. The first three chapters in this section are devoted to monetary policy and the Federal Reserve System. In terms of day-to-day financial market activity the Fed—the central bank of the United States—probably has more impact on the American financial system than any other agency of government. A brief history of the Federal Reserve System is presented along with an analysis of the operating structure of the Fed, its major policy tools, and its policy indicators. Recent problems in the pursuit of the nation's major economic goals are examined, and their implications for the future considered.

The fiscal operations of federal, state, and local governments are examined in Chapters 25 and 26 of the text. Fiscal policy—the taxing and spending activities of the federal government—and the management of the huge public debt of the U.S. government are reviewed in Chapter 25. State and local government financial affairs are the subject of Chapter 26.

Finally, Part Eight of the text is devoted to the international financial system. Topics covered here include the economic benefits of international trade and finance, the history of changing monetary standards, and the balance-of-payments accounts. The markets for foreign currencies are examined in considerable detail, including the mechanics of modern foreign exchange trading. Part Eight concludes with a discussion of international banking institutions.

Throughout this book there is a strong emphasis on the innovative character of modern financial systems and institutions. There has been a virtual explosion of new instruments and trading techniques within the financial system in recent years. Examples include financial futures, new types of home mortgages and tax-exempt revenue bonds, instant electronic transfer of funds and other financial information, and major changes in laws and regulations affecting financial services offered, prices charged, and returns paid to savers. Moreover, the pace of innovation in financial services and methods appears to be accelerating under the combined pressure of increased competition, rising costs, and burgeoning demand. As we will see in the pages that follow, these forces of innovation, competition, rising costs, and growing demand are profoundly reshaping the structure and operations of our whole financial system today.

STUDY QUESTIONS

1. Why is it important to understand how the financial system operates? In what ways is the financial system linked to the economy as a whole?

2. What are the principal functions of the financial system? How do the financial markets fulfill those functions?

3. Explain what is meant by saving and by investment. Why are they important to economic growth and the nation's standard of living?

4. Describe the payments function performed by the financial system. In recent years a number of new payments devices have been developed. Describe some of these.

5. Distinguish between the money market and the capital market, between open and negotiated markets, primary and secondary markets, and spot, forward, and futures markets. What are the principal divisions of each?

6. Why do interest rates and security prices in the various segments of the financial system tend to move in the same direction? What forces seem to bind the various parts of the financial system together?

7. What is a *perfect* market? An *efficient* market? Identify some features of real-world markets which in your judgment limit their efficiency.

SELECTED REFERENCES

Dougall, Herbert E., and Jack E. Gaumnitz. *Capital Markets and Institutions.* 4th ed. Englewood Cliffs, N.J.: Prentice-Hall, 1980.

Fama, Eugene F., and Merton H. Miller. *The Theory of Finance.* New York: Holt, Rinehart & Winston, 1972.

Polakoff, Murray E., and Thomas A. Durkin et al. *Financial Institutions and Markets.* 2d ed. Boston: Houghton Mifflin, 1981.

Van Horne, James C. *Financial Market Rates and Flows.* 2d ed. Englewood Cliffs, N.J.: Prentice-Hall, 1984.

2

Financial Assets, Money, and Financial Transactions

PURPOSE OF THIS CHAPTER

To examine the methods by which funds flow in the nation's financial system from lenders of funds to borrowers of funds. This borrowing and lending process, made possible by the system of financial markets, is described in terms of the creation and destruction of *financial assets*— financial claims having unique properties. The chapter concludes with a discussion of the vitally important role of financial intermediaries which simultaneously acquire and issue financial assets in pursuit of their borrowing and lending activities.

KEY TERMS AND CONCEPTS IN THE CHAPTER

contractual institutions
debt securities
deficit-budget units
depository institutions
direct finance

disintermediation
equities
financial assets
financial intermediaries
indirect finance

investment institutions
money
real assets
semidirect finance
surplus-budget units

The financial system is the mechanism through which loanable funds reach borrowers. Through the operation of the financial markets, money is exchanged for financial claims in the form of stocks, bonds, and other securities. And, through the exchange of money for financial claims, the economy's capacity to produce goods and services is increased. This happens because the money and capital markets provide the financial resources needed for investment. While it is true that the financial markets deal mainly in the exchange of paper claims and bookkeeping entries, these markets provide an indispensable conduit for the conversion of savings into investment, accelerating the economy's growth and development.

This present chapter looks closely at the essential role played by the financial markets in converting savings into investment and how that role has changed over time. We begin by observing that nearly all financial transactions between buyers and sellers involve the creation or destruction of a special kind of asset—a financial asset. Financial assets perform a vital role in the behavior and decision making of businesses, consumers, and governments. Moreover, financial assets possess a number of characteristics which make them unique among all the assets held by individuals and institutions. In the next section we consider the nature of financial assets and how they are created and destroyed through the workings of the financial system.

THE CREATION OF FINANCIAL ASSETS

What is a *financial asset?* It is a claim against the income or wealth of a business firm, household, or unit of government, represented usually by a certificate, receipt, or other legal document and is usually created by the lending of money. Familiar examples include stocks, bonds, insurance policies, and deposits held in a commercial bank, credit union, or savings bank.

Characteristics of Financial Assets

Financial assets do *not* provide a continuing stream of services to their owner as does a home or an apartment, an automobile, or a washing machine. These assets are sought after because they promise *future* returns to the holder and serve as a store of value (purchasing power). As noted later in this chapter, money too is a financial asset.

A number of other features make financial assets unique. They cannot be depreciated because they do not wear out like physical goods. Moreover, their physical condition or form is generally not relevant in determining their market value (price). A stock certificate is not more or less valuable, for example, because of the size or quality of paper it is printed on or whether it is frayed around the edges. Because financial assets are generally represented by a piece of paper (certificate or contract) or, increasingly, by information stored in a computer file, they have little or no value as a commodity and their cost of transport and storage is low. Finally, financial assets are *fungible*—they can be easily changed in form and interchanged with or substituted for other assets. Thus, a bond or stock usually can be quickly converted into cash at low cost and then subsequently converted into any other asset the holder desires.

Different Kinds of Financial Assets

While there are thousands of different financial assets outstanding at any one time, they generally fall into one of three categories: money, equities, or debt securities.

Any financial asset that is generally accepted in payment for purchases of goods and services is *money*. Thus, checking accounts and Federal Reserve currency are clearly financial assets serving as payment media and, therefore, are forms of money. Later in this chapter we will discuss more fully the special features and importance of money as a financial asset. *Equities* (more commonly known as stock) represent ownership in a business firm and, as such, are claims against the firm's profits and against proceeds from the sale of any of its assets. We usually further subdivide equities into *common stock*, which entitles its holder to vote for the members of a firm's board of directors and therefore determine company policy, and *preferred stock*, which normally carries no voting privilege but does entitle its holder to a fixed share of the firm's net earnings ahead of any dividends that might be paid to common stockholders.

Debt securities include such familiar financial claims as *bonds, notes,* and *accounts payable.* Legally these financial assets entitle their holder to a priority claim over the holders of equities to the assets and income of an individual, business firm, or unit of government. Usually that claim is fixed in amount and time (maturity) and, depending on the terms of the *indenture* (contract) accompanying most debt securities, may be backed up by the pledge of specific assets as collateral. Financial analysts usually divide debt securities into two broad classes: (1) *negotiable* which can easily be transferred from holder to holder as a marketable security; and (2) *nonnegotiable* which cannot legally be transferred to another party. Passbook savings accounts and U.S. Savings Bonds are good examples of nonnegotiable debt securities. In this text our primary focus is on negotiable (marketable) instruments such as Treasury bills, commercial paper, and corporate notes and bonds.

The Creation Process for Financial Assets

How are financial assets created? We may illustrate this process using a very rudimentary financial system in which there are only two economic units—a household and a business firm.

Assume that this financial system is *closed* so that no external transactions with other units are possible. Each unit holds certain assets accumulated over the years as a result of its saving out of current income. The household, for example, may have accumulated furniture, an automobile, books, clothes, and other items needed to provide entertainment, food, shelter, and transportation. The business firm holds inventories of goods to be sold, raw materials, machinery and equipment, a building, and other assets required to produce its product and sell it to the public.

The financial position of these two economic units is presented in the form of balance sheets, shown in Exhibit 2–1. A balance sheet, of course, is a financial statement prepared as of a certain date, showing a particular

EXHIBIT 2–1

Balance Sheets of Units in a Simple Financial System

HOUSEHOLD
Balance Sheet

Assets*		Liabilities and Net Worth†	
Cash	$ 13,000	Net worth	
Furniture	1,000	(accumulated	
Clothes	1,500	savings)	$ 20,000
Automobile	4,000		
Other assets.	500		
		Total liabilities	
Total assets	$ 20,000	and net worth	$ 20,000

BUSINESS FIRM
Balance Sheet

Assets*		Liabilities and Net Worth†	
Inventories		Net worth	
of goods	$ 10,000	(accumulated	
Machinery and		savings)	$100,000
equipment.	25,000		
Building	60,000		
Other assets.	5,000		
		Total liabilities	
Total assets	$100,000	and net worth	$100,000

* Accumulated uses of funds.
† Accumulated sources of funds.

unit's assets, liabilities, and net worth. Assets represent the accumulated uses of funds made by economic units, while liabilities and net worth represent the various sources of funds that economic units have drawn upon to acquire the assets they now hold. The net worth account represents total savings accumulated over time by each economic unit. A balance sheet must always balance, meaning the total assets (accumulated uses of funds) must equal total liabilities plus net worth (accumulated sources of funds).

The household in our example holds total assets valued at $20,000, including an automobile, clothes, furniture, and cash. Because the household's financial statement must balance, total liabilities and net worth also add up to $20,000, all of which in this instance happens to come from net worth (accumulated savings). The business firm holds assets amounting to $100,000, including a building housing the firm's offices, equipment, and machinery, and an inventory of unsold goods. The firm's only source of funds currently is net worth (accumulated savings), also valued at $100,000.

By today's standards the two balance sheets shown in Exhibit 2–1 are most unusual. Neither the household nor the business firm has any outstanding liabilities. Each unit is entirely self-financed, because each has acquired its assets by saving and spending within its current income and not by borrowing. In the terminology of finance, both the household and the business firm have engaged in *internal financing*—the use of current income and accumulated savings to acquire assets.[1] For most businesses and households, internally generated funds are the most important resources for acquiring assets. For example, in the U.S. economy half or more of all investment in plant, equipment, and inventories carried out by business firms each year is financed internally rather than by borrowing. Households as a group save substantially more than they borrow each year, with the savings flowing into purchases of real assets, such as homes, automobiles, appliances, and clothing, and into sizable purchases of stocks, bonds, and other financial assets.

Suppose the business firm in our rudimentary financial system wishes to purchase new equipment in the form of a drill press. Due to inflation and shortages of key raw materials, however, the cost of the new drill press has been increasing rapidly. Internal sources of funds are not suffi-

---

[1] In the case of the household, it has accumulated savings by taking some portion of each period's income and setting money aside rather than spending all of its income on current consumption. The business firm has abstained from paying out all of its revenues in expenses (including stockholder dividends). Instead, some portion of the firm's cash inflow each period has been set aside in the form of retained earnings (accumulated savings).

cient to cover the equipment's full cost. What can be done? There are four likely alternatives: (1) postpone the purchase of the new equipment until sufficient savings can be accumulated to cover its cost; (2) sell off some existing assets to raise the necessary funds; (3) borrow all or a portion of the needed funds; or (4) issue new stock (equity securities).

Time is frequently a determining factor here. Postponement of the equipment purchase probably will result in lost sales and lost profits. In the real world where there is not one business firm, as in our example, but many serving the same market, a competitor may rush ahead to expand operations and capture some share of this firm's market. Then, too, in an environment of inflation, the new drill press surely will cost even more in the future than it does now. While selling some existing assets to raise the necessary funds is a distinct possibility, this may take time, and there is the risk of substantial loss, especially if fixed assets must be sold. The third alternative—borrowing—has the advantage of raising funds quickly, and the interest cost on the loan is tax deductible.[2] The firm could sell additional stock if it hesitated to take on a debt obligation, but equity financing is usually much more expensive than borrowing and requires more time to arrange.

If the business firm decides to borrow, who will lend the funds that it needs? Obviously, in this two-unit financial system the household must provide the needed funds. The firm must engage in external financing by issuing to the household securities evidencing a loan of money. In general, if any economic unit wishes to add to its holdings of assets but lacks the necessary resources to do so, it can raise additional funds by issuing financial liabilities (borrowing)—provided a buyer of those IOUs can be found. The buyer will regard the IOUs as an asset—a financial asset—which may earn income unless the borrower goes out of business and defaults on his or her loan.

Suppose the business firm decides to borrow by issuing a liability in the amount of $10,000 in order to pay for its new drill press. Because the firm is promising an attractive interest rate on this new IOU, the household willingly acquires it as a financial asset. This asset is intangible— a mere promise to pay $10,000 at maturity plus a promised stream of

---

[2] An added advantage associated with issuing debt is the "leverage effect." If the firm can earn more from purchasing and using the new equipment than the cost of borrowing funds, the surplus return will flow to the stockholders in the form of increased earnings. Earning per share of stock will rise, increasing the value of the company's stock and the value of the stockholder's investment. The result is favorable financial leverage. Unfortunately, leverage is a two-edged sword. If the firm earns less than the cost of borrowed funds, the stockholders' losses will be magnified as a result of unfavorable (negative) financial leverage.

interest payments over time. The borrowing and creation of this financial asset may be shown on the balance sheets of these two economic units. As shown in Exhibit 2–2, the household has purchased the firm's IOU by using some of its accumulated cash. Its total assets are unchanged. Instead of holding $13,000 in noninterest-bearing cash, the household now holds an interest-bearing asset in the form of a $10,000 security and $3,000 in cash. The business firm has increased its stock of machinery and equipment from $25,000 to $35,000 after purchasing the new equipment but also has incurred new debt amounting to $10,000. The firm's total assets and total liabilities *increase* due to the combined effects of borrowing and the acquisition of a productive real asset.

EXHIBIT 2–2

Unit Balance Sheets Following the Purchase of Equipment and the Issuance of a Financial Asset

HOUSEHOLD
Balance Sheet

Assets*		Liabilities and Net Worth†	
Cash	$ 3,000	Net worth	$ 20,000
Financial asset	10,000		
Furniture	1,000		
Clothes	1,500		
Automobile	4,000		
Other assets	500		
		Total liabilities	
Total assets	$ 20,000	and net worth	$ 20,000

BUSINESS FIRM
Balance Sheet

Assets*			Liabilities and Net Worth†	
Inventories of goods		$ 10,000	Liabilities	$ 10,000
Machinery and			Net worth	100,000
equipment:				
Existing equipment	$ 25,000			
New equipment	10,000			
Total machinery				
and equipment		35,000		
Building		60,000		
Other assets		5,000		
			Total liabilities	
Total assets		$110,000	and net worth	$110,000

* Accumulated uses of funds.
† Accumulated sources of funds.

FINANCIAL ASSETS AND THE FINANCIAL SYSTEM

This simple example illustrates several important points concerning the operation and role of the financial system in the economy. First, the act of borrowing simultaneously gives rise to the creation of an equal volume of financial assets. In the foregoing example, the $10,000 financial asset held by the household lending money is exactly matched by the $10,000 liability of the business firm borrowing money. This suggests another way of defining a financial asset: *Any asset held by a business firm, government, or household that is also recorded as a liability or claim on some other economic unit's balance sheet is a financial asset.* As we have seen, many different kinds of assets satisfy this definition, including common and preferred stock, corporate and government bonds, and deposits and loans held with a financial institution.

For the entire financial system the sum of all financial assets must equal the total of all financial liabilities and claims outstanding. In contrast, real assets, such as automobiles, furniture, machinery, and buildings, are not necessarily matched by claims or liabilities somewhere in the financial system.

This distinction between *financial assets* and *liabilities,* on the one hand, and *real assets,* on the other, is worth pursuing with an example. Suppose you borrow $4,000 from the bank to purchase an automobile. Your balance sheet will now contain a liability in the amount of $4,000. The bank from which you borrowed the funds will record the transaction as a loan—an interest-bearing financial asset—appearing on the asset side of its balance sheet in the like amount of $4,000. On the asset side of your balance sheet appears the market value of the automobile—a real asset. The value of the real asset probably exceeds $4,000 since most banks expect a borrower to supply some of his or her own funds rather than lending the full purchase price. Let's say the automobile was sold to you for $5,000 with $1,000 of the cost coming out of your savings account and $4,000 from the bank loan. Then, your balance sheet would contain a new real asset (automobile) valued at $5,000, a liability (bank loan) of $4,000, and your savings account (a financial asset) would decline by $1,000.

Clearly, there are two equalities which hold for this transaction and also hold whenever money is loaned and borrowed in the financial system. First,

$$\begin{array}{rcl} \text{Volume of financial} & = & \text{Volume of liabilities} \\ \text{assets created} & & \text{issued by borrowers} \\ \\ \text{In this case, a bank} & = & \text{A borrower's IOU} \\ \text{loan of } \$4,000 & & \text{of } \$4,000 \end{array} \qquad (2\text{--}1)$$

Second,

$$\text{Total uses of funds} = \text{Total sources of funds}$$

$$\text{Purchase of a \$5,000} = \text{Issue of a \$4,000} \qquad (2\text{--}2)$$
$$\text{automobile} \qquad \text{borrower IOU} + \$1,000$$
$$\text{drawn from a savings}$$
$$\text{account}$$

Every financial asset in existence represents the lending or investing of money transferred from one economic unit to another.

Because the sum of all financial assets created must always equal the amount of all liabilities and claims outstanding, the amount of lending in the financial system must always equal the amount of borrowing going on. In effect, *financial assets and liabilities (claims) cancel each other out across the whole financial system.* We can illustrate this fact by reference to the balance sheet of any unit in the economy—business firm, household, or government. The following must be true for all balance sheets:

$$\text{Total assets} = \text{Total liabilities} + \text{Net worth} \qquad (2\text{--}3)$$

Because all assets may be classified as either real assets or financial assets, it follows that

$$\text{Real assets} + \text{Financial assets} = \text{Total liabilities} + \text{Net worth} \quad (2\text{--}4)$$

Because the volume of financial assets outstanding must always equal the volume of liabilities and claims in existence, it follows that the aggregate volume of real assets held in the economy must equal the total amount of net worth. Therefore, for the economy and financial system as a whole:

$$\text{Total financial assets} = \text{Total liabilities} \qquad (2\text{--}5)$$

$$\text{Total real assets} = \text{Net worth (i.e., accumulated savings)} \qquad (2\text{--}6)$$

This means that the value of all buildings, bridges, highways, machinery, schools, and other real assets in existence matches the total amount of saving carried out by all businesses, households, and units of government.[3]

---

[3] This statement does *not* imply that total real assets must equal net worth (accumulated savings) for each individual, firm, or institution or for each sector of the economy. We will see why this is so shortly.

We are not better off in real terms by the mere creation of financial assets and liabilities. These are only pieces of paper evidencing a loan or investment of money. Rather, society increases its wealth only by saving and thus increasing the quantity of real assets, for these assets enable the economy to produce more goods and services in the future.

Does this suggest that the creation of financial assets and liabilities— one of the basic functions of the financial system—is a useless exercise? Not at all. The mere act of saving by one economic unit does not guarantee that those savings will be used to build or purchase real assets which add to society's stock of wealth. In modern economies saving and investment usually are carried out by different groups. In the U.S. economy, for example, the bulk of saving is carried out by households, while business firms account for the majority of investments in productive real assets. Some mechanism is needed to ensure that savings flow from those who save to those who invest in real assets.

The *financial system* provides the essential channel necessary for the creation and exchange of financial assets between savers and borrowers so that real assets can be acquired. Without that channel for savings, the total volume of investment in the economy surely would be reduced, and the growth of investment and production would be diminished. All investment by individual economic units would have to depend on the ability of those same units to save (i.e., engage in internal financing). Many promising investment opportunities would have to be foregone or postponed due to insufficient savings. Society's scarce resources would be allocated less efficiently than is possible with a system of financial markets. Growth in the nation's income, employment, and standard of living would be seriously impaired.

LENDING AND BORROWING IN THE FINANCIAL SYSTEM

Business firms, households, and governments play a wide variety of roles in modern financial systems. It is quite common for an individual or institution to be a lender of funds in one period and a borrower in the next, or to do both simultaneously. Indeed, financial intermediaries, such as banks and insurance companies, are in the business of operating on both sides of the financial markets borrowing funds from their customers by issuing attractive financial claims and simultaneously making loans available to other customers. Virtually all of us at one point or another in our lifetime will be involved in the financial system as a borrower or lender of funds and probably both.

A number of years ago two economists, Gurley and Shaw (1956, 1960), pointed out that each business firm, household, or unit of government active in the financial system must conform to the following identity:

Expenditures out of   Change in holdings of debt and equity
current income   = − Change in holdings of financial
− Current income   assets during the current period
receipts

In symbols,

$$E - R = \Delta D - \Delta FA \qquad (2\text{-}7)$$

If our current expenditures (E) exceed our current receipts (R), we usually make up the difference by: (1) reducing our holdings of financial assets (−ΔFA)—for example, by drawing money out of a savings account; (2) issuing debt or stock (ΔD); or (3) using some combination of both. On the other hand, if our receipts (R) in the current period are larger than current expenditures (E), we can (1) build up our holdings of financial assets (+ΔFA)—for example, by placing money in a savings account or buying a few shares of stock; (2) pay off some outstanding debt or retire stock previously issued by our business firm (− ΔD); or (3) do some combination of both.

It follows that for any given period of time (i.e., week, month, or year) the individual economic unit must fall into one of three groups:

Deficit-budget unit   E > R; and so ΔD > ΔFA
(net borrower of funds)

Surplus-budget unit   R > E; and thus, ΔFA > ΔD
(net lender of funds)

Balanced-budget unit   R = E; and therefore, ΔD = ΔFA
(neither net lender
nor net borrower)

A net lender of funds is really a net supplier of funds to the financial marketplace. He or she accomplishes this function by purchasing financial assets, paying off debt, or retiring equity claims (stock). In contrast, a net borrower of funds is a net demander of funds from the money and capital markets, selling financial assets, issuing new debt, or selling new stock. The business and government sectors of the economy tend to be net borrowers (demanders) of funds, while the household sector, composed of all families and individuals, tends to be a net lender (supplier of funds). This is shown clearly in data on purchases of financial assets and increases in liabilities compiled each year by the Federal Reserve System for the U.S. Flow-of-Funds accounting system.[4] For example, as

---

[4] See Chapter 3 for a description of the method of construction and uses of the Federal Reserve System's Flow of Funds Accounts.

Exhibit 2–3 reveals, in 1984 households acquired about $433 billion in financial assets and issued about $244 billion in liabilities, making this sector of the U.S. economy a net lender of funds to the financial markets in the amount of almost $190 billion. In contrast, nonfinancial businesses were net borrowers of $86 billion, while the federal government borrowed net almost $197 billion during the year.

EXHIBIT 2–3

Net Acquisitions of Financial Assets and Liabilities by Major Sectors of the U.S. Economy, 1984 ($ billions)

	Net Acquisition of Financial Assets during Year	Net Increase in Liabilities during Year	Net Lender (+) or Net Borrower (−) of Funds
Households	$433.4	$243.5	+189.9
Nonfinancial businesses	85.8	171.8	−86.0
State and local governments	46.5	33.9	+12.6
Federal government	28.3	224.9	−196.6

SOURCE: Board of Governors of the Federal Reserve System, *Flow of Funds Accounts,* 4th quarter 1984, Statistical Release of the Division of Research and Statistics.

Of course, over any given period of time any one household, business firm, or unit of government may be a deficit, surplus-, or balanced-budget unit. In fact, from day to day and week to week, our major institutions in the business and government sectors fluctuate from being deficit-budget units to surplus-budget units and back again. Consider a large corporation such as General Motors or Exxon. One week such a firm may be a net lender, supplying monies for short periods of time through purchases of U.S. Treasury bills, bank CDs, and other financial assets. The following week a dividend payment may be due company stockholders, bonds must be refunded, or purchases made to increase inventories and expand plant and equipment. At this point the firm may become a net borrower of funds, drawing down its holdings of financial assets, securing loans by issuing financial liabilities, or selling equity securities. Most of the large institutions that interact in the nation's financial markets continually fluctuate from one side of the market to the other. This is also true of most households today. One of the most important contributions of the financial system to our daily lives is in permitting businesses, households, and governments to adjust their financial position from that of net borrower to net lender and back again, smoothly and efficiently.

MONEY AS A FINANCIAL ASSET

What Is Money?

The most important financial asset in the economy is money. All financial assets are valued in terms of money and flows of funds between lenders and borrowers occur through the medium of money. Money itself is a true financial asset because all forms of money in use today in the United States and in most countries are a claim against some institution, public or private, and are issued as debt. For example, one of the largest components of the U.S. money supply today is the checking account, which is the debt of a commercial bank. Another important component of the money supply is currency and coin, or pocket money held by the public. The bulk of currency in use today in the United States consists of Federal Reserve notes, representing debt obligations of the 12 Federal Reserve banks. In fact, if the Federal Reserve ever closed its doors (a highly unlikely event), Fed notes held by the public would be a first claim against the assets of the Federal Reserve banks. As we will see in Chapter 24, some definitions of the nation's money supply today include savings accounts at banks and credit unions, shares in money market mutual funds, and even overnight loans between financial institutions and their customers—all forms of debt, giving rise to financial assets.

The Functions of Money

Money performs a wide variety of important services. It serves as a *standard of value* for all goods and services. Without money the price of every good or service we might wish to trade would have to be expressed in terms of exchange ratios with all other goods and services—an enormous information burden for both buyers and sellers. We would need to know, for example, how may loaves of bread would be required to purchase a quart of milk or what quantity of firewood might exchange for a suit of clothes. To trade just 12 different goods and services, we would have to remember 66 different exchange ratios. In contrast, the existence of money as a common standard of value permits us to express the prices of all goods and services in terms of only one good—the monetary unit. In the United States that unit is, of course, the dollar. But, whatever the monetary unit is called, it always has a constant price in terms of itself (i.e., a dollar always exchanges for a dollar). The prices of all other goods and services are expressed in multiples or in fractions of the monetary unit.

Money also serves as a *medium of exchange*. It is usually the only financial asset which virtually every business, household, and unit of government will accept in payment for goods and services. By itself, money typically has little or no use as a commodity (except when gold or silver, for example, is used as the medium of exchange). People accept money only because they know they can exchange the monetary medium at a later date for goods and services. The monetary unit itself need have little or no intrinsic value as a commodity once it is widely accepted. This is why modern governments have been able to separate the monetary unit from precious metals like gold and silver bullion and successfully issue fiat money (i.e., pieces of paper) not tied to any particular commodity. Money's service as a medium of exchange frees us from the terrible constraints of barter, allowing us to separate the act of selling goods and services from the act of buying goods and services. With a medium of exchange, buyers and sellers no longer need to have an exact coincidence of wants in terms of quality, quantity, time, and location.

Money serves also as a *store of value*—a reserve of future purchasing power. We need not spend dollars right away but can hold them until circumstances are right and our need for goods or services is imminent. Purchasing power can be stored in currency or in a checking account until the time is right to buy. Of course, money is not always a good store of value. The value of money, measured by its purchasing power, can experience market fluctuations. For example the prices of consumer goods represented in the U.S. cost-of-living index more than tripled between 1967 and 1984. If individuals or families had purchased in each of these years the identical market basket of goods and services represented in the U.S. cost-of-living index, they would have found that the purchasing power of each dollar of their money had decreased by about two thirds during this period.

Money functions as the only *perfectly liquid asset* in the financial system. An asset is liquid if it can be converted into cash quickly with little or no loss in value.[5] All assets—real and financial—differ in their degrees of liquidity. Generally, financial assets, especially U.S. Treasury bills, bank deposits, and stocks and bonds issued by major corporations, tend to be highly liquid, while real assets, such as a home, an automobile, clothing, furniture, and diamonds, may be extremely difficult to sell in a hurry without taking a substantial loss. Money is, of course, the most liquid of all assets since it need not be converted into any other form in order to be spent. Unfortunately, the most liquid assets, including money, tend to carry the lowest rates of return. One measure of the "cost" of holding money is the income foregone by the owner who fails to convert his or her money balances into more profitable investments in real or financial

---

[5] A liquid asset possesses three essential characteristics: price stability, ready marketability, and reversibility. An asset must be considered *liquid* if its price tends to be reasonably stable over time, if it has an active resale market, and if it is reversible so that investors can recover their original investment without loss.

assets. The rate of interest, which is the price of obtaining credit in the financial system, is a measure of the penalty suffered by an investor for not converting money into earning assets.

TYPES OF FINANCIAL TRANSACTIONS

Financial markets are never static but change constantly in response to shifting demands from the public, the development of new technology, and changes in laws and regulations. Competition in the financial market-place forces financial institutions to respond to public need by developing new, better quality, and more convenient financial services. Over time, the system of financial markets has evolved from simple to more complex ways of carrying out financial transactions. The growth of industrial centers with enormous capital investment needs and the emergence of a huge middle class of savers have played major roles in the gradual evolution of the financial system.

Whether simple or complex, all financial systems perform at least one basic function. They move scarce funds from those who save and lend (surplus-budget units) to those who wish to borrow and invest (deficit-budget units). In the process, money is exchanged for financial assets. However, the transfer of funds from savers to borrowers can be accomplished in at least three different ways. We label these methods of funds transfer: (1) direct finance, (2) semidirect finance, and (3) indirect finance. Most financial systems have evolved gradually over time so as to place less and less reliance on the direct and semidirect financing techniques and greater emphasis on the indirect financing approach.

Direct Finance

With the direct financing technique, borrower and lender meet each other and exchange funds in return for financial assets. You engage in *direct finance* when you borrow money from a friend and give him or her your IOU or when you purchase stocks or bonds directly from the company issuing them (often called a private placement). We usually call the claims arising from direct finance *primary securities* since they flow directly from the borrower to the ultimate lender of funds. (Figure 2–1 illustrates the process of direct financing between borrowing units and lending units.)

Direct finance is the simplest method of carrying out financial transactions. However, it has a number of serious limitations. For one thing, both borrower and lender must desire to exchange the same amount of funds at the same time. More important, the lender must be willing to accept the borrower's IOU which may be quite risky, illiquid, or slow to mature. Clearly, there must be a coincidence of wants between surplus-

FIGURE 2–1

Direct Finance

and deficit-budget units in terms of the amount and form of a loan. Without that fundamental coincidence, direct finance breaks down.

Another problem is that both lender and borrower must frequently incur substantial information costs simply to find each other. The borrower may have to contact many lenders before finding the one surplus-budget unit with just the right amount of funds and a willingness to take on the borrower's IOU. Not surprisingly, direct finance soon gives way to other methods of carrying out financial transactions as money and capital markets develop.

Semidirect Finance

Early in the history of most financial systems, a new form of financial transaction appears, which we call *semidirect finance.* Some individuals and business firms become securities brokers and dealers whose essential function is to bring surplus- and deficit-budget units together, thereby reducing information costs (see Figure 2–2).

We must distinguish here between a broker and a dealer in securities. A *broker* is merely an individual or financial institution who provides

FIGURE 2–2

Semidirect Finance

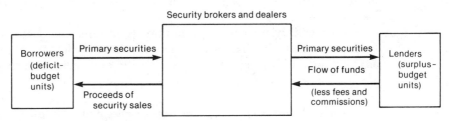

information concerning possible purchases and sales of securities. Either a buyer or a seller of securities may contact a broker, whose job is simply to bring buyers and sellers together. A *dealer* also serves as a middleman between buyers and sellers, but the dealer actually acquires the seller's securities in the hope of marketing them at a later time at a more favorable price. Dealers take a "position of risk" because, by purchasing securities outright for their own portfolios, they are subject to risk of loss if the securities decline in value.[6]

Semidirect finance is an improvement over direct finance in a number of ways. It lowers the search (or information) costs for participants in the financial markets. Frequently a dealer will split up a large issue of primary securities into smaller units affordable by even buyers of modest means and thereby expand the flow of savings into investment. In addition, brokers and dealers facilitate the development and growth of secondary markets where securities can be offered for resale.

Despite the important contribution of brokers and dealers to the functioning of the financial system, the semidirect finance approach is not without its limitations. The ultimate lender still winds up holding the borrower's securities, and therefore the lender must be willing to accept the risk, liquidity, and maturity characteristics of the borrower's IOU. There still must be a fundamental coincidence of wants and needs between surplus- and deficit-budget units for semidirect financial transactions to take place.

Indirect Finance

The limitations of both direct and semidirect finance stimulated the development of indirect financial transactions, carried out with the help of *financial intermediaries.* Financial intermediaries active in today's financial markets include commercial banks, insurance companies, credit unions, finance companies, savings and loan associations, mutual savings banks, pension funds, mutual funds, and similar organizations. (See Exhibit 2–4.) Their fundamental role in the financial system is to serve as intermediaries between ultimate lenders and borrowers, but in a much more complete way than brokers and dealers do. Financial intermediaries issue securities of their own—*secondary securities*—to ultimate lenders and at the same time accept IOUs from borrowers—*primary securities* (see Figure 2–3).

The secondary securities (sometimes called indirect securities) issued by financial intermediaries include such familiar financial instruments as checking and saving accounts; health, life and accident insurance poli-

---

[6] The meaning of the term *position of risk* is discussed in greater detail in Chapter 13, where the activities of U.S. government securities dealers are examined.

EXHIBIT 2–4

Major Financial Institutions Active in the Money and Capital Markets

Financial Intermediaries

Depository institutions:
   Commercial banks
   Nonbank thrifts:
      Savings and loan associations
      Mutual savings banks
      Credit unions
      Money market funds
Other financial intermediaries:
   Finance companies
   Government pension funds
   Government credit agencies

Contractual institutions:
   Life insurance companies
   Property-casualty insurers
   Private pension funds

Investment institutions:
   Investment companies
   Real estate investment trusts

Other Financial Institutions

Investment bankers
Mortgage bankers

Security dealers
Security brokers

cies; pension plans; and shares in a mutual fund. For the most part these securities share a number of common characteristics. They generally carry low risk of default. For example, most deposits held in U.S. banks and credit unions are insured by an agency of the federal government up to $100,000. Moreover, the majority of secondary securities can be acquired in small denominations, affordable by savers of limited means. For the most part secondary securities are liquid and therefore can be converted quickly into cash with little risk of significant loss for the purchaser. Financial intermediaries in recent years have tried to make savings as convenient as possible through mail transactions services and trans-

FIGURE 2–3

Indirect Finance

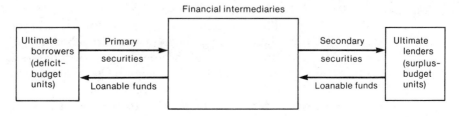

fer of funds by plastic card, computer terminal, and telephone in order to reduce transactions costs to the saver.

Financial intermediaries accept primary securities from those who need credit, and in doing so, take on financial assets which many savers, especially those with limited funds, and limited knowledge of the market, would find unacceptable. For example, many large corporations require billions of dollars in credit financing each year—sums which would make it impractical to deal directly with thousands of small savers. By pooling the resources of scores of small savings accounts, however, a large commercial bank or other intermediary frequently can service the credit needs of several large firms simultaneously. In addition, many primary securities, even those issued by some of the largest borrowers, are not readily marketable and carry sizable risk of borrower default—a situation usually not acceptable to the small saver. By issuing its own securities, which are attractive to ultimate lenders (savers), and accepting primary securities from borrowers, the financial intermediary acts to satisfy the financial needs of both surplus- and deficit-budget units in the economy.

RELATIVE SIZE AND IMPORTANCE OF MAJOR FINANCIAL INSTITUTIONS

Financial institutions differ greatly in their relative importance within the U.S. financial system. Measured by total financial assets, *commercial banks* dominate the financial system, as shown in Exhibit 2–5. The more than $1.5 trillion in financial assets held by U.S. banks at year-end 1983 represented about two fifths of the total resources of all American financial institutions. A distant second in relative size are *savings and loan associations*—another deposit-type financial intermediary active in the nation's mortgage market. Very similar in sources and uses of funds to savings and loans are *mutual savings banks,* headquartered mainly along the Atlantic seaboard and in the New England area, that attract small-denomination savings deposits from individuals and families. The fourth major kind of deposit-type financial intermediary, the *credit union,* was also created to attract small savings deposits from individuals and families and make loans to credit union members.

When the assets of all four deposit-type intermediaries—commercial banks, savings and loans, mutual savings banks, and credit unions—are combined, they represent about two thirds of the total financial assets of all U.S. financial institutions. The remaining third of the sector's total financial assets are held by a highly diverse group of financial institutions. *Life insurance companies,* which protect their policyholders against the risks of premature death and disability, lead the list of nondeposit financial institutions. The other type of insurance firm—*property-casualty insurers*—offer a far wider array of policies to reduce risk associated with

EXHIBIT 2–5

Total Financial Assets Held by U.S. Financial Institutions, Selected Years
($ billions at year-end)

Financial Institution	1960	1970	1980	1983
Financial intermediaries:				
Commercial banks	$224.2	$488.9	$1,247.9	$1,595.4
Savings and loan associations	70.3	173.1	621.9	828.6
Life insurance companies	115.8	200.9	464.2	633.3
Private pension funds	38.1	110.4	412.7	607.8
State and local government pension funds	19.7	60.3	198.1	316.1
Finance companies	27.6	64.0	198.7	259.8
Property-casualty insurance companies	26.2	49.9	174.3	255.3
Money market funds	—	—	74.4	162.5
Mutual savings banks	41.0	79.3	171.5	194.4
Investment companies	17.0	46.8	63.5	129.3
Credit unions	6.3	18.0	71.6	102.5
Real estate investment trust	—	3.9	5.8	7.9
Other financial institutions:				
Security brokers and dealers	6.7	16.2	36.1	49.1

SOURCE: Board of Governors of the Federal Reserve System, *Flow of Funds Accounts, Assets and Liabilities Outstanding 1960–83,* September 1984.

loss of property, ill health related to disease and injury, crime and vandalism, weather damage, and personal negligence. Among the fastest-growing financial institutions are *pension funds* which, like insurance companies, protect their customers against risk; for example, the risk of living too long following retirement and outlasting the individual's accumulated savings.

Other important financial institutions include finance companies, investment companies, money market funds, and real estate investment trusts. *Finance companies* lend money to both businesses and consumers to meet short-term working-capital needs and for long-term investment. *Investment companies* pool the funds contributed by thousands of investors by selling shares and then invest in securities sold in the open market. A specialized type of investment company is the *money market fund* which accept savings (share) accounts from businesses and individuals and places those funds in high-quality, liquid money market securities.

Also related to investment companies are *real estate investment trusts*, the smallest member of the financial institutions' sector, investing mainly in commercial and residential real estate projects.

CLASSIFICATION OF FINANCIAL INSTITUTIONS

Financial institutions may be grouped in a variety of different ways. One of the most important distinctions is between *depository institutions* (commercial banks, savings and loan associations, mutual savings banks, and credit unions), *contractual institutions* (insurance companies and pension funds), and *investment institutions* (investment companies or mutual funds, money market funds, and real estate investment trusts). Depository institutions derive the bulk of their loanable funds from deposit accounts sold to the public, while contractual institutions attract funds by offering legal contracts to protect the saver against risk. Investment institutions sell shares to the public and invest the proceeds in stocks, bonds, and other securities.

Some authorities find it useful to distinguish between *local* financial institutions and *regional* or *national* institutions. A financial institution is local in character if it receives the bulk of its funds and acquires the majority of its financial assets from the surrounding community (usually a city or county area). Most credit unions, savings and loans, and smaller commercial banks are locally oriented institutions. Other financial institutions, especially insurance companies, finance companies, larger commercial banks, pension funds, and investment companies, tend to be regional or national in scope. Their sources of funds and financial assets tend to cover wide geographic areas and may even reach into foreign markets. This distinction between local, regional, national, or international institutions is especially important in trying to assess the degree of competition prevailing in the financial institutions' sector and in evaluating how well each institution is serving the public in its chosen market area.

PORTFOLIO DECISIONS BY FINANCIAL INTERMEDIARIES AND OTHER FINANCIAL INSTITUTIONS

The management of a financial institution is called upon daily to make portfolio decisions; that is, what financial assets to buy or sell, what the institution's sources and uses of funds should be. A number of factors affect these critical decisions. For example, the *relative rate of return and risk attached to different financial assets* will affect the composition of the institution's portfolio. Obviously, if management is interested in maximizing profits and has minimal aversion to risk, it will tend to pursue the highest-yielding financial assets available, especially corporate bonds and stocks. A more risk-averse institution, on the other hand, is likely to surrender some yield in return for the greater safety available in acquiring government bonds and high-quality money market instruments.

The *cost, volatility,* and *maturity of incoming funds* provided by surplus-budget units also has a significant impact upon the loans and securities acquired by a financial institution. Commercial banks, for example, derive a substantial proportion of their funds from checking accounts, which are relatively inexpensive but highly volatile. Such an institution will tend to concentrate its lending activities in short- and medium-term loans in order to avoid an embarrassing and expensive shortage of cash (liquidity). On the other hand, a financial institution such as a pension fund, which receives a stable and predictable inflow of savings, is largely freed from concern over short-run liquidity needs. It is able to invest heavily in long-term financial assets. Thus, the *hedging principle*—the approximate matching of the maturity of assets held with liabilities taken on—is an important guide for choosing those financial assets that a financial institution will hold in its portfolio.[7]

Decisions on what loans and securities to acquire and what sources of funds to draw upon are also influenced by the *size* of the individual financial institution. Larger institutions frequently can take advantage of greater diversification in sources and uses of funds than smaller institutions. This means that the overall risk of a portfolio of securities can be reduced by acquiring securities from many different borrowers. Similarly, a larger institution can contact a broader range of savers and achieve greater stability in its incoming flows of funds. At the same time, through economies of scale (size), larger financial institutions can often sell financial services to both borrowers and ultimate lenders at lower cost per unit and pass those savings along to their customers.

Finally, regulations and competition, two external forces, play major roles in shaping both the sources and uses of funds for a financial institution. Because they hold the bulk of the public's savings and are so crucial to economic growth and investment activity, financial intermediaries are among the most heavily regulated of all business firms. Examples abound. Commercial banks are prohibited from investing in corporate stock or in speculative debt securities. Insurance companies must restrict any security purchases to those a "prudent man" would most likely choose. Most regulations in this sector pertain to prices charged, assets that can be acquired, adequacy of net worth, and services that can be offered to

---

[7] See Chapters 9 and 14 for further discussion of the hedging principle.

the public. In theory, at least, such regulations are designed to promote competition and ensure the safety of the public's funds.

DISINTERMEDIATION OF FUNDS

One factor which has had a profound influence on the financial assets selected by financial institutions for their portfolios in recent years is the phenomenon of *disintermediation*. Exactly opposite from the intermediation of funds, disintermediation means the withdrawal of funds from a financial intermediary by ultimate lenders (savers) and the lending of those funds directly to ultimate borrowers. In other words, disintermediation involves the shifting of funds from indirect finance to direct and semidirect finance (see Figure 2–4).

FIGURE 2–4

Financial Disintermediation

You engage in disintermediation when you remove funds from a savings account at the local bank and purchase common stock or Treasury bills through a broker. The phenomenon is more likely to occur during periods of high and rapidly rising interest rates when the higher returns demanded by savers may outpace the interest rates offered by financial intermediaries. Clearly, disintermediation forces a financial institution to surrender funds and, if severe, may lead to losses on assets and ultimate failure. While intermediaries are forced to be more liquid and reduce their credit-granting activities during periods of disintermediation, there is no evidence that the total flow of credit through the financial system is reduced during such periods. Moreover, disintermediation has become far less a problem for financial intermediaries now that federal interest-rate ceilings on deposits have been almost entirely phased out, allowing financial intermediaries to respond more freely to movements in market interest rates. Correspondingly, however, financial intermediaries today are faced with greater uncertainty about funds flows and costs than ever before.

CONCLUSIONS

In the next section of the book we will explore in more depth the role of financial institutions in the money and capital markets. We will discover that their role has been expanding rapidly in recent years in response to the rise of the small saver and the massive needs for credit coming from businesses, consumers, and governments today. In most years the process of indirect finance (financial intermediation) accounts for about four fifths of all savings flows in the American economy. Thus, while direct financing and semidirect financing techniques are still important ways of carrying out financial transactions, indirect financing through financial intermediaries is clearly the most important route for financial transactions in the modern world.

STUDY QUESTIONS

1. What is a financial asset? How does it arise within the workings of the financial system? Why must the volume of financial assets outstanding equal the volume of liabilities?

2. Explain the difference between internal and external finance. When an economic unit, such as business, household, or government, needs funds, what are its principal alternatives? What factors enter into the choice among different sources of funds?

3. How is the creation of financial assets and liabilities linked to saving and investment activity in the economy?

4. Define lending and borrowing for an economic unit. Are these two necessarily equal to each other?

5. Define the term deficit-budget unit, surplus-budget unit, and balanced-budget unit. Which were you last month? Why?

6. What is money? What are its principal functions within the financial system?

7. Distinguish between direct finance, semidirect finance, and indirect finance. Which is most important today in the financial system? Explain why.

8. What are primary securities? Secondary securities? Give examples of each. Why is the distinction between these two kinds of securities important? What are the principal characteristics of each?

9. List the major kinds of financial intermediaries in the American economy. Which ones on your list can be classified as depository intermediaries? Contractual intermediaries? Investment intermediaries? Local? National or regional?

10. Distinguish between security brokers and dealers. What is the essential difference between the two?

11. What is disintermediation? What are its principal causes and possible cures?

SELECTED REFERENCES

Dougall, Herbert E., and Jack E. Gaumnitz. *Capital Markets and Institutions.* 4th ed. Englewood Cliffs, N.J.: Prentice-Hall, 1980.

Goldsmith, Raymond W. *Financial Institutions.* New York: Random House, 1968.

Gurley, John G., and Edward S. Shaw. "Financial Intermediaries and the Saving-Investment Process." *Journal of Finance,* May 1956, pp. 257–66.

————. *Money in a Theory of Finance.* Washington, D.C.: Brookings Institution, 1960.

Jacobs, Donald P.; C. Farwell Loring; and Edwin Neave. *Financial Institutions.* 5th ed. Homewood, Ill.: Richard D. Irwin, 1966.

Polakoff, Murray E., Thomas A. Durkin, et al. *Financial Institutions and Markets.* 2d ed. Boston: Houghton Mifflin, 1981.

Pyle, David H. "On the Theory of Financial Intermediation." *Journal of Finance,* June 1971, pp. 737–47.

Smith, Paul F. *Economics of Financial Institutions and Markets.* Homewood, Ill.: Richard D. Irwin, 1971.

3

Sources of Information for Financial Decision Making in the Money and Capital Markets

PURPOSE OF THIS CHAPTER

To acquaint the reader with the most important sources of financial data and information. Five different types of financial information are discussed: (1) debt security prices and yields; (2) stock prices and dividend yields; (3) the financial condition of individual issuers of securities; (4) general economic and financial conditions; and (5) social accounting data. The chapter concludes with a discussion of the Flow of Funds Accounts—a key source of data on financial institutions and the saving, investment, borrowing, and lending activities of major sectors of the economy.

KEY TERMS AND CONCEPTS IN THE CHAPTER

bid and asked prices
bonds and notes
economic and
* financial conditions*
financial decisions
flow of funds accounts

flow of funds matrix
national income
* accounts*
security issuer
* information*

social accounting data
sources and uses of
* funds statements*
stock price listings

Every day in the money and capital markets, individuals and institutions must make important financial decisions. For those who plan to borrow funds, for example, key decisions must be made concerning the timing of a request for credit and exactly where the necessary funds should be raised. Lenders of funds must make decisions on when and where to invest their limited resources, considering such factors as the risk, marketability, and expected return on securities available in the financial marketplace. Government policymakers also are intimately involved in the financial decision-making process. It is the responsibility of government to ensure that the financial markets function smoothly in channeling savings into investment and in creating a volume of credit sufficient to support business and commerce. Government financial policy is aimed at stabilizing the financial system while, at the same time, promoting full employment, price stability, satisfactory economic growth, and a sustainable balance-of-payments position with the rest of the world. Central banks around the world, including the Federal Reserve System in the United States, must make decisions each day on whether to enter the financial marketplace in order to influence interest rates and credit availability.[1]

Sound financial decisions require adequate and accurate financial information. Borrowers, lenders, and those who make financial policy require data on the prices and yields attached to individual money and capital market securities today and the prices and yields likely to prevail in the future. A borrower, for example, may decide to postpone the taking out of a loan or to shorten the maturity of current borrowings if it appears that the cost of credit will be significantly lower six months from now than it is today. Those who wish to forecast future interest rates and security prices need information concerning the expected supply of new securities brought to market and the expected demand for those securities. Since economic conditions exert a profound impact upon the money and capital markets, the financial decision maker must also be aware of vital economic data series which reflect employment, prices, industrial output, spending on goods and services, the volume of savings flows, changes in business inventories, business capital expansion plans, and related types of information.

What are the principal sources of financial information? Where do financial decision makers go to find the data they need? We may divide the sources of information relied upon by financial decision makers into five broad groups: (1) debt security prices and yields, (2) stock prices and dividend yields, (3) information on security issuers, (4) general economic and financial conditions, and (5) social accounting data. In the

---

[1] We discuss central banking and the operations of the Federal Reserve System in Chapters 22 through 24.

following sections we discuss some of the most important sources of these kinds of financial and economic information.

DEBT SECURITY PRICES AND YIELDS

Among the most important securities traded in the financial system are *bonds* and *notes*. As noted in Chapter 2, bonds and notes are debt obligations issued by governments and corporations, usually in units (par values) of $1,000. A *note* is a short-term written promissory olbigation, usually not exceeding 5 years to maturity while a bond is a long-term promissory note, usually at least 5 to 10 years to maturity and often much longer. While bonds and notes generally pay a fixed rate of return to the investor in the form of coupon income, their prices fluctuate widely as interest rates change. Therefore, while bonds and notes are often referred to as "fixed-income securities," the investor may experience significant capital gains or losses on these securities as their prices change. Bonds and notes issued in the United States generally carry a set maturity date, at which time the issuer must pay the holder the security's par value. These securities are generally identified by the name of the issuing company or governmental unit, their coupon (fixed-interest) rate, and their maturity date.

Quotations of prices and yields on bonds and notes actively traded in the financial markets are available from a wide variety of published sources. Major securities dealers trading in bonds and notes publish *quote sheets* showing the market prices, yields, and amounts outstanding. A portion of a sample page from a major bond dealer's quote sheet is shown in Exhibit 3–1. This particular exhibit presents price quotations on U.S. Treasury bonds and notes posted by First Boston Corporation, one of the nation's leading securities dealers.[2] The prices shown for each security issue—identified by its coupon rate and date of maturity—are quoted in terms of a $100 par value.

The market prices of bonds and notes generally are expressed in 32ds of a dollar and sometimes in 64ths, indicated by a plus (+) sign. Both bid and asked prices are posted by the dealer, who will purchase securities at the *bid* price but sell to customers at the *asked* price.[3] Yields are computed against the asked price and are generally figured to maturity when the security is selling at a discount. When the security is selling

---

[2] As we will see in Chapter 25, Treasury notes carry original maturities of 1 to 10 years while bills must mature within 1 year. Treasury bonds can carry any maturity, but usually exceed 10 years.

[3] Dealer quotations like those shown in Exhibit 3–1 are generally for purchases and sales of *round lots,* consisting of at least 100 securities. Additional service charges or price adjustments are made for smaller (odd-lot) transactions.

EXHIBIT 3–1

Dealer Quotation Sheet for U.S. Treasury Securities

United States Treasury Securities

First Boston
Park Avenue Plaza   New York, N Y 10055

NEW YORK (212) 909-2000   ATLANTA (404) 658-9009   BOSTON (617) 542-7700   CHICAGO (312) 372-8640   CLEVELAND (216) 696-8822   DALLAS (214) 742-2900   LOS ANGELES (213) 485-9898   PHILADELPHIA (215) 972-1700   SAN FRANCISCO (415) 981-0700

U.S. TREASURY NOTES AND BONDS

Coupon	Maturity	Bid	Asked	Chg	Yield to Mat	Corp After Tax Equiv	Yield Value Par 1/32	1981 Range High	Low	Amt Pub Held	Dated Date
N 8	2-15-85	88- 0	88-16 +16	.....13.39	8.20 15.19	.0158	89- 4	83-20	2755	2-15-78
N14 5/8	2-15-85	101- 6	101-10 + 8	.....13.98	7.55 13.98	.0146	102- 6	98-24	5593	2-16-82
N13 3/8	3-31-85	98-20	98-28 + 8	.....13.86	7.57 14.02	.0142	99-22	95-16	3408	3-31-81
**B 3 1/4	5-15-85	84- 0	85- 0	..... 9.39	6.18 11.44	.0141	85- 0	82- 0	369	6- 3-58
**B 4 1/4	5-15-85/75	84- 0	85- 0	.....10.50	6.79 12.58	.0143	85- 0	82- 0	515	4- 5-60
N10 3/8	5-15-85	92- 0	92- 4 +12	.....13.81	8.07 14.95	.0144	92-24	68-16	2501	12- 4-72
N14 1/8	5-15-85	100- 8	100-12 + 6	.....13.94	7.53 13.94	.0136	101-12	98- 2	5250	5-17-82
N14 3/8	5-15-85	101- 8	101-12 + 8	.....13.75	7.42 13.75	.0135	102- 4	98-24	2458	3- 3-80
N14	6-30-85	98-24	98-28	.....14.47	7.90 14.63	.0134	101- 4	97- 4	3143	6-30-81
N 8 1/4	8-15-85	86-16	86-24 +20	.....13.64	8.34 15.46	.0139	87- 8	82-16	3213	8-15-78
N 9 5/8	8-15-85	89-24	90- 0 +24	.....13.70	8.13 15.05	.0136	90-12	86- 0	3209	6- 5-60
N15 7/8	9-30-85	104- 8	104-16 +16	.....14.06	7.59 14.06	.0120	105-24	101-14	3656	9-30-81
N11 3/4	11-15-85	94-12	94-20 +24	.....13.80	7.82 14.48	.0124	95-12	91- 0	3082	9- 3-80
N14 1/8	12-31-85	100-16	100-24 +20	.....13.84	7.47 13.84	.0116	101-14	97- 8	3276	12-31-81
N13 1/2	2-15-86	96-20	98-28 +20	.....13.89	7.57 14.03	.0114	100- 8	95-20	3171	12- 0-80
N14	3-31-86	100- 8	100-12 +20	.....13.85	7.46 13.65	.0110	102- 2	97- 6	3817	3-31-82
N 7 7/8	5-15-86	83- 6	83-16 +24	.....13.52	8.32 15.40	.0119	84- 0	78-12	4061	5-17-76
N13 3/4	5-15-86	99-20	99-28 +24	.....13.77	7.44 13.76	.0107	100-24	96- 4	3434	3- 4-01
N14 7/3	6-30-86	102-16	102-20 +16	.....13.98	7.55 13.96	.0103	102-20	100- 8	4008	7- 6-82

DECIMAL EQUIVALENTS of 32nds and 64ths per 1/100

+ $ .015625	5 + $ .171875	10 + $ .328125	15 + $ .484375	20 + $ .640625	25 + $ .796875	30 + $ .953125	
1 .031250	6 .187500	11 .343750	16 .500000	21 .656250	26 .812500	31 .968750	
1+ .046875	6+ .203125	11+ .359375	16+ .515625	21+ .671875	26. .828125	31+ .984375	
2 .062500	7 .218750	12 .375000	17 .531250	22 .687500	27 .843750	32 1.00000	
2+ .078125	7+ .234375	12+ .390625	17+ .548875	22+ .703125	27+ .859375		
3 .093750	8 .250000	13 .406250	18 .562500	23 .718750	28 .875000		
3+ .109375	8+ .265625	13+ .421875	18+ .578125	28+ .890625			
4 .125000	9 .281250	14 .437500	19 .593750	24 .750000	29 .906250		
4+ .140625	9+ .296875	14+ .453125	19+ .809375	24+ .765625	29+ .921875		
5 .156250	10 .312500	15 .468750	20 .625000	25 .781250	30 .937500		

Coupon Rate %	Interest Per Million Per Day	Nbr Days to Equal 1/32nd	Coupon Rate %	Interest Per Million Per Day	Nbr Days to Equal 1/32nd	Coupon Rate %	Interest Per Million Per Day	Nbr Days to Equal 1/32nd
1½	$ 41.09589	7.6	8¼	$171.23288	1.8	9¼	$253.42466	1.2
2	54.79452	5.7	6⅛	178.08219	1.8	9½	260.27397	1.2
2½	68.49315	4.6	8⅜	184.93151	1.7	9¾	267.12329	1.2
3	82.19178	3.8	7	191.78082	1.6	10	273.97260	1.1
3½	95.89041	3.2	7⅛	198.63014	1.6	10¼	280.82192	1.1
4	109.58904	2.9	7½	205.47945	1.5	10½	287.67123	1.1
4½	123.28767	2.6	7⅝	212.32877	1.5	10¾	294.52055	1.1
5	136.98630	2.3	8	219.17808	1.4	11	301.36986	1.0
5¼	143.83562	2.2	8¼	226.02740	1.4	11¼	308.21918	1.0
5½	150.68493	2.1	8½	232.87871	1.3	11½	315.06849	1.0
5¾	157.53425	2.0	8¾	239.72603	1.3	11¾	321.91781	1.0
6	164.38356	1.9	9	246.57534	1.3	12	328.76712	1.0

365 day basis

CLOSING QUOTATIONS— MON., JULY 12, 1982 **YIELDS FOR DELIVERY—** WED., JULY 14, 1982

U.S. Treasury Notes and Bonds are exempt from state and local income tax. B Bonds, N Notes. WI When Issued. Yield to first call for callable issues quoted at a premium.

◇ As of 2/26/82 Issue Date if later. Amounts in millions

■ Yield after corporate tax of 46%. For obligations selling at a discount from par, and which are more than twelve months from maturity, effect is given to the corporate capital gains tax of 28%.

SOURCE: The First Boston Corporation, *Handbook of the Securities of the United States Government and Federal Agencies,* 30th ed., 1982, p. 202.

at premium over par and has various possible maturity dates, the yield is generally figured to the nearest maturity date.[4] New prices and yields must be posted daily by dealers because demand and supply factors continually alter the price and return on individual securities.

To illustrate the kinds of information displayed in a dealer's quote sheet, let us examine the first entry in Exhibit 3–1. The security represented there is a U.S. Treasury note bearing an 8 percent coupon rate. It was issued February 15, 1978, and matured on February 15, 1985. On July 12, 1982, the dealer was willing to buy (bid) the note at 88

---

[4] The yield to maturity concept assumes the investor will hold the security until final maturity. (See Chapter 8 for a discussion of the concept of yield to maturity.) After-tax yields generally are figured using a 46 percent corporate profits tax rate on coupon income and a 28 percent corporate tax rate on long-term capital gains.

0/32 and sell it at 88 16/32. Because each 32d equals $0.03125 per $100, this coupon security would sell for $88.50 assuming a par value of $100 or $885 for a $1,000 par-value security. Its yield to maturity at that price would be 15.19 percent before federal income taxes and 8.20 percent after taxes for a corporation subject to maximum federal tax rates. A total of about $2,755 million of these Treasury notes was held by the public at the time these price and yield quotations were published. An investor interested in this particular note would, of course, want to compare one dealer's asked price with the prices posted by other dealers.

Financial newspapers report daily quotations on the most actively traded bonds and other securities. Most daily newspapers contain a list of prices for bonds traded on the New York and American stock exchanges. One of the most complete listings of daily price and yield quotations appears in *The Wall Street Journal* (WSJ), published by Dow Jones. WSJ reports the prices of securities traded on the major securities exchanges and also issues sold over the counter (OTC). Exhibit 3–2 shows the prices of corporate bonds traded on the New York Stock Exchange on March 27, 1985, as reported in *The Wall Street Journal.* In these quotations, bonds are priced in dollars and fractions of a dollar (in this case, down to one eighth of a dollar or $0.125), assuming a $100 par value. For example, we note that bonds issued by American Natural Resources (ANR), carrying a coupon rate of 8⅝ percent and due to mature in 1993, traded the previous business day at a high price of 83½ and a

EXHIBIT 3–2

Bond Price and Yield Quotations from *The Wall Street Journal* low price of 83½ and closed at that same price. This means that, when trading ended on the date indicated, the ANR bonds were selling for $835 for a $1,000 par-value security. This closing price was 1½ points above the closing price for these bonds the previous business day, which was 82 or $820 per $1,000 par-value bond. The ANR bond's current yield—or ratio of interest (coupon) income to its current price—was 10 percent.[5]

The bulk of bond trades on the major securities exchanges, such as the New York Stock Exchange, are small-volume, odd-lot transactions. Purchases and sales of large quantities of bonds between dealers and major institutional investors generally take place off the major exchanges through direct negotiation or with the aid of security brokers. Prices and yields on such large transactions (round lots) must be gathered from other sources of information, including dealer quote sheets such as the one shown in Exhibit 3–1.

Several other sources of information on bond yields and prices are readily available to investors in published form. *The Daily Bond Buyer*, for example, gives a detailed breakdown of daily prices and yields for a large number of actively traded bond issues, as does the *Commercial and Financial Chronicle*, a financially oriented newspaper. Moreover, a number of bond-yield *indexes* have been compiled in recent years; they pool several bond issues of similar quality and report the average rate of return (yield) to the investor for the entire pool of bonds. In this way bond market investors and companies planning to issue new bonds can read the "drift" of recent price and yield changes and decide if their plans need to be altered to reflect the latest market developments.

Among the most popular bond-yield indexes are those compiled by Moody's Investor Service and the *Bond Buyer* newspaper for both corporate and state and local government bonds. In addition, the U.S. Treasury makes available estimated average yields for its notes and bonds, arrayed by maturity (e.g., 1-year, 2-year, 3-year, 5-year, 10-year, and 20-year Treasury securities). Dow Jones publishes a daily index of prices for some of the most actively traded corporate bonds, including 10 utility and 10 industrial issues. The Dow bond averages date back to 1915.

These various bond-yield indicators appear in numerous publications, including both private and governmental sources. *The Federal Reserve Bulletin*, published by the Board of Governors of the Federal Reserve System, and the *Survey of Current Business*, published by the U.S. Department of Commerce, report weekly, monthly, and annual average bond yields. Recent changes in various bond-yield indexes as reported in the *Federal Reserve Bulletin* are shown in Exhibit 3–3. We note the marked

---

[5] Current yields are not shown in the case of convertible bonds. These are designated cv. See Chapter 10 for a description of convertible bonds.

EXHIBIT 3–3

Indicators of Average Bond Yields (Average annual yields in percent)

Yield Series	1981	1982	1983	1984	1985*
State and local government notes and bonds:					
Aaa—Moody's Series	10.43	10.88	8.80	9.61	8.80
Bond Buyer Series	11.33	11.66	9.51	10.10	9.37
Corporate bonds:					
Seasoned issues, all industries—	15.06	14.94	12.78	13.49	12.47
Moody's classified by rating:					
Aaa	14.17	13.79	12.04	12.71	11.85
Aa	14.75	14.41	12.42	13.31	12.29
A	15.29	15.43	13.10	13.74	12.59
Baa	16.04	16.11	13.55	14.19	13.13

* For the week ended February 1.
SOURCE: Board of Governors of the Federal Reserve System, *Federal Reserve Bulletin,* April 1985.

fluctuations in bond yields between 1981 and 1985, reflecting significant changes in economic conditions and credit demands during this period.

STOCK PRICES AND DIVIDEND YIELDS

Of all securities traded in the money and capital markets, stocks are among the most popular with investors. Stock prices can be extremely volatile, offering the prospect of substantial capital gains if prices rise but also significant capital losses if prices fall. Most corporations issuing stock pay dividends regularly, thus giving the investor a reasonably steady source of income as well as the opportunity to achieve "windfall" gains if the value of the stock rises. Unlike a bond, however, a share of stock is a certificate of ownership in a corporation and not a debt obligation. No corporation need pay dividends to its stockholders, and some never do, preferring to retain all after-tax earnings in the business.

As in the case of bonds, price and yield data on the most actively traded stocks are reported daily in the financial press. Most daily newspapers list current stock prices, especially for those equities traded on the New York and American stock exchanges. *The Wall Street Journal* contains an extensive list of the daily prices and dividend yields of major stocks sold over the counter and on the major securities exchanges, including the New York, American, Midwest, Pacific, Philadelphia, Boston, and Cincinnati stock exchanges. An example of WSJ stock price quotations is shown in Exhibit 3–4.

We note that each stock price quotation is identified by the abbreviated name of the company using it. High and low prices at which the stock

EXHIBIT 3–4

Stock Price Quotations from *The Wall Street Journal*

NEW YORK STOCK EXCHANGE COMPOSITE TRANSACTIONS

Wednesday, March 27, 1985

Quotations include trades on the Midwest, Pacific, Philadelphia, Boston and Cincinnati stock exchanges and reported by the National Association of Securities Dealers and Instinet

52-week High	Low	Stock	Div.	Yld.	PE	Sales 100s	High	Low	Last	Chg.
66	37¾	BankTr	2.70	4.3	7	x497	63¼	62⅜	62⅝	…
24¾	19¼	BkTr pf	2.50	11.	..	x11	23½	23	23	− ½
12⅞	7½	Banner	.03e	.3	18	5	11⅛	11⅛	11⅛	+ ¼
30¼	19	Bard	.44	1.5	13	816	29½	29⅛	29¼	+ ¼
24½	18	BarnGp	.80	3.6	9	40	22⅜	22½	22¼	..
50	32½	Barnet	1.36	2.8	9	438	49⅝	49½	49¼	− ¼
33⅜	19½	BaryWr	.60	2.5	14	183	24	23⅜	23¾	…
13¾	8¾	BASIX	.12b	1.0	12	342	12⅛	12	12⅛	+ ⅛
28¼	17½	Bausch	.78	3.1	16	422	25⅛	24¾	25	− ⅛
18⅝	11¾	BaxtTr	.37	2.3	76	3824	16	15¾	15⅞	..
25½	17¾	BayFin	.20e	1.0	19	154	21⅜	21	21	− ⅜
31½	19¾	BayStG	2.60	8.3	9	22	u31⅜	30⅞	31¼	…
38¾	29¾	Bearing	1	3.0	11	28	33⅞	33½	33½	− ¼
33¼	24¾	BeatCo	1.80	5.9	9	3203	30¾	29½	30¼	+ 1⅛
62	46½	Beat pf	3.38	6.0	..	5	55⅞	55	55⅞	+ 1⅛
48	30¾	BectnD	1.20	2.5	15	650	u48¼	47¼	48¼	+ ¾
11¾	4¾	Beker				169	5⅞	5⅜	5⅜	− ¼
10¾	9⅞	Beker pf	1.70	17.	..	23	10⅛	10	10⅛	+ ⅛
18¼	12½	BeldnH	.40	3.1	7	5	12⅞	12⅞	12⅞	…
30½	21⅜	BelHwl	.56	2.2	9	340	27	26¼	26¾	+ ⅜
30	21¼	BelHw pf	.67	2.5	..	3	26½	26¼	26½	+1
85⅛	66	BellAtl	6.80	8.2	8	1350	83⅝	82½	82¾	+ 1⅞
28⅞	22⅜	BCE g	2.28		..	237	u29½	28¾	29	+ ¼
27¼	19⅝	BellInd	.32	1.4	12	11	23⅜	23⅜	23⅜	+ ⅛
37⅜	27¼	BellSo	s2.80	7.8	8	7515	35¾	35½	35¾	+ ⅛
55	35¾	BeloAH	.80	1.5	22	24	53¾	53¼	53¼	− ⅜
29⅞	20⅜	Bemis	1	3.6	11	29	28⅛	28	28⅛	− ⅛
90⅜	73	Bndx	pf4.04	4.7	..	18	86½	86½	86½	− ⅛
37½	23	BenfCp	2	5.5	9	109	36⅜	36⅜	36½	…
36¼	30¼	Benef	pf4.30	13.	..	74	35	33¾	33¾	− ¾
166¼	104½	Benef	pf5.50	3.4	..	y40	162	162	162	+ 1⅞
20⅞	17	Benef	pf2.50	13.	..	z100	20	20	20	…
7¾	5¾	BengtB	.22e	3.8	24	534	5⅝	5⅝	5¾	…
23½	7¼	BergEn			14	47	23	22¾	22⅞	+ ⅛
6⅜	3⅞	Berkey			29	113	5¾	5⅜	5½	+ ⅛
17¼	10⅜	BestPd	.24	2.0	12	415	12⅛	11⅞	11⅞	− ⅛
27⅜	14¼	BethStl	.40	2.3	..	544	17⅜	17¼	17¼	+ ⅛
57¾	37¼	BethSt pf	5	12.	..	39	42¼	41¾	41⅞	…
28¾	18⅝	BethSt	pf2.50	12.	..	36	21⅛	20⅞	20⅞	+ ⅛
36⅞	21	Beverly	.32	1.0	18	474	32½	31¾	32	− ¼
24⅞	19¾	BigThr	.80	3.5	16	209	22⅝	22¾	22⅝	+ ⅛
14	13⅛	Bioctt n		..	..	660	13¾	13¼	13¼	+ ¼
26⅞	17¼	BlackD	.64	2.6	12	940	24¼	23¾	24¼	+ ¼
30¼	20	BlckHP	1.92	6.6	8	33	29¼	29	29¼	+ ⅜
40	14¼	BlairJn	.56	2.6	17	276	21¾	21½	21¾	+ ¼
50¾	37	BlckHR	2.40	4.7	13	394	u51¾	50	51⅛	+ 1¼
66⅞	36	Boeing	1.40	2.3	8	1341	62¼	61¾	61⅞	+ ¼
44⅜	32½	BoiseC	1.90	4.9	17	263	38⅜	38⅛	38⅛	− ¼
57	46	BoiseC pf	5	9.3	..	2	54	54	54	+ ¼
29⅞	15¾	BoltBer	.10	.4	29	852	26¼	26	26	…
70¼	52	Borden	2.72	3.9	10	598	u70⅝	69½	70⅜	+ 1⅜
24⅞	16⅞	BorgWa	.92	4.5	9	1186	20⅞	20⅛	20½	− ⅛
8⅜	4¼	Bormns					6½	6½	6½	…
38	25	BosEd	3.24	8.5	8	136	u38⅜	37¾	38⅛	+ ⅜
75½	63	BosE	pf8.88	12.	..	z100	74¼	74¼	74¼	…
10⅝	9	BosE	pr1.17	12.	..	4	10⅛	10	10⅛	+ ⅛
25⅜	10½	BosE	pr1.46	12.	..	32	12½	12¼	12¼	− ⅛
25⅞	14⅞	Bowtr n	.72	3.3	8	1776	22⅛	21¼	21¼	…
31⅛	25½	BrigSt	1.60	5.5	8	129	29	28¾	29	…
56¼	43	BristM	1.88	3.3	17	2732	u57½	56¾	57½	+ 1¼
117½	91	BrstM pf	2	1.7	..	2	u120	120	120	+ 3½

52-week High	Low	Stock	Div.	Yld.	PE	Sales 100s	High	Low	Last	Chg.
23½	13¼	Conair	.24b	1.1	12	63	22¾	22¼	22¾	..
187⅝	13¾	ConnE	s1.60	9.5	8	41	17	16⅜	16⅞	+ ⅛
26	19½	CnnNG	2.40	9.8	9	18	24⅝	24¼	24⅝	− ¼
17¾	10⅜	Conrac	.40	3.0	6	107	13¼	12⅞	13⅛	− ⅛
31¼	23⅜	ConsEd	2.40	7.7	7	1744	u31⅜	31⅛	31¼	+ ⅛
43	35	ConE	pf4.65	11.	..	z2550	41¼	40½	41¼	..
44¾	38	ConE pf	5	11.	..	11	44⅜	44¼	44⅜	+ ⅜
38¾	26⅛	ConsFd	1.44	3.9	11	181	37½	37⅛	37⅜	− ⅛
36	20⅛	CnsFrt	s 1	3.3	11	212	30⅜	30	30¼	− ⅝
44½	31	CnsNG	2.32	5.1	9	291	u45⅞	43¾	45⅞	+2
11		ConsPw			6	1504	6½	6¼	6½	+ ⅛
26	13	CnP	pfA4.16	17.	..	z230	24	23½	24	+ ½
28½	13¼	CnP	pfB4.50	17.	..	z120	25¾	25¼	25¼	..
45½	23¼	CnP	pfD7.45	18.	..	z130	42	41½	41½	− 1½
46½	25	CnP	pfG7.76	18.	..	z20	42	42	42	..
25⅞	11½	CnP	prV4.40	19.	..	35	23¼	23	23⅜	+ ⅜
21⅜	9¼	CnP	prU3.60	18.	..	51	19¾	19¼	19¾	+ ⅜
22⅜	10¼	CnP	prT3.78	19.	..	19	20	19⅞	20	+ ¼
45¾	25⅜	CnP	prH7.68	19.	..	z230	42	41	41	..
23⅞	11¼	CnP	prR 4		..	8	21⅛	20¾	21⅛	+ ⅛
23½	10⅞	CnP	prP3.98	19.	..	12	21⅛	20⅞	20⅞	+ ⅛
22⅞	10¼	CnP	prN3.85	19.	..	11	20¼	20⅜	20⅜	..
15½	7¼	CnP	prM2.50	18.	..	10	14¼	14	14¼	+ ¼
14⅛	7	CnP	prL2.23	17.	..	1	13	13	13	− ¼
24½	11	CnP	prS4.02	19.	..	6	21¼	21	21⅛	+ ¼
15	7¼	CnP	prK2.43	18.	..	11	13¾	13⅜	13¾	+ ⅜
43	23½	CntlCp	2.60	6.6	7	405	39½	39¼	39¼	− ¼
10¼	4⅜	Contil		..	..	75	8¾	8⅝	8¾	…
4¼	⅜	Contil	rt		..	492	3½	3	3½	..
48½	12	Cntlll	pf		..	53	44	43⅝	43⅝	− 1⅛
4½	⅜	CtllHd	n		..	460	1½	1	1½	+ ⅛
9⅞	4½	Cntinfo			6	38	8	7¾	7¾	− ⅜
24	18	ContTel	1.72	7.6	8	1913	22⅝	22¼	22⅜	− ⅛
39¼	24⅜	CtData	.72	2.4	37	11197	30⅜	29¾	29⅞	− ⅛
33⅞	23⅜	Conwd	1.10	3.7	11	108	29⅞	29½	29½	− ⅜
3½	1	viCookU		..	..	65	1¾	1½	1¾	..
34½	26⅞	Coopr	1.52	5.2	14	418	29¼	28¾	29	+ ⅛
37⅜	30	Coopl	pf2.90	8.8	..	173	33	32¾	33	+ ¼
27	11¾	CoopLb	.03e	.2	3	97	14¾	14½	14¾	..
20⅝	12⅜	CoprTr	.40	2.0	8	179	19⅞	19¾	19⅞	+ ⅛
24⅜	12⅛	Coopvis	.40	1.8	16	570	22⅝	22½	22⅝	+ ⅛
21½	11⅜	Copwld	.44	3.6	..	30	12½	12½	12⅜	..
27¼	19¼	Cpwld	pf2.48	11.	..	1	21⅞	21⅞	21⅞	..
27⅜	17½	Cordura	.84	3.2	17	69	26⅛	26⅜	26⅜	..
15¼	10⅞	CoreIn	.56	4.1	13	224	13¾	13¼	13¼	+ ⅜
30	30	CorhG	s1.28	3.7	15	532	35¾	34¾	34⅞	− ¼
45	22¾	CorBlk	1		2.3	109	42½	42½	42⅞	+ ⅜
64½	40⅜	CoxCm	.34	.6	20	380	61	60	60¾	+ ¼
9½	4¼	Craig			..	20	8⅞	8¾	8⅞	+ ⅛
37	32	Crane	1.60b	4.7	11	22	34	33¾	33¾	− ⅛
78½	38½	CrayRs		..	22	543	67	65¾	66½	+ ⅜
27½	16¼	CrockN	.40	1.6	..	73	25⅞	25½	25⅝	+ ⅛
22	15¼	CrckN	pf2.18	11.	..	2	19	19	19	..
52¾	34¾	CrwnCk			11	100	u52⅞	52¼	52⅞	+ ½
42⅞	27¾	CrwZel	1	2.4	16	2589	41¾	41¼	41⅜	+ ⅜
51½	43	CrZel	pf4.63	9.3	..	16	50	49½	49⅜	+ ⅜
28	19¼	Culbro	.80	2.9	6	25	27¾	26⅝	27¾	+ ¼
33¾	12½	Culinet	s		37	1261	28½	27¾	28	+ ¾
88½	61¼	CumEn	2.20	3.0	4	371	74	72¾	74	+ 1⅛
10⅜	8¼	CurrInc	1.10a	11.	..	11	9⅞	9¾	9¾	..
40½	30¼	CurtW	1.20	3.5	10	21	34⅞	34⅜	34⅜	..
52¼	27½	Cyclops	1.10	2.2	10	123	50	48⅞	50	+ 1½

has been traded during the past year and the most recent annual dividend declared by the issuing company are given.[6] The dividend yield, or ratio

---

[6] The occasional letters which appear beside certain stocks in the list of quotations refer to footnotes which give special information. All stocks shown are common equity shares unless the symbol pf appears, indicating an issue of preferred stock. The symbol u indicates a 52-week high in price while d reflects a new 52-week low. The letter s refers to a stock split or stock dividend of 25 percent or more in the past 52 weeks.

of dividends to current price, appears next, along with the ratio of the stock's current price to the past 12 months of company earnings, or the P-E ratio. All remaining entries provide a summary of the previous business day's transactions in the markets where that particular stock is bought and sold. The one-day sales volume, expressed in hundreds of shares, is shown, as well as the highest and lowest prices at which the stock was exchanged that day. The closing price for which the stock was traded in the last sale of the day is reported, expressed in dollars and fractions of a dollar down to eighths. The final entry gives the net change between the day's closing price and the closing price one business day earlier.

Stock prices for individual companies, covering a period of several years, are provided by *The Value Line Investment Survey*, published weekly by Arnold Bernhard & Company of New York. Each company's business is described and basic financial information, such as sales, net earnings, long-term indebtedness, and return on invested capital, is provided for at least a decade. Similar financial and price data for more than 1,100 actively traded stocks are published in the monthly series *3-Trend Security Charts* and in the quarterly series *3-Trend Cycli-Graphs*, both published by Securities Research Company of Boston. Extensive charts showing weekly stock price ranges, earnings, dividends, and number of shares traded appear in each issue.

Stock prices and basic internal financial data for individual companies are also presented in comprehensive reports compiled by Standard & Poor's Corporation (S&P) and published as *Stock Reports*. This monthly S&P series covers shares traded on the New York and American stock exchanges and over the counter. Information is provided subscribers on dividends paid by each company, its principal products, significant income and balance sheet items, and an analysis of management performance. Daily and weekly stock price movements are also reported in S&P's quarterly publication, the *Daily Stock Price Record*.

The stock market is watched closely by investors as a barometer of expectations in the business community. A rising trend in stock prices generally signals an optimistic assessment of future business prospects and expectations of higher corporate earnings. A declining market, on the other hand, is often a harbinger of adverse economic news and may signal a cutback in business investment and lower corporate earnings.

Many students of the financial markets follow several broad stock price indexes which reflect price movements in groups of similar quality securities. One of the most popular indexes is the Dow-Jones Industrial Average of 30 stocks, including such major companies as American Telephone & Telegraph, Exxon, General Motors, Sears Roebuck, and U.S. Steel. Dow Jones also reports a Transportation Average of 20 stocks (including such industry leaders as American Airlines and Southern Pacific Company) and a Utility Average of the shares of 15 leading utility companies (such

FIGURE 3–1

The Dow Jones Industrial Stock Price Average

SOURCE: *The Wall Street Journal*, March 28, 1985.

as Consolidated Edison and Pacific Gas and Electric). The Utility Average is of special importance to many investors because it appears to be highly sensitive to interest-rate fluctuations, and some analysts regard it as a barometer of interest-rate expectations. Recent movements in the Dow Jones Industrial Average reported in *The Wall Street Journal* are shown in Figure 3–1. Daily reports on the performance of all the Dow series also may be found in local newspapers as well as in Standard & Poor's *Daily Stock Price Record.*[7]

---

[7] The Dow Industrial, Transportation, and Utility averages are combined to form a fourth market indicator—the 65 stock Composite Average. The Dow Industrial Average is the oldest of the four series, dating back to 1897, when it contained share prices for just 12 major industrial firms. Probably the most widely followed stock market index in the world, the Dow Industrials is constructed by adding up the current prices of 30 industrial stocks represented and dividing by an adjustment factor designed to account for stock splits and changes in the list of companies represented in the average. (For example, June 1979, IBM and Merck were substituted for Esmark and Chrysler.) The current adjustment factor for all four Dow stock price averages may be found in the latest issue of *Barron's* magazine.

EXHIBIT 3–5

Daily Stock Market Diary

STOCK MARKET DATA BANK — March 27, 1985

Major Indexes

HIGH	LOW (12 MOS)		CLOSE	NET CH	% CH	12 MO CH	%	FROM 12/31	%
DOW JONES AVERAGES									
1299.36	1086.57	30 Industrials	1264.91	+ 5.19	+ 0.41	+ 90.29	+ 7.69	+ 53.34	+ 4.40
635.30	444.03	20 Transportations	599.53	+ 3.87	+ 0.65	+ 91.20	+17.94	+ 41.40	+ 7.42
151.36	122.25	15 Utilities	151.36	+ 1.18	+ 0.79	+ 23.04	+17.96	+ 1.84	+ 1.23
528.78	421.36	65 Composite	512.97	+ 2.72	+ 0.53	+ 53.73	+11.70	+ 23.11	+ 4.72
NEW YORK STOCK EXCHANGE									
106.08	85.13	Composite	103.93	+ 0.65	+ 0.63	+ 12.03	+13.09	+ 7.55	+ 7.83
122.55	99.73	Industrials	119.41	+ 0.74	+ 0.62	+ 11.63	+10.79	+ 8.83	+ 7.99
54.65	42.94	Utilities	54.65	+ 0.41	+ 0.76	+ 10.30	+23.22	+ 3.08	+ 5.97
103.38	73.11	Transportation	97.05	+ 0.71	+ 0.74	+ 9.91	+11.37	+ 6.44	+ 7.11
111.44	76.44	Finance	107.35	+ 0.45	+ 0.42	+ 16.39	+18.02	+ 9.72	+ 9.96
STANDARD & POOR'S INDEXES									
183.35	147.82	500 Index	179.54	+ 1.11	+ 0.52	+ 19.66	+12.30	+ 12.30	+ 7.35
205.15	168.88	400 Industrials	200.42	+ 1.29	+ 0.65	+ 19.52	+10.79	+ 14.06	+ 7.54
162.54	117.20	20 Transportations	152.16	+ 0.53	+ 0.35	+ 12.39	+ 8.86	+ 8.25	+ 5.73
79.84	62.90	40 Utilities	79.84	+ 0.50	+ 0.63	+ 15.08	+23.29	+ 3.95	+ 5.20
21.50	14.09	40 Financials	20.59	+ 0.09	+ 0.44	+ 2.92	+16.53	+ 1.79	+ 9.52
NASDAQ									
288.35	225.30	OTC Composite	277.56	+ 1.38	+ 0.50	+ 26.55	+10.58	+ 30.21	+12.21
312.43	250.18	Industrials	295.80	+ 1.88	+ 0.64	+ 12.49	+ 4.41	+ 35.07	+13.45
328.55	226.87	Insurance	321.98	+ 1.89	+ 0.59	+ 64.17	+24.89	+ 38.87	+13.73
253.59	192.51	Banks	253.55	+ 0.31	+ 0.12	+ 49.79	+24.44	+ 23.78	+10.35
123.14	93.94	Nat. Mkt. Comp.	116.79	+ 0.65	+ 0.56	No Comparison		+ 12.07	+11.53
118.23	92.55	Nat. Mkt. Indus.	109.81	+ 0.80	+ 0.73	No Comparison		+ 11.78	+12.02
OTHERS									
231.22	187.61	AMEX	225.98	+ 1.57	+ 0.70	+ 15.84	+ 7.54	+ 21.72	+10.63
1024.5	755.3	Fin. Times Indus.	979.3	− 2.7	− 0.27	+ 104.1	+11.89	+ 27.0	+ 2.84
12550.82	9703.35	Nikkei Dow Jones	12550.82	+64.67	+ 0.52	+1849.95	+17.29	+1008.2	+ 8.73
201.18	162.46	Value-Line	193.08	+ 1.12	+ 0.58	+ 11.16	+ 6.13	+ 15.10	+ 8.48
1890.37	1508.83	Wilshire 5000	1847.30	+11.36	+ 0.62	+ 211.06	+12.90	+145.30	+ 8.54

Most Active Issues

NYSE	VOLUME	CLOSE		CH
Unocal	8,535,300	47⅝	+	⅞
McGraw Ed	2,033,000	64	+	¼
Phil Pet wd	1,699,200	38½	−	⅛
Diam Shm	1,623,800	19¼	+	1½
Texaco Inc	1,287,900	35		
Amer T&T	1,198,400	21⅝	+	¼
Johnsn Cn	1,185,200	42⅛	+	2
Sony Corp	1,167,000	18	+	⅛
Contr Data	1,119,700	29⅞	−	1⅛
IBM	1,098,400	126⅞	+	1
Rowan	1,022,000	8⅞	+	¼
Gen Elec	1,019,100	60	+	¼
Am Express	934,800	42⅝	+	¼
Searle GD	922,300	48⅜	+	1¾
City Invest	776,600	37⅛	+	⅛

NASDAQ				
MCI Comm	1,261,200	8¾	+	⅛
Beecham Cp	788,700	4⁹⁄₁₆	+	⁵⁄₁₆
Graph Scan	726,800	6¼	+	⅜
Int Thrbred	705,200	10⅜	+	¾
De Beers	694,600	5⅛	+	⁹⁄₃₂
Sensormtc	685,800	7⅞	+	½
Glaxo Hold	606,100	13⅝	+	¼

AMEX				
BAT Ind	2,652,600	4⅛	−	¹⁄₁₆
Dome Ptrl	763,700	2⅛	+	¹⁄₁₆
Echo Bay g	746,100	11¼	+	½
Wang Lab B	522,900	19⅜	+	½
Data Prod	306,900	13⅛	−	⅞
Brown For B	177,100	33⅜	+	⅛
Dillard s	143,200	60	+	2⅜

Diaries

NYSE	WED	TUE	WK AGO
Issues traded	1,990	1,996	2,028
Advances	1,042	814	709
Declines	532	692	853
Unchanged	422	484	466
New highs	97	50	61
New lows	10	12	10
Adv Vol (000)	70,093	47,603	41,924
Decl Vol (000)	20,865	29,936	52,111
Total Vol (000)	101,040	89,930	107,530
Block trades	1,958	1,761	2,217

NASDAQ			
Issues traded	4,123	4,123	4,121
Advances	976	826	804
Declines	712	890	915
Unchanged	2,435	2,407	2,402
New highs	84	68	88
New lows	31	30	25
Adv Vol (000)	37,602	28,431	25,063
Decl Vol (000)	14,547	17,364	30,386
Total Vol (000)	77,712	70,930	87,319
Block trades	941	897	1,013

AMEX			
Issues traded	768	765	805
Advances	284	222	242
Declines	259	281	303
Unchanged	225	262	260
New highs	21	15	21
New lows	11	10	12
Adv Vol (000)	4,092	2,587	2,199
Decl Vol (000)	3,099	1,873	5,856
Total Vol (000)	8,630	6,540	10,280
CompVol (000)	11,311	7,437	11,919
Block trades	96	101	114

SOURCE: *The Wall Street Journal,* March 28, 1985, p. 61. Reprinted by permission of *The Wall Street Journal* © Dow Jones & Company, Inc. 1985. All rights reserved.

Two of the most comprehensive stock market indicators available are Standard & Poor's 400 Industrial Stock Price Index and 500 Composite Stock Price Index, both including the most actively traded U.S. corporate equity shares. The S&P 500 includes the shares of 40 utility companies, 20 transportation firms, and 40 financial stocks not present in the S&P 400 industrial index. All five S&P stock series—the 400 Index, Utility Index, Transportation Index, Financial Stock Index, and the 500 Composite Index—are widely followed and regarded as sensitive barometers of general stock price movements in the United States.[8] An even broader price index than the S&P 500 Composite is the New York Stock Exchange Composite Index, which gives greatest weight to stocks having the highest market values. Considered a useful indicator of total market performance, the NYSE Composite is often used to compare the performance of major institutional investors, such as investment companies and pension funds, against the market as a whole.[9]

Many newspapers, including *The Wall Street Journal,* and financially oriented magazines contain a daily stock market diary similar to that shown in Exhibit 3–5. Such summaries of recent market developments indicate both price movements and the volume of trading on the major exchanges. Market diaries usually report the total number of shares traded on a given day or week, the number of stocks advancing or declining in price, and those whose price remains unchanged after recent trading. Many stock analysts chart movements in the ratio of advances to declines as an indicator of "oversold" or "overbought" conditions in the market.

INFORMATION ON SECURITY ISSUERS

Lenders of funds have a pressing need to secure accurate financial information on those individuals and institutions who seek to borrow funds or sell their stock. Fortunately, financial information on individual companies and other security issuers is available from a wide variety of published sources. Two of the most respected sources of information on major security issuers are Moody's Investors Service, Inc., and Standard & Poor's Corporation, both headquartered in New York City. In a series of annual volumes, Moody's provides financial data on industrial corporations, commercial banks, insurance companies, investment funds, real estate companies, utilities, and state and local units of government. The most widely known Moody's volumes include the *Industrial Manual,*

---

[8] See Chapter 21 for a discussion of the market for corporate stocks and the factors which influence stock prices.

[9] Two other broad market indicators are the AMEX Index, a weighted average of all stocks traded on the American Stock Exchange, and the NASDAQ OTC Composite, which measures price movements in stocks sold over the counter.

Bank and Finance Manual, Public Utility Manual, Transportation Manual, and *Municipal and Government Manual.* In the case of individual corporations, Moody's provides information on the history of each firm, including any recent acquisitions or mergers, names of key officers, and recent financial statements. In addition, Moody's assigns credit ratings to selected issuers of corporate and municipal bonds, commercial paper, and preferred stock as a guide for investors. These ratings are published monthly in Moody's *Bond Record.* Standard & Poor's provides similar credit ratings for corporate and municipal bonds, assessing the likelihood of default on a security issue and the degree of protection afforded the investor. The S&P *Bond Guide,* containing relevant financial information on more than 6,000 bond issues, appears once a month.[10]

Even more extensive financial data are provided by the reports and registration statements which corporations must file with the Securities and Exchange Commission (SEC). These SEC reports and statements are available in many libraries on microfiche or microfilm. One company, Disclosure Incorporated, which is under contract with the SEC, provides its subscribers with microfiche copies of more than 100,000 corporate documents filed each year by approximately 11,000 U.S. companies.

The most important of these corporate documents is the SEC's *10-K Report*—an annual business and financial report which must be filed by most companies within 90 days after their fiscal year-end. 10-K reports identify the principal products or services and markets served by a firm, provide a summary of its operations for the past five years, note any securities outstanding, include complete audited financial statements, and list the names of key officers. SEC regulations pursuant to the Securities Act of 1933 and the Securities Exchange Act of 1934 also require corporations offering securities for public sale to file registration statements. While these statements vary in content with the type of organization selling the securities, registration statements generally include a prospectus outlining the terms of sale of new securities, marketing arrangements, issue and distribution expenses, and company financial reports.

Another useful source of data on business firms seeking credit is the Business Information Report prepared by Dun & Bradstreet, Inc. This credit-rating company collects information on approximately 3 million Canadian and U.S. firms, making detailed financial reports available to its subscribers. A sample page from a Dun & Bradstreet Business Information Report is presented in Exhibit 3–6. Dun & Bradstreet also provides industrywide financial data so the financial condition of an individual business borrower can be compared with that of other firms in the same

---

[10] Moody's and Standard & Poor's investment ratings are discussed in Chapter 10 and presented in detail in Appendix A.

EXHIBIT 3–6

The Dun & Bradstreet Business Information Report

```
Dun & Bradstreet, Inc.                              This report has been prepared for:
  BE SURE NAME, BUSINESS AND          ANSWERING         SUBSCRIBER: 008-001042
  ADDRESS MATCH YOUR FILE             INQUIRY
        THIS REPORT MAY NOT BE REPRODUCED IN WHOLE OR IN PART IN ANY MANNER WHATEVER
  CONSOLIDATED REPORT                                         {FULL REVISION}
```

```
DUNS:  06-647-3261                 DATE PRINTED                 SUMMARY
RETTINGER PAINT CORP.              AUG 13, 197-          RATING     CC2

727 WHITMAN WAY                    WHOL PAINTS &         STARTED    1950
BENSON, MI  48232                  VARNISHES            PAYMENTS    DISC-PPT
    TEL 313 961-0720                                    SALES       $ 424,612
                                   SIC NO.              WORTH       $ 101,867
CARL RETTINGER, PRES.              51 98                EMPLOYS     5
                                                        HISTORY     CLEAR
                                                        CONDITION   GOOD
                                                        TREND       STEADY
```

SPECIAL EVENTS   Business burglarized July 3 but $18,000 loss is fully insured.

```
PAYMENTS  {Amounts may be rounded to nearest figure in prescribed ranges}
REPORTED  PAYING      HIGH      NOW       PAST     SELLING      LAST SALE
          RECORD     CREDIT     OWES      DUE      TERMS        WITHIN
07/7-     Disc       30000     17000      -0-      2 10 30      1-2 mos.
          Disc       27000     14000      -0-      1 10 30      2-3 mos.
          Disc-Ppt   12000      4400      200      2 10 30      1 mo.
          Ppt         9000      8000      -0-      30           1 mo.
06/7-     Disc       16000      7500      -0-      2 10 30      2-3 mos.
05/7-     Disc        9000      3800      -0-      2 10 30      1 mo.
          Ppt         1500       -0-      -0-      30           1-2 mos.
```

```
FINANCE
06/22/7-          Fiscal statement dated May 31, 197-:
          Cash          $  20,623    Accts Payable      $  47,246
          Accts Rec        55,777    Owing Bank            34,000
          Merchandise      92,103    Notes Pay {Trucks}     7,020
                        ---------                        ---------
          Current         168,503    Current               88,266
          Fixts. & Equip.  13,630    Common Stock          35,000
          Trucks            8,000    Earned Surplus        66,867
                        -------                         ---------
          Total Assets    190,133    Total                190,133
          SALES {Yr}: $424,612.  Net profit $17,105.  Fire ins. mdse $95,000;
          equipt $20,000.  Mo. rent: $3500.  Prepared by Steige Co., CPAs, Detroit, MI.
                                --0--
                06/22/7- Lawson defined monthly payments: $3000 to bank, $400 on notes.
          Admitted collections slow but losses insignificant.  Said inventory will drop
          to $60,000 by December.  Expects 5% sales increase this year.
PUBLIC FILINGS
03/25/7-        March 17, 197- financing statement #741170 named subject as debtor and
          NCR Corp., Dayton, O. as secured party.  Collateral: equipment.
05/28/7-        May 21, 197- suit for $200 entered by Henry Assoc., Atlanta, Ga. Docket
          #27519.  Involves merchandise which Lawson says was defective.
BANKING
06/25/7-        Account, long maintained, carries average balances low to moderate five
          figures.  Unsecured loans to moderate five extended and now open.
HISTORY
06/22/7-  CARL RETTINGER, PRES.             JOHN J. LAWSON, V PRES.
          DIRECTORS:  The Officers
                Incorporated Michigan February 2, 1950.  Authorized capital 3500 shares,
          no par common.  Paid in capital $35,000, officers sharing equally.
                RETTINGER, born 1920, married.  Employed by E-Z Paints, Detroit 12 yrs,
          five as manager until starting subject early 1950.
                LAWSON, born 1925, married.  Obtained accounting degree 1946 and then
          employed by Union Carbide, Chicago until joining Rettinger at inception.
OPERATION
06/22/7-        Wholesales paints and varnishes {85%}, wallpaper and supplies.  500
          local accounts include retailers {75%} and contractors.  Terms: 2 10 30.  Peak
          season spring thru summer.  EMPLOYEES:  Officers active with three others.
          LOCATION: Rents 7500 sq ft. one-story block structure, good repair.
```

SOURCE: Dun & Bradstreet.

industry. D&B's Key Business Ratios series calculates 14 key operating and financial ratios for more than 800 lines of business, grouped by SIC Code. Similar industrywide performance indicators are prepared and published in *Troy's Alamanac,* in Robert Morris & Associates' *Annual Statement Studies,* and in Standard & Poor's *Industry Surveys* and the *Analysts Handbook.* This information can be supplemented with news information on individual industries and firms by checking *The Wall Street Journal Index,* the *New York Times Index,* the *Business Periodicals Index,* and *Barron's Index.*

Information on banks and other financial institutions is available from a wide variety of sources, starting with trade associations in each industry and federal and state regulatory agenices. For example, the American Bankers Association, Life Insurance Association of America, Insurance Information Institute, League of U.S. Savings Associations, and Credit Union National Association frequently will provide annual reports, pamphlets, or brochures describing recent industry trends and new services being developed. Studies and commentaries on financial institutions' problems are found in specialized journals and magazines, such as the *Journal of Commercial Bank Lending, Journal of Bank Research, Bankers Magazine, Savings Bank Journal, Financial Analysts Journal,* the *Institutional Investor,* and *Euromoney.*

Among key government agenices providing annual reports and special studies of financial institutions' trends and problems are the Federal Deposit Insurance Corporation, Federal Reserve Board and Federal Reserve Banks, Federal Home Loan Board and Banks, National Credit Union Administration, and the Comptroller of the Currency. For example, the Federal Reserve Banks publish annually the results of their Functional Cost Analysis study which presents data on bank costs and returns for a wide variety of bank services and sizes. The Federal Deposit Insurance Corporation provides periodic reports on the growth of bank offices and branches, aggregate financial statements, and bank failures.

Information on individuals and families who seek credit is assembled and disseminated to institutional lenders such as banks and finance companies by nearly 2,000 credit bureaus in the United States. The files of these bureaus include such information as the individual's place of residence and occupation, marital status, loans and credit charges outstanding, and the promptness with which the individual pays his or her bills. A typical credit file for an individual will indicate whether he or she has filed for bankruptcy or has judgments or liens against either assets or income. Most credit bureaus maintain files on an individual's bill-paying records for up to seven years and may release that information only to those lenders, debt collectors, employers, or licensing agencies who have a legitimate right to know the individual's credit standing. As discussed in Chapter 18, the Fair Credit Reporting Act, passed in 1971, gives individuals access to their credit files and the right to dispute information contained therein.

GENERAL ECONOMIC AND FINANCIAL CONDITIONS

A number of different sources provide market participants with information on developments in the economy, prevailing trends in the money and capital markets, and actions by the government which may affect economic and financial conditions. For example, many of the nation's major commercial banks publish monthly and weekly newsletters for the benefit of their smaller correspondent banks and customers. These newsletters frequently contain discussions of recent changes in employment, prices, industrial output, the nation's money supply, security prices, and interest rates.

The Federal Reserve System releases large quantities of financial information to the public upon request. Statistical releases available on a weekly or monthly basis cover such items as interest rates, money-supply measures, assets and liabilities held by commercial banks and nonbank thrift institutions, the federal government's fiscal and debt-financing operations, and reports on corporate earnings, consumer borrowing, industrial output, and international transactions. Information of this sort is summarized each month in the *Federal Reserve Bulletin* published by the Board of Governors of the Federal Reserve System in Washington, D.C. The board also publishes the results of internal staff studies which examine in detail recent financial trends or address major issues of public policy.

Within the Federal Reserve System, the Federal Reserve Bank of St. Louis publishes large quantities of financial data in its weekly, monthly, and quarterly news releases. One of the most popular is *U.S. Financial Data,* which appears weekly and contains a summary of week-to-week changes in interest rates and in the components of the nation's money supply. Another regular St. Louis Fed publication is *Monetary Trends,* summarizing monthly changes in the money supply and bank reserves. These data series are watched closely by many investors because they often foreshadow broad movements in interest rates, security prices, and national economic conditions.

A number of published sources regularly report on the status of the national economy, particularly as reflected in employment, prices, and production. Newsletters published by banks in major money centers, and daily financial newspapers, such as *The Wall Street Journal,* nearly always include important economic data. The Federal Reserve Bank of St. Louis publishes a monthly news release, *National Economic Trends,* which tracks changes in U.S. employment, consumer and wholesale prices, industrial production, productivity, and labor cost. The *Survey of Current Business,* a monthly magazine published by the U.S. Department of Commerce, contains one of the most up-to-date and comprehensive collections of U.S. economic data available anywhere. The *Survey* reports the latest consumer spending, government expenditures at all levels, changes in business inventories, business capital spending, and exports and imports. The *Survey* contains a detailed breakdown of U.S. production volume by market and industrial groupings, and it tracks movements in manufacturer's sales, inventories, and new orders. Other economic data series found in the *Survey* cover residential and commercial construction, mortgage lending, wholesale and retail trade, employment, and prices of consumer, farm, and producer goods. Information on international economic and financial developments is provided by the St. Louis Federal Reserve Bank's monthly publication, *International Economic Conditions,* and the Federal Reserve Bank of Chicago's biweekly *International Letter.*

Forecasts of future economic and financial developments are available from a wide variety of private financial institutions and management consulting firms. For example, Salomon Brothers, a leading investment banking firm and New York Stock Exchange member, provides annual estimates of the supply and demand for credit in the U.S. economy and a forecast of the trend in long- and short-term interest rates for the ensuing year. Other major investment/brokerage houses usually make economic and financial forecasts available upon request. Forecasts of annual capital spending in the U.S. economy based on repeated industry surveys are prepared regularly by the U.S. Department of Commerce (published quarterly), McGraw-Hill Publication Company Department of Economics, Merrill Lynch Economics, Inc., and Rinfret Associates, Inc. Banks and other businesses often subscribe to one or more of a number of economic consulting firms that prepare detailed forecasts of the nation's GNP and its components, inflation, unemployment, and interest rates. Among the more prominent of these economic consulting firms are Chase Econometrics Associates, Inc., Data Resources, Inc., and Wharton Econometric Forecasting Associates, Inc.[11]

SOCIAL ACCOUNTING DATA

Students of the economy and the financial markets also make use of social accounting systems to keep track of broad trends in national economic and financial conditions. Social accounting refers to a system of recordkeeping which reports transactions between the principal sectors of the economy, such as households, financial institutions, corporations,

---

[11] For a list of major econometric forecasting models and their comparative performance, see McNees and Ries (1983).

and units of government. The two most widely accepted and closely followed social accounting systems are the National Income Accounts and the Flow of Funds Accounts.

National Income Accounts

The National Income Accounts (NIA) are compiled and released quarterly by the U.S. Department of Commerce. The NIA accounting system presents data on the nation's production of goods and services, income flows, investment spending, consumption, and savings. Probably the best-known account in the NIA series is gross national product (GNP), which is a measure of the market value of all goods and services newly produced in the U.S. economy within a year's time. GNP may be broken down into the uses to which the nation's output of goods and services is put. For example, Exhibit 3–7, drawn from the *Survey of Current Business*, indicates the size of the U.S. GNP and its major components in 1984.

EXHIBIT 3–7

National Income and Product Accounts: The Components of U.S. GNP, 1984 (Billions of current dollars)

Personal consumption expenditures:		$2,342.0
Durable goods	$ 318.5	
Nondurable goods	856.8	
Services	1,166.7	
Gross private domestic investment:		637.0
Fixed investment	579.1	
Change in business inventories	57.9	
Net exports of goods and services:		−62.5
Exports	364.8	
Imports	427.3	
Government purchases of goods and services:		747.7
Federal	295.6	
State and local	452.1	
Gross national product of the United States		$3,664.2

SOURCE: U.S. Department of Commerce, *Survey of Current Business;* and Board of Governors of the Federal Reserve System, *Federal Reserve Bulletin,* April 1985.

Clearly, the National Income Accounts provide valuable information on the level and growth of the nation's economic activity. However, these accounts provide little or no information on financial transactions and the money and capital markets. For example, one component of the NIA system reports the annual amount of personal savings, but it does not show how those savings are allocated among purchases of bonds, bank deposits, stocks, and other financial assets. This task is left to the Flow of Funds Accounts, prepared by the Board of Governors of the Federal Reserve System.

The Flow of Funds Accounts

Flow of funds data have been prepared and published quarterly by the Federal Reserve System since 1955 and some data series go back to 1945. Monthly issues of the *Federal Reserve Bulletin* contain the latest summary reports of flow of funds transactions, while detailed breakdowns of financial transactions among major sectors of the economy are readily available on both a quarterly and an annual basis from the Federal Reserve Board in Washington, D.C.

Purposes of the Flow of Funds Accounts.   The basic purposes of the Flow of Funds Accounts are to: (1) trace the flow of savings by businesses, households, and governments into purchases of financial assets; (2) show how the various parts of the financial system are related to and interact with each other; and (3) highlight the interconnections between the financial sector and the rest of the economy.

Flow of Funds Construction and Sector Balance Sheets.
Construction of the Flow of Funds Accounts takes place in four basic steps. First, the economy is divided into several broad *sectors,* each consisting of economic units (transactors) with similar balance sheets. The 13 major sectors in the current account series include:

Households, including personal trusts, foundations, private schools and hospitals, labor unions, churches, and charitable organizations.

Farm businesses.

Nonfarm noncorporate businesses, including partnerships and proprietorships engaged in nonfinancial activities.

Nonfinancial corporations.

State and local governments.

U.S. government, including government-owned agencies.

Federally sponsored credit agencies, such as the Federal Land Banks and Federal National Mortgage Association.

Monetary authorities, including the Federal Reserve System and certain monetary accounts of the U.S. Treasury.

Commercial banks.

Foreign banking agencies.

Savings institutions, including savings and loans, property-casualty insurers and private and government pension funds.

Other financial institutions, such as finance companies, investment companies, and security brokers and dealers.

The second step in assembling the Flow of Funds Accounts is to construct *balance sheets* for each of the sectors listed above at the end of each quarter. Like any balance sheet prepared for a business firm or household, sector balance sheets contain estimates of the total assets, liabilities, and net worth held by each sector as of a single point in time. Assets are divided into financial assets and real (nonfinancial) assets. Detailed breakdowns of total financial assets and liabilities outstanding for each sector are made available to the public once a year.

An example of such a partial balance sheet containing financial assets and liabilities for the household sector for the years 1972 through 1983 is shown in Exhibit 3–8. We note, for example, that households held total financial assets of more than $6 trillion at year-end 1983 (shown in line 1)—more than double their financial asset holdings of a decade before. A substantial part of this total was represented by holdings of demand deposits, currency, and time and savings deposits at commercial banks and nonbank savings institutions. These liquid financial assets totaled nearly $2.2 trillion in 1983 (line 3). The next most important financial asset held by households was corporate stock (equities), totaling almost $1.5 trillion in 1983 (line 18), or about one quarter of the household sector's total financial resources. Holdings of debt securities (credit market instruments), including U.S. Treasury notes and bonds, federal agency securities, state and local government bonds, mortgages and similar assets, amounted to about $739 billion (line 8) as of year-end 1983. It is interesting that the total indebtedness of individuals and families in the United States is far less than their holdings of financial assets.[12] Exhibit 3–8 indicates that the household sector's liabilities totaled nearly $2 trillion in 1983 (line 25)—roughly a third of its total financial assets. Most of the household sector's indebtedness was in the form of home mortgages (line 27) and installment debt (line 28).

Sources of Data.   Data needed to construct sector balance sheets in the Flow of Funds Accounts come from a wide variety of public and private sources. For example, the U.S. Treasury provides monthly statements of its receipts and expenditures and selected data on state and local government financial activity. Information on lending, borrowing, and acquisition of securities by nonfinancial businesses is derived from

---

[12] The relationship between household debt and holdings of financial assets is examined in more detail in Chapter 18.

the Securities and Exchange Commission, the Internal Revenue Service, the U.S. Department of Agriculture, the Commerce Department, the Bureau of the Census, and the Federal Reserve itself. The National Association of Mutual Savings Banks, the Institute of Life Insurance, the Investment Company Institute, the National Association of Real Estate Investment Trusts, and the National Credit Union Administration provide financial data on their respective industries, while the Securities Industry Association provides selected information on gross offerings of securities.

As the Federal Reserve Board observed recently:

> Flow of funds accounting consists of absorbing and digesting a wide variety of financial information, both flows and balances, each part of which has been constructed in isolation from the others with its own accounting procedures, timing classifications, and institutional coverages.[13]

Inevitably, inconsistencies arise in classifying financial transactions due to differences in accounting procedures used by agencies and groups contributing data to the accounts. Moreover, in an economy as vast and complex as that of the United States, some financial transactions are lost "between the cracks." To deal with these problems of consistency and coverage, the Federal Reserve includes a Statistical Discrepancy account which brings each sector into balance.

Preparation of Sources and Uses of Funds Statement.   After balance sheets are constructed for each sector of the economy, the third step in the construction of the Flow of Funds Accounts is to prepare a sources and uses of funds statement for each sector. The sources and uses of funds statement shows changes in net worth and changes in holdings of financial assets and liabilities taken from each sector's balance sheet at the beginning and end of a calendar quarter or year. Thus:

Sources and Uses of Funds Statement

Uses of Funds	Sources of Funds
Change in real assets (or net real investment)	Change in liabilities outstanding (or net borrowing)
Change in financial assets (or net financial investment)	Change in net worth (or net current savings)
Change in total assets = Total uses of funds	Change in liabilities and net worth = Total sources of funds

---

[13] See Board of Governors of the Federal Reserve System, *Introduction to the Flow of Funds,* February 1975, p. 51.

EXHIBIT 3–8

Statement of Financial Assets and Liabilities for the Household Sector, 1972–1983 ($ billions; year-end outstandings)

Households, Personal Trusts, and Nonprofit Organizations

		1972	1973	1974	1975	1976	1977	1978	1979	1980	1981	1982	1983
1	Total financial assets	2,382.4	2,296.8	2,201.0	2,558.9	2,899.7	3,076.5	3,364.5	3,850.0	4,532.0	4,826.3	5,377.3	6,057.5
2	Deposits + credit market instruments	967.1	1,077.9	1,178.2	1,294.8	1,438.9	1,596.2	1,767.5	1,975.1	2,181.0	2,433.9	2,645.6	2,916.4
3	Deposits	710.6	787.1	847.8	940.1	1,062.0	1,189.5	1,321.5	1,450.4	1,620.7	1,830.2	1,983.3	2,177.6
4	Checkable deposits + currency	142.5	156.4	163.6	170.4	186.2	205.2	228.3	249.4	264.0	299.4	315.9	355.7
5	Small time + savings deposits	545.3	585.3	622.6	719.6	835.8	930.9	996.9	1,056.9	1,140.2	1,187.1	1,323.8	1,537.6
6	Money market fund shares	—	—	2.4	3.7	3.7	3.9	10.8	45.2	74.4	181.9	206.6	162.5
7	Large time deposits	22.8	45.4	59.2	46.4	36.4	49.5	85.5	98.8	142.0	161.7	137.0	121.7
8	Credit market instruments	256.5	290.8	330.4	354.7	376.9	406.7	446.0	524.8	560.4	603.7	662.3	738.8
9	U.S. government securities	91.9	108.7	127.2	138.7	145.5	163.4	184.1	226.8	240.2	264.8	277.3	328.3
10	Treasury issues	78.9	95.2	111.3	126.2	129.8	142.3	156.8	181.6	188.2	208.2	226.2	268.7
11	Savings bonds	57.7	60.4	63.3	67.4	72.0	76.8	80.7	79.9	72.5	68.2	68.3	71.5
12	Other Treasury	21.3	34.9	48.0	58.9	57.8	65.5	76.1	101.8	115.6	140.0	157.9	197.2
13	Agency issues	12.9	13.4	15.8	12.5	15.6	21.2	27.3	45.2	52.1	56.5	51.1	59.5
14	Tax-exempt obligations	48.4	53.7	61.9	68.1	70.1	70.1	72.7	83.2	89.9	100.8	132.8	173.8
15	Corporate and foreign bonds	51.2	51.5	54.6	60.9	71.6	71.4	65.2	64.0	58.3	50.4	45.7	45.0
16	Mortgages	59.5	63.1	70.0	76.2	83.6	91.7	105.9	125.9	148.1	171.2	191.7	183.8
17	Open-market paper	5.5	13.8	16.9	10.9	6.1	10.0	18.1	24.7	23.8	16.5	14.7	7.9

18	Corporate equities	908.7	705.7	498.5	646.9	766.0	723.4	741.0	892.3	1,188.2	1,134.3	1,274.8	1,466.2
19	Mutual fund shares	58.9	46.6	35.2	43.0	46.5	45.4	45.8	51.2	63.5	63.8	89.5	129.3
20	Other corporate equities	849.8	659.1	463.3	603.9	719.5	678.1	695.2	841.1	1,124.8	1,070.5	1,185.4	1,336.9
21	Life insurance reserves	143.9	151.3	158.4	166.5	175.3	184.8	196.0	206.7	216.4	225.6	232.8	240.8
22	Pension fund reserves	326.4	322.8	325.2	405.6	467.2	513.8	592.6	699.6	859.1	941.2	1,122.7	1,322.3
23	Security credit	5.0	4.9	3.9	4.5	6.3	5.3	7.8	9.6	14.8	12.7	16.0	19.3
24	Miscellaneous assets	31.3	34.1	36.8	40.6	46.0	52.9	59.5	66.7	72.4	78.5	85.3	92.5
25	Total liabilities	621.1	697.7	752.2	808.0	907.4	1,051.7	1,225.8	1,409.8	1,544.3	1,679.3	1,778.7	1,975.7
26	Credit market instruments	591.0	670.9	725.5	778.8	871.2	1,012.1	1,182.5	1,362.5	1,487.0	1,619.2	1,712.1	1,887.5
27	Home mortgages	358.0	404.5	442.3	482.9	544.3	635.1	746.5	869.2	967.5	1,051.0	1,096.9	1,200.1
28	Installment consumer credit	133.2	155.1	164.6	172.3	193.8	230.6	273.6	312.0	314.9	335.7	355.8	396.1
29	Other consumer credit	44.5	48.6	49.0	50.9	54.8	58.6	64.3	71.3	74.8	80.7	85.9	96.9
30	Tax-exempt debt	—	.4	1.3	2.7	4.7	8.1	10.7	13.6	16.7	21.1	29.4	40.6
31	Other mortgages	21.5	22.6	23.7	24.8	25.6	26.7	28.1	29.6	31.5	33.8	36.4	38.9
32	Bank loans NEC	10.1	13.5	15.2	13.7	14.6	17.4	19.9	20.8	26.8	31.2	34.4	38.4
33	Other loans	23.6	26.2	29.4	31.5	33.4	35.7	39.5	45.9	54.7	65.8	73.2	76.5
34	Security credit	17.5	13.2	11.4	12.1	17.2	18.5	19.7	20.7	27.2	25.6	28.8	48.1
35	Trade credit	6.6	7.3	8.3	9.4	10.5	11.7	13.2	14.9	17.2	19.8	22.2	24.0
36	Deferred and unpaid life insurance premiums	6.0	6.4	7.1	7.7	8.4	9.3	10.3	11.7	12.9	14.7	15.5	16.1

* Excludes corporate equities.
SOURCE: Board of Governors of the Federal Reserve System, *Flow of Funds Accounts, Assets and Liabilities Outstandings, 1960–83.*

An example of such a statement for the U.S. commercial banking sector for 1980–84 is shown in Exhibit 3–9. The first portion of the sources and uses statement (lines 1–17) shows changes in the banking sector's net worth (i.e., current surplus, representing net current savings), real assets (net investments in plant and equipment), and net acquisitions of financial assets. The second portion of the statement (lines 18–36) reflects net borrowing as reflected in an increase in the liabilities carried by U.S. commercial banks and their affiliates.[14] We note, for example, that U.S.-chartered commercial banks added net $168 billion in various kinds of financial assets to their portfolios during 1984 (line 3). The bulk of this addition came in the form of loans to consumers, businesses, and other borrowers, totaling $158 billion (line 10). Commercial bank holdings of U.S. government securities rose just $3.5 billion (line 5); banks also acquired $9.5 billion in state and local government debt obligations (line 8) and $3.2 billion in corporate bonds (line 9) during 1984. The nation's commercial banks invested $14.7 billion in plant and equipment (line 2) during the course of that year.

Where did the banking sector get the funds it needed to make loans, purchase securities, and increase its investment in plant and equipment during 1984? A small portion of the necessary funds came from retained earnings as reflected in the current surplus account (line 1), which rose $12.8 billion during 1984. Most of the required funds, however, were derived from issuing liabilities. Liabilities of the banking sector rose more than $163 billion during 1984 (line 18), net of repayments of outstanding debt. Exhibit 3–9 shows that the bulk of the borrowed funds were derived by selling time deposits to the public in the form of CDs, passbook savings accounts, and other attractive savings instruments. Checking accounts (demand deposits) increased net $23.4 billion (line 19) in 1984. Banks also raised funds by selling stocks and bonds (lines 31 and 32), borrowing reserves from other banks and selling securities under agreements to repurchase them at a future date (line 25), and borrowing from the Federal Reserve banks and foreign banking organizations (lines 28 and 30).

Balancing Out a Sources and Uses of Funds Statement.   As we have seen, sources and uses of funds statements in the Flow of Funds Accounts are derived from the aggregated balance sheets of each sector

---

[14] All changes on a sources and uses of funds statement are shown *net* of purchases and sales. When purchases of an asset exceed sales of that asset, the resulting figure is reported as a *positive* increase in the asset. When sales exceed purchases, an asset item will carry a *negative* sign. A nonnegative liability item on the sources and uses statement indicates that net borrowing (i.e., total borrowings minus debt repayments) has occurred during the period under study. If a liability item is negative, debt repayments exceed new borrowings during the period covered by the statement.

of the economy. Because balance sheets must always balance out, with total assets equal to total liabilities plus net worth, we would also expect a sources and uses of funds statement to balance out (except, of course, for discrepancies due to gaps or inaccuracies in the underlying data). In a sources and uses statement,

$$
\begin{matrix}
\text{Net investment} & & \text{Net acquisitions} & & \text{Net increase in} \\
\text{in plant} & + & \text{of financial} & = & \text{liabilities} + \text{Change} \\
\text{and equipment} & & \text{assets} & & \text{in current surplus account}
\end{matrix} \quad \text{(3–1)}
$$

Net acquisitions of financial assets are frequently referred to as financial investment, while net pruchases of plant and equipment may be labeled real investment. Both are *uses of funds* for a sector or economic unit. Net increases in liabilities represent "borrowing" in the current period. And changes in the current surplus account reflect current saving. Both of these latter items are *sources of funds*. Therefore, the relationship shown above may be written simply as:

$$
\begin{aligned}
\text{Net real investment} + \text{Net financial investment} \\
= \text{Net borrowing} + \text{Net current saving}
\end{aligned} \quad \text{(3–2)}
$$

or,

$$
\text{Total uses of funds} = \text{Total sources of funds} \quad \text{(3–3)}
$$

For each unit—business, household, or government—and for each sector of the economy, the above statements must hold true. For example, in the commercial banking sector during 1984 we have, as shown in Exhibit 3–9:

Uses of Funds ($ billions)		Sources of Funds ($ billions)	
Net investment in plant and equipment (line 2)	$ 14.7	Net borrowing (line 18)	$163.3
Net financial investment (line 3)	167.8	Net current saving (line 1)	12.8
		Statistical discrepancy (line 35)	6.4
Total uses	$182.5	Total sources	$182.5

Once the statistical discrepancy is taken into account, total uses and sources of funds should be equal for this and for all other sectors in the economy.

EXHIBIT 3-9

Sources and Uses of Funds Statement for the U.S. Banking Sector, 1980–1984 ($ billions)

U.S. Chartered Commercial Banks

| | Seasonally Adjusted Annual Rates | | | | | 1983 | | 1984 | | | |
	1980	1981	1982	1983	1984	III	IV	I	II	III	IV
1 Current surplus	7.6	8.9	10.0	14.3	12.8	14.4	15.2	14.2	14.3	12.0	10.8
2 Plant and equipment	9.8	10.7	12.4	14.9	14.7	15.8	15.2	14.6	15.2	15.2	14.0
3 Net acquisition of financial assets	84.2	106.3	112.1	133.7	167.8	120.9	167.2	203.3	163.9	160.5	143.4
4 Total bank credit	84.2	100.3	106.7	136.6	174.3	122.5	175.7	212.5	160.6	156.4	167.7
5 U.S. government securities	25.0	11.4	26.7	44.2	3.5	36.3	10.5	16.0	−24.9	16.3	6.5
6 Treasury issues	15.3	1.8	19.4	43.5	4.1	38.4	16.5	22.4	−26.0	14.4	5.5
7 Agency issues	9.7	9.6	7.3	.7	−.6	−2.1	−6.0	−6.4	1.2	1.9	1.1
8 Tax-exempt obligations	13.2	5.7	4.6	3.8	9.5	6.8	11.5	7.4	1.7	22.0	6.9
9 Corporate bonds	.5	*	1.7	3.6	3.2	2.1	1.5	8.0	−.2	3.3	1.8
10 Total loans	45.6	83.2	73.7	85.0	158.1	77.2	152.2	181.2	184.0	114.9	152.4
11 Mortgages	17.7	21.4	14.5	28.6	46.2	35.4	34.2	55.8	51.2	42.9	35.0
12 Consumer credit	−6.2	4.0	6.7	22.7	46.0	27.7	45.3	45.7	65.0	35.7	37.4
13 Bank loans NEC	31.9	53.4	51.0	33.2	58.9	21.4	67.2	73.3	70.5	23.5	68.1
14 Open-market paper	1.0	−.2	1.0	−1.5	1.3	−.9	2.5	−5.8	7.5	5.5	−1.8
15 Security credit	1.2	4.7	.5	2.0	5.7	−6.3	3.0	12.1	−10.1	7.3	13.7
16 Vault cash and member bank reserves	−1.0	−3.4	2.2	−3.6	−2.0	−1.8	2.2	−3.7	4.2	12.8	−21.2

17 Miscellaneous assets	.9	9.4	3.2	.7	−4.5	.2	−10.7	−5.6	−.9	−8.6	−3.0
18 Net increase in liabilities	76.7	100.1	107.5	125.9	163.3	113.5	155.7	199.7	160.6	151.6	141.3
19 Checkable deposits	10.7	14.8	20.9	15.6	23.4	−28.4	−18.6	66.8	13.6	−10.8	23.9
20 U.S. government	−2.6	−1.1	6.1	−5.3	3.8	−21.7	−19.8	14.0	−12.1	23.3	−9.8
21 Foreign	−.2	−3.0	−2.2	1.4	2.0	.3	.8	−.5	−1.3	3.0	6.8
22 Private domestic	13.4	18.9	17.1	19.5	17.5	−6.9	.3	53.3	27.1	−37.0	26.8
23 Small time and savings deposits	44.8	40.3	97.0	130.0	70.7	100.9	80.7	−4.6	110.4	92.3	84.6
24 Large time deposits	39.3	43.9	2.3	−38.7	35.9	−9.2	12.5	71.3	44.7	22.1	5.6
25 Fed funds and security RPs	17.8	13.1	10.7	10.2	9.2	29.0	6.6	27.4	−30.4	5.4	34.5
26 Net interbank liabilities	−36.7	−18.8	−27.6	7.6	17.1	25.5	78.8	37.5	15.0	34.0	−18.0
27 Federal Reserve float	−2.3	−2.7	1.0	−1.2	−.7	.7	−.8	.5	−7.8	9.1	−4.6
28 Borrowing at Federal Reserve banks	.4	−.2	−.9	.2	2.7	−6.1	−.4	−5.2	15.4	9.9	−9.5
29 To domestic banks	−12.4	−9.7	−9.5	−1.0	8.1	−2.1	24.0	25.2	−1.6	1.5	7.3
30 To foreign banks	−22.3	−6.2	−18.2	9.6	7.1	33.0	56.0	17.0	9.0	13.4	−11.2
31 Corporate equities	.4	.5	.6	.7	.8	.7	.8	.8	.8	.8	.9
32 Corporate bonds	.2	−.1	.6	−.2	1.9	.1	−1.2	−.8	8.9	−2.9	2.4
33 Profit taxes payable	−.5	−.4	−.1	−.1	*	−.1	*	*	*	*	*
34 Miscellaneous liabilities	.8	6.7	3.1	.9	4.2	−5.0	−3.7	1.4	−2.4	10.5	7.4
35 Discrepancy	−9.7	−7.9	−7.0	−8.4	−6.4	−8.9	−11.4	−4.0	−4.2	−12.1	−5.3
36 Memo: Credit market funds advanced	83.1	95.6	106.2	134.6	168.6	128.8	172.7	200.5	170.7	149.1	154.0

SOURCE: Board of Governors of the Federal Reserve System, *Flow of Funds Accounts*, fourth quarter 1984.

Constructing a Flow of Funds Matrix for the Economy as a Whole. The final step in the construction of the Federal Reserve's Flow of Funds Accounts is to combine the sources and uses of funds statement for each sector into a Flow of Funds Matrix for the whole economy. An example of such a matrix for the U.S. economy in recent years is shown in Exhibit 3–10, which shows borrowings by each major sector of the economy and total borrowings by all sectors combined, and Exhibit 3–11, which shows funds loaned by each major sector to domestic nonfinancial borrowers and total credit extended by all sectors. The majority of funds sought by businesses, consumers, and governments in the nation's financial markets clearly were raised by issuing debt instruments, as shown in Exhibit 3–10. The sum total of all debt instruments outstanding rose a net $843.5 billion (line 50) in 1984. The U.S. Treasury and various federal agencies were among the heaviest borrowers of funds, issuing about $273 billion in debt instruments (line 51). Next in line for the most borrowed funds were issuers of residential and commercial mortgages who borrowed more than $201 billion in 1984 (line 54). State and local governments borrowed net $54.6 billion (line 52), while domestic corporations and foreign borrowers issued $49.4 billion net in bonds during 1984 (line 53). Installment credit extended to consumers totaled just over $100 billion (line 55).

Exhibit 3–11 looks at borrowing in the economy from the lenders' point of view—for whatever is borrowed by one sector must be credit extended by other sectors. For example, line 1 in Exhibit 3–11 shows that total funds advanced in U.S. credit markets in the form of loans to domestic nonfinancial sectors amounted to $715.3 billion in 1984. This amount exactly matches the total net borrowing by domestic nonfinancial sectors shown in line 1 of Exhibit 3–10. Similarly, Exhibit 3–10 shows that corporations retired a net $29.8 billion in outstanding stock (corporate equity shares) in 1984 (line 59), which corresponds exactly to the decline in total funds advanced through stock sales in the U.S. economy during 1984 as shown in Exhibit 3–11 (line 51). The Flow of Funds Matrix reminds us that, for all sectors of the economy combined into one, the amount of saving must equal the total amount of real investment in the economy and the amount of borrowing in total must equal total financial investment (i.e., the total amount of financial assets acquired by all sectors).

Limitations and Uses of the Flow of Funds Accounts. It should be clear by now that the Flow of Funds Accounts provide a vast amount of information on current and past trends in the financial system. They are an indispensable aid in tracing the flow of savings and other funds through the nation's money and capital markets. Moreover, as we will see later in Chapter 11, estimates of flow of funds data can be used

EXHIBIT 3–10

Funds Raised in U.S. Credit Markets ($ billions; half-yearly data are at seasonally adjusted annual rates)

Transaction category, sector	1979	1980	1981	1982	1983	1984	1982 H1	1982 H2	1983 H1	1983 H2	1984 H1	1984 H2
							Nonfinancial sectors					
1 Total net borrowing by domestic nonfinancial sectors	386.0	344.6	380.4	404.1	526.4	715.3	358.1	450.1	448.9	563.8	697.9	732.6
By sector and instrument												
2 U.S. government..........................	37.4	79.2	87.4	161.3	186.6	198.8	104.1	218.4	222.0	151.1	177.4	220.2
3 Treasury securities.....................	38.8	79.8	87.8	162.1	186.7	199.0	105.5	218.8	222.1	151.2	177.6	220.3
4 Agency issues and mortgages..............	-1.4	-.6	-.5	-.9	-.1	-.2	-1.4	-.4	-.1	-.1	-.2	-.1
5 Private domestic nonfinancial sectors........	348.6	265.4	293.1	242.8	339.8	516.5	254.0	231.7	266.9	412.7	520.5	512.4
6 Debt capital instruments	211.2	192.0	159.1	158.9	239.3	288.4	140.7	177.2	214.4	264.2	280.4	296.4
7 Tax-exempt obligations...............	30.3	30.3	22.7	53.8	56.3	54.6	43.9	63.7	62.8	49.7	37.9	71.3
8 Corporate bonds....................	17.3	26.7	21.8	18.7	15.7	32.2	12.0	25.3	23.0	8.4	24.1	40.3
9 Mortgages........................	163.6	135.1	114.6	86.5	167.3	201.5	84.8	88.2	128.6	206.0	218.3	184.8
10 Home mortgages.................	120.0	96.7	76.0	52.5	108.7	128.9	53.6	51.3	83.8	133.6	140.9	116.9
11 Multifamily residential............	7.8	8.8	4.3	5.5	8.4	13.8	5.1	5.8	2.8	13.9	17.1	10.4
12 Commercial....................	23.9	20.2	24.6	23.6	47.3	57.3	19.7	27.5	40.3	54.3	58.5	56.1
13 Farm........................	11.8	9.3	9.7	5.0	2.9	1.6	6.5	3.5	1.6	4.1	1.8	1.3
14 Other debt instruments	137.5	73.4	134.0	83.9	100.5	228.1	113.2	54.6	52.5	148.5	240.2	216.1
15 Consumer credit..................	45.4	6.3	26.7	21.0	51.3	100.6	20.6	21.4	35.9	66.6	103.0	98.2
16 Bank loans n.e.c.................	51.2	36.7	54.7	55.5	27.3	71.5	69.0	42.0	13.3	41.2	83.2	59.7
17 Open market paper...............	11.1	5.7	19.2	-4.1	-1.2	23.8	10.0	-18.2	-10.6	8.3	31.5	16.0
18 Other.........................	29.7	24.8	33.4	11.5	23.1	32.3	13.6	9.4	13.9	32.3	22.4	42.1
19 By borrowing sector.................	348.6	265.4	293.1	242.8	339.8	516.5	254.0	231.7	266.9	412.7	520.5	512.4
20 State and local governments............	17.6	17.2	6.2	31.3	36.7	33.0	24.1	38.5	41.9	31.6	18.9	47.0
21 Households.....................	179.3	122.1	127.5	94.5	175.4	241.6	94.7	94.3	134.8	216.0	236.6	246.6
22 Farm.........................	21.4	14.4	16.3	7.6	4.3	-2.2	9.6	5.6	.8	7.9	.6	1.8
23 Nonfarm noncorporate.............	34.4	33.7	40.2	39.5	63.9	76.3	36.6	42.3	50.1	77.6	86.1	66.5
24 Corporate......................	96.0	78.1	102.9	70.0	59.5	163.5	89.0	51.0	39.3	79.6	178.3	148.6
25 Foreign net borrowing in United States........	20.2	27.2	27.2	15.7	18.9	1.7	10.2	21.2	15.3	22.5	17.9	-15.7
26 Bonds...........................	3.9	.8	5.4	6.7	3.8	2.7	2.4	11.0	4.6	2.9	1.1	4.4
27 Bank loans n.e.c....................	2.3	11.5	3.7	-6.2	4.9	-6.2	-7.6	-4.7	11.3	-1.5	-6.0	-6.3
28 Open market paper.................	11.2	10.1	13.9	10.7	6.0	.4	12.5	9.0	-4.6	16.5	18.9	-18.1
29 U.S. government loans	2.9	4.7	4.2	4.5	4.3	4.8	3.0	6.0	3.9	4.6	5.3	4.4
30 Total domestic plus foreign	406.2	371.8	407.6	419.8	545.3	717.0	368.3	471.4	504.2	586.3	717.1	717.0
							Financial sectors					
31 Total net borrowing by financial sectors	82.4	62.9	84.1	69.0	90.7	126.5	84.2	53.8	74.0	107.3	121.0	131.9
By instrument												
32 U.S. government related....................	47.9	44.8	47.4	64.9	67.8	74.2	60.0	69.7	66.2	69.4	69.1	79.2
33 Sponsored credit agency securities	24.3	24.4	30.5	14.9	1.4	30.0	22.4	7.5	-4.1	6.9	30.8	29.2
34 Mortgage pool securities	23.1	19.2	15.0	49.5	66.4	44.2	36.8	62.2	70.3	62.5	38.3	50.0
35 Loans from U.S. government...............	.6	1.2	1.9	.4	.4		.8					
36 Private financial sectors....................	34.5	18.1	36.7	4.1	22.9	52.3	24.2	-16.0	7.8	38.0	51.9	52.7
37 Corporate bonds	7.8	7.1	-.8	2.5	17.1	14.5	-2.5	7.6	15.2	18.9	14.9	14.1
38 Mortgages.......................	*	-.1	-.5	.1	*		.1					
39 Bank loans n.e.c...................	-.5	-.9	.9	1.9	-.2	.9	3.2	.6	-2.5	2.2	.1	1.7
40 Open market paper.................	18.0	4.8	20.9	-1.2	13.0	21.2	12.3	-14.7	7.2	18.8	21.2	21.1
41 Loans from Federal Home Loan Banks..........	9.2	7.1	16.2	.8	-7.0	15.7	11.1	-9.5	-12.1	-2.0	15.7	15.7
By sector												
42 Sponsored credit agencies	24.8	25.6	32.4	15.3	1.4	30.0	23.2	7.5	-4.1	6.9	30.8	29.2
43 Mortgage pools....................	23.1	19.2	15.0	49.5	66.4	44.2	36.8	62.2	70.3	62.5	38.3	50.0
44 Private financial sectors..............	34.5	18.1	36.7	4.1	22.9	52.3	24.2	-16.0	7.8	38.0	51.9	52.7
45 Commercial banks	1.6	.5	.4	1.2	.5	2.7	.7	1.7	.8	.2	4.8	.6
46 Bank affiliates	6.5	6.9	8.3	1.9	8.6	10.8	9.7	-5.8	-6.1	11.1	20.0	1.5
47 Savings and loan associations.........	12.6	7.4	15.5	2.5	-2.7	20.1	14.3	-9.3	-10.0	.4.5	18.2	21.9
48 Finance companies	16.5	5.8	12.8	-.9	17.0	19.5	*	-1.9	11.4	22.7	9.6	29.4
49 REITs	-1.3	-2.2	-.2	.1	.2	.1	.1	.1	.2	.2	.1	.1
							All sectors					
50 Total net borrowing.................	488.7	434.7	491.8	488.8	635.9	843.5	452.5	525.1	578.2	693.6	838.1	848.9
51 U.S. government securities............	84.8	122.9	133.0	225.9	254.4	273.1	163.5	288.3	288.4	220.5	246.7	299.5
52 State and local obligations...........	30.3	30.3	22.7	53.8	56.3	54.6	43.9	63.7	62.8	49.7	37.9	71.3
53 Corporate and foreign bonds	29.0	34.6	26.4	27.8	36.5	49.4	11.8	43.8	42.8	30.3	40.1	58.8
54 Mortgages.......................	163.5	134.9	113.9	86.5	167.2	201.5	84.8	88.2	128.5	206.0	218.2	184.7
55 Consumer credit..................	45.4	6.3	26.7	21.0	51.3	100.6	20.6	21.4	35.9	66.6	103.0	98.2
56 Bank loans n.e.c..................	52.9	47.3	59.3	51.2	32.0	66.2	64.6	37.9	22.1	41.9	77.3	55.1
57 Open market paper................	40.3	20.6	54.0	5.4	17.8	45.3	34.8	-23.9	-8.0	43.6	71.5	19.0
58 Other loans......................	42.4	37.8	55.8	17.2	20.3	52.8	28.5	5.9	5.7	35.0	43.4	62.2
							External corporate equity funds raised in United States					
59 Total new share issues...............	-3.8	22.2	-4.1	35.3	67.8	-29.8	23.3	47.2	83.5	52.0	-43.3	-16.4
60 Mutual funds....................	.1	5.2	6.3	18.4	32.8	38.1	12.5	24.3	36.8	28.9	39.0	37.2
61 All other.......................	-3.9	17.1	-10.4	16.9	34.9	-67.9	10.9	22.9	46.8	23.1	-82.3	-53.6
62 Nonfinancial corporations	-7.8	12.9	-11.5	11.4	28.3	-72.1	7.0	15.8	38.2	18.4	-84.5	-59.6
63 Financial corporations	3.2	2.1	.8	4.0	2.7	3.0	3.9	4.1	2.8	2.5	2.9	3.2
64 Foreign shares purchased in United States	.8	2.1	.3	1.5	4.0	1.1	-.1	3.0	5.7	2.2	-.7	2.9

SOURCE: Board of Governors of the Federal Reserve System, *Federal Reserve Bulletin,* April 1985, Table 1.57, p. A-42.

EXHIBIT 3–11

Direct and Indirect Sources of Funds to Credit Markets ($ billions, except as noted: half-yearly data are at seasonally adjusted annual rates)

Transaction category, or sector	1979	1980	1981	1982	1983	1984	1982 H1	1982 H2	1983 H1	1983 H2	1984 H1	1984 H2
1 **Total funds advanced in credit markets to domestic nonfinancial sectors**	**386.0**	**344.6**	**380.4**	**404.1**	**526.4**	**715.3**	**358.1**	**450.1**	**488.9**	**563.8**	**697.9**	**732.6**
By public agencies and foreign												
2 Total net advances	75.2	97.0	97.7	109.1	117.1	142.6	100.8	117.3	119.7	114.6	123.7	161.5
3 U.S. government securities	-6.3	15.7	17.2	18.0	27.6	35.8	9.7	26.2	40.5	14.6	33.4	38.2
4 Residential mortgages	35.8	31.7	23.5	61.0	76.1	56.5	47.6	74.4	80.1	72.0	52.0	61.1
5 FHLB advances to savings and loans	9.2	7.1	16.2	.8	-7.0	15.7	11.1	-9.5	-12.1	-2.0	15.7	15.7
6 Other loans and securities	36.5	42.4	40.9	29.3	20.5	34.6	32.4	26.2	11.1	29.9	22.6	46.6
Total advanced, by sector												
7 U.S. government	19.0	23.7	24.1	16.0	9.7	16.7	14.8	17.1	9.1	10.3	6.1	27.2
8 Sponsored credit agencies	53.0	45.6	48.2	65.3	69.5	71.8	61.8	68.7	68.2	70.7	73.0	70.6
9 Monetary authorities	7.7	4.5	9.2	9.8	10.9	8.4	3.8	15.7	15.6	6.2	17.1	-.3
10 Foreign	-4.6	23.2	16.3	18.1	27.1	45.7	20.4	15.8	26.8	27.4	27.5	64.0
Agency and foreign borrowing not in line 1												
11 Sponsored credit agencies and mortgage pools	47.9	44.8	47.4	64.9	67.8	74.2	60.0	69.7	66.2	69.4	69.1	79.2
12 Foreign	20.2	27.2	27.2	15.7	18.9	1.7	10.2	21.2	15.3	22.5	19.2	-15.7
Private domestic funds advanced												
13 Total net advances	379.0	319.6	357.3	375.6	495.9	648.6	327.5	423.8	450.8	541.1	662.5	634.7
14 U.S. government securities	91.1	107.2	115.8	207.9	226.9	237.3	153.7	262.0	247.8	205.9	213.2	261.3
15 State and local obligations	30.3	30.3	22.7	53.8	56.3	54.6	25.2	63.7	62.8	49.7	37.9	71.3
16 Corporate and foreign bonds	18.5	19.3	18.8	14.8	14.6	17.4	-.1	29.6	22.9	6.3	18.0	16.9
17 Residential mortgages	91.9	73.7	56.7	-3.2	40.9	86.1	11.0	-17.4	6.4	75.5	105.9	66.2
18 Other mortgages and loans	156.3	96.2	159.5	103.2	150.2	268.9	130.2	76.3	98.7	201.7	303.2	234.7
19 Less: Federal Home Loan Bank advances	9.2	7.1	16.2	.8	-7.0	15.7	11.1	-9.5	-12.1	-2.0	15.7	15.7
Private financial intermediation												
20 Credit market funds advanced by private financial institutions	313.9	281.5	323.4	285.6	376.7	541.9	274.4	296.7	323.2	430.1	522.2	561.6
21 Commercial banking	123.1	100.6	102.3	107.2	136.1	176.1	99.9	114.5	121.6	150.6	192.8	159.4
22 Savings institutions	56.5	54.5	27.8	31.3	136.8	147.7	25.2	37.4	128.9	144.6	157.0	138.4
23 Insurance and pension funds	85.9	94.3	97.4	108.8	98.8	113.2	111.4	106.3	89.5	108.1	95.6	130.8
24 Other finance	48.5	32.1	96.0	38.3	5.0	104.9	37.9	38.6	-16.8	26.8	76.7	133.1
25 Sources of funds	313.9	281.5	323.4	285.6	376.7	541.9	274.4	296.7	323.2	430.1	522.2	561.6
26 Private domestic deposits and RPs	137.4	169.6	211.9	174.7	203.5	283.9	147.6	201.9	192.7	214.2	277.0	290.7
27 Credit market borrowing	34.5	18.1	36.7	4.1	22.9	52.3	24.2	-16.0	7.8	38.0	51.9	52.7
28 Other sources	142.0	93.9	74.8	106.7	150.4	205.8	102.6	110.8	122.8	177.9	193.2	218.3
29 Foreign funds	27.6	-21.7	-8.7	-26.7	22.1	20.8	-28.3	-25.1	-14.2	58.5	15.7	25.9
30 Treasury balances	.4	-2.6	-1.1	6.1	-5.3	3.8	-2.0	14.1	10.1	-20.8	.9	6.8
31 Insurance and pension reserves	72.8	83.9	90.4	104.6	99.2	108.2	111.4	97.8	90.0	108.4	107.6	108.9
32 Other, net	41.2	34.2	-5.9	22.8	34.4	72.9	21.5	24.1	36.8	31.9	69.0	76.8
Private domestic nonfinancial investors												
33 Direct lending in credit markets	99.6	56.1	70.6	94.2	142.1	159.0	77.3	111.0	135.3	148.9	192.3	125.7
34 U.S. government securities	52.5	24.6	29.3	37.4	88.7	114.0	35.3	39.5	95.9	81.4	139.4	88.6
35 State and local obligations	9.9	7.0	10.5	34.4	42.5	31.8	30.1	38.7	52.7	32.3	21.5	42.1
36 Corporate and foreign bonds	-1.4	-5.7	-8.1	-5.2	2.0	-6.2	-17.7	7.3	-1.7	5.7	7.8	-20.1
37 Open market paper	8.6	-3.1	2.7	-.1	3.9	1.0	3.5	-3.7	-8.1	15.9	3.0	-1.0
38 Other	30.0	33.3	36.3	27.8	5.0	18.4	26.2	29.3	-3.4	13.5	20.7	16.2
39 Deposits and currency	146.8	181.1	221.9	181.9	222.6	294.6	152.1	211.7	214.5	230.7	290.2	299.0
40 Currency	8.0	10.3	9.5	9.7	14.3	14.2	6.7	12.7	14.8	13.8	17.7	10.7
41 Checkable deposits	18.3	5.2	18.0	15.7	21.7	16.4	1.9	29.5	48.0	-4.7	36.6	-3.9
42 Small time and savings accounts	59.3	82.9	47.0	138.2	219.1	148.0	83.2	193.1	278.6	159.7	124.9	171.2
43 Money market fund shares	34.4	29.2	107.5	24.7	-44.1	47.2	39.4	10.0	-84.0	-4.2	30.2	64.2
44 Large time deposits	18.8	45.8	36.9	-7.7	-7.5	69.8	21.9	-37.3	-61.0	45.9	80.0	59.7
45 Security RPs	6.6	6.5	2.5	3.8	14.3	2.4	1.1	6.6	11.0	17.5	5.3	-.5
46 Deposits in foreign countries	1.5	1.1	.5	-2.5	4.8	-3.4	-2.2	-2.9	7.0	2.7	-4.5	-2.3
47 **Total of credit market instruments, deposits and currency**	**246.5**	**237.2**	**292.5**	**276.1**	**364.7**	**453.6**	**229.4**	**322.7**	**349.8**	**379.6**	**482.5**	**424.8**
48 Public holdings as percent of total	18.5	26.1	24.0	26.0	21.5	19.9	27.4	24.9	23.7	19.5	17.2	22.5
49 Private financial intermediation (in percent)	82.8	88.1	90.5	76.0	76.0	83.5	83.8	70.0	71.7	79.5	78.8	88.5
50 Total foreign funds	23.0	1.5	7.6	-8.6	49.2	66.5	-7.9	-9.3	12.6	85.9	43.1	89.9
Memo: Corporate equities not included above												
51 Total net issues	-3.8	22.2	-4.1	35.3	67.8	-29.8	23.3	47.2	83.5	52.0	-43.3	-16.4
52 Mutual fund shares	.1	5.2	6.3	18.4	32.8	38.1	12.5	24.3	36.8	28.9	39.0	37.2
53 Other equities	-3.9	17.1	-10.4	16.9	34.9	-67.9	10.9	22.9	46.8	23.1	-82.3	-53.6
54 Acquisitions by financial institutions	12.9	24.9	20.1	19.2	57.5	19.4	11.0	67.3	75.9	39.2	7.6	31.3
55 Other net purchases	-16.7	-2.7	-24.2	-3.9	10.2	-49.2	12.3	-20.1	7.6	12.8	-50.8	-47.6

NOTES BY LINE NUMBER.
1. Line 1 of table 1.58.
2. Sum of lines 3–6 or 7–10.
6. Includes farm and commercial mortgages.
11. Credit market funds raised by federally sponsored credit agencies, and net issues of federally related mortgage pool securities.
13. Line 1 less line 2 plus line 11 and 12. Also line 20 less line 27 plus line 33. Also sum of lines 28 and 47 less lines 40 and 46.
18. Includes farm and commercial mortgages.
26. Line 39 less lines 40 and 46.
27. Excludes equity issues and investment company shares. Includes line 19.
29. Foreign deposits at commercial banks, bank borrowings from foreign branches, and liabilities of foreign banking agencies to foreign affiliates.
30. Demand deposits at commercial banks.
31. Excludes net investment of these reserves in corporate equities.
32. Mainly retained earnings and net miscellaneous liabilities.
33. Line 12 less line 20 plus line 27.
34–38. Lines 14–18 less amounts acquired by private finance. Line 38 includes mortgages.
40. Mainly an offset to line 9.
47. Lines 33 plus 39, or line 13 less line 28 plus line 40 and 46.
48. Line 2/line 1.
49. Line 20/line 13.
50. Sum of lines 10 and 29.
51, 53. Includes issues by financial institutions.
NOTE. Full statements for sectors and transaction types in flows and in amounts outstanding may be obtained from Flow of Funds Section, Division of Research and Statistics, Board of Governors of the Federal Reserve System, Washington, D.C. 20551.

SOURCE: Board of Governors of the Federal Reserve System, *Federal Reserve Bulletin,* April 1985, Table 1.58, p. A-43.

to make forecasts of savings and investment, lending and borrowing, and interest-rate changes. However, these social accounts have a number of limitations which must be kept firmly in mind.

First, the Flow of Funds Accounts present no information on transactions among economic units within each sector. If a household sells stock to another household, this transaction will not be picked up in the accounts since both units are in the same sector. However, if a household sells stock to a business firm, this transaction will be captured by the flow of funds bookkeeping system. Moreover, the accounts show only *net* flows over the period under study, not changes or fluctuations which occur between beginning and ending points of the study period.

Finally, all flow of funds data are expressed in terms of current market values. Therefore, these accounts measure not only the flow of savings in the economy but also fluctuations in the prices of stocks, bonds, and other financial assets (i.e., capital gains and losses). This market-value bias distorts estimates of the amount of saving and investment activity occurring from quarter to quarter and from year to year.

Despite these limitations, however, the Flow of Funds Accounts are one of the most comprehensive sources of information available to students of the financial system. The Flow of Funds Accounts provide vital clues on the demand and supply forces which shape movements in interest rates and security prices. The Flow of Funds Accounts indicate which types of securities are growing or declining in volume and which sectors finance other sectors within the economic system. One of the principal uses of flow of funds data today is to forecast interest rates and build econometric models to simulate future conditions in the credit markets. Coupled with the National Income Accounts and other sources of information, flow of funds accounting provides us with the raw material out of which financial decisions can be made.

CONCLUSIONS

An unimpeded flow of relevant information is vital to the functioning of the financial system. If the scarce resource of credit is to be allocated efficiently and an ample flow of savings made available for investment, financial information must be easily and instantly accessible to market participants. There are really two types of markets within the financial system—an information market and a market for financial claims, evidencing loans and investments. The two markets must work together in coordinated fashion to accomplish the desired end result—a smooth flow of scarce loanable funds toward their most profitable and beneficial uses.

In this chapter we have examined the information market in some detail. Our principal focus has been upon five broad categories of financial information available today—debt security prices and yields, stock prices and dividend yields, the financial condition of security issuers, general conditions in the nation's economy and financial system, and social accounting data. The purpose of this chapter has been to give the student of the financial system a broad overview of the kinds and quality of information currently available. Knowing where to find relevant and up-to-date information is an essential ingredient in the process of solving economic and financial problems.

STUDY QUESTIONS

1. Why is the availability of financial information important to borrowers and lenders of funds? Government policymakers?

2. List several major sources of financial information, and discuss which types of information each contains.

3. If you needed to gather information for a possible stock or bond purchase, where would you look? What information is available on the financial condition of major U.S. companies.

4. What is social accounting? Compare and contrast the Flow of Funds Accounts with the National Income Accounts. What type of information does each provide that might be useful for financial decisions?

5. Explain how the Flow of Funds Accounts are constructed. What is a sources and uses of funds statement?

6. Discuss the principal limitations of flow of funds data and the implications of those limitations.

PROBLEMS

1. Construct sources and uses of funds statements for each sector of the economy and for the whole economy using the following information:

	Households ($ billion)	Business Firms ($ billion)	Banks and Other Financial Institutions ($ billion)	Governmental Units ($ billion)
Current saving	$428.8	$280.0	$35.0	−$35.0
Current real investment	332.5	350.0	17.5	—
Current financial investment	306.3	78.8	43.8	8.8
Current borrowing	210.0	148.8	26.3	43.8

Assume that the four sectors listed above are the only sectors in the economy and there are no international transactions. Referring back to the discussion in Chapter 2, which sectors are deficit-budget and which surplus-budget sectors?

2. Suppose you are given the data listed below for the household sector of the economy. From this information construct a statement of financial assets and liabilities for the household sector.ds,4

($ billion)		($ billion)	
Deposits in banks and savings institutions. . .	$540	U.S. government securities.	$110
Home mortgages	290	Credit extended by nonbank lending institutions . . .	40
Installment loans extended by banks	110	Trade credit	5
Holdings of currency and coin	120	Corporate and foreign bonds	30
Security credit owed . . .	10	Corporate equities	680
State and local government bonds	50	Life insurance reserves	130
Deferred and unpaid life insurance premiums . .	10	Pension fund reserves	420
Holdings of miscellaneous financial assets	50	Miscellaneous liabilities	35

3. Construct a sources and uses of funds statement for the commercial banking sector for the year immediately concluded. A check of the Federal Reserve's Flow of Funds Accounts indicates that U.S. banks reported a current earnings surplus of $12 billion and made investments in plant and equipment of $11 billion. They acquired net $120 billion in loans to their customers and purchased $3 billion in corporate bonds, $13 billion in state and local government bonds, and $25 billion in U.S. government securities. Miscellaneous assets rose $10 billion. There was a statistical discrepancy in the Flow of Funds Accounts of $8 billion in the banking sector's sources of funds.

SELECTED REFERENCES

Cohen, J. "Copeland's Moneyflows after Twenty-Five Years: A Survey." *Journal of Economic Literature,* March 1972, pp. 1–25.

Freund, William C., and Edward D. Zinbarg. "Applications of Flow of Funds to Interest-Rate Forecasting." *Journal of Finance,* May 1963, pp. 231–48.

Goldsmith, Raymond W. *Capital Market Analysis and the Financial Accounts of the Nation.* Morristown, N.J.: General Learning Press, 1982.

McNees, Stephen K., and John Ries. "The Track Record of Macroeconomic Forecasts." *New England Economic Review,* Federal Reserve Bank of Boston, November/December 1983, pp. 5–18.

National Bureau of Economic Research. *The Flow-of-Funds Approach to Social Accounting.* New York, 1962.

Ritter, Lawrence S. *The Flow of Funds Accounts: A Framework for Financial Analysis.* New York: Institute of Finance, New York University, 1968.

Part Two

Financial Institutions in the Financial System

4

Commercial Banks and Money Creation

PURPOSE OF THIS CHAPTER

To trace the important functions of commercial banks in the financial system in granting loans, purchasing securities, making payments, and holding the public's savings. The chapter examines recent changes in the structure of the banking industry and the key regulatory agencies that oversee bank operations. Bank financial statements are reviewed along with an analysis of how banks have the capacity to create and destroy money.

KEY TERMS AND CONCEPTS IN THE CHAPTER

ATMs
bank holding
  company
Bank Holding
  Company Act
banking structure
branch banking
commercial bank

Comptroller of the
  Currency
demand deposits
deregulation
DIDC
excess reserves
Federal Reserve
  System

FDIC
Glass-Steagall Act
legal reserves
national banks
primary reserves
secondary reserves
state-chartered banks
transaction accounts

The dominant privately owned financial institution in the United States and in the economies of most major industrialized countries is the *commercial bank*. This institution offers the public both deposit and credit services and is the major financial intermediary involved in making payments on behalf of the public for purchases of goods and services. The name *commercial* implies that banks devote a substantial portion of their resources to meeting the financial needs of business firms. In recent years, however, commercial banks have significantly expanded their offerings of financial services to consumers and units of government. The result is the emergence of a financial institution which has rightly been called a "financial department store" because it satisfies a broad spectrum of credit and deposit needs in the economy.

The dominant importance of commercial banks may be measured in a number of ways. Banks hold about two fifths of the total assets of all financial institutions headquartered in the United States. While this is significantly less than the 70 to 80 percent share of total assets held by commercial banks during the 19th century, it actually reflects a gradual rise in recent years as banks have become more innovative and more aggressive in pursuit of the customer's business. Commercial banks are still the principal means of making payments in the U.S. economy— through the checking accounts (demand deposits) they offer. And banks are important because of their ability to create money from excess reserves made available from the public's deposits. The commercial banking system can take a given volume of excess cash reserves and, through the making of loans and investments, generate a multiple amount of credit—a process explained later in this chapter.

Banks today are the principal channel for government monetary policy. In the United States, the Federal Reserve System carries out its policies to affect interest rates and the availability of credit mainly through altering the level and rate of growth or reserves held by banks and nonbank depository institutions. Today, U.S. commercial banks are the most important source of consumer credit and one of the major sources of loans to small- and medium-sized businesses. In most years, banks are the principal purchasers of debt securities issued by state and local governments and are one of the major buyers of new security issues by the U.S. Treasury. For all of these reasons commercial banks play a dominant role in the money and capital markets and are worthy of detailed study if we are to understand more fully how the financial system operates.

THE STRUCTURE OF U.S. COMMERCIAL BANKING

The structure of U.S. banking is unique in comparison with other banking systems around the globe. The term *structure* focuses on the number and different sizes of commercial banks operating in thousands of local communities across the nation. While the banking systems of most other nations consist of a few large banking organizations operating hundreds or thousands of branch offices, the U.S. banking system is dominated by thousands of relatively small commercial banks. For example, in 1985 there were about 15,000 commercial banking institutions headquartered in the United States, compared to only 11 domestically chartered banks in Canada and less than three dozen domestically owned banks in the United Kingdom.

Not surprisingly, most U.S. banks are modest in size compared to banks in other countries. Nearly two thirds of all American commercial banks have total assets of under $50 million each, while less than 2 percent hold assets of a billion dollars or more and actively compete in global markets for loans and deposits (see Exhibit 4–1). While smaller banks predominate in numbers, the larger banks have a disproportionate share of the industry's assets. For example, the roughly 2 percent of all U.S. banks with a billion or more dollars in total assets hold nearly two thirds of all assets in the industry. In contrast, the numerically dominant small banks with less than $50 million in assets hold less than 10 percent of the banking industry's total assets.

EXHIBIT 4–1

Number and Size of Insured U.S. Commercial Banks, December 31, 1983

Asset Size Group	Number of Banks	Percent of Total	Total Amount of Assets ($ millions)	Percent of Total*
Less than $25 million	5,814	40.2%	$ 82,181	3.5%
$25 to $50 million	3,744	25.9	133,964	5.7
$50 to $100 million	2,624	18.1	181,064	7.7
$100 to $500 million	1,833	12.7	346,590	14.8
$500 million to $1 billion	194	1.3	134,382	5.7
Over $1 billion	256	1.8	1,463,921	62.5
Totals	14,465	100.0%	$2,342,102	100.0%

* Columns may not add to totals due to rounding.
SOURCE: Federal Deposit Insurance Corporation, *Bank Operating Statistics,* 1983.

Most commercial banks in the United States are chartered by the states rather than by the federal government. As shown in Exhibit 4–2, of the almost 15,000 commercial banks in operation at year-end 1983, close to 10,000 were state chartered. The remaining one third, classified as national banks, were chartered by the federal government. National banks, on average, are much larger and include nearly all of the nation's

EXHIBIT 4–2

Number of Operating Commercial Banks and Branches in the United
States, December 31, 1983

Category	Number of Commercial Banks	Number of Branch Offices
Insured banks:		
National banks	4,751	21,329
State-chartered member banks	1,052	4,814
Members of the Federal Reserve System:		
Total	5,803	26,143
Nonmember state-chartered banks	8,666	14,714
Total	14,469	40,857
Noninsured banks	455	37
Total	14,924	40,894

SOURCE: Federal Deposit Insurance Corporation, *1983 Statistics on Banking,* Washington, D.C.

billion-dollar banking institutions. All national banks must be insured by
the Federal Deposit Insurance Corporation (FDIC) and be members of
the Federal Reserve System. State-chartered banks may elect to become
members of the Fed and also elect to have their deposits insured by
the FDIC if they are willing to conform to the regulations of these two
federal agencies. The vast majority of U.S. banks (about 97 percent) are
FDIC insured, but only a minority have elected to join the Federal Reserve System. Nevertheless, Fed member banks hold more than two thirds
of all bank deposits and assets in the United States. We will have more
to say about the roles of the Fed, the FDIC, and other bank regulatory
agencies at a later point in this chapter.

A Trend toward Consolidation

A number of interesting structural changes have affected the banking
industry in recent years. One of the most important is the drive toward
consolidation of industry assets and deposits into larger and larger organizations.

As we noted above, the United States is still essentially a nation of
small banks. But great pressures are operating to form larger banking
organizations in order to make more efficient use of resources. Research
studies by Bell and Murphy (1968), Benston (1965), Daniel, Longbrake,
and Murphy (1973), and others suggest that as banks grow, their costs
increase more slowly than output, resulting in cost savings. In general,
a 100 percent rise in deposit and loan accounts results in only about a
92 percent increase in the cost of bank operations. When automated

bookkeeping and computer processing of accounts are used, substantial economies of size characterize bank installment and real estate lending and the offering of checking accounts. Under pressure from a cost squeeze, declining profit margins, and increased competition from bank and nonbank financial institutions, many U.S. bankers view the strategy of growing into larger-sized banking organizations as an "escape" from these pressures.

We must hasten to add, however, that these scale economies resulting from growth appear to be modest—once a bank reaches perhaps $100 million or so in total assets its unit production costs appear to stop falling and level out. In fact, some analysts argue that production costs begin rising when banks approach the billion-dollar size because of the difficulty management has in controlling such a large and diverse organization and because of the tendency of larger banks to proliferate their service offerings. Others argue, however, that rising unit production costs are more than offset by the lower costs of raising capital and the stabilizing effects of diversification that large banks enjoy.

Branch Banking

The drive toward consolidation of banks into larger organizations is most evident in the shift toward branch banking. Until the 1940s and 1950s, the United States was basically a nation of unit banks, each housed in only a single office. For example, in 1900 there were 12,427 banks, but only 87 of these had any branches. By 1983, however, there were almost 15,000 commercial banks of which just slightly over 7,000 (47 percent) were branch-banking organizations. And the number of branch offices has increased dramatically in recent years. In 1950 there were approximately 4,700 branch-banking offices in operation; by 1983 the total reached almost 41,000 (see Exhibit 4–2).

The growth of branching has been aided by the liberalization of many state laws to permit greater use of branch offices as a means of growth. Prominent examples of states liberalizing their branch-banking laws in recent years include Florida, New Jersey, New York, and Virginia. Another factor is the massive shift of the U.S. population over the last three decades to suburban and rural areas. Many of the nation's largest banks have followed their customers to outlying markets through branching and merger in order to protect their sources of funds.

In the decade of the 1980s expansion of branch offices across state lines has become a key issue in American banking. Although the McFadden Act of 1927 and the Banking Act of 1933 (Glass-Steagall) prohibited full-service interstate branching, individual states could vote to allow out-of-state banking organizations to branch into their territory if they so chose. (See Exhibit 4–3.) Few states endorsed such "invasions" until the

EXHIBIT 4–3

Key Federal Laws Affecting the Structure of the U.S. Banking Industry

National Bank Act (1863–64)	Set up a procedure for federal chartering of new banks and their supervision and examination by the Office of the Comptroller of the Currency.
Federal Reserve Act (1913)	Created the Federal Reserve System as a central bank and guarantor of the banking system's liquidity.
McFadden Act (1927)	Vested the states with authority to determine the limits of branch banking within their borders and prohibited interstate branching unless the states involved specifically okayed outside entry.
Banking Act of 1933 (Glass-Steagall Act)	Created the FDIC, prohibited commercial banks from paying interest on demand deposits and from underwriting corporate securities, and strengthened prohibitions against interstate branching.
Bank Holding Company Act (1956)	Multibank holding companies controlling two or more banks were required to register with the Federal Reserve Board and be subject to its rules. Acquisitions of 5 percent or more of the stock of an out-of-state bank was prohibited (Douglas Amendment).
Bank Merger Act (1960)	Mergers involving federally supervised banks must have the approval of their principal federal regulatory agency.
Bank Merger Act and Bank Holding Company Act Amendments (1966)	Merger or holding-company acquisitions could be approved by federal banking agencies if their anticompetitive effects were outweighed by public convenience and needs.
Bank Holding Company Act Amendments (1970)	Holding companies controlling only one bank are subject to Federal Reserve regulation; nonbank business ventures acquired or started by holding companies are confined to fields closely related to commercial banking.
International Banking Act (1978)	Foreign banks operating in the United States were brought under federal regulation for the first time, restricting their interstate branching activities, requiring federal licensing of branch and agency offices, imposing deposit reserve requirements, and providing FDIC insurance for retail deposits.
Depository Institutions Deregulation and Monetary Control Act (1980)	Granted nonbank thrift institutions broader deposit and credit powers, began the phasing out of federal deposit rate ceilings and imposed uniform deposit reserve requirements on banks and nonbank thrifts.
Garn–St Germain Depository Institutions Act (1982)	Authorized banks and savings and loans to offer money market deposit accounts, granted savings and loans additional commercial and consumer lending powers, and provided for mergers or government-backed loans for troubled deposit-type financial institutions.

1980s when several, such as Florida, Kentucky, South Dakota, and the six New England states, approved entry by out-of-state banks provided their banks were extended the same privilege. This new trend toward "reciprocal branching" put great pressure on Congress to repeal or amend federal restrictions against interstate branching.

Further pressure for greater bank branching and service powers arose during the 1970s and 1980s with the expansion of financial conglomerates, such as Sears, Roebuck Co., Prudential-Bache, and Shearson-American Express, and so-called nonbank banks. The latter are limited-service depository institutions that manage to avoid regulations as commercial banks either by ceasing to make commercial loans or by refusing to accept checkable deposits—the two key services which, under federal law, constitute commercial banking. Many of the nonbank banks and financial conglomerates have elected to concentrate their service offerings in the consumer area, selling credit, insurance, real estate, security brokerage, and savings plans, either by mail or through conveniently located branch offices that are not restricted by antibranching laws. The rise of this form of "outside competition" for commercial banks has brought forth strong protests from inside the banking community and from some federal regulatory agencies who fear loss of control over the banking system and loss of public confidence in banking institutions due to increased failures and a blurring of the traditional distinctions between banking and commerce.

Bank Holding Companies

Paralleling the rapid growth of branch banking has been the growth of bank holding companies. The bank holding company is a relatively old organizational form in the industry, having its origins in the 19th century. A *bank holding company* is simply a corporation organized to acquire and hold the stock of one or more banks. The company may also hold stock in certain nonbank business ventures. Holding companies have become popular as vehicles to avoid laws prohibiting or restricting branch banking and as a way to offer services that commercial banks themselves cannot offer.

Fearing danger to the safety of banks, Congress first attempted to regulate the bank holding company movement during the 1930s but was largely unsuccessful. Then in 1956 the Bank Holding Company Act was passed. The new law required all holding companies controlling at least 25 percent of the stock of two or more banks to register with the Federal Reserve Board. In addition, a holding company seeking to acquire additional shares of a bank was required to obtain Fed approval.

The Bank Holding Company Act left an unregulated opening for holding companies which held stock in only one bank. As a result, many of the nation's largest commercial banks formed one-bank holding companies during the late 1960s and began to reach out and acquire nonbank businesses far removed from the business of banking, including steel mills and meat-packing plants. Congress closed this loophole with passage of the 1970 amendments to the Bank Holding Company Act. From this point on, all holding companies seeking to acquire even a single bank had to register with the Federal Reserve Board and gain Fed approval before purchasing or starting any new bank or nonbank business. Nonbank business ventures acquired must now be so "closely related" to banking as to be "a proper incident thereto."

What business activities are "closely related" to banks? To date, the Federal Reserve Board has approved for holding company acquisition businesses engaged in the making of loans (such as finance, mortgage, or credit card companies), the writing of full-payment leases for personal or real property (e.g., equipment-leasing companies), insuring the repayment of credit (such as firms selling credit life insurance), the recording and transfer of financial information (such as data processing firms), and the giving of financial advice (i.e., through a trust company, management consulting firm, or investment adviser)—to name the principal permissible nonbank activities.

Bank holding companies have grown rapidly in the United States. In 1960 there were just 47 registered bank holding company organizations controlling only about 8 percent of the total assets of U.S. insured commercial banks. By 1983, holding companies numbered more than 5,000 and held well over 87 percent of total insured bank assets, according to the Federal Reserve Board. Most of this dramatic growth was due to the requirement after 1970 that one-bank companies register with the Federal Reserve Board. The growth of nonbanking business activities of holding companies also has been extremely rapid. Insurance agencies, finance companies, mortgage companies, leasing firms, factoring companies, data processing facilities, consulting firms, and other financially related businesses have been started or acquired in substantial numbers by bank holding companies in recent years. These ventures represent an attempt to diversify banking operations geographically and by product line in order to reduce risk and gain access to a broader market, often outside a bank's home state. In fact, the offices of out-of-state nonbank business ventures operated by U.S. bank holding companies numbered more than 5,000 in 1984.

International Banking

The growth of larger U.S. banking organizations at home has been paralleled by substantial growth of American banks abroad. This expansion overseas has not been confined to the largest institutions in such established money centers as New York, Chicago, Los Angeles, and San

Francisco, but today includes leading banks in regional financial centers, such as Atlanta, Dallas, Houston, and Miami. Several of the nation's largest banks receive half or more of their net income from foreign sources.

These big U.S. banks have penetrated overseas markets for a wide variety of reasons. In many cases their corporate customers expanding abroad have needed multinational banking facilities. The huge Eurodollar market which spans the globe offers an attractive source of bank funds when domestic sources of funds are less available or more costly. In most instances, foreign markets have also offered fewer regulatory barriers and less banking competition than are found in the United States. On the other side of the coin, foreign banks have grown rapidly in the United States, with many of the largest European, Middle Eastern, and Asian banks viewing the 50 states as a huge, economically and politically stable common market. Congress responded to this "invasion" by foreign banks by passing the International Banking Act of 1978, bringing foreign banks under federal regulation for the first time.[1]

Bank Failures

One undesirable side effect of all these recent changes in the banking community is an apparent rise in the bank failure rate. For most of its history, the banking industry has experienced an extremely low failure rate due to extensive government regulations, and conservative management practices. Studies show that the long-term failure rate in U.S. banking is between 1 and 2 percent of the total banking population, compared to about 10 times that figure for private industry as a whole. However, the number of commercial bank failures and the average size of failing banks have advanced sharply in recent years. For example, a postwar record for the number of bank failures in a single year was set in 1983, when 48 insured U.S. banks closed their doors. However, this record was beaten in 1984 when nearly 80 collapsed. Moreover, bank failures occurring in the 1970s and 1980s included the largest in U.S. history. Among the most notable were Franklin National Bank of New York in 1974 and Penn Square Bank in Oklahoma City in 1982, both billion-dollar institutions. In addition, several major money-center banks recently got into deep financial trouble and had to be merged with a healthy institution or backstopped by federal loans and guarantees. Most notable in this case was Continental Illinois Bank of Chicago which in 1984 was propped up by approximately $4.5 billion in federal insurance funds.

The reasons behind this apparent acceleration in bank failures are numerous. Many bankers today are willing to accept greater risk in their

---

[1] The provisions of the International Banking Act and the recent growth of international banking are discussed more fully in Chapter 29.

operations, in part because of intensified competition from other banks, thrift institutions, and nonbank financial conglomerates and because of government insurance of bank deposits. More leniency in the interpretation and enforcement of banking regulations, such as standards for the maintenance of equity capital, has also been a factor in the overall trend of increased bank failures. The movement toward banking *deregulation* in the 1980s gave banks greater opportunities to market new services and expand geographically without such strict controls, but also increased their opportunities for failure. Some analysts argue that even more important is the increased volatility of *economic* and *financial conditions,* especially interest rates and the prices of foreign currencies. Related to the economic factors are the many loans to energy companies, farm operators, and cash-strapped developing nations which have become delinquent in the wake of falling energy and commodity prices. A growing fear of many bankers as failure rates increased was that the hard-won progress toward deregulation might be overturned by public and congressional concern over the safety of the nation's banking system.

Changing Technology

Banking today is passing through a technological revolution. Computer terminals and high-speed information processing are transforming the industry, stressing convenience and speed in handling such routine banking transactions as making deposits, withdrawing cash, repaying loans, and cashing checks. Most of the new technology is designed to reduce labor and paper costs, making the industry less labor intensive and more capital intensive.

Among the most important pieces of technology in the industry are automated teller machines (ATMs). ATMs accept deposits, dispense cash and information, and accept payments. For many banking transactions they perform just as human tellers do, with the added advantage of 24-hour availability. Initially most ATMs were placed on bank premises, but their future growth probably will be centered in retail stores, shopping centers, airports, and train terminals. In these locations they are known as remote service units (RSUs) and serve to lower transactions costs for the customer and to reduce the need for conventional branch offices.

Related to ATMs are point-of-sale terminals (POS) located in retail stores and other commercial establishments. Connected on-line to the bank's computer, POS terminals accept plastic credit and debit cards, permitting the customer to pay instantly for a purchase without the necessity of cashing a check. For those customers who do want to cash checks, a store can use the POS terminal to verify that a check is good. Customers have not accepted POS terminals as enthusiastically as they have ATMs. Part of the problem is the customer's loss of checkbook float when payments are made instantly. Further, POS terminals have faced serious legal challenges on grounds that they violate antibranching laws in several states.

Another important new piece of machinery in the industry is the automated clearinghouse (ACH). An ACH transfers information from one financial institution to another and from account to account via computer tape. More than 10,000 banks and other institutions are members of nearly three dozen ACHs that serve the nation. They are used principally for handling payrolls, dispensing welfare payments, and processing federal government transactions. In the near future, check truncation systems will be used extensively alongside the ACH. Such a system transmits images of checks electronically from one financial institution to another, eliminating the need to transfer paper.

On the near horizon is in-home banking via TV screen and telephone, probably coupled with retail shopping information and other convenience services. Using a special keyboard the customer can punch in a request for information or conduct transactions over the telephone. Even arrangements for a loan could be made by telephone and remote video screen. Such systems, in effect, make every customer a branch, provide greater convenience, and cut down on paper flow. Telephone bill-paying services are also expected to proliferate in great numbers in the years to come.

These recent technological changes have profound implications for bank costs, employment, and profitability. In the future, customers will have less need to enter a bank building, and the need for brick-and-mortar branches will decline. Indeed, hundreds of branch offices have recently been closed in a move toward greater economy and efficiency. Higher energy costs suggest that future banking needs will be met mainly by transferring information rather than by requiring people to move from one location to another. The banker's principal function will be one of providing the necessary equipment and letting customers conduct their own financial transactions. This development implies fewer, but more highly skilled bank employees and more equipment per dollar of deposits. A heavy investment of bank funds in computers and money machines will result in substantial fixed costs, requiring a large volume of transactions and favoring the largest banking organizations in the nation. The new technology of banking should further intensify pressures for consolidation of the industry into banks smaller in number but much larger in average size.

THE REGULATORY FRAMEWORK FOR BANKS

Commercial banks, due to their dominant importance in the financial system, are closely regulated. Moreover, in the United States banking is more heavily regulated than is true in most other industrialized countries. From this nation's earliest history there has been a fear of concentrated power in banking, because bank credit is so vital to the economic well-being of businesses and households. During colonial times several banks were burned to the ground because of public mistrust and misunderstanding of their basic function in the economy. During the 19th century and again early in this century severe restrictions were placed on the growth of banks through branching and holding companies.

Another significant restriction on banking's growth and development occurred in 1933 when Congress passed the Glass-Steagall Act, forbidding commercial banks from acquiring or underwriting corporate stock. This step effectively prevented banks from gaining control of nonfinancial corporations through purchases of stock. When banks skirted around this prohibition in the late 1960s through the formation of holding companies, Congress again applied the brakes by passing the 1970 amendments to the Bank Holding Company Act. However, as the 1980s began a significant *deregulation* trend set in, marked by the passage of two landmark pieces of legislation—the Depository Institutions Deregulation and Monetary Control Act of 1980 (DIDMCA) and the Garn-St Germain Depository Institutions Act of 1982 (Garn bill). As we shall see in this and the following chapter these new laws granted major new asset and deposit powers to commercial banks and to their principal competitors—savings banks, savings and loans, and credit unions. The net result was to place banks and nonbank thrift institutions on more equal footing, leveling the competitive playing field for all depository institutions.

Responsibility for regulating U.S. banks is divided among three federal banking agencies and the state banking commissions of each of the 50 states. These regulatory agencies have overlapping responsibilities, so that most banks are subject to multiple jurisdictions. This division of authority and responsibility has stimulated a number of reform proposals in recent years to consolidate the regulatory process and make it more efficient. The regulatory agencies responsible for enforcing banking's ground rules include the Federal Reserve System, the Comptroller of the Currency, and the Federal Deposit Insurance Corporation—all at the federal level—and the state banking commissions of the 50 states. Figure 4–1 provides a brief summary of the principal regulatory powers exercised by these federal and state agencies.

The Federal Reserve System

The Federal Reserve System is responsible for examining and supervising the activities of all its member banks. When a member bank wishes to merge with another bank or establish a branch office, it must notify the Fed. The Fed must review and approve the formation of all bank

FIGURE 4–1

Principal Bank Regulatory Agencies

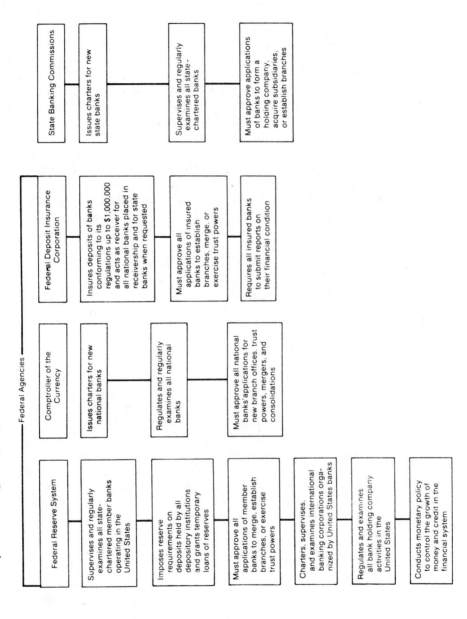

Federal Agencies			State Banking Commissions
Federal Reserve System	**Comptroller of the Currency**	**Federal Deposit Insurance Corporation**	Issues charters for new state banks
Supervises and regularly examines all state-chartered member banks operating in the United States	Issues charters for new national banks	Insures deposits of banks conforming to its regulations up to $1,000,000 and acts as receiver for all national banks placed in receivership and for state banks when requested	Supervises and regularly examines all state-chartered banks
Imposes reserve requirements on deposits held by all depository institutions and grants temporary loans of reserves	Regulates and regularly examines all national banks	Must approve all applications of insured banks to establish branches, merge, or exercise trust powers	Must approve applications of banks to form a holding company, acquire subsidiaries, or establish branches
Must approve all applications of member banks to merge, establish branches, or exercise trust powers	Must approve all national banks' applications for new branch offices, trust powers, mergers, and consolidations	Requires all insured banks to submit reports on their financial condition	
Charters, supervises, and examines international banking corporations organized by United States banks			
Regulates and examines all bank holding company activities in the United States			
Conducts monetary policy to control the growth of money and credit in the financial system			

holding companies active in the United States and approve the acquisition of nonbank businesses by holding companies. The Federal Reserve is responsible for certain U.S.-based international banking corporations (known as Edge Act subsidiaries) and for supervising member bank operations in foreign countries. It is responsible for regulating credit extended by banks and by security brokers and dealers for the purchasing or carrying of corporate stocks or convertible securities.

The Fed sets reserve requirements on both transactions deposits (such as checking accounts and NOW accounts) and time and savings deposits for all depository institutions. Moreover, the chairman of the Federal Reserve Board is a voting member of the Depository Institutions Deregulation Committee (DIDC), a regulatory body set up with passage of the DIDMCA of 1980. The DIDC is charged with responsibility for phasing out federal interest-rate ceilings on deposits offered by commercial banks and nonbank thrift institutions by 1986, allowing these institutions to offer competitive market interest rates on any deposit plans offered the public. This committee consists of the chairman of the Federal Reserve Board, the Secretary of the Treasury, the chairman of the Federal Deposit Insurance Corporation, the Comptroller of the Currency (a nonvoting member), the chairman of the Federal Home Loan Bank Board, and the chairman of the National Credit Union Administration.

The Comptroller of the Currency

The Comptroller of the Currency—also known as the Administrator of National Banks—is a division of the U.S. Treasury, established under the National Banking Act of 1863. The Comptroller has the power to issue federal charters for the creation of new *national banks.* These banks, once chartered, are subject to an impressive array of regulations, most of which pertain to the kinds of loans and investments that may be made and the amount and types of capital which each bank must hold. All national banks are examined at least once each year by the Comptroller's staff and may be liquidated, merged, or consolidated with another financial institution if deemed to be in the public interest.

Federal Deposit Insurance Corporation

The Federal Deposit Insurance Corporation insures deposits of U.S. commercial banks which meet its regulations; the coverage provides up to $100,000 per depositor. Roughly 98 percent of all U.S. banks are insured, and approximately 60 percent of all commercial bank deposits are covered by the FDIC's insurance program. Each participating bank is assessed annually a fraction of its eligible deposits to build and maintain a national insurance fund.

One of the most important functions of the FDIC is to act as a check on the state banking commissions, because few banks today—even those with state charters—will open their doors without FDIC insurance. The FDIC reviews the adequacy of capital, earnings prospects, the character of management, and the public convenience and needs aspects of each application before granting deposit insurance. This agency is also charged with examining insured banks that are not members of the Federal Reserve System. The FDIC acts as receiver for all national banks placed in receivership and as receiver for state banks when requested by a state banking commission. In most cases an insolvent bank will be merged with or absorbed by a healthy one. The FDIC often purchases some of the bankrupt institution's weaker assets to support such a merger.

State Banking Commissions

The regulatory powers of the federal banking agencies overlap with those of the state banking agencies which regularly examine all state-chartered banks. The states also have rules prescribing the minimum amount of equity capital for individual *state-chartered banks* and issue charters for new banks. One of the areas in which state banking law currently is supreme is that concerning branch banking. Since the McFadden Act of 1927, the federal government has allowed the states to determine whether commercial banks operating within their borders will be permitted to establish any branch offices and, if so, under what circumstances. In 1982, nine states prohibited multiple full-service branch offices. These so-called unit-banking states are situated mainly in the Midwest and South and include Texas, Kansas, Missouri, Nebraska, Oklahoma, and Colorado. However, as we saw earlier, there is a definite trend toward greater use of branching and holding company activity in most parts of the United States. Recent examples include Florida, which until 1978 was a unit-banking state and now permits statewide branching. The state of New York converted to statewide branching in 1976, following an experiment with limited branching in designated regions. Most experts predict that in future years interstate branching in one form or another will spread across the United States as the need for larger banking organizations and new financial services increases.

PORTFOLIO CHARACTERISTICS OF COMMERCIAL BANKS

Commercial banks are the "financial department stores" of the nation's financial system. They offer a wider array of financial services than any other form of institution, meeting the credit, payments, and savings needs of individuals, businesses, and governments. This characteristic of financial diversity is reflected in the basic financial statement of the industry—its balance sheet (or statement of condition). Exhibit 4–4 provides a list of the uses of funds (assets) and major sources of funds (liabilities and equity capital) for all FDIC-insured commercial banks for selected years.

Cash and Due from Banks (Primary Reserves)

All commercial banks hold a substantial part of their assets in *primary reserves*, consisting of cash and deposits due from other banks. These reserves are the banker's first line of defense against withdrawals by depositors, customer demand for loans, and immediate cash needs to cover expenses. Banks generally hold no more in cash than is absolutely required to meet short-run contingencies, however, since the yield on cash assets is minimal or nonexistent. The deposits held with other banks do provide an implicit return, though, because they are a means of "paying" for correspondent banking services. In return for the deposits of smaller banks, the larger U.S. correspondent banks provide such important services as clearing of checks, management of security portfolios, tax advice, and computer processing of records. Thousands of smaller banks across the United States invest their excess cash reserves in loans to other banks (usually called federal funds) with the help of their larger correspondents.[2] Primary reserves also include reserves held behind deposits as required by the Federal Reserve System.

Security Holdings and Secondary Reserves

Commercial banks hold securities acquired in the open market as a long-term investment and also as a secondary reserve to help meet short-run cash needs. For many banks municipal securities—bonds and notes issued by state, city, and other local governments—represent the largest portion of security investments. Commercial banks are subject to the same tax rates as most nonfinancial corporations and therefore find the tax-exempt interest income paid by municipal securities to be extremely attractive.[3]

About equal to municipals in amount are bank holdings of U.S. Treasury obligations (including bills, notes, and bonds). Banks generally favor Trea-

---

[2] A more complete discussion of the operations of the federal funds market is presented in Chapter 14.

[3] Purchase of tax-exempt state and local government bonds is the most important method used by banks today to tax shelter their earnings. Banks also tax shelter their income through the purchase and leasing of equipment to business firms. Another bank tax shelter consists of setting aside a portion of current income as an operating expense for protection against possible losses on loans.

EXHIBIT 4-4

Assets, Liabilities, and Capital of Insured Commercial Banks in the United States (year-end figures)

	1970		1980		1983	
	Millions of Dollars	Percent Total Assets	Millions of Dollars	Percent Total Assets	Millions of Dollars	Percent Total Assets
Assets						
Cash and due from banks (primary reserves)	$ 93,948.1	16.1%	$ 331,909.3	17.9%	$ 341,849.6	14.6%
Security holdings:						
U.S. Treasury securities	61,617.0	10.7	104,466.2	5.6	168,095.3	7.2
Federal agency securities	13,277.7	2.3	59,078.3	3.2	76,525.7	3.3
Municipal securities	69,390.3	12.0	146,263.4	7.9	158,384.9	6.8
Other securities	2,933.9	0.5	24,637.3	1.3	38,341.6	1.6
Federal funds sold and securities purchased under agreements to resell	15,952.3	2.8	70,321.8	3.8	93,484.0	4.0
Loans:						
Real estate loans	73,053.4	12.7	269,111.6	14.5	327,430.1	14.0
Loans to farmers	11,153.6	1.9	32,259.8	1.7	39,292.6	1.7
Commercial and industrial loans	112,215.0	19.5	309,930.8	21.1	524,748.1	22.4
Loans to individuals	66,005.7	11.5	187,375.7	10.1	218,081.6	9.3
All other loans	35,771.9	6.2	48,940.8	2.6	208,681.8	8.9
Less: Unearned income on loans	*	*	21,031.7	1.1	19,112.5	0.8
Less: Allowance for possible loan losses	*	*	10,053.0	0.5	15,471.7	0.7
Direct lease financing	*	*	13,993.2	0.8	17,064.5	0.7
Real estate owned	9,550.3	1.7	2,208.4	0.1	41,779.0	1.8
Other assets	12,381.6	2.1	110,394.6	5.9	122,331.8	5.2
Total assets	$576,350.8	100.0%	$1,855,687.8	100.0%	$2,342,100.2	100.0%

Exhibit 4–4 (concluded)

	1970		1980		1983	
	Millions of Dollars	Percent Total Assets	Millions of Dollars	Percent Total Assets	Millions of Dollars	Percent Total Assets
Liabilities						
Demand deposits	$247,170.4	42.9%	$ 431,539.4	23.3%	$ 389,526.9	16.6%
Savings deposits	98,815.9	17.1	200,869.8	10.8	462,567.6	19.8
Time deposits	136,527.5	23.7	554,740.0	29.9	682,009.5	29.1
Deposits in foreign offices . .	*	*	294,011.6	15.8	308,398.5	13.2
Total deposits	482,513.9	83.7	1,481,160.7	79.8	1,842,502.5	78.7
Federal funds purchased and securities sold under agreements to repurchase .	16,609.0	2.9	133,290.7	7.2	178,533.7	7.6
Other liabilities	28,359.1	4.9	127,086.3	6.8	173,425.1	7.4
Total liabilities	527,482.0	91.5	1,741,537.7	93.8	2,194,461.2	93.7
Subordinated notes	2,091.9	0.4	6,553.6	0.4	7,092.8	0.3
Equity Capital						
Preferred stock—par value. . .	107.3	0.0†	134.6	0.0†	663.8	0.0†
Common stock—par value. . .	11,137.8	1.9	21,672.0	1.2	25,723.3	1.1
Undivided profits, surplus, and reserves . .	29,229.4	5.1	85,789.9	4.6	114,159.0	4.9
Total equity capital. . . .	40,474.5	7.0	107,596.5	5.8	140,546.1	6.0
Total liabilities and capital . .	$576,350.8	100.0%	$1,855,687.8	100.0%	$2,342,100.0	100.0%

Note: figures may not add to totals due to rounding.
* Not available as a separately reported item.
† Less than 0.1 percent.
SOURCE: Federal Deposit Insurance Corporation, *Bank Operating Statistics*, 1980 and 1983, and *Annual Report*, 1970.

sury bills (which must mature within one year) and shorter-term Treasury notes and bonds because these securities can be marketed readily to cover short-run cash needs. Moreover, Treasury securities are free of default risk. A closely related form of federal debt—securities issued by federal agencies such as the Federal Land Banks—has rapidly increased its share of bank portfolios. These securities carry yields slightly above those on direct Treasury obligations; yet they appear to involve little additional risk. Commercial banks also hold small amounts of corporate bonds, notes, and debentures, though they generally prefer to make direct loans to businesses as opposed to purchasing their securities in the open market. Under existing regulations, commerical banks are forbidden to purchase corporate stock. However, banks do hold small amounts of corporate stock as collateral for loans.

Loans

The principal business of commercial banks is to make loans to qualified borrowers. Loans are among the highest-yielding assets a bank can add to its portfolio, and they provide the largest portion of operating revenue.

Banks make loans of reserves to other banks through the federal funds market and to securities dealers through repurchase agreements. Far more important in dollar volume, however, are direct loans to both businesses and individuals. These loans arise from negotiation between the bank and its customer and result in a written agreement designed to meet the specific credit needs of the customer and the requirements of the bank for adequate security and income.

As shown in Exhibit 4–4, most bank credit is extended to commercial and industrial customers. Historically, commercial banks have preferred to make short-term loans to businesses, principally to support purchases of inventory. In recent years, however, banks have lengthened the maturity of their business loans to include term loans (which have maturities over one year) to finance the purchase of buildings, machinery, and equipment. Because the longer-term loans carry greater risk due to unexpected changes in interest rates, banks have also required a much greater proportion of new loans to carry variable interest rates that can be changed in response to shifting market conditions.

Moreover, longer-term loans to business firms have been supplanted to some extent in recent years by equipment leasing plans available from larger banks and the subsidiaries of bank holding companies. These leases are the functional equivalent of a loan: the customer not only makes the required lease payments for using the equipment but is responsible for repairs and maintenance and for any taxes due. Lease financing carries not only significant cost and tax advantages for the customer but also substantial tax advantages for a bank because it can depreciate leased equipment and write off a portion of the cost as an investment tax credit.

Commercial banks are also important lenders in the real estate field, supporting the construction of residential and commercial structures and even carrying out a limited volume of permanent mortgage financing for higher-priced residential and commercial ventures. Major types of loans in the real estate category include farm real estate credit, conventional and government-guaranteed (FHA and VA), single-family residential loans, conventional and government-guaranteed loans on multifamily residences, and mortgage loans on nonfarm commercial properties. Indeed, commercial banks are the most important source of construction financing in the U.S. economy.

Probably the most dynamic area in bank lending today is the making of installment loans to individuals and families. The number of new households has expanded rapidly in recent years, and commercial banks have moved to answer this need by offering longer maturities on installment loans and new types of credit arrangements, especially credit card plans. As a result, the commercial banking industry has become the major consumer installment lending institution in the United States. Banks finance the purchase of automobiles, mobile homes, recreational vehicles, home furnishings and appliances, and provide funds to modernize homes and other properties.

Deposits

In order to carry out their extensive lending and investing operations, banks draw upon a wide variety of deposit and nondeposit sources of funds. The bulk of commercial bank funds (80 percent or more) comes from deposits. There are three main types of deposits. *Demand deposits,* more commonly known as checking accounts, are the principal means of making payments because they are safer than cash and widely accepted. *Savings deposits* generally are in small dollar amounts; they bear a relatively low-interest rate but may be withdrawn by the depositor with little or no notice. *Time deposits* carry a fixed maturity and offer the highest interest rates a bank can pay. Time deposits may be divided into nonnegotiable certificates of deposit (CDs), which are usually small, consumer-type accounts, and negotiable CDs that may be traded in the open market and are purchased mainly by corporations.

During the 1970s and early 1980s new forms of checkable (demand) deposits appeared, combining the essential features of both demand and savings deposits. These *transaction accounts* include negotiable orders of withdrawal (NOWs) and automatic transfer services (ATS). NOW accounts may be drafted to pay bills but also earn interest subject to regulation, while ATS is a preauthorized payments service in which the bank transfers funds from an interest-bearing savings account to a checking account as necessary to cover checks written by the customer. Two relatively new transaction accounts—money market deposits accounts (MMDAs) and Super NOWs—were offered in 1983, following passage of the Garn bill in 1982. MMDAs, designed to compete directly with the high-yielding share accounts offered by money market mutual funds,[4] and Super NOWs may carry prevailing market rates on short-term liquid funds with no federal interest-rate ceilings. Both can be drafted by check, automatic withdrawal, or telephone transfer, but the number of permissible withdrawals from MMDAs is limited. MMDAs may be held by an individual, business firm, or unit of government, but Super NOWs can be held only by individuals, governments, and nonprofit organizations. The new accounts, especially the MMDAs, proved to be tremendously popular; within four months the volume of MMDAs exceeded $300 billion.[5]

The mix of bank deposits has changed dramatically in recent years. Demand deposits and low-yield savings deposits have declined as a percentage of bank funds, while more costly interest-bearing accounts such as MMDAs have grown rapidly. This shift toward more expensive deposits reflects, in part, the growing sophistication of bank customers, especially large corporations, who have developed efficient cash management practices and insist on maximum returns on their funds. Banks are well aware today that their customers are more financially sophisticated and have a greater tendency to "shop around" for the highest returns available on both transactions and savings deposits. As a result, both the cost and volatility of bank deposits has increased.

Moreover, the cost of attracting customer funds has been further increased in recent years by the tendency of bankers to expand services, offering their customers "one-stop" financial convenience. Thus, to retain old deposits and attract new ones many banks have developed or franchised: (1) security brokerage services so that customers can purchase stocks and bonds and pay by charging their deposit accounts; (2) insurance counters to make life, health, and property-casualty policies available; (3) networking agreements with other banks so that customers can access their deposit accounts while traveling; (4) account relocation services and real estate brokerage for customers who move; and (5) financial and tax counseling centers to aid customers with important personal and business decisions. These new services may have opened up new markets for banks, but they have also created new complexities for bank management and demanded greater efficiency and greater emphasis on marketing and customer analysis.

---

[4] See Chapter 5 for a discussion of the nature and growth of money market mutual funds.

[5] See especially Furlong (1983).

Nondeposit Sources of Funds

One of the most marked trends in banking in recent years is greater use of nondeposit borrowed funds to meet bank cash needs, especially as competition for deposits has increased. Principal nondeposit sources of funds for banks today include purchases of reserves (federal funds) from other banks, security repurchase agreements, and the issuance of capital notes. Capital notes are of particular interest because these securities are eligible under federal regulations and the laws of most states to be counted as equity capital for purposes of determining a bank's loan limit. Both state and federal laws limit the amount of money a commercial bank can lend to any one borrower to a fraction of the bank's equity capital (net worth).[6] In order to be counted as equity capital, however, capital notes must be subordinated to deposits, so that if a bank is liquidated the depositors have a first claim on its assets.

Equity Capital

Equity capital (or net worth) supplied by a bank's stockholders provides only a minor portion (about 6 percent, on average) of total funds for most banks today. In fact, the ratio of equity capital to bank loans and deposits has been falling for several decades, due to declining profit margins, inflation, and efforts by bank managers to employ greater financial leverage. This development has many financial experts concerned, because one of the most important functions of equity capital is to keep a bank open even in the face of operating losses until management can correct its problems.

Revenues and Expenses

The majority of bank revenues come from interest and fees on loans, as shown in Exhibit 4–5. Interest and dividends on security holdings are the second most important source of bank revenue after loans. Other minor sources of income include earnings from trust (fiduciary) activities and service charges on deposit accounts (mainly checking accounts).

Bank expenses have risen rapidly in recent years, putting a "squeeze" on operating income. Greater competition from bank and nonbank financial institutions for sources of funds, especially CDs and transaction accounts, has resulted in dramatic increases in the cost of raising funds. Interest on deposits is the principal expense item for commercial banks,

---

[6] For national banks the limit is a maximum of 15 percent of equity capital and surplus. Most states are more lenient, allowing loans to a single borrower up to a larger maximum percentage—25 percent is common—of equity capital.

EXHIBIT 4-5

Earnings and Expenses of Insured Commercial Banks in the United States—1970, 1980, and 1983

	1970		1980		1983	
	Millions of Dollars	Percent Total Revenues	Millions of Dollars	Percent Total Revenues	Millions of Dollars	Percent Total Revenues
Sources of revenue:						
Interest and fees on loans	$22,967.4	66.2%	$126,953.5	66.5%	$151,781.8	63.2%
Interest on balances with depository institutions	*	—	16,256.3	8.5	17,008.0	7.1
Interest on federal funds sold and securities purchased under agreement to resell	1,006.4	2.9	8,763.8	4.6	9,216.5	3.8
Interest on U.S. Treasury and federal agency securities	3,767.1	10.9	13,463.8	7.1	24,309.7	10.1
Interest on municipal securities	2,620.3	7.5	8,170.1	4.3	10,665.7	4.4
Income from other securities	151.8	0.4	1,442.6	0.8	1,980.7	0.8
Income from direct lease financing	*	—	1,370.6	0.7	1,966.7	0.8
Income from fiduciary activities	1,132.2	3.3	2,739.2	1.4	4,189.9	1.7
Service charges on deposit accounts	1,178.2	3.4	3,186.9	1.7	5,417.2	2.3
Other operating income	1,189.2	3.4	8,422.2	4.4	13,641.3	5.7
Total operating income	$34,716.4	100.0%	$190,768.3	100.0%	$240,178.1	100.0%

Exhibit 4–5 *(concluded)*

	1970		1980		1983	
	Millions of Dollars	Percent Total Revenues	Millions of Dollars	Percent Total Revenues	Millions of Dollars	Percent Total Revenues
Expenses:						
Salaries and employee benefits	$ 7,717.1	22.2%	$ 24,673.2	12.9%	$ 33,795.5	14.1%
Interest on deposits	10,483.8	30.2	98,419.4	51.6	120,269.9	50.1
Expense of federal funds purchased and securities sold under agreements to resell	1,400.8	4.0	16,770.6	8.8	16,488.3	6.9
Interest on other nondeposit borrowings	569.3	1.6	4,932.7	2.6	6,964.5	2.9
Occupancy, furniture and fixture	1,254.5	3.6	7,353.6	3.9	11,144.5	4.6
Provision for possible loan losses	703.2	2.0	4,478.6	2.3	10,643.8	4.4
Other operating expenses	5,459.9	15.7	14,635.5	7.7	21,752.9	9.1
Total operating expenses	$27,588.6	79.5%	$171,263.8	89.8%	$221,067.3	92.0%
Income before taxes and security transactions	7,127.8	20.5	19,504.6	10.2	19,110.7	8.0
Applicable income taxes	2,173.8	6.3	5,019.7	2.6	4,104.0	1.7
Income before securities gains or losses	4,954.0	14.3	14,484.9	7.6	15,006.7	6.2
Securities gains, gross	−224.0	0.6	−854.5	−0.4	−26.3	0.0†
Applicable income taxes	−120.3	0.3	−362.1	−0.2	−15.0	0.0†
Securities gains, net	−103.7	0.3	−492.0	−0.3	−11.7	0.0†
Net income before extraordinary items	4,850.3	14.0	13,992.8	7.3	14,994.9	6.2
Extraordinary items, net of tax	−12.8	—	16.8	0.0†	69.9	0.0†
Net income after taxes	$ 4,837.3	13.9%	$ 14,009.6	7.3%	$ 15,064.9	6.3%

Note: Figures may not add to totals due to rounding.
* Not reported as a separate item in the indicated year.
† Figure is less than 0.1 percent.
SOURCE: Federal Deposit Insurance Corporation, *Bank Operating Statistics*, 1980 and 1983 and *Annual Report*, 1970.

followed by the salaries and wages of their employees. Rising rapidly in importance is the interest cost on nondeposit sources of funds, such as borrowing in the federal funds market or long-term borrowing in the form of mortgages and capital notes. Commercial banks must be more conscious of expense control and tax management in future years if they are to protect their profit margins, generate sufficient capital to grow, and provide a greater array of financial services to the public.

MONEY CREATION AND DESTRUCTION BY BANKS

Commercial banks differ from most other financial institutions in one critical respect: *banks have the power to create money in the form of new checkable deposits.* The banking system creates and destroys billions of dollars in money each year at the stroke of a pen. Now an individual bank cannot create any more money in the form of checkable deposits than the volume of excess reserves that it holds. However, the banking system as a whole can create a volume of money equal to a multiple of any excess reserves deposited with it simply by extending credit (i.e., making loans and purchasing securities).

Reserve Requirements and Excess Reserves

Money creation by banks is made possible because the public readily accepts claims on bank deposits (mainly checks) in payment for goods and services. In addition, the law requires individual banks to hold only a fraction of the amount of deposits received from the public as reserves, thus freeing up a majority of incoming funds for the making of loans and the purchasing of securities. We need to look more closely at these so-called reserve requirements banks must meet because they play a key role in the money-creation process.

Under current federal law, banks and other depository institutions must hold reserves in cash or in deposit form behind their transactions accounts and nonpersonal time deposits. These reserve requirements are linked to the size of the depository institution and require that a specified percentage (ranging from 3 to 12 percent) of all deposits must be placed either in an account at the Federal Reserve bank in the region or as cash in the bank's vault.[7] Vault cash and deposits at the Fed constitute

---

[7] As a practical matter, banks hold most of their reserves in the form of deposits with the regional Federal Reserve banks. Vault cash holdings are kept to a minimum; insurance rates increase significantly when large amounts of vault cash are held on bank premises. The current reserve requirements of commercial banks and the important role which reserve requirements play in government monetary policy are discussed in Chapter 23.

a bank's holdings of *legal reserves*—those assets acceptable for meeting reserve requirements behind the public's deposits.

Each bank's legal reserves may be divided into two categories—required reserves and excess reserves. *Required reserves* are equal to the legal reserve requirement ratio times the volume of deposits subject to reserve requirements. For example, if a bank holds $20 million in transaction accounts and $30 million in nonpersonal time deposits and the law requires it to hold 3 percent of its transaction accounts and 3 percent of its nonpersonal time deposits in legal reserves, the required reserves for this bank are $20 million $\times$ 3% + $30 million $\times$ 3%, or $1.5 million.

Excess reserves equal the difference between the total legal reserves actually held by a bank and the amount of its required reserves. For example, if a bank is required to hold legal reserves equal to $1.5 million, but finds on a given date that it has $500,000 in cash on the premises and $1.5 million on deposit with the Federal Reserve bank in its region, this bank clearly holds $500,000 in *excess* reserves. Because legal reserve assets earn little or no interest income, most commercial banks try to keep their holdings of excess reserves as close to zero as possible.

The Creation of Money and Credit

The distinction between excess and required reserves is important because it plays a key role in the growth of credit in the economy and the creation of money by the commercial banking system. To understand why, we need to make certain assumptions concerning how banks behave and the rules and regulations they face. To simplify the arithmetic, assume that the Federal Reserve has set a basic reserve requirement of 20 percent behind the public's deposits. Therefore, for every dollar that the public deposits in the banking system, each commercial bank must put aside in either vault cash or deposits at the Federal Reserve 20 cents as required reserves. Assume also that, initially, the banking system is "loaned up"—that is, bankers, in attempting to increase their profits, have loaned out all excess legal reserves available to them. No additional reserves are made available to the banking system from some external source. In addition, assume that all bankers are profit maximizers and will attempt to loan out immediately any excess funds available to them in order to earn the maximum interest income possible.

Suppose that a deposit of $1,000 is made from some source outside the banking system. Perhaps the Federal Reserve has purchased securities from a dealer and paid for its purchase by providing $1,000 in additional reserves to the dealer's bank. Alternatively, the public may have decided to convert a portion of its currency and coin holdings ("pocket money") into bank deposits for greater convenience and safety. Either way, a deposit of $1,000 appears at Bank A as shown in Exhibit 4–6. This exhibit contains an abbreviated balance sheet (T account) for Bank A with changes in assets shown on the left-hand side and changes in liabilities and net worth shown on the right-hand side.

Under the assumed Federal Reserve regulations, Bank A would be required to place $200 aside as required reserves (i.e., 20 percent of the $1,000 deposit), leaving excess legal reserves of $800. Because the $800 in cash earns no interest income, the banker will immediately try to loan out these excess reserves. Banks make loans today by bookkeeping entry. The borrower signs a note indicating how much is borrowed at what rate of interest and when the note will come due. In return, the banker creates a checking account in the borrower's name. In our example, assume that Bank A has received a loan request from one of its customers and decides to grant the customer a loan of $800—exactly the amount of excess legal reserves it holds.

Commercial banks find that, when they make loans, the borrowed funds are withdrawn rapidly as borrowers spend the proceeds of their loans. Moreover, it is likely that most of the borrowed funds will wind up as deposits in other banks as loan customers write checks against their accounts. For this reason, Bank A will not loan out any more than the $800 in excess legal reserves it currently holds. This way, when the borrower spends the funds and the money flows to other banks, Bank A will have sufficient funds in reserve to cover the cash letters demanding payment which it will receive from other banks.

Assume that the $800 loaned by Bank A eventually winds up as a deposit in Bank B. As indicated in Exhibit 4–6, Bank B must place $160 of this deposit in required reserves and then has excess reserves of $640, which are quickly loaned out. As this borrower spends the funds, the $640 loan finds it way into deposits at Bank C. After setting aside required reserves of $128, Bank C has excess reserves of $512. It too will move rapidly to loan out these funds if a suitable borrower can be found.

The pattern of these changes in deposits, loans, and required reserves should now be fairly clear. The results are summarized in the bottom portion of Exhibit 4–6. Note that the total volume of bank deposits has been considerably expanded by the time it reaches the third or fourth bank. Similarly, the total volume of new loans grows rapidly as funds flow from bank to bank within the system. If the credit-creation process works through the entire banking system and there are no leakages, then with a 20 percent reserve requirement, the banking system ultimately will hold $5,000 in deposits and will have created loans in the amount of $4,000. Clearly, by making loans whenever and wherever excess reserves appear, the banking system eventually creates total depos-

EXHIBIT 4–6

The Creation of Credit and Deposits by the Banking System

1. Bank A Receives New Deposit			4. Loan Made by Bank B		
Assets		Liabilities	Assets		Liabilities
Required		Deposits 1,000	Required		Deposits 800
reserves	200		reserves	160	
Cash	800		Loans	640	

2. Loan Made by Bank A			5. Deposit of Loan Funds in Bank C		
Assets		Liabilities	Assets		Liabilities
Required		Deposits 1,000	Required		Deposits 640
reserves	200		reserves	128	
Loans	800		Cash	512	

3. Deposit of Loan Funds in Bank B			6. Loan Made by Bank C		
Assets		Liabilities	Assets		Liabilities
Required		Deposits 800	Required		Deposits 640
reserves	160		reserves	128	
Cash	640		Loans	512	

By making loans whenever there are excess reserves, the banking system will ultimately generate a volume of deposits several times larger than the amount of the initial deposit received by Bank A.

Transactions within the Banking System

Name of Bank	Deposits Received	Loans Made	Required Reserves
A	$1,000	$ 800	$ 200
B	800	640	160
C	640	512	128
D	512	410	102
—	—	—	—
—	—	—	—
Final amounts for all banks in the system	$5,000	$4,000	$1,000

its and total loans several times larger than the original volume of funds received.[8]

Destruction of Deposits and Reserves

Not only can the money supply expand by a multiple amount as a result of the injection of new reserves, but it can also *contract* by a multiple amount when reserves are withdrawn from the banking system. This is illustrated in Exhibit 4–7, where a depositor has decided to withdraw $1,000 from a transaction account at Bank A. Recall that behind the $1,000 deposit Bank A holds only $200 in required reserves. This means that when the deposit is withdrawn, that bank will have a deficiency of $800. If Bank A is loaned up and has used all of its cash in making loans and investments, it will have to raise the necessary funds through the sale of securities or through borrowing.

Suppose Bank A decides to sell securities in the amount of $800. As indicated in Exhibit 4–7, the sale of securities increases Bank A's required reserves by the necessary amount. However, the individuals and institutions who purchase those securities pay for them by writing checks against their deposits in other banks, reducing the legal reserves of those institutions.

For example, assume that Bank B loses deposits of $800 and required reserves of $800 as Bank A gains these funds. Considering Bank A and Bank B together, total deposits have fallen by $1,800. This deposit contraction has freed up about $360 ($200 + $160) in required reserves. However, if Bank B is also loaned up and has no excess reserves, the $800 lost to Bank A means Bank B has a net reserve deficiency of $640. Further contraction of deposits will occur as Bank B attempts to cover its reserve deficiency by drawing reserves from other banks. In fact, with a 20 percent reserve requirement and no other leakages from the banking system, deposits will contract by a full $5,000 as banks try to cover their reserve deficits by raising funds at the expense of other banks.

---

[8] In the foregoing example each dollar of required reserves supports $5 in deposits, due to the fact that the legal reserve requirement is 20 percent. That is, total deposits created by the banking system are equal to the initial amount of legal reserves deposited in the system—in this example $1,000—times the reciprocal of the reserve requirement ratio—in this case 1/0.20, or 5. The reciprocal of the reserve requirement ratio is known as the *deposit multiplier,* a concept we will discuss more fully in Chapter 23.

In the real world, leakages from the banking system greatly reduce the size of the deposit multiplier—probably to no more than two. Among the most important leakages are the public's desire to convert some portion of new demand deposits into currency and coin (pocket money) or into time and savings deposits, and the presence of unutilized lending capacity, which results because banks either cannot find qualified borrowers or wish to hold a protective "cushion" of reserves.

EXHIBIT 4–7

Deposit and Credit Destruction in the Banking System

Depositor withdraws funds:

Federal Reserve Bank		Bank A	
Assets	Liabilities	Assets	Liabilities
	Member bank reserves −1,000	Required reserves −1,000	Deposits −1,000

If Bank A was loaded up when the withdrawal occurred, it will now have a reserve deficiency of $800 as indicated below.

Total reserves lost at Bank A when depositor withdrew funds	$1,000
Required reserves no longer needed due to deposit withdrawal	−200
Total reserve deficit at Bank A	$ 800

Bank A sells securities to acquire additional reserves:

Bank A		Bank B	
Assets	Liabilities	Assets	Liabilities
Securities −800 Required reserves +800		Required reserves −800	Deposits −800

The sale of securities in the amount of $800 enables Bank A to cover its reserve deficits. However, customers of Bank B bought those securities and that bank was already loaned up. Therefore, Bank B now has a reserve deficiency of $640. Thus:

Total reserves lost at Bank B after deposit withdrawals to purchase Bank A's securities	$800
Required reserves no longer needed due to deposit withdrawals	−160
Total reserve deficit at Bank B	$640

The actions taken by Bank B to cover its reserve deficit will cause other banks to lose reserves and incur deficits. Deposits will continue to contract until total reserves available to the banking system are sufficient for *all* banks to meet their legal reserve requirements.

Implications of Money Creation and Destruction

This capacity of banks to create and destroy money has a number of important implications for the financial system and for the economy. Creation of money by banks is one of the most important sources of credit funds in the economy—an important supplement to the supply of savings in providing funds for investment so the economy can grow faster. Money created by banks is instantly available for spending and, therefore, unless carefully controlled by government action, can fuel inflation. That is why the Federal Reserve System, the nation's central bank, regulates the growth of the money supply principally through controlling the growth of bank reserves—a subject dealt with at length in Chapter 23.

SUMMARY AND CONCLUSIONS

It is clear that the banking industry has undergone significant financial and structural changes in recent years. These changes have been brought about by shifts in regulations and by strong economic and financial pressures. High interest rates, soaring operating costs, and intense competition from nonbank financial institutions have propelled bankers into a new scenario in which the character of their loans, investments, and sources of funds has changed markedly. Moreover, there is no end in sight to many of these trends. Costs of labor and funds continue to rise or remain at high levels. Indeed, many experts looking at the age composition of the U.S. population and the expected rate of family formations ahead expect relatively high interest rates and continued pressure on bankers to find higher-yielding uses for their funds in order to offset rising costs. A key factor in the industry's response to these demand and cost pressures, of course, will be the willingness of federal and state regulatory authorities and the Congress to permit banks to respond freely to new and changing public demands.

The drive toward larger and larger banking organizations centered around branch banks and bank holding companies appears to be a continuing trend for the future. Again, a key issue is whether the Congress and the states will readily permit greater branching and holding-company activity. One area of growing concern to the banking industry is the proliferation of "near-banks" which offer credit services and recently have begun to attract the public's funds through sales of deposit-like IOUs. These organizations include such well-known names as Sears, Roebuck Co., Prudential-Bache, Shearson-American Express, and various stock brokerage firms. These organizations offer financial services to customers and yet are not subject to the extensive regulations which commercial banks must satisfy. The future, therefore, promises to foster intense competition not only within the banking industry but from without. In line with economic theory, stronger competition should mean lower profit margins and a more efficient use of financial resources within the banking system.

STUDY QUESTIONS

1. Why are commercial banks frequently labeled "financial department stores"?

2. In what ways are commercial banks of special importance to the functioning of the money and capital markets and the economy?

3. Why are banks so heavily regulated? List the principal bank regulatory agencies. What areas of bank operations are subject to regulation?

4. What are the principal uses of commercial bank funds? Major sources of funds?

5. What has happened in recent years to bank liquidity? Capital adequacy? The composition of loans and deposits? What forces have brought about these changes?

6. Two dominant postwar movements in the structure of U.S. banking have been the spread of branch banking and the growth of bank holding companies. Explain what has happened in these two areas and why.

7. Why have the number and average size of failing banks increased in recent years?

8. Why and how are banks able to create money? Does the ability of banks to create money have important implications for public policy? Please explain.

PROBLEMS

1. Given the following information on the revenues and expenses of First National Bank determine the bank's net income after taxes for the year just concluded:

Salaries and employee benefits	$ 80,000	Occupancy costs	$11,000
Interest on deposits	170,000	Provision for loan losses	22,000
Interest on loans	320,000	Miscellaneous expenses	8,000
Income from U.S. Treasury securities	75,000	Interest on municipal securities	86,000
Extraordinary items, net	0	Service charges on deposits	10,000
Interest on nondeposit borrowings	30,000	Miscellaneous operating revenues	13,000
Net securities gains	0		
Applicable income taxes	50,000		

2. Construct the Report of condition (balance sheet) for First National
    Bank for December 31st of the year just ended from the information
    below:

Equity capital	$ 50 million	Other assets	$ 50 million
Demand deposits	100 million	Real estate loans	60 million
Savings deposits	150 million	U.S. Treasury	
Time deposits	200 million	securities	25 million
Federal funds		Commercial and industrial	
borrowings	12 million	loans	300 million
Cash and due from		Other liabilities	38 million
banks	20 million	Municipal securities	55 million
		Loans to individuals	40 million

3. A commercial bank holds $120 million in transaction accounts and
    $240 million in nonpersonal time deposits. Current reserve require-
    ments set by the Federal Reserve Board stipulate that 3 percent of
    the first $30 million in transaction deposits and 12 percent of any
    excess transaction deposits over $30 million must be held in a legal
    reserve account. Similarly, 3 percent of nonpersonal time deposits
    must be placed in the legal reserve account. What is the bank's total
    reserve requirement based on the above deposit totals? Suppose the
    bank's legal reserve account has a current average balance of $20
    million. Does the bank have any excess reserves? If so, how much?

SELECTED REFERENCES

Bell, R. W., and Neil B. Murphy. *Costs in Commercial Banking: A Quantitative
    Analysis of Bank Behavior and Its Relation to Bank Regulations*, Research
    Report No. 41, Federal Reserve Bank of Boston, 1968.

Benston, George J. "Economies of Scale and Marginal Costs in Banking Opera-
    tions." *The National Banking Review*, June 1965, pp. 507–49.

————. "The Optimal Banking Structure: Theory and Evidence." *Journal of
    Bank Research*, Winter 1973, pp. 220–37.

Boltz, Paul W., and Tim S. Campbell. *Innovations in Bank Loan Contracting:
    Recent Evidence*, Staff Study 104, Board of Governors of the Federal Reserve
    System, May 1979.

Buser, Stephen A. "Efficient Risk-Return Management in Commercial Banking."
    Journal of Bank Research, Winter 1980, pp. 235–47.

Chase, Samuel, and John Mingo. "The Regulation of Bank Holding Companies."
    Journal of Finance, May 1975, pp. 282–92.

Daniel, Donnie L.; William A. Longbrake; and Neil B. Murphy. "The Effects of
    Technology on Bank Economies of Scale for Demand Deposits." *Journal of
    Finance*, March 1973, pp. 131–46.

Eisenbeis, Robert A. "Regulation and Financial Innovation: Implications for Financial Structure and Competition among Depository and Nondepository Institutions." *Issues in Bank Regulation,* Winter 1981.

Furlong, Frederick T. "New Deposit Instruments." *Federal Reserve Bulletin,* May 1983, pp. 319–26.

Martin, John D.; Arthur J. Keown; and David F. Scott, Jr. "Bank Leverage Really Does Pay." *The Bankers Magazine,* 160 no. 2 (Spring 1977) pp. 70–76.

Rose, Peter S. "People, Machines and the Future of Banking." *The Canadian Banker and ICB Review.* December 1980, pp. 56–61.

White, George C. "Electronic Banking and Its Impact on the Future." *The Magazine of Bank Administration,* December 1979, pp. 39–42.

5

Nonbank Thrift Institutions: Credit Unions, Savings and Loan Associations, Mutual Savings Banks, and Money Market Mutual Funds

PURPOSE OF THIS CHAPTER

To increase our understanding of the important role played by nonbank thrift institutions—credit unions, savings and loan associations, mutual savings banks, and money market mutual funds—in the financial system. This important role is highlighted by examining how these institutions attract savings (principally from individuals and families) and channel those funds into credit, mainly in the form of mortgages, installment loans, and government securities.

KEY TERMS AND CONCEPTS IN THE CHAPTER

credit unions	*FDIC*	*money market*
DIDC	*FHLB*	*securities*
DIDMCA	*Garn bill*	*mutual savings banks*
family financial	*MMDA*	*savings and loans*
center	*money market fund*	*share accounts*

There is a tendency in discussions of the financial system to minimize the role of nonbank financial institutions and emphasize the part played by commercial banks in the flow of money and credit. For many years financial experts did not consider the liabilities of nonbank financial institutions, including deposits in savings and loan associations, mutual savings banks, and credit unions, as really close substitutes for bank deposits. It was argued that interindustry competition between commercial banks and other financial institutions was slight and, for all practical purposes, could be ignored. Beginning in the 1960s and continuing to the present day, however, a new view has emerged concerning the relative importance of nonbank financial institutions. We now recognize that these institutions play a vital role in the flow of money and credit within the financial system and are particularly important in selected markets, such as the mortgage market, and in the markets for corporate bonds, stocks, and consumer savings.

This new awareness of the critical importance of nonbank financial institutions in the economy and financial system stems from a number of sources. One is the rapid growth of selected nonbank financial intermediaries in recent years; some have outstripped commercial banks in the growth of their loans and total resources. For example, credit unions and money market mutual funds have been the fastest-growing financial institutions in the United States over the past three decades.

Still another factor is the increasing penetration of traditional financial service markets by nonbank institutions. For example, credit unions, mutual savings banks, money market mutual funds, and savings and loan associations offer share accounts, NOWs, and other interest-bearing payments services that compete head to head with bank checking account plans. For a number of years credit unions have marketed credit cards, many of which have carried lower interest charges than those levied by banks. Moreover, the *Depository Institutions Deregulation and Monetary Control Act of 1980 (DIDMCA)* authorized federally chartered savings and loan associations to issue credit cards and make credit card loans. That law along with a second bill—the Garn-St Germain Depository Institutions Act of 1982 *(Garn bill)*—greatly expanded the powers of nonbank thrifts to make both consumer installment loans and business loans comparable to many forms of bank credit. Insurance companies, savings banks, and credit unions today are offering new savings plans with fixed or floating interest rates that compete directly with commercial bank certificates of deposit (CDs) and other savings plans.

On both the asset and liability sides of the balance sheet, then, nonbank financial institutions are becoming increasingly like commercial banks and competing for many of the same customers. This is why financial analysts today stress the importance of studying the whole sector of financial institutions—bank and nonbank financial intermediaries—in order to understand how the financial system works. In this chapter and the next we examine the major types of nonbank financial institutions that channel savings into loans and investments.

CREDIT UNIONS

Growth of Credit Unions

The characteristics and operations of *credit unions* have been a neglected area of research in the financial system. Recently, however, there has been a strong revival of interest in credit union behavior and growth. One reason is the rapid growth of this financial intermediary. For example, credit union assets have expanded more than fivefold since 1970 (see Exhibit 5–1). Today U.S. credit associations are the third-largest institutional supplier of consumer installment credit, behind commercial banks and finance companies, and account for about one sixth of all consumer installment loans in the United States. These institutions are exclusively household-oriented intermediaries—offering their deposit plans and credit resources only to individuals and families. Their rapid growth stems mainly from offering low loan rates and high deposit interest rates to individuals and families.

EXHIBIT 5–1

Credit Unions in the United States

Years	Number of Credit Unions	Number of Members	Total Assets ($ millions)
1940	9,023	2,826,612	$ 253
1950	10,591	4,610,278	1,005
1960	20,456	12,037,533	5,653
1970	23,699	22,797,193	17,960
1980	21,930	45,420,000	72,250
1983*	19,203	48,359,000	98,287

* 1983 figures are preliminary.
SOURCE: Credit Union National Association, Inc., *Credit Union Report 1983* (Madison, Wis., 1984).

Credit unions are really cooperative, self-help associations of individuals rather than profit-motivated financial institutions. Savings deposits and loans are offered only to members of each association, and the members are technically the *owners,* receiving dividends and sharing in any losses that occur. Credit unions were first begun early in the 20th century to serve low-income individuals and families by providing inexpensive credit and an outlet for savings. The early growth of credit unions was modest until the decade of the 1950s, when these institutions broadened their appeal to middle-income individuals by offering many new financial services and engaging in aggressive advertising campaigns.

The credit union sector remains relatively small compared to other major financial institutions. However, the industry's potential for future growth appears excellent due to its innovative character and growing public acceptance. For both savings deposits and consumer installment loans, the credit union has become an aggressive competitor with commercial banks, savings and loan associations, and mutual savings banks. Beginning in 1978 credit unions were authorized to offer money market certificates (MMCs) which can carry the same terms as money market deposit plans sold by commercial banks and savings banks. In addition, many credit unions offer payroll savings plans where employees of a company can conveniently set aside a portion of their salary in a savings account.

Credit union loans have kept pace with the growth of their deposits. Consumer loan rates charged by credit unions are fully competitive with rates charged by the other two major consumer lenders—commercial banks and finance companies. For example, a recent study found that both banks and credit unions were then charging approximately 10½ percent on new car loans. However, credit unions granted their borrowing members interest refunds up to 20 percent of the amount of their loans.[1] Thus, credit unions often accept a smaller spread between their loan and deposit interest rates, made possible because their operating costs are usually so low. Many associations provide credit life insurance free to their customers—a service charged for by most other lending institutions. Data released by the Federal Reserve Board show that credit unions accounted for only 4 percent of total consumer installment loans outstanding in 1950 but that by 1982 this figure had risen to 14 percent. Both commercial banks and credit unions have gained a larger share of the consumer credit market at the expense of other lenders.

Chartering and Regulation

In the United States credit unions are chartered and regulated at both state and federal levels (see Exhibit 5–2). Today about 58 percent of all credit unions are chartered by the federal government and the remainder by the states. Federal credit unions have been regulated since 1970 by

---

[1] See, for example, Flannery (1974) and Cargill (1977).

EXHIBIT 5-2

Government Agencies Regulating the Nonbank Thrifts

Nonbank Thrift Institution	Chartering and Licensing of Thrifts	Setting Up Branches		Mergers and Acquisitions		Deposit Insurance	Supervision and Examination
		Intrastate	Interstate	Intrastate	Interstate		
Credit unions	National Credit Union Administration/State Banking Departments	No approval required		National Credit Union Administration/State Banking Department	National Credit Union Administration/State Banking Departments	National Credit Union Share Insurance Fund/State Departments	National Credit Union Administration/State Banking Departments
Savings and loan associations	Federal Home Loan Bank Board/State Banking or Savings and Loan Departments	Federal Home Loan Bank Board/Federal Savings and Loan Insurance Corporation/State Savings or State Savings and Loan Departments	*	Federal Home Home Loan Bank Board/State Banking Departments/State Savings and Loan Departments	Federal Savings and Loan Insurance Corporation	Federal Savings and Loan Insurance Fund/State Insurance Funds	Federal Home Loan Bank Board/State Banking or Savings and Loan Departments
Mutual savings banks	Federal Home Loan Bank Board/State Banking Departments	Federal Home Loan Bank Board/State Banking Departments	*	Federal Home Loan Bank Board/State Banking Departments	Federal Deposit Insurance Corporation	Federal Deposit Insurance Corporation/State Insurance Funds	Federal Deposit Insurance Corporation/State Banking Departments
Money market funds	Securities and Exchange Commission	No approval required		No approval required		No government programs/some employ private plans	None

* Generally prohibited for federal thrift institutions.
SOURCE: Based on *Depository Institutions and Their Regulators*, Federal Reserve Bank of New York.

the National Credit Union Administration (NCUA), an independent agency within the federal government. Deposits are insured by the National Credit Union Share Insurance Fund (NCUSIF) up to $100,000. State-chartered credit unions may qualify for federal insurance if they conform to NCUA's regulations. About 99 percent of all savings in U.S. credit unions are insured by federal or state insurance programs.

Credit Union Membership

Credit unions are organized around a common affiliation or common bond among their members. Most credit union members work for the same employer or for one of a group of related employers. In most cases if one family member belongs to a credit union, other family members are eligible as well. Occupation-related credit unions account for about four fifths of all U.S. credit unions. About one sixth of American credit unions are organized around a nonprofit association, such as a labor union, a church, or a fraternal or social organization. Common area of residence, such as a city or state, has also been used in recent years as a base from which to get credit unions started.

Size of Credit Unions

There is a strong shift today toward fewer, but larger credit unions. For example, the number of associations reached an all-time high in 1969 at almost 24,000 and now totals only about 19,000 (see Exhibit 5-1). However, in 1970 only about one sixth of the nation's credit unions held more than $1 million in assets, but today that figure exceeds 40 percent. The average-size credit union still remains very small compared with other depository institutions, however. Nevertheless, credit union membership continues to grow rapidly, increasing 1 to 2 million a year. There were fewer than 5 million U.S. credit union members in 1950, but this total exceeded 48 million in 1983. Worldwide, there are about 60 million members associated with 45,000 credit unions operating in about 70 countries.

New Services Offered

Credit unions are rapidly expanding the number of services they offer. Some sell life insurance today, while others act as brokers for group insurance plans where state law permits. Many credit unions are active in offering 24-hour teller services, traveler's checks, travel-planning services, and money orders. Larger credit unions compete directly with commercial banks for transactions accounts by offering *share drafts*—interest-bearing checkbook deposits. The share draft was first authorized by several states in 1974 and made legal for all federally insured credit unions when the DIDMCA law was passed in 1980 (see Exhibit 5–3). About 3,500 credit unions across the nation now offer share-draft services. Roughly another 500 offer credit cards and automated teller machines, many of which are linked nationwide through an electronic exchange network.

U.S. credit unions have been under intense pressure to develop new services and penetrate new markets, due to increasing competition from other financial institutions and a decline in the demand for their most important credit service—automobile loans. The auto loan accounted for about a third of the volume of credit union loans until recently, when consumers began buying fewer new cars and more used cars. In addition, a substantially larger proportion of family income today is spent on food,

EXHIBIT 5–3

Provisions of the Depository Institutions Deregulation and Monetary
Control Act (DIDMCA) of 1980 Applying to Credit Unions, Savings and
Loan Associations, and Mutual Savings Banks

New Deposit Powers

1. Interest-rate ceilings on deposits will be phased out over a six-year period, permitting rates offered the public to respond to competition in the marketplace.
2. NOW accounts which bear interest and can be used to make payments may be offered to individuals and nonprofit organizations by all federally insured depository institutions beginning December 31, 1980.
3. Federally insured credit unions are authorized to offer share drafts (i.e., interest-bearing checking accounts) beginning March 31, 1980.
4. Mutual savings banks are empowered to offer demand deposits to their business customers.

New Loan and Investment Powers

1. Federally insured credit unions can offer real estate loans.
2. Federally chartered savings and loan associations may issue credit cards, offer trust services, and make investments in consumer loans, commercial paper, and corporate bonds up to 20 percent of their assets.
3. Mutual savings banks with federal charters may invest up to 5 percent of their total assets in commercial, corporate, and business loans within the home state of the bank or within 75 miles of the bank's home office.

fuel, and other necessities; credit unions have begun shifting their loan programs into these areas.

Government Regulation of Loans, Investments, and Dividends

Credit unions, like commercial banks, are heavily regulated in the services they are permitted to offer, the rates charged for credit, and dividends paid on members' deposits. Under current federal regulations, these institutions are permitted to make unsecured loans to members, including credit card loans, not exceeding 5 years to maturity, or secured loans out to 30 years. The 1982 Garn bill significantly expanded their real estate lending powers, including their ability to accept second-mortgage loans (see Exhibit 5–4).

Associations' permissible investments in securities are limited to a list prescribed by either state or federal regulations. In the main, credit unions are permitted to acquire U.S. government securities, hold savings deposits at commercial banks, savings and loans associations, savings banks, and federally insured credit unions, and purchase selected federal agency securities. Credit unions rely heavily on U.S. government securities and on savings deposits in other financial institutions to provide liquidity in order to meet deposit withdrawals and accommodate member credit needs.

Credit unions pay dividends to their members, but are considered nonprofit associations doing business only with their owners. Therefore, credit unions are classified as tax-exempt mutual organizations. To qualify for tax exemption, however, all earnings except those flowing to equity reserves must be paid out to their members.

A Strong Competitive Force

Credit unions today represent stiffer competition for commercial banks, savings banks, finance companies, and other financial institutions serving the consumer than was true in the past. Today, one out of every six Americans belongs to a credit union—roughly double the proportion a decade earlier. The industry has repeatedly demonstrated its capacity for innovation and the ability to compete successfully for both installment loans and small savings accounts. With the authority recently granted credit unions by the DIDMCA law of 1980, the Garn bill of 1982, and by other federal and state laws to make more flexible real estate loans and offer credit cards, transaction accounts, and higher-yielding savings certificates, these nonbank thrifts are likely to be an even more significant competitive force in offering consumer credit and savings plans in the years ahead.

EXHIBIT 5–4

Provisions of the Garn-St Germain Depository Institutions Act of 1982
(Garn bill; HR-6267) Applying to Credit Unions, Savings and Loan
Associations, and Mutual Savings Banks

New Deposit Powers

1. Depository Institutions Deregulation Commission (DIDC) is authorized to develop a deposit account for banks and nonbank thrifts "directly equivalent to and competitive with money market mutual funds" no later than December 15, 1982.
2. Interest-rate differentials between commercial banks' and nonbank depository institutions' time and savings deposits will be phased out by January 1, 1984.
3. Federally chartered savings associations may accept regular checkbook deposits from businesses having a loan relationship to the associations or as a repository for payments.
4. All deposit-type financial institutions are permitted to offer NOW accounts to governmental units.

New Loan and Investment Powers

1. Federal savings associations may make secured or unsecured loans to businesses up to 10 percent of their total assets starting in 1984.
2. Commercial real estate loans may be increased from 20 to 40 percent of total assets at federal savings associations and required loan-value minimum ratios are eliminated. Federal credit unions are granted broader real estate loan powers with longer maximum maturities, the ability to lend against residential real estate regardless of price, and the ability to grant refinancing loans and second mortgages.
3. Federal savings associations may purchase municipal revenue bonds (up to 10 percent of capital limitation) as well as general-obligation municipal bonds and invest in time deposits at depository institutions insured by the Federal Savings and Loan Insurance Corporation (FSLIC).
4. Federal savings associations may invest in consumer loans up to 30 percent of their total assets (including loans to businesses to acquire consumer goods inventories).
5. Federal savings associations may lease or lend against personal property up to 10 percent of their assets.
6. State laws and court decisions restricting enforcement of due-on-sale clauses in real property loans (such as home mortgages) are preempted (except for loans originated or assumed during the period between applicable state law and passage of the Garn bill).

Other Provisions of Garn-St Germain

1. Qualified insured depository institutions may issue net worth certificates to their federal insurance agency in return for promissory notes from the agency which can be held as assets to strengthen the depository institution's net worth. The issuing institution must have net worth equal to or less than 3 percent of its assets, a consistent loss record, and at least 20 percent of its loans in the mortgage area.
2. Depository institutions can freely change organizational form from mutual to stockholder owned and change their federal or state supervisory agency.

SAVINGS AND LOAN ASSOCIATIONS

Savings and loan associations are similar to credit unions because they extend financial services to households. They differ from credit unions, however, in their heavy emphasis on long-term rather than short-term lending. In particular, *savings and loans* are the major source in the United States of mortgage loans to finance the purchase of single-family homes and multifamily dwellings. And, like credit unions, savings and loans today are developing many new financial services to attract new deposit and credit accounts and protect their earnings.

The first savings and loans were started early in the 19th century as "building and loan associations." Money was solicited from individuals and families so that certain members of the group could finance the building of new homes. The same individuals and families who provided the funds were also borrowers from the association. Today, however, savers and borrowers from S&Ls are frequently different individuals.

Savings and loan associations began as basically a single-product industry—accepting savings deposits from middle-income individuals and families and lending those funds to home buyers—and this persisted until the 1970s. More recently, however, competition from commercial banks and credit unions, coupled with high and unstable interest rates, have forced savings and loans to diversify their operations and aggressively advertise for new accounts. Favorable regulatory decisions at federal and state levels have aided the industry recently in developing new financial services.

Chartering and Regulation

Currently savings associations receive their charters either from the states or from the federal government. Today about one half receive their charters from state authorities who supervise their activities and regularly examine their books. The remainder of all S&Ls have federal charters, and these associations are insured (up to a maximum of $100,000 per depositor) by the Federal Savings and Loan Insurance Corporation (FSLIC) (see Exhibit 5–2). S&Ls chartered by the states also may qualify for FSLIC insurance and, in fact, three quarters of the state associations have done so. Both federally chartered and federally insured state associations are supervised and examined by the Federal Home Loan Bank System—the principal regulator of the industry.

Most savings and loans are *mutual* organizations and therefore have no stockholders. Technically, they are owned by their depositors and borrowers. However, a growing number of associations are converting to stock form. Stockholder-owned S&Ls can issue capital stock to increase their net worth—a privilege that is particularly important when a savings and loan is growing rapidly and needs an additional source of capital. Nationwide, close to one fourth of all S&Ls are stock associations. The stockholder-owned associations, on average, are much larger in size than the mutuals, however, holding about 40 percent of the industry's total assets.

How Funds Are Raised and Allocated

Savings and loans, like credit unions, are gradually broadening their role with many choosing to offer a full line of financial services for individuals and families, while other S&Ls are branching out into business credit and commercial real estate lending.

Asset Portfolios.   Residential mortgage loans still dominate the asset side of the savings and loan business. Exhibit 5–5, showing the industry's assets and liabilities for year-end 1983, indicates that mortgage credit (predominantly residential loans) accounted for about two thirds of total industry assets. But, the current era has brought rapid growth in other housing-related investments, such as mortgage-backed securities, mobile home loans, and investments in service corporations which provide funds for land development, mobile home parks, and housing-rehabilitation projects. Mortgage-backed securities include pass-throughs issued by the Government National Mortgage Association and participation certificates (PCs) issued by the Federal Home Loan Mortgage Corporation. Both pass-throughs and PCs are investor shares in a pool of mortgages that are backed by the issuing government agency.

In certain states, savings and loans are allowed to extend *consumer credit* for nonhousing purposes, such as the purchase of automobiles and home appliances. In addition, as shown in Exhibits 5–3 and 5–4, the 1980 DIDMCA law and the 1982 Garn bill, both passed in the early 1980s, granted federal savings associations the power to issue credit cards and invest a substantial portion of their assets in consumer loans, commercial paper, and corporate debt securities. Restrictions on home mortgage lending were eased to allow adjustable-rate mortgages (ARMS) whose returns vary with market conditions and S&Ls were granted power to invest in mutual funds and offer trust services. Acquisitions of municipal revenue bonds and time deposits of other S&Ls were also added to the permissible list. The essence of all these changes was to allow associations to become more like commercial banks with flexible asset portfolios, better able to withstand fluctuations in interest rates and economic conditions.

Liabilities of S&Ls.   Savings deposits provide the bulk of funds available to the savings and loan industry. However, there has been a significant shift in deposit mix in recent years from those savings accounts

EXHIBIT 5–5

Assets and Liabilities of All Savings and Loan Associations in the United States, December 31, 1983*

Item	Amount (millions)	Percentage of Total
Assets:		
Mortgage loans outstanding	$521,308	63.6%
Insured mortgages and mortgage-backed securities	90,902	11.1
Mobile home loans	3,857	0.5
Home improvement loans	5,490	0.7
Loans on savings accounts	3,195	0.4
Education loans	2,465	0.3
Other consumer loans	14,091	1.7
Cash and investments eligible for liquidity	84,958	10.4
Other investments	24,965	3.0
Federal Home Loan Bank stock	6,100	0.7
Investment in service corporations	8,196	1.0
Buildings and equipment	11,347	1.4
Real estate owned	6,800	0.8
All other assets	35,494	4.3
Total assets	$819,168	100.0%
Liabilities and Net Worth:		
Savings deposits:		
Accounts with no fixed term	$203,656	24.9%
Certificates of deposit	467,401	57.1
Federal Home Loan Bank advances	57,253	7.0
Other borrowed money	41,258	5.0
All other liabilities	16,620	2.0
Net worth	32,980	4.0
Total liabilities and net worth	$819,168	100.0%

Note: Components may not add to totals due to rounding.
* Preliminary.
SOURCES: Federal Home Loan Bank Board; United States League of Savings Institutions, '84 Savings Institutions Sourcebook, Table 70, p. 54.

earning the low passbook interest rate to deposits earning much higher and more flexible returns. Particularly important among the new higher-rate savings deposit plans offered by the industry are money market CDs (MMCs), small-saver certificates (SSCs), and Keogh and IRA-plan retirement accounts—all developed during the 1970s. MMCs, first authorized in June 1978, carry an interest rate tied to the yield on new six-month U.S. Treasury bills, SSCs, authorized in January 1980, offer a rate tied to the latest yield on 2½-year U.S. Treasury notes. A further major step was taken in late 1982 and early 1983 when Money Market Deposit Accounts (MMDAs) and Super NOWs were authorized with passage of the Garn bill. Both of these new deposit accounts are draftable by check or preauthorized transfer and carry interest rates that change with money market conditions. One unfortunate side effect of these newer deposit plans is that savings and loans today are faced with both a more costly and a more volatile deposit base.

Savings and loans also rely upon several nondeposit sources of funds to support their loans and investments. One of the most important consists of advances (loans) from the Federal Home Loan Bank System, which provides extra liquidity in periods when deposit withdrawals are heavy or when loan demand exceeds incoming deposits.[2] Equity capital or net worth (i.e., the retained earnings and the general reserves held by individual associations) makes up about 5 percent of total funds sources, but is very important to the public. It is the net worth account which absorbs operating losses and keeps the doors open until management can correct any serious problems.

Trends in Revenues and Costs

As the 1980s began, savings and loans were experiencing one of the darkest periods in their history. In fact, 1980 was the least profitable year for S&Ls since World War II and profits turned negative in both 1981 and 1982. For example, in 1982 the industry's average return on equity was −16.1 percent. While subsequent years brought modest profitability for the S&L industry, many savings associations clung to desperately thin net worth positions. Dozens of ailing associations were helped into mergers by the FSLIC, which purchased sizable quantities of questionable industry assets. Some observers feared that a continuation of this adverse trend would eventually swamp the FSLIC's insurance fund, perhaps bringing on an emergency bailout by the federal government. Quickly, Congress moved in the fall of 1982 with passage of the Garn bill to authorize the FSLIC (as well as the FDIC) to head off outright failures with agency-assisted mergers. A troubled S&L could be merged with another, stronger association (even one in another state if suitable in-state associations were in short supply) or with another depository institution (such as a commercial bank) if suitable S&L merger partners could not be found.

For those associations apparently headed toward serious trouble, as reflected in continuing losses and declining net worth, the FSLIC could

---

[2] In recent years, savings associations have turned in growing numbers to the secondary mortgage market for funds, especially in periods when loan demand is high and deposit growth is impaired. Older, lower-yielding mortgages are sold to other investors during such periods, generating additional funds which may be invested in new, higher-yielding mortgages.

provide emergency assistance to restore an S&L's net worth to acceptable levels. This could be accomplished by an exchange of notes. The agency could issue insurance corporation notes and exchange these for net worth certificates of the troubled association. Both the total assets and the net worth of the aided S&L would increase.

What circumstances put the industry in such a dismal state? One cause is the fact that S&Ls historically have issued mortgage loans with fixed-interest rates, while accepting deposits whose interest rates are sensitive to changing market conditions. In short, the bulk of their assets are rate insensitive, while a growing portion of their liabilities are highly rate sensitive. In periods of rapidly rising interest rates, the industry's net interest margin—the difference between its interest earnings on assets and its interest costs on borrowed funds—has been severely squeezed. Indeed, in several recent periods, short-term interest rates paid on deposits exceeded interest rates earned on long-term loans; the industry's net interest margin turned negative.

Other recent trends have also hurt the industry's profitability. The individuals and families whose savings provide the bulk of association funds have become more financially sophisticated, withdrawing their deposits whenever higher returns are available elsewhere or whenever there is even a hint of trouble in the thrift industry. The fragile nature of public confidence was demonstrated dramatically in 1985, for example, when 70 Ohio savings and loans were threatened with collapse due to the failure of a Cincinnati-based savings association that appeared to threaten the viability of Ohio's state-sponsored private deposit insurance fund. Unquestionably the savings and loan industry was damaged severely in the late 1970s and early 1980s by the rapid growth of money market mutual funds—aggressive institutions that offered small savers higher and more flexible yields than the returns on savings and loan deposits. We will discuss the characteristics of money market funds later in this chapter.

Legal Interest-Rate Ceilings

Added to this situation is the problem of legal interest-rate ceilings. For decades the deposits at commercial banks, mutual savings banks, and savings and loan associations have been subject to legal ceilings which specify the maximum rate that can be paid on each type of deposit. The ceiling rates are now set by the Depository Institutions Deregulation Committee (DIDC), composed of the heads of the major federal financial regulatory agencies. Shares offered by money market funds and other securities sold in the open market have never been subject to these legal ceilings. When interest rates on these alternative investments rose above the ceilings, many savers opted to disintermediate their funds from S&Ls

and seek higher yields elsewhere. With passage of the DIDMCA law in 1980 the phasing out of these deposit-rate ceilings was mandated by 1986. And the DIDC moved rapidly to implement the rate ceiling phase out. A further rate deregulation move occurred in 1982 when the Garn bill required the elimination of different deposit-rate ceilings for commercial banks versus S&Ls and mutual savings banks. The basic idea was to allow *all* depository institutions to compete freely for savings accounts at going market rates of interest.

Trends in Industry Structure

The pressure of rising costs and the resulting squeeze on earnings have caused many savings and loans to merge or be absorbed by larger associations. As a result, the number of associations in the United States has been declining since 1960. The S&L population decreased from about 6,300 in 1960 to less than 3,400 in 1984. Not surprisingly, with declining numbers, the average-size S&L has increased tremendously in recent years, from about $11 million in assets in 1960 to $265 million by year-end 1984. Still there are numerous small associations—about 2,000 have assets of less than $100 million each. With large numbers of relatively small S&Ls, continuing increases in costs and competition, and downward pressure on earnings, more savings and loans will be absorbed into larger financial institutions in the future.

Possible Remedies for the Industry's Problems

If savings and loans are to be viable institutions in the future, they will need help from at least two sources: (1) sound decision making by management to diversify their operations, identifying innovative new services to offer the public; and (2) a further relaxation of government regulations to permit the offering of new services and the merging of smaller associations into larger ones. The classical model of a savings and loan association—investing the bulk of its assets in fixed-rate mortgages and offering relatively low-yielding savings accounts to the public—cannot survive in today's volatile economic environment.

More aggressive S&Ls are branching out in at least three different directions. Some have followed a *real estate* model, literally becoming mortgage banking firms. These savings associations are selling off their long-term mortgages and converting into real estate service organizations, managing and developing property, and brokering mortgages. Many have become *family financial centers,* offering a full range of retail banking services to the consumer. Services offered range from NOW accounts and credit cards to financial counseling and even assistance in preparing income tax returns. While home mortgages continue to dominate their asset portfolios, most of these S&Ls offer principally adjustable-rate mortgages (ARMs) whose yield adjusts more readily to changing financial market conditions. Other S&Ls have adopted a *diversified* model, becoming holding-company organizations with ownership and control over commercial banks, retail-oriented consumer banks, mortgage banking firms, and commercial credit affiliates. Only time will tell which of these models can adapt successfully to the changing character of the nation's financial system.

MUTUAL SAVINGS BANKS

Mutual savings banks were started in the United States approximately 150 years ago to meet the financial needs of the small saver. Unlike credit unions, savings and loans, and other depository institutions that have spread nationwide, mutuals have remained essentially rooted along the eastern seaboard of the United States where they began. These institutions play an active role in the residential mortgage market, as do savings and loans, but are much more diversified in their investments, purchasing corporate bonds and common stock, making consumer loans, and investing in commercial mortgages.[3]

From their earliest origins mutual savings banks have designed their financial services to appeal to individuals and families. Deposit accounts can be opened for amounts as small as $1, with transactions carried out by mail or, in many instances, through 24-hour automated tellers in convenient locations. Mutual savings banks in Massachusetts and New Hampshire were the first to develop the interest-bearing NOW account, perhaps the most important new consumer financial service of the past two decades. Many savings banks advertise the availability of family financial counseling services, low-cost insurance, and travel planning as well as a wide variety of savings instruments.

Number and Distribution of Savings Banks

The number of mutuals operating today is small—about 600. Through most of this century the savings bank population has been on the decline. For example, in 1900 there were 626 mutuals operating in the United States, but the number had fallen to only 424 by 1982. Then, legislation

---

[3] The Garn bill of 1982 permitted S&Ls to convert readily into federal savings banks and savings banks to convert readily into S&Ls. For this reason the technical distinction between savings and loans and mutual savings banks will become less relevant in future years. In fact, in 1983 the National Association of Mutual Savings Banks and the United States League of Savings Institutions, representing the savings and loan industry, agreed to consolidate their activities and form one National Council of Savings Institutions— a trade group committed to supporting the thrift industry.

was passed to allow the chartering of federal savings banks (FSBs), resulting in a dramatic increase in the numbers of savings banks to just over 600 by year-end 1984. Savings bank assets and deposits also have grown rapidly in recent years. In 1950 total assets of all mutuals stood at $22 billion, but industry assets had reached nearly $290 billion in 1984. Of course, as a result of the long-term decrease in the number of savings banks coupled with their rapidly expanding assets the average mutual savings bank grew tremendously in size and now exceeds $400 million in total assets—far larger than most credit unions and savings and loan associations, and even most commercial banks. This increase in average size has aided mutuals in offering a greater variety of services and in slowing somewhat the growth of their operating costs.

Mutual savings banks are not evenly distributed across the United States but rather are located primarily in New England and the Middle Atlantic states. Massachusetts leads the list followed by New York. Other states which have mutuals headquartered within their borders include Alaska, Connecticut, Delaware, Indiana, Maine, Maryland, Minnesota, New Hampshire, New Jersey, Oregon, Pennsylvania, Rhode Island, Vermont, Washington, and Wisconsin.

Charters and Regulations

Mutuals can be chartered by either the states or the federal government.[4] Moreover, state and federal governments also share responsibility for insuring their deposits. (See Exhibit 5–2.) Most savings banks have their deposits insured by the Federal Deposit Insurance Corporation (up to $100,000); the remainder are covered by state insurance programs or by the Federal Savings and Loan Insurance Corporation. Today, only 16 states charter mutuals, but these institutions are not bound by geography in raising funds or making loans and investments. Their mortgage-lending activities reach nationwide and occasionally even abroad to support the building of commercial and residential projects.

How Funds Are Raised and Allocated

Technically, mutual savings banks are owned by their depositors. All net earnings available after funds are set aside to provide adequate reserves must be paid to the depositors as owners' dividends. Regulations

---

[4] Federal chartering of savings banks was authorized by Congress in 1978. Previous to that time all mutuals were chartered by the states and only by those few states, located principally along the eastern seaboard, that made explicit provision for them in their statutes. The advent of federally chartered savings banks (FSBs) opens up the possibility of the eventual nationwide spread of these institutions, overcoming their narrow geographic origins.

exercised primarily by the states are designed to insure maximum safety of deposits. This is accomplished principally through close control over the types of *assets* which a savings bank is permitted to acquire. For example, state law and the "prudent man" rule enforced by the courts generally limit mutuals' investments to first-mortgage loans (the majority of which must come from the home state), U.S. government and federal agency securities, high-grade corporate bonds and stocks, and municipal bonds.

The industry's role in the financial system can be seen by looking at its balance sheet. On the asset side, the key investment is mortgages and mortgage-related instruments, accounting for about half of their total assets. (See Exhibit 5–6.) Most of the mortgage total represents direct mortgage loans to build single-family homes, apartments, shopping centers, office facilities, and other commercial and residential structures. The remainder is devoted to Government National Mortgage Association (GNMA) pass-through securities (also known as Ginnie Maes), backed by a government-guaranteed pool of mortgages.[5]

A distant second in importance to mortgages are savings bank investments in corporate bonds, corporate stock, and government bonds and notes. The volume of corporate bonds held by the industry outnumbers its investments in corporate stock about five to one. Due to the pressures of inflation and higher deposit costs, however, many states have liberalized their regulations to allow mutuals increased purchases of common and preferred stock. Another factor favoring investments in stock has been the industry's growing federal tax burden, especially following the Tax Reform Act of 1969 which reduced mutuals' tax shelters. Since 85 percent of stock dividend income is exempt from federal taxation, mutuals have taken greater interest in the stock market. State law and tradition, however, severely limit the growth potential of savings bank investments in the stock market. Savings banks also make loans for the support of education, to fund home improvements, and to cover personal expenses.

The principal source of funds for savings banks is *deposits*, representing close to 90 percent of total funds available. Savings deposits carry no specific maturity but may be withdrawn at any time by the customer and carry the lowest rate of interest. Time deposits, on the other hand, have fixed maturities, and savings banks are allowed to pay higher maximum rates on these accounts, depending on their maturity date.

Industry deposits have grown rapidly over the past three decades, reflecting the ability of mutual savings banks to appeal to the financial needs of individuals and families. The larger savings banks have established extensive branch office systems and have been highly innovative

---

[5] See Chapter 19 for a discussion of GNMA pass-throughs and other mortgage-related securities.

EXHIBIT 5–6

Balance Sheet of the Savings Bank Industry, December 31, 1983*
(amounts in millions of dollars for all FDIC-insured savings banks)

Item	Amount (millions)	Percentage of Total
Assets:		
Real estate loans	$ 91,057	50.7%
Commercial and industrial loans	4,633	2.6
Loans to individuals	7,982	4.4
Loans to financial institutions	1,284	0.7
Other loans	89	†
Cash and due from depository institutions	5,870	3.3
U.S. Treasury and federal agency securities	28,335	15.8
State and local government securities	2,167	1.2
Corporate bonds	17,588	9.8
Other bonds, notes, and debentures	3,573	2.0
Corporate stock	3,240	1.8
Buildings and equipment	1,657	0.9
Real estate owned	430	0.2
All other assets	11,627	6.5
Total assets	$179,532	100.0%
Liabilities and Surplus Accounts:		
Demand deposits	$ 2,910	1.6%
Savings deposits	69,850	38.9
Time deposits	88,807	49.5
All other liabilities	8,388	4.7
Subordinated notes and debentures	701	0.4
Surplus accounts	8,876	4.9%
Total liabilities and surplus accounts	$179,532	100.0%

Note: Columns may not add to totals because of rounding.
* Preliminary data.
† Item is less than 0.05 percent.
SOURCE: Federal Deposit Insurance Corporation.

in offering new services. Nearly all savings banks today offer checkable NOW accounts, money orders, Christmas club accounts, loans against passbook savings accounts, traveler's checks, and home-improvement loans. Many savings banks also offer life insurance policies to their customers where permitted by state law.

Like savings and loan associations, mutuals have discovered that the customers they serve have become more financially sophisticated in recent years. The highest-yielding time deposit accounts have grown much faster than lower-yielding savings plans. The most pronounced shift has been out of regular passbook savings accounts to fixed-maturity time deposits which, in many instances, carry contract rates that float with conditions in the money market. Nondeposit borrowings also have grown rapidly. The net result of all these changes has been to push interest costs higher, put pressure on earnings, and increase the volatility of funds flows. Savings banks today must be more concerned with their liquidity (cash) position than has been true in the past. Their relatively new checkable NOW and money market accounts in particular are more volatile than savings deposits and require increased investments in liquid assets to back them up.

Current Trends and Future Problems

The savings bank industry faces a number of problems which will significantly affect its future growth and viability as a conduit for savings and investment. One factor is increasing competition with credit unions, savings and loan associations, and commercial banks offering similar services. Because of the heavy concentration of savings bank assets in mortgage-related investments, mutuals are less flexible than commercial banks in adjusting to changing financial conditions and to the changing service needs of their customers. Many still have severe earning problems due to their inflexible asset structures coupled with sharply higher deposit interest costs.

On the other hand, many savings banks have countered this relative inflexibility in their asset structure with aggressive competition for funds and innovative new services. For example, mutuals have been among the leading institutions in developing new types of variable-rate mortgages, in order to introduce greater flexiblity into their revenue flows. The future growth of this industry, like that of most other financial institutions, will depend heavily on the ability of savings banks to gain the necessary changes in federal and state regulations to allow them to expand their services on both the credit and the deposit side of their business.

MONEY MARKET FUNDS

A fourth major nonbank thrift institution appeared on the scene as recently as 1972. In that year the first money market mutual fund—a financial intermediary pooling the savings of thousands of individuals and businesses and investing those monies in short-term, high-quality money market instruments—opened for business. Taking advantage of the fact that the interest rates on most deposits offered by commercial and savings banks, savings and loans, and credit unions were restrained by federal ceilings, the money fund offered "share accounts" whose yields reflected prevailing interest rates in the nation's money market. Thus, the money fund represents the classic case of profit-seeking entrepreneurs finding a loophole around ill-conceived government regulations.

The growth of money market funds was explosive. As of year-end
1973 there were only four in existence with assets totaling about $100
million. By the end of 1980 there were about 80 funds with assets approaching $75 billion. Their high watermark was reached in 1982 when
more than 200 funds held over $200 billion in assets. (See Exhibit 5–7.)
Beginning in late 1982 and 1983, however, a decline set in as banks
and other depository institutions fought back with Super NOWs and
Money Market Deposit Accounts (MMDAs), both authorized to carry unregulated interest rates by the Garn bill in October 1982. However, even
in 1983 money market funds held assets of about $160 billion and subse-
quently resumed their growth, though at a much more modest pace.

EXHIBIT 5–7

Money Market Funds: Assets Held and Total Shares Outstanding,
1974–1983

Item	1974	1975	1976	1977	1978	1979	1980	1981	1982	1983
Assets:										
Demand deposits and currency	—	*	*	*	$ 0.1	$ 0.1	$ 0.2	$ −0.5	$ 0.3	$ −0.3
Time deposits	1.6	2.1	1.5	1.8	4.5	12.0	21.0	43.9	40.8	24.0
Security RPs	0.1	0.1	0.1	0.3	0.3	2.4	5.6	14.5	16.2	13.0
Foreign deposits	—	—	—	*	0.5	5.1	6.8	18.8	23.8	21.9
U.S. government securities	0.1	0.9	1.1	0.9	1.5	5.6	8.2	31.9	54.6	36.2
Open-market paper	0.6	0.5	0.9	1.1	3.7	19.3	31.6	70.4	69.1	66.2
Miscellaneous assets	−0.1	−0.1	−0.1	−0.2	0.3	0.7	1.1	2.9	1.8	1.5
Total assets	$2.4	$3.7	$3.7	$3.9	$10.8	$45.2	$74.4	$181.9	$206.6	$162.5
Total shares outstanding	$2.4	$3.7	$3.7	$3.9	$10.8	$45.2	$74.4	$181.9	$206.6	$162.5

Note: Columns may not add to totals because of rounding.
* Less than $50 million.
SOURCE: Board of Governors of the Federal Reserve System, *Flow of Funds Accounts, Asset and Liabilities Outstanding,*
1960–83.

What factors explain the initial rapid growth and continuing viability
of this newest nonbank thrift institution? One is the absence of regulatory
restrictions. There are no interest-rate ceilings and, unless the funds themselves impose it, no mandatory penalties for early withdrawals as is required by law with many deposit plans offered by banks and thrifts. Another factor is the high quality of assets acquired by the funds. The typical
money market fund invests primarily in U.S. Treasury bills, bank certifi-

cates of deposit, bankers' acceptances, commercial paper, and securities issued by federal government agencies.[6] All are the highest quality financial instruments with low or nonexistent risk of borrower default and limited fluctuations in price (i.e., low market risk). Contributing to the low-risk character of money fund investments is their short-average maturity. Most funds limit the average maturity of their security holdings to less than four months. The short maturity of fund investments results in a highly liquid security portfolio which can be adjusted quickly to changing market conditions. Many funds declare dividends on a daily basis, crediting the earnings to customer accounts and often notifying the customer by mail monthly of additional shares purchased with the dividends earned. Most are "no load" funds which do *not* charge their customers commissions for opening an account, purchasing additional shares, or redeeming shares for cash.

One of the outstanding advantages of the money funds for many investors is the ease with which their accounts can be accessed. Most funds allow the customer to write checks in order to redeem shares, provided the amount of each check exceeds a designated minimum ($500 is common). The customer is issued a book of checks and can merely write out and deposit the check in his or her local bank account, often receiving credit for the deposited check from the local bank or thrift the same day, even though it may take several days for the money fund check to be collected from the fund's bank of deposit (in most cases, a major New York bank). Meantime, daily interest is still being earned on the monies waiting in the customer's share account. Most money funds also offer their customers the option of purchasing or redeeming shares by wire or telephone. A toll-free phone number is usually maintained to provide transfer services as well as to answer customer inquiries concerning transactions and the latest money market yields.

Despite their numerous advantages for customers interested in professional management of short-term funds, the money funds today possess some competitive disadvantages which many financial analysts believe will limit their future growth. Their share accounts are not federally insured as are bank and thrift deposits. And, with the recent rise in bank and corporate business failures this deficiency concerns some investors. Many of the funds have attempted to deal with this problem by arranging for private insurance and spreading their holdings of bank CDs around to qualify many of their CDs for federal insurance coverage.

While the money funds attracted billions of dollars in deposits from banks and nonbank thrifts (especially savings and loans) due to federal deposit-rate ceilings, these ceilings are being phased out, as we noted

---

[6] These various money market securities are discussed in depth in Part Four of the text.

earlier in this chapter. Thus, a key competitive advantage originally possessed by money market funds has been reduced significantly. Their posted yields on share accounts still generally average higher than on money market deposits at banks, however, because of lower operating costs and more flexible asset portfolios. But, of course, the yield differential between money fund shares and bank and thrift deposits has narrowed sharply since 1982—a key factor explaining the much more modest growth of the funds in recent years. In brief, the money funds are not likely to "go away"; they are an established and potent competitor for both small individual savings accounts and institutions' liquid funds. However, barring further restrictive federal regulation of bank and thrift deposits, all bank and nonbank thrift institutions, including money funds, will continue to compete for savings and interest-bearing transactions accounts on more equal terms. The relative growth of all these competing financial institutions should be more balanced and stable in the period ahead.

SUMMARY AND CONCLUSIONS

Nonbank thrift institutions—that is, credit unions, savings and loans, mutual savings banks, and money market funds—are expected to grow rapidly in the coming years. But it will not be an era of trouble-free growth and expansion. The volatility in funds flows experienced by nonbank thrifts during the 1970s and early 1980s may be accentuated in the years ahead by another powerful force—competition. An intense competitive battle for savings deposits, transaction accounts, and consumer loans is now under way between commercial banks and nonbank thrifts in thousands of local markets across the United States.

This fierce competitive battle is not likely to end in the near future: it should in fact intensify as electronic systems are further developed for the automated transfer of funds. Savings and loans, savings banks, credit unions, and money funds are determined to be a part of the growing "electronic money" network which moves funds almost instantly nationwide via computer tape and terminal. In fact, savings and loans in the Midwest have taken the lead in developing point-of-sale (POS) terminals in retail stores, automated tellers in shopping centers, and branch offices to service their customers' financial needs. Investment in these devices is motivated by the desire to bid transaction accounts away from commercial banks. As Professor Nadler (1974) has observed:

The savings organizations recognize that the days when they could survive as specialized thrift institutions are gone, and that for them to survive they must also offer the variety of services that banks can offer. They expect that in a few years there will be full-service banks for families, and they have the motive of fear of not surviving otherwise to spur them on to newer and newer innovation.

Moreover, federal and state authorities which oversee nonbank thrift institutions have shown a willingness in recent years, however belatedly, to liberalize operating rules so that these institutions can expand and improve their services to the public.

STUDY QUESTIONS

1. Credit unions are one of the fastest-growing financial intermediaries in the United States. What are the factors that have contributed to this rapid growth?

2. What are the principal differences between savings and loan associations and mutual savings banks? How are these institutions similar to each other?

3. How and why did money market funds begin in the 1970s? What factors contributed to their rapid growth in the late 1970s and early 1980s? Why did that growth subsequently slow?

4. Competition between commercial banks, credit unions, mutual savings banks, money market funds, and savings and loan associations is increasing rapidly, especially in the markets for savings deposits, payments accounts, and consumer credit. Explain the reasons for this trend toward increasing competition. What are the probable consequences for the consumer? For these thrift institutions?

5. Discuss the factors that are most likely to affect the future growth of nonbank deposit-type financial institutions. Explain how each of these factors is related to the types of services and the viability of these institutions in future years.

6. Why is the savings and loan industry in trouble? What solutions have been offered to deal with the problem?

7. What has happened in recent years to the number of nonbank thrift institutions in operation? Can you explain why?

8. What effect would you expect NOW accounts, MMDAs, and share drafts to have on the loan and investment policies of nonbank thrift institutions? Please explain the reasoning behind your answer.

SELECTED REFERENCES

Cargill, Thomas F. "Recent Research on Credit Unions: A Survey." *Journal of Economics and Business,* Winter 1977, pp. 155–62.

Credit Union National Association. *1983 Yearbook,* Madison, Wis.

Dunham, Constance. "The Growth of Money Market Funds." *New England Economic Review,* Federal Reserve Bank of Boston, September–October 1980, pp. 20–34.

Eisenbeis, Robert A. "New Investment Powers for S&Ls: Diversification or Specialization?" *Economic Review,* Federal Reserve Bank of Atlanta, July 1983, pp. 53–62.

Flannery, Mark J. "Credit Unions as Consumer Lenders in the United States." *New England Economic Review,* Federal Reserve Bank of Boston, July–August 1974, pp. 3–12.

Harless, Doris E. *Nonbank Financial Institutions.* Federal Reserve Bank of Richmond, October 1975.

Longrehr, Frederick W. "Money Market Mutual Fund Investors' Savings Account Holdings and Demographic Profile." *Journal of Bank Research,* Autumn 1982, pp. 202–6.

Moran, Michael J. "Thrift Institutions in Recent Years." *Federal Reserve Bulletin,* December 1982, pp. 725–38.

Nadler, Paul S. "As Savings and Loans Fight for Survival." *Banker's Monthly,* April 15, 1974, pp. 11–13 and 39.

National Association of Mutual Savings Banks. *Annual Report of the President.* New York, May 1982.

United States League of Savings Associations. *Savings and Loan Sourcebook.* Chicago, 1983.

6

Insurance Companies, Pension Funds, and Other Financial Institutions

PURPOSE OF THIS CHAPTER

To explore the roles played and the financial services offered by a variety of financial institutions, including life insurance companies, property-casualty insurance companies, pension funds, finance companies, investment companies, security dealers, investment bankers, mortgage banks, real estate investment trusts, leasing companies, and financial conglomerates (symbiotics). The principal sources of funds drawn upon and principal uses of funds made by each institution are discussed along with a review of the current trends and problems in each financial industry.

KEY TERMS AND CONCEPTS IN THE CHAPTER

bond funds
buy and hold
consolidation
consumer finance
  companies
corporate bond
corporate stock
diversification
ERISA
finance companies
insurance
  underwriting
investment banking

investment companies
lease companies
life insurance
  companies
load funds
mortgage bankers
mutual funds
open-end companies
pension funds
policy loans
property-casualty
  insurance companies

prudent man
REITs
sales finance
  companies
security dealers
separate account
symbiotics
the insurance
  principle
universal life
  insurance

We now turn to a highly diverse group of financial institutions that attract savings mainly from individuals and families and, for the most part, make long-term loans in the capital market. Included in this group are life insurance companies, pension funds, and property-casualty insurance companies, which today are leading institutional buyers of bonds and stocks. Finance companies, another member of the group, are active lenders to both business firms and consumers and borrow heavily in the nation's money market from commercial banks, insurance companies, and other financial institutions. While not generally providing new capital to businesses and other borrowers, investment companies (often called mutual funds) are active traders in corporate stocks and bonds and state and local government securities. As we will soon see, the majority of these financial institutions provide important services to participants in the markets for business and consumer credit.

LIFE INSURANCE COMPANIES

Life insurance companies were present early in the history of the United States. In fact, they were one of the first financial institutions founded in the American colonies. The Corporation for Relief of Poor and Distressed Presbyterian Ministers and of the Poor and Distressed Widows and Children of Presbyterian Ministers, established in 1759, was the first life insurance company in the United States. Life insurance companies offer their customers a hedge against the risk of earnings losses that often follow death, disability, or retirement. Policyholders receive risk protection in return for the payment of policy premiums that are set high enough to cover estimated benefit claims against the company, operating expenses, and a target profit margin. Additional funds to cover claims and expenses are provided by investments made by life insurance companies in bonds, stocks, mortgages, and other assets approved by law and government regulation. Figures on the volume of insurance in force in the United States are shown in Exhibit 6-1, while the principal kinds of insurance policies sold by U.S. life insurers are listed in Exhibit 6-2.

The Insurance Principle

The insurance business is founded upon the Law of Large Numbers. This mathematical principle states that a risk that is not predictable for one person can be forecasted accurately for a sufficiently large group of people. No insurance company can accurately forecast when any one person will die, but its actuarial estimates of the total number of policyholders who will die in any given year are usually quite accurate.

Life insurance companies today insure their policyholders against three basic kinds of risk: premature death, the danger of living too long and

EXHIBIT 6-1

Life Insurance in Force in the United States, 1973–1983 ($ billions)

Category	1973	1983
Total amount:		
Ordinary	$ 928	$ 2,544
Group	708	2,220
Industrial	41	31
Credit	101	171
	$ 1,778	$ 4,966
Average amount:		
Per family	$24,400	$54,200
Per insured family	28,800	63,000

Note: Columns may not add to totals due to rounding.
SOURCE: American Council of Life Insurance, *1984 Life Insurance Fact Book.*

outlasting one's accumulated assets, and serious illness or accident. Many of their policies combine financial protection against death, disability, and retirement with savings plans to help the policyholder prepare for some important future financial need, such as the purchase of a home or meeting the costs of a college education. Actually, most of their benefit payments are made to living, rather than deceased, policyholders who receive annuities, disability checks, and other health insurance benefits. U.S. life companies are among the leading sources of retirement (pension) benefit payments for older Americans and today more than 30 million U.S. citizens are enrolled in pension programs managed by life insurance companies. These companies are heavily regulated by the states to guarantee adequate compensation to the companies themselves and to ensure that the public is not overcharged or poorly served.

Investments of Life Insurance Companies

Life insurance companies invest the bulk of their funds in long-term securities—bonds, stocks, and mortgages. They are inclined to commit their funds long term due to the high predictability of their cash inflows and outflow. Moreover, this high cash-flow predictability normally would permit a life insurance company to accept considerable risk in the securities it acquires. However, both law and tradition require a life insurer to act as a "prudent man." This restriction is imposed to ensure that sufficient funds are available to meet all legitimate claims from policyholders or their beneficiaries at precisely the time those claims mature.

Life companies pursue income certainty and safety of principal in their investments. In most years at least 90 percent of the corporate securities

EXHIBIT 6–2

The Principal Kinds of Insurance Policies Sold by Life Insurance Companies

Ordinary or whole-life insurance	Insurance protection covers the entire lifetime of the policyholder whose designated beneficiaries are paid whenever the policyholder dies. Premiums are either payable throughout the policyholder's lifetime—a straight life policy—or for a limited time period—a limited pay policy—and build up cash values that may be borrowed by the policyholder.
Term life insurance	Insurance coverage for a certain number of years so that the policyholder's beneficiaries receive benefit payments only if death occurs within the period of coverage.
Endowment policy	Benefits are payable to the living policyholder on a specified future date or to the policyholder's beneficiaries if death occurs before the date specified in the policy. Premium payments build up cash value for the policyholder as with whole life insurance.
Group life insurance	Master insurance policy covering a group of people (usually all working for the same employer or members of the same organization) and sold normally without a required health examination.
Industrial life insurance	Small-denomination life policies with premium payments collected monthly or weekly by a company agent calling at the insured's place of residence.
Universal life insurance	Insurance protection with premium payments whose amount or timing can be changed by the policyholder to increase or decrease the policy benefit. These policies include a savings account built up through premium payments with a flexible rate of return.
Variable life insurance	Insurance protection whose benefits vary in amount with the value of assets pledged behind the policy contract (though in most cases the beneficiaries receive at least a guaranteed minimum death benefit payment).
Adjustable life insurance	A flexible form of insurance protection which permits the policyholder to alter some of the policy contract's terms, such as the premium payments, the time period of coverage, or the face value of the policy.
Credit life insurance	A type of term insurance contract pledged to pay off a loan or other form of debt in the event the borrower dies before the debt is paid off.

they purchase are in the top four credit-rating categories.[1] Moreover, life insurers frequently follow a "buy and hold" strategy, acting as long-term holders of securities rather than rapidly turning over their portfolios. This investment approach reduces the risk of fluctuations in income and avoids having to rely on forecasting interest rates. We should note, however, that in recent years some life companies have become more active traders and speculators in securities. Emphasizing *performance* more than permanency in their investments, the larger life companies have set up trading rooms to more closely monitor the performance of their investment holdings, selling out and reinvesting in higher-yielding alternatives when circumstances warrant. Because this new investment strategy creates additional risk, some of the larger companies have begun to trade in financial futures contracts to protect themselves against losses from fluctuating interest rates.

Exhibit 6–3 shows the kinds of investments held by U.S. life insurance

EXHIBIT 6–3

Assets of U.S. Life Insurance Companies, 1983

Item	Amounts ($ billions)	Percent of Total Assets
Government securities:		
U.S. Treasury obligations	$ 28.6	
Federal agency securities	25.9	
State and local debt obligations	10.0	
Debt of foreign governments and international agencies	12.1	
Total government securities	$ 76.6	11.7%
Corporate securities:		
Bonds	$218.8	
Common stocks	51.8	
Preferred stocks	13.0	
Total corporate securities	$297.0	45.3
Mortgages:		
Farm	$ 12.7	
Nonfarm	138.3	
Total mortgages	$151.0	23.1
Loans to policyholders	$ 54.1	8.3
Real estate owned	22.2	3.4
Miscellaneous assets	54.0	8.3
Total assets	$588.2	100.0%

Note: Columns may not add to totals due to rounding.
SOURCE: American Council of Life Insurance, *1984 Life Insurance Fact Book.*

---

[1] See Chapter 10 and Appendix A for an explanation of security ratings.

EXHIBIT 6–4

Recent Trends in Acquisitions of Financial Assets by U.S. Life Insurance Companies, 1980–1984

Financial Assets Acquired	Annual Net Acquisitions of Financial Assets ($ billions)				
	1980	1981	1982	1983	1984
Demand deposits and currency	$ 0.5	$ 1.1	$ 0.3	$−0.6	$−0.5
Corporate stock (equities)	0.5	2.9	3.4	3.1	*
U.S. Treasury securities	1.0	2.3	8.4	12.1	12.9
Federal agency securities	1.8	3.1	4.3	7.2	7.3
State and local government securities (municipals)	0.3	0.5	1.9	0.9	−0.6
Corporate bonds	8.7	7.3	16.2	16.7	21.6
Mortgages (residential and commercial)	12.3	6.7	4.2	9.6	5.7
Open-market paper	2.2	7.4	4.2	3.4	6.8
Policy loans	6.6	7.3	4.3	1.1	0.5
Miscellaneous assets	3.6	7.3	8.1	6.1	6.4
Total acquisitions of financial assets (net for the year)	$37.4	$45.9	$55.4	$59.7	$60.2

* Less than 0.1 percent.
SOURCE: Board of Governors of the Federal Reserve System, *Flow of Funds Accounts, Fourth Quarter 1984*, February 1985.

companies as of year-end 1983, while Exhibit 6–4 indicates the most important kinds of financial assets life insurers have added to their investment portfolios in recent years. The primary investment is in corporate bonds, the majority of which are issued by domestic companies, though purchases of foreign bonds (mainly from Canada) are also important. Holdings of common and preferred stock, though much smaller, have become significant in recent years. Life insurance companies have shown renewed interest in corporate stock due to inflation and the growing importance of variable annuity policies and variable life insurance plans in their sales programs.

The second most important asset held by life insurance companies comprises mortgages on farm, residential, and commercial properties.

Substantial changes have occurred in life insurance company mortgage investments in recent years. The industry has reduced its holdings of single-family and multifamily residential mortgages and increased its holdings of farm and commercial mortgages, including loans on retail stores, shopping centers, office buildings, hospitals, and factories. The higher yields and absence of legal interest-rate restrictions on nonresidential mortgages explain much of the recent rapid growth of commercial mortgage lending by the life insurance industry.[2] However, life insurers continue to provide indirect support to the residential mortgage market by making heavy purchases of federal agency securities, most of which come from government agencies aiding the home mortgage market.

Government securities play a secondary but still important role in the portfolios of life insurance companies. These securities serve the important function of providing a reservoir of *liquidity*, because they may be sold with little difficulty when funds are required. Recently investments in government securities have been rising as industry cash flows have become more volatile, increasing demands for liquid reserves. Life insurance companies buy mostly federal government securities rather than state and local government obligations. The industry has only a limited need for the tax-exempt income provided by state and local bonds because its tax rate is still relatively low. When life insurance companies do purchase local government securities, they generally prefer revenue bonds, which carry the highest yields.

One asset whose importance increased dramatically during the 1960s and 1970s is loans to policyholders. The holder of an ordinary (whole-life) insurance policy usually is entitled to borrow against the accumulated cash value of the policy, which increases every year. The interest rate on such loans is stated in the contract accompanying the policy and is usually quite low. For example, many policies issued not long ago carry an 8 percent loan rate. Policy loans tend to follow the business cycle, rising significantly in periods when economic activity and interest rates are increasing rapidly and declining when the economy or interest rates are headed down or growing more slowly as was true in the early 1980s.

---

[2] In granting mortgage credit, life insurance companies usually employ *advance commitments*. These consist of promises to provide long-term mortgage funds to a real estate developer before a residential or commercial construction project begins. The developer will use that financing commitment as an aid in obtaining short-term cash (usually from commercial banks) to complete construction. Later, when the project is completed, the insurance company will loan the funds promised and the proceeds of the long-term loan will be used to repay any short-term borrowings. Recently, pressured by inflation and high-interest rates, insurance companies have been insisting on short-term advance commitments, floating rather than fixed rates on mortgage loans, and a share in any net earnings from a residential or commercial project.

Because of this cyclical characteristic, policy loans are a volatile claim on the industry's resources. When loan demand is high, life insurance companies frequently are forced to reduce their purchases of bonds and stocks.[3]

Sources of Life Insurance Company Funds

The industry's main sources of funds have changed little since World War II. The primary income source is premium receipts from sales of life insurance policies, annuity contracts, and health and liability insurance policies. Annual net income from investments in bonds, stocks, and other securities average only about a third of premium receipts. The industry's net earnings after expenses roughly equal its investment income each year because virtually all premiums from the sale of policies are ultimately returned to policyholders or their beneficiaries. This means that, on balance, the industry hopes to "break even" from its insurance-underwriting operations (with premiums flowing in balanced by benefits paid out) while earning profits from its investment income. (See Exhibit 6–5 for a statement of sources and uses of life insurance industry funds.)

Regulating the Industry

The life insurance business has been heavily regulated by the states since its inception. It is generally thought to be "vested with the public interest," and therefore its activities are carefully monitored by state insurance commissions and the courts. Field representatives must be licensed and policy forms and premium rates approved by state agencies. All funds must be invested in accordance with court decisions and with state laws and regulations. Only commercial banking appears to be as heavily regulated as the life insurance business, though unlike banks, life insurers face little federal regulation. In fact, they are one of the few American financial institutions free from direct federal supervision.

Structure and Growth of the Life Insurance Industry

More than 90 percent of the 2,000-plus American life insurance companies are corporations owned by their stockholders. The rest are mutuals,

---

[3] The sensitivity of life insurance policyholders to interest rates, as demonstrated by the importance of policy loans, is also mirrored in the apparent sensitivity of life insurance customers to variations in *policy prices*. For example, a recent study by Babbel (1985) finds that inflation-adjusted U.S. life insurance sales were negatively correlated to a statistically significant degree with the real cost of insurance coverage over the 1953–79 period. However, the author could not find statistically significant evidence that customers readily shift from high- to low-cost insurance companies on the basis of policy prices alone.

EXHIBIT 6–5

The U.S. Life Insurance Company Dollar: Sources and Uses of Funds in 1983 (in cents)

Sources of income:	
Policyholder premiums	69.0¢
Earnings from investments and other income	31.0
	100.0¢
How used:	
Benefit payments during year	50.6¢
Additions to policy reserves	28.8
Additions to special reserves and surplus funds	1.8
	81.2¢
Operating expenses:	
Commissions paid to agents	5.7¢
Home and field office expenses	9.9
	15.6¢
Taxes*	2.0¢
Dividends to stockholders of stock life insurance companies†	1.2
	100.0¢

* Direct investment taxes (such as real estate) are excluded from taxes and are deducted, with other investment expenses, from investment income. Federal income taxes, however, are included in total taxes.
† If only stockholder-owned companies are included, then the dividend ratio becomes 2 cents per dollar.
SOURCE: Adapted from the American Council of Life Insurance, *1984 Life Insurance Fact Book.*

which issue ownership shares to their policyholders. However, mutual firms are much bigger on average and generally were established much earlier. In total, mutual life insurers hold about three fifths of industry assets, with stock companies accounting for the remaining 40 percent. Most new companies in recent years have been stockholder owned, and a few mutuals have converted to stockholder organizations to gain greater financial flexibility.

Until recently, the number of life insurance companies had been declining. Many smaller companies were absorbed by other insurers to counteract growing expenses and provide a broader range of services. However, in recent years many new companies have been formed to meet specialized local and regional insurance needs, leaving the older and larger companies to cover the national and international market for insurance. Then, too, the U.S. life insurance industry has grown rapidly in the 1980s as millions of Americans from the post–World War II baby boom have reached the middle-aged group where most life insurance purchases are made. In 1983 alone life insurance purchases exceeded $1 trillion for the first time in history—a volume of business that has supported both the growth of older, established companies and many new companies as well.

New Services

Life insurers are under increasing pressure to originate and market new services to the public. Increasing competition from other financial intermediaries and rising costs have played major roles in encouraging the development of new services. Among the most important new developments are the creation of separate accounts, universal and adjustable life insurance, variable premium and variable life insurance, mutual funds, tax shelters, venture-capital loans, and corporate cash-management systems.

A *separate account* is an asset account which a life insurance company holds on behalf of a customer (usually a pension fund) apart from its other assets. Funds stored in the account are subject to more liberal investment rules, permitting a larger portion of these monies to be placed in common stock and other more risky investments. Begun in 1979, *universal life insurance* allows the customer to change the face amount of his or her policy and the size and timing of the premium payments as well as earn higher investment returns from any premiums paid in. Premium payments on a universal life insurance policy usually are invested in a money market fund. Universal life is just one example of the more *flexible* types of insurance policies developed by life companies in recent years, each designed to deal with inflation and changing economic conditions. Another example of the newer flexible life insurance products is *adjustable life insurance* which permits the policyholder to change periodically from an ordinary (whole-life or permanent) insurance policy to term insurance (which offers protection only for a designated period) and back again in order to match the customer's changing curcumstances. Adjustable policies allow the policyholder to increase or decrease the face value of his or her policy, the period of insurance protection, and the size of premium payments within the limits spelled out in the policy contract. A variation on this idea is *variable premium life insurance* which grants the policyholder lower premium payments when investments made by the life insurance company earn a greater return due to rising interest rates.

Variable life insurance pays benefits according to the value of assets pledged behind the policy (primarily common stock) rather than paying a fixed amount of money. There is, however, normally a guaranteed minimum benefit for the policyholder's designated beneficiary with variable life policies. It is a form of inflation-hedged life insurance now authorized in all 50 states and growing rapidly. Universal and variable life insurance sales combined accounted for a fifth of all policy sales in the United

States in 1983, compared to just 10 percent the year before. New services offered by life insurance companies in future years will depend heavily on changes in government laws and regulations, something that is also true of other financial intermediaries.

PROPERTY–CASUALTY INSURANCE COMPANIES

Property-casualty insurers offer protection against fire, theft, bad weather, negligence, and other acts and events which result in injury to persons or property. So broad is the range of risk for which these companies provide protection that property-casualty insurers are sometimes referred to as "insurance supermarkets." In addition to their traditional insurance lines—automobile, fire, marine, personal liability, and property coverage—many of these firms have branched into the health and medical insurance fields, clashing head-on with life insurance companies offering the same services. (See Exhibit 6–6 for a list of the major types of policies written by property-casualty insurers.)

EXHIBIT 6–6

Principal Lines of Insurance Coverage Provided by U.S. Property-Casualty Companies, 1983 ($ millions)

Insurance Lines	Net Premiums Written by U.S. Companies*	Insurance Lines	Net Premiums Written by U.S. Companies*
Auto liability	$28,080	Worker's compensation	$14,005
Auto physical damage	19,748	Accident and health	4,348
Medical malpractice	1,568	Inland marine	2,649
Other nonauto liability		Ocean marine	1,096
insurance	5,679	Surety and fidelity	1,649
Fire insurance and		Boilers and machinery	356
allied lines†	4,608	Aircraft insurance	302
Homeowners multiple		Burglary and theft	106
peril insurance	12,512	Glass	27
Commercial multiple			
peril insurance	7,293		
Farm owners' multiple			
peril insurance	692		

* Net premiums written represent premium income earned by insurance companies, direct or through reinsurance, less payments made for business reinsured.
† Allied lines include crop-hail insurance premiums.
SOURCE: Insurance Information Institute, *Insurance Facts,* 1984–85 edition.

Makeup of the Property-Casualty Insurance Industry

The property-casualty insurance business has grown rapidly in recent years due to the effects of inflation, rising crime rates, and a growing volume of lawsuits arising from product liability and professional negligence claims. There were almost 3,500 property-casualty companies in the United States in 1985, holding about $270 billion in assets. Stockholder-owned companies are dominant, holding about three fourths of the industry's total resources. Mutual companies—owned by their policyholders—hold roughly a fourth of all industry resources.

Changing Risk Patterns in Property-Liability Coverage

Property-casualty insurance is a riskier business than life insurance. The risk of policyholder claims arising from crime, fire, bad weather, personal negligence, and similar causes is much less predictable than is the risk of death. Moreover, inflation has had a potent impact on the cost of property and services for which this form of insurance pays. For example, the cost of medical care and for repair of automobiles has more than doubled over the past decade.

Equally important, basic changes now seem to be under way in the risk patterns of many large insurance programs, creating problems in forecasting policyholder claims and new premium rates. Examples include much larger settlements awarded by the courts on policyholder claims, a rapid rise in medical malpractice suits, a virtual explosion in product liability claims against manufacturers of automobiles, tires, home appliances, and other goods and services, and the emergence of billions of dollars in claims from so-called *toxic torts*. These are claims arising from civil court decisions favoring individuals suffering from illness or injury caused by exposure to asbestos, nuclear radiation, and other hazardous substances. In order to reduce risk, more property-casualty insurers have become *multiple-line companies,* diversifying into many different lines of insurance.

Investments by Property-Casualty Companies

The majority of funds received by property-casualty companies are invested in state and local government bonds and common stock. Property-casualty companies, unlike most financial institutions, are subject to the full federal corporate income tax rate (except that policyholder dividends are tax deductible). Faced with a potentially heavy tax burden, these companies find tax-exempt state and local government bonds an

EXHIBIT 6–7

Financial Assets and Liabilities of U.S. Property-Casualty Insurance
Companies, December 31, 1983

Asset and Liability Items	Amounts ($ billions)	Percent of Total Assets or Liabilities
Demand deposits and currency	$ 2.6	3.4%
Security repurchase agreements (RPs)	13.7	
Corporate stock	48.1	18.8
U.S. government securities	17.4	12.0
Federal agency obligations	10.7	4.6
State and local government securities	86.7	42.5
Corporate and foreign bonds	21.6	12.6
Commercial mortgages	2.3	0.8
Trade credit	22.2	9.9
Total financial assets	$225.3	100.0%
Policy payables	$156.0	99.0%
Profit taxes payable	0.2	0.1
Total liabilities	$156.2	100.0%

Note: Columns may not add to totals due to rounding.
SOURCE: Board of Governors of the Federal Reserve System, *Flow of Funds Accounts: Assets and Liabilities Outstanding,* 1960–83.

attractive investment. As shown in Exhibit 6–7, industry holdings of state and local bonds represented close to half of total financial assets, although as indicated in Exhibit 6–8, property-casualty insurers have placed less emphasis on purchases of municipal bonds in recent years due, in part, to their sluggish earnings. Their second most important asset, common stock, is intended to protect industry earnings and net worth against inflation. Other important investments include U.S. government securities, federal agency securities, and corporate bonds. As Exhibit 6–7 shows, property-casualty insurers have stepped up their purchases of federal government securities in recent years due to their high yields (reflecting the government's large deficits) and their high degree of safety.

It is interesting to compare the distribution of the assets held by life insurance companies and by property-casualty companies. The net cash flows of the two industries—their annual premium income—are roughly comparable. Yet life insurers hold about three times the assets of property-casualty insurers. Much of the difference is explained by the fact that life insurance is a highly predictable business, while property and personal injury risks are not. Most life insurance policies are long-term contracts, and claims against the insurer are not normally expected for several years. In contrast, property-casualty claims are payable from the day the policy is written, because an accident or injury may occur at any time. Therefore,

EXHIBIT 6–8

Recent Trends in Acquisitions of Financial Assets by U.S. Property-
Casualty Insurers, 1980–1984

Financial Assets Acquired	Annual Net Acquisitions of Financial Assets ($ billions)				
	1980	**1981**	**1982**	**1983**	**1984**
Demand deposits and currency	$ 0.1	$ 0.1	*	$−0.4	*
Security repurchase agreements (RPs)	—	0.1	4.0	9.6	4.3
Corporate stock (equities)	3.1	2.0	3.0	3.2	2.0
U.S. Treasury securities	1.6	1.4	0.6	3.3	3.5
Federal agency securities	0.2	0.8	1.5	2.2	2.3
State and local government securities (municipals)	7.7	4.0	3.0	−0.3	0.5
Corporate bonds	*	2.8	−0.5	−4.2	0.2
Commercial mortgages	0.3	0.4	0.3	0.7	0.3
Trade credit	2.0	2.6	2.1	2.0	2.0
Total acquisitions of financial assets, net for the year	$37.4	$45.9	$55.4	$59.7	$60.2

* Less than 0.05 billion.
SOURCE: Board of Governors of the Federal Reserve System, *Flow of Funds Accounts, Fourth Quarter 1984*, February 1985.

while life insurance companies can stay almost fully invested, property-casualty insurers must be ready at all times to meet the claims of their policyholders. In addition, claims against property-casualty companies are directly affected by inflation, which drives up repair costs. In contrast, most life insurance policies pay the policyholder or his or her designated beneficiary a fixed sum of money.

Sources of Income

Like life insurance firms, property-casualty insurers plan to break even on their insurance product lines and earn most of their net return from investments. Achieving the break-even point in insurance underwriting has been difficult in recent years, however, due to rising costs, increased litigation, and new forms of risk. For example, in 1983 the industry ran a net underwriting loss of $13.3 billion. Investment income, however, usually more than offsets underwriting losses. For example, during 1983 U.S. property-casualty insurers reported investment income of $16 billion, resulting in net income before taxes of about $2.7 billion. This represented a return on net worth of about 9 percent for the year; property-casualty insurers return on net worth has declined every year since 1977. Industry profits are highly volatile from year to year, however, due to unexpected losses, growing litigation expenses, and the refusal of many state insurance commissions to let policy premiums rise as fast as industry expenses.

Business Cycles, Inflation, and Competition

This is an industry whose earnings, and sales revenue reflect the ups and downs of the business cycle. This cyclical sensitivity, coupled with the vulnerability of property-casualty insurers to inflation, has created a difficult environment for insurance managers. Inflation has pushed up claims costs, while intense competition holds premium rates down. Foreign insurance underwriters are more active in domestic markets today, and many U.S. corporations recently have started their own "captive" insurance companies. In order to improve their situation in future years, property-casualty insurers must become more innovative in developing new services and more determined to eliminate those services which have resulted in underwriting losses. This will not be easy due to extensive state government regulations and public pressure for lower insurance rates.

PENSION FUNDS

Pension funds protect individuals and families against loss of income in their retirement years by allowing workers to set aside and invest a portion of their current income. A pension plan will place current savings in a portfolio of stocks, bonds, real estate, and other assets in the expectation of building an even larger pool of funds in the future. In this way, the pension plan member can balance his or her planned consumption after retirement with the amount of savings set aside today.

Growth of Pension Funds

Pension funds have been among the most rapidly growing of all American financial intermediaries. Between 1970 and 1983 the assets of all private and public pension funds more than quadrupled (see Exhibit 6–9). Approximately one half of all full-time workers in commerce and industry and three quarters of all government civilian employees are protected

EXHIBIT 6–9

Total Assets of U.S. Private and Public Pension Funds, Selected Years
($ billions)

Type of Pension Plan or Program	1940	1950	1960	1970	1980	1983
Private pension programs:	$2.0	$12.1	$ 52.0	$138.2	$422.7	$ 673.9
Insured plans	0.6	5.6	18.8	41.2	165.8	264.6
Noninsured plans	1.4	6.5	33.2	97.0	286.8	409.3
Government pension programs:	$4.3	$25.8	$ 56.1	$125.9	$289.6	$ 429.4
State-local retirement systems	1.6	5.3	19.3	60.3	185.2	289.7
Federal civilian programs	0.6	4.2	10.5	23.1	75.8	114.2
Railroad retirement program	0.1	2.6	3.7	4.4	2.1	0.6
Social security program (OASDI)	$2.0	$13.7	$ 22.6	$ 38.1	$ 26.5	$ 24.9
Total assets of all funds	$6.3	$37.9	$108.2	$262.0	$712.3	$1,103.3

Note: Columns may not add to totals due to rounding.
SOURCES: Securities and Exchange Commission: Railroad Retirement Board; U.S. Department of Health and Human Services; and the American Council of Life Insurance, *Pension Facts,* 1983 update.

by pension plans other than the social security program (OASDI). Nearly 170 million persons are insured under social security.

Pension fund growth in the United States has been spurred on by the relatively few retirees drawing pensions compared to the number of people working and contributing to a pension program. That situation is changing rapidly, however; individuals over 65 years of age now represent about 12 percent of the U.S. population, and analysts project this percentage will rise much higher in the years ahead. The growing proportion of retired individuals will threaten the solvency of many private pension funds and has, in fact, already created major funding problems for the social security program.[4]

Intense competition among employers for skilled management person-

---

[4] The present ratio of working adults to retired persons in the U.S. population is about three to one. This ratio is projected to shrink to about two to one by 1995. When the Social Security Act was passed in 1935, there were 11 working adults for each retired individual. Substantial changes will be needed in the way in which social security is funded, in its promised benefits to retirees, or more likely in both if this social insurance program is to remain actuarially sound on a long-term basis. Current proposals to reform the system include increasing the eligible age for full retirement benefits from 65 to 68 and encouraging retired persons to stay in the labor force as long as their health and productivity permit.

nel has also spurred pension fund growth as firms have tried to attract top-notch employees by offering attractive fringe benefits. This growth factor is likely to persist in the 1980s and beyond due to a developing shortage of young, skilled entry-level workers. Some experts foresee a real problem in this area, however, stemming from the recent difficulties pension plans have had in keeping up with inflation. Workers in the future are likely to demand both better performance from their pension plans and greater control over how their long-term savings are invested.

Investment Strategies of Pension Funds

Pension funds are long-term investors with limited need for liquidity. Their incoming cash receipts are known with considerable accuracy because a fixed percentage of each employee's salary is usually contributed to the fund. At the same time, cash outflows are not too difficult to forecast because the formula for figuring benefit payments is stipulated in the contract between the fund and its members. This situation encourages pensions to purchase common stock, long-term bonds, and real estate and hold these assets on a more or less permanent basis. In addition, interest income and capital gains from investments are exempt from federal income taxes, while pension plan members are not taxed on their contributions unless cash benefits are paid out.

While favorable taxation and predictable cash flows favor longer-term, somewhat riskier investments, the pension fund industry is closely regulated in all of its activities, including the investing of funds. The Employee Retirement Income Security Act of 1974 (ERISA) requires all private plans to be *funded*, which means that any assets held plus anticipated investment income must be adequate to cover all promised benefits. ERISA also requires that investments must be made in a "prudent" manner, which is usually interpreted to mean highly diversified holdings of high-grade common stock, corporate bonds, and government securities with only limited real estate investments.

While existing regulations do emphasize caution and conservatism in pension fund investments, the private plans have been under intense pressure in recent years by both management and employees of sponsoring companies to be more liberal in their investment policies. The sponsoring employer has a strong incentive to encourage its affiliated pension plan to reduce operating expenses and earn the highest possible returns on its investments. This permits the company to minimize its contributions to the plan. Both sponsoring employers and employees have a keen interest in seeing that the pension plan earns a high enough return on its investments to at least keep pace with inflation. Otherwise, the employees will tend to seek other jobs whose pension programs offer more lucrative returns.

Pension Fund Assets

The particular assets held as investments by pension funds depend heavily on whether the fund is government controlled or private. As shown in Exhibit 6–10, private funds emphasize investments in corporate stock, which represent about half of their assets. Corporate bonds ranked a distant second, accounting for about one sixth of all private pensions' financial investments. With few liquidity needs, private pensions held relatively small amounts of cash and bank deposits, though their holdings of U.S. government securities have increased significantly in recent years due to the relatively high yields and safety of these investments (see Exhibit 6–11).

Corporate stock is far less important in the portfolios of government pensions than among private plans. As Exhibit 6–10 shows, state and local government pension programs held about one quarter of their financial assets in corporate stock. Stock investments were outweighed in government pension plans by holdings of corporate bonds, which represented more than a third of their assets. Thus, the pressure of strict regulation falls more heavily upon government (public) pension plans than on private plans and, as a result, their investments tend to be more conservative

EXHIBIT 6–10

Financial Assets Held by Private, Noninsured Pension Funds and State and Local Government Employee Retirement Funds, December 31, 1983 ($ billions at year-end)

Asset Items	Private Noninsured Pension Funds		State and Local Government Employee Retirement Funds	
	Amount	Percent	Amount	Percent
Cash assets	$ 3.4	0.6%	$ 10.4	3.3%
Time deposits	21.6	3.6	—	—
Corporate stock	306.2	50.4	89.6	28.3
U.S. government securities	101.1	16.6	50.2	15.9
Federal agency securities	51.2	8.4	37.7	12.9
State and local government securities	—	—	1.8	0.6
Corporate and foreign bonds	92.3	15.2	111.5	35.3
Mortgages	5.2	0.9	14.8	4.7
Miscellaneous assets	26.7	4.4	—	—
Totals	$607.8	100.0%	$316.1	100.0%

Note: Columns may not add to totals due to rounding.
SOURCE: Board of Governors of the Federal Reserve System, *Flow of Funds Accounts—Assets and Liabilities Outstanding,* September 1984.

EXHIBIT 6–11

Recent Trends in Acquisitions of Financial Assets by Private and State
and Local Government Pension Funds, 1980–1984

Financial Assets Acquired	Annual Net Acquisitions of Financial Assets ($ billions)				
	1980	1981	1982	1983	1984
	Private Pension Funds				
Demand deposits and currency	$ 0.1	$ 0.2	$−0.2	$ 0.6	$ 0.7
Time deposits	0.4	1.2	−1.3	4.4	3.0
Corporate stock (equities)	17.7	5.4	20.1	15.3	−2.5
U.S. Treasury securities	19.5	26.2	35.7	15.5	18.6
Federal agency securities	6.5	10.3	10.3	5.3	6.7
Corporate bonds	10.7	3.4	1.1	5.8	2.2
Mortgages	0.6	0.1	0.4	1.1	0.4
Miscellaneous assets	−0.1	1.3	−1.5	4.5	3.7
Total acquisitions of financial assets	$48.9	$37.6	$54.3	$47.3	$26.1
	State and Local Government Employee Pension Plans				
Demand deposits and currency	$ 0.3	$ 0.2	$ 2.5	$ 3.2	$ 3.8
Corporate stock (equities)	5.3	8.3	10.1	22.2	8.4
U.S. Treasury securities	6.2	6.6	9.3	13.6	19.5
Federal agency securities	3.7	5.2	9.5	3.9	5.3
State and local government debt securities	0.1	−0.2	−0.7	−1.2	−0.5
Corporate bonds	9.5	9.1	5.2	1.9	2.4
Mortgages	1.3	1.8	1.3	0.8	0.4
Total acquisitions of financial assets	$26.5	$31.0	$37.3	$44.5	$39.3

Note: Columns may not add to totals due to rounding.
SOURCE: Board of Governors of the Federal Reserve System, *Flow of Funds Accounts, Fourth Quarter 1984,* February 1985.

with corporate and government bonds preferred over more risky stock. Government pensions also place moderate amounts of funds in state and local government securities—often IOUs issued by their own governmental units.

Factors Affecting the Growth of Pension Funds in the Years Ahead

Most experts feel that pension fund growth is likely to slow significantly in future years. One reason is the rising proportion of pension beneficiaries to working contributors, related to the gradual aging of the general population. At the same time, the cost of maintaining pension programs has increased dramatically. The full funding of a plan to cover all promised benefits may place extreme pressure on corporate profits, particularly if declining stock and bond markets diminish investment returns.

Even more significant is the rapidly rising cost of government regulation. ERISA, passed by Congress in 1974, imposed costly reporting requirements on the industry and granted employees the right to join a pension program, in most cases, after only one year on the job. More rapid *vesting* of accumulated benefits was also required so that employees can recover a higher proportion of their past contributions should they decide to retire early or move to another job. Trying to eliminate the danger that pensions may not have adequate funds to pay future claims against them, Congress now requires employers to eventually cover any past liabilities not fully covered at present. In addition, a federal agency—the Pension Benefit Guaranty Corporation (PBGC)—was created in 1974 to insure some part of all vested employee benefits. PBGC is supported by premiums contributed annually by participating employers and can borrow up to $100 million from the U.S. Treasury in an emergency.

These new government regulations have forced many private pension plans to close. The control of others has been turned over to a financial institution—typically a bank trust department or life insurance company—better able to deal with the current rules and more knowledgeable about profitable investment opportunities. The pension sector faces troubled times and considerable uncertainty in the period ahead.

FINANCE COMPANIES

Finance companies are sometimes called "department stores of consumer and business credit." These institutions grant credit to businesses and consumers for a wide variety of purposes, including the purchase of inventories, business equipment, automobiles, home repairs, vacations, medical care, mobile homes, and home appliances. Most authorities divide firms in the industry into one of three groups: consumer finance companies, sales finance companies, and commercial finance companies.

Different Finance Companies for Different Purposes

Consumer finance companies, also known as small-loan companies, make personal cash loans available to many individuals. The majority of their loans support the purchase of passenger cars, home appliances, recreational vehicles, and mobile homes. However, a growing proportion of consumer finance company loans center on aiding customers with medical and hospital expenses, educational costs, vacations, home repair and maintenance, and energy bills. Loans made by small-loan companies are considered to be more risky than other consumer installment loans and therefore generally carry steeper finance charges than those assessed by banks, credit unions, savings and loan associations, and other installment lenders.

Sales finance companies make indirect loans to consumers by purchasing installment paper from dealers selling automobiles and other consumer durables. Many of these firms are "captive" finance companies controlled by a dealer or manufacturer. Their principal function is to promote sales of the sponsoring firm's goods and services by providing credit. Companies having captive finance affiliates include General Electric, Motorola, Sears, Wards, and International Harvester. Generally, sales finance companies will specify in advance to retail dealers the terms (i.e., maturities, minimum down payments, and finance charges) of installment contracts they are willing to accept. Frequently they will give the retail dealer a supply of contract forms which the dealer will fill out when the sale is made. The contract is then sold immediately to the finance company.

Commercial finance companies, as their name implies, focus principally on extending credit to business firms. Most of these companies provide "accounts receivable financing" or "factoring" services to small- or medium-sized manufacturers and wholesalers. With accounts receivable financing, the commercial finance company may extend credit against the borrower's receivables in the form of a direct cash loan. Alternatively, a factoring arrangement may be used in which the finance company acquires the borrowing firm's credit accounts at an appropriate discount rate to cover the risk of loss. Most commercial finance companies today do not confine their credit-granting activities to the financing of receivables but also make loans secured by business inventories, machinery, and other fixed assets. In addition, they offer lease financing for the purchase of capital equipment and rolling stock (such as airplanes and railroad cars) and make short-term unsecured cash loans.

We should not overdramatize the differences between these three types of finance companies. The larger companies are active in all three areas. In addition, most finance companies today are extremely diversified in their credit-granting activities, offering a wide range of installment and working-capital loans, leasing plans, and long-term credit to support capital investment. Exhibit 6–12 shows that consumer loans are the most important financial assets held by finance companies, accounting for almost half their total assets. Business loans were also significant and, in fact, have grown faster than consumer loans in finance company portfolios in the most recent period, as shown in Exhibit 6–13. Much smaller amounts of funds are committed by the industry to real estate mortgages or held in cash to provide liquidity.

EXHIBIT 6–12

Financial Assets and Liabilities Held by Finance Companies,
December 31, 1983

Asset and Liability Items	Amount ($ billions)	Percent of Total
Assets:		
Demand deposits and currency	$ 5.0	1.9%
Mortgages	17.8	6.9
Consumer credit	123.9	47.7
Loans to businesses	113.0	43.5
Total financial assets	$259.8	100.0%
Liabilities:		
Corporate bonds issued	$ 70.3	27.1%
Bank loans, n.e.c.	15.4	5.9
Open-market paper issued	83.7	32.2
Profit taxes payable	*	*
Funds from parent companies	47.0	18.1
Miscellaneous liabilities	49.3	19.0
Total liabilities	$259.8	100.0%

Note: Columns may not add to totals due to rounding.
* Less than $50 million.
SOURCE: Board of Governors of the Federal Reserve System, *Flow of Funds Accounts—
Assets and Liabilities Outstanding, 1960–83.*

Growth of Finance Companies

Finance companies have been profoundly affected by recent changes
in the character of competition among financial intermediaries. Their
lack of an extensive network of branch offices has put them at a disadvantage in reaching the household borrower who values convenience. As a
result, both commercial banks and nonbank thrifts have been able to
capture a larger share of the consumer installment loan market at the
expense of finance companies. For example, data compiled by the Federal
Reserve Board show that finance companies held about 45 percent of
consumer installment loans extended by financial institutions in 1950,
but only 35 percent in 1983. Over the same interval of time, credit unions
tripled their share of the consumer installment loan market.

While finance companies dominated the auto-loan market for many
years, this service line may be "drying up" due to higher energy costs,
higher prices for both new and used automobiles, and intense competition
from banks and credit unions. Many experts now feel that the fastest-
growing market for finance companies in future years will be business-
oriented rather than consumer-oriented financial services. Revolving
credit, second mortgages on real property, and equipment leasing are

among the fastest-growing forms of credit extended by finance companies today.

Methods of Industry Financing

Finance companies are heavy users of debt in financing their operations. Principal sources of borrowed funds include bank loans, commercial paper, and long-term debentures (bonds) sold primarily to banks, insurance companies, and nonfinancial corporations. (See Exhibit 6–12.) Which source of funds these companies emphasize most heavily at any given time depends essentially on the structure of interest rates. When long-term rates are high, these companies tend to emphasize commercial paper and shorter-term bank loans as sources of funds. On the other hand, in years when long-term rates are relatively low, usually during a business recession, long-term bonds will be drawn upon more heavily, as can be seen in Exhibit 6–13.

EXHIBIT 6–13

Recent Trends in Acquisitions of Financial Assets by Finance Companies, 1980–1984

Financial Assets Acquired	Annual Net Acquisitions of Financial Assets ($ billions)				
	1980	1981	1982	1983	1984
Demand deposits and currency	$ 0.1	$ 0.1	$0.1	$ 0.1	$ 0.1
Mortgages	0.6	2.9	1.1	1.4	1.0
Consumer credit	9.9	14.6	5.3	6.0	11.6
Loans to businesses	3.4	9.5	−1.4	16.9	20.0
Total acquisition of financial assets	$14.0	$27.1	$5.1	$24.3	$32.6
Corporate bonds issued	$ 5.4	$−0.8	$1.2	$12.1	$ 8.1
Bank loans n.e.c.	0.9	−0.3	0.3	−4.7	−3.7
Open-end market paper issued	−0.5	13.9	−2.5	9.6	15.1
Profit taxes payable	−0.2	−0.2	*	*	*
Investments by parent companies	4.4	7.9	7.8	4.5	5.2
Miscellaneous liabilities	3.5	5.0	1.2	4.9	5.0
	$14.0	$27.1	$5.1	$24.3	$32.6

Note: Columns may not add to totals due to rounding.
* Less than $50 million.
SOURCES: Board of Governors of the Federal Reserve System, *Flow of Funds Accounts, Fourth Quarter 1984*, February 1985.

Recent Changes in the Character of the Finance Company Industry

The structure of the finance industry has changed markedly in recent years. As in the case of credit unions, savings and loans, and savings banks, the number of finance companies has been trending downward, although the average size of such companies has grown considerably. A survey by the Federal Reserve Board revealed that in 1960 there were more than 6,400 finance companies operating in the United States, but by 1980 only about 2,000 independent companies could be found. A modest rise in the number of new firms occurred during the 1970s, however, as bank holding companies centered around some of the nation's largest banks organized new finance company subsidiaries.

This long-term downtrend in the industry's population reflects a number of powerful economic forces at work. Rising cost pressures, the broadening of markets, the need to innovate, and intensified competition from other financial institutions have encouraged finance companies to strive for larger size and greater efficiency. Many smaller companies have sold out to larger conglomerates as high-interest rates squeezed earnings. Despite their declining numbers, however, finance companies rank among the fastest-growing financial intermediaries in the United States and continue to be a potent force in the markets for business and consumer credit.

INVESTMENT COMPANIES

Investment companies provide an outlet for the savings of thousands of individual investors, directing their funds into bonds, stocks, and money market securities. These companies are especially attractive to the small investor to whom they offer continuous management services for a large and highly varied security portfolio. By purchasing shares offered by an investment company, the small saver gains greater price stability and reduced risk, opportunities for capital gains, and indirect access to higher-yielding securities that can only be purchased in large blocks. In addition, most investment company stock is highly liquid, since many companies stand ready at all times to repurchase their outstanding shares at current market prices.

The Background of Investment Companies

Investment companies made their appearance in the United States after World War I as a vehicle for buying up and often for monitoring subsidiary corporations. Many were unsuccessful in the early years, and the Great Depression of the 1930s forced scores of these new firms into bankruptcy. New life was breathed into the industry after World War II, however, when investment companies began to appeal to a rapidly growing middle class of savers. They were also buoyed by rising stock prices which attracted millions of investors, most of whom had only modest amounts to invest and little knowledge of how the financial markets work. The industry launched an aggressive advertising campaign which ultimately attracted more than 40 million shareholders during the 1960s.

Then the roof fell in as the long postwar bull market in stocks collapsed in the late 1960s. During the 1970s the stock market staged modest recoveries, only to be thrown back each time as it neared highs set during the 60s. Small investors began to pull out of the stock market in droves. Total assets of the most important kind of investment company—the mutual fund—reached nearly $48 billion in 1970 but five years later had dropped to less than $46 billion. In all but three years during the 1970s, redemptions of mutual funds' shares exceeded their sales.

Many investment companies disappeared in this shakeout period, most of them consolidated into larger firms. The future of the industry seemed very much in doubt until a new element appeared—*innovation*. Owners and managers began to develop new types of investment companies designed to appeal to groups of investors with specialized financial needs. By custom and tradition investment companies had stressed investments in common stock, offering investors capital appreciation as well as current income. With the stock market performing poorly, however, these firms turned their focus increasingly to other markets, especially to bonds and money market instruments. The new *bond funds*, which first became prominent in the 1960s, direct the majority of their funds into either corporate debt obligations or tax-exempt municipal bonds. Their principal objectives are to generate current income and, in the case of the municipal bond fund, a higher after-tax rate of return for the investor. Capital appreciation is normally a secondary consideration to these particular investment companies.

Money market funds, discussed earlier in Chapter 5, began in 1972 with the announced intent of holding money market securities—mainly bank certificates of deposit (CDs), commercial paper, and U.S. Treasury bills. They were created in response to record-high interest rates in U.S. money markets and the desire of the small investor to skirt around federal interest-rate ceilings on time and savings deposits offered by banks and nonbank thrift institutions. In addition, the money funds have offered corporations and other institutional investors professional management of their liquid funds and reduced risk through diversification.

Interestingly enough, the traditional equity (stock)-investing mutual funds began to grow rapidly again in the 1980s, particularly after the deep recession of 1982. While money market funds rescued the investment companies during the turbulent 1970s, the equity funds generally outpaced the money market funds in the early 1980s with money flowing in from individual retirement accounts (IRAs) and from investors enamored with bargain stock prices. Moreover, several of the stock funds have outperformed the market as a whole (as measured, for example, by the behavior of Standard & Poor's 500 Stock Index) by purchasing stocks from smaller, rapidly growing firms dealing in high-tech products or specialty items. Nevertheless, most stock funds did *not* outperform the market which increased the popularity of so-called *index funds* that invest in a portfolio of stock and bonds reflective of the whole market portfolio and tend to move synchronously with the market.[5]

Regulation of Investment Companies

Investment companies are heavily regulated at the federal level through such laws as the Investment Company Act and the Investment Advisers Act, both passed by Congress in 1940. Registration of investment company securities and periodic reports to the Securities and Exchange Commission (SEC) are mandatory. Policies for investing funds are determined by the investment company's shareholders, who also elect at least two thirds of the company's directors. The portfolio held by an investment company is managed by a separate management company or investment advisory service, which levies a substantial fee for its services. The management fee is typically a small percentage (perhaps 1 to 2 percent) of the fund's total assets and is *not* based on the fund's performance. Any contractual arrangements between the investment advisory service and the investment company must be approved by the latter's stockholders and must come up for renewal or revision every two years. Most investment advisory services are provided by either life insurance firms or security specialists.

Tax Status of the Industry

Investment companies have a highly favorable tax situation. As long as they conform to certain rules to qualify as an investment company, they do *not* pay federal taxes on income generated by their security holdings. However, no less than half their resources must be devoted to securities and cash assets. Investment companies must maintain a

---

[5] *Index funds* are based on the theory of *efficient markets* which argues that, in the long-run, active money managers cannot "beat the market" (i.e., outperform the market as a whole). Thus, index funds tend to hold their investments longer and charge lower brokerage and service fees than do investment companies that turn over their security portfolios more rapidly.

highly diversified portfolio—a maximum of one quarter of their total resources can be devoted to securities issued by any one firm. Only a small portion of their net income (no more than 10 percent) can be retained in the business. The rest must be distributed to their shareholders.

Open-End and Closed-End Investment Companies

There are two basic kinds of investment companies. *Open-end companies*—often called mutual funds—will buy back (redeem) their shares any time the customer wishes and sell open shares in any quantity demanded. Thus, the amount of their outstanding shares changes continually in response to public demand. The price of each open-end company share is equal to the net asset value of the fund, that is, the difference between the values of its assets and liabilities divided by the volume of shares issued.

Open-end companies may be either *load* or *no-load* funds. Load funds, which are in the majority, offer their shares to the public at net asset value plus a commission to brokers marketing the shares. No-load funds sell their shares purely at net asset value. The investor must contact the no-load company directly, however. Whether load or no-load, open-end investment companies are heavily invested in common stock, with corporate bonds running a distant second. As Exhibit 6–14 shows, corporate stock represents more than half the industry's total financial assets with state and local government (municipal) bonds and corporate bonds

EXHIBIT 6–14

Financial Assets Held by Open-End Investment Companies (mutual funds), December 31, 1983

Asset Items	Amount ($ billions)	Percent of Total
Demand deposits and currency	$ 1.7	1.3%
Corporate stock (equities)	73.5	56.8
Credit instruments:		
U.S. government securities	5.7	4.4
State and local government securities	31.5	24.4
Corporate and foreign bonds	13.0	10.1
Open-end market paper	4.0	3.1
Total financial assets	$129.3	100.0%

Note: Columns may not add to totals due to rounding.
SOURCE: Board of Governors of the Federal Reserve System, *Flow of Funds Accounts—Assets and Liabilities Outstanding, 1960–83.*

accounting for the bulk of the remaining industry portfolio. However, mutual funds have added substantially to their holdings of fixed-income securities (federal, state and local government bonds and corporate bonds) in recent years, as indicated in Exhibit 6–15, due to the higher yields and relative stability of these investments compared to their traditional investments in stock (equities).

Closed-end investment companies sell only a specific number of ownership shares. An investor wanting to acquire closed-end shares must find another investor who wishes to sell. The investment company does not take part in the transaction. In addition to selling equity shares, closed-end companies issue a variety of debt and equity securities to raise funds, including preferred stock, regular and convertible bonds, and stock warrants. In contrast, open-end companies rely almost exclusively on the sale of equity shares to the public to raise the funds they require.

Goals and Earnings of Investment Companies

Investment companies adopt many different goals. *Growth funds* are interested primarily in long-term capital appreciation and tend to invest mainly in common stocks offering strong growth potential. *Income funds* stress current income in their portfolio choices rather than growth of capital, and they typically purchase stocks and bonds paying high dividends and interest. *Balanced funds* attempt to bridge the gap between growth and income, acquiring bonds, preferred stock, and common stock which offer both capital gains (growth) and adequate current income.

EXHIBIT 6–15

Recent Trends in Acquisitions of Financial Assets by Open-End Investment Companies (mutual funds), 1980–1984

Financial Assets Acquired	Annual Net Acquisitions of Financial Assets ($ billions)				
	1980	1981	1982	1983	1984
Demand deposits and currency	$0.1	*	$ 0.3	$ 0.6	$ 0.4
Corporate stock (equities)	−1.8	−0.6	3.5	13.7	5.6
U.S. government securities	0.3	0.9	2.3	0.6	7.4
State and local government securities (municipals)	2.0	2.9	10.9	10.3	13.4
Corporate bonds	1.3	1.6	0.2	2.7	2.3
Open-market paper	1.2	−0.1	−0.6	1.0	2.7
Net share issues	$5.2	$6.3	$18.4	$32.8	$38.1

* Less than $50 million.
SOURCE: Board of Governors of the Federal Reserve System, *Flow of Funds Accounts, Fourth Quarter 1984*, February 1985.

On average, balanced funds place about two thirds of their resources in stocks and about one third in bonds.

The majority of investment companies give priority to growth in capital over current income due to the tax advantages of capital gains to their investors.[6] However, the industry's growth in recent years has centered primarily in funds that stress current income. Prominent examples include bond funds, money market funds, and option income funds (which issue options against a portfolio of common stocks). While most investment companies hold a highly diversified portfolio of securities, a few specialize in stocks or bonds from a single industry or sector (such as precious metals or oil and natural gas).

It is not at all clear that investment companies hold a significant advantage over other investors in seeking out the highest returns available in the financial marketplace. Moreover, there is evidence that these companies may roll over their portfolios too rapidly, which runs up the cost of managing the fund and reduces net earnings. Less frequent trading activity on the part of investment companies might well result in greater long-run benefits for the saver. Research evidence has been mounting for a number of years that security markets are highly efficient. Overvaluation or undervaluation of securities is, at most, a temporary phenomenon.[7] In this kind of environment it is doubtful that investment companies are of significant benefit to the large investor, though they may indeed aid the small investor in reducing information and transactions costs and opening up investment opportunities not otherwise available.

OTHER FINANCIAL INSTITUTIONS

In addition to the foregoing a number of other financial institutions have developed over the years to provide services to the meet specialized financial needs of their customers. For example, *security dealers* provide a conduit for buyers and sellers of marketable securities (such as U.S government bills and bonds, corporate and municipal bonds, and federal agency notes and certificates) to adjust their holdings of those securities. These dealer houses stand ready at all times to buy selected private and government securities or sell from a list of securities to their customers on demand at posted "bid" and "asked" prices. The most well known of the dealers are the 36 primary government securities dealers that aid the U.S. Treasury in selling new issues of federal debt and trade securities with the Federal Reserve System.

---

[6] See Chapter 10 for a discussion of the favorable federal tax rates applicable to capital gains.

[7] See especially the studies by Blume, Crockett and Friend (1974) and Malkiel (1975) and the discussion of efficient markets in Chapters 7 and 21.

Many of these dealers also serve as *investment bankers,* who market large amounts of new securities on behalf of governments, governmental agencies, and corporations. These "banks" are especially prominent in the offering of new corporate securities, state and local government bonds and notes, and securities issued by federal government agencies such as the Federal National Mortgage Association ("Fannie Mae") and the Farm Credit System. They *underwrite* new offerings of these securities, purchasing them from the original issuer and placing them in the hands of interested investors at a higher price. (Thus, in terms of the classifications of financial transactions discussed in Chapter 2, investment banks, like security dealers, engage in semidirect finance.) When a new issue of securities involves substantial risk, several investment banking firms will usually band together to form a *syndicate* to bid for and market the issue, thus spreading market risk. Investment banks also give financial advice on the best terms and times to sell new securities and on how to finance corporate mergers and acquisitions. Investment banking firms are among the best-known names on Wall Street, including such prominent companies as Salomon Brothers, Goldman Sachs, First Boston Corporation, Merrill Lynch Capital Markets, Morgan Stanley, Drexel Burnham Lambert, Kidder Peabody, Blyth Eastman Paine Webber, Lehman Brothers, Shearson-American Express, and E. F. Hutton.

A related type of dealer firm is the *mortgage banking* institution. Mortgage bankers commit themselves to take on new mortgage loans used to fund the building of homes, apartments, office buildings, shopping centers, and other structures. They will carry these loans for a short time—perhaps weeks or months—until the mortgages can be sold to a long-distance (permanent) lender of mortgage funds, such as an insurance company or savings bank. As is the case with other dealer operations, the financial risks to the mortgage banker are substantial. A rise in interest rates will sharply reduce the market value of existing fixed-rate mortgage loans, presenting the mortgage banker with a loss when he sells the loans out of his portfolio. This risk of rising interest rates and falling mortgage prices encourages mortgage banks to turnover their portfolios rapidly and to arrange lines of credit from commercial banks to backstop their operations.

Specialized financial institutions active in the mortgage market include real estate investment trusts and mortgage companies. Authorized by federal law in 1960, *real estate investment trusts* (REITs) are publicly held, tax-exempt corporations that must receive at least three quarters of their gross income from real estate transactions (such as rental income, mortgage interest, and sales of property) and devote at least three quarters of their assets to real estate property or loans, cash, and U.S. government securities. Raising funds by selling stock and debt securities, REITs invest most of their available funds in mortgage loans to finance the building of apartments and other multifamily housing developments and commercial structures, such as office buildings and shopping centers. In contrast, mortgage companies (some of which sponsor REITs) loan funds for real estate projects and then offer the resulting mortgage IOUs to other investors (such as life insurance companies and mutual savings banks). Thus, these companies typically provide temporary financing to real estate brokers and builders for commercial and residential construction projects and then attempt to find permanent financing of these same projects from "long-distance" investors. They also service mortgage loans for other lenders by collecting loan payments and inspecting mortgage property to see that all the terms of the loan contract are being honored. Mortgage bankers raise funds by borrowing from banks, from parent holding companies, and from sales of notes.

Leasing companies represent still another kind of specialized financial institution that provides their customers with access to productive assets, such as airplanes, automobiles, equipment, furniture, and real estate, through the writing of leases. These leases allow a business or household to use assets, sometimes at a lower cost than borrowing and owning these same assets without having to raise money for a down payment. Moreover, the lease payments are a current operating expense and, therefore, tax deductible for the business lessee. The leasing company, on the other hand, benefits from the stream of lease payments and gains substantial tax benefits in the form of an investment tax credit from purchasing the asset for its customer and from depreciating the asset. These tax benefits have been especially attractive to commercial banks in recent years who often tax shelter a significant proportion of their earnings via leasing activities. While there are numerous independent leasing companies serving national, regional and local markets, competition is intense in this industry because of the entry of scores of commercial banks and bank holding companies, insurance companies, pension funds, and manufacturing firms which have either opened leasing departments or formed captive and subsidiary leasing companies.

Finally, a unique financial institution emerged in the 1970s and 1980s that combined several different institutions under the same corporate umbrella. This dynamic and increasingly important financial institution is the *symbiotic*—a conglomerate financial firm that frequently merges insurance sales, security brokerage, real estate brokerage, financial counseling, and credit services under the same roof in an effort to become a "financial department store." Usually each unit within the symbiotic attempts to sell not only its own services, but to cross-sell services offered by other units in the conglomerate to its customers. Moreover, the same top-management team may oversee all or most parts of the conglomerate organization. Prominent examples include Sears, Roebuck & Company, which in 1981 acquired control of Coldwell Banker, the leading U.S.

real estate brokerage firm, and major security broker, Dean Witter Reynolds; Prudential Insurance Company, which acquired Bache Group, Inc., a leading security broker; and the well-known credit card company, American Express, which acquired broker Shearson Loeb Rhodes. We could also add to this list of prominent financial conglomerates General Motors, General Electric, International Harvester, Ford Motor Company, and J. C. Penney—all of which control major finance companies designed to help finance and sell their manufactured products and gain a share of the rapidly expanding market for financial services. The symbiotics possess a distinct advantage over banks, investment companies, and other financial institutions with which they compete because they are largely *unregulated.* However, a major uncertainty that surrounds their operations is whether their management can successfully control and market such a diverse range of products and services.

TRENDS AFFECTING ALL FINANCIAL INSTITUTIONS TODAY

The emergence of the symbiotics is but a reflection of the major trends which affect all financial institutions today. One of these trends is *increasing cost pressures,* due to the rising expense of raising funds for lending and investing and burgeoning labor and equipment costs that have narrowed profit margins. Another trend is *consolidation* in which each financial institution tries to expand its size in order to improve efficiency and ease its growing cost burden. Certainly the new symbiotics represent a move to consolidate financial resources into a large conglomerate organization and utilize existing managerial talent, labor, and physical facilities more efficiently. A key result of the consolidation movement is declining numbers of independent financial institutions, but institutions that average much larger in size and organizational complexity.

Still a third trend is *service diversification* as all major financial institutions have invaded each other's traditional markets with new services in an effort to offset rising costs, open up new sources of revenue, and protect thinning profit margins. Thus, service diversification has led to a blurring of functions among the different institutions so that it becomes increasingly difficult to distinguish between different financial institutions. The symbiotics are a good example of this trend toward service diversification, but so are commercial banks, nonbank thrifts, insurance companies, finance companies, mutual funds, and many other financial institutions today.

The offering of many new services over wider market areas has been made possible by another trend in the financial institutions' sector—a *technological revolution,* particularly in the growing adoption of computers and automated electronic equipment for making payments and transferring financial information. Soon there may be little need to walk into the offices of most financial institutions with many transactions handled more accurately and efficiently via home and office computers linked on-line to each financial institution's electronic computer network.

Many of the new services and technological innovations have come into existence because of a fifth trend—*deregulation,* in which the content and prices of financial services increasingly are being determined by the marketplace rather than by government rules. As we noted in Chapter 5, most of the deregulation movement has centered, thus far, in banking and among nonbank depository institutions. However, as depository institutions continue to receive new powers and expand their markets, it is quite likely that the whole panoply of financial institutions, such as insurance companies, pension funds, and finance and investment companies, will seek to loosen the regulatory rules that bind them as well. And, hopefully, the public will be the ultimate beneficiary in terms of more and better financial services at lower cost.

STUDY QUESTIONS

1. Against what kinds of risk do life insurance companies protect their policyholders? How about property-casualty insurers?

2. What is the "Law of Large Numbers?" What is its relationship to the insurance business?

3. Compare and contrast the asset portfolios of life insurance companies and property-casualty insurers. Try to explain any differences you observe.

4. What are the principal lines of insurance offered by property-casualty insurance companies? Have the risks faced by this industry changed in recent years? Why?

5. What is the principal function of pension funds? Explain why these institutions have been among the most rapidly growing financial institutions in recent years. Do you expect their growth to be faster or slower in the future? Why?

6. What are the principal assets acquired by pension funds? What factors guide their selection of securities?

7. What role do finance companies play in providing funds to the financial markets? How many different kinds of finance companies are there?

8. Major changes have occurred in the structure of the finance company industry in recent years. Explain how these changes resemble those going on in other financial industries, such as credit unions and savings banks, and what the principal causes appear to be.

9. What advantages do investment companies offer the small saver? Why has their growth been so erratic in recent years?

10. Define the following terms:
    a. Open-end company.
    b. Closed-end company.
    c. Bond fund.
    d. Money market fund.
    e. Growth funds.
    f. Balanced fund.

11. What is an REIT? A mortgage bank? A leasing company? Why do you think these specialized financial institutions came into being? In your opinion are they likely to survive as independent entities in an era when most financial institutions appear to be invading each other's territory with new services? Why or why not?

12. How do symbiotics (financial conglomerates) differ from more traditional financial institutions? What advantages do they have in the race for customer financial accounts?

13. In the concluding section of this chapter five major trends affecting all financial institutions today are discussed. Identify these trends. Which ones do you expect to continue over the next decade and which do you think might be short lived? Explain your reasoning.

PROBLEMS

1. The manager of a life insurance company is trying to decide what annual premium to charge a group of policyholders, each of whom has just reached their 40th birthday. A check of mortality tables indicates that, for every million persons born 40 years ago, 3 percent die, on average, sometime during their 40th year. If the company has 10,000 policyholders in this age bracket and each has taken out a $50,000 life insurance policy, estimate the probable amount of death benefit claims against the company. How much must be charged in premiums from each policyholder just to cover these expected claims? Suppose the company has operating expenses (plus a target profit) on sales to these policyholders of $500,000. What annual premium must be charged each policyholder to recover expenses and meet expected benefit claims?

2. A pension fund has accumulated $1 million in a retirement plan for James B. Smith, who retires this month at age 65. If Mr. Smith has a life expectancy of 75 years, what is the minimum-size annual annuity check that the pension plan will be able to send him each year (assuming that the value of the pension fund's investments remain stable)? Should he insist on receiving that size payment each year? Why or why not? What other kinds of information would be helpful in analyzing Mr. Smith's financial situation at retirement. (Note: see Chapter 8 for a discussion of annuity payments.)

SELECTED REFERENCES

American Council of Life Insurance. *1983 Life Insurance Fact Book,* 1984.

Antoncil, Madelyn, and Paul Bennet. "Corporate Use of Pension Overfunding." *Quarterly Review,* Federal Reserve Bank of New York, Spring 1984, pp. 17–30.

Babble, David F. "The Price Elasticity of Demand for Whole Life Insurance." *The Journal of Finance,* 40, no. 1 (March 1985), pp. 225–39.

Blume, Marshall E., Jean Crockett; and Irwin Friend. "Stock Ownership in the United States: Characteristics and Trends." *Survey of Current Business,* Department of Commerce, November 1974.

Board of Governors of the Federal Reserve System. "Survey of Finance Companies, 1980." *Federal Reserve Bulletin,* May 1981, pp. 398–409.

Friend, Irwin, Marshall Blume, and Jean Crockett. *Mutual Funds and Other Institutional Investors.* New York: McGraw-Hill, 1970.

Harless, Doris. *Nonbank Financial Institutions.* Federal Reserve Bank of Richmond, 1975.

Insurance Information Institute. *Insurance Facts,* 1983–84 Edition.

Malkiel, Burton G. *A Random Walk down Wall Street.* New York: W. W. Norton, 1975.

Morrison, Ann M. "Boom Time for Equity Mutual Funds." *Fortune,* July 25, 1983, pp. 80–81.

The Private Pension Controversy. New York: Bankers Trust Co., 1973.

Rose, Peter S. "Symbiotics: Financial Supermarkets in the Making." *The Canadian Banker & ICB Review,* April 1982, pp. 77–84.

Snellings, Aubrey N. "The Financial Services Industry: Recent Trends and Future Prospects." *Economic Review,* Federal Reserve Bank of Richmond, January–February 1980.

Part Three

Interest Rates and Security Prices

7

Interest Rates in the Financial system

THE PURPOSE OF THIS CHAPTER

To highlight the importance of interest rates in the economy by emphasizing their critical function in stimulating savings, in rationing credit to the most promising investment projects, in bringing the public's demand for money into line with the available money stock, and in acting as a policy tool for government to control the economy. The chapter discusses several popular views of the forces that cause interest rates to rise or fall, including the classical, liquidity preference, loanable funds, and rational expectations theories of interest.

KEY TERMS AND CONCEPTS IN THE CHAPTER:

classical theory	*loanable funds*	*risk-free rate*
efficient markets	*money creation*	*savings*
hoarding	*net investment*	*speculative motive*
income effect	*price expectations*	*substitution effect*
interest rate	*effect*	*time preference*
liquidity effect	*precautionary motive*	*transactions motive*
liquidity preference	*rational expectations*	*wealth effect*

In the opening chapter we described the money and capital markets as one vast pool of funds, depleted by the borrowing activities of households, businesses, and governments and replenished by the savings which these sectors of the economy also provide. The financial markets make saving possible by offering the individual saver a wide menu of choices where funds may be placed at attractive rates of return. By committing funds to one or more securities, the saver, in effect, becomes a lender of funds. The financial markets also make borrowing possible by giving the borrower a channel through which securities can be issued to lenders. And the financial markets make investment and economic growth possible by providing the funds needed for the purchase of machinery and equipment and the construction of buildings, highways, and other productive facilities.

Clearly, then, the acts of saving and lending, borrowing and investment are intimately linked with each other through the financial system. And one factor which significantly influences all of them is the *rate of interest*. The rate of interest is the "price" a borrower must pay to secure scarce loanable funds from a lender for an agreed-upon period. It is the *price of credit*. But unlike other prices in the economy, the rate of interest is really a *ratio* of two quantities—the money cost of borrowing funds to the amount of money actually borrowed, usually expressed on an annual percentage basis.

Interest rates send *price signals* to borrowers, lenders, savers, and investors. For example, higher interest rates generally bring forth a greater volume of savings and stimulate the lending of funds. Lower rates, on the other hand, tend to dampen the flow of savings and reduce lending activity. Higher interest rates tend to reduce the volume of borrowing and capital investment, while lower rates stimulate borrowing and investment spending. In the ensuing sections of this chapter we will discuss in more detail the forces which are believed by economists and financial analysts to determine prevailing rates of interest in the financial system.

FUNCTIONS OF THE RATE OF INTEREST IN THE ECONOMY

The rate of interest performs several different and highly important roles or functions in the economy:

> It helps guarantee that current savings will flow into investment to promote economic growth.

> The rate of interest rations the available supply of credit, generally providing loanable funds to those investment projects with the highest expected returns.

It brings into balance the nation's supply of money with the public's demand for money.

The rate of interest is also an important tool of government policy through its influence upon the volume of saving and investment. If the economy is growing too slowly and unemployment is rising, the government can use its policy tools to lower interest rates in order to stimulate borrowing and investment. On the other hand, an overheated economy experiencing rapid inflation has traditionally called for a government policy of higher interest rates to slow both borrowing and spending.

In the pages of the financial press, the phrase "the interest rate" is frequently used. In truth, there is no such thing as "the interest rate," for there are thousands of different interest rates in the financial system. Even securities issued by the same borrower will often carry a variety of interest rates. In Chapters 9 and 10 the most important factors which cause rates to vary among different securities and over time are examined in detail. In this chapter our focus is upon those basic forces that influence the level of *all* interest rates.

To uncover these general and pervasive rate-determining forces, however, we must make a simplifying assumption. We will assume in this chapter that there is one fundamental interest rate in the economy known as the *pure* or *risk-free* rate of interest, which is a component of *all* rates. The closest approximation to this pure rate in the real world is perhaps the market yield on U.S. Treasury bills. It is a rate of return presenting no risk of financial loss to the investor and represents the true "opportunity cost" of holding idle money because the investor can always invest in riskless Treasury bills and earn this minimum rate of return.

Once the pure rate of interest is determined, all other interest rates may be determined from it by examining the special characteristics of the securities issued by individual borrowers. For example, only the government can borrow at approximately the pure, risk-free interest rate; other borrowers pay higher rates than this due, in part, to the greater risk of loss attached to their securities. Differences in liquidity, marketability, and maturity are other important factors causing various interest rates to differ from the pure, risk-free rate. First, however, we must examine the forces which determine the pure, risk-free rate itself.

THE CLASSICAL THEORY OF INTEREST RATES

One of the oldest theories concerning the determinants of the risk-free-interest rate is the classical theory, developed originally during the 18th and 19th centuries by a number of British economists, refined by the Austrian economist Bohm-Bawerk, and elaborated by Irving Fisher early in this century.[1] The classical theory argues that the rate of interest is determined by two forces: (1) the supply of savings, derived mainly from households, and (2) the demand for investment capital from the business sector. Let us examine these rate-determining forces of saving and investment demand in more detail.

Saving by Households

What is the relationship between the rate of interest and the volume of saving in the economy? Most saving in modern industrialized economies is carried out by individuals and families. For these households, saving is simply abstinence from consumption spending. *Current savings, therefore, are equal to the difference between current income and current consumption expenditures.*

In making the decision on the timing and amount of saving to be done, households typically consider several factors: the size of current and long-run income; the desired savings target; and the desired proportion of income to be set aside in the form of savings (i.e., the propensity to save). Generally, the volume of household savings rises with income. Higher-income families and individuals tend to save more and consume less relative to their total income than families with lower incomes do.

While income levels probably dominate savings decisions, interest rates also play an important role. Interest rates affect an individual's choice between current consumption and saving for future consumption. The classical theory of interest assumed that individuals have a definite *time preference* for current consumption over future consumption. A rational individual, it was assumed, would always prefer current enjoyment of goods and services over future enjoyment. Therefore, the only way to encourage an individual or family to consume less now and save more was to offer a higher rate of interest on current savings. If more were saved in the current period at a higher rate of return, future consumption and future enjoyment would be increased. For example, if the current rate of interest is 10 percent and a household saves $100 instead of spending it on current consumption, it will be able to consume $110 in goods and services a year from now.

The classical theory thus considers the payment of interest a *reward for waiting*—that is, the postponement of current consumption in favor of greater future consumption. Higher interest rates presumably increase the attractiveness of saving relative to consumption spending, encouraging more individuals to substitute saving (and future consumption) for

---

[1] See especially Bohm-Bawerk (1891) and Fisher (1930).

some quantity of current consumption relative to savings. This so-called *substitution effect* calls for a *positive* relationship between interest rates and the volume of saving. Higher interest rates bring forth a greater volume of saving. Figure 7–1 illustrates the substitution effect: if the rate of interest in the financial markets rises from 5 percent to 10 percent, the volume of current saving by households is assumed to increase from $100 billion to $200 billion.

Saving by Business Firms

Our principal focus to this point has been on the determinants of saving by households. Businesses also save, however, and direct a portion of their savings into the financial markets to purchase securities and make loans. Most business firms have temporary cash surpluses from week to week or month to month, and these frequently will be invested in money market instruments, such as U.S. Treasury bills or bank certificates of deposit. Most businesses hold long-run savings balances in the form of retained earnings (as reflected in their equity or net worth accounts). In fact, the increase in retained earnings reported by business corporations each year is a key measure of the volume of current business saving. And these retained earnings supply most of the money for annual investment spending by businesses.

FIGURE 7–1

The Substitution Effect Relating Saving and Interest Rates

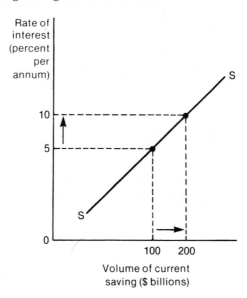

Volume of current
saving ($ billions)

The volume of business saving depends upon two key factors—the level of business profits and the dividend policies of corporations. These two factors are summarized in the *retention ratio*—the ratio of retained earnings to net income after taxes. This ratio indicates the proportion of business profits retained in the business for investment purposes rather than paid out as dividends to the owners. Experience has shown that dividend policies of major corporations change infrequently. Many corporations prefer to keep their dividend payments level or increase them slightly each year, regardless of current earnings. Any shortfalls in earnings needed for dividend payments are made up through borrowing or by drawing upon previously accumulated funds. The critical element in determining the amount of business saving is, therefore, the level of business profits.

If profits are expected to rise, businesses will be able to draw more heavily upon earnings retained in the firm and less heavily upon the money and capital markets for funds. The result is a reduction in the demand for credit and a tendency toward lower interest rates. On the other hand, when profits fall but firms do not cut back on their investment plans, they are forced to make heavier use of the money and capital markets for investment funds. The demand for credit rises, and interest rates usually increase as well.

While the principal determinant of business saving is profits, interest rates also play a role in the decision of what proportion of a business's current operating costs and long-term investment expenditures should be financed internally and what proportion externally. Higher rates in the money and capital markets typically encourage firms to use internally generated funds more heavily in financing their projects. Conversely, lower interest rates encourage greater use of external funds from the money and capital markets.

Saving by Government

Governments also save, though less frequently and generally in smaller amounts than the household and business sectors. In fact, most government saving (i.e., a budget surplus) appears to be unintended saving that arises when government receipts unexpectedly exceed the actual amount of government expenditures. Income flows in the economy (out of which government tax revenues arise) and the pacing of government spending programs are the dominant factors affecting government saving; interest rates are probably *not* a key factor here.

The Demand for Investment Funds

Business, household, and government saving are important determinants of interest rates according to the classical theory of interest, but

not the only ones. The other critical rate-determining factor in the classical theory is *investment spending by business firms.*

Businesses require huge amounts of funds each year for the purchase
of equipment, machinery, and inventories and to support the construction
of new buildings and other physical facilities. The majority of business
expenditures for these purposes consists of what economists call *replacement investment;* that is, expenditures to replace equipment and facilities
which are wearing out or are technologically obsolete. A smaller, but
more dynamic, form of business capital spending is labeled *net investment*—expenditures to acquire additional equipment and facilities in order to increase output. The sum of replacement investment plus net
investment equals *gross investment.*

Replacement investment usually is more predictable and grows at a
more even rate than does net investment. This is due to the fact that
such expenditures are financed almost exclusively from inside the firm
and frequently follow a routine pattern based on depreciation formulas.
Expenditures for new equipment and facilities (net investment), on the
other hand, depend on the business community's outlook regarding future
sales, changes in technology, industrial capacity, and the cost of raising
funds. Because these factors are subject to frequent changes, it is not
surprising that net investment (particularly inventory investment) is
highly volatile.

Net investment, because of its total size and volatility, is a driving
force in the economy. Changes in net investment are closely linked to
fluctuations in the nation's output of goods and services, employment,
and prices. A significant decline in net investment frequently leads to
a business recession, a decline in productivity, and a rise in unemployment
unless offset by increased consumer or government spending. In fact,
substantial cutbacks in inventory investment and long-term capital spending occur, on average, every three to four years in the United States,
usually precipitating a recession. Two recent examples occurred in 1980
and 1982 when sharply higher interest rates and other factors combined
to slow the pace of domestic net investment, leading to significant declines
in industrial production and a sharp rise in the U.S. unemployment rate.

The Investment Decision-Making Process.   The process of investment decision making by business firms is complex and depends on
a host of qualitative and quantitative factors. The firm must compare
its current level of production with the capacity of its existing facilities
and decide whether it has sufficient excess capacity to handle anticipated
demand for its product. If expected future demand will strain the firm's
existing facilities, it will consider expanding operating capacity through
net investment.

Most business firms have several investment projects under consideration at any one time. While the investment decision-making process varies from firm to firm, each business generally makes some estimate of net cash flows (i.e., revenues minus all expenses including taxes) which each project will generate over its useful life. From this information plus knowledge of each investment project's acquisition cost, management can calculate its expected rate of return and compare that projected return with anticipated returns from alternative projects.

One of the more popular methods of performing this calculation is the *internal rate of return method,* which equates the total cost of an investment project with the future net cash flows (NCF) expected from that project discounted back to their present values. Thus,

$$\text{Cost of project} = \frac{\text{NCF}_1}{(1+r)^1} + \frac{\text{NCF}_2}{(1+r)^2} + \cdots + \frac{\text{NCF}_n}{(1+r)^n} \qquad (7\text{--}1)$$

where each NCF represents the expected annual net cash flow from the project and r is its expected internal rate of return. The internal rate performs two functions: (1) it measures the annual yield the firm expects from an investment project; and (2) it reduces the value of all future cash flows expected over the useful economic life of the project down to their present value to the firm. In general, if the firm must choose among several mutually exclusive projects, it will choose the one with the *highest* expected internal rate of return.

While the internal rate of return provides a yardstick for selecting potentially profitable investment projects, how does a business executive decide how much to spend on investment at any point in time? How many projects should be chosen? It is here that the financial markets play a key role in the investment decision-making process.

Suppose a business firm is considering the following projects with their associated expected internal rates of return:

Project	Expected Annual Rate of Return (internal)
A	15%
B	12
C	10
D	9
E	8

How many of these projects will be adopted? The firm must compare each project's expected rate of return with the cost of raising capital to finance the project.

Assume that funds must be borrowed in the financial marketplace to complete any of the above projects and the current cost of borrowing is 10 percent. Then which projects are acceptable from an economic standpoint? As shown in Figure 7–2, projects A and B clearly are acceptable because their expected returns exceed the cost of borrowing capital to finance them. The firm would be indifferent about project C because its expected return is no more than the cost of borrowed funds. Projects D and E, on the other hand, are unprofitable at this time.[2]

It is through changes in the cost of raising funds that the financial markets can exert a powerful influence on the investment decisions of business firms. As credit becomes scarcer and more expensive, the cost of borrowed capital rises, eliminating some investment projects from consideration. For example, if the cost of borrowed funds rises from 10 percent to 13 percent, it is obvious that only project A in our earlier example would then be economically viable. On the other hand, if credit becomes more abundant and less costly, the cost of capital for the individual firm will tend to decline and more projects will become profitable. In our example, a decline in the cost of borrowed funds from 10 percent to 8½ percent would make all but project E economically viable and probably acceptable to the firm.

Investment Demand and the Rate of Interest.   This reasoning explains, in part, why the demand for investment capital by business firms was regarded by the classical economists as *negatively* related to the rate of interest. Figure 7–3 depicts the business investment demand curve as drawn in the classical theory. This demand curve slopes downward and to the right, reflecting the declining net marginal productivity

---

[2] The internal-rate-of-return method for evaluating investment projects is only one of several capital-budgeting techniques in use today. Another popular technique is net present value (NPV), which determines the net contribution in total after-tax dollars of a project by discounting all expected cash flows back to their present value using the individual firm's minimum required rate of return. Financial analysts generally consider the NPV method to be superior to the internal-rate method because the latter does not consider the scale of investment and uses a different reinvestment rate for every project.

The payback period (PP) approach determines the number of years required for the firm to recover fully the cost of a project. If expected cash flows from a project pay the firm back more rapidly than the minimum length of time acceptable to management, the project is likely to be adopted.

Recent studies indicate that major corporations use a wide variety of capital-budgeting techniques and may apply several different methods to the same project. There is clearly a trend, however, toward greater use of discounted cash flow techniques (such as net present value and internal rate of return), especially among larger firms. See, for example, the studies by Petty, Scott, and Bird (1975) and Klammer (1972).

FIGURE 7–2

The Cost of Capital and the Investment Decision

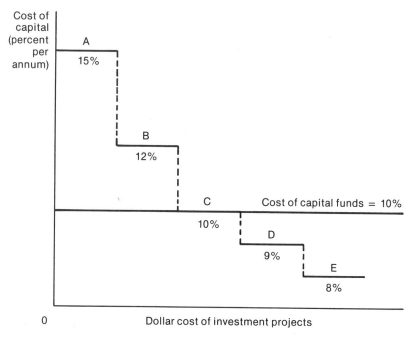

FIGURE 7–3

The Investment Demand Schedule in the Classical Theory of Interest Rates

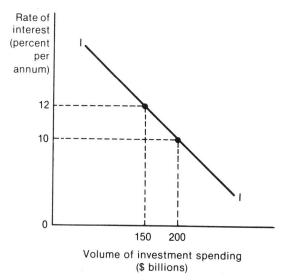

of capital as more and more capital funds are invested by firms.[3] At low rates of interest more investment projects become economically viable and firms require more funds to finance a longer list of projects. On the other hand, if the rate of interest rises to high levels, fewer investment projects will be pursued and less funds will be required from the financial markets. For example, at a 12 percent rate of interest only $150 billion in funds for investment spending might be demanded by business firms in the economy. If the rate of interest drops to 10 percent, however, the volume of desired investment by firms might rise to $200 billion.[4]

The Equilibrium Rate of Interest in the Classical Theory of Interest

The classical economists believed that interest rates in the financial markets were determined by the interplay of the supply of saving and the demand for investment. Specifically, the equilibrium rate of interest is determined at the point where the quantity of savings supplied to the market is exactly equal to the quantity of funds demanded for investment. As shown in Figure 7–4, this occurs at point E, where the equilibrium rate of interest is i_E and the equilibrium quantity of capital funds traded in the financial markets and invested is Q_E.

To illustrate, suppose the total volume of savings supplied by businesses, households, and governments in the economy at an interest rate of 10 percent is $200 billion. Moreover, at this same 10 percent rate businesses would also demand $200 billion in funds for investment purposes. Then 10 percent must be the equilibrium rate of interest and $200 billion is

---

[3] As the quantity of investment capital is increased relative to land, labor, and other productive factors, the laws of production in economics suggest that output will increase at a decreasing rate. Therefore, with technology held constant, the marginal cost of capital rises as more of it is employed by the individual firm and the net marginal productivity of additional capital declines. As a firm spends more funds for investment purposes, it expects its return to capital to decline. For this reason the investment demand schedule shown in Figure 7–3 slopes downward with an increasing volume of investment spending.

[4] The foregoing discussion implies that changes in interest rates affect predominantly *long-term investment projects,* which typically involve substantial borrowing over long periods of time. What about short-term investments, particularly purchases of inventories? Are they affected by changing interest rates? Until recently, the best answer appeared to be no. But, recent studies with better-designed research models tend to find the expected *negative* relationship between interest rates and business inventories— a rise in the cost of credit to carry inventories causes business firms to reduce their inventory levels. See, for example, Bechter and Pollock (1980).

FIGURE 7–4

The Equilibrium Rate of Interest in the Classical Theory

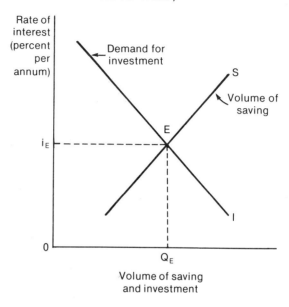

the equilibrium quantity of funds that would be traded in the money and capital markets.

The market rate of interest always moves toward its equilibrium level. However, supply and demand forces change so fast that the interest rate rarely has the opportunity to "settle in" at a specific equilibrium level. At any given time the rate is probably above or below its true equilibrium level, but moving *toward* that equilibrium. If the market rate is temporarily above equilibrium, then the volume of savings exceeds the demand for investment capital, creating an excess supply of savings. Savers will offer their funds at lower and lower rates until the market interest rate approaches equilibrium. Similarly, if the market rate lies temporarily below equilibrium, investment demand exceeds the quantity of savings available. Business firms bid up the interest rate until it approaches the level at which the quantity saved equals the quantity of funds demanded for investment purposes.

Limitations of the Classical Theory of Interest

The classical theory sheds considerable light on the factors affecting interest rates. However, it has some serious limitations.

The central problem is that the theory ignores several factors other than saving and investment which affect interest rates. For example, commercial banks have the power to create money by making loans to the public. When borrowers repay their bank loans, money is destroyed. The amount of money created or destroyed affects the total amount of credit available in the financial marketplace and therefore must be considered in any explanation of the factors determining interest rates. In addition, the classical theory assumes that interest rates are the principal determinant of the quantity of savings available. Today, economists recognize that *income* is far more important in determining the volume of saving. Finally, the classical theory contends that the demand for borrowed funds comes principally from the business sector. Today, however, both consumers and governments are important borrowers, significantly affecting credit availability and cost. As we will see in the balance of this chapter, more recent theories of the interest rate address a number of these limitations of the classical theory.

THE LIQUIDITY PREFERENCE THEORY

The classical theory of interest has been called a long-run explanation of interest rates because it focuses upon the public's thrift habits and the productivity of capital—factors which tend to change slowly. During the 1930s British economist John Maynard Keynes developed a short-run theory of the rate of interest which, he argued, was more relevant for policymakers and for explaining near-term changes in interest rates. This theory of interest-rate determination is known as liquidity preference.[5]

The Demand for Liquidity

Keynes argued that the rate of interest is really a payment for the use of a scarce resource—money. Businesses and individuals prefer to hold money for carrying out daily transactions and also as a precaution against future cash needs even though its yield is low or nonexistent. Investors in fixed-income securities, such as corporate and government bonds, frequently desire to hold money as a haven against declining security prices. Interest rates, therefore, are the "price" that must be paid to induce money holders to surrender a perfectly liquid asset and hold other assets that carry more risk. At times the preference for liquidity grows very strong. Unless the government expands the nation's money supply, interest rates will rise.

In the theory of liquidity preference, only two outlets for investor

---

[5] See especially J. M. Keynes (1936).

funds are considered—bonds and money (including bank deposits). Money provides perfect liquidity (i.e., instant spending power) while bonds pay interest but cannot be spent until converted into cash. If interest rates rise, the market value of bonds paying a fixed rate of interest will fall; the investor would suffer a capital loss if those bonds were converted into cash. On the other hand, a fall in interest rates results in higher bond prices; the bondholder will experience a capital gain if his or her bonds are sold for cash. To the classical theorists it was irrational to hold money because it provided little or no return. To Keynes, however, the holding of money could be a perfectly rational act if interest rates were expected to rise because rising rates could result in substantial losses from investing in bonds.

Motives for Holding Money.   Keynes observed that the public demands money for three different purposes (motives). The *transactions motive* represents the demand for money in order to purchase goods and services. Because inflows and outflows of money are not perfectly synchronized in either timing or amount and it is costly to shift back and forth between money and other assets, businesses, households, and governments must keep some cash in the till or in demand accounts simply to meet daily expenses. Some money also must be held as a reserve for future emergencies and to cover extraordinary expenses. This *precautionary motive* for holding money arises because we live in a world of uncertainty and cannot predict exactly what expenses or what opportunities will arise in the future.

Keynes assumed that money demanded for transactions and precautionary purposes was dependent upon the level of national income, business sales, and prices. Reflecting money's role as a medium of exchange, higher levels of income, sales, or prices increased the need for money to carry out transactions and to respond to future expenses and opportunities. However, neither the precautionary nor the transactions demand for money was assumed to be affected by changes in interest rates. In fact, Keynes assumed money demand for precautionary and transactions purposes to be fixed in the short run. In a longer-run period, however, transactions and precautionary demands change as national income changes.

Short-run changes in interest rates were attributed by Keynes to a third motive for holding money—the *speculative motive* which stems from uncertainty about the future prices of bonds. As noted earlier, rising interest rates result in falling prices for bonds. To illustrate, suppose an investor has recently purchased a corporate bond for $1,000. The company issuing the bond promises to pay $100 a year in interest income. In order to simplify matters, assume the bond is a *perpetual security*. This means the investor will receive $100 a year for as long as he or she wishes to hold the security. The annual rate of return (or yield) on the bond, then, is 10 percent ($100/$1,000). Suppose now that the interest rate on bonds of similar quality rises to 12 percent. What happens to the price of the 10 percent bond? Obviously, its price in the marketplace will fall because its annual yield is less than 12 percent.

How far will the bond's price fall? It will approach $833 because at this price the $100 annual interest payment gives the investor an approximate annual yield of 12 percent ($100/$833). In the reverse situation, if interest rates were to decline—say, to 9 percent—the 10 percent bond would become more attractive and its market price would rise.[6]

If investors expect rising interest rates, many of them will demand money or near-money assets instead of bonds because they believe bond prices will fall. As the expectation that interest rates will rise grows stronger and stronger in the marketplace, the demand for money as a secure store of value increases. We may represent this speculative demand for money by a curve which slopes downward and to the right, as shown in Figure 7–5, reflecting a *negative* relationship between the speculative demand for money and the level of interest rates. At low rates of interest, many investors feel that interest rates are soon to rise (i.e., bond prices are going to fall), and therefore more money is demanded. At high rates of interest, on the other hand, many investors will conclude that rates soon will fall and bond prices rise, so the demand for money decreases while the demand for bonds increases.

From another vantage point, when interest rates are high, the opportunity cost (loss) from holding idle cash increases. Thus, high interest rates encourage investors to reduce their cash balances and buy bonds. In contrast, when interest rates are low, the opportunity cost of holding idle cash is also low, but the expected capital loss from holding bonds is high should interest rates rise. Thus, there is more incentive to hold money rather than buy bonds when interest rates are low.

Total Demand for Money.   The total demand for money in the economy is simply the sum of transactions, precautionary, and speculative demands. Because the principal determinant of transactions and precautionary demands is income, not interest rates, these money demands

---

[6] The price of a perpetual bond (P) is related to its market interest rate (r) by the formula

$$P = R/r$$

where R is the annual income in dollars paid by the security. Clearly, as interest rate r increases, market price P falls. As we will see in Chapter 8, the same *inverse* relationship between the price and interest yield on a fixed-income security holds even if we assume that the security is not perpetual but has a finite maturity.

FIGURE 7–5

Speculative Demand for Money

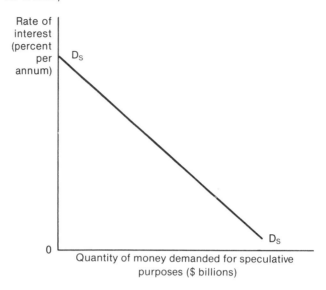

are fixed at a certain level of national income. Let this demand be represented by the quantity OK shown along the horizontal axis in Figure 7–6. Then, any amount of money demanded in excess of OK represents speculative demand. The total demand for money is represented along curve D_T. Therefore, if the rate of interest at the moment is at i, Figure 7–6 shows that the speculative demand for money is KJ and the total demand for money is OJ.

The Supply of Money

The other major element determining interest rates in liquidity preference theory is the supply of money. In modern economies the money supply is controlled or at least closely regulated by government. Because government decisions concerning the size of the nation's money supply presumably are guided by the public welfare and not by the level of interest rates, we assume that the supply of money is *inelastic* with respect to the rate of interest. Such a money-supply curve is represented in Figure 7–7 by the vertical line M_S.

The Equilibrium Rate of Interest in Liquidity Preference Theory

The interplay of the total demand for money and the supply of money determines the equilibrium rate of interest in the short run. As shown

FIGURE 7–6

The Total Demand for Money in the Economy

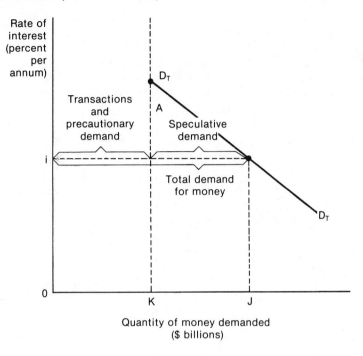

FIGURE 7–7

The Equilibrium Rate of Interest in the Liquidity Preference Theory in Figure 7–7, the equilibrium rate of interest is found at point i_E where the quantity of money demanded by the public equals the quantity of money supplied. Above this equilibrium rate, the supply of money exceeds the quantity demanded, and some businesses, households, and units of government will try to dispose of their unwanted money balances by purchasing bonds. The prices of bonds will rise, driving interest rates down toward equilibrium at i_E. On the other hand, at rates below equilibrium, the quantity of money demanded exceeds the supply. Some decision makers in the economy will sell their bonds to raise additional cash, driving bond prices down and interest rates up toward equilibrium.

Liquidity preference theory provides some useful insights into investor behavior and the influence of government policy on the economy and financial system. For example, it suggests that it is rational at certain times for the public to hoard money and at other times to "dishoard" (spend away) unwanted cash. If the public disposes of some of its cash balances by purchasing securities, this action increases the quantity of loanable funds available in the nation's financial markets. Other things equal, interest rates will fall. On the other hand, if the public tries to hoard more money, expanding its cash balances by selling securities, less money will be available for loans. Interest rates will rise, *ceteris paribus.*

Liquidity preference illustrates how central banks such as the Federal Reserve System can influence interest rates in the financial markets, at least in the short run. For example, if higher interest rates are desired, the central bank can contract the size of the nation's money supply and rates will tend to rise, assuming the demand for money is unchanged. If the demand for money is increasing, then the central bank can bring about higher interest rates by ensuring that the money supply grows more slowly than money demands. In contrast, if the central bank expands the nation's money supply, interest rates will decline in the short run if the demand for money does not increase as well.

Subsequent research by Friedman (1968), Cagan (1972), and others suggests that three dynamic effects on the equilibrium interest rate follow when the money supply changes: (1) an initial *liquidity effect;* (2) a subsequent *income effect;* and, over a longer time horizon, (3) a *price expectations* effect. For example, an increase in the nation's money supply creates excess liquidity, at least temporarily, and interest rates fall. However, the excess liquidity will generate additional spending in the economy, driving up income and increasing the demand for money. Unless the money supply expands further, the downward trend in rates will be reversed and interest rates will begin rising. Finally, an increasing money supply coupled with rising incomes may generate inflationary expectations. Businesses and consumers come to expect rising prices as do lenders of funds who, therefore, increase interest rates on loans. Thus, it is argued, given sufficient time the liquidity effect of money-supply changes will be offset by income and price-expectations effects. Interest rates may end up higher or lower than their initial level after a money-supply change, depending on the relative strengths of these three effects.

Limitations of the Liquidity Preference Theory

Like the classical theory of interest, liquidity preference theory has important limitations. It is a short-run approach to interest-rate determination because it assumes that income remains stable. As we have seen in the longer run, interest rates are affected by changes in the level of income and price (inflationary) expectations. Indeed, it is impossible to have a stable equilibrium interest rate without also reaching an equilibrium level of income, saving, investment, and prices in the economy. Then, too, liquidity preference considers only the supply and demand for the stock of money, whereas business, consumer, and government demands for credit clearly have an impact upon the cost of credit to these borrowers. A more comprehensive view of interest rates is needed which considers the important roles played by all actors in the financial system, that is, businesses, households, and governments.

THE LOANABLE FUNDS THEORY

An explanation of interest rates that overcomes many of the limitations of earlier theories is the loanable funds approach. This view argues that the risk-free interest rate is determined by the interplay of two forces— the demand for and the supply of loanable funds. The demand for loanable funds consists of credit demands from businesses, consumers, and units of government. The supply of loanable funds stems from three sources: saving, hoarding demand for money, and money creation by the banking system. We consider each of these demand and supply factors in turn.

Consumer Demand for Loanable Funds

Consumers demand loanable funds in order to purchase a wide variety of goods and services on credit. Recent research indicates that consumers are not particularly responsive to the rate of interest when they seek credit but focus instead principally on the "nonprice" terms of a loan, such as the down payment, maturity, and size of installment payments. This implies that consumer demand for credit is relatively *inelastic* with respect to the rate of interest. Certainly a rise in interest rates leads to some reduction in the quantity of consumer demand for loanable funds (particularly where home mortgage credit is involved), while a decline in rates stimulates some additional consumer borrowing. However, along the consumer's relatively inelastic demand schedule, a substantial change in the rate of interest must occur before the quantity of consumer demand for funds changes significantly.

Business Demand for Loanable Funds

The credit demands of businesses generally are more responsive to changes in the rate of interest than is consumer borrowing. Most business credit is for such investment purposes as the purchase of inventories and new plant and equipment. As noted earlier in our discussion of the classical theory of interest, a high interest rate eliminates some business investment projects from consideration because their expected rate of return is lower than the cost of funds. On the other hand, at lower rates of interest, many investment projects look profitable, with their expected returns exceeding the cost of funds. Therefore, the quantity of loanable funds demanded by the business sector increases as the rate of interest falls.

Government Demand for Loanable Funds

Government demand for loanable funds is a growing factor in the nation's financial markets but does not depend significantly on the level of interest rates. This is especially true of borrowing by the federal government. Federal decisions on spending and borrowing are made by Congress in response to social needs and the public welfare, not the rate of interest. Moreover, the federal government has the power both to tax and to create money in order to pay its debts. State and local government demand, on the other hand, is slightly interest elastic because many local governments are limited in their borrowing activities by legal interest-rate ceilings. When open-market rates rise above these legal ceilings, some state and local units of government are prevented from offering their securities to the public.

Total Demand for Loanable Funds

The total demand for loanable funds is the sum of consumer, business, and government credit demands. This demand curve slopes downward and to the right with respect to the rate of interest, as shown in Figure 7–8. Higher rates of interest lead some businesses, consumers, and governments to curtail their borrowing plans, while lower rates bring forth more credit demand. However, the demand for loanable funds does not determine the rate of interest by itself. The supply of loanable funds must be added to complete the picture.

FIGURE 7–8

Total Demand for Loanable Funds

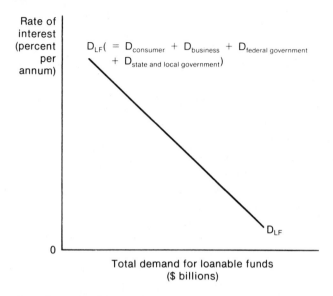

$D_{LF}(= D_{consumer} + D_{business} + D_{federal\ government} + D_{state\ and\ local\ government})$

Rate of interest (percent per annum)

D_{LF}

0

Total demand for loanable funds
($ billions)

The Supply of Loanable Funds

Loanable funds flow into the money and capital markets from at least three different sources: (1) saving by businesses, consumers, and governments; (2) dishoarding (spending down) of excess money balances held by the public; and (3) creation of money by the banking system. We consider each of these sources of funds in turn.

Saving.   The supply of savings is the principal source of loanable funds. As noted earlier, most saving is done by households and is simply the difference between current income and current consumption. Businesses, however, also save by retaining a portion of current earnings and by adding to their depreciation reserves. Government saving, while relatively rare, occurs when current revenues exceed current expenditures.

Earlier in the chapter we noted that most economists today believe that income levels, rather than interest rates, are the dominant factor in the decision of how much and when to save.[7] There is also evidence

---

[7] There is, however, considerable controversy as to just what measure of income determines the annual volume of savings. Some economists argue that current saving is determined, not by current income levels, but by a long-run view of income, perhaps adjusted for the stage of life of the income recipient. See, for example, Ando and Modligiani (1963).

that business and household saving may be goal oriented—the so-called *income effect*. That is, some business firms and households set target levels of total savings as a long-run goal. For example, suppose an individual wishes to accumulate $100,000 in anticipation of his or her retirement. Interest rates subsequently rise from 5 percent to 10 percent. Will this individual save more out of each period's income or less? Probably less, because the higher interest rate will enable the saver to reach his or her goal with less sacrifice of current income. On the other hand, a lower interest rate might lead to a greater volume of saving because a business or household must accumulate more funds to achieve its savings goal.

Clearly, then, the goal or income effect would have the opposite effect on the volume of saving from the substitution effect, described earlier in our discussion of the classical theory of interest. These two effects pull aggregate saving in opposite directions as interest rates change. It should not be surprising, therefore, that the annual volume of saving in the economy is an extremely difficult quantity to forecast.

Recent research using econometric models of the U.S. economy has suggested the importance of another factor—the *wealth effect*—in influencing savings decisions.[8] Individuals accumulate wealth in many different forms, such as real assets (automobiles, furniture, houses, land), and financial assets (stocks, bonds). What happens to the value of financial assets as interest rates change? If rates rise, the market value of financial assets will fall until their yield approaches market-determined levels. On the other hand, with a decline in interest rates the market value of financial assets will rise until their yield approaches market-determined levels. Then again, a decline in interest rates tends to increase the value of financial assets, especially long-term bonds. In general, then, a rise in interest rates will result in decreases in the value of wealth held in financial assets, forcing the individual to save more to protect his or her wealth position. Conversely, a decrease in interest rates will increase the value of financial assets, increasing wealth and perhaps necessitating a lower volume of current saving.

For businesses and individuals heavily in debt, however, the opposite effects may ensue. When interest rates rise, debt contracted in earlier periods, when interest rates were lower, seems less of a burden now. For example, a home mortgage taken on by a family when rates in the mortgage market were 10 percent seems a less burdensome drain on family income when rates on new mortgages have risen to 15 percent. Therefore, a rise in interest rates tends to make those economic units carrying a large volume of debt relative to their financial assets feel better off, and they may tend to save less as a result. A decrease in interest

---

[8] See especially Boskin (1978), Feber (1973), and Justen and Taylor (1975).

rates, on the other hand, may result in more savings due to the wealth effect.

The net effect of savings goals, substitution, and wealth effects leads to a relatively interest-inelastic supply-of-savings curve. Substantial changes in interest rates usually are required to bring about any significant changes in the volume of aggregate saving in the economy.

Dishoarding of Money Balances.   Still another source of loanable funds is centered on the public's demand for money relative to the available supply of money. As noted in our earlier discussion of liquidity preference theory, the public's demand for money varies with interest rates and income levels. The supply of money, on the other hand, is closely controlled by government. Clearly the two—money demand and money supply—need not be the same. The differences between the public's total demand for money and the money supply is known as *hoarding.* When the public's demand for money exceeds the supply, *positive hoarding* of money takes place as individuals and businesses attempt to increase their money holdings at the expense of others. Hoarding *reduces* the volume of loanable funds available in the financial markets. On the other hand, when the public's demand for money is less than the supply available, *negative hoarding* (dishoarding) occurs. Some individuals and businesses will dispose of their excess money holdings, increasing the supply of loanable funds available in the financial system.

Creation of Credit by the Banking System.   Commercial banks and nonbank thrift institutions offering payments accounts have the unique ability to create credit by lending and investing their excess reserves. Credit created by the banking system represents an additional source of loanable funds, which must be added to the amount of savings and dishoarding of money balances (or minus the amount of hoarding demand) to derive the total supply of loanable funds in the economy. The total supply-of-loanable-funds curve is depicted in Figure 7–9. This curve rises with higher rates of interest, indicating that a greater supply of loanable funds will flow into the financial marketplace when the returns from lending increase.

The Equilibrium Rate of Interest in the Loanable Funds Theory

The two forces of supply and demand for loanable funds determine not only the volume of lending and borrowing going on in the economy, but also the rate of interest. The interest rate tends toward the equilibrium point at which the supply of loanable funds equals the demand for loanable funds. This point of equilibrium is shown in Figure 7–10 at i_E.

FIGURE 7–9

Supply of Loanable Funds

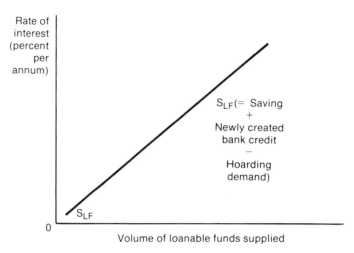

If the interest rate is temporarily *above* equilibrium, the quantity of loanable funds supplied by savers, by the banking system, and from the dishoarding of money balances (or minus hoarding demand) exceeds the total demand for loanable funds, and the rate of interest will be bid down. On the other hand, if the interest rate is temporarily *below* equilib-

FIGURE 7–10

The Equilibrium Rate of Interest in the Loanable Funds Theory

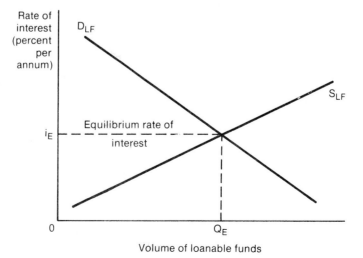

rium, loanable funds demand from businesses, consumers, and governments will exceed the supply. The interest rate will be bid up by borrowers until it settles at equilibrium once again.

The equilibrium depicted in Figure 7–10 is only a *partial* equilibrium position, however. This is due to the fact that interest rates are affected by conditions in the economy as a whole. For the economy to be in equilibrium, planned saving must equal planned investment across the whole economic system. For example, if planned investment exceeds planned saving at the equilibrium rate shown in Figure 7–10, investment demands will push interest rates higher in the short run. However, as additional investment spending occurs, incomes will rise, generating a greater volume of savings. Eventually, interest rates will fall. Only when the economy, the money market, and the loanable funds market are *simultaneously* in equilibrium will interest rates remain stable. Thus a stable equilibrium interest rate will be characterized by planned savings in the economy equal to planned investment, money supply equal to money demand (zero hoarding), and the quantity of loanable funds supplied to the financial markets equal to the total demand for loanable funds.

This simple demand-supply framework is useful for analyzing broad movements in interest rates. For example, if the supply of loanable funds from savings and other sources is increasing and the demand for loanable funds remains unchanged or rises more slowly, the volume of credit extended in the financial markets must increase, and interest rates will fall. This is illustrated in Figure 7–11A, which shows the supply curve sliding downward and to the right when S_{LF} increases to S'_{LF}, resulting in a decline in the equilibrium rate of interest from i_1 to i_2. The equilibrium quantity of loanable funds traded in the financial system increases from C_1 to C_2.

What happens when the demand for loanable funds increases with no change in the supply of funds available? In this instance, the volume of credit extended will increase, but loans will be made at higher interest rates. Figure 7–11B illustrates this. The loanable funds demand curve rises from D_{LF} to D'_{LF}, driving the interest rate upward from i_1 to i_2.

THE RATIONAL EXPECTATIONS THEORY

In recent years a fourth major theory on the forces determining interest rates has appeared and now appears to be rapidly gaining supporters. This is the *rational expectations* view. It builds upon a growing body of research evidence that the money and capital markets are highly "efficient" institutions in digesting and reacting to new information affecting interest rates and security prices.

For example, when new data appears about business investment,

FIGURE 7–11

Changes in the Demand for and Supply of Loanable Funds

A. Effects of increased supply of loanable funds with demand unchanged

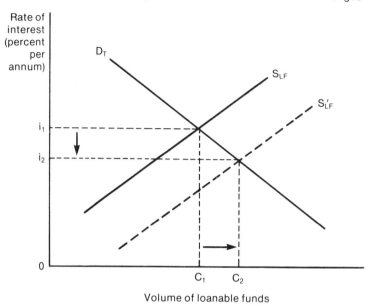

Volume of loanable funds

B. Effects of increased demand for loanable funds with supply unchanged

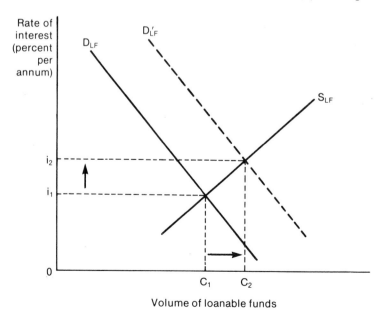

Volume of loanable funds

household saving, or growth in the nation's money supply, investors begin immediately to translate that new information into decisions to buy or sell securities, borrow or lend funds. In a short space of time—perhaps in minutes or seconds—security prices and interest rates change to reflect the new information. So rapid is this process of the market digesting and using new information that security prices and interest rates presumably already impound the new data from virtually the moment that data appears. In a perfectly efficient market it is impossible to snare excess profits by trading on publicly available information. Interestingly enough, this concept of the rapid response of interest rates and security prices to new information runs counter to much of the traditional interest-rate literature and counter to many interest-rate forecasting models today which assume that weeks or months must pass before a new development affecting rates and prices will exert its full effect on the financial marketplace.[9]

If the money and capital markets are highly efficient in the way we have described above, this implies that interest rates will always be at or very near their equilibrium levels. Any deviation from the equilibrium rate level dictated by demand and supply forces will be almost instantly eliminated. Security traders or speculators who hope to *consistently* earn "windfall" profits from correctly guessing whether interest rates are "too high" and, therefore, will probably fall or are "too low" and, therefore, will probably rise are unlikely to be successful in the long run. Interest-rate fluctuations around equilibrium are likely to be random and momentary. Moreover, knowledge of *past* interest rates—for example, those

---

[9] The important assumptions and implications of the rational expectations-efficient markets view are that: (1) the prices of securities and interest rates should reflect all available information and the market uses this information correctly in establishing the probability distribution of future prices and rates; (2) changes in rates and security prices are correlated only with unanticipated, not anticipated information; (3) the serial correlation between rates of return in successive time periods is zero; (4) no unexploited opportunities for profit (above a normal return) can be found in the securities' markets; (5) transactions and storage costs for securities are negligible and information costs are small relative to the value of securities traded; and (6) expectations concerning future security prices and interest rates are formed rationally and used efficiently. This last assumption means that businesses and individuals are assumed to be *rational agents* who form expectations about the distribution of future security prices and interest rates that do not differ significantly from optimal forecasts made from using all the available information the marketplace provides. Rational agents attempt to make optimal use of the resources at their disposal in order to maximize their returns. They do not ignore or inefficiently employ available information in their attempts at return maximization. A rational agent would tend to make unbiased forecasts of future security prices, interest rates, and other variables rather than make systematic forecasting errors.

that prevailed yesterday or last month—will *not* be a reliable guide to where those rates are likely to be today or in the future.

The rational expectations view also suggests that interest rates do *not* stray permanently from their current equilibrium levels *unless new information appears.* Old news will not affect today's interest rates because those rates already have impounded that information. Rates will only change if entirely *new* and *unexpected* information appears. For example, if the federal government announces for several weeks running that it must borrow an additional $10 billion next month, interest rates probably reacted to that information only the first time it appeared. In fact, interest rates probably *increased* at that time because many investors would view the government's additional need for credit as adding to other demands for credit in the economy and, with the supply of credit unchanged, interest rates would be expected to move higher. However, if the government merely repeated that same announcement again, interest rates probably wouldn't change a second time; it would be *old* information already reflected in today's interest-rate level.

Imagine a new scenario, however. The government suddenly reveals that, contrary to expectations, tax revenues are now being collected in greater amounts than first forecast and, therefore, no new borrowing will, in fact, be needed next month. Interest rates probably will fall immediately as market participants are forced to revise their borrowing and lending plans to deal with a new situation. How do we know which *direction* rates will move? Clearly the path rates will take depends on *what market participants expected to begin with.* Thus, if market participants were expecting increased demand for credit (with supply unchanged), an unexpected announcement of reduced credit demand implies *lower* interest rates in the future. Similarly, a market expectation of less credit demand in the future (again, supply unchanged), when confronted with an unexpected announcement of higher credit demand, implies that interest rates will *rise.*

The rational expectations view, then, argues that forecasting interest-rate changes requires knowledge of the public's *current set of expectations.* If new information is sufficient to alter those expectations, interest rates must change. If correct, this portion of the rational expectations theory creates significant problems for government policymakers. It implies that policymakers cannot cause interest rates to move in any particular direction without knowing what the public already expects to happen and, indeed, cannot change interest rates at all unless government officials can convince the public that a new set of expectations is warranted.

A growing number of studies today imply that at least some elements of the rational expectations-efficients markets view do show up in actual market behavior. For example, studies by Mishkin (1978) and Phillips and Pippenger (1976) find that past interest-rate movements are *not* significantly related to current rates of return for bonds or for stock, as the theory predicts. Other studies [e.g., Rozeff (1974)] find that *past* information on economic conditions and money-supply movements also appear to bear little correlation to today's interest-rate levels or to observed changes in current interest rates. However *unanticipated* growth in the nation's money supply and in income, production, and the price level do appear to be correlated with bond and stock returns. Moreover, adjustments in interest rates and security prices to new information appear to be very rapid—far more rapid than implied by econometric models based upon the more traditional interest-rate theories.

Nevertheless, the rational expectations view still is in the development stage and provides, at this time, little help for such practical problems as trying to forecast interest rates. One key problem here is that we do not know very much about how the public *forms* its expectations—what data is used, what weights are applied to individual bits of data, and so on. Moreover, there are several characteristics of real-world markets that seem at odds with the assumptions of the expectations theory. For example, the cost of gathering and analyzing information relevant to the pricing of loans and securities is not always negligible, as assumed by the theory, tempting many lenders and borrowers of funds to form their expectations by rules of thumb (trading rules) that are not fully rational. While rationally formed expectations appear to exist in large auction markets (such as the markets for U.S. government securities or listed common stock), it is not clear that such is the case for other financial markets such as those for consumer and small business loans. Finally, some current interest rates—for example, those on short-term securities such as Treasury bills—do exhibit correlations with past interest-rate movements. Thus, not all interest rates and security prices appear to approximate a "random walk" as implied by the expectations theory.

CONCLUSIONS

Each theory of the determinants of interest rates reviewed in this chapter offers useful insights into the functioning of the financial system. Collectively, the various views of interest-rate determination point to those forces in the economy which should be studied carefully if we are to understand current trends in interest rates and anticipate future trends. In the next two chapters we consider various factors that cause the interest rate on one security or loan to be different from the rate on another security or loan. These factors include expectations of inflation, the maturity or length of a security or loan, the risk of borrower default, the risk of calling in a security in advance of its maturity, taxes, and security convertibility. We will find that a thorough understanding of the entire structure of interest rates in the economy requires us to be aware of *all* of these factors as well as the interest-rate theories we have reviewed in this chapter.

STUDY QUESTIONS

1. What are the different roles of the rate of interest in the economy?

2. What is the risk-free, or pure, interest rate? Explain its relationship to other interest rates in the economy.

3. What factors determine the rate of interest in the classical theory? Explain why the supply-of-savings curve has a positive slope. What determines the shape of the demand curve in this theory?

4. Compare and contrast the liquidity preference and classical theories of interest. What are the principal limitations of each?

5. Define the following: transactions motive, precautionary motive, and speculative motive. How is the total demand for money determined in the liquidity preference theory? Why does the demand-for-money curve slope downward and to the right?

6. What is the liquidity effect associated with changes in the money supply? The income effect? The price-expectations effect? Explain how these effects cause interest rates to change when the money supply expands (demand for money unchanged). Suppose the money supply contracts (again with money demand unchanged).

7. What factors make up the demand for loanable funds? The supply of loanable funds? How is the equilibrium rate of interest determined in the loanable funds theory?

8. Trace through what happens to the equilibrium rate of interest when the demand for loanable funds increases with supply unchanged. What happens to the equilibrium rate if the supply of loanable funds expands with demand unchanged?

9. Describe the rational expectations theory of interest-rate determination. What is assumed in this theory? Can you see any problems in trying to use this theory to anticipate future trends in rates?

PROBLEMS

1. Construct a supply of savings curve (with all curves and axes correctly labeled) which illustrates the *income effect*. Do the same to illustrate the *wealth effect*. Explain the differences you observe.

2. Suppose the going market rate of interest on high-quality (AAA-rated) corporate bonds is 12 percent. FORTRAN Corporation is considering an investment project which will last 10 years, requires an initial cash outlay of $1.5 million, but will generate estimated revenues of $500,000 per year for 10 years. Would you recommend that this project be adopted? Explain why.

3. A government securities dealer has purchased a Treasury long-term bond bearing a coupon rate of 9 percent. The bond was purchased at par ($1,000). Interest rates on *new* bonds with comparable terms rise to 11 percent. What will happen to the 9 percent bond's market price? What price will it approach? Answer these same questions in the case where bond rates decline to 7 percent. Explain the price changes you have calculated.

4. The statements listed below were gathered from recent issues of financial newssheets. Read each statement carefully and then *(a)* identify which theory or theories of interest-rate determination is implicit in each statement; and *(b)* indicate which *direction* interest rates should move if the statement is a correct analysis of the current market situation. Use appropriate supply-demand diagrams, where possible, to show the reasoning behind your answers to part b.

    "The factor which is likely to dominate interest-rate changes in the weeks ahead is a tighter credit policy at the Federal Reserve."

    "The White House unexpectedly disclosed today that budget negotiations with Capitol Hill have broken down. Market analysts are fearful of the effects on the bond and stock markets when trading begins tomorrow morning."

    "Corporate profits have declined significantly in the quarter just concluded, following a year of substantial growth. Financial experts expect this negative trend to continue for at least the next six months."

    "Personal consumption expenditures are rising rapidly, fueled by an unprecedented level of borrowing. Personal savings is up in real dollar terms, but the national savings rate dropped significantly this past year and further declines are expected. Economists believe this recent change in the savings rate explains the current trend in interest rates—a trend likely to continue into next autumn."

SELECTED REFERENCES

Ando, A., and Franco Modigliani. "The Life Cycle Hypothesis of Saving." *American Economic Review*, March 1963, pp. 55–84.

Bechter, Don M., and Stephen H. Pollock. "Are Inventories Sensitive to Interest Rates?" *Economic Review*, Federal Reserve Bank of Kansas City, April 1980, pp. 18–27.

Bohm-Bawerk, Eugen von. *The Positive Theory of Capital.* New York: Macmillan, 1891.

Boskin, M. J. "Taxation, Savings and the Rate of Interest." *Journal of Political Economy*, April 1978, pp. S3–S27.

Cagan, Phillip. *The Changes of Monetary Effects on Interest Rates.* New York: National Bureau of Economic Research, 1972.

DeFina, Robert H. "The Link between Savings and Interest Rates: A Key Element in the Tax Policy Debate." *Business Review*, Federal Reserve Bank of Philadelphia, November–December 1984, pp. 15–21.

Fama, Eugene F., and Merton H. Miller. *The Theory of Finance.* New York: Holt, Rinehart & Winston, 1972.

Feber, R. "Consumer Economics: A Survey." *Journal of Economic Literature*, December 1973, pp. 1303–42.

Fisher, Irving. *The Theory of Interest.* New York: Macmillan, 1930.

Friedman, Milton. "Factors Affecting the Level of Interest Rates." *Proceedings of the Conference on Savings and Residential Financing*, U.S. League of Savings Associations, 1968, pp. 11–27.

Justen, F. T., and L. D. Taylor. "Towards a Theory of Saving Behavior." *American Economic Review*, May 1975, pp. 203–9.

Keynes, John M. *The General Theory of Employment, Interest and Money.* New York: Harcourt Brace Jovanovich, 1936.

Klammer, Thomas. "Empirical Evidence of the Adoption of Sophisticated Capital Budgeting Techniques." *Journal of Business*, July 1972, pp. 387–97.

Mishkin, Frederick. "Efficients-Markets Theory: Implications for Monetary Policy." *Brookings Papers on Economic Activity*, 3 (1978), pp. 707–52.

———, "Monetary Policy and Long-Term Interest Rates: An Efficient-Markets Approach." *Journal of Monetary Economics*, January 1981, pp. 29–55.

Petty, J. William; David F. Scott; and Monroe M. Bird. "The Capital Expenditure Decision-Making Process of Large Corporations." *Engineering Economist*, Spring 1975, pp. 159–72.

Phillips, Llad, and John Pippenger. "Preferred Habitat vs. Efficient Market: A Test of Alternative Hypotheses." *Review*, Federal Reserve Bank of St. Louis (May 1976), pp. 11–19.

Poole, William. "Rational Expectations in the Macro Model." *Brookings Papers on Economic Activity,* 2(1976).

Rozeff, Michael S. "Money and Stock Prices: Market Efficiency and the Lag in Effect of Monetary Policy." *Journal of Financial Economics,* 1 (September 1974), pp. 245–302.

8

Relationships between Interest Rates and Security Prices

THE PURPOSE OF THIS CHAPTER

To illustrate the principal ways in which interest rates and security prices are measured in the financial markets and to examine the relationships between interest rates and security prices. The chapter is designed to give investors, lenders, and borrowers different ways to evaluate returns and costs associated with different financial instruments.

KEY TERMS AND CONCEPTS IN THE CHAPTER

add-on rate
annual percentage
  rate (APR)
basis points
bond prices
bond-yield tables

coupon rate
current yield
discount method
holding-period yield
present value tables
rate of interest

simple interest
stock price
yield approximation
  formula
yield to maturity

Theories of the rate of interest help us to understand the forces that cause interest rates and prices of securities to change. They provide clues on the future direction of interest rates. However, these theories provide little or no information on how interest rates should be *measured in the real world.* As a result, many different measures of interest rates on securities and loans have been developed, leading to some confusion, especially for small borrowers and investors. In this chapter the methods most frequently used to measure interest rates and security prices in today's financial markets are examined. We also consider the relationship between security prices and interest rates and how they influence each other.

UNITS OF MEASUREMENT FOR INTEREST RATES AND SECURITY PRICES

Definition of Interest Rates

The interest rate is, of course, the price charged a borrower for the loan of money. As noted in Chapter 7, this "price" is unique because it is really a *ratio* of two quantities—the total required fee that a borrower must pay a lender to obtain the use of credit for a stipulated period to the amount of credit actually made available to the borrower. By convention, the interest rate is usually expressed in *percent per annum.* Thus:

$$\begin{matrix} \text{Annual rate} \\ \text{of interest} \\ \text{on loanable} \\ \text{funds} \\ \text{(in percent)} \end{matrix} = \frac{\begin{matrix} \text{Fee required by the} \\ \text{lender in order for the} \\ \text{borrower to obtain credit} \end{matrix}}{\begin{matrix} \text{Amount of credit made} \\ \text{available to the borrower} \end{matrix}} \times 100 \qquad (8\text{--}1)$$

For example, an interest rate of 10 percent per annum on a $1,000 one-year car loan implies that the lender of funds has received a borrower's promise to pay a fee of $100 (10 percent of $1,000) in return for the use of $1,000 credit for a year. The promised fee of $100 is in addition to the repayment of the loan principal ($1,000) which must occur sometime during the year.

Interest rates are usually expressed as *annualized percentages* even for investments that are shorter than a year. For example, in the federal funds market commercial banks frequently loan reserves to each other overnight, with the loan being repaid the next day. Even in this market the interest rate quoted daily by lenders is expressed in percent per annum as though the loan were for a year's time. As we will soon see, however, various types of loans and securities carry important differences in how interest fees and amounts borrowed are valued or accounted for, leading to several different methods for determining interest rates. In addition, some interest-rate measures use a 360-day year and others, a 365-day year. Some employ compound rates of return, with interest income earned on accumulated interest, and some do not use compounding.[1]

Basis Points

Interest rates on securities traded in the open market rarely are quoted in whole percentage points, such as 5 percent or 8 percent. The typical case is a rate expressed in hundredths of a percent, for example, 5.36 percent or 7.62 percent. Moreover, most interest rates change by only fractions of a whole percentage point in a single day or week. To deal with this situation the concept of the basis point was developed. A *basis point* equals 1/100 of a percentage point. Thus an interest rate of 10.5 percent may be expressed as 10 percent plus 50 basis points, or 1,050 basis points. Similarly an increase in a loan or security rate from 5.25 percent to 5.30 percent represents an increase of 5 basis points.

Security Prices

The prices of common and preferred stock in the United States are measured in dollars and eighths of a dollar. Thus, a stock price of 5⅛ is a quote of $5.125 (because one eighth of a dollar = $0.125), while 40¼ means each share of a particular stock is selling for $40.25.

Bond prices are expressed in points and fractions of a point, with each point equal to $1 on a $100 basis. Thus, a U.S. government bond with a price quotation of 97 points is selling for $97 for each $100 in par (face) value. A $1,000 par-value bond, therefore, would be selling for $970. Fractions of points are typically measured in 32ds, 8ths, quarters, or halves, and occasionally even 64ths. Note that one-half point equals $0.50, while 1/32 equals $0.03125 on a $100 basis. Thus, a price quote on a bond of 97 4/32 (sometimes expressed as 97.4 or 97–4) is $97.125 for each $100 or $971.25 for a $1,000 bond. Quotations expressed in 64ths usually will be indicated by a plus (+) sign added to the nearest 32d. Thus, 100.2+ means 100 5/64.

As we noted in Chapter 3, security dealers quote *two* prices for a security rather than one. The higher of the two is the *asked* price, which indicates what the dealer will *sell* the security for. The *bid* price is the

---

[1] Interest rates on U.S. Treasury bills, commercial paper, and few other short-term financial instruments are based on a 360-day year and do not compound interest. See Part Four, on the money market, for a discussion of these instruments and the basis for calculating their rates of return to the investor.

price at which the dealer is willing to purchase the security. The difference between bid and asked prices—known as the *spread*—provides the
dealer's return for creating a market for the security. Generally, the
longer the maturity of a security, the greater the *spread* between its
bid and asked prices. This is due to the added risks associated with trading
in longer-term securities. Short-term securities may trade with a spread
as low as ⅟₃₂ (equal to $312.50 for a sale of $1 million in securities).
Purchases and sales of intermediate maturities may carry spreads of ⁴⁄₃₂
(equal to $1,250 on a $1 million trade), while long-term bonds may be
trading on spreads of ⁸⁄₃₂ (or about $2,500 for every $1 million sold).
For small transactions, a commission fee is usually added to cover the
cost of executing the transaction. On very large sales, however, dealers
often forgo commissions and quote a "net price."

MEASURES OF THE RATE OF RETURN, OR YIELD, ON A LOAN OR SECURITY

The interest rate on a loan is the annual rate of return *promised* by
the borrower to the lender as a condition for obtaining the loan. However,
that rate is not necessarily a true reflection of the yield or rate of return
actually earned by the lender during the life of the loan. Some borrowers
will default on all or a portion of their promised payments. The market
value of the security evidencing the loan may rise or fall, adding to or
subtracting from the lender's total rate of return (yield) on the transaction.
Thus, while the interest rate measures the "price" the borrower has promised to pay for a loan, the actual *yield* or rate of return on the loan
from the lender's viewpoint may be quite different. In this section a
number of the most widely used measures of the yield or rate of return
on a loan or security are discussed.

Coupon Rate

One of the best-known measures of the rate of return on a debt security
is the *coupon rate* which appears on corporate, U.S. government, and
municipal bonds and notes. The coupon rate is the contracted rate which
the security issuer agrees to pay at the time a security is issued. If, for
example, a company issues a bond with a coupon rate printed on its
face of 9 percent, the borrower has promised the investor an annual
interest payment of 9 percent of the bond's par value. Most bonds are
issued with $1,000 par values, and interest payments are semiannual.

The .amount of promised annual interest income paid by a bond
is called its *coupon.* The annual coupon may be determined from the
formula

$$\text{Coupon rate} \times \text{Par value} = \text{Coupon} \qquad (8\text{–}2)$$

Thus, a bond with par value of $1,000 bearing a coupon rate of 9 percent pays an annual coupon of $90.

The coupon rate is not an adequate measure of the return on a bond or other debt security unless the investor purchases the security at a price equal to its par value, the borrower makes all of the promised payments on time, and the investor sells or redeems the bond at its par value. However, the prices of bonds fluctuate with market conditions; rarely will a bond trade exactly at par.

Current Yield

Another popular measure of the return on a loan or security is its *current yield.* This is simply the ratio of the annual income (dividends or interest) generated by the loan or security to its current market value. Thus a share of common stock selling in the market for $30 and paying an annual dividend to the shareholder of $3 would have a current yield calculated as follows:

$$\text{Current yield} = \frac{\text{Annual income}}{\begin{array}{c}\text{Market price}\\\text{of security}\end{array}} = \frac{\$3}{\$30} = 0.10, \text{ or } 10\% \qquad (8\text{–}3)$$

Frequently, the yields reported on stocks and bonds in the financial press are current yields. Like the coupon rate, the current yield is usually a poor reflection of the rate of return actually received by the lender or investor. It ignores the stream of actual and anticipated payments associated with a loan or security and the price at which the investor will be able to sell or redeem it.

Yield to Maturity

The most widely accepted measure of the rate of return on a loan or security is its *yield to maturity.* It is the rate of interest that the market is prepared to pay for a financial asset in order to exchange present dollars for future dollars. Specifically, the yield to maturity is the rate which equates the purchase price of a security or other financial asset (P) with the present value of all its expected annual net cash inflows (income). In general terms,

$$P = \frac{I_1}{(1+y)^1} + \frac{I_2}{(1+y)^2} + \cdots + \frac{I_n}{(1+y)^n} \qquad (8\text{–}4)$$

where y is the yield to maturity and each I represents the expected annual income from the security, presumed to last for n years and terminate when the financial asset is retired. The I terms in the above formula include both receipts of income and repayments of principal.

To illustrate the use of this formula, assume the investor is considering the purchase of a bond due to mature in 20 years, carrying a 10 percent coupon rate. This security is available for purchase at a current market price of $850. If the bond has a par value of $1,000 which will be paid to the investor when the security reaches maturity, the bond's yield to maturity, y, may be found by solving

$$\$850 = \frac{\$100}{(1+y)^1} + \frac{\$100}{(1+y)^2} + \cdots + \frac{\$100}{(1+y)^{20}} + \frac{\$1,000}{(1+y)^{20}} \qquad (8\text{--}5)$$

In this instance y equals 12 percent—a rate higher than its 10 percent coupon rate because the bond is currently selling at a *discount* from par.

Suppose this same $1,000, 10 percent coupon bond were selling at a *premium* over par. For example, if this 20-year security has a current market price of $1,200, its yield to maturity would be

$$\$1,200 = \frac{\$100}{(1+y)^1} + \frac{\$100}{(1+y)^2} + \cdots + \frac{\$100}{(1+y)^{20}} + \frac{\$1,000}{(1+y)^{20}} \qquad (8\text{--}6)$$

In this case y equals 8 percent. Because the investor must pay a higher current market price than par value (the amount the investor will receive back when the bond matures), this bond's yield to maturity must be *less* than its coupon rate.

From the two examples above it should be clear that the value of a debt security depends on the size of its promised rate of return (coupon rate) relative to prevailing market interest rates on securities of comparable quality and terms. If a security's coupon rate equals the current market interest rate on comparable securities that security will trade at *par*. If the security's coupon rate is less than the prevailing market rate it will sell at a *discount* from par. Finally, if the security's coupon rate exceeds the current interest rate in the market it will sell at a *premium* above its par value.

The yield to maturity carries a number of significant advantages as a measure of the rate of return or yield on a financial asset. In fact, security dealers and brokers typically use the yield to maturity in quoting rates of return to investors. Unlike the current yield, this return measure considers the time distribution of expected cash flows from a security or other financial asset. Of course, the yield-to-maturity measure does assume the investor will hold a security until it reaches final maturity. Moreover, yield to maturity is not an appropriate yield measure for stocks, which are perpetual instruments, and even for some bonds, because the investor may sell them prior to their termination date or the bonds may pay a variable return each year which is unpredictable. Another problem is that this yield measure assumes all cash flowing to the investor can be reinvested at the computed yield to maturity.[2] And, we have not yet considered the impact of taxes on the investor's true return from a security—a subject taken up in Chapter 10.

Holding-Period Yield

A slight modification of the yield-to-maturity formula results in a return measure for those situations where an investor holds a security or other financial asset for a time and then sells it to another investor in advance of the asset's maturity. This so-called holding-period yield is simply

$$P = \frac{I_1}{(1+h)^1} + \frac{I_2}{(1+h)^2} + \cdots + \frac{I_m}{(1+h)^m} + \frac{P_m}{(1+h)^m} \qquad (8\text{--}7)$$

where h is the holding-period yield, and the total length of the investor's holding period covers m time periods. Thus, the holding-period yield is simply the rate of discount (h) equalizing the market price of a financial asset (P) with all net cash flows between the time the asset is purchased and the time it is sold (including the selling price, P_m). If the asset is held to maturity, its holding-period yield equals its yield to maturity.

Calculating Yields to Maturity and Holding-Period Yields

Holding-period yields and yields to maturity can be calculated in several different ways. One method is to employ present value tables identical to those presented in most basic finance and accounting texts.[3]

Suppose, for example, that an investor is contemplating the purchase of a corporate bond, $1,000 par value, with a coupon rate of 10 percent. Currently the bond is selling for $900. The investor plans to hold the bond to maturity, which occurs in five years. We have:

---

[2] The examples shown above assume that interest is paid once a year; however, most bonds sold in the United States pay interest semiannually and some even more frequently. In this instance the yield to maturity formula needs to be modified slightly with the inclusion of the parameter k—the number of times during the year that interest is paid to the bondholder. The formula then becomes:

$$\text{Purchase price} = \frac{I_1/k}{(1+y/k)^1} + \frac{I_2/k}{(1+y/k)^2} + \cdots + \frac{I_{nk}/k}{(1+y/k)^{nk}} + \frac{\text{Final price}}{(1+y/k)^{nk}}$$

Thus, for a 10-year government bond paying $50 interest twice each year, k = 2 and there would be 20 periods (n × k = 10 × 2) in which the investor receives $50 in interest income. Solution of the yield-to-maturity formula proceeds the same way as before except that you need to look up y/k percent in the present value and annuity tables (instead of y) and discount over n × k rather than n time periods.

[3] See, for example, Weston and Brigham (1985) or any other good basic finance or accounting textbook.

$$\$900 = \frac{\$100}{(1+y)^1} + \frac{\$100}{(1+y)^2} + \frac{\$100}{(1+y)^3}$$
$$+ \frac{\$100}{(1+y)^4} + \frac{\$100}{(1+y)^5} + \frac{\$1,000}{(1+y)^5} \tag{8-8}$$

It is useful at this point to consider what each term in Equation 8–8 means. Both the yield-to-maturity and holding-period yield formulas are based on the concept of *present value*—funds to be received in the future are worth less than funds received today. Present dollars may be used to purchase and enjoy goods and services today, but dollars to be received in the future are only *promises* to pay and force us to postpone consumption until the funds actually are received. Equation 8–8 indicates that a bond promising to pay $100 for five successive years in the future plus a lump sum of $1,000 at maturity is worth only $900 in present value dollars. The yield, y, serves as a rate of discount reducing each payment of future dollars back to its present value in today's market. The further in the future the payment is to be made, the larger the discount factor, $(1 + y)^n$, becomes.

Turning the concept around, the purchase of a security in today's market represents the investment of present dollars in the expectation of a greater return in the form of future dollars. The familiar *compound interest formula* applies here. This formula,

$$A_n = P(1 + y)^n \tag{8-9}$$

indicates that the amount of funds accumulated n years from now (A_n) depends on the principal originally invested (P), the investor's expected rate of return or yield (y), and the number of years the funds are invested (n). Thus, a principal of $1,000 invested today at a 10 percent annual rate will amount to $1,100 a year from now [i.e., $1,000 \times (1 + 0.10)$]. Rearrangement of the compound interest formula gives

$$P = \frac{A_n}{(1 + y)^n} \tag{8-10}$$

Equation 8–10 states that the present value of A_n dollars to be received in the future is P if the promised interest rate is y. If we expect to receive $1,100 one year from now and the promised interest rate is 10 percent, the present value of that $1,100 must be $1,000.

Each term on the right-hand side of the yield-to-maturity and holding-period yield formulas is a form of Equation 8–10. Solving Equation 8–8 for the yield to maturity of a bond simply means finding a value for y, which brings both right- and left-hand sides of the yield formula into balance, equating the current price (P) of a security or other financial asset with the stream of future dollars it will generate for the investor.

When all expected annual cash flows are not the same in amount, trial and error may be used to find the solution. Fortunately, in the case of the bond represented in Equation 8–8, the solution is not complicated. Rewrite Equation 8–8 in the following form:

$$\$900 = \$100 \left[\frac{1}{(1+y)^1} + \frac{1}{(1+y)^2} + \cdots + \frac{1}{(1+y)^5} \right] \\ + \$1,000 \left[\frac{1}{(1+y)^5} \right] \tag{8-11}$$

This indicates that the bond will pay an annuity of $1 per year (multiplied by $100) for five years, plus a lump-sum payment of $1 (multiplied by $1,000) at the end of the fifth year.

Use of Present Value Tables. What is the yield on this bond? A reasonable initial guess is 10 percent. To determine how accurate a guess it is, we need to consult the present value and annuity tables in Appendix B. The annuity table in Appendix B indicates that the present value of $1 received annually for five years at a discount yield of 10 percent is $3.791. The present value table in Appendix B shows that the present value of $1 to be received five years from today at 10 percent is $0.621. Inserting these figures into Equation 8–11 yields

$$\$100[3.791] + \$1,000[0.621] = \$1,000.1 > \$900 \tag{8-12}$$

An annual yield of 10 percent is obviously too small because it results in a present value for the bond far in excess of $900. A 12 percent yield gives a present value of $927.50, while a 14 percent yield results in a present value for the bond of $862.30. Clearly, the true yield to maturity of this $900 bond lies between 12 percent and 14 percent, but closer to 12 percent. Linear interpolation fixes this yield at 12.84 percent.[4] The investor interested in maximizing return would compare this yield to maturity with the yields available on other assets of comparable risk.

---

[4] The present value and annuity tables in Appendix B provide the following information:

Difference in Yield to Maturity	Difference in Present Value of Bond
14%	$862.3
12	927.5
2%	$−65.2

There is a difference of $27.5 between the current $900 price of the bond and its present value at a yield of 12 percent, which is $927.50. Therefore, the bond's actual yield to maturity may be found from:

EXHIBIT 8–1

Bond Yield Table (prices of a bond with a 10 percent coupon rate)*

Yield to Maturity in Percent	Maturity of a Bond in Years				
	5	10	15	20	25
5%	121.88	138.97	152.33	162.76	170.91
6	117.06	129.75	139.20	146.23	151.46
7	112.47	121.32	127.59	132.03	135.18
8	108.11	113.59	117.29	119.79	121.48
9	103.96	106.50	108.14	109.20	109.88
10	100.00	100.00	100.00	100.00	100.00
11	96.23	94.02	92.73	91.98	91.53
12	92.64	88.53	86.24	84.95	84.24
13	89.22	83.47	80.41	78.78	77.91
14	85.95	78.81	75.18	73.34	72.40
15	82.84	74.51	70.47	68.51	67.56

* Prices expressed on the basis of $100 par value.

Present value tables may also be used to calculate the holding-period yield on corporate stock. To illustrate, suppose an investor is considering the purchase of common stock issued by Gulf Oil Corporation currently selling for $40 per share. He plans to hold the stock for two years and sell out at an expected price of $50 per share. If dividends of $2 per share are expected each year, what holding-period yield does the investor expect to earn? Following the form of Equation 8–6 we have

$$\$40 = \frac{\$2}{(1+h)^1} + \frac{\$2}{(1+h)^2} + \frac{\$50}{(1+h)^2} \qquad (8\text{–}13)$$

The reader may wish to verify from the present value and annuity tables that the holding-period yield on Gulf Oil's stock is 16.54 percent.

Bond Yield Tables.   Present value tables provide an accurate method for calculating maturity and holding-period yields. However, use of the tables is a trial-and-error process and can be quite time-consuming. To save time, securities dealers and experienced investors use bond yield tables, which give the appropriate yield for bonds of a given coupon rate, maturity, and price. An example of a page from a bond yield table is shown in Exhibit 8–1.

$$12\% + \frac{27.5}{65.2} \times 2\% = 12\% + 0.8436\% = 12.84\%$$

Linear interpolation of this sort must be used with care, especially where yield differentials are substantial, because the yield-price relationship is *not* linear.

To illustrate, suppose the investor holds a corporate bond, bearing a 10 percent coupon rate, with 10 years remaining until maturity. The bond's purchase price may be found in the table under the correct number of years (or, for more detailed bond yield tables, number of months and years) to maturity. The correct yield to maturity will then be found along the same line as the price in the extreme left-hand column of the table. For example, if the 10-year bond's purchase price were $88.53 (on a $100 basis), then its yield to maturity would be 12 percent.

The Yield Approximation Formula.   When tables are unavailable, the yield approximation formula can be used to estimate the rate of return on a security. This formula simply assumes that

$$\text{Average annual yield on a security} = \frac{\text{Average annual income from the security}}{\text{Average amount of funds invested in the security}} \quad (8\text{–}14)$$

In the case of a bond, for example, the yield would be composed of annual interest income plus the average amount of price appreciation (or minus price depreciation) which occurs each year. The average amount of funds invested can be represented by the simple arithmetic average of the purchase price and the expected selling price of the security. That is,

$$\text{Average annual yield} = \frac{\text{Annual interest income} \pm \dfrac{\text{Capital gain or loss}}{\text{Years remaining until sold or redeemed}}}{\dfrac{\text{Purchase price} + \text{Selling price}}{2}} \quad (8\text{–}15)$$

To illustrate the use of this formula, suppose an investor is considering the purchase of a bond with a current market price of $900, a coupon rate of 10 percent, and the bond will be sold or redeemed in 10 years at an expected price of $1,000. The approximate expected yield would be:

$$\text{Average annual yield on bond} = \frac{\$100 + \dfrac{(\$1,000 - 900)}{10}}{\dfrac{\$900 + \$1,000}{2}} = \frac{\$110}{\$950} = 11.58\% \quad (8\text{–}16)$$

Note that the investor expects a capital gain of $100 over the remaining life of this bond because it sells currently for $900 and will be redeemed in 10 years for $1,000. The average annual gain in price, therefore, is $10.

The same formula may be used in the case of a security that is expected to experience a capital loss between time of purchase and time of sale or redemption. Suppose, for example, the investor wishes to purchase a $1,000 par-value bond currently selling for $1,200 with a coupon rate of 10 percent. If the bond matures in 10 years and is held to maturity,

$$\text{Average annual yield on bond} = \frac{\$100 + \dfrac{(\$1,000 - \$1,200)}{10}}{\dfrac{\$1,200 + \$1,000}{2}} \qquad (8\text{--}17)$$

$$= \frac{\$100 - \$20}{\$1,100} = 7.27\%$$

The expected capital loss on the bond partially offsets the annual interest income it will pay to the investor, thus reducing the investor's average yield.

YIELD–PRICE RELATIONSHIPS

The yield-to-maturity and holding-period yield formulas illustrate a number of important relationships between security prices and yields or interest rates which prevail in the financial system. One of these important relationships is:

> The price of a security and its yield or rate of return are inversely related—a rise in yield implies a decline in price; conversely, a fall in yield is associated with a rise in the security's price.

Recall that investing funds in financial assets can be viewed from two different perspectives—the borrowing and lending of money or the buying and selling of securities. As noted in Chapter 7, the rate of interest from the lending of funds is determined by the interaction of the supply of loanable funds and the demand for loanable funds. Demanders of loanable funds (borrowers) supply securities to the financial marketplace, while suppliers of loanable funds (lenders) demand securities as an investment. Therefore, the rate of return or yield on a security and the price of that security are determined at one and the same instant and are simply different aspects of the same phenomenon—the borrowing and lending of loanable funds.

This point is depicted in Figure 8–1, which shows demand and supply curves for both the rate of interest (yield) and the price of securities. The supply of loanable funds curve (representing lending) in the interest-rate diagram (Figure 8–1A) is analogous to the demand for securities

FIGURE 8–1

Equilibrium Security Prices and Interest Rates (yields)

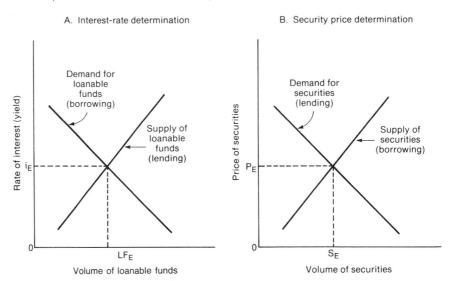

curve (also representing lending) in the price of securities diagram (Figure 8–1B). Similarly, the demand for loanable funds curve (representing borrowing) in the interest-rate diagram is analogous to the supply of securities curve (also representing borrowing) in the price of securities diagram.

We note in Figure 8–1B that borrowers are assumed to issue a larger volume of securities at a higher price and that lenders will demand more securities at a lower price. In Figure 8–1A, on the other hand, borrowers demand a smaller quantity of loanable funds at a higher interest rate (yield) while lenders supply fewer loanable funds at a lower interest rate. The *equilibrium interest rate* (yield) in Figure 8–1A is determined, as discussed in Chapter 7, at point i_E where the demand for loanable funds equals the supply of loanable funds. Similarly, in Figure 8–1B the *equilibrium price* for securities lies at point P_E, where the demand for and supply of securities are equal. Only at the equilibrium interest rate and equilibrium security price will both borrowers and lenders be content with the volume of lending and borrowing taking place.

The *inverse* relationship between interest rates and security prices can be seen quite clearly when we allow the supply and demand curves depicted in Figure 8–1 to change. This is illustrated in Figure 8–2. For example, suppose that, in the face of continuing inflation, consumers and business firms accelerate their borrowings, increasing the demand for loanable funds. As shown in the upper left-hand portion of Figure 8–2, the demand for loanable funds curve slides upward and to the right

FIGURE 8-2

Effects of Changing Supply and Demand on Security Rates (yields) and Prices

A. Effects of an increase in the demand for loanable funds:
higher interest rates and lower security prices

B. Effects of an increase in the supply of loanable funds:
lower interest rates and higher security prices

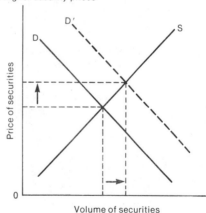

with the supply of loanable funds unchanged. This increasing demand for loanable funds also means that the supply of securities must expand, shown in the upper right-hand portion of Figure 8–2 by a shift in the supply curve from S to S′. Both a new *lower* equilibrium price for securities and a *higher* equilibrium interest rate for loanable funds result.

Conversely, suppose consumers decide to save more, expanding the supply of loanable funds. As shown in the lower left-hand panel of Figure 8–2, the supply of loanable funds curve slides downward and to the right from S to S'. But, with more savings, the demand for securities curve must rise, sliding upward and to the right from D to D', as those added savings are invested in securities. The result is a *rise* in the equilibrium price of securities and a *decline* in the equilibrium interest rate (yield) on loanable funds.

INTEREST RATES CHARGED BY INSTITUTIONAL LENDERS

In this chapter we have examined several different measures of the rate of return, or yield, on securities traded in the financial marketplace. Our list is not complete, however, for institutional lenders of funds—commercial banks, credit unions, savings banks, insurance companies, and finance companies, to name the most important—often employ very different methods to calculate the rate of interest charged on their loans. Four commonly used methods for calculating institutional loan rates are discussed below.

The Simple-Interest Method

The widely used simple-interest method assesses interest charges on a loan only for the period of time the borrower actually has use of borrowed funds. The total interest bill *decreases* the more frequently a borrower must make payments on a loan.

For example, suppose you borrow $1,000 for a year at simple interest. If the interest rate is 10 percent, your interest bill will be $100 for the year. This figure is derived from the well-known formula

$$I = P \times r \times t \qquad (8\text{--}18)$$

where I represents the interest charge (in dollars), P is the principal amount of the loan, r is the annual rate of interest, and t is the term (maturity) of the loan expressed in years or fractions of a year. (In this example, $1,000 \times 0.10 \times 1 = 100).

If the $1,000 loan is repaid in one lump sum at the end of the year, you will pay a total of

$$\frac{\text{Principal} + \text{Interest} = \text{Total payment}}{\$1,000 + \$100 \quad = \quad \$1,100}$$

Suppose, however, that this loan is paid off in two equal installments of $500 each every six months. Then, you will pay

$$\underline{\text{Principal} + \text{Interest}} \qquad = \text{Total payment}$$

First installment: $500 + $50 (i.e., 6 months' interest = $ 550
                                  on $1,000 at 10%)

Second installment: $500 + $25 (i.e., 6 months' interest = $ 525
                                  on $500 at 10%) $1,075

Clearly, you pay a lower interest bill ($75 versus $100) with two install-ment payments instead of one. This happens because with two installment payments on the loan's principal you effectively have use of the full $1,000 for only six months. For the remaining six months of the year, you have use of only $500. A shorthand formula for determining the total payment (interest plus principal) on a simple-interest loan is

$$\text{Total payment due} = P + P \times r \times t = P(1 + r \times t) \qquad (8\text{--}19)$$

The simple-interest method is still popular with many mortgage lenders, credit unions, and commercial banks.

Add-On Rate of Interest

A method of calculating loan interest rates often used by finance com-panies and commercial banks is the *add-on* approach. In this instance, interest is calculated on the full principal of the loan, and the sum of interest and principal payments is divided by the number of payments to determine the dollar amount of each payment. For example, suppose you borrow $1,000 for one year at an interest rate of 10 percent. You agree to make two equal installment payments, six months apart. The total amount to be repaid is, then, $1,100 ($1,000 principal + $100 inter-est). At the end of the first six months you will pay half ($550), and the remaining half will be paid at the end of the year.

If the money is borrowed and repaid in one lump sum (i.e., a single-payment loan), the simple-interest and add-on methods give the same interest rate. However, as the number of installment payments increases, the borrower pays a higher effective interest rate under the add-on method. This happens because the average amount of money borrowed for the term of the loan declines with the greater frequency of installment payments, yet the borrower pays the *same* total interest bill. In fact, the effective rate of interest nearly doubles when monthly installment payments are required. For example, if you borrow $1,000 for a year at 10 percent simple interest but repay the loan in 12 equal monthly installments, you have only about $500 available for use, on average, over the course of the year. Because the total interest bill is $100, the interest rate exceeds 18 percent.

Discount Method

Many commercial loans, especially those used to raise working capital, are extended on a discount basis. This means that the total interest bill is calculated on the basis of the amount to be repaid, and the borrower receives as proceeds of the loan the *difference* between the total amount owed and the interest bill. For example, suppose you borrow $1,000 for one year at 10 percent, for a total interest bill of $100. Using the discount method, you actually receive $900 (i.e., $1,000 − $100) in net loan proceeds. The effective interest rate, then, is

$$\frac{\text{Interest paid}}{\text{Net loan proceeds}} = \frac{\$100}{\$900} \times 100 = 11.11\% \qquad (8\text{--}20)$$

Some lenders will grant the borrower the full amount of money required, but add the amount of discount to the face amount of the borrower's note. For example, if you need the full $1,000, the lender under this method will multiply the effective interest rate (11.11 percent) times $1,000 to derive a total interest bill of $111.11. The face value of the borrower's note and, therefore, the amount that must be repaid becomes $1,111.11. However, the borrower actually receives only $1,000 for use during the year. Most discount loans are for terms of one year or less and usually do not require installment payments. Instead, these loans generally are settled in lump sum when the note comes due.

Annual Percentage Rate (APR)

The wide diversity of rates quoted by lenders is often confusing and discourages "shopping around" for credit. With this in mind, Congress passed the Consumer Credit Protection Act in 1968. More popularly known as Truth in Lending, this law requires institutions regularly extending credit to consumers to tell the borrower what interest rate he or she is actually paying and to use a prescribed method for calculating that rate.[5] Specifically, banks, credit unions, and other lending institutions are required to calculate an annual percentage rate (APR) and inform the loan customer what this rate is before the loan contract is signed. The actuarial method is used to determine the APR, and loan officers usually have tables at hand to translate simple interest or add-on rates into the APR.

The constant ratio formula, shown below, usually gives a good approximation to the true APR:

---

[5] See Chapter 18 for a discussion of consumer credit laws.

$$APR = \frac{\begin{array}{c}2 \times \text{Number of payment periods in a year} \\ \times \text{Annual interest cost in dollars}\end{array}}{\begin{array}{c}(\text{Total number of loan payments} + 1) \\ \times \text{Principal of the loan}\end{array}} \times 100 \quad \text{(8–21)}$$

To illustrate, suppose you borrow \$1,000 at 10 percent simple interest but must repay your loan in 12 equal monthly installments. The APR for this loan is calculated as follows:

$$APR = \frac{2(12)(\$100)}{(12 + 1)(\$1,000)} \times 100 = 18.46\% \quad \text{(8–22)}$$

This computational formula slightly overstates the true APR. The actual APR on this loan is closer to 18 percent.

Congress expected that introduction of the APR would encourage consumers to exercise greater care in the use of credit and to "shop around" to obtain the best terms on a loan. It is not at all clear that either goal has been realized, however. Most consumers continue to give primary weight to the size of their installment payments in deciding how much, when, and where to borrow. If their budget can afford the principal and interest charges on a loan, most consumers seem little influenced by the reported size of the APR and are not usually inclined to ask other lenders for their rates on the same loan. While consumer education is vital to intelligent financial decision making, progress in that direction has been slow in coming.

Compound Interest

Some lenders and loan situations require the borrower to pay *compound interest* on a loan. In addition, most interest-bearing deposits at banks, savings and loans, and credit unions pay compound interest on the balance in the account as of a certain date. The compounding of interest simply means that the lender or depositor earns interest income on both the principal amount and on any accumulated interest. Thus, the longer the period of time over which interest earnings are compounded, the more rapidly does interest earned on interest and interest earned on principal grow.

The conventional formula for calculating the future value of a loan or deposit earning compound interest is simply

$$FV = P(1 + r)^t \quad \text{(8–23)}$$

where FV is the sum of principal plus all accumulated interest over the life of the loan or deposit, P is the loan or deposit's principal value, r is the annual rate of interest or APR, and t is the time expressed in years. For example, suppose \$1,000 is borrowed for three years at 10 percent a year, compounded annually. Using an electronic calculator or a compound interest table (see Appendix B) to find the compounding factor, $(1 + r)^t$, gives

$$FV = \$1,000(1 + 0.10)^3 = \$1,000(1.331) = \$1,331 \qquad (8\text{--}24)$$

which is the lump-sum amount the borrower must pay back at the end of three years.[6] The amount of accumulated compound interest on this loan must be

$$\text{Compound interest} = FV - P = \$1,331 - \$1,000 = \$331 \quad (8\text{--}25)$$

Increased competition in the financial institution's sector in recent years has encouraged many deposit-type institutions to offer their depositors interest compounded more frequently than annually, as assumed in the formula above. To determine the future value of accumulated interest from such a deposit two changes must be made in the formula: (1) the quoted annual interest rate (r) must be divided by the number of periods during the year for which interest is compounded; and (2) the number of years involved (t) must be multiplied by the number of compounding periods within a year. For example, suppose you hold a \$1,000 deposit, earning a 12 percent annual rate of interest, with interest compounded monthly and you plan to hold the deposit for three years. At the end of three years you will receive back the lump sum of

$$\begin{aligned} FV = P(1 + r/12)^{t \times 12} &= \$1,000(1 + 0.12/12)^{3 \times 12} \\ &= \$1,000(1.431) = \$1,431 \end{aligned} \qquad (8\text{--}26)$$

Total interest earned clearly will be \$1,431 − \$1,000 or \$431. Compounding on a more frequent basis increases the depositor's total accumulated interest and, therefore, the deposit's future value.[7]

---

[6] The compound interest table in Appendix B may be used to easily derive the compound interest factor in this problem. Simply check along the top row of the table for the appropriate annual percentage rate (10 percent in the above problem) and then check the number of time periods (in this case, three years) in the extreme left-hand column. The figures in the body of the compound interest table indicate the total future value (FV)—principal plus interest—repaid or earned per \$1 of principal at alternative annual interest rates and time periods.

[7] The reader can look up the 1.431 compounding factor in the compound interest table, Appendix B, simply by checking under the 1 percent (i.e., 12%/12 months) annual percentage rate column and checking the row for 36 (3 × 12 months) periods.

Many financial institutions quote deposit rates compounded *daily*. In this case the

CONCLUSIONS

Interest rates and security prices are among the most important ingredients of financial decisions. Over the years a number of methods have been developed for measuring interest rates and security prices. The intelligent investor must learn to distinguish one method from another. From a conceptual point of view the yield-to-maturity and holding-period-yield methods are among the best ones for measuring the true return from lending and investing funds because both consider the time value of money. From the borrower's point of view, the annual percentage rate (APR) is an effective technique for measuring the true cost of credit.

In this chapter we have highlighted one of the fundamental principles of finance. This is the mandatory *inverse* relationship between the prices of debt securities and interest rates. Falling bond prices, for example, are associated with rising interest rates, while rising bond prices imply falling interest rates. We also frequently observe stock prices falling during a period of rising interest rates, though this is not always the case because stock prices are also sensitive to other factors such as the size of corporate earnings. In the next two chapters various factors that significantly influence the interest rate attached to a loan or security are reviewed. These factors—inflation, maturity, marketability, default risk, taxation, and other influences—have a significant impact on the price of credit in the nation's money and capital markets.

STUDY QUESTIONS

1. What is a basis point? How are stock and bond prices measured?

2. Do you think the coupon rate and the current yield are good measures of the true rate of return on a bond? Why?

3. What is the difference between yield to maturity and holding-period yield? Why are bond yields typically quoted on a yield-to-maturity basis? Why are stock yields usually expressed in terms of current yield?

---

annual interest rate (r) is divided by 360 for simplicity and the number of years (t) in the formula is multiplied by 365. Thus, the formula for *daily* interest rate compounding is simply

$$FV = P(1 + r/360)^{t \times 365}$$

4. Explain why debt-security prices and interest rates are *inversely* related. Illustrate with a diagram.

5. Explain the meaning of the following terms:
   a. Simple interest.
   b. Add-on interest.
   c. Discount method.
   d. APR.
   e. Compounding of interest.

PROBLEMS

1. Suppose a bond is issued with a coupon rate of 8 percent when the market rate of interest is also 8 percent. If the market rate rises to 9 percent, what happens to the price of this bond? What happens to the bond's price if the market rate falls to 6 percent? Explain why.

2. An issue of preferred stock for XYZ corporation is issued at par for $50 per share. If stockholders are promised an 8 percent annual dividend, what was the stock's current yield at time of issue? If the stock's market price has risen to $60 per share, what is its new current yield?

3. An AAA-rated corporate bond has a current market price of $800 and will pay $100 in interest for 10 years. If its par value is $1,000, what is its yield to maturity? Suppose the investor plans to sell it in five years for $900. What would his holding-period yield be?

4. Using the yield approximation formula, calculate the average yield on a $1,000 bond six years from final maturity with a 12 percent coupon rate, selling today for $1,100. What would the bond's yield be if it were selling for $940?

5. You plan to borrow $2,000 in order to take a vacation and want to repay the loan in a year. The banker offers you a simple-interest rate of 12 percent with repayment in two equal installments, 6 months and 12 months from now. What is your total interest bill? What is the APR? Would you prefer an add-on interest rate with one payment at the end of the year? If the bank applies the discount method to your loan, what are the net proceeds of the loan? What is your effective rate of interest?

6. An investor is interested in purchasing a new 20-year government bond carrying a 10 percent coupon rate. The bond's current market price is $875 for a $1,000 par-value instrument. If the investor buys

the bond at the going price and holds to maturity what will be his yield to maturity? Suppose the investor sells the bond at the end of 10 years for $950. What is the investor's holding-period yield?

7. You discover a $1,000 par-value bond just issued by XYZ corporation that pays interest *semiannually* at a coupon rate of 12 percent. The bond will mature in 10 years and can be purchased today at a price of $900 including the broker's commission. What is the bond's yield to maturity if all interest payments are made on time?

8. You borrow $2,500 for five years at a rate of 12 percent per annum, compounded annually. What is the lump-sum amount due at the end of five years? What is the total amount of interest that must be paid?

9. In problem 8 above, if interest were compounded monthly, instead of annually, what lump-sum amount would be due in five years and how much total interest must be paid?

10. You have just placed $1,500 in a bank savings deposit and plan to hold that deposit for eight years, earning 5½ percent per annum. If the bank compounds interest *daily* what will be the total value of the deposit in eight years? How does your answer change if the bank switches to monthly compounding? Quarterly compounding?

SELECTED REFERENCES

Cook, Timothy Q. "Some Factors Affecting Long-Term Yield Spreads in Recent Years." *Monthly Review*, Federal Reserve Bank of Richmond, September 1973, pp. 2–14.

The First Boston Corporation. *Handbook of Securities of the U.S. Government and Federal Agencies.* 30th ed. New York: The First Boston Corporation, 1978.

Freund, William C. *Investment Fundamentals.* Washington, D.C.: American Bankers Association, 1970.

Homer, Sidney. *A History of Interest Rates.* New Brunswick, N.J.: Rutgers University Press, 1963.

Homer, Sidney, and Martin L. Leibowitz. *Inside the Yield Book.* Englewood Cliffs, N.J.: Prentice-Hall, 1972.

LaPorte, Anne Marie. "ABCs of Figuring Interest." *Business Conditions*, Federal Reserve Bank of Chicago, September 1973, pp. 3–11.

Trainer, Richard D. C. *The Arithmetic of Interest Rates*, Federal Reserve Bank of New York, 1980.

Weston, J. Fred, and Eugene F. Brigham. *Essentials of Managerial Finance.* 7th ed. New York: CBS College Publishing, 1985.

9

Inflation and Yield Curves

PURPOSE OF THIS CHAPTER

To explain the linkages between changes in the rate of inflation and changes in interest rates in the nation's financial markets. The chapter also explores the relationship between the maturity (or term) of a security and the size of its yield to maturity. This relationship is explored through a study of the yield curve and the factors that determine the yield curve's slope as well as through a study of duration—a value-weighted maturity measure.

KEY TERMS AND CONCEPTS IN THE CHAPTER

coupon effect
depreciation effect
duration
expectations
  hypothesis
Fisher effect
income effect
income tax effect

inflation
inflation premium
liquidity premium
market segmentation
nominal rate
portfolio
  immunization

preferred habitat
price elasticity
real rate
wealth effect
yield curve

In Chapter 7 we examined the demand and supply forces believed to determine the rate of interest on a loan or security. We know, however, that there is not just one interest rate in the economy—there are thousands. And many of these rates differ substantially from one another. For example, in May 1985 the going market rate on one-year U.S. Treasury bills averaged 8.10 percent, while the market rate on seasoned corporate bonds was 12.06 percent. At the same time, major U.S. commercial banks were quoting average loan rates to their largest and most financially sound customers of 10 to 11 percent. Meanwhile, investors in the market for high-grade state and local government bonds were receiving an annual rate of return of about 9.4 percent.

Why are all these rates so different from one another? Are these rate differences purely random, or can we attribute them to a limited number of factors that can be studied and perhaps predicted? Understanding the factors that cause interest rates to differ among themselves is an indispensable aid to the investor in choosing securities for a portfolio. It is not always advisable, for example, to reach for the highest rate available in the financial marketplace. The investor who does so may assume unacceptable levels of risk, have the securities called in by the issuer in advance of their maturity, pay an unacceptably high tax bill, accept a rate of return whose value is seriously eroded by inflation, or suffer other undesirable consequences. Without question, the intelligent investor must have a working knowledge of the factors affecting interest rates and be able to anticipate future changes in those factors.

For example, what role does inflation play in accounting for differences between one interest rate and another? What influence do changes in the maturity (term) of a loan or security have on the rate of return that a financial instrument pays to the investor? Why are default risk and marketability important determinants of relative interest rates? What is call risk and how does it influence the interest rate (yield) on callable securities? What role do taxes and convertibility play in accounting for rate differences? In this chapter and the next we address each of these important questions.

INFLATION AND INTEREST RATES

One of the most serious problems confronting the U.S. economy and, indeed, many economies in recent years is *inflation*. Inflation is defined as a rise in the average level of prices for all goods and services. Some prices of individual goods and services are always rising, while others are declining. However, inflation occurs when the *average* level of all prices in the economy rises.[1] Interest rates represent the "price" of credit. Are they also affected by inflation? The answer is yes, though there is considerable debate as to exactly *how* and by *how much* inflation affects interest rates.

The Correlation between Inflation and Interest Rates

To be sure, the *apparent* correlation in recent years between the rate of inflation in the United States and both long- and short-term interest rates is high. Exhibit 9–1, which tracks two popular measures of the rate of inflation—the consumer price index and the GNP deflator—and a money market interest rate—the yield on six-month prime commercial paper—suggests a close association between inflation and interest rates, especially during the 1970s. Note, for example, the sharp run-up in the rate of inflation between 1971 and 1974 and the parallel upward surge in the commercial paper rate, which reached an average yield of nearly 10 percent in 1974. Similarly, between 1974 and 1980 the inflation rate soared into double digits before falling back in the early 1980s and interest rates did the same.

In reality, however, the correlation between these two data series has not always been so high. During the 1950s and early 1960s, for example, a relatively calm economic environment prevailed with modest annual price increases. Interest rates, too, were more stable and the simple correlation between inflation and interest rates was not statistically significant. Late in the 1960s and during the 1970s, however, spurred by the Vietnam War, increasing government deficits, and rising price expectations, inflation soared and so did interest rates before both cooled off during the 1980s. Thus, more recently interest rates and inflation have tended to become more closely correlated with each other.

The Nominal and Real Interest Rate

To explore the relationship between inflation and interest rates, several key terms must be defined. First, we must distinguish between nominal and real interest rates. The *nominal rate* is the published or quoted interest rate on a security or loan. For example, an announcement in the financial press that major commercial banks have raised their prime lending rate to 15 percent per annum indicates what nominal interest rate is now being quoted by banks to their best customers. In contrast, the *real rate* of interest is the return to the lender or investor measured in terms of its actual purchasing power. In a period of inflation, of course,

---

[1] See Chapter 24 for a discussion of the nature, causes, and recent public policy responses to inflation.

EXHIBIT 9–1

Inflation and Interest Rates (annual rates; percent)

Year	Rate of Inflation Measured by Percentage Change in		Interest Rate on Prime Commercial Paper (six-month maturities)
	Consumer Price Index	GNP Deflator	
1960	1.6%	1.7%	3.85%
1961	1.0	0.0	2.97
1962	1.1	1.8	3.26
1963	1.2	1.5	3.55
1964	1.3	1.6	3.97
1965	1.7	2.2	4.38
1966	2.9	3.3	5.55
1967	2.9	2.9	5.10
1968	4.2	4.5	5.90
1969	5.4	5.0	7.83
1970	5.9	5.4	7.72
1971	4.3	5.1	5.11
1972	3.3	4.1	4.69
1973	6.2	5.9	8.15
1974	10.7	9.7	9.84
1975	9.4	9.5	6.32
1976	5.8	5.3	5.35
1977	6.5	5.8	5.60
1978	7.6	7.3	7.99
1979	11.5	8.8	10.91
1980	13.5	8.8	12.29
1981	8.9	8.9	14.76
1982	3.9	4.4	11.89
1983	3.8	3.8	10.16
1984	4.0	3.6	10.16
1985*	4.1	5.2	9.05

* Consumer price index for 1985 measured from year-end 1984 through March 1985. GNP deflator is measured from the fourth quarter 1984 through the end of the first quarter in 1985. The commercial paper rate is for week ending March 1, 1985.
SOURCES: U.S. Department of Commerce, *Survey of Current Business,* selected issues; and Board of Governors of the Federal Reserve System, *Federal Reserve Bulletin,* selected issues.

the real rate will be *lower* than the nominal rate. Another important concept is the *inflation premium,* which measures the rate of inflation *expected* by investors in the marketplace during the life of a financial instrument.

These three concepts are all related to one another. Obviously, a lender of funds is most interested in the real rate of return on a loan; that is, the purchasing power of any interest earned. For example, suppose you loan $1,000 to a business firm or an individual for a year and expect prices of goods and services to rise 10 percent during the year. If you charge a nominal interest rate of 12 percent on the loan, your real rate of return on the $1,000 face amount of the loan is only 2 percent, or $20. However, if the actual rate of inflation during the period of the loan turns out to be 13 percent, you have actually suffered a real decline in the purchasing power of the monies loaned. In general, lenders will attempt to charge nominal rates of interest that give them desired *real* rates of return on their loanable funds. And nominal interest rates will change as frequently as lenders alter their expectations regarding inflation.

The Fisher Effect

In a classic article written just before the turn of the century, economist Irving Fisher (1896) argued that the nominal interest rate was related to the real rate by the following equation:

$$\begin{array}{l}\text{Nominal} \\ \text{interest} \\ \text{rate}\end{array} = \begin{array}{l}\text{Expected} \\ \text{real} \\ \text{rate}\end{array} + \begin{array}{l}\text{Inflation} \\ \text{premium}\end{array} + \begin{array}{l}\text{Expected} \\ \text{real} \\ \text{rate}\end{array} \times \begin{array}{l}\text{Inflation} \\ \text{premium}\end{array} \qquad \textbf{(9-1)}$$

Clearly if the expected real interest rate is held fixed, changes in nominal rates would reflect shifting inflation premiums (i.e., changes in the public's views on expected inflation). The cross-product term in the above equation is often eliminated because it is usually quite small except in countries experiencing very severe inflation.

Does the above equation suggest that an increase in expected inflation *automatically* increases nominal interest rates? Not necessarily. There are several different views on the matter. Fisher argued that the expected real rate of return tended to be stable over time because it depends on such long-run factors as the productivity of capital and the volume of savings in the economy. Therefore, a change in the inflation premium is likely to influence only the nominal interest rate, at least in the short run. The nominal rate will rise by the full amount of the expected increase in the rate of inflation and decline by the full amount of any expected decline in inflation. For example, suppose the expected real rate is 3 percent and the expected rate of inflation is 10 percent. Then the nominal rate would be:

$$\text{Nominal interest rate} = 3\% + 10\% = 13\% \qquad \textbf{(9-2)}$$

According to Fisher's hypothesis, if the expected rate of inflation now rises to 12 percent, the expected real rate will remain unchanged at 3 percent, but the nominal rate will rise to 15 percent.

If this view (known today as the *Fisher effect*) is correct, it suggests a method of judging the *direction* of future interest-rate changes. To the extent that a rise in the actual rate of inflation causes investors to expect greater inflation in the future, higher nominal interest rates will soon result. Conversely, a decline in the actual rate of inflation may cause investors to revise downward their expectations of future inflation, leading to lower nominal interest rates.

Alternative Views on Inflation and Interest Rates

The simple one-to-one relationship between the expected inflation rate and the nominal rate of interest posited by Irving Fisher was the majority view for several decades until researchers began to find problems with it. For example, the Fisher effect assumes that inflation is *fully antici-pated*. As an example, let us imagine that both borrowers and lenders of funds expect that the inflation rate for the next year will be 10 percent and the real interest rate is 3 percent. Then the supply and demand curves for loanable funds will both shift upward just enough to ensure that the going nominal interest rate on a one-year loan is 3 percent plus 10 percent, or 13 percent. Lenders would be unwilling to lend out money at any lower rate than 13 percent because they expected the prices of goods and services they plan to purchase to increase by 10 percent during the life of the loan. Suppose, however, that all or a portion of the increase in inflation is *unanticipated*. In this case there is no way to be certain about what the equilibrium nominal interest rate will be, for the nominal rate may not fully reflect the full amount of inflation. The simple one-for-one change in the nominal rate in response to chang-ing inflationary expectations breaks down.

The Wealth Effect.   Another problem with the Fisher effect cen-ters on its assumption that people will borrow and lend the *same* amount of funds at any expected real interest rate, regardless of the expected inflation rate. However, inflation can affect incomes, wealth holdings, the attractiveness or unattractiveness of business investment, the burden of taxes, and so on. Suppose, for example, that people come to expect a higher inflation rate and they perceive this change as lowering the value of their inflation-adjusted (real) wealth. In response to this inflation-caused wealth effect people may decide to save more, lowering the equilibrium expected real rate of interest. Therefore, the nominal interest rate would rise *less* than the expected increase in inflation because of the offsetting decline in the expected real interest rate. Similarly, a decrease in expected inflation might lead to a perceived increase in the real value of wealth holdings, reduce current saving, and cause the real interest rate to rise. Thus, the nominal interest rate will fall by *less* than the decrease in expected inflation. Clearly, with the wealth effect there is *less* than a one-to-one relationship between changes in expected inflation and nomi-nal interest rates.

The Income Effect.   The wealth effect of changing inflation may be joined by an *income effect*. A rise in the expected inflation rate, for example, may lead to an increase in real (inflation-adjusted) income. This may happen because a declining real interest rate associated with the reduced value of wealth may cause consumers to reduce their supply of savings to the financial markets and to step up their spending on goods and services. At the same time businesses borrow more heavily to increase production and stock their shelves with additional goods to sell. The expanded consumption and production increases employment, and both businesses and consumers experience a rise in their income. Out of the higher income more savings will eventually flow into the financial system, expanding the aggregate supply of loanable funds. Other factors held equal, borrowing and lending will take place at a lower real rate of interest and the nominal rate will again rise by *less* than the increase in expected inflation.

Similarly, a decrease in expected inflation may stimulate more saving and less consumption, reducing business investment, employment, and incomes. Eventually savings flowing into the financial markets will begin to fall, the real interest rate will rise even as nominal rates fall due to lower expected inflation. As before, there is *less* than a one-to-one relationship between changes in the expected rate of inflation and nominal interest rates.

Both the income effect and the wealth effect take *time* to exert their influence on real and nominal rates and this time factor can distort the inflation-interest rate linkage. Unless we adopt a pure rational expectations-efficient markets approach to explaining interest rates (as discussed in Chapter 7) nominal interest rates will reach final equilibrium only after a series of rate-determining adjustments have been made. For example, suppose the Federal Reserve increases the nation's money supply. The liquidity preference theory of interest discussed in Chapter 7 suggests that nominal rates will fall at first due to the expansion in the available money stock relative to the public's money demand. However, the growing money stock may kindle both expectations of inflation and rising incomes, putting upward pressure on nominal rates. Thus, the nominal interest rate we observe at any point in time may not fully reflect inflationary expectations in the financial system because it is being buffeted by several other factors in its journey toward equilibrium.

The Depreciation Effect.   Still another factor possibly leading to smaller changes in nominal rates than occur in the expected inflation rate is the *depreciation effect*. Inflation drives up the cost of new capital goods, such as buildings, machinery, equipment, cars, trucks, and ships, which must be purchased to replace old capital items that are wearing out. However, old capital must be depreciated by formulas (such as straight-line or sum-of-the-years' digits methods) dictated by federal and state tax laws. Thus, in periods of rapid inflation the true cost of using up existing capital equipment is understated, so that taxable business income is inflated. As a result, *after-tax* income from business investment projects is less than would be true with lower or no inflation. Experiencing reduced real returns after taxes, businesses cut back on their plans to purchase new capital goods and the resulting fall in the demand for loanable funds decreases the equilibrium real interest rate. Clearly, then, if the expected rate of inflation rises and the real rate falls at the same time, the nominal interest rate is likely to rise by *less* than the increase in expected inflation. The exact opposite effects ensue if the expected rate of inflation declines, with nominal rates dropping by *less* than the decrease in expected inflation.

Income Tax Effect.   The depreciation effect brings *taxes* into the picture. Recent research suggests that the tax impact may work in both directions; that is, while the depreciation effect tends to dampen changes in the nominal rate, the *income tax effect* may so widen movements in the nominal rate that it changes by *more* than any given change in the rate of inflation. The heart of this argument is that lenders and investors not exempt from federal and state income taxes make lending and investing decisions on the basis of their expected real rate of return after taxes. If an investor desires to protect (i.e., hold constant) his or her expected real after-tax rate of return, then the nominal rate has to increase by a *greater* amount than any rise in the expected inflation rate because, otherwise, the investor's real after-tax return will decline when inflation increases.

To see the validity of this argument we observe that

$$\begin{array}{l}\text{Expected after-tax}\\ \text{real rate of return}\\ \text{earned by a taxpaying}\\ \text{investor}\end{array} = \begin{array}{c}\text{Nominal}\\ \text{rate}\end{array} - \begin{array}{c}\text{Nominal}\\ \text{rate}\end{array} \times \begin{array}{c}\text{Taxpayer's income}\\ \text{tax bracket rate}\end{array} \quad (9\text{-}3)$$

$$- \text{ Inflation premium}$$

Suppose an individual investor is in the top 50 percent income tax bracket so that half of any additional income he earns is taxed away. Moreover, suppose the current nominal interest rate on a one-year taxable security this investor is interested in buying is 12 percent, and the inflation premium (expected inflation rate) over the coming year is 5 percent. Then, this investor's expected real after-tax return from the security must be

$$\begin{array}{l}\text{Expected after-tax}\\ \text{real rate of return}\\ \text{earned by a tax-}\\ \text{paying investor}\end{array} = 12\% - 12\%(0.50) - 5\% = 1\% \quad (9\text{-}4)$$

Now suppose the expected rate of inflation rises from 5 percent to 6 percent. By how much must the *nominal interest rate* on the taxable security rise to yield this investor the *same* expected real rate of return after taxes? The answer must be 14 percent for

$$\begin{matrix} \text{Expected after-tax} \\ \text{real rate of return} \\ \text{earned by a tax-} \\ \text{paying investor} \end{matrix} = 14\% - 14\%(0.50) - 6\% = 1\% \qquad (9\text{--}5)$$

Thus, a change of 1 percent in the expected inflation rate required a 2 percent change in the nominal rate to leave this top-tax-bracket investor in the same place in terms of a real (purchasing-power) return from his or her investment.

Clearly the arithmetic shown above works both ways—a *reduction* in expected inflation by 1 percent requires a 2 percent *decline* in the nominal rate to leave the real after-tax return where it is. While investors in lower tax brackets would not require as numerically large a change in nominal rates to leave after-tax real returns unaltered, inflation tends to force most investors into higher and higher tax brackets as both prices and nominal incomes rise, unless government tax schedules are indexed to change with changing inflation—something the Congress mandated for U.S. taxpayers beginning in 1985.

Conclusions from Recent Research. With all of the foregoing possible effects from inflation, what actually happens to nominal rates when the expected rate of inflation shifts? Do nominal rates rise more or less than the change in expected inflation? The bulk of recent research suggests *nominal rates rise by less than any given increase in the expected inflation rate and decline by less than any given decrease in the expected inflation rate.* In essence, the income, wealth, and depreciation effects appear to outweigh those influences pulling in the opposite direction, such as the income tax effect. Estimates vary from study to study but generally suggest that nominal rates change by 60 to perhaps 90 percent of the calculated change in the expected inflation rate, depending on the period examined and the particular measure of expected inflation chosen.[2]

While it is reassuring to embrace such a sweeping conclusion, the reader should retain a healthy skepticism about research in this field. The topic of inflation and interest rates is plagued by numerous problems

---

[2] Prominent studies in the field include those by Fama (1975), Friedman (1980), Gibson (1972), Mundell (1963), Pindyck (1984), Sargent (1982), Tanzi (1980), and Taylor (1982).

of methodology and measurement. For example, there are no direct, widely accepted measures of two key actors in the drama—the real rate and the expected rate of inflation. Because the underlying theory speaks of *expected* inflation and the *expected* real market-clearing rate of return, there is the obvious problem of measuring people's expectations. We cannot, as a practical matter, survey all investors and the results of such a survey soon would be irrelevant anyway because expectations change. Most research studies have represented expected inflation by a survey of market experts or by employing a weighted average of past inflation rates. Both are, admittedly, crude proxies for the underlying concept. Note, too, that we cannot automatically derive the expected real interest rate merely by subtracting the current inflation rate from the current nominal rate; this gives us a measure of the *actual* real rate at a single point in time, not necessarily the *expected* rate. Moreover, none of the foregoing approaches takes into account the impact of *time lags* as interest rates, buffeted by numerous forces, strive to reach long-run equilibrium. In brief, we know for sure only that the relationship between inflation and interest rates is a *positive* one—more rapid inflation tends to push interest rates higher; however, the *magnitude* of that relationship remains in dispute.[3]

THE MATURITY OF A LOAN

One of the most important factors causing interest rates to differ from one another is differences in the *maturity* (or term) of securities and loans. Financial assets traded today in the nation's financial markets have a wide variety of maturities. In the federal funds and U.S. government securities markets, for example, some loans are overnight or over-the-weekend transactions, with the borrower repaying the loan in a matter of hours. At the other end of the spectrum, many mortgages used to finance the purchase of new homes stretch out 25 to 30 years. Corporate stocks are perpetual securities and will be traded as long as the issuing corporation continues to operate or until the stock is repurchased by the issuer and retired. In between these extremes lie thousands of securities issued by large and small borrowers with a tremendous variety of maturities.

---

[3] An interesting controversy has emerged in recent years concerning the linkages between inflation and *stock prices*. While the conventional wisdom views stock as a hedge against rising inflation, recent research, looking at data from the 1960s and 1970s, frequently reaches an opposite conclusion: increasing inflation rates often lead to falling stock prices. As Pindyck (1984) suggests, this may be due to increases in corporate earnings risk in an inflationary environment. If investors feel that inflationary conditions have either lowered expected corporate profits or increased the variability (risk) of those profits, stock prices must fall with all other factors held fixed.

The Yield Curve and the Term Structure of Interest Rates

The relationship between the rates of return (or yield) on financial instruments and their maturity is called the term structure of interest rates. This term structure may be represented visually by drawing a *yield curve* for all securities having the same credit quality. An example of a yield curve for U.S. government securities as it appeared in a recent issue of the *Treasury Bulletin* is shown in Figure 9–1. We note that yield to maturity (measured by the annual percentage rate of return) is plotted along the vertical axis, while the horizontal scale shows the length of time (term) to final maturity (measured in months and years).

The yield curve considers only the relationship between the maturity or term of a loan or security and its yield at one moment in time, with all other possible influential factors held constant. For example, we cannot draw a yield curve for securities bearing different degrees of risk or subject to different tax laws because both risk and tax laws affect relative yields

FIGURE 9–1

Yields of Treasury Securities, March 31, 1980 (based on closing bid quotations)

SOURCE: *Treasury Bulletin,* April 1980, p. 84.

along with maturity. We may, however, draw a yield curve for U.S. government securities of varying maturity because they all have minimal default risk, the same tax status, and so on. Similarly, yield curves could be constructed for all corporate bonds or for all municipal bonds having the same credit rating.

Types of Yield Curves

Yield curves change their shape over time in response to changes in the public's interest-rate expectations, fluctuations in the demand for liquidity in the economy, and other factors. Several different shapes have been observed, but most yield curves may be described as upward sloping, downward sloping, or horizontal (flat). An upward-sloping yield curve, of course, indicates that borrowers must pay higher interest rates for longer-term loans than for shorter-term loans. A downward-sloping yield curve means that longer-term loans and securities presently carry lower interest rates than shorter-term financial assets. Figure 9–1 illustrates a

FIGURE 9–2

Yields of Treasury Securities, April 30, 1980 (based on closing bid quotations)

SOURCE: *Treasury Bulletin*, May 1980, p. 86.

FIGURE 9–3

Yields of Treasury Securities, December 30, 1983 (based on closing bid quotations)

SOURCE: *Treasury Bulletin,* First Quarter, Fiscal 1984, Winter Issue, p. 33.

downward-sloping yield curve, while Figure 9–3 pictures an upward-sloping curve. Figure 9–2 depicts a recent horizontal or flat yield curve. Each shape of the yield curve has important implications for lenders and savers, borrowers and investors, and the financial institutions that serve them.

The Expectations Hypothesis

What determines the shape or slope of the yield curve? One view (with considerable research evidence to support it) is the expectations hypothesis, which argues that investor expectations regarding future changes in short-term interest rates determine the shape of the curve.[4] For example, a rising yield curve is presumed to be an indication that investors expect short-term interest rates to rise above their current levels in the future. A declining yield curve suggests declining short-term rates in the future. Finally, a horizontal yield curve implies that investors in the market expect interest rates to remain essentially unchanged from their present levels. If the expectations hypothesis is true, then the yield curve becomes an important forecasting tool for the investor because it suggests the direction of future movements in short-term interest rates.

The *unbiased expectations hypothesis* assumes that investors act as *profit maximizers* over their planned holding periods and have no maturity preferences. All securities in a given risk class, regardless of their maturity, are perfect substitutes for each other in the minds of investors. Each investor will seek those individual securities or combinations of securities offering the highest rates of return. For example, it is immaterial to investors with a planned 10-year investment horizon whether they buy a 10-year security, two 5-year securities, or a series of 1-year securities until the 10-year holding period terminates. Each investor will pursue that investment strategy which offers the greatest rate of return or yield over the length of his or her planned holding period.

Profit-maximizing behavior on the part of many thousands of investors interacting in the marketplace ensures that holding-period yields on all securities move toward equality. Once equilibrium is achieved, and assuming no transactions costs, the investor should earn the same yield from buying a long-term security as from purchasing a series of short-term securities whose combined maturities equal that of the long-term security. If the rate of return on long-term securities rises above or falls below the return the investor would receive from buying and selling several short-term securities, forces are quickly set in motion to restore equilibrium. Investors at the margin will practice *arbitrage* (i.e., moving funds from one security market to another) until long-term yields once again are brought into balance with short-term yields.

The Role of Expectations in Shaping the Yield Curve

How can a factor as intangible as expectations determine the shape of the yield curve? Expectations are a potent force in the financial marketplace because investors *act* on their expectations. For example, if interest rates are expected to rise in the future, this is disturbing news to investors

---

[4] Key research studies in the development and testing of the expectations hypothesis include works by Buse (1965), Fisher (1896), Hicks (1946), Kessel (1965), Lutz (1940), Malkiel (1966), Meiselman (1962), and Walsh (1985).

in long-term bonds. As we noted in Chapter 8, rising interest rates mean falling prices for bonds and other debt securities. Moreover, the longer the term of a bond, the more sensitive its price is to changes in rates. Faced with the possibility of falling bond prices, many investors will sell their long-term bonds and buy short-term securities or hold cash. As a result, the prices of long-term bonds will plummet, driving their rates (yields) higher. At the same time, increased investor purchases of short-term securities will send the prices of these securities higher and their yields lower. With rising long-term rates and falling short-term rates, the yield curve will gradually assume an upward slope. The yield curve's prophecy of rising interest rates will have come true simply because investors responded to their expectations by making changes in their security portfolios.

Relative Changes in Long-Term Interest Rates

The expectations theory does help to explain an interesting phenomenon in the financial markets. Long-term rates tend to change slowly over time, while short-term interest rates are highly volatile and often move over wide ranges. The expectations hypothesis argues that the long-term interest rate may be represented as a *geometric* average of a series of rates on current and future (forward) short-term loans whose combined maturities equal that of the long-term loan. In terms of conventional symbols,

$$(1 + {}_tR_n)^n = (1 + {}_tR_1)(1 + {}_{t+1}r_{1t})(1 + {}_{t+2}r_{1t}) \ . \ . \ . \ (1 + {}_{t+n-1}r_{1t}) \quad (9\text{--}6)$$

where

$\quad {}_tR_n =$ The rate of interest prevailing at time t on a long-term loan covering n periods of time.

$\quad {}_tR_1 =$ The one-period loan rate prevailing at time period t.

$\quad {}_{t+1}r_{1t} =$ Forward interest rate as quoted at time t on a one-period loan to start in time period t + 1.

$\quad {}_{t+2}r_{2t} =$ Forward interest rate as quoted at time t on a one-period loan to start in time period t + 2.

$\quad\quad\quad\quad .$

$\quad\quad\quad\quad .$

$\quad\quad\quad\quad .$

$\quad {}_{t+n-1}r_{1t} =$ Forward interest rate as quoted at time t on a one-period loan to start in time period t + n − 1.

The expectations hypothesis presumes that each of the forward rates—${}_{t+1}r_{1t}, {}_{t+2}r_{2t}, \ . \ . \ . \ , {}_{t+n}r_{1t}$—are equal to the future interest rates the market *expects* to exist at each indicated future time period from t + 1 through t + n − 1. Equation 9–6 illustrates a fundamental principle in the expectations theory: *an investor expects the same holding-period yield regardless of whether he or she purchases one long-term security or a series of short-term securities whose combined maturities make up the long-term security. This is true because all markets are presumed to be perfectly competitive without significant barriers between them and all securities, whatever their maturity, are presumed to be perfect substitutes for each other.*

According to the expectations theory, the rate of interest on a 20-year bond, for example, may be viewed as equivalent to the geometric average of the interest rate on a current 1-year loan plus the rates expected to be attached in future periods to a series of 19 1-year loans, altogether adding up to 20 years. Experience teaches us that an average changes much more slowly than the individual components making up that average. If the long-term interest rate is really a geometric *average* of current and expected future short-term rates, then this helps to explain why in real-world markets long-term rates tend to lag behind short-term rates and are less volatile. As we will see more fully in Chapter 11, the assumption that the long-term interest rate embodies the market's expectation regarding expected future short-term interest rates suggests an important clue on forecasting future rate movements in the financial marketplace.

Policy Implications of the Expectations Hypothesis

The expectations hypothesis has important implications for public policy. The theory clearly implies that changes in the relative amounts available of long-term versus short-term securities do not influence the shape of the yield curve *unless* investor expectations also are affected. For example, suppose the U.S. Treasury decided to refinance $100 billion of its maturing short-term IOUs by issuing $100 billion in long-term bonds. Would this government action affect the shape of the yield curve? Certainly the supply of long-term bonds would be significantly increased, while the supply of short-term securities would be sharply reduced. However, according to the expectations theory, the yield curve itself would not be changed *unless* investors altered their expectations about the future course of short-term interest rates.

To cite one more example, the Federal Reserve System buys and sells U.S. government securities almost daily in the money and capital markets in order to promote the nation's economic goals.[5] Can the Fed influence the shape of the yield curve by buying one maturity of securities and selling another? Once again, the answer is *no* unless the Federal Reserve can influence the interest-rate expectations of investors. Why? The reason lies in the underlying assumption of the unbiased expectations hypothesis:

---

[5] Federal Reserve open-market operations are discussed at length in Chapter 23.

investors regard all securities, whatever their maturity, as perfect substitutes. Therefore, the relative amounts of long-term bonds versus short-term securities simply should not matter to investors.

The Liquidity Premium View of the Yield Curve

The strong assumptions underlying the unbiased expectations theory coupled with the real-world behavior of investors have caused many financial analysts to question the theory's veracity. Securities dealers and analysts who trade actively in the financial markets frequently argue that other factors besides rate expectations also exert a significant impact on the character and shape of the yield curve.

For example, in recent years most yield curves have sloped *upward.* Is there a built-in bias toward positively sloped yield curves due to factors other than interest-rate expectations? The liquidity premium view of the yield curve suggests that such a bias exists.

Longer-term securities tend to have more volatile market prices than short-term securities. Therefore, the investor faces greater risk of capital loss when buying long-term financial instruments. To overcome this risk, it is argued, investors must be paid an extra return in the form of an interest-rate premium to encourage them to purchase long-term issues. If it exists, this additional rate or yield premium for giving up liquidity—known as the *liquidity premium*—would tend to give yield curves a bias toward a positive slope.

Why then do some yield curves slope downward? In such instances, expectations of declining interest rates plus other factors simply overcome the liquidity premium effect. The liquidity premium view does not preclude the important role of interest-rate expectations in influencing the shape of the yield curve. Even though expectations may be the dominant factor influencing the yield curve, however, other factors such as liquidity play an important role as well.

Moreover, the liquidity argument may help explain why yield curves tend to "flatten out" at the longest maturities. (Note that this flattening out at the long-term end of the maturity spectrum is characteristic of all three yield curves shown in Figures 9–1, 9–2, and 9–3.) There are obvious differences in liquidity between a 1-year and 10-year bond, but it is not clear that major differences in liquidity exist between a 10-year bond and a 20-year bond, for example. Therefore, the size of the required liquidity premium paid to long-term investors may decrease for securities of the longest maturities.

The Segmented-Markets or Hedging-Pressure Argument

A strong theoretical and empirical challenge to the expectations theory of the yield curve appeared in the 1950s and 1960s in the form of the *market segmentation argument* or *hedging-pressure theory* of the term structure of interest rates.[6] The underlying assumption is that all securities are *not* perfect substitutes in the minds of investors. Maturity preferences exist among major investor groups. Moreover, these investor groups will not stray away from their desired maturity spectrum unless induced to do so by higher yields or other favorable terms on longer- or shorter-term securities.

Why would certain investors strongly prefer one maturity of security over another? Market segmentation theorists find the answer in a fundamental assumption concerning investor behavior, especially the investment behavior of financial intermediaries such as investment companies, savings and loan associations, pension funds, and commercial banks. These investor groups, it is argued, often act as *risk minimizers* rather than as profit maximizers as assumed in the expectations hypothesis. They prefer to *hedge* against the risk of fluctuations in the prices and yields of securities by balancing the maturity structure of their assets with the maturity structure of their liabilities.

For example, pension funds have stable and predictable long-term liabilities. Therefore, these intermediaries prefer to invest in bonds, stocks, and other long-term assets. Credit unions and commercial banks, on the other hand, with volatile deposits and volatile short-term money market liabilities, prefer to confine the majority of their investments to short-term loans and securities. These important investor groups use the *hedging principle of* portfolio management—that is, correlating the maturity of their liabilities with the maturity of their assets to ensure the ready availability of liquid funds when those funds are needed. This portfolio strategy reduces the risks of fluctuating income and loss of principal.

The existence of maturity preferences among important investor groups implies that the financial markets are *not* one large pool of loanable funds but rather are segmented or divided into a series of submarkets. Thus, the market for securities of medium maturity (e.g., 5- to 10-year securities) attracts different investor groups than the market for long-term (e.g., over 10-year) securities. And demand and supply curves within each maturity range are held to be the dominant factors shaping the level and structure of interest rates within that maturity range. However, interest rates prevailing in one maturity range are little influenced by demand and supply forces at work setting rates in other maturity ranges. The segmented-markets or hedging-pressure theory does not rule out the possible influence of expectations in shaping the term structure of

---

[6] Important research studies contributing to the development and investigation of the segmentation or hedging-pressure theory include: Culbertson (1957), Dobson, Sutch and Vanderford (1976), Elliott and Echols (1976), Kessel (1965), Malkiel (1966), and Modigliani and Sutch (1966).

interest rates, but it argues that other factors related to maturity-specific demand and supply forces are of dominant importance.

Policy Implications of the Segmented-Markets Theory

The segmented-markets theory, like the expectations theory, has significant implications for public policy. If markets along the maturity spectrum are relatively isolated from each other due to investor preferences, government policymakers can alter the shape of the yield curve merely by influencing supply and demand curves in one or more market segments.

For example, if a positively sloped yield curve were desired, with long-term interest rates higher than short-term rates, the government and the central bank could flood the market with long-term bonds. Simultaneously, the government could purchase large quantities of short-term securities. The expanded supply of bonds would drive long-term rates higher, while purchases of short-term securities would push short-term rates down, other factors held equal. Therefore, government economic policy could alter the shape of the yield curve merely by shifting the supplies available of different maturities of securities relative to the demand for those securities. This policy conclusion directly contradicts the expectations hypothesis.

The Preferred Habitat or Composite Theory of the Yield Curve

During the 1960s and 70s an expanded theory of the yield curve appeared which attempted to combine the expectations, liquidity premium, and market segmentation arguments into a single theory. This composite view argues that investors, particularly institutional investors, such as insurance companies or pension funds, seek out their "preferred habitat" along the scale of varying maturities of securities that matches their risk preferences, tax exposure, liquidity needs, regulatory requirements, and other investment policy stipulations. Normally an investor will not stray from his or her preferred habitat unless rates of return on longer- or shorter-term securities are high enough to overcome each investor's menu of preferences. The result is that security markets are divided up into distinct submarkets by these multifaceted investor preferences. Thus, factors other than just expectations play a key role in shaping the character of the yield curve at any given moment.[7]

---

[7] Key research studies either developing the theory of preferred habitat or testing its implications include: Dobson, Sutch, and Vanderford (1976), Elliott and Echols (1976), Malkiel (1966), Modigliani and Sutch (1966), and Terrell and Frazer (1972).

Proponents of the preferred habitat view typically argue that investors derive their expectations about future interest rates on the basis of *historical experience*—the recent trend of rates and what history suggests is a "normal" range for interest rates. In the short run the majority of investors generally expect current rate trends to persist into the future; thus, rising interest rates in recent weeks often lead to the expectation that rates will continue to rise in the near-term. However, investors generally expect that, given sufficient time (months or years), interest rates will return toward their historical averages. An important research implication here is that more recent movements in interest rates and yield spreads are linked to *past* interest-rate behavior—a conclusion which tends to contradict the expectations and efficient markets theories of how the financial markets operate.

Research Evidence on Yield-Curve Theories

Which view of the yield curve is correct? Existing research evidence tends to support the *expectations* view. Studies by Sargent (1982), Meiselman (1962), Buse (1965), and others find rate expectations to be a significant factor in shaping the maturity structure of interest rates. While all investors clearly do not regard all maturities of securities as perfect substitutes, there are sufficient numbers of traders in the financial marketplace who do not have specific maturity preferences. These investors are guided principally by relative yields on different securities. They bring about the results generally predicted by the expectations theory.

Nevertheless, there is evidence that other factors, especially the demand for liquidity, do affect the shape of the yield curve. Studies by Kessel (1965), Van Horne (1965), Walsh (1985), and others suggest the existence of a liquidity premium attached to the yields on longer-term securities, compensating investors for the risks associated with all but the shortest-term investments. The size of the liquidity premium does appear to decline (though not necessarily at an even rate) with increasing maturity, however. There is also evidence provided by Elliott and Echols (1976), Modigliani and Sutch (1966), Terrell and Frazer (1972) and others that changes in the supply of securities in any particular maturity range can, at least temporarily, alter the shape of the yield curve, offering some support for the segmented-markets or hedging-pressure argument. For example, at certain phases of the business cycle, commercial banks become heavy sellers of medium-term U.S. government securities in order to raise cash and make more loans. During these periods, the yield curve frequently has a bowed or "humped" shape, with the highest yields offered by medium-term securities. In this instance, a sudden and massive increase in the supply of medium-term bonds appears to change the yield curve's overall shape for a brief period of time.

Uses of the Yield Curve

The controversy surrounding the determinants of the yield curve should not obscure the fact that this curve can be an extremely useful tool for investors.

Forecasting Interest Rates.   First, if the expectations hypothesis is correct, the yield curve gives the investor a clue concerning the future course of interest rates. If the curve has an upward slope, for example, the investor may be well advised to look for opportunities to move away from bonds and other long-term securities into investments whose market price is less sensitive to interest-rate changes. A downward-sloping yield curve, on the other hand, suggests the likelihood of near-term declines in interest rates and a rally in bond prices if the market's forecast of lower rates turns out to be true. Under the terms of the pure or unbiased expectations hypothesis the yield curve prevailing at any given point in time actually generates a very precise forecast of what the market expects interest rates to be in any future period. We will see exactly how in Chapter 11.

Uses for Financial Intermediaries.   The slope of the yield curve is critical for financial intermediaries, especially commercial banks, savings and loan associations, and savings banks. A rising yield curve is generally favorable for these institutions because they borrow most of their funds by selling short-term deposits and lend a major portion of those funds long term. The more steeply the yield curve slopes upward, the wider the spread between borrowing and lending rates and the greater the potential profit for a financial intermediary. However, if the yield curve begins to flatten out or slope downward, this should serve as a warning signal to portfolio managers of these institutions.

A flattening or downward-sloping yield curve squeezes the earnings of financial intermediaries and calls for an entirely different portfolio-management strategy than an upward-sloping curve. For example, if an upward-sloping yield curve starts to flatten out, portfolio managers of financial institutions might try to "lock in" relatively cheap sources of funds by getting long-term commitments from depositors and other funds-supplying customers. Borrowers, on the other hand, might be encouraged to take out long-term loans at fixed rates of interest. Of course, the financial institution's customers also may be aware of impending changes in the yield curve and resist taking on long-term loans or deposit contracts at unfavorable interest rates.

Detecting Overpriced and Underpriced Securities.   Yield curves can be used as an aid to investors in deciding which securities are temporarily overpriced or underpriced. This use of the curve derives from the fact that, in equilibrium, the yields on all securities of comparable risk should come to rest along the yield curve at their appropriate maturity level. In an efficiently functioning market, however, any deviations of individual securities from the yield curve will be short lived, so the investor must act quickly to profit from the deviations.

If a security's rate of return lies *above* the yield curve, this sends a signal to investors that that particular security is temporarily *underpriced* relative to other securities of the same maturity. Other things equal, this is a *buy* signal which some investors will take advantage of, driving the price of the purchased security upward and its yield back down toward the yield curve. On the other hand, if a security's rate of return is temporarily *below* the yield curve, this indicates a temporarily *overpriced* financial instrument, because its yield is below that of securities bearing the same maturity. Some investors holding this security will *sell* it, pushing its price down and its yield back up toward the curve.

Indicating Trade-Offs between Maturity and Yield.   Still another use of the yield curve is to indicate the current trade-off between maturity and yield confronting the investor. If the investor wishes to alter the maturity of a portfolio, the yield curve indicates what gain or loss in rate of return may be expected for each change in the portfolio's average maturity.

With an upward-sloping yield curve, for example, an investor may be able to increase a bond portfolio's expected annual yield from 9 percent to 11 percent by extending the portfolio's average maturity from six to eight years. However, the prices of longer-term bonds are more volatile, creating greater risk of capital loss. Moreover, longer-term securities tend to be less liquid and less marketable than short-term securities. Therefore, the investor must weigh the gain in yield from extending the maturity of his or her portfolio against added price, liquidity, and marketability risk. Because yield curves tend to flatten out for the longest maturities, the investor bent on lengthening the average maturity of a portfolio eventually discovers that gains in yield get smaller and smaller for each additional unit of maturity. At some point along the yield curve it clearly does *not* pay to further extend the maturity of a security portfolio.

Riding the Yield Curve.   Finally, some active security investors, especially dealers in U.S. government securities, have learned to "ride" the yield curve for profit. If the curve is positively sloped, with a slope steep enough to offset transactions costs from buying and selling securities, the investor may gain by timely portfolio switching.

For example, if a security dealer purchases U.S. Treasury bills six months from maturity, holds them for three months, converts the bills into cash, and buys new six-month bills, he or she can profit in two ways from a positively sloped yield curve. Because the yield is lower on three-month than on six-month bills, the dealer experiences a capital gain on the sale. Second, the purchase of new six-month bills replaces a lower-yielding security with a higher-yielding one at a lower price. Riding the yield curve can be risky, however, because yield curves are constantly changing their shape. If the curve gets flatter or turns down, a potential gain can be turned into a realized loss. In this case a rise in interest rates may make riding the yield curve less profitable than a simple "buy and hold" strategy. Experience and good judgment are indispensable in using the yield curve for profitable investment decision making.

DURATION: A DIFFERENT APPROACH TO MATURITY

The Price Elasticity of a Debt Security

Theories of the yield curve remind us that longer-maturity debt securities tend to be more volatile in price. That is, for the same change in interest rates, the price of a longer-term bond generally changes more than the price of a shorter-term bond. A popular measure of how responsive a debt security's price is to changes in interest rates is its price elasticity—thus,

$$\text{Price elasticity of a debt security (E)} = \frac{\begin{array}{c}\text{Percentage change over time in a security's price}\end{array}}{\begin{array}{c}\text{Percentage change over time in a security's yield}\end{array}} = \frac{\dfrac{P_1 - P_0}{P_0}}{\dfrac{y_1 - y_0}{y_0}} \qquad (9\text{--}7)$$

where P_0 and y_0 represent a security's price and yield at some initial point in time, while P_1 and y_1 represent the security's price and yield at a subsequent point in time. Price elasticity is generally measured from the security's par value and coupon rate and is larger for downward price movements than for upward price movements.[8] Security price elasticity must be *negative* because rising interest rates (yields) result in falling security prices and conversely.

For example, suppose we are interested in purchasing a 10-year bond, par value of $1,000, promising its holder a 10 percent annual coupon rate (i.e., $100 a year in interest). Looking this bond up in a bond-yield

---

[8] That is, for the same change in yield, capital gains generally are larger than capital losses on the same debt security.

table (see Chapter 8) tells us that if interest rates on comparable securities sold in the open market are at 10 percent, this bond will sell for exactly $1,000. If rates fall to 5 percent, the 10 percent bond will have a price of $1,389.70 and if rates climb to 15 percent, the bond's price will drop to just $745.10. What is the price elasticity of this bond, measured from par? From Equation 9–7 we have for the downward movement in interest rates from 10 to 5 percent:

$$\text{Price elasticity of 10 percent bond (E)} = \frac{\dfrac{(\$1,389.70 - \$1,000)}{\$1,000}}{\dfrac{5\% - 10\%}{10\%}} = \frac{0.3897}{-0.5} = -0.779 \quad (9\text{–}8)$$

On the other hand, for an upward movement in rates from 10 to 15 percent this bond's elasticity is −0.510. (The reader should verify this.) Clearly E is greater in absolute terms for the downward movement in interest rate or yield (from 10% to 5%) than it is for the rise in rate or yield (from 10% to 15%).

Greater price elasticity means a security goes through a greater price change for a given change in market rates of interest. And, as we noted above, longer-term securities generally carry greater price risk (i.e., their price elasticity, E, is larger) than for shorter-term securities. However, this relationship between time to maturity and price elasticity is *not* linear (i.e., strictly proportional). It is *not* true, for example, that 10-year bonds are twice as price elastic (and price volatile) as 5-year bonds. One important reason for this nonlinear relationship is that the price volatility and elasticity of a security depend upon the size of its *coupon rate—* the annual rate promised by the borrower—as well as its maturity.

The Impact of Varying Coupon Rates

The lower a security's annual coupon rate, the more volatile (and elastic) its price tends to be; thus, investors buying lower-coupon securities generally take on greater risk of price fluctuations. In effect, a security promising lower annual coupon payments to the holder behaves as though it has a longer maturity even if it is due to mature on the same date as a security carrying a higher-coupon rate. With a low-coupon (promised) rate the investor must wait longer for a substantial return of his or her funds because a greater proportion of the low-coupon security's total dollar return lies in the final payment at maturity when the bond's face value is returned to the investor. And, the longer in the distant future cash payments are to be received, the more sensitive is the present value of that stream of payments to changes in interest rates.

The relationship we have been describing is usually called the *coupon effect.* It says simply that the prices of low-coupon rate securities tend to rise *faster* than the prices of high-coupon rate securities when market interest rates decline. Similarly, a period of rising interest rates will cause the prices of low-coupon securities to fall *faster* than the prices of high-coupon securities. Thus, the potential for capital gains and capital losses is greater for low-coupon than for high-coupon securities.

An Alternative Maturity Index for a Security: Duration

Knowledge of the impact of varying coupon rates on security price volatility and elasticity resulted in the search for a new index of maturity other than simply straight calendar time (years and months)—the maturity measure used in conventional yield curves. What was needed was a measure of the term or length of a bond that would allow financial analysts to construct a *linear* (i.e., strictly proportional) relationship between term to maturity and security price volatility or elasticity, regardless of differing coupon rates. Such a measure would have the property, for example, that a doubling of the term to maturity would mean a doubling of a security's price elasticity, thereby giving us a direct measure of the interest-rate risk faced by the individual investor. This maturity measure is known today as *duration:*

$$D = \frac{\begin{array}{c}\text{Present value of interest and}\\\text{principal payments from a}\\\text{security weighted by the timing}\\\text{of those payments}\end{array}}{\begin{array}{c}\text{Present value of the security's}\\\text{promised stream of interest and}\\\text{principal payments}\end{array}} = \frac{\sum\limits_{t=1}^{n} \dfrac{I_t(t)}{(1+y)^t}}{\sum\limits_{t=1}^{n} \dfrac{I_t}{(1+y)^t}} \qquad (9\text{–}9)$$

In the above formula I represents each expected payment of principal (face value) and interest income from the security and t represents the time period in which each payment is to be received. The discount factor, y, is the security's yield to maturity with final maturity reached at the end of n periods. As the above formula indicates, D is a *weighted average* measure of term to maturity in which each payment of interest and principal is multiplied by the time period in which it is received by the investor. Strictly speaking, duration measures the price elasticity of a debt instrument with respect to changes in the instrument's yield to maturity.

We can explain the use of the duration formula by examining a simple numerical example. Let us imagine that an investor is interested in purchasing a $1,000 par-value bond that has a term to maturity of 10 years, a 10 percent annual coupon rate (with **interest paid once a year**), and a 12 percent yield to maturity based on its current price. Then its duration must be:

$$\text{Duration (D)} = \frac{\dfrac{\$100(1)}{(1.12)} + \dfrac{\$100(2)}{(1.12)^2} + \cdots + \dfrac{\$100(10)}{(1.12)^{10}} + \dfrac{\$1{,}000(10)}{(1.12)^{10}}}{\dfrac{\$100}{(1.12)} + \dfrac{\$100}{(1.12)^2} + \cdots + \dfrac{\$100}{(1.12)^{10}} + \dfrac{\$1{,}000}{(1.12)^{10}}} \qquad (9\text{--}10)$$

or,

$$D = \frac{5810.90}{887.10} = 6.55 \text{ years}$$

A number of duration's features are evident from this example. For example, duration is always *less* than the time to maturity for a coupon-paying security.[9] Moreover, duration increases with a longer stream of future payments (i.e., when the time until final cash payment is longer), but the rate of increase in D decreases as time to maturity stretches out. Finally, the larger a security's yield to maturity, y, the lower its duration.

As Equation 9–10 shows, duration reflects the amount and timing of *all* payments expected during the life of a security, unlike the conventional measure of maturity—calendar time—which shows only the length of time until the final cash payment. In simplest terms, duration is an index of the average amount of time required for the investor to recover the original cash outlay used to buy the security. It has the essential property that securities with higher values of D are more volatile in price and, therefore, carry increased price risk. Moreover, lower-coupon bonds have longer duration and, therefore, display more price risk than higher-coupon bonds.

Uses of Duration

Today duration has aroused great interest among portfolio managers for major financial institutions, such as commercial banks. The reason is its possible usefulness as a device to insulate (or, in the terminology of finance, "immunize") security portfolios against the risk of changing inter-

---

[9] See Chapter 8 for a discussion of yield to maturity and calculating discounted present value such as required in this duration formula. Any security carrying installment payments of principal and/or interest will have a duration shorter than its calendar maturity. Only for zero-coupon bonds or for any loan where principal and accumulated interest are paid in a lump sum at maturity, without any intervening installment payments, will duration and maturity be the same.

est rates. In theory, *portfolio immunization against interest-rate changes can be achieved by simply acquiring a portfolio of securities whose average duration equals the investor's desired holding period.* If this is done, the effect is to hold the investor's earnings *constant* regardless of whether interest rates rise or fall. In the absence of borrower default the investor's realized return can be no less than the return he or she has been promised by the borrower. Only if the future course of interest-rate movements is known for certain would portfolio immunization be a less-than-optimal investor strategy.[10]

How does portfolio immunization work? Suppose an investor buys a portfolio of bonds with an average yield to maturity of 12 percent and an average duration of six years which exactly matches the investor's planned holding period. If interest rates rise *above* 12 percent and remain there over this six-year period, the market value of the bonds will decline and must be sold at a capital loss at the end of the holding period. However, the investor will be able to reinvest the periodic interest payments from the bonds at the higher interest rates. In this case added interest earnings during the holding period will offset the capital loss suffered on the sale of the bonds *if* the portfolio's average duration equals six years, the same length as the investor's holding period. Conversely, if interest rates fall *below* 12 percent and remain low for the six-year period, the investor will be forced to reinvest the interest earnings from the bonds at lower rates. Thus, interest income will decline; *but,* the lower interest rates mean the 12 percent bonds will rise in market value and can be sold for a capital gain at the conclusion of the investor's holding period. Again, if portfolio duration equals the length of the investor's holding period, the lower interest income will be fully offset by the capital gain on the bonds and the investor's total dollar return will be protected.

All of this sounds easy: *To protect the return from a portfolio of securities against changes in interest rates merely select a portfolio whose duration equals the time remaining in your planned holding period.* In practice it does not work out quite this easily, however. For example, it is usually very difficult to identify and purchase a collection of securities whose average portfolio duration exactly matches the investor's holding period. And, because many bonds are callable in advance of maturity, investors may find themselves with a sudden and unexpected change in their portfolios' average duration. Moreover, duration is sensitive to the particular tax treatment of capital gains. Another problem arises if the slope of the yield curve changes over the holding period. In general,

---

[10] Important studies dealing with the development of the duration and immunization concepts and the exploration of their properties and uses include: Bierwag, Kaufman, and Toevs (1983), Marshall and Yawitz (1982), Kalotay (1985), Kolb and Chiong (1982), and Macaulay (1938).

different patterns of interest-rate movements require somewhat different measures of duration—an exceedingly complex problem. However, there is evidence that investors can achieve reasonably accurate immunization against changing interest rates by *approximately* matching portfolio durations with their planned holding periods.

SUMMARY AND CONCLUSIONS

While theories of interest-rate determination typically assume there is a single interest rate in the economy, there are, in fact, thousands of different interest rates confronting investors at any one time. This chapter has focused upon two major factors: (1) the maturity, term, or duration of a loan; and (2) inflationary expectations, which cause interest rates to vary on different types of securities. Knowledge of each of these factors is of critical importance to security investors in making intelligent portfolio decisions.

One key factor affecting interest rates considered in this chapter is *inflation.* Increases in the general level of prices for all goods and services affect interest rates because lenders are unwilling to commit their funds to borrowers unless they are adequately protected against any expected future losses in purchasing power. If lenders expect a higher rate of inflation during the life of a credit contract, they will adjust upward the nominal rate on a loan in order to achieve their desired real rate of return. Modern financial theory argues that the nominal (published) rate on a loan or security equals the sum of the expected real rate of return (measured in terms of the real purchasing power of any income earned from the financial instrument) and the inflation premium (or expected rate of inflation). According to the so-called Fisher effect, if the expected inflation rate rises, the nominal interest rate on a loan or security must also rise by exactly the same amount, point for point. Lesser-known views usually referred to as the wealth, income, and depreciation effects contend that a rise in the expected inflation premium reduces the real rate of return to lenders as well as pushing nominal rates higher. However, because of the offsetting decline in the real rate, nominal rates rise *less* than the increase in expected inflation. A contrasting view argues that taxation of interest income from loans and securities forces the nominal interest rate to rise more than expected inflation in order for lenders and investors to protect their expected after-tax real rate of return. Existing research tends to give support to the idea that interest rates do respond to inflation in the *direction* predicted by the Fisher effect, but by *less* than the change in the inflation rate due to income, wealth, and other effects. However, dispute over the true magnitude of the inflation effect points to the need for further research in future years.

This chapter also emphasizes the key importance of the *yield curve* in explaining and predicting interest-rate movements. The yield curve expresses the relationship between the annual rate of return on a financial instrument and its term to maturity when all other factors are held constant. Yield curves reflect the interest-rate *expectations* of the market-place and hint at the direction, if not the magnitude, of future rate movements. They are a key tool in the management of financial intermediaries who borrow a substantial proportion of their funds at the short end of the maturity spectrum and lend heavily at the long-term end. Knowledge of what and how the yield curve is determined is vital, therefore, to the long-term profitability of financial institutions.

In recent years financial analysts have become somewhat dissatisfied with one of the two key variables making up the yield curve relationship— the term to maturity, or number of months and years until a security must finally be paid off. After all, the term to maturity of a security conveys no information on the timing or size of payments received by an investor over the life of a security, but only gives the date of the final payment. An alternative measure of maturity called *duration* has become popular in recent years because it is a weighted average capturing both the size and timing of all cash payments from an individual security or portfolio of securities. Duration has grown in popularity among portfolio managers because it can be used to at least partially "immunize" a portfolio of securities against changing interest rates.

STUDY QUESTIONS

1. Explain how inflation affects interest rates. What is the Fisher effect? The income effect? The wealth effect? The depreciation effect? The tax effect?

2. The correlation between the inflation rate and market interest rates appears to have increased considerably in recent years. Can you explain why?

3. Explain the meaning of the phrase "term structure of interest rates." What is a yield curve? What assumptions are necessary to construct a yield curve?

4. Explain the differences between the expectations, market-segmentation, preferred habitat, and liquidity-premium views of the yield

curve. Depending upon which of these views is correct, what are the implications of each for investors? For public policy?

5. What is the *coupon effect*? How does it relate to the concept of *security price elasticity*? What is the relationship between the coupon rate on a security and the volatility of its price as interest rates change?

6. Explain the meaning and importance of the concept of *duration*. How can duration be used to aid a security portfolio manager in protecting investments against fluctuating interest rates?

PROBLEMS

1. According to the Fisher effect if the real interest rate is presently equal to 3 percent and the nominal interest rate is 8 percent, what rate of inflation is the financial marketplace predicting? Explain the reasoning behind your answer. If the nominal rate rises to 11 percent and following the assumptions of the Fisher effect, what would you conclude about the expected inflation rate? The real rate?

2. Suppose the real interest rate in the economy is 4 percent and the nominal interest rate is 9 percent. Now investors in the financial marketplace expect a sudden doubling in the rate of inflation. According to the Fisher effect what new rate of inflation is expected? If the depreciation, income, or wealth effects are at work, what do you conclude is the new expected rate of inflation? Explain your answer.

3. Calculate the expected after-tax real rate of return for an investor in the 40 percent marginal income tax bracket if he or she purchases a bond whose nominal rate is 12 percent and the expected rate of inflation is 4 percent.

4. An investor buys a U.S. Treasury bond whose current yield to maturity as reported in the daily newspaper is 10 percent. The investor is subject to a 45 percent federal income tax rate on any new income received. His real after-tax return from this bond is 2 percent. What is the expected inflation rate in the financial marketplace?

5. Calculate the price elasticity of a 15-year bond around its $1,000 par value and 10 percent coupon rate if market interest rates on comparable securities drop to 6 percent. The market price of the bond at a 6 percent yield to maturity is $1,392. Suppose now the yield to maturity climbs to 14 percent. If the bond's price falls to $751.80, what is the bond's price elasticity?

6. Calculate the value of duration for a 20-year, $1,000 par-value U.S. government bond purchased today at a yield to maturity of 15 per-

cent. The bond's coupon rate is 12 percent and it pays interest once a year at year's end.

SELECTED REFERENCES

Bierwag, G. O.; George G. Kaufman; and Alden Toevs. "Duration: Its Development and Use in Bond Portfolio Management." *Financial Analysts Journal,* July–August 1983, pp. 15–35.

Buse, A. "The Expectations Hypothesis, Yield Curves, and Monetary Policy." *Quarterly Journal of Economics,* November 1965, pp. 666–68.

Chew, I. Keong, and Ronnie J. Clayton. "Bond Valuation: A Clarification." *The Financial Review,* 18, no. 2 (May 1983), pp. 234–36.

Culbertson, John M. "The Term Structure of Interest Rates." *Quarterly Journal of Economics,* November 1957, pp. 485–517.

Dobson, Steven W.; Richard C. Sutch; and David E. Vanderford. "An Evaluation of Alternative Empirical Models of the Term Structure of Interest Rates." *Journal of Finance,* September 1976, pp. 1035–65.

Elliott, J. W., and M. E. Echols. "Market Segmentation, Speculative Behavior, and the Term Structure of Interest Rates." *Review of Economics and Statistics,* February 1976, pp. 40–49.

Fama, Eugene F. "Short-Term Interest Rates as Predictions of Inflation." *American Economic Review,* 65 (June 1975), pp. 269–82.

Fisher, Irving. "Appreciation and Interest." *Publication of the American Economic Association,* August 1896.

Friedman, Benjamin M. "Price Inflation, Portfolio Choice, and Nominal Interest Rates." *American Economic Review,* 70 (March 1980), pp. 12–21.

Gibson, William E. "Interest Rates and Inflationary Expectations: New Evidence." *American Economic Review,* December 1972, pp. 854–65.

Hicks, John R. *Value and Capital.* 2d ed. New York: Oxford University Press, 1946.

Kalotay, Andrew J. "The After-Tax Duration of Original Issue Discount Bonds." *Journal of Portfolio Management,* Winter 1985, pp. 70–72.

Kessel, Reuben H. *The Cyclical Behavior of the Term Structure of Interest Rates.* New York: National Bureau of Economic Research, 1965.

Kolb, Robert W., and Raymond Chiong. "Duration, Immunization, and Hedging with Interest Rate Futures." *The Journal of Financial Research,* 5, no. 2 (Summer 1982), pp. 161–70.

Lutz, Friedrich A. "The Structure of Interest Rates." *Quarterly Journal of Economics,* November 1940, pp. 36–63.

Macaulay, Frederick R. *Some Theoretical Problems Suggested by the Movements of Interest Rates, Bond Yields, and Stock Prices in the United States Since 1856.* New York: National Bureau of Economic Research, 1938.

Malkiel, Burton G. *The Term Structure of Interest Rates.* Princeton, N.J.: Princeton University Press, 1966.

Marshall, William J., and Jess B. Yawitz. "Lower Bounds on Portfolio Performance: An Extension of the Immunization Strategy." *Journal of Financial and Quantitative Analysis,* 17, no. 1 (March 1982), pp. 101–70.

Meiselman, David A. *The Term Structure of Interest Rates.* Englewood Cliffs, N.J.: Prentice-Hall, 1962.

Modigliani, Franco, and Richard Sutch. "Innovations in Interest Rate Policy." *American Economic Review,* May 1966, pp. 178–97.

Mundell, Robert. "Inflation and Real Interest," *Journal of Political Economy,* June 1963.

Pindyck, Robert S. "Risk, Inflation, and the Stock Market." *The American Economic Review,* June 1984, pp. 335–51.

Sargent, Thomas J. "Anticipated Inflation and Nominal Interest." *Quarterly Journal of Economics,* May 1982.

Tanzi, Vito. "Inflationary Expectations, Economic Activity, Taxes and Interest Rates." *American Economic Review,* 70 (March 1980), pp. 12–21.

Taylor, Herbert. "Interest Rates: How Much Does Expected Inflation Matter?" *Business Review,* Federal Reserve Bank of Philadelphia, July–August 1982, pp. 3–12.

Terrell, William T., and William J. Frazer, Jr. "Interest Rates, Portfolio Behavior, and Marketable Government Securities." *Journal of Finance,* March 1972, pp. 1–35.

Van Horne, James. "Interest-Rate Risk and the Term Structure of Interest Rates." *Journal of Political Economy,* August 1965, pp. 344–51.

Walsh, Carl E. "A Rational Expectations Model of Term Premia with Some Implications for Empirical Asset Demand Equations." *The Journal of Finance,* 60, no. 1 (March 1985), pp. 63–83.

10

Marketability, Default Risk, Call Privileges, Taxes, and Other Factors Affecting Interest Rates

PURPOSE OF THIS CHAPTER

To examine the impact of marketability, default risk, call privileges, taxation, and convertibility on the interest rate or yield attached to different securities. This chapter continues the theme begun in the preceding chapter which attempts to explain why there are so many different interest rates—literally thousands of them—in the economy.

KEY TERMS AND CONCEPTS IN THE CHAPTER

*anticipated default
  loss*
bond ratings
call penalty
call premium
call privilege
*capital gains and
  losses*

capital-gains effect
convertibility
debenture
default risk
default risk premium
expected yield
investment value

marginal tax rates
marketability
promised yield
*structure of interest
  rates*
tax-exempt securities

In the preceding chapter we examined several factors which cause the interest rate or yield on one security to be different from the rate or yield on another security. These factors included the maturity or term of a loan and expected inflation. In this chapter our focus is on a different collection of elements influencing relative interest rates: (1) marketability, (2) default risk, (3) call privileges, (4) taxation of income from securities, and (5) convertibility. While the impact on each of these factors is analyzed separately, it should be noted that yields on securities typically are influenced by several factors acting simultaneously. For example, the market yield on a 20-year corporate bond may be 12 percent, while the yield on a 10-year municipal bond may be 7 percent. The difference in yield between these two securities reflects not only the difference in their maturities, but also any differences in their degree of default risk, marketability, callability prior to maturity, and tax status. To analyze yield differentials between securities, therefore, we must understand thoroughly *all* the factors which shape and direct interest rates in the money and capital markets.

MARKETABILITY

One of the most important considerations for an investor is: Does a market exist for those assets he or she would like to acquire? Can an asset be sold quickly, or must the investor wait some time before suitable buyers can be found? This is the question of marketability, and financial instruments vary widely in terms of the ease and speed with which they can be sold and converted into cash.

For example, U.S. Treasury bills, notes and bonds have one of the most active and deepest markets in the world. Large lots of marketable Treasury securities in multiples of a million dollars are bought and sold daily, with the trades taking place in a matter of minutes. Small lots (under $1 million) of these same securities are more difficult to sell. However, there is usually no difficulty in marketing even a handful of Treasury securities provided the seller can wait a few hours or a few days. Similarly, common stock actively traded on the New York and American exchanges typically can be moved in minutes, hours, or overnight, depending on the number of shares being sold and how far removed the investor is from the center of trading activity. In active markets like these, negotiations are usually conducted by telephone and confirmed by wire, and frequently payment for any securities purchased is made the same day by wire or within one or two days by check.

For the thousands of lesser-known securities not actively traded each day, however, marketability is frequently a problem. For example, stocks, bonds, and notes issued by smaller companies usually have a narrow market, often confined to the local community or region. Trades occur infrequently, and it is difficult to establish a consistent market price. A seller may have to wait weeks or months to secure a desired price or, if the security must be sold immediately, its price may have to be discounted substantially from the expected figure. Marketability is *positively* related to the size (total sales or total assets) and reputation of the institution issuing the securities and to the number of similar securities outstanding. Not surprisingly, stocks and bonds issued in large blocks by the largest corporations and governmental units tend to find more ready acceptance in the market. With a greater number of similar securities available, buy-sell transactions are more frequent, and a consistent market price can be established.

Marketability is a decided advantage to the security purchaser (lender of funds). In contrast, the issuer of securities is not particularly concerned about any difficulties the purchaser may encounter in the resale (secondary) market unless lack of marketability significantly influences security sales in the primary market. And where marketability is a problem, it does influence the yield the issuer must pay in the primary market. In fact, there is a negative, or inverse, relationship between marketability and yield. More marketable securities generally carry *lower* expected returns, other things equal. Purchasers of securities that can be sold in the secondary market only with difficulty must be compensated for this inconvenience by a higher promised rate of return.

DEFAULT RISK AND INTEREST RATES

Another important factor causing one interest rate to differ from another is the degree of default risk carried by individual securities. Investors in securities face many different kinds of risk,[1] of course, but one of the most important is *default risk*, that is, the risk that a borrower will not meet all promised payments at the times agreed upon. All securities except U.S. government securities are subject to varying degrees of default risk. If you purchase a 10-year corporate bond with $1,000 par value and a coupon rate of 9 percent, the issuing company promises in the indenture (i.e., bond contract) that it will pay you $90 a year (or more commonly, $45 every six months) for 10 years plus $1,000 at the end of the 10-year period. Failure to meet *any* of these promised payments on time puts the borrower in default, and the investor may have to go to court to recover at least some of the monies owed him or her.

---

[1] See Chapter 12 for a discussion of the principal types of risk confronting investors in financial instruments.

The Premium for Default Risk

The yield on a risky security is *positively* related to the risk of borrower default as perceived by investors. Specifically, the yield on a risky security is composed of at least two elements:

$$\text{Yield on risky security} = \text{Risk-free interest rate} \atop + \text{Default risk premium} \qquad (10\text{--}1)$$

where:

$$\text{Default risk premium} = \text{Promised yield on a risky security} \atop - \text{Risk-free interest rate} \qquad (10\text{--}2)$$

The *promised yield* on a risky security is the yield to maturity that will be earned by the investor if the borrower makes all the payments that are pledged when they are due. The higher the degree of default risk associated with a risky security, the higher the default-risk premium on that security and the greater the required rate of return (yield) that must be attached to that security as demanded by investors in the marketplace. Any adverse development, such as a downturn in the economy, a natural disaster, ill health, serious financial difficulties, that makes a borrower appear more risky will lead the market to assign a higher default risk premium to his or her security. And, if the risk-free rate remains unchanged, the security's risky yield must rise and its price must decline.

The Expected Rate of Return or Yield on a Risky Security

Increasingly in recent years, some of the nation's largest firms (such as Braniff Airlines and Franklin National Bank of New York) and even some local government units (such as the huge Washington Public Power Supply System) have been forced into bankruptcy and into default on their bonds. Others, like Chrysler Corporation and Continental Illinois Corporation, have experienced highly publicized financial problems. Volatile changes in business and consumer spending, interest rates, and commodity prices frequently have led to serious miscalculations by both large and small firms with sometimes fatal results. For this reason, many investors today have learned to look at the *expected* rate of return, or yield, on a security as well as its *promised* yield.

The *expected yield* is simply the weighted average of all possible yields to maturity from a risky security. Each possible yield is weighted by the probability that it will occur. Thus, if there are m possible yields from a given risky security,

$$\text{Expected yield} = \sum_{i-1}^{m} p_i y_i \qquad (10\text{--}3)$$

where y_i represents the ith possible yield on a risky security and p_i is the probability that the ith possible risky yield will be obtained.

Anticipated Loss and Default-Risk Premiums

For a risk-free security held to maturity, the expected yield equals the promised yield. However, in the case of a risky security, the promised yield may be greater than the expected yield, and the yield spread between them is usually labeled the anticipated loss due to default. That is,

$$\text{Anticipated loss due to default on a risky security} = \text{Promised yield} - \text{Expected yield} \quad (10\text{--}4)$$

The concept of *anticipated loss due to default* is important because it represents each investor's view of what the appropriate risk premium on a risky security should be. To illustrate, let's suppose that an investor carries out a careful financial analysis of a company in preparation for purchasing its bonds and decides that the firm is a less risky borrower than perceived by the market as a whole. Perhaps the market has assigned the firm's bonds a default-risk premium of 4 percent; however, the investor feels the true anticipated loss due to default is only 3 percent. Because the market's default-risk premium exceeds this investor's anticipated loss, he would be inclined to *buy* that security. As he sees it, the risky security's yield (including its market-assigned default-risk premium) is too high and, therefore, its price is too low. To this investor the security appears to be a bargain—a temporarily underpriced financial asset.

Consider the opposite case. An investor calculates the anticipated loss due to default on bonds issued by a state toll road project. She concludes that a default-risk premium of 5 percent is justified because of a significant number of uncertainties associated with the future success of the project. However, the current yield on the risky security is only 10 percent, and the risk-free interest rate is 6 percent. Because the market has assigned only a 4 percent default-risk premium, while the investor prefers a 5 percent premium, it is unlikely that she will purchase the toll road bond. As the investor views this bond, its risky yield is too low, and therefore its price is too high.

Major financial institutions, especially insurance companies and commercial banks, employ large number of credit analysts for the express purpose of assessing the anticipated loss due to default on a wide range of securities they would like to acquire. These institutions feel they have a definite advantage over the average investor in assessing the true degree of default risk associated with any particular security. This high level of technical expertise may permit major institutional investors to take advantage of underpriced securities where, in their judgment, the market has overestimated the true level of default risk.

EXHIBIT 10–1

Bond-Rating Categories Employed by Moody's Investor Service and
Standard & Poor's Corporation

Quality Level of Bonds	Moody's Rating Category	Standard & Poor's Rating Category	Risk Premium
High-quality or high-grade bonds	Aaa	AAA	Lowest
	Aa	AA	
	A	A	
Medium-quality or medium-grade bonds	Baa	BBB	
	Ba	BB	
	B	B	
Lowest grade, speculative or poor-quality bonds	Caa	CCC	
	Ca	CC	
	C	C	
Defaulted bonds and bonds issued by bankrupt companies	—	DDD	Highest
	—	DD	
	—	D	

Factors Influencing Default-Risk Premiums

What factors influence the risk premiums assigned by the market to
different securities? For many years in the United States, privately owned
investment-rating companies have exercised a dominant influence on
investor perceptions of the riskiness of individual security issues. The
two most widely consulted investment-rating companies are Moody's Investor Service—a division of Dun and Bradstreet, Inc., and Standard &
Poor's Corporation—a subsidiary of McGraw-Hill, Inc. Both companies
rate individual security issues according to their perceived probability
of default (based on the borrower's financial condition and business prospects) and publish the ratings as letter grades. A summary of the letter
grades used by these companies for rating corporate and municipal bonds
is shown in Exhibit 10–1.[2]

---

[2] While Moody's and Standard & Poor's currently dominate the security-rating business, a number of smaller but rapidly growing rating agencies have come into prominence
recently. The oldest of these is Fitch Investors Service, Inc., of New York, but in 1982
Duff & Phelps, Inc. of Chicago was recognized as an acceptable nationwide credit-
rating firm by the Securities and Exchange Commission (SEC). SEC recognition was
also granted to McCarthy, Crisanti & Maffei, Inc. of New York in 1983. The recent
rapid growth of these smaller national credit-rating firms is a reflection of the increased

FIGURE 10–1

Long-Term Bonds Yields (Quarterly Averages)

SOURCE: Board of Governors of the Federal Reserve System, *Historical Chart Book,* 1984.

Moody's investment ratings range from Aaa for the highest-quality securities, with negligible default risk, to C for those securities deemed to be speculative and carrying a significant prospect of default. Quality ratings assigned by Standard & Poor's range from AAA for high-grade ("gilt-edged") securities to those financial instruments actually in default (D) or issued by bankrupt firms. Bonds falling in the four top-rating categories—Aaa to Baa for Moody's and AAA to BBB for Standard & Poor's—are called *investment-grade issues.* State and federal laws frequently require commercial banks, insurance companies, and other financial institutions to purchase only those securities rated in these four categories. Lower-rated securities are referred to as *speculative issues.*

Figure 10–1 illustrates how the yield on bonds in two different Moody's categories—Aaa and Baa—have fluctuated in recent years, and it high-

number of corporate bankruptcies and near-bankruptcies over the last few years which has led many investors to seek multiple credit opinions on any given security before committing their funds.

lights the spread between the yields on these risky securities and those on riskless long-term U.S. government bonds. Exhibit 10–2 compares market yields on 20-year U.S. Treasury bonds with those on corporate bonds in the four top-rating categories—Aaa to Baa. It is interesting to note that these yield relationships are all in the direction theory would lead us to expect. For example, the yield on Aaa corporate bonds—the least risky of the securities rated by Moody's and Standard & Poor's—is consistently lower than yields attached to lower-rated (Baa) bonds. Moreover, the graph lines representing Aaa and Baa bonds in Figure 10–1 never cross each other; this suggests that investors in the marketplace tend to rank securities in the same relative default-risk order as the rating agencies do. This is perhaps an appropriate strategy because there is evidence of a high correlation between the ratings assigned by the agencies and the actual default record of marketable corporate bonds.

We note, however, that the spreads between yields in different rating categories vary significantly over time. There is, for example, a pronounced association between market-assigned default-risk premiums and fluctuations in business activity between recessions and expansions or boom periods. The yield spread between Aaa- and Baa-rated securities shown in Figure 10–1 tends to increase during recessions and tends to decrease during periods of economic expansion. Note, for example, the marked increase in the yield spread between Aaa and Baa corporate bonds at the time of the 1969–70, 1974–75, and 1980–82 recessions and the significant decrease in that spread after these recessions ended. The correlation is not perfect, of course. Fluctuations in the nation's output and income do not always influence the default-risk premium on one security versus another in the same way or to the same degree. But it is evident that, when economic and financial conditions suggest to inves-

EXHIBIT 10–2

Market Yields on Rated Corporate Bonds and 20-Year U.S. Treasury Bonds, 1981–1985

Type of Bond*	Average Yields (percent per annum)				
	1981	1982	1983	1984	1985†
20-year U.S. Treasury	13.72%	12.92%	11.34%	12.48%	12.06%
Aaa corporate	14.17	13.79	12.04	12.71	12.47
Aa corporate	14.75	14.41	12.42	13.31	12.47
A corporate	15.29	15.43	13.10	13.74	13.06
Baa corporate	16.04	16.11	13.55	14.19	13.51

* Corporate bond ratings are from Moody's Investor Service.
† Figures are for March 1985.
SOURCE: Board of Governors of the Federal Reserve System. *Federal Reserve Bulletin*, selected issues.

tors that uncertainty has increased and that business prospects are less robust, the market translates these opinions into higher default-risk premiums.[3]

Several studies in recent years have addressed the question of what factors influence default-risk premiums on securities (especially corporate bonds) and the factors which security-rating companies use to evaluate default risk. Among the factors identified for corporate securities are *variability in company earnings, the period of time a firm has been in operation,* and the *amount of leverage employed* (i.e., the amount of debt relative to equity).[4] A company with volatile earnings runs a greater risk of experiencing periods when losses will exceed the firm's ability to raise funds. Moreover, the longer a firm has been operating without a default, the more investors come to expect continued successful performance. Greater use of financial leverage (debt) in the capital structure of a firm offers the potential for greater earnings per share of stock, because debt is a relatively cheap source of funds (measured on an after-tax basis). However, financial leverage is a two-edged sword. As the proportion of borrowed funds rises relative to equity, the risk of significant declines in earnings is increased.

In summary, careful study of the relationship between default risk and interest rates points to a fundamental principle in the field of finance: *default risk and expected return are positively related.* The investor seeking higher expected returns must also be willing to accept greater risk of ruin. Moreover, default risk is correlated with both *internal* (borrower-specific) factors associated with a loan and *external* factors, especially the state of the economy and changing demands for a particular industry's product or service.

CALL PRIVILEGES

Nearly all corporate bonds and mortgages, most municipal revenue bonds, and some U.S. government bonds issued in today's financial mar-

---

[3] This conclusion is supported by research studies prepared by Hickman (1958), Fisher (1959), and Jaffee (1975).

[4] See especially the study by Fisher (1959). While we do not know for sure what factors the security-rating companies use to assign default-risk ratings, we do know that they consider at least three levels of factors: (1) condition of the economy; (2) industry conditions; and (3) borrower-specific factors, including coverage ratios (i.e., earnings before interest and taxes to interest and principal payments owed), leverage ratios (i.e., debt to equity ratios), liquidity indicators (such as the current ratio), and profitability measures (such as return on assets and return on equity). Recent studies of corporate bankruptcy, as noted by Scott (1981), have found some of these factors—especially liquidity or cash flow variables, earnings, debt exposure, and stock prices—to be effective discriminators between corporations declaring bankruptcy and healthy firms.

kets carry a *call privilege*. This provision of the bond contract, or indenture, permits the borrower to retire all or a portion of a bond issue by
buying back the securities in advance of their maturity. Bondholders
usually are informed of a call through a notice in a newspaper of general
circulation, while holders of record of registered bonds are notified directly. For most bonds there is usually a period of *call deferment* (often
5 to 10 years) during which the security cannot be called in, thus giving
the bondholder some call protection. Normally, when the *call privilege*
is exercised, the security issuer will pay the investor the call price, which
equals the securities' face value plus a call penalty. The size of the *call
penalty* is set forth in the indenture (contract) and generally varies inversely with the number of years remaining to maturity and the length
of the call deferment period. In the case of a bond, one year's worth of
coupon income is often the minimum call penalty required.

Calculating the Yields on Called Securities

Bonds may be callable immediately or the privilege may be deferred
(postponed) for a time. In the corporate sector, bonds usually are not
eligible for call for a period of 5 to 10 years after issue in order to give
investors at least some protection against early redemption. Of course,
calling a security at any point in advance of its final maturity has an
impact on the investor's effective yield.

To demonstrate this, we recall from Chapter 8 that the yield to maturity
of any security is that discount rate, y, which equates the security's price,
P, with the present value of all future cash flows, I_i, expected from holding
the security. In symbols,

$$P = \frac{I_1}{(1+y)^1} + \frac{I_2}{(1+y)^2} + \cdots + \frac{I_n}{(1+y)^n} \qquad (10\text{--}5)$$

where n is the number of periods until maturity. Suppose that after k
periods (with k < n) the borrower exercises the call option and redeems
the security. The investor will receive the call price (C) for the security,
which can be reinvested at the current market interest rate, i. If the
investor's planned holding period ends in time period n, the expected
holding-period yield (h) can be calculated using the following formula:

$$P = \frac{I_1}{(1+h)^1} + \frac{I_2}{(1+h)^2} + \cdots + \frac{I_k}{(1+h)^k} + \frac{i \times C_{k+1}}{(1+h)^{k+1}}$$

$$+ \frac{i \times C_{k+2}}{(1+h)^{k+2}} + \cdots + \frac{i \times C_n}{(1+h)^n} + \frac{C}{(1+h)^n} \qquad (10\text{--}6)$$

Using summation signs, this reduces to:

$$P = \sum_{j=1}^{k} \frac{I_j}{(1+h)^j} + \sum_{j=k+1}^{n} \frac{i \times C_j}{(1+h)^j} + \frac{C}{(1+h)^n} \qquad (10\text{-}7)$$

The first term in Equation 10-7 gives the present value of all expected cash flows (I) from the security until it is called in time period, k. The second term captures the present value of income received by the investor after he or she reinvests at interest rate i the call price (C) received from the security issuer. The third and final term in the equation shows the current discounted value of the call price which the investor expects to receive when the holding period ends in time period n.

To take an example of the above formula's use let's suppose that a corporate bond, originally offering investors an 8 percent coupon rate for 10 years and issued at $1,000 par, is called 5 years after issue date when going market interest rates on investments of comparable risk are 6 percent. What is this bond's 10-year holding-period yield (h), if its call price equals par plus two years' worth of coupon income? We have

$$\$1,000 = \sum_{t=1}^{5} \frac{\$80}{(1+h)^t} + \sum_{t=6}^{10} \frac{\$1,160 \times .06}{(1+h)^t} + \frac{\$1,160}{(1+h)^{10}} \qquad (10\text{-}8)$$

The reader, using the present value and annuity tables in Appendix B, should verify that h, the 10-year holding-period yield, is 8.70 percent in this instance.

Equation 10-7 shows quite clearly that the investor in callable securities encounters two major uncertainties:

1. The investor does not know if or when the securities might be called (i.e., the value of k).
2. The investor does not know the market yield (reinvestment rate, i) that might prevail at the time the security is called.

Therefore, how aggressively the investor chooses to bid for a callable instrument will depend on:

1. The investor's expectations regarding future changes in interest rates, especially decreases in rates, during the term of the security.
2. The length of the deferment period before the security is eligible to be called.
3. The call price (face value plus call penalty) the issuer is willing to pay to redeem the security.

Advantages and Disadvantages of the Call Privilege

Clearly, the call privilege is an advantage to the security issuer because it grants greater financial flexibility and the potential for reducing future interest costs. On the other hand, the call privilege is a distinct disadvantage to the security buyer, who may suffer a decline in the expected holding-period yield if the security is, in fact, called. The issuer will call in a security if the market rate of interest falls far enough so that the savings from issuing a new security at lower interest rates more than offset the call penalty plus flotation costs of a new security issue. This means, however, that the investor who is paid off will be forced to reinvest the call price in lower-yielding securities.

Another disadvantage for the investor is that call privileges limit the potential increase in a security's market price. In general, the market price of a security will not rise significantly above its call price, even when interest rates fall. The reason is that the issuer can call in a security at its call price, presenting the investor with a loss equal to the difference between the prevailing market price and the call price. Thus, callable securities have a more limited potential for capital gains than noncallable securities.

The Call Premium and Interest-Rate Expectations

For all of the foregoing reasons, securities that carry a call privilege generally sell at lower prices and higher interest rates than noncallable securities. Moreover, there is an inverse relationship between the length of the call deferment period and the required rate of interest on callable securities. The longer the period of deferment and, therefore, the longer the investor is protected against early redemption, the lower the interest rate that the borrower must pay. Issuers of callable securities must pay a call premium in the form of a higher rate of interest for the option of early redemption and for a shorter period of deferment.

The key determinant of the size of the call premium is the *interest-rate expectations* of investors in the marketplace. If interest rates are expected to rise over the term of a security, the risk that the security will be called is low. Borrowers are highly unlikely to call in their securities and issue new ones at higher interest rates. As a result, the yield differential between callable and noncallable securities normally will be minimal. The same conclusions apply even if interest rates are expected to decline moderately but not enough to entice borrowers to call in their securities and issue new ones.

It is when interest rates are *expected to fall* substantially that securities are most likely to be called. In this instance security issuers can save large amounts of money—more than enough to cover the call penalty plus flotation costs of new securities—by exercising the call privilege.

Thus, the call premium is likely to be significant as investors demand a higher yield on callable issues to compensate them for increased call risk. Moreover, the yield spreads between bonds with long call deferments versus those with short or no call deferments widen during such periods as investors come to value more highly the deferment feature.

Research Evidence

Is there evidence of an *inverse* relationship between interest-rate expectations and the value of the call privilege? Recent research answers in the affirmative. For example, Cook (1973) finds that, when interest rates are high, the call premium rises because investors expect interest rates to fall in the future. Moreover, he points out that call provisions also influence yield spreads between corporate bonds, nearly all of which have the call privilege attached, and municipal and U.S. government bonds, which generally are not subject to call. For example, when interest rates are expected to fall, the spread between corporate and U.S. government bond rates tends to widen. Pye (1966, 1967) and Jen and Wert (1966, 1967, 1968) find additional evidence that bonds carrying a call deferment have lower rates of return than bonds that are callable immediately.

Effect of Coupon Rates on Call Risk

Finally, we should note that the coupon rate on a bond is closely related to the investor's call risk. We recall from Chapter 8 that a bond's coupon rate is the rate of return against the security's par value promised by the borrower. High coupon rates mean that a bond issuer is forced to pay high interest costs as long as the bond is outstanding. Therefore, there is a strong incentive to call in such bonds and replace them with lower coupon securities.

Another problem is that bonds bearing high coupons have less opportunity for capital gains than bonds carrying lower coupon rates. This is true because the market value of a high coupon security is usually close to its call-price ceiling. In contrast, bonds with more-modest coupon rates sell at lower prices and carry considerably more potential for capital gains before hitting the call price. This means there is more risk of call and less potential capital gain to the investor who chooses high coupon securities. As a result, the issuer of such securities must pay a higher yield to induce investors to buy them and accept greater call risk.

TAXATION OF SECURITY RETURNS

Taxes imposed by federal, state, and local governments have a profound effect on the returns earned by investors in financial assets. The income from most securities—interest or dividends and capital gains—is subject to taxation at the federal level and by many state and local governments as well. Government uses its taxing power to encourage purchases of certain financial assets and thereby redirect the flow of savings and investment toward areas of critical social need. Today U.S. tax laws heavily favor two kinds of financial transactions: (1) long-term lending and investing of funds, as opposed to short-term lending and investing; and (2) fund raising by those sectors of the economy considered to be *disadvantaged* in the competition for loanable funds. Prominent among these "disadvantaged" groups are state and local governments and buyers and sellers of real estate, especially residential properties.

The Tax Treatment of Capital Gains

Short-Term Capital Gains.   Governments frequently use tax laws to encourage greater long-term investment in capital goods in order to accelerate the economy's rate of growth. For example, the federal government imposes lower tax rates on long-term capital gains than on short-term capital gains.

Under current tax rules administered by the Internal Revenue Service, an increase in the value of a capital asset (including stocks and bonds) which the taxpayer converts into cash is subject to federal income taxation. For example, if you had purchased stock in **XYZ** Corporation for $1,900 and then sold it at a later date for $3,100, you would have experienced a capital gain of $1,200. Under the Tax Reform Act of 1984, if you held the stock for six months or less before selling it, the $1,200 increase in value would be defined as a short-term capital gain. Such gains are taxable as ordinary income at your current income tax rate. Thus, a $1,200 short-term capital gain for an investor in the 50 percent tax bracket would result in a tax liability of $600 ($1,200 × 0.50).

Long-Term Capital Gains.   Current tax policy calls for much *lower* tax rates, however, if **XYZ** Corporation's stock is held for a longer period before it is sold. For example, if the investor holds the stock for more than six months before selling it, the result is a long-term capital gain of $1,200. For individual taxpayers, only 40 percent of this long-term gain ($480) is taxable. A taxpayer in the top 50 percent federal tax bracket, for example, would have a resulting tax liability of just $240 ($480 × 0.50). Under the terms of the Economic Recovery Tax Act of 1981, the maximum tax rate on long-term capital gains is 20 percent.

Treatment of Capital Losses.   Net losses on security investments are deductible for tax purposes within well-defined limits. For the individual taxpayer, a net short-term capital loss is deductible up to the amount of the capital loss, the size of ordinary income, or $3,000, whichever is smaller. For example, suppose an investor experiences a net loss on securities held for less than six months of $8,000. By definition, this is a short-term capital loss. Suppose this person receives other taxable income of $20,000. How much of the short-term loss can be deducted? What is this taxpayer's total taxable income? The maximum loss deduction in this case is $3,000, and therefore the taxpayer's net taxable income is $17,000 (i.e., $20,000 minus the $3,000 in deductible losses). Current federal law does allow the taxpayer to carry forward into subsequent years the remaining portion of the loss (i.e., $5,000 in this example) until all of the short-term loss has been deducted from ordinary income, but the loss cannot be carried backward.

In the case of net long-term capital losses, federal tax rules allow the individual taxpayer to recognize only 50 percent of the loss as a deduction from current taxable income. For example, suppose an investor purchased securities at a cost of $5,000 and sold them two years later in a declining market for $3,000. Then only $1,000 of the $2,000 long-term capital loss could be charged against other income in the current year. But the other $1,000 could be carried forward into future years' deductions. As in the case of short-term losses, a maximum amount of $3,000 can be carried forward into future years but not backward into past years.

Netting Out Losses and Gains.   What happens when the taxpayer has a mixture of short- and long-term capital gains and losses? First, the long-term losses must be deducted from the long-term gains to yield the taxpayer's net long-term capital gain or loss. Next, short-term losses must be deducted from any short-term gains to derive the taxpayer's net short-term gain or loss.

When both net figures are *positive,* the investor pays the ordinary marginal income tax rate appropriate for his or her income bracket (see Exhibit 10–3) on the net short-term gain. In contrast, the lower capital gains tax rate applies to the long-term net gain.

When both the net long- and short-term gains are *negative,* 50 percent of the long-term loss can be used to offset ordinary income up to $3,000. In contrast, all of the net short-term loss may be used to offset ordinary income up to $3,000. If the combined sum of a short-term loss and 50 percent of a long-term capital loss for a particular year exceeds $3,000, the taxpayer may carry the loss forward until all of it is written off.

When there is a net short-term capital loss and a long-term gain, the two are netted out. Any excess long-term gain over short-term loss is taxed at the lower capital gains rate. If there is a short-term gain exceeding a long-term capital loss, however, the net gain is taxed at the individual's marginal income tax rate.

EXHIBIT 10–3

Examples of Marginal Federal Income Tax Rates (Tax Brackets) Applicable
to Married Taxpayers Filing a Joint Return, 1980 and 1984

	Applicable Marginal Tax Rate (bracket)	
Taxable Income	1980	1984
$ 15,000	21%	16%
25,000	32	25
35,000	37	28
50,000	49	38
75,000	54	42
100,000	59	45
150,000	64	49
200,000	70	50

Note: Marginal tax rates for 1980 were as specified in the
Revenue Act of 1978, while those for 1984 reflect changes
brought about by the Economic Recovery Tax Act of 1981. The
1981 law provided for a gradual reduction of individual tax rates
over a period of 33 months.

The Capital Gains Effect.   The low capital gains tax rate clearly
favors those securities with the strongest capital gains potential. In particular, bonds have less appeal than common stock, especially growth stocks
which often pay limited dividends but offer the prospect of significant
capital appreciation. Capital gains tax rules also favor bonds bearing low
coupon rates over those with high coupon rates. This is true because in
a period of relatively high interest rates low coupon bonds would be
selling at a substantial discount from their par values. As a low coupon
security approaches maturity, its price rises toward par. Therefore, the
investor will earn interest income as determined by the coupon rate
on the bond and a capital gain.

An excellent example of this so-called *capital gains effect* occurred
recently in the U.S. Treasury bond market. For example, U.S. Treasury
bonds bearing a 4 percent coupon were issued in 1961 to mature in
1981. With interest rates during 1978, 1979, and into early 1980 rising
to record double-digit levels, these low coupon bonds were selling for
about 60 percent of their face value. However, demand for these Treasury
bonds was extremely heavy due to their expected capital gain at maturity.
(The Treasury must redeem its bonds at full face value on the maturity
date.) As a result, while other interest rates in the economy were climbing
rapidly, market yields on the low coupon Treasuries moved up much
more slowly than those on higher coupon securities in return for the
prospect of significant capital gains, taxable at a highly favorable rate.

Planning for Capital Gains and Losses.   The favorable tax treatment of long-term capital gains and short-term capital losses encourages investors to carefully *plan* their purchases and sales of financial instruments. For example, many investors today hold securities for periods longer than normally desired in order to take advantage of the lower tax rate on long-term capital gains. Often capital gains are taken in years of depressed income, while capital losses are sought during high-income years in order to avoid reaching a higher tax bracket and to even out fluctuations in annual income. Capital losses may be taken early in order to offset capital gains earned later on.[5] Frequently, securities are sold via the "installment method" to defer realized capital gains in a given year and keep the investor out of a higher tax bracket. Due to the extreme complexity and constantly changing character of modern tax laws, the wise investor today seeks professional advice from competent tax attorneys and accountants when planning future security sales and purchases.

Tax-Exempt Securities

One of the most controversial tax rules affecting securities is the tax-exemption privilege granted investors in state and local government (municipal) bonds. The *interest income* earned on municipal bonds is exempt from federal income taxes, and most states exempt interest on their own securities from state income taxes.[6] The tax-exempt privilege is a subsidy

---

[5] The fact that long-term capital gains are more favorably taxed than short-term gains creates a dilemma for the investor when the market price of a security has made a short-term gain but is now declining. Should he or she sell now and take the short-term gain, which will be taxed as ordinary income (like salary, interest, and dividends), or hold the security for the required six months to secure a long-term gain? As we noted above, 60 percent of a long-term capital gain is excluded from taxable income. If the security's price is dropping, when should the investor sell out to maximize his or her after-tax return?

A formula which has proved useful to many investors is:

$$\begin{array}{l}\text{After-tax} \\ \text{short-term} \\ \text{capital gain}\end{array} = \begin{array}{l}\text{Long-term} \\ \text{capital} \\ \text{gain}\end{array} - 0.40 \text{ (Long-term capital gain)} \times \begin{array}{l}\text{Investor's} \\ \text{marginal tax} \\ \text{rate}\end{array}$$

The investor knows what the short-term capital gain will be if he sells now and knows his current marginal tax rate. It is a relatively simple matter to solve for the long-term gain which will make the above equation balance. The investor will benefit by holding the security as long as the gain does not drop below the calculated long-term capital gain.

[6] Capital gains earned on municipals are taxable at the capital gains rate. An exception to this rule occurs if a municipal bond is issued at a price below its par value. The appreciation between the original purchase price and par is tax exempt. However, if the price of the bond rises above par, that portion of the gain is fully taxable.

to induce investors to support local government by financing the construction of schools, highways, bridges, airports, and other needed public projects. The exemption privilege shifts the burden of federal taxation from buyers of municipal bonds to other taxpayers.

What investors benefit from buying municipals? The critical factor here is the marginal tax rate (tax bracket) of the investor—the rate he or she must pay on the last dollar of income received during the tax year. For individual investors, these marginal tax rates range from zero for nontaxpayers to as high as 50 percent for the highest income earners. (See Exhibit 10–3 for an example of marginal tax rates applying to married taxpayers filing a joint tax return.) The marginal rate for corporations is 15 percent on the first $25,000 in taxable profits; 18 percent for taxable profits over $25,000 but less than $50,000; 30 percent for taxable corporate earnings over $50,000 but less than $75,000; 40 percent for earnings exceeding $75,000 but below $100,000; and 46 percent for all taxable profits in excess of $100,000. In recent years, marginal tax rates in the 25 to 50 percent range have represented a break-even level for investors interested in municipal bonds. Investors carrying marginal tax rates above this range generally receive higher after-tax yields from buying tax-exempt securities instead of taxable securities. Below this range, taxable securities generally yield a better after-tax return.

The Effect of Marginal Tax Rates on After-Tax Yields.   To illustrate the importance of knowing the investor's marginal tax rate in deciding whether to purchase tax-exempt securities, consider the following example. Assume the current yield to maturity on taxable corporate bonds is 12 percent, while the current tax-exempt yield on municipal bonds of comparable quality and rating is 7 percent. The after-tax yield on these two securities can be compared by using the following formula:

$$\text{Before-tax yield } (1 - \text{Investor's marginal tax rate}) = \text{After-tax yield} \quad \textbf{(10–9)}$$

For an investor in the 28 percent tax bracket (see Exhibit 10–3), the after-tax yields on these bonds are:

Taxable Corporate Bond	Tax-Exempt Municipal Bonds
$12\% \ (1 - 0.28) = 8.64\%$	7% before and after taxes

On the basis of yield alone, the investor in the 28 percent tax bracket would prefer the taxable corporate bond.[7]

---

[7] It is important to note that the particular tax brackets favoring the purchase of municipals versus taxable securities change over time due to changes in tax laws and variations in the yield spread between taxable and tax-exempt securities.

At what rate would an investor be *indifferent* to whether securities are taxable or tax exempt? In other words, what is the break-even point between these two types of financial instruments?

This point is easily calculated from the formula

$$\text{Tax-exempt yield} = (1 - t) \times \text{Taxable yield} \qquad (10\text{--}10)$$

where t is the investor's marginal tax rate. Solving for the break-even tax rate gives

$$t = 1 - \frac{\text{Tax-exempt yield}}{\text{Taxable yield}} \qquad (10\text{--}11)$$

Clearly, if the current yield on tax-exempt securities is 6 percent and it is 10 percent on taxable issues, the break-even tax rate is $1 - 0.60$, or 40 percent. An investor in a marginal tax bracket *above* 40 percent would prefer a tax-exempt security to a taxable one, other factors held equal.

Comparing Taxable and Tax-Exempt Securities. The existence of both taxable and tax-exempt securities complicates the investor's task in trying to choose a suitable portfolio to buy and hold. In order to make valid comparisons between taxable and tax-exempt issues the investor must convert all expected security yields to an after-tax basis.

In the case of the yield to maturity on a security, this can be done by using the following formula:

$$P_o = \sum_{i=1}^{n} \frac{I_i(1 - t)}{(1 + a)^i} + \frac{(P_n - P_o)(1 - cg)}{(1 + a)^n} + \frac{P_o}{(1 + a)^n} \qquad (10\text{--}12)$$

which equates the current market value (P_o) of the security to the present value of all after-tax returns promised in the future. If the security is to be held for n years, I_i is the amount of interest or other income expected each year and t is the marginal income tax rate of the investor. If we assume the security will be sold or redeemed for price P_n at maturity, then ($P_n - P_o$) measures the expected capital gain on the instrument which, of course, will be taxed at the appropriate capital gains rate, cg. Provided investors know their marginal income tax rate, the capital gains tax rate, the current price of the security, and the expected distribution of future income from the security, they can easily calculate discount rate, a—the after-tax yield to maturity.

For example, consider the case of a $1,000 corporate bond selling for $900 (with par equal to $1,000), maturing in 10 years, with a 10 percent coupon rate. If an investor in the 40 percent federal income tax bracket buys and holds the bond to maturity, his after-tax yield, a, could be found from evaluating

$$\$900 = \sum_{t=1}^{10} \frac{\$100(1-0.40)}{(1+a)^t} + \frac{(\$1,000 - \$900)(1 - 0.4 \times 0.4)}{(1+a)^{10}} + \frac{\$900}{(1+a)^{10}}$$

In this instance the reader should verify, using the annuity and present value tables in Appendix B, that the after-tax yield, a, is 7.37 percent. Note that the capital gains tax rate, cg, for an individual taxpayer is the product of the taxpayer's income tax bracket (in this case, 0.40) times the 40 percent of a long-term capital gain that is subject to federal taxation.

Certainly the tax-exempt privilege has lowered the interest rates at which municipals can be sold in the open market relative to taxable bonds, and therefore the amount of interest cost borne by local taxpayers. For example, in April 1984, Aaa-rated municipal bonds carried an average yield to maturity of 9.54 percent compared to 12.81 percent on comparable quality seasoned (taxable) corporate bonds—a yield spread of more than 3 full percentage points. However, the primary beneficiaries of the exemption privilege are *investors* who can profitably purchase municipals and escape some portion of the federal tax burden. Other taxpayers must pay higher federal taxes in order to make up for those lost tax revenues. Moreover, by limiting the municipal market to these high tax bracket investors, the tax-exemption feature has probably increased the unpredictability of municipal bond interest rates and made the job of state and local government fiscal management more difficult.

CONVERTIBLE SECURITIES

Another factor which affects relative rates of return on different securities is *convertibility*. Convertible securities consist of special issues of corporate bonds or preferred stock which entitle the holder to exchange these securities for a specific number of shares of the issuing firm's common stock. Convertibles are frequently called "hybrid securities" because they offer the investor the prospect of both stable income in the form of interest or dividends plus capital gains on common stock once conversion takes place. The timing of a conversion is purely at the option of the investor; however, the contract agreed to at time of purchase specifies the terms under which conversion may take place. An issuing firm often can "force" conversion of its securities by encouraging a rise in the price of its common stock (such as by announcing a merger offer), because conversion is most likely to occur in a rising market. Conversion is a one-way transaction—once convertibles are exchanged for common stock there is no way back for the investor.

Investors generally pay a premium for convertible securities over non-convertible securities in the form of a higher price and reduced yield. Thus, convertibles will carry a lower rate of return than other securities of comparable quality and maturity issued by the same company. This occurs because the investor in convertibles is granted a hedge against future risk. If security prices fall, the investor still earns a fixed rate of return in the form of interest income from a convertible bond or dividend income from each share of convertible preferred stock. On the other hand, if stock prices rise, the investor can exercise his or her option and share in any capital gains earned on the company's common stock. Of course, convertibles are most attractive in a period of rising stock prices and declining interest rates.

Bonds with the convertible feature are nearly always issued as debentures. A *debenture* is a long-term corporate IOU that is unsecured in the sense that no specific collateral is pledged to support the security in the event of financial problems. Instead, the debenture is backed by the general earning power of the issuing corporation, which promises to pay interest at specified times and return the principal (par) value of the security at maturity. The interest and principal amount owed on a convertible bond must be paid before any dividends are paid on the issuing company's preferred and common stock. Most convertibles are callable bonds and, like other callable bonds, are worth no more than their call price on the day of redemption.

Convertible bonds offer several significant advantages to the issuing company. Due to the conversion feature they can be issued at a lower net interest cost than conventional (nonconvertible) bonds. Convertibles offer an alternative to issuing more common stock which a firm may wish to avoid because the additional stock could dilute the equity interest of current stockholders and reduce earnings per share. Moreover, dividends on stock are not deductible from federal income taxes but interest on convertible bonds *is* a tax-deductible expense.

Key advantages to the investor include the fact that convertible bonds guarantee the payment of interest (as long as the issuing company remains solvent) and generally appreciate in value when the company's common stock is rising in price. Moreover, there is a floor under the price of a convertible bond—known as its *investment value*—below which its price normally will not fall. This is the price which would produce a yield on the convertible equal to the yield on nonconvertible bonds of the same quality and credit rating. However, investors are often counseled by financial analysts not to buy convertibles unless they would be happy holding the issuing company's *stock* because the issuer may call in the securities early, thereby forcing conversion. (Many convertible issues are accompanied by a sinking-fund provision that allows the issuer to call in a few securities each year.) This situation may present the investor with a substantially reduced return on his investment, especially if the convertibles are called within a few years of their issue date, because, when new, they usually sell at substantial premiums above their conversion value. It normally takes at least a few months and sometimes a few years for the investor to recover the purchase premium.

Convertible bonds have been exceedingly popular securities in recent years. The number of convertibles listed on the New York Stock Exchange nearly doubled during the 1970s, for example. Firms issuing convertible bonds in recent years number among the largest corporations in the United States, including such firms as Alcoa, American Motors, Chase Manhattan Corporation, General Telephone, RCA, U.S. Steel Corporation, and United Airlines. Innovative types of convertibles have appeared in recent years, including floating-rate securities with interest returns linked to dividends on the issuing company's stock. Convertibles are generally regarded as a more conservative investment than purchasing the stock of the same company because they offer less risk than stock. They also provide less potential return than stock, of course; nevertheless, convertibles permit an investor to get "a piece of the action" in the stock market without actually holding stock.

THE STRUCTURE OF INTEREST RATES

As we conclude this chapter, it is important to gain some perspective on the fundamental purpose of this section of the book. In reality, Chapters 7, 8, 9, and 10 should be viewed as a unit, tied together by a common subject—what determines the level of and changes in interest rates and security yields. In Chapter 7 we argued that there is *one* interest rate which underlies all interest rates and is a component of all rates. This is the *risk-free* (or pure) rate of interest, which is a measure of the opportunity cost of holding money and a measure of the reward for saving money rather than spending all of our income on consumption. All other interest rates are scaled *upward* by varying degrees from the risk-free rate, depending on such factors as the term (maturity) of a loan, the risk of borrower default, and the marketability, callability, convertibility, and tax status of the securities to which those rates apply. However, the interest rates attached to *all* securities have the risk-free rate in common.

There is, then, a *structure* to interest rates whose foundation is the risk-free rate (as determined by the demand and supply for loanable funds described in Chapter 7). Perhaps one *picture* of that interest-rate structure is worth a thousands words. Recently, the yield to maturity on long-term U.S. Treasury bonds was reported as 11.39 percent, while corporate BAA bonds were quoted at an average yield of 13.40 percent. As Exhibit 10–4 indicates, each of these rates, like *all* interest rates, is really a summation of rewards (premiums) paid to investors (lenders of

EXHIBIT 10–4

An Example of the Structure of Interest Rates in the Financial System—
Estimated Components of the Market Interest Rate on Risky (BAA-rated)
Corporate Bonds

		Interest-Rate Premiums Offered to Security Buyers

Long-term U.S. Treasury bond rates during the week of May 10, 1985 averaged 11.39%:

Estimated components of the 11.39% rate on long-term U.S. Treasury bonds	Risk-free real rate of interest	7.00%	Rate premium for foregoing consumption and saving money, earning the risk-free rate
	Expected rate of inflation	+ 3.00%	Rate premium for bearing inflation risk
	Liquidity premium	+ 1.39% / 11.39%	Rate premium for the risk of accepting a long-term security rather than a short-term security

Corporate BAA bond rates in the same period averaged 2.01% higher than the long-term Treasury bond rates:

Estimated components of the 2.01% rate *spread* between the corporate BAA bond rate and long-term U.S. Treasury bond rate	Premium for lower marketability	0.26% +	Rate premium for accepting a less marketable security
	Call risk premium	0.25% +	Rate premium for accepting risk security might be called
	Default-risk premium	1.50% / 2.01%	Rate premium for accepting risk of borrower default

Corporate BAA bond rates for that week averaged 13.40%, or 11.39% + 2.01%.

SOURCE: Interest rates on corporate and U.S. Treasury bonds from the Federal Reserve Bank of St. Louis, *U.S. Financial Data,* May 9, 1985. Rate premium estimates by the author.

funds) to get those investors to hold a particular security. Each reward or premium is merely compensation for bearing some kind of *risk;* for example, (1) the risk of giving up liquidity and accepting greater price risk from buying a longer maturity security; (2) the risk of inflation over the term of a security; (3) the risk the borrower will default on some or all of his or her promised payments; (4) the risk that some securities can be called in before they mature and the investor may have to reinvest his or her money at a lower interest rate; and (5) the risk of taking on a security with a weak resale market (i.e., low marketability). Each interest rate or yield that we see in today's market is the *sum* of some or all of these risk-premium factors plus the real risk-free interest rate. And, when interest rates *change,* that change may be due to a change in the risk-free rate or to a change in *any* of the risk-premium factors cited above.

Truly, interest rates are a *complex* phenomenon, affected by many factors and influences. We need to keep this complexity in mind as we proceed on to the next chapter and take on the difficult task of trying to anticipate and forecast interest-rate changes.

STUDY QUESTIONS

1. Define the term *marketability.* Explain its importance to the securities investor and its relationship to the yield on a financial instrument.

2. Do interest rates appear to display consistent, well-defined seasonal patterns? If so, briefly describe these patterns. Why are these patterns not more pronounced in your opinion?

3. Explain the meaning of the phrase *default risk.* What factors appear to influence the degree of default risk displayed by a security? In what ways are security ratings designed to reflect default risk?

4. What is a *call privilege?* Why is this privilege an advantage to the security issuer and a disadvantage to the investor?

5. What types of risk are encountered by the investor in callable securities? Does the coupon rate on a bond influence its call risk?

6. What is the principal determinant of the size of the call premium on callable securities?

7. Which kinds of securities are favored by current U.S. tax laws? Explain why these particular financial instruments are given favorable tax treatment.

8. What is a capital gain, and how exactly is it treated for tax purposes? How are net losses on security investments treated for tax purposes?

9. What portion of the income generated by municipal bonds is tax exempt, and what portion is taxable under federal law? Why do you think the law is structured in this way? Should it be?

10. Explain the relationship between the investor's marginal tax rate and after-tax yields on corporate and municipal bonds. Would municipal bonds be a worthwhile investment for you today? Why?

11. Define the term *convertibility*. Why are convertibles sometimes called "hybrid securities"? Convertible bonds typically carry lower yields than nonconvertible bonds of the same maturity and risk class. Explain why this is true.

PROBLEMS

1. In a recent Federal Reserve publication the following market interest rates or yields were reported:

Three-month Treasury bills	10.22%
One-year Treasury bills	10.38
Five-year Treasury bonds	12.52
Long-term Treasury bonds	12.38
Corporate Baa bonds	14.24
Aaa municipal bonds	10.15

Calculate the difference in percentage points and basis points between these rates. *Explain* the rate differences you derive in terms of the factors discussed in Chapters 9 and 10.

2. The market yield to maturity on a risky bond is currently listed at 14.50 percent. The risk-free interest rate is estimated to be 9.25 percent. What is the default-risk premium, all other factors removed? The promised yield on this bond is 15 percent. A certain investor, looking at this bond, estimates there is a 25 percent probability the bond will pay 15 percent at maturity, a 50 percent probability it will pay a 10 percent return, and a 25 percent probability it will yield only 5 percent. What is the bond's expected yield? What is this investor's anticipated default loss? Will the investor buy this bond?

3. A 10-year corporate bond was issued on January 1, 1982 with call privilege attached. The bond was sold to investors at $1,000 par value with a 10 percent coupon rate. The bond was called on January 1,

1985, at a price to holders of par plus one year's coupon income. At the time prevailing market interest rates on securities of comparable quality and term was 8 percent. If a holder of this bond reinvested the call price at 8 percent for 7 years, calculate this investor's holding-period yield for the entire period of 10 years.

4. Aaa-rated municipal bonds are carrying a market yield today of 5.25 percent, while Aaa-rated corporate bonds have current market yields of 11.50 percent. What is the break-even tax rate that would make a taxable investor indifferent between these two types of bonds?

5. An investor purchases a 10-year U.S. government bond for $800. The bond's coupon rate is 10 percent and at time of purchase it still had five years remaining till maturity. If the investor holds the bond until it matures and collects the $1,000 par value from the Treasury and his marginal tax rate remains at 40 percent, what will be his after-tax yield to maturity?

SELECTED REFERENCES

Altman, Edward I. "The Success of Business Failure Prediction Models." *Journal of Banking and Finance,* 8 (1984), pp. 171–98.

Cook, Timothy Q. "Some Factors Affecting Long-Term Yield Spreads in Recent Years." *Monthly Review,* Federal Reserve Bank of Richmond, September 1973, pp. 2–14.

Fisher, Lawrence. "Determinants of Risk Premiums on Corporate Bonds." *Journal of Political Economy,* June 1959, pp. 217–37.

Hickman, W. Braddock. *Corporate Bond Quality and Investor Experience.* New York: National Bureau of Economic Research, 1958.

Jaffee, Dwight M. "Cyclical Variations in the Risk Structure of Interest Rates." *Journal of Monetary Economics,* July 1975, pp. 309–25.

Jen, Frank C., and James E. Wert. "The Value of the Deferred Call Privilege." *The National Banking Review,* March 1966, pp. 269–78.

————. "The Effect of Call Risk on Corporate Bond Yields." *Journal of Finance,* December 1967, pp. 637–51.

————. "The Deferred Call Provision and Corporate Bond Yields." *Journal of Financial and Quantitative Analysis,* June 1968, pp. 157–69.

Mehra, Yash. "The Tax Effect, and the Recent Behavior of the After-Tax Real Rate: Is It Too High?" *Economic Review,* Federal Reserve Bank of Richmond, July/August 1984, pp. 8–20.

Mitchell, Karlyn. "Taxation of Corporate Income." *Economic Review,* Federal Reserve Bank of Kansas City, September–October 1983, pp. 7–23.

Pye, Gordon. "The Value of Call Deferment on a Bond: Some Empirical Results." *Journal of Finance,* December 1967, pp. 623–36.

_____. "The Value of the Call Option on a Bond." *Journal of Political Economy,* April 1966, pp. 200–205.

Scott, James. "The Probability of Bankruptcy: A Comparison of Empirical Predictions and Theoretical Models." *Journal of Banking and Finance,* 5 (1981), pp. 317–44.

Wakeman, Lee Macdonald. "The Real Function of Bond Rating Agencies." *Chase Financial Quarterly,* 1, no. 1 (Fall 1981), pp. 18–25.

11

Interest-Rate Patterns, Forecasting, and Hedging in a Dynamic Economy

PURPOSE OF THIS CHAPTER

To examine additional factors, including the business cycle and seasonal fluctuations, that influence interest rates and cause them to change over time. In addition, the chapter reviews various methods used in recent years to predict or forecast interest-rate movements—their strengths and limitations. Finally, the chapter concludes with a brief overview of various techniques developed in recent years to protect lenders and borrowers against losses due to interest-rate fluctuations.

KEY TERMS AND CONCEPTS IN THE CHAPTER

business cycle	flow-of-funds	liquidity effect
consensus forecast	approach	market expectations
duration	forward calendar	rate forecasting
econometric models	gap management	seasonality
expectations effect	hedging	yield curve
financial futures	income effect	
Fisher effect	interest-rate SWAPs	

In this section of the book we have looked at a few of the most important factors that cause interest rates and security prices to change over time. Included in our survey have been such powerful rate- and price-determining factors as savings, investment demand, inflation, maturity, default risk, taxes, marketability, convertibility, and call features. Yet even this impressive list of influential factors does not account for all of the changes in interest rates and security prices that we observe daily in the real world. Political developments at home and abroad, changes in government economic policy, news reports of changes in corporate earnings or business conditions, announcements of new security offerings, and thousands of other bits of information flood the financial markets daily and bring about fluctuations in interest rates and security prices. In fact, for actively traded securities (such as stocks listed on the New York Stock Exchange or U.S. government bonds) demand and supply forces are continually shifting, minute by minute, so that investors interested in these securities must constantly stay abreast of the latest developments in the financial marketplace. Prices and interest rates sometimes change so fast that even a few minutes' delay in receiving new information can mean substantial losses for the uninformed investor.

THE INFLUENCE OF THE BUSINESS CYCLE IN SHAPING INTEREST RATES

Amidst the turmoil of daily movements in interest rates and security prices there are certain long-run factors that seem to create trends or *patterns* in both rates and prices. One of the most obvious of these patterns relates to the *condition of the nation's economy*—whether the economy is in a period of *expansion,* with production, jobs, and income rising (often accompanied by rising inflation) or in a period of *recession,* with falling production and rising unemployment. These phases of the business cycle may last for months or years, in some cases, and interest rates tend to move with them (with short leads or lags), because the demand for and supply of loanable funds changes with the business cycle. *Interest rates tend to fall* (and the prices of bonds and other debt securities rise) *during a business recession, while interest rates typically rise* (and debt security prices fall) *during a period of economic expansion.*[1]

None of this should be particularly surprising. An expansion period encourages both businesses and consumers to borrow more relative to the available supply of loanable funds, and the resulting increase in the demand for loanable funds drives up interest rates. In contrast, during recessions business and consumers become more cautious, reducing their

---

[1] For corroboration of this cyclical pattern of market interest rates, particularly with respect to real interest rates, see especially Holland (1984).

borrowings relative to the available supply of loanable funds and building up their savings as a precaution against possible unemployment, declining sales, and loss of income. Interest rates usually fall during such periods, then, under the combined pressure of reduced credit demands and a larger supply of savings.

This typical cyclical movement in interest rates is illustrated in Exhibit 11–1, which tracks changes in rates (yields) on long-term U.S. Treasury, corporate, and municipal bonds. The U.S. economy entered a recession as the 1970s began, and bonds yields declined sharply after mid-1970, reaching a low point in late 1971. As business sales and employment recovered from this recession, interest rates climbed to new highs, peak-

EXHIBIT 11–1

Average Yields of Long-Term Treasury, Corporate, and Municipal Bonds

SOURCE: *U.S. Treasury Bulletin,* Third Quarter, Fiscal 1983, p. 33.

ing in mid-1974 just after the Oil Embargo. There followed in 1975 one of the worst business recessions since World War II. Declining industrial production and a sharp rise in unemployment were accompanied by a long-term decline in interest rates, which did not cease until the latter half of 1977 in the market for municipal bonds. Then a sharp rebound in economic activity during 1978 and 1979, accompanied by soaring, double-digit inflation, sent interest rates to unprecedented highs early in 1980. However, reflecting once again the powerful influence of the business cycle upon the nation's financial markets, interest rates plummeted rapidly beginning in the spring of 1980 as the economy entered the next business recession, rising during the brief recovery in 1981 before declining sharply in 1982 as another recession occurred. Then interest rates rose in 1983 and through most of 1984 as the economy recovered and grew rapidly. However, interest rates began to retreat in late 1984 and early 1985 as the economy's growth rate slowed, inflation moderated, and loan demand tapered off. More rapid economic growth then set in, and interest rates correspondingly edged higher once again.

Relative Movements in Short- and Long-Term Interest Rates and Security Prices over the Business Cycle

The cyclical movements in the economy do not fall evenly across the broad spectrum of interest rates. In general, short-term interest rates (especially those attached to money market securities) are more volatile and sensitive to business cycle changes than are long-term interest rates on bonds and other capital market securities. Figure 11–1 depicts the typical pattern displayed by long- and short-term interest rates during the course of the business cycle.

During an expansion period, when the economy is growing at a rapid pace, *all* interest rates—both long- and short-term—tend to rise. However, short-term interest rates typically rise faster than long-term rates and at some point, in the later stages of the expansion, may climb *above* long-term rates. This means, of course, that at certain phases of the business cycle, especially around cyclical peaks, borrowers negotiating a loan for, say, six months will actually pay higher annual interest rates than were the same loan to be stretched over 5 or 10 years. Thus, the yield curve typically has a *positive* slope during most of the expansion phase of the business cycle, probably due to expectations of rising interest rates on the part of investors. Around the cyclical peak and in the early stages of the ensuing business recession, however, yield curves usually assume a *negative* slope as investors come to expect declining interest rates. Once the expansion phase of the cycle is over and the economy starts down into a recession, however, *all* rates begin to fall. But, short-term interest rates typically drop faster than long-term rates and fall below

FIGURE 11–1

Interest Rates over the Course of a Business Cycle

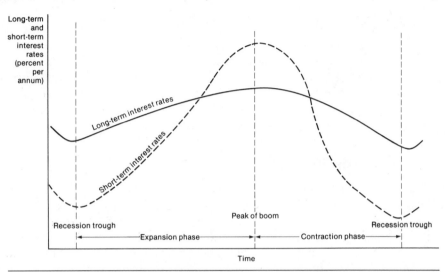

long-term rates as the recession deepens. Thus, at some point midway in a recession the yield curve typically will again assume a *positive* slope. Once the trough (low point) of the recession is reached and recovery begins, the process is repeated with short-term interest rates rising more rapidly than long-term rates.

Why do long-term and short-term interest rates behave in this way? Their behavior reflects another important relationship which exists between security prices and interest rates in the financial system:

> Long-term security prices tend to be more volatile than the prices of short-term securities. In contrast, short-term interest rates tend to be more volatile than long-term interest rates.

Fluctuations in market prices, then, will tend to be greater the longer is the maturity of a security. This conclusion follows logically if we examine closely the yield-to-maturity formula discussed in Chapter 8. This formula indicates that the market price of any security equals the present value of all its promised future payments, but each future payment is discounted by the security's yield. With a long-term security there are more future payments affected by any change in yield than is true for a short-term security. Therefore, a given increase in interest rates will bring about a greater decrease in the price (present value) of a long-term security than in the price of a short-term security. Similarly, for the same decrease in interest rates, the price (present value) of a short-term security will be less affected than the price of a long-term security.

The greater volatility of long-term security prices means that investors in bonds and other long-term financial instruments face greater risk of capital loss (i.e., increased *principal risk*) than investors in short-term securities. Partly as a result, interest rates charged on long-term loans are usually higher than those charged for short-term credit, other things being equal. Lenders must be compensated for the added risk of price fluctuations associated with long-term financial instruments. Of course, the long-term investor has the advantage of receiving a more stable rate of return (i.e., reduced *income risk*) than the short-term investor. Long-term securities generally provide a stable cash flow over an extended period until they are sold or redeemed.

SEASONALITY

Just as interest rates change with cycles in business activity there is some evidence that interest rates also display *seasonal patterns*—tending to be higher at some times of the year than at others. If seasonal rate patterns were consistent and predictable this would be extremely important information for both borrowers and lenders for it would suggest the best times of the year to borrow and lend money. While there is a diversity of opinion on the subject, most studies seem to agree that interest rates *do* display seasonal patterns. In particular, short-term rates tend to be pushed higher through the summer and fall months due to rising seasonal demand for short-term funds, especially as businesses stock their shelves with inventory for the fall. From January through May, on the other hand, slackening demand for short-term credit encourages short-term interest rates to fall, *other factors held equal*. Long-term interest rates, on the other hand, tend to experience upward pressure in the late spring through midsummer (June or July), perhaps related to the higher level of construction activity normally occurring during this time of the year, and then long-term rates approach seasonal lows in the winter months.

Several notes of caution should be added here, however. First, these seasonal patterns are easily overridden by other factors such as changes in the economy or in government economic policy. For example, the Federal Reserve System frequently uses its monetary policy tools to counteract seasonal changes in the supply and demand for loanable funds. Second, limited evidence suggests the observed seasonal patterns are not stable over time.[2] Third, unpredictable events, such as droughts, changes in laws and regulations, political turmoil, and energy crises, often create false signals of seasonal interest-rate pressures. In general, we can

---

[2] See, for example, Kohn (1974) and Barth and Bennett (1975).

say that seasonal interest-rate patterns probably exist, but they are usually of *minor* importance in explaining interest-rate changes.

FORECASTING INTEREST RATES: ADVANTAGES AND PROBLEMS[3]

The tendency of interest rates to move up and down with the business cycle and to some extent with seasonal pressures has led economists and financial analysts to believe that many rate movements can be predicted. By using variables that reflect changing economic conditions—GNP, employment, industrial production, savings flows, consumer prices, and so on—it seems logical to expect that at least broad, longer-term interest-rate movements can be forecast successfully (assuming, of course, that the forecaster has confidence in his forecast of the economy itself).

Advantages of Rate Forecasting

Clearly it would be an advantage to almost everyone (i.e., businesses, consumers, and governments) to be able to accurately forecast interest rates. Borrowers could plan ahead to seek loans at those times when rates were supposed to be the lowest, saving hundreds or thousands of dollars in interest costs. A family considering the purchase of a new home with a variable-rate mortgage would be able to estimate how its monthly payments would change over time and whether the family budget could withstand future rate shifts. The same advantage would accrue to a business firm seeking a variable-rate bank loan to purchase inventories or fund a new warehouse. Banks and other lenders of funds could reduce their exposure to earnings risk and default risk by charging loan rates that were in line with their forecast of deposit rates. They would also be able to assess their borrowing customers' ability to service (i.e., meet future payments on) new floating-rate loans. When a large borrowing customer cannot repay a loan because of rising interest charges, *both* the customer and the bank are subject to greater risk of failure.

Problems in Forecasting Interest Rates

Unfortunately, while the ability to forecast interest rates would be enormously useful to almost everyone at one time or another, the problem is far from easy to solve. For one thing, as we saw in Chapter 7, there is a continuing controversy over which of several possible theories—loanable funds, rational expectations, and so on—explains how and why rates change. Clearly this matters greatly because each theory suggests that

---

[3] This section is based, in part, on Rose's earlier article in the *Canadian Banker* (1984) and is used with the permission of that journal.

we gather somewhat different information about the economy in order to predict which way rates are headed and suggests a different structuring of our forecasting equations. Moreover, if our financial markets are "highly efficient," as much research evidence suggests, all data relevant to where security prices and rates should be is already captured in those prices and rates. The theory of efficient markets implies that to be consistently "right," the forecaster must either have access to data the market does not now possess or "outguess" the market on the implications of new information that has not yet been revealed. This is a most difficult assignment!

An added problem is that the statistical forecasting tools currently at our disposal may be too crude to generate a consistently accurate forecast of rate movements. The reason should be obvious: we live in an economy composed of millions of households, businesses, and units of government who borrow money and generate savings. Each year tens of thousands of these individuals and institutions enter the financial markets to save (i.e., supply loanable funds) or borrow money (i.e., demand loanable funds). Each and every individual financial decision affects either the demand for or supply of loanable funds and, therefore, influences the "price of credit." To really know *for sure* which way interest rates are headed we would need a working model which incorporates those thousands of individual financial decisions. Even the largest most sophisticated econometric forecasting models today—some of which contain several hundred equations and forecast 1,000 or more variables—cannot consistently deal with the enormity of detail in today's financial markets.[4] Perhaps as business and household computers are increasingly linked to each other and a majority of money flows in the economy are handled electronically we may be better able to track credit demand and supply forces and anticipate future rate changes; but that era still lies ahead of us.

APPROACHES TO MODERN INTEREST-RATE FORECASTING

The inherent difficulties in interest-rate and security-price forecasting have not stopped economists and financial analysts from attempting to predict the future. They are impressed by the continual presence of

---

[4] Another problem plaguing forecasters of interest rates is measurement errors in economic data, especially in national income and production data and money-supply statistics. Often large errors are not picked up until revisions are made months later. Unfortunately, the largest econometric forecasting models in use today probably face the most serious data measurement problems because they rely on such huge amounts of current economic data.

broad trends in interest rates, particularly those related to the business cycle and to Federal Reserve monetary policy. A number of forecasting models have been developed in recent years and some have performed at least better than pure chance for short periods of time. Several of the more popular rate forecasting models are reviewed below.

Money-Supply Approaches

Many financial analysts attempt to forecast short-run changes in interest rates, particularly short-term money market rates, by tracking weekly, monthly, and quarterly money-supply figures. Each week the Federal Reserve System releases estimates of recent rates of growth in its various measures of the U.S. money supply. The most prominent of these money-supply measures are: (1) M1, the sum of currency and coin held by the public plus transaction (payments) accounts (such as noninterest-bearing checkbook (demand) deposits and interest-bearing NOW accounts); M2, the sum of M1 plus passbook savings deposits and other small-denomination thrift accounts and deposits; and M3, the sum of M2 plus large-denomination (over $100,000) savings accounts at banks, savings and loans, money market funds, and other nonbank institutions.[5]

We recall from Chapter 7 that changes in the money-supply can be linked in theory to interest-rate changes in several different ways. For example, the so-called *liquidity effect* suggests that an increase in money-supply growth (relative to money demand) results in lower interest rates in the short run. On the other hand, slower money growth (relative to money demand) should lead to short-run increases in interest rates. A contrary force, the *expectations effect,* argues that, when the actual money-supply growth rate exceeds the public's expected rate of money growth, interest rates will tend to *rise,* perhaps due to the public's fear of more inflation. Conversely, a slower-than-expected money growth rate will lead to *lower* interest rates. Many financial analysts believe the expectations effect has become more important than the liquidity effect since the Federal Reserve System announced in October 1979 that it would begin to concentrate its efforts on hitting preannounced money-supply targets during the year. Thus, when actual money growth exceeds the Fed's announced target growth range, the public may fear that the Fed will attempt to slow future money growth and drive up interest rates. In contrast, actual money-supply growth below the Fed's target range may lead the public to predict lower interest rates in the future as the Federal Reserve accelerates money growth to catch up to its target.

---

[5] See Chapter 24 for a more complete discussion of these and other measures of the nation's money supply or money stock.

Which of these effects—the liquidity effect or the expectations effect—better explain observed rate movements? One very rough test of these two competing views is provided in Exhibit 11–2 which compares the monthly rate of growth in the M1 and M2 measures of the U.S. money supply during 1984 and early 1985 with the monthly average interest rate on federal funds loans that banks make to each other.[6] In this case money-supply growth is lagged one month behind the federal funds rate to provide a lead rate forecast of one month. If the liquidity effect predominated over this particular time period, the federal funds rate should rise when money-supply growth falls and decline when money growth increases. A dominant expectations effect, on the other hand, would result in money-supply growth and the federal funds interest rate rising and falling together. And, indeed, in 6 of 14 months reported in Exhibit 11–2 lagged money growth and the federal funds rate do, in fact, change in the *same* direction (as shown by the arrows drawn in the exhibit), consistent with the expectations effect. However, in 8 of those 14 months money growth and the funds rate moved in opposite directions as suggested by the liquidity effect. A strong note of caution is appropriate here, however, because both the strength and direction of the money-interest rate relationship may vary over time.

We may recall from our discussion of interest-rate theories in Chapter 7 that money-supply changes can also influence interest rates through an *income effect*. Specifically, an increase in total spending and income in the economy increases the public's demand for money, other factors held constant. If the nation's money supply remains fixed or grows more slowly than money demand, the relative increase in money demand will lead to higher interest rates. Conversely, a decline or slower growth in money demand—perhaps related to a slowing of income growth in the economy—will put downward pressure on interest rates, other factors held constant. Clearly, there should be a *positive* correlation between income and spending in the economy and market interest rates through income-caused changes in the demand for money if the income effect is controlling. And, such a positive relationship between total spending and interest rates *does* seem to hold over the course of most business cycles, as we noted at the beginning of this chapter.

How might an interest-rate forecaster use the *income effect?* Let's suppose the federal government or a professional forecasting firm has just released an estimate that nominal GNP—a widely used barometer

---

[6] See Chapter 14 for a discussion of the federal funds market and federal funds loans. For a recent investigation and corroboration of the short-term liquidity effect between money-supply changes and interest rates, see Hafer and Hein (1982).

EXHIBIT 11–2

Money-Supply Growth Rates and the Interest Rate on Federal Funds Loans, 1984 and 1985 (All figures are expressed in annualized percentage rates)

Money-supply growth rates:

	Jan. 1984	Feb. 1984	Mar. 1984	Apr. 1984	May 1984	June 1984	July 1984	Aug. 1984	Sept. 1984	Oct. 1984	Nov. 1984	Dec. 1984	Jan. 1985	Feb. 1985
M1, lagged 1 month	8.0	6.5	7.2	4.3	7.6	11.1	−0.9	4.5	5.8	−7.0	12.0	10.2	9.0	14.1
M2, lagged 1 month	2.6	8.3	6.8	6.2	7.8	2.8	6.0	6.8	8.4	5.5	14.0	13.1	13.6	10.5

Interest rate on federal funds loans, current month:

	Feb. 1984	Mar. 1984	Apr. 1984	May 1984	June 1984	July 1984	Aug. 1984	Sept. 1984	Oct. 1984	Nov. 1984	Dec. 1984	Jan. 1985	Feb. 1985	Mar.* 1985
	9.59	9.91	10.29	10.32	11.06	11.23	11.64	11.30	9.99	8.83	8.38	8.35	8.50	8.40

* Average for week ending March 1, 1985.
SOURCE: Board of Governors of the Federal Reserve System, *Federal Reserve Bulletin*, various monthly issues; and Federal Reserve Bank of St. Louis, *Monetary Trends*, various monthly issues.

of total spending in the economy—will increase at an 8 percent annual rate next year. However, the Federal Reserve System has just announced that its target range for growth in the nation's money supply (something they must reveal at least twice a year) is going to be just 4 to 6 percent next year. If the money supply does, in fact, grow this slowly while the public plans to increase its aggregate spending (GNP) by 8 percent, what must happen to interest rates? Clearly, they must *rise* to bring about a faster rate of turnover (velocity) in the money supply in order to accommodate the higher volume of planned spending.[7]

Of course, if the Fed achieves its relatively low money growth target, it is highly unlikely that GNP will be able to increase a full 8 percentage points because the resulting higher interest rates will discourage some borrowing and spending by the public. However, the point is that we can get a clue about the *direction* of future interest-rate changes by comparing money-supply growth estimates for a future period with forecasts of economic activity for that same period (assuming, of course, that we have confidence in *both* the money-supply and economic forecasts). Thus,

1. If projected money-supply growth > projected GNP growth, interest rates are likely to *fall*.
2. If projected money-supply growth < projected GNP growth, interest rates are likely to *rise*.

Inflation and the Fisher Effect

In Chapter 9 we discussed still another possible approach to interest-rate forecasting; that is, the *Fisher effect,* which asserts that *the nominal (published) interest rate charged by a lender of funds must equal the lender's expected real rate of return on the loan plus the expected rate of inflation over the life of the loan.* Many economists, including Irving Fisher, have argued that the expected real rate is relatively constant—perhaps in the 3 to 3.5 percent range—in the long run. If true, observed changes in nominal interest rates will tend to reflect changes in the rate of inflation expected by lenders in the financial marketplace.

The table below suggests a simple rate-forecasting strategy using the Fisher effect:

---

[7] For a detailed discussion of the theoretical and empirical linkages between money-supply growth and fluctuations in income and production in the economy, see especially Poole (1975).

Forecasting Interest Rates Using the Fisher Effect (percent)

If lenders in the marketplace expect the inflation rate over the coming year to average	And the real rate of interest is expected to be	Then the nominal interest rate on a one-year loan according to the Fisher effect will be
1%	3 to 3.5%	4 to 4.5%
2	3 to 3.5	5 to 5.5
3	3 to 3.5	6 to 6.5
4 ·	3 to 3.5	7 to 7.5
5	3 to 3.5	8 to 8.5
6	3 to 3.5	9 to 9.5

Of course, a key problem with this approach is estimating the rate of inflation *expected* by lenders over the life of a loan or security. Unfortunately there is little agreement at this point on the most accurate method of making such an estimate. One commonly used approach is to calculate a weighted average of past rates of inflation (often with declining weights so that more recent inflation news is more heavily weighted) and use that average as a proxy for expected inflation. This is a crude approximation because we do not know exactly what factors the public considers in formulating its inflation forecast. Undoubtedly, past rates of inflation do influence public expectations concerning future inflation, but other factors (such as the outcome of presidential elections, unemployment, and the performance of the stock market) also are likely to play a role in such forecasts. More recently, periodic surveys of economists and investors have been used to represent inflationary expectations in the marketplace, but such an approach suffers from being both incomplete and irrelevant. Expectations often change so fast that any opinion survey can be outdated even before its results are published.

Econometric Models

The four interest-rate relationships we have discussed to this point—the liquidity, expectations, income, and Fisher effects—have been used in a large number of interest-rate forecasting models consisting of one or more equations. These so-called *econometric models* developed by economists and financial analysts over the years often employ current and lagged values of money, income or total spending, and past rates of inflation to predict short- and long-term interest rates through the application of least-squares regression techniques.[8] The larger models

---

[8] For readers unfamiliar with the regression technique, see Cooley and Lohnes (1971) or any comprehensive statistics text.

EXHIBIT 11–3

Linking Interest Rates to the Economy in Major Econometric Models

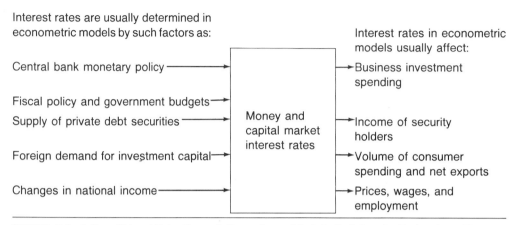

Interest rates are usually determined in econometric models by such factors as:

Central bank monetary policy ⟶

Fiscal policy and government budgets ⟶
Supply of private debt securities ⟶

Foreign demand for investment capital ⟶

Changes in national income ⟶

Money and capital market interest rates

Interest rates in econometric models usually affect:

⟶ Business investment spending

⟶ Income of security holders

⟶ Volume of consumer spending and net exports

⟶ Prices, wages, and employment

SOURCE: Peter S. Rose, "Interest Rates, Economic Forecasting and Bank Profits," *Canadian Banker,* June 1984.

simultaneously measure changes in total spending for goods and services, consumption and investment, inflation, government policy, exports and imports, employment, wages and salaries, credit demands, supplies of securities and capital goods, and a broad spectrum of interest rates, forecasting several variables simultaneously and considering interactions among both predictor and predicted variables. Among the best-known of such models are those used by Chase Econometric Associates (CHASE), Data Resources, Inc. (DRI), and Wharton Econometric Forecasting Associates, Inc. (WEFA). Such models are truly impressive in their complexity and detail; for example, the DRI model forecasts approximately 1,000 financial and economic variables, while the Wharton model in use since 1963 forecasts about 10,000 different variables. The complex interactions in such models between forecast variables (such as interest rates and the nation's income) and causal factors (such as government monetary and fiscal policy, and the supply of securities) are illustrated in Exhibit 11–3.

An example of a relatively simple econometric model prepared by the Federal Reserve Bank of St. Louis is shown in Exhibit 11–4. This simple model contains only eight basic equations and generates quarterly forecasts for seven essential economic and financial variables: *(a)* the level of nominal (current dollar) GNP; *(b)* the annual rate of change in nominal GNP; *(c)* the annual rate of change in real (constant dollar) GNP; *(d)* the annual rate of change in the general price level; *(e)* the U.S. unemployment rate; and two interest rates—*(f)* the rate (or yield) on Aaa corporate bonds; and *(g)* the four- to six-month commercial paper rate. The type of interest-rate forecasting equations used in this short econometric model is illustrated by the equation below which tracks the long-term Aaa corporate bond rate—a key capital market interest rate:

$$
\begin{array}{l}
\text{Moody's seasoned} \\
\text{corporate Aaa} \\
\text{bond rate in} \\
\text{quarter t}
\end{array}
= 1.28 - .06
\left[
\begin{array}{l}
\text{Annual rate} \\
\text{of change in} \\
\text{money stock, t}
\end{array}
\right]
+ 1.42
\left[
\begin{array}{l}
\text{Dummy variable} \\
\text{representing} \\
\text{specific time} \\
\text{periods}
\end{array}
\right]
$$

$$
+ \sum_{}^{16} a_i
\left[
\begin{array}{l}
\text{Annual rate of} \\
\text{change in real} \\
\text{output in the} \\
\text{economy, t-i}
\end{array}
\right]
+ \sum_{i=0}^{16} b_i
\left[
\begin{array}{l}
\text{Annual rate of} \\
\text{change in the U.S.} \\
\text{price level (GNP} \\
\text{deflator) divided} \\
\text{by the U.S.} \\
\text{unemployment} \\
\text{rate index, t-i}
\end{array}
\right]
$$

Careful inspection of the above equation reveals the prominent role that changes in the nation's money stock (reflecting primarily the liquidity effect), changes in the nation's income or output (reflecting primarily the income effect), and changes in the price level relative to unemployment (reflecting expectations and Fisher effects among other influences) are believed to play today in influencing interest rates.

While econometric models are all somewhat different from one another and their forecasts are often at odds with each other, a few generalizations can be made about their content and interest-rate predictions. For example, econometric models nearly always contain a money-supply or monetary policy variable and show that an easier money and credit policy by the government leads to lower interest rates for periods stretching from about six months to one year. In contrast, when credit tightens up, interest rates (especially money market rates) climb higher for roughly 6 to 12 months. In most models interest rates (particularly short-term rates) react quickly, if not immediately, to the change toward tight or easy money policy, but as the months go by rates begin to move back toward their original levels. And, if the public believes inflation will increase, interest rates may rebound higher than they were at the beginning of the forecast period. Much depends on how much excess capacity there is in the economy at the time a government policy change occurs. And, of course, there are always feedback effects from the economy to the financial markets. Thus, higher interest rates reduce business investment spending, the building and buying of new homes, and spending by consumers (especially for durable items); however, a slowdown in spending generally reduces credit demands and eventually leads to lower interest rates, according to the structure of most major econometric models.

It is difficult to generalize concerning the track record of econometric forecasting models. As McNees (1981) notes, different models have had different degrees of success depending on which variable is being forecast. Moreover, some are superior at forecasting short-run changes and others perform better over the long range. However, there has been much dissatisfaction in the business community in recent years with the models' poor track record at spotting major turning points in the economy and at handling external shocks, such as the Oil Embargo of 1973–74. Despite the enormous complexity of some of these models, the economy and

EXHIBIT 11–4

An Example of an Econometric Forecasting Model: The Monetarist Model
of the Federal Reserve Bank of St. Louis

Equations Making up the Model

1. Total spending:

$$\Delta Y_t = f_1 [\Delta M_t, \cdots, \Delta M_{t-n}, \Delta E_t, \cdots, \Delta E_{t-n}]$$

2. Price equation:

$$\Delta P_t = f_2 [D_t, \cdots, D_{t-n}, \Delta P_t^A]$$

3. Demand pressure identity:

$$D_t = \Delta Y_t - (X_t^F - X_{t-1})$$

4. Total spending identity:

$$\Delta Y_t = \Delta P_t + \Delta X_t$$

5. Interest-rate equation:

$$R_t = f_3 (\Delta M_t, \Delta X_t, \cdots, \Delta X_{t-n}, \Delta P_t, \Delta P_t^A)$$

6. Anticipated price equation:

$$\Delta P_t^A = f_4 (\Delta P_{t-1}, \cdots, \Delta P_{t-n})$$

7. Unemployment rate equation:

$$U_t = f_5 (G_t, G_{t-1})$$

8. GNP gap identity:

$$G_t = \frac{X_t^F - X_t}{X_t^F}$$

Endogenous (Forecast) Variables	**Exogenous Variables**
ΔY_t = Change in total spending (nominal GNP)	ΔM_t = Change in nation's money stock
ΔP_t = Change in price level (GNP price deflator)	ΔE_t = Change in high-employment federal expenditures
D_t = Demand pressure	X_t^F = Potential (full-employment) output of goods and services in the U.S.
ΔX_t = Change in the nation's output (real GNP)	
R_t = Market interest rate	
ΔP_t^A = Anticipated change in price level	
U_t = Unemployment rate	
G_t = GNP gap	

EXHIBIT 11–4 *(concluded)*

Flow Diagram of the St. Louis Econometric Model

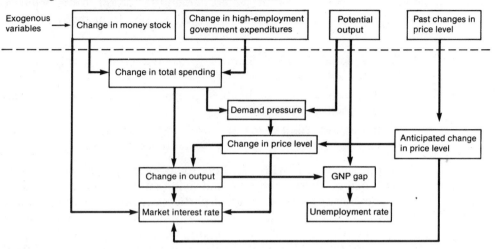

SOURCE: Leonall C. Anderson and Keith M. Carlson, "A Monetarist Model for Economic Stabilization," *Review*, Federal Reserve Bank of St. Louis, April 1970, pp. 7–25.

the financial markets they are designed to mirror are infinitely more complex. As the U.S. experience with the 1973–74 Oil Embargo suggests, the real-world economy is subject to unexpected political and social changes that no mathematical model can adequately duplicate. Indeed, it is surprising that many econometric models work as well as they do.

The Flow of Funds Accounts as a Source of Forecasting Information

Still another rate-forecasting approach which depends upon forecasts of other variables is the loanable-funds or flow of funds approach. The basic idea is to *estimate* total demand for credit from different borrowing sectors in the economy *assuming that interest rates remain at current levels.* This might be done, for example, by extrapolating past growth trends in the volume of business loans, consumer loans, government borrowing, and foreign borrowing into future time periods. The Flow of Funds Accounts (discussed in Chapter 3) can be used to provide historical data with which to make such future estimates. Similarly, we can estimate the projected supply of credit from key financial institutions such as commercial banks, savings and loan associations, insurance companies, finance companies, and pension funds. An example of such estimates is shown in Exhibit 11–5.

Once derived, the total projected demand for credit in the economy can be compared to total estimated credit supply. If, at today's level of interest rates,

1. Projected credit demand > projected credit supply, interest rates will tend to *rise.*
2. Projected credit demand < projected credit supply, interest rates will tend to *fall.*
3. Projected credit demand = projected credit supply implies that interest rates will remain essentially *unchanged.*

This approach is used with variations today by such well-known institutions as Bankers Trust Company and Salomon Brothers. It provides a useful benchmark for other forecasts, particularly in suggesting the direction of future rate changes, and can be used to predict yield spreads between various sectors of the economy. One obvious drawback of this forecasting method is that numerous estimates of various sources of credit supply and credit demand must be made, increasing the forecaster's opportunities for error.

Following the Forward Calendar of New Security Offerings

One of the rate-determining variables included in the larger econometric models is the supply of debt securities being offered in the open market at any given time. Theory suggests that an increase in offerings of *new* corporate, municipal, or U.S. Treasury notes and bonds would drive interest rates higher because these offerings represent additional demand for credit. Conversely, when the volume of new debt offerings declines, the lessened demand for credit should lead to lower interest rates, *ceteris paribus.*

This is the reason many market analysts follow the announced *forward calendar* of new security offerings expected to come to market in coming weeks. Such information is regularly reported in *The Wall Street Journal* and other leading financial newssheets and magazines. Indeed, Exhibit 11–6 gives an example of a recent forward calendar of planned security offerings as it appeared in *The Wall Street Journal.* Any indication that the market is becoming "clogged" with increased quantities of yet to be sold notes and bonds, especially when security dealers are reporting heavy inventories of already issued but unsold securities, usually triggers a forecast of rising interest rates and falling security prices in the near-term. Similarly, the huge federal government budget deficits in recent

EXHIBIT 11–5

Using the Loanable Funds Theory of Interest Rates and the Federal
Reserve's Flow of Funds Accounts to Forecast Interest Rates

	Predicted Amounts ($ billions)
1. Estimate ex ante *demands* for credit in the economy at today's interest rates from:	
a. Dometic business firms:	
Estimated short-term (working capital) loans	$ 70
Estimated long-term (plant and equipment) loans	40
Nonresidential mortgage credit demand	30
b. Households:	
Estimated nonmortgage installment loans	50
Estimated residential mortgage credit demand	100
c. Governmental units:	
Estimated federal government credit demand	160
Estimated federal agency borrowings	20
Estimated state and local government borrowings	50
d. Foreign units (businesses and governments)	
Estimated foreign borrowing in U.S. financial markets	60
Total estimated credit demands	$580
2. Estimate ex ante *supplies* of credit in the economy at today's interest rates from:	
a. Depository institutions:	
Estimated commercial bank credit supplied	$100
Estimated savings and loan and savings bank credit	50
Estimated credit union loans	10
b. Pension funds and insurance companies:	
Estimated credit provided by private and public pensions	40
Estimated credit provided by life and property-casualty insurers	50
c. Estimated credit supplied by other financial institutions:	
Investment company credit supplied	30
Finance company credit supplied	20
Miscellaneous lending institutions	30
d. Estimated direct loans from nonfinancial sectors of the economy	120
e. Estimated residual funds sources and statistical discrepancy	50
Total estimated credit supplies	$500
3. Estimated excess credit demand (+) or excess credit supply (−) at today's interest rates	+$ 80

Interpretation: Excess credit demand (+) implies *rising* interest rates; excess credit supply
(−) implies *falling* interest rates.

EXHIBIT 11–6

An Example of a Forward Calendar of New Security Offerings from
The Wall Street Journal

Record Refinancing By Treasury to Take New-Issue Spotlight

By a WALL STREET JOURNAL *Staff Reporter*

NEW YORK—The Treasury's record $20.5 billion quarterly financing operation will take center stage in the new-issue markets this week.

The package consists of $8 billion of three-year notes to be auctioned tomorrow, $6.5 billion of 10-year notes to be sold Wednesday, and $6 billion of 29¾-year bonds scheduled for sale Thursday.

A heavy volume of new state and local government bond offerings is also slated for sale this week. A report by Salomon Brothers estimates about $2.3 billion of new municipal issues this week, compared with nearly $2.2 billion last week.

The following U.S. Treasury, corporate and municipal offerings are tentatively scheduled for sale this week, as compiled by Dow Jones Capital Markets Report:

U.S. TREASURY

Today

$14 billion of 13-week and 26-week bills.

Tuesday

$8 billion of three-year notes.

Wednesday

$6.5 billion of 10-year notes.

Thursday

$6 billion of 29¾-year bonds.

CORPORATE

One Day This Week

Americare Health Corp.—initial offering of 2.5 million common shares, via First Boston Corp.

Applied Data Research Inc.—one million common shares, via Dean Witter Reynolds Inc.

Denmark—150 million European currency units of floating-rate notes, due May 15, 1990, via Salomon Brothers Inc.

Mobile Communications Corp. of America—$30 million of convertible debentures, due 2005, via Bear, Stearns & Co.

Sbarro Inc.—initial offering of one million common shares, via Prudential-Bache Securities Inc.

Simmons Airlines Inc.—one million common shares, via Prudential-Bache.

Staley Continental Inc.—$300 million of convertible, zero-coupon notes, due 2001, to raise about $75 million for the company, via Merrill Lynch Capital Markets.

Textron Inc.—$125 million of notes, due 1995, and separately, $125 million of debentures, due 2010, via Morgan Stanley & Co.

Today

Tempe Union High School District No. 213, Maricopa County, Ariz.—$25 million of school improvement bonds.

Tomorrow

New Jersey—$455 million of various-purpose bonds, rated triple-A by Moody's Investors Service Inc.

Florida State Board of Education—$100 million of public education capital outlay bonds, rated double-A by Standard & Poor's Corp.

Wednesday

Mesa, Ariz.—$67.5 million of improvement and utility systems revenue bonds.

Dallas—$43.3 million of improvement bonds, rated triple-A by both Moody's and S&P.

Thursday

Connecticut—$50 million of various-purpose bonds.

One Day This Week

Puerto Rico Public Finance Corp.—$400 million of fixed-rate and variable-rate bonds, via Chase Manhattan Capital Markets Corp.

New York (State) Triborough Bridge and Tunnel Authority—$400 million of refunding revenue bonds, via Lazard Freres & Co.

Florida Housing Finance Authority—$150 million of single-family mortgage revenue bonds, via E.F. Hutton & Co.

Dade County, Fla., Housing Finance Agency—$56.3 million of single-family mortgage revenue bonds, via Shearson Lehman Brothers Inc.

Pima, Ariz., Industrial Development Authority—$52 million of single-family mortgage revenue bonds, via Rauscher Pierce Refsnes Inc.

Nevada Housing Finance Agency—$33 million of multifamily mortgage revenue bonds, via Goldman, Sachs & Co.

SOURCE: *The Wall Street Journal,* May 6, 1985, p. 47.

years have led many financial analysts to carefully scrutinize congressional reports, press releases, and budget data from the U.S. Treasury (as reported, for example, in *The Treasury Bulletin*) to estimate whether the government's need for new cash appears to be rising or falling. Increased Treasury borrowing requirements frequently lead to near-term increases in government security rates and increases in other market yields as well.

Market Expectations and Rate Forecasting

Our discussion of the rational expectations theory of interest rates in Chapter 7 and the expectations hypothesis of the yield curve in Chapter 9 suggests the critical role that shifting public opinion about the future can play in influencing the financial markets. We recall from our earlier discussion of the expectations hypothesis, for example, that the slope of the yield curve itself implies a forecast of interest-rate changes expected by the public.

For example, suppose that 30-day maturity U.S. Treasury bills are currently selling in the market to yield 10 percent, while 60-day bills carry current yields of 10.5 percent. This obvious upward slope in the short-term yield curve carries an implied forecast of what investors in the market expect Treasury bill rates to be in the next 30 days. Specifically, the 30-day bill rate 30 days from now is expected to be

$$\frac{\text{Current 30-day Treasury bill rate} + \text{30-day forward (expected) Treasury bill rate}}{2} = \text{Current 60-day Treasury bill rate}$$

or

$$\frac{10.0\% + \text{30-day forward (expected) Treasury bill rate}}{2} = 10.50\%$$

and, thus,

$$\text{30-day forward (expected) rate on bills} = 11.00\%$$

The yield curve is forecasting an 11 percent, 30-day Treasury bill rate one month from today. Why? Because, according to the expectations hypothesis about the yield curve, investors in an efficient market should earn the same average return over the next 60 days whether they buy a 10.5 percent, 60-day Treasury bill today or a 10 percent, 30-day Treasury bill today followed by an 11 percent, 30-day bill purchased one month from now.

Actually a more accurate forecast of the forward rate implied by the current slope of the yield curve can be found by using the formula

$$_{t+n}r_{kt} = \left[\frac{(1 + _tR_{n+kt})^{n+k}}{(1 + _tR_{nt})^n}\right]^{1/k} - 1$$

where the security whose rate is being forecast covers k periods and the loan to the borrower begins at time t + n. (This formula is derived from solving Equation 9–4 in Chapter 9 for any future k-period loan rate.) For the Treasury bill whose rate we were trying to forecast in the example above, we are working with a loan period of length 30 days, beginning 30 days from now. Therefore we can let k = 1, meaning one 30-day loan period, and n = 1, meaning the 30-day loan whose rate we wish to forecast begins one 30-day period after the current 30-day loan period. Thus:

$$_{t+1}r_{1t} = \left[\frac{(1.1050)^2}{(1.10)^1}\right]^{1/1} - 1 = \frac{1.221}{1.10} - 1 = 0.11 \text{ or } 11\%$$

Another implied market forecast of future changes in interest rates is conveyed by current prices on *financial futures contracts*—a subject discussed more fully in Chapter 17. A financial futures contract is an agreement between a buyer and a seller to deliver a designated amount and type of securities days, weeks, or months in the future but at a price agreed upon today. Thus, we might assume that current prices on such contracts reflect security traders' and investors' expectations about the levels of interest rates and security prices around the future delivery date of the securities mentioned in the futures contract. In general, the interest rate (or yield) in the futures market will be higher than the interest rate (or yield) on the same security in the cash market if interest rates are expected to rise; conversely, the futures market rate (or yield) will be below the rate (or yield) on the same security in the cash market if interest rates are expected to fall.

For example, *The Wall Street Journal* reported that contracts for the delivery of $1 million in U.S. Treasury bills in December 1984 were selling for $88.65 (assuming a $100 face value) on July 18, 1984. This price translated into an interest yield of 11.35 percent if the Treasury bill were held to maturity. In contrast, Treasury bills of comparable maturity available for immediate (cash) delivery were selling in the open market on July 18 for a yield of 10.30 percent. Clearly, investors in bill futures contracts were signaling an expectation of *rising* short-term interest rates between July and December 1984.

The Consensus Forecast

While expectations models are useful barometers of current market opinion, the financial market forecaster must recognize their inherent limitations. They give us a reading only on what the marketplace—the average investor—expects, but not necessarily on what *will* happen. Expectations are often disappointed; other factors often intrude to upset the most convincing of forecasts. Indeed, no one rate-forecasting method has yet demonstrated its consistent superiority over the others. Perhaps the safest approach is for the forecaster to use several different methods, checking to see if there is a *consensus forecast* that emerges from a variety of different approaches. Still, the forecasting process is laden with difficulties and uncertainties. Many analysts today confine their forecasts to rate predictions only one or two months in advance, with constant checking and revision as new information appears.

INTEREST–RATE HEDGING STRATEGIES

The increasingly volatile interest rates in recent years coupled with the inherent difficulties of rate forecasting have led many individuals and institutions to find ways to *insulate* themselves from interest-rate changes. If rate changes cannot be accurately or reliably forecast, it may be possible to *hedge* against the damaging effects of increasing or decreasing interest rates. While several rate hedging methods have been developed, there is a "price" for such interest-rate insurance: *hedging lowers interest-rate risk, but also reduces the potential profits that could be earned by correctly anticipating the direction and magnitude of interest-rate changes.*

Duration

In Chapter 9 we discussed the concept of duration—a time-weighted, present value measure of the maturity of a loan or security portfolio. In that chapter we pointed out that an investor could *immunize* his or her portfolio against interest-rate changes simply by setting the

$$\begin{array}{l} \text{Duration of} \\ \text{a loan or} \\ \text{security} \\ \text{portfolio} \end{array} = \begin{array}{l} \text{Length of the} \\ \text{investor's} \\ \text{planned holding} \\ \text{period} \end{array}$$

With this investment strategy a rise in interest rates will reduce the market value of our investor's portfolio, but the interest return on reinvested cash flows from the portfolio will increase by a corresponding amount. Thus, the investor's total return from the loan or security portfolio will be stabilized. Similarly, falling interest rates reduce interest returns from reinvesting the earnings from loans or securities, but with duration set equal to holding-period length the market value of those loans or securities will rise by a corresponding amount. Again, the total return will be stabilized. For a financial institution (such as a bank) which both borrows and lends funds simultaneously, a good immunizing strategy is to set:

$$\text{Asset duration} = \text{Liability duration}$$

In this case changes in interest rates should affect both the institution's assets and liabilities *equally*.

Unfortunately, as we also saw in Chapter 9, duration has its limitations. It is often difficult to find desirable loans or securities with durations exactly matching the investor's holding period. Moreover, the theory of duration assumes parallel changes in all interest rates (both short and long term) and it is not clear how effective this hedging strategy will be if interest rates don't behave in such lock-step fashion. Fortunately there are other hedging devices which can serve as a backstop to duration.

GAP Management

A very popular interest-rate hedging strategy among banks and other financial institutions is known as interest-sensitivity analysis (ISA) or GAP management. The basic strategy is to set

$$\begin{array}{c}\text{Interest-sensitive} \\ \text{asset holdings}\end{array} = \begin{array}{c}\text{Interest-sensitive} \\ \text{liabilities}\end{array}$$

For example, a commercial bank holding deposits whose interest rates rise along with increases in market rates could hold an equal volume of floating-rate loans. Thus, when the bank's deposit interest costs increased in a rising-rate period, interest revenues from loans would increase by a similar amount, thereby protecting the bank's *net interest margin* (or gap) between its revenues and its expenses.

There are several problems with "gapping," however. Borrowers may resist accepting loans whose rate continually fluctuates with market conditions. In practice, it is often difficult (if not impossible) to exactly match interest-sensitive assets with interest-sensitive liabilities at every maturity. And, any mismatches threaten the investor's net return from lending.

Moreover, the choice of the time horizon over which to measure the interest-rate sensitivity of assets and liabilities seems to affect significantly the measurement of each institution's exposure to interest-rate changes and, therefore, management's response to the problem.

Financial Futures Contracts

In the middle and late 1970s still another interest-rate hedging device was developed—trading in financial futures. The basic futures rate-hedging strategy calls for offsetting purchases (sales) of securities in the cash (spot) market with sales (purchases) of an equal amount of contracts on a futures exchange. Then, if interest rates rise, securities purchased in the cash market will fall in price, but an offsetting profit will be made in the futures market because the futures contract can be honored with lower-priced securities or canceled out with a lower-priced futures contract. We will explore the delicate "ins" and "outs" of futures trading in Chapter 17.

Interest-Rate SWAPs

Finally, early in the 1980s a new interest-rate hedging strategy—the interest-rate SWAP—became popular. SWAPs are based on the fact that rate spreads related to default risk are generally *greater* in the long-term capital market than they are in the short-term money market. Interest-rate SWAPs enable a lender to earn a stable net interest return merely for "intermediating" a credit deal between borrowers with different credit ratings without committing large amounts of funds to a full-scale loan.

Consider the case where a top-rated corporation can borrow in the bond market at the lowest AAA bond rate, while a lower credit-rated company is charged perhaps prime or LIBOR plus a full 1 percent or more on a short-term loan from a bank.[9] A bank or other lending institution might aid these two firms by helping the top-rated firm sell long-term bonds in the open market at a low coupon rate and getting the lower-rated company to agree to make the top-rated firm's bond interest payments. At the same time the top-rated firm pays the lower-rated company's LIBOR or prime-based borrowing rate which, because it is a short-term interest rate, often is lower than bond rates and certainly is more flexible. Thus, *both* firms may wind up with lower interest costs and the lower-rated company has, in effect, replaced a variable loan rate

---

[9] LIBOR stands for London Interbank Offer Rate and is the basic deposit interest rate in the Eurodollar market, used as the basis for setting loan rates to major corporations. See Chapter 16 for a discussion of the Eurodollar loan and deposit markets.

with a fixed loan rate. And, the lending institution bringing the two firms together earns a fee based on the difference in loan rates between the top-rated and lower-rated firms.

SUMMARY AND CONCLUSIONS

In this chapter we have discussed the close relationship that exists between changes in interest rates and the cycle of business expansion and recession in the economy. Interest rates tend to rise in periods of economic expansion with short-term rates generally increasing faster than long-term rates. Conversely, recessions typically bring falling interest rates with, again, short-term rates declining more rapidly than long-term rates. This cyclical pattern in rates suggests to many economists and financial analysts that interest rates can be forecast by looking at factors reflecting the state of the economy plus other determining variables. However, as we have discovered in this chapter, interest-rate forecasting is at best a difficult art. No single theory of interest rate changes and no single factor accounts for *all* the changes in security prices and rates we observe all the time. And no forecast, however well constructed, is likely to be completely accurate or totally reliable. The economy and the millions of individual decision-making units—businesses, households, and governments—that make it up offer too many opportunities for the most carefully drawn assumptions to go awry.

Still, interest-rate theory focuses our attention upon a limited set of factors that need to be watched in conjunction with any rate forecast. These key rate-influencing factors include the *liquidity effect* of changes in the nation's money supply, suggesting that money-supply expansion may produce lower rates in the near-term if money demand is fixed or changes slowly. The *expectations effect* of money-supply changes contends that, if money growth exceeds the public's expectations, interest rates may well rise because the public may fear worsening inflation and more restrictive government policies. The *income effect* of money-supply changes suggests that the growth of income and spending raises money demand and ultimately interest rates. The *supply effect* of new security offerings argues that an increase in planned new security offerings is an indicator of added credit demands and, other things equal, tends to push interest rates higher in the short run.

Expected inflation also affects interest rates because, according to the *Fisher effect*, a rise in the rate of inflation expected by lenders of funds over the life of a loan or security causes a rise in the nominal (published) rate of interest attached to that security or loan, especially for longer-term financial instruments. Another factor in rate forecasting is *estimated credit demands* captured by changes in gross national product, personal income, factory output, retail sales, consumption spending, business investment plans, and other measures of spending and production in the economy. Rising credit demands suggest the onset of higher interest rates unless offset by an increasing supply of credit funds. Finally, *public expectations* regarding future interest rates, security prices, unemployment, spending, and future government policies all exert powerful effects on the bond and stock markets and must be weighed in the forecasting process.

The great difficulties inherent in forecasting interest rates have led many borrowers and lenders of funds to practice *interest-rate hedging,* thereby insulating themselves at least partially from the ravages of fluctuating interest costs and returns. Among the more popular rate-hedging devices are the use of *duration* analysis, which weights the maturity of loans and securities by the timing of their cash payments, and GAP management. Interest-rate hedging with duration requires that a lender match the length of his or her holding period to the duration of the securities he or she holds. GAP management, on the other hand, requires an individual or institution to match the volume of their interest-sensitive assets to the volume of liabilities they hold that are also sensitive to interest-rate changes. The goal of GAP management is to protect a lender's net interest margin, that is, the difference between his or her returns on assets and the cost of borrowed funds. Interest-rate hedging may also be done using *financial futures contracts* in which cash transactions are matched by futures contracts calling for the future sale or purchase of the same securities. Finally, hedging has also been used by banks making large corporate loans through *interest-rate SWAPs* which give the lender a fixed return no matter which way interest rates move in the financial marketplace. Each hedging strategy has important limitations, but those limitations may be outweighed in those cases where borrowers and lenders are significantly exposed to the vagaries of a volatile financial marketplace.

STUDY QUESTIONS

1. Describe the relationship between changes in economic activity and interest rates. Why do interest rates often rise during a period of economic expansion and fall when the economy is in a recession?

2. How do long- and short-term rates usually behave over the course of a business cycle? Which rises or falls at a faster rate? Can you explain why?

3. Why are interest rates so difficult to forecast? What advantages can you identify from being able to forecast rates successfully?

4. Explain the meaning of the following terms:
   a. Liquidity effect.
   b. Expectations effect.
   c. Income effect.
   d. Fisher effect.
   Describe how each might be used to forecast or predict future increases or decreases in the level of interest rates.

5. What factors or variables are used most frequently to forecast interest rates in econometric models? What are some of the weaknesses or limitations of these models?

6. What is the forward calendar? Explain how it could be useful as an indicator of future security prices and rates.

7. How can market expectations be used as a guide to future changes in interest rates? What pitfalls are there in such an approach?

8. Explain the meaning of the term *consensus forecast.*

9. What is hedging? Explain how or why hedging works when duration, gap management, or interest-rate SWAPs are used.

PROBLEMS

1. Suppose that today the one-year U.S. Treasury bond rate is 6 percent, the two-year Treasury bond rate is 7 percent, and the three-year bond rate is 8 percent. Plot a yield curve from this data. What interest rate is this yield curve forecasting on a one-year loan one year from now? What is the expected one-year loan rate two years from now? What is the expected two-year bond rate one year from now?

2. Current interest rates in the corporate bond market on AAA rated bonds are as follows: one-year bonds, 8 percent; two-year bonds, 9 percent; three-year bonds, 10 percent; four-year bonds, 11 percent; and five-year bonds, 12 percent. What is the slope of the yield curve in the one-to-five year range? Calculate the implied one-year expected rate one year from now? What one-year loan rate is expected two years from now? three years from now? four years from now?

SELECTED REFERENCES

Anderson, Leonall C. and Keith M. Carlson. "A Monetarist Model for Economic Stabilization." *Review*, Federal Reserve Bank of St. Louis, April 1970, pp. 7–25.

Barth, James R., and James T. Bennett. "Seasonal Variation in Interest Rates." *Review of Economics and Statistics*, February 1975, pp. 80–83.

Brick, John R., and Howard E. Thompson. "Time-Series Analysis of Interest Rates: Some Additional Evidence." *Journal of Finance* 33, no. 1 (March 1978), pp. 93–103.

Cooley, William W., and Paul R. Lohnes. *Multivariate Data Analysis*. New York: John Wiley & Sons, 1971.

Cooper, Kathleen M. "Re-Thinking the Fundamentals of Interest Rate Determination." *Business Economics*, January 1983, pp. 25–30.

Elliott, J. Walter, and Jerome R. Baier. "Econometric Models and Current Interest Rates: How Well Do They Predict Future Rates?" *Journal of Finance* 34, no. 4 (September 1979), pp. 975–86.

Emory, John T., and Robert H. Scott. "Evidence on Expected Yields Implied from the Term Structure and the Futures Market." *Business Economics*, May 1979.

Hafer, R. W., and Scott E. Hein. "Monetary Policy and Short-Term Real Rates of Interest." *Review*, Federal Reserve Bank of St. Louis, March 1982, pp. 13–19.

Holland, A. Steven. "Real Interest Rates: What Accounts for Their Recent Rise?" *Review*, Federal Reserve Bank of St. Louis, December 1984, pp. 18–29.

Kohn, Donald L. "Causes of Seasonal Variation in Interest Rates." *Monthly Review*, Federal Reserve Bank of Kansas City, February 1974, pp. 3–12.

Lang, Richard W. "Using Econometric Models to Make Economic Policy: A Continuing Controversy." *Business Review*, Federal Reserve Bank of Philadelphia, January–February 1983, pp. 3–13.

McNees, Stephen K. "The Optimists and the Pessimists: Can We Tell Whose Forecast Will Be Better?" *New England Economic Review*, Federal Reserve Bank of Boston, May–June 1981, pp. 5–14.

———. "The Recent Record of Thirteen Forecasters." *New England Economic Review*, Federal Reserve Bank of Boston, September–October 1981, pp. 5–21.

———, and Nicholas S. Perma. "Forecasting Macroeconomic Variables: An Eclectic Approach." *New England Economic Review*, Federal Reserve Bank of Boston, May–June 1981, pp. 15–30.

Murphy, J. E., and M. F. M. Osborne. "Predicting the Volatility of Interest Rates." *Journal of Portfolio Management*, Winter 1985, pp. 66–69.

Poole, William. "The Relationship of Monetary Decelerations to Business Cycle Peaks: Another Look at the Evidence." *The Journal of Finance,* June 1975, pp. 697–712.

Roley, V. Vance, and Rick Troll. "The Impact of New Economic Information on the Volatility of Short-Term Interest Rates." *Economic Review,* Federal Reserve Bank of Kansas City, February 1983, pp. 3–15.

Rose, Peter S. "Interest Rates, Economic Forecasting, and Bank Profits." *Canadian Banker* 91, no. 3 (June 1984), pp. 38–44.

Schott, Francis H. "Interest Rate Forecasting in Theory and Practice." *Business Economics,* September 1977, pp. 55–60.

Walmsley, Julian K. "Understanding Interest-Rate SWAPs?" *The Bankers Magazine,* June 1984, pp. 44–47.

Part Four

The Money Market

12

Characteristics of the Money Market

PURPOSE OF THIS CHAPTER

To illustrate how important the money market is within the nation's financial system and to explain the many roles and functions performed by the money market. The chapter also describes the key characteristics of money market institutions, including banks, corporations, dealers, and units of government.

KEY TERMS AND CONCEPTS IN THE CHAPTER

actual maturity	dealers	opportunity cost
bankers' acceptances	default risk	original maturity
cash deficits	Eurodollars	political risk
cash surpluses	federal funds	reinvestment risk
CDs	inflation risk	safety
clearinghouse funds	liquidity	telephone market
commercial paper	market risk	Treasury bills
currency risk	money market	wholesale market

To the casual observer, the nation's financial markets appear to be one vast cauldron of borrowing and lending activity in which some individuals and institutions are seeking credit while others supply the funds needed to make lending possible. All transactions carried out in the financial markets seem to be basically the same—borrowers issue securities which lenders purchase. When the loan is repaid, the borrower retrieves the securities and returns funds to the lender. Closer examination of our financial institutions reveals, however, that beyond the simple act of exchanging securities for funds, there are major differences between one financial transaction and another. For example, you may borrow $100,000 for 30 years to purchase a new home, whereas my financing need may be for a six-month loan of $3,000 to cover my federal income-tax obligation. A corporation may enter the financial markets this week to offer a new issue of 20-year bonds to finance the construction of an office building, and next week, find itself in need of funds for 60 days to purchase raw materials so that production can continue without interruption.

Clearly, then, the *purposes* for which money is borrowed within the financial system vary greatly from person to person, institution to institution, and transaction to transaction. And the different purposes for which money is borrowed result in the creation of different kinds of financial assets, having different maturities, yields, default risks, and other features. In this chapter and others in Part Four, we will be focusing on a collection of financial markets which share a common purpose in their trading activity and deal in financial instruments with similar features. Our particular focus is on the *money market*—the market for short-term credit.

In the nation's money market, loans have an original maturity of one year or less. Money market loans are used to help corporations and governments pay the wages and salaries of their workers, make repairs, purchase inventories, pay dividends and taxes, and satisfy other short-term, working-capital needs. In this respect the money market stands in sharp contrast to the capital market. The capital market deals in long-term credit, that is, loans and securities over a year to maturity typically used to finance capital investment projects. There are important similarities between the money and capital markets, as we will see in subsequent chapters, but also important differences which make these two markets unique.

CHARACTERISTICS OF THE MONEY MARKET

The money market, like all financial markets, provides a channel for the exchange of financial assets for money. However, it differs from other parts of the financial system in its emphasis upon loans to meet purely short-term cash needs. *The money market is the mechanism through which holders of temporary cash surpluses meet holders of temporary cash deficits.* It is designed, on the one hand, to meet the short-run cash requirements of corporations, financial institutions, and governments, providing a mechanism for granting loans as short as overnight and as long as one year to maturity. At the same time, the money market provides an investment outlet for those spending units (also principally corporations, financial institutions, and governments) who hold surplus cash for short periods of time and wish to earn at least some return on temporarily idle funds. The essential function of the money market, of course, is to bring these two groups into contact with each other in order to make borrowing and lending possible.

The Need for a Money Market

Why is such a market needed? There are several reasons. First, for most individuals and institutions inflows of cash and outflows of cash are rarely in perfect harmony with each other. Governments, for example, collect taxes from the public only at certain times of the year, such as in April, when personal and corporate income tax payments are due. Disbursements of cash must be made throughout the year, however, in order to cover such items as wages and salaries of government employees, office supplies, repairs, and fuel costs as well as unexpected expenses. When taxes are collected, governments usually are flush with funds which far exceed their immediate cash needs. At these times they frequently enter the money market as lenders of funds and purchase U.S. Treasury bills, bank deposits, and other attractive financial assets. Later on, however, as cash runs low relative to current expenditures, these same governmental units must once again enter the money market as borrowers of funds, issuing short-term notes attractive to money market investors.

Business firms, too, collect sales revenue from their customers at one point in time and dispense cash at other points in time to cover wages and salaries, make repairs, and meet other operating expenses. The checking account of an active business firm fluctuates daily between large surpluses and low or nonexistent balances. A surplus cash position frequently brings such a firm into the money market as a net *lender* of funds, investing idle funds in the hope of earning at least a modest rate of return. Cash deficits force it onto the *borrowing* side of the market, however, seeking other institutions with temporary cash surpluses. Clearly, then, the money market serves to bridge the gap between receipts and expenditures of funds, covering cash deficits with short-term borrowings when current expenditures exceed receipts and providing an investment outlet to earn some interest income for those units whose current receipts exceed their current expenditures.

To fully appreciate the workings of the money market, we must remember that money is one of the most perishable of all commodities. The holding of idle surplus cash is expensive, because cash balances earn little or no income for the owner. When idle cash is not invested, the holder incurs an opportunity cost in the form of interest income which is foregone.[1] Moreover, each day that idle funds are not invested is a day's income lost forever. When large amounts of funds are involved, the income lost from not profitably investing idle funds for even 24 hours can be substantial. For example, the interest income from a loan of $10 million for one day at a 10 percent annual rate of interest amounts to about $2,800.[2] In a week's time close to $20,000 in interest would be lost from not investing $10 million in idle funds. Many students of the financial system find it hard to believe that investment outlets exist for loans as short as one day or even two or three days. However, billions of dollars in credit are extended in the American money market for as little as 24 hours to securities dealers, commercial banks, and nonfinancial corporations to cover temporary shortfalls of cash. As we will see in Chapter 14, one important money market instrument—the federal funds loan—is designed mainly for extending credit overnight or over a weekend.

Borrowers and Lenders in the Money Market

Who are the principal lenders of funds in the money market? Who are the principal borrowers? These questions are difficult to answer because the same institutions frequently operate on *both sides* of the money market. For example, a large commercial bank operating in the New York money market (such as Chase Manhattan or Manufacturers Hanover) will be borrowing short-term funds aggressively in the market through CDs, federal funds, and Eurodollars, while simultaneously lending short-

---

[1] The nationwide spread of interest-bearing checking accounts (such as NOW accounts) has reduced the opportunity cost of holding cash balances for some units in the economy. However, the yields on these transactions balances are still among the lowest available in the financial system and some interest-bearing payments accounts such as NOWs may be held only by individuals and nonprofit institutions. Thus, the money market offers a convenient, low-risk way to earn competitive interest returns on money needed in the near-term for transactions.

[2] As we saw in Chapter 8, the amount of interest income from a simple-interest loan may be calculated from the formula:

$$I = P \times r \times t$$

where I is interest income, P is the principal amount loaned, r is the annual rate of interest, and t is the maturity of the loan. In the example given above, we have:

$$I = (\$10,000,000)(0.10)(1/360) = \$2,777.78$$

Note that for purposes of simplifying the calculation we have assumed a 360-day year—a common assumption made in determining the yields on money market instruments.

term funds to corporations who have temporary cash shortages. Frequently, large nonfinancial corporations borrow millions of dollars on a single day only to come back into the money market later in the week as a lender of funds due to a sudden upsurge in cash receipts. Institutions which typically play both sides of the money market include large commercial banks, major nonfinancial corporations, state and local units of government, finance companies, and savings banks. Even the nation's central bank, the Federal Reserve System, may be an aggressive supplier of funds to the money market on one day and reverse itself the day following, demanding funds through the sale of securities in the open market. One institution that is virtually always on the demand side of the market, however, is the U.S. Treasury—the largest of all money market borrowers.

The Goals of Money Market Investors

Investors in the money market seek mainly *safety* and *liquidity* plus the opportunity to earn some interest income. This is because funds invested in the money market represent only temporary cash surpluses and are usually needed in the near future to meet tax obligations, cover wage and salary costs, pay stockholder dividends, and so on. For this reason, *money market investors are especially sensitive to risk.*

The strong aversion to risk among money market investors is especially evident when there is even a hint of trouble concerning the financial condition of a major money market borrower. For example, when the huge Penn Central Transportation Company collapsed in 1970 and defaulted on its short-term commercial notes, the short-term commercial paper market virtually ground to a halt because many investors refused to buy even the notes offered by top-grade companies. Similarly, in 1974 when Franklin National Bank of New York, holding nearly $4 billion in assets, closed its doors, the rates on short-term certificates of deposit (CDs) issued by other big New York banks surged upward due to fears on the part of money market investors that all large-bank CDs had become more risky.

Types of Investment Risk

What kinds of risk do investors face in the financial markets? And how do money market instruments rank in terms of these different kinds of risk?

First, all securities, including money market instruments, carry *market risk* (sometimes called interest-rate risk), which refers to the danger that their prices will fall (and interest rates rise), subjecting the investor to a capital loss. Even U.S. Treasury notes and bonds decline in price when interest rates rise. Only the dollar bill escapes market risk in the domestic economy because, of course, a dollar always exchanges for a dollar.

Not only can security prices fall, but interest rates can also decline. This latter development increases an investor's *reinvestment risk;* that is, the risk that earnings from a loan or security will have to be reinvested in lower-yielding loans and securities at some point in the future. Even government securities carry reinvestment risk.

Securities issued by private firms and state and local governments carry *default risk.* For such securities there is always some positive probability that the borrower will fail to meet some or all of his promised principal and/or interest payments.

Lenders of funds face the possibility that increases in the average level of prices for all goods and services will reduce the purchasing power of their income; this is known as *inflation risk* (sometimes called purchasing-power risk). Of course, lenders usually attempt to offset anticipated inflation by charging higher contract rates on their loans.[3]

International investors also face *currency risk*—possible loss due to unfavorable changes in the value of foreign currencies. For example, if an American investor purchases British treasury bills in the London money market, the return from these bills may be severely reduced if the value of the British pound falls relative to the dollar during the life of the investment.[4]

Finally, *political risk* refers to the possibility that changes in government laws or regulations will result in a diminished rate of return to the investor or, in the extreme case, a total loss of invested capital. For example, the windfall profits tax on U.S. petroleum companies levied by Congress in 1980 generally reduced the earnings of petroleum stockholders. Investors in industries that are closely regulated, such as banking, insurance, and public utilities, continually run the risk that new price controls, output or service quotas, or other restrictions will be imposed, reducing their earnings potential. In some foreign countries, facilities and equipment owned by U.S. corporations have been expropriated by national governments, resulting in total loss for the investors involved. A summary of each of the foregoing kinds of risk is shown in Exhibit 12–1.

Money market instruments generally offer more protection against such risks than most other investments. For example, the prices of money market securities tend to be remarkably stable over time compared to

---

[3] Inflation risk and default risk are discussed in greater detail in Chapters 9 and 10.

[4] See Chapters 27 and 28 for a further examination of currency or exchange-rate risk.

EXHIBIT 12–1

Types of Risks Confronting Investors in the Money and Capital Markets

Type of Risk	Definition
Market risk	The risk that the market price (value) of an asset will decline, resulting in a capital loss when sold. Sometimes referred to as interest-rate risk.
Reinvestment risk	The risk that an investor will be forced to place earnings from a loan or security into a lower-yielding investment because interest rates have subsequently fallen.
Default risk	The probability that a borrower will fail to meet one or more promised principal or interest payments on a loan or security.
Inflation risk	The risk that increases in the general price level will reduce the purchasing power of investor earnings from a loan or security.
Currency risk	The risk that adverse movements in the price of one national currency vis-à-vis another will reduce the net rate of return from a foreign investment. Sometimes called exchange-rate risk.
Political risk	The probability that changes in government laws or regulations will reduce the investor's expected return from an investment.

the prices of bonds, stocks, real estate, and actively traded commodities, such as wheat, corn, gold, and silver. Money market instruments generally do not offer the prospect of significant capital gains for the investor, but neither do they normally raise the specter of substantial capital losses. Similarly, default risk is minimal in the money market. In fact, money market borrowers must be well-established institutions with impeccable credit ratings before their securities can even be offered for sale in this market.

Few investments today adequately protect the investor against inflation risk. Money market securities are no exception. However, they do offer the investor superior *liquidity,* allowing him to quickly cash them in when a promising inflation-hedged investment opportunity comes along.

Currency risk concerns the international investor who frequently must convert one currency into another. That risk has dramatically increased in recent years due to the advent of foreign exchange rates that float with market conditions. Investors who purchase securities in foreign markets cannot completely escape currency risk, but they are probably less prone to such losses when buying money market instruments, due to the short-term nature of these securities. Money market instruments also provide some hedge against political risk because they are short-term investments and fewer changes in government policy are likely over brief intervals of time.

Money Market Maturities

Despite the fact that money market securities cover a narrow range of maturities—one year or less—there are maturities available within this range to meet just about every short-term cash and investment need. We must distinguish here between original maturity and actual maturity, however. The interval of time between the issue date of a security and the date on which the borrower promises to redeem it is the security's *original maturity. Actual maturity,* on the other hand, refers to the number of days, months, or years between today and the date the security is actually redeemed or retired.

Original maturities on money market instruments range from as short as one day on many federal funds transactions and loans to security dealers out to a full year on some Eurodollar deposits, bank certificates of deposit, and U.S. Treasury bills. Obviously, once a money market instrument is issued, it grows shorter in actual maturity every day. Because there are thousands of money market securities outstanding, some of which reach maturity each day, investors have a wide menu from which to select the precise number of days they need to invest cash.

Depth and Breadth of the Money Market

The money market is extremely "broad and deep," meaning it can absorb a large volume of transactions with only small effects on security prices and interest rates. Investors can easily sell most money market instruments on short notice, often in a matter of minutes. This is one of the most *efficient* markets in the world, containing a vast network of securities dealers, major banks, and funds brokers in constant touch with one another and alert to any "bargains." The slightest hint that a security is underpriced (i.e., carries an exceptionally high yield) usually brings forth a flood of buy orders, while money market traders are quick to dump or avoid overpriced securities. This market is dominated by active traders who constantly search their video display screens for opportunities to arbitrage funds; that is, they move money from a corner of the market with relatively low yields to one where investments offer the highest returns available. And overseeing the whole market is the Federal Reserve System, which tries to ensure that trading is orderly and prices are reasonably stable.

There is no centralized trading arena in the money market as there is on a stock exchange, for example. The money market is a *telephone market,* in which participants arrange trades over the phone and usually confirm by wire. Speed is of the essence in this market because, as we observed earlier, money is a highly perishable commodity. Each day that passes means thousands of dollars in lost interest income if newly received funds are not immediately invested. Most business between traders, therefore, is conducted in seconds or minutes, and payment is made almost instantaneously.

Federal Funds versus Clearinghouse Funds

How can funds move so fast in the money market? The reason is that money market traders usually deal in *federal funds.* These funds are mainly deposit balances of commercial banks held at the regional Federal Reserve banks and at larger correspondent banks across the nation. When a dealer firm buys securities from an investor, for example, it immediately contacts its bank and requests that funds be transferred from its account to the investor's account at another bank. Many of these transactions move through the Federal Reserve's wire transfer network. In this case the Fed removes funds from the reserve account of the buyer's bank and transfers these reserves to the seller's bank. The transaction is so quick that the seller of securities has funds available to make new investments, pay bills, or for other purposes the same day a trade is carried out or a loan is made. Federal funds are often called "immediately available funds" because of the speed with which money moves from one bank's reserve account to that of another.

Contrast this method of payment with that used generally in the capital market and by most businesses and households. When most of us purchase goods and services—especially purchases involving a large amount of money—the *check* is the most desirable means of paying the bill. Funds transferred by check are known as *clearinghouse funds.* This is because, once the buyer writes a check, it goes to the seller's bank, which forwards that check eventually to the bank upon which it was drawn. If the two banks are in the same community, they exchange bundles of checks drawn against each other every day through the local clearinghouse—an agreed-upon location where checks and other cash items are delivered and passed from one bank to another.

Clearinghouse funds are an acceptable means of payment for most purposes, but *not* in the money market, where speed is of the essence. It takes at least a day to clear local checks and two to three days for checks moving between cities. For money market transactions this is far too slow, because no interest can be earned until the check is collected. Clearinghouse funds also have an element of risk because a check may be returned as fraudulent or for insufficient funds. Federal funds transactions, however, are not only speedy but safe.

A Market for Large Borrowers and Lenders

The money market of the United States is dominated by a relatively small number of large financial institutions. No more than a hundred commercial banks in New York, Chicago, San Francisco, Dallas, and a handful of other money centers are at the heart of the market. These large banks account for the bulk of federal funds trading through which money market transactions are carried out. In addition, securities move readily from sellers to buyers through the market-making activities of about three dozen major government security dealers and a handful of dealers and brokers in commercial paper, bankers' acceptances, certificates of deposit, and federal funds. And, of course, the U.S. government plays a major role in this market as the largest borrower and as regulator, setting the "rules of the game." The Federal Reserve System, operating principally through the trading desk at the Federal Reserve Bank of New York, is in the market nearly every day, either supplying funds to banks and security dealers or absorbing funds through security sales.

Individual transactions in the money market involve huge amounts of funds. Most trading occurs in multiples of a million dollars. For this reason the money market is often referred to as a "wholesale" market for funds, as opposed to the "retail" market where consumers and small businesses borrow and save.

THE VOLUME OF MONEY MARKET SECURITIES

The principal financial instruments traded in the money market are U.S. Treasury bills, federal agency securities, dealer loans, repurchase agreements, bank certificates of deposit (CDs), federal funds, commercial paper, bankers' acceptances, financial futures, and Eurodollar deposits. Each of these instruments is discussed in detail in the next several chapters, but it is useful at this point to examine the relative importance, measured by the dollar volume outstanding, of each of these instruments in the American money market.

In fact, the volume of money market securities has grown rapidly in recent years. One reason is the economy's growing need for liquid, readily marketable investment securities. Another factor in the money market's growth has been the attractive yields offered investors. Frequently in recent years money market yields have risen above rates available on longer-term securities, causing many investors to shift their savings into the money market. In 1981, for example, market rates on three-month Treasury bills averaged about 14 percent, while the average yield on long-term Treasury bonds was less than 13 percent. Then, too, in a period of severe inflation, such as characterized the late 1970s and early 1980s, many investors are hesitant to commit their funds to long-term securities, particularly those with fixed rates of return. In an inflationary environment, investors often prefer the superior marketability and liquidity of money market securities.

As shown in Exhibit 12–2, two of the most important money market instruments (measured by dollar volume) are U.S. Treasury bills and certif-

EXHIBIT 12–2

Volume of Selected Money Market Instruments, 1981–1985
($ billions at year-end)

Financial Instruments	1981	1982	1983	1984	1985*
U.S. Treasury bills	$245.0	$311.8	$343.8	$374.4	NA
Federal agency securities	211.9	237.1	239.7	261.3	$260.8
Commercial paper	165.8	166.7	185.9	239.1	245.3
Bankers' acceptances	69.2	79.5	78.3	75.5	72.5
Federal funds borrowings and repurchase agreements	111.8	127.7	140.5	140.9	138.7
Net Eurodollar borrowings by domestic banks from their own foreign branches	18.1	47.7	42.7	31.4	34.9
Certificates of deposit ($100,000 or more)	325.4	347.9	283.1	325.8	324.8

NA = not available.
* Figures are for January 1985.
SOURCE: Board of Governors of the Federal Reserve System, *Federal Reserve Bulletin,* selected issues.

icates of deposit (CDs). By the beginning of 1985 about $375 billion in Treasury bills were outstanding, representing about one quarter of the federal government's debt. Somewhat less in total amount were $100,000-plus certificates of deposit issued by U.S. banks and thrift institutions. These large-denomination CDs totaled close to $325 billion as 1985 began. We should note, however, that the volume of CDs fluctuates widely with credit market conditions, corporate earnings, and changes in interest rates available on other securities.

Nearly as large as Treasury bills and CDs is the total volume of securities issued by federal agencies. These high-quality securities, nearly half of which fall due within a year and therefore are true money market instruments, exceeded $260 billion in 1985. Three quarters of all agency IOUs are issued by just three federally sponsored organizations—the Federal Home Loan Banks, the Federal National Mortgage Association, and the Farm Credit Banks. The remaining agency issues come from a variety of government-related enterprises and organizations, including the Department of Defense, Export-Import Bank, Postal Service, Tennessee Valley Authority, and Student Loan Marketing Association.

Commercial paper issued by top-flight U.S. corporations totaled $245 billion early in 1985 and represented one of the most rapidly growing money market instruments. Many large corporations have found the commercial paper market a cheaper and more flexible place to obtain credit than borrowing from banks. Bankers' acceptances—time drafts against large multinational banks—have also fluctuated with the growth of world trade, but exceeded $70 billion in 1985.

The volume of federal funds loans—the principal means of payment in the money market—is difficult to estimate because thousands of U.S. banks are active in this market every day and not all transactions are reported. Moreover, the federal funds market is extremely volatile, reflecting wide swings in the flow of funds through the banking system. Estimates by the Federal Reserve System indicate that Fed funds loans outstanding (including repurchase agreements) totaled around $140 billion in 1985.

The true size of the Eurodollar market (i.e., dollar deposits in banks abroad) is also unknown, principally because this market spans so many nations and is not regulated. The amount shown in Exhibit 12–2 of about $35 billion in 1985 includes only the net amount of Eurodollar borrowings by U.S. banks from their foreign branches. Conservative estimates of total Eurodollar deposits worldwide place the net figure well over $500 billion and perhaps in the neighborhood of $1 trillion.

THE PATTERN OF INTEREST RATES IN THE MONEY MARKET

The rates of return on money market securities vary over time and among different securities. The foundation of the market's structure is the level of yields on U.S. Treasury bills. These securities are considered to have zero default risk and minimal market risk as well. Moreover, the resale market for Treasury bills is the most active and deep of all securities markets, making bills readily marketable should the investor need cash in a hurry. Because of this combination of low risk and ready marketability, Treasury bills carry the lowest yields in the American money market.

Other yields in the money market are scaled upward from Treasury bill rates. One set of yields which hovers very close to T bill rates is the yield on federal agency securities, considered virtually riskless by many investors. Nevertheless, agency securities are less marketable than bills, though their quantity has increased rapidly in recent years. As a result, the yield spread between agencies and bills in recent periods averages about 1 percentage point in favor of agency securities.

Another yield in the money market which stays fairly close to the Treasury bill rate is the rate charged on federal funds loans. The low risk of these loans coupled with their short maturities helps to explain their relatively low yields. As shown in Exhibit 12–3, the Federal funds rate in March 1985 was slightly below (by $\frac{7}{100}$ of a percentage point or 7 basis points) the market rate of return on three-month Treasury bills.

The interest rates on two bank-related financial instruments—negotiable CDs and bankers' acceptances—also tend to follow changes in the market yield on Treasury bills and hover close to prevailing bill rates for the same maturities. As shown in Exhibit 12–3, the secondary market

EXHIBIT 12–3

Yield Relationships in the Money Market, Week of March 1, 1985

Security	Yield (percent per annum)	Yield Spread over Three-Month U.S. Treasury Bills (basis points)
U.S. Treasury bills:*		
Three-month	8.47%	—
Six-month	8.80	+23
One-year	8.84	+37
Federal funds rate	8.40	−7
Commercial paper (prime):†		
One-month	8.55	+8
Three-month	8.75	+28
Six-month	9.05	+58
Certificates of deposit (CDs) ($100,000 or more):‡		
One-month	8.62	+15
Three-month	8.91	+44
Six-month	9.47	+100
Bankers' acceptances, three-month†	8.80	+33
Eurodollars	9.35	+88
Prime bank lending rate§	10.50	+203
Federal Reserve discount rate	8.00	−47

* Based on daily closing bid prices in the secondary market and the bank discount method.
† Interest yield figured by the bank discount method which is explained in Chapter 13.
‡ Secondary market as quoted by five dealers.
§ Average for February 1985.
SOURCE: Board of Governors of the Federal Reserve System, *Federal Reserve Bulletin,* May 1985.

yield on three-month CDs was about one half percentage point (44 basis points) higher than the three-month T bill rate, while the spread between this bill rate and the rate of return on three-month bankers' acceptances was about one third of a percentage point (33 basis points). CDs issued by the largest U.S. banks are rated *prime* and carry the lowest yields in the CD market. The same is true of prime-rated bankers' acceptances. Acceptances are considered to be a high-quality investment nearly as riskless as U.S. Treasury bills. However, the resale market for acceptances is not as active or as deep as the T bill market, and this difference in marketability helps to explain why acceptances must carry a slightly higher yield.

Large, well-established corporations in need of credit can, of course, draw upon many different sources of funds. However, when short-term credit is needed, two of the most popular funds sources are borrowing from commercial banks and issuing marketable IOUs in the commercial paper market. The largest and best-known corporations generally qualify for the prime bank lending rate. Thus, the market for prime-rate bank loans is a direct competitor with the commercial paper market. As shown in Exhibit 12–3, for those corporations able to tap either market, it is generally cheaper to borrow in the commercial paper market. This spread in rates on short-term corporate loans favoring commercial paper helps explain why the commercial paper market has been one of the most rapidly growing segments of the U.S. money market in recent years.

The final money market interest rate shown in Exhibit 12–3 is the discount rate charged member banks when they borrow from the Federal Reserve banks. In contrast to the other yields discussed to this point, the discount rate is not determined by demand and supply forces in the marketplace but is set by the Federal Reserve banks with the approval of the Board of Governors of the Federal Reserve System. The level of the discount rate is governed by the Federal Reserve's assessment of the state of the economy and credit market conditions. Where possible, however, the Fed tries to keep the discount rate reasonably close to rates on U.S. Treasury bills. An unusually low discount rate may result in excessive borrowing at the Fed's "discount window." In contrast, an excessively high discount rate forces banks to borrow heavily in the open market, increasing the volatility of interest rates and sometimes creating unstable market conditions.

SUMMARY AND CONCLUSIONS

In this chapter we have presented a broad overview of one of the most important components of any financial system—the money market. By convention, money markets are defined as the collection of institutions and trading relationships that move short-term funds from lenders to borrowers. All money market loans have an original maturity of one year or less. Most loans extended in the money market are designed to provide short-term working capital to businesses and governments so they can purchase inventories, meet payrolls, pay dividends and taxes, and deal with other immediate needs for cash. These short-run cash needs arise from the fact the inflows and outflows of cash are not perfectly synchronized. In the real world, even with the best of planning, temporary cash deficits and temporary cash surpluses are more the rule rather than the exception.

The money market at one and the same time answers the needs of borrowers for short-term credit and the needs of lenders for temporary interest-bearing outlets for their surplus funds. In a period of rapid inflation and high interest rates, it is too costly to let cash lie idle for even a few days. At the same time, however, money market investors are extremely conservative when it comes to investing their funds. They will accept little or no risk of borrower default, prefer financial instruments whose prices are stable, and usually require an investment where their funds can be recaptured quickly as the need arises. For this reason nearly all money market instruments are of prime quality—among the safest, most liquid, and most readily marketable in the financial system. In the remaining chapters of this section we examine in detail the characteristics of each of the money market's key financial instruments.

STUDY QUESTIONS

1. What is the money market? Explain why there is a critical need for money market instruments.

2. Who are the principal lenders and borrowers active in the U.S. money market?

3. Define the following:
    a. Money risk.
    b. Credit risk.
    c. Inflation risk.
    d. Currency risk.
    e. Political risk.
    Which of these risks are minimized by investing in money market instruments? Does a money market investor avoid all of the above risk factors? Why or why not?

4. Why do interest rates on the various money market instruments tend to move together in the same direction at approximately the same time?

5. What are federal funds? Clearinghouse funds? Explain which is more important in the money market and why.

6. Who is the principal borrower in the money market? What is the role of the Federal Reserve System in the money market?

7. Describe the structure of interest rates in the U.S. money market. Which instrument anchors the market and appears to be the foundation for other interest rates? Can you explain why this is so?

PROBLEMS

1. How much interest would be earned (on a simple-interest basis) from a three-day money market loan for $1 million at an interest rate of 12 percent (annual rate)? Suppose the loan were extended on the third day for an additional day at the going market rate of 11 percent. How much total interest income would the money market lender receive?

2. Check the most recent issue of *The Wall Street Journal* you can find. Calculate the *yield spreads* in basis points between U.S. Treasury bills of varying maturity, the Federal funds rate, and commercial paper, CD, and bankers' acceptance rates. How do your calculated yield spreads compare with those shown in Exhibit 12–3? Can you explain the observed differences in yield spreads using your knowledge of the factors explaining movements in interest rates as discussed in Chapters 7–11?

SELECTED REFERENCES

Banks, Lois. "The Market for Agency Securities." *Quarterly Review,* Federal Reserve Bank of New York, Spring 1978.

Federal Reserve Bank of Richmond. *Instruments of the Money Market,* 1977.

Lucas, Charles M.; Marcos T. Jones; and Thom B. Thurston. "Federal Funds and Repurchase Agreements." *Quarterly Review,* Federal Reserve Bank of New York, Summer 1977, pp. 33–48.

McCurdy, Christopher J. "The Dealer Market for U.S. Government Securities." *Quarterly Review,* Federal Reserve Bank of New York, Winter 1977–78.

Melton, William C. "The Market for Large Negotiable CDs." *Quarterly Review,* Federal Reserve Bank of New York, Winter 1977–78, pp. 22–34.

Polakoff, Murray E. and others. *Financial Institutions and Markets.* 2d ed. Boston: Houghton Mifflin Co., 1981.

Robinson, Roland I., and Dwayne Wrightsman. *Financial Markets: The Accumulation and Allocation of Wealth.* 2d ed. New York: McGraw-Hill, 1980.

13

Treasury Bills, Dealer Loans, and Repurchase Agreements

PURPOSE OF THIS CHAPTER

To examine the characteristics and functions of two key elements of the money market—trading in U.S. Treasury bills and the activities of government security dealers. The chapter discusses why Treasury bills are important to money market investors, how they are auctioned each week, how T bill yields are calculated, and how the dealer houses that lie at the heart of the bill market raise funds and carry out their essential market-making activities.

KEY TERMS AND CONCEPTS IN THE CHAPTER

auction technique
bank discount method
brokers
carry income
cash-management
  bills
competitive tenders

continuing contracts
dealer loans
long position
noncompetitive
  tenders
position profits
regular-series bills

repurchase
  agreements (RPs)
reverse RPs
short position
spread
strip bills
U.S. Treasury bills

As we noted in the previous chapter, the money market is an institution designed to supply the cash needs of short-term borrowers and provide investors who hold temporary cash surpluses with an interest-bearing outlet for their funds. In this chapter we focus on one of the most important of all money market instruments—the U.S. Treasury bill. Purchases and sales of Treasury bills represent the largest volume of daily transactions in the money market. Interest rates on bills are the anchor for all other money market interest rates. Trading in T bills, as these instruments are usually called "on the street," is one component of a vast domestic and international market for securities issued by the U.S. government. These government IOUs, which include bills, notes, and long-term bonds, carry great weight in the financial system due to their zero default risk, ready marketability, and high liquidity. At the heart of the market for Treasury bills, notes, and bonds is a handful of securities dealers who make the market "go" and aid the federal government in selling billions of dollars in new securities each year. In this chapter we examine the activities of these securities dealers and how they finance their daily trading operations in T bills and other financial instruments.

U.S. TREASURY BILLS

Treasury bills are direct obligations of the U.S. government. By law, they must have an original maturity of one year or less. T bills were first issued by the U.S. Treasury in 1929 in order to cover the federal government's frequent short-term cash deficits.

The federal government's fiscal year runs from October 1 to September 30. However, individual income taxes—the largest single source of federal revenue—are not fully collected until April of each year. Therefore, even in those rare years when a sizable federal budget surplus is expected, the government is likely to be short of cash during the fall and winter months and often in the summer as well. During the spring, personal and corporate tax collections are usually at high levels, and the resulting inflow of funds can be used to retire some portion of those securities issued earlier in the fiscal year. T bills are well suited to this seasonal ebb and flow of Treasury cash since their maturities are short, they find a ready market among banks and other investors, and their prices adjust readily to changing market conditions.

Volume of Bills Outstanding

The volume of U.S. Treasury bills outstanding has grown rapidly in recent years, especially since the mid-1960s. As shown in Exhibit 13–1, the total volume of bills outstanding climbed to more than $380 billion in 1985, compared to only $216 billion in 1980, and just $88 billion in

EXHIBIT 13–1

U.S. Treasury Bills: Total Amount Outstanding and Their Proportion of
the Marketable Public Debt, 1960–1985

End of Year	Volume of Bills Outstanding ($ billions)	Total Marketable Public Debt of the United States ($ billions)	T Bills as a Percent of the Marketable Public Debt
1960	$ 39.4	$ 189.0	20.8%
1965	60.2	214.6	28.1
1970	87.9	247.7	35.5
1975	157.5	363.2	43.4
1980	216.1	623.2	34.7
1984	374.4	1,247.4	30.0
1985*	381.9	1,310.7	29.1

* Figures are for second quarter of 1985.
SOURCE: Board of Governors of the Federal Reserve System, *Federal Reserve Bulletin*, selected issues.

1970. The major factors behind the recent growth of T bills have been record federal budget deficits, deep recessions which reduced government tax revenues, and the rapid expansion of certain federal government programs such as national defense. Moreover, the U.S. economy has grown rapidly at times in recent years, creating a greater need for liquid assets such as bills to aid commercial banks and other investors in the efficient management of their cash positions.

Types of Treasury Bills

There are several different types of Treasury bills. *Regular-series* bills are issued routinely every week or month in competitive auctions. Bills issued in the regular series have original maturities of three months, six months, and one year. New three- and six-month bills are auctioned weekly, while one-year bills normally are sold once each month. Of these three bill maturities, the six-month bill provides the largest amount of revenue for the Treasury.

On the other hand, *irregular-series* bills are issued only when the Treasury has a special cash need. These instruments include strip bills and cash management bills. A "package offering" of bills requiring investors to bid for an entire series of different bill maturities is known as a *strip bill.* Investors who bid successfully must accept bills at their bid price each week for several weeks running. *Cash-management* bills, on the other hand, consist simply of reopened issues of bills that were sold in prior weeks. The reopening of a bill issue normally occurs when there is an unusual or unexpected Treasury need for more cash.

How Bills Are Sold

Treasury bills are sold using the *auction* technique. The marketplace, not the U.S. Treasury, sets bill prices and yields. A new regular bill issue is announced by the Treasury on Thursday of each week, with bids from investors due the following Monday at 12 noon, Central Standard Time, for three- and six-month bills and every fourth Thursday at noon for one-year bills (unless a federal holiday intervenes). Interested investors fill out a form tendering an offer to the Treasury for a specific bill issue at a specific price. These forms must be filed by the Monday deadline with one of the 37 regional Federal Reserve banks or branches. The interested investor can appear in person at a Federal Reserve bank or branch to fill out a tender form, submit the form by mail, or place an order through a security broker, bank, or other depository institution.

The Treasury will entertain both competitive and noncompetitive tenders for bills. *Competitive* tenders typically are submitted by large investors, including commercial banks and government securities dealers, who buy several million dollars worth at one time. Institutions submitting competitive tenders bid aggressively for bills, trying to offer the Treasury a price high enough to win an allotment of bills but not too high, because the higher the price bid, the lower the rate of return. *Noncompetitive* tenders (normally less than $500,000 each) are submitted by small investors who agree to accept the average price set in the weekly or monthly bill auction. The investor must pay the full par-value price of the bill at the time the tender is made and, on the issue date, receives a refund check from the Federal Reserve representing the difference between the amount paid in by the investor and the auction price. Generally, the Treasury tries to fill *all* noncompetitive tenders for bills.

In the typical bill auction, Federal Reserve officials open all the bids at the designated time and array them from the highest down to the lowest price. For example, a typical series of bids in a Treasury bill auction might appear as follows:

Hypothetical Bid Prices
for Three-Month U.S. Treasury Bills

$99.115
99.113
98.985
98.982
.
.
.
97.729
97.664
97.657

Note that all bids are expressed on a $100 basis as though T bills have a $100 par value.[1] In fact, the minimum denomination for bills is $10,000, and they are issued in multiples of $5,000 above that minimum. The highest bidder (in this case the one offering to pay $99.115) receives his or her bills, and those who bid successively lower prices also receive their bills until all available securities have been allocated.

The lowest price at which at least some bills are awarded is called the *stop-out price*. Let's suppose that this is a price of $97.729, the third price from the bottom in the array of prices shown above. No one bidding less than the stop-out price will receive any bills in this particular auction. However, once bills are acquired by successful bidders, many of them will be sold right away in the secondary market, giving the unsuccessful bidders a chance to add to their own T bill portfolios. Payments for bills won in the auction must be made in federal funds, cash, by redeeming maturing Treasury securities or coupon payments, cashier's check, certified personal check, or when permitted by the Treasury, through crediting Treasury tax and loan accounts at banks.[2] All bills today are issued only in *book-entry form*—a computerized record of ownership maintained in Washington, D.C.—with the owner receiving a statement of account about four to six weeks after purchase. The Treasury Department automatically sends a check to the investor the day the bill matures unless reinvestment of the maturing bill's proceeds into new Treasury securities has been requested.

Results of a Recent Bill Auction

A summary of the results from each T bill auction is published in *The Wall Street Journal.* The results from an actual bill auction are presented in Exhibit 13–2. We note that in this particular auction, held during August 1980, two maturities of bills—13 and 26 weeks—were offered to the public, and both issues were heavily oversubscribed. More than $7.1 billion in 13-week bills and almost $6.5 billion in 26-week bills were requested; however, the Treasury awarded only $3.8 billion of each. Sixty-five percent of the bids offering the low (or stop-out) price on the 13-week issue received bills, while 95 percent of the bids offering the low

---

[1] Treasury regulations require that competitive tenders carry a price expressed on the basis of 100 and contain not more than three places to the right of the decimal point.

[2] These so-called T&L accounts are Treasury deposits kept in about 12,000 of the nation's 15,000 commercial banks. The purpose of these accounts is to minimize the impact on the financial system of Treasury tax collections and debt-financing operations. As taxes are collected or securities are sold, the Treasury deposits the funds received in these T&L accounts and gradually withdraws money from them as needed into its checking accounts held at the Federal Reserve banks.

EXHIBIT 13–2

Report of Results from a Typical Weekly Auction of U.S. Treasury Bills,
August 14, 1980

Item	13-Week Bill Issue	26-Week Bill Issue
Applications for bills	$7,140,370,000	$6,497,475,000
Accepted bids	3,800,465,000	3,800,885,000
Percent accepted at low price	65%	95%
Noncompetitive bids accepted	$ 811,115,000	$ 437,815,000
Average auction price (rate)	97.795 (8.723%)	95.505 (8.891%)
High price (rate)	97.810 (8.664%)	95.554 (8.794%)
Low price (rate)	97.785 (8.763%)	95.480 (8.941%)
Coupon-equivalent yield	9.04%	9.44%

Notes: The 13-week bills mature November 13, 1980, and the 26-week bills mature February 12, 1981. The interest rates (yields) reported under each price are determined by the difference between the purchase price and the face value and assume a 360-day year. The coupon-equivalent yield is based on a 365-day year.
SOURCE: *The Wall Street Journal,* August 12, 1980.

price for the 26-week issue were awarded some bills. Noncompetitive tenders in the amount of $811 million for the 13-week issue and almost $438 million for the 26-week issue received their bills.

The dollar-weighted average auction price for the 13-week bills was $97.795 per $100, or $9,779.50 for a $10,000 denomination bill. The 26-week issue sold for an average price of $9,550.50. This works out to an 8.72 percent rate of return on the 13-week bill and an 8.89 percent return on the 26-week issue.[3] On a yield to maturity (or coupon-equivalent) basis, the 13-week bill carried an average return of 9.04 percent, while the 26-week bill had an average return of 9.44 percent. The highest competitive bidders paid a price of $9,781 for the 13-week security and $9,555.40 for the 26-week, $10,000 par-value instrument. The lowest successful bidders received their 13-week bills for only $9,778.50 and 26-week bills for $9,548 per $10,000 par bill. Those who bid less than these prices underbid in the auction and received no bills. If these unsuccessful bidders wish to purchase bills in this particular issue they must buy them in the secondary market, usually from a government securities dealer.

Calculating the Yield on Bills

Treasury bills do not carry a promised interest rate but instead are sold at a discount from par. Thus, their yield is based on their appreciation

---

[3] These rates of return are figured on a bank discount basis, as discussed below.

in price between the time the bills are issued and the time they mature or are sold by the investor. Any price gain actually realized by the investor is treated, not as a capital gain, but as ordinary income received during the year the bill matures for federal tax purposes.[4] We saw in Chapter 8 that the rate or yield on most debt instruments is calculated as a yield to maturity. However, bill yields are determined by the *bank discount method*, which ignores the compounding of interest rates and uses a 360-day year for simplicity.

The bank discount rate (DR) on bills is given by the following formula:

$$DR = \frac{\text{Par value} - \text{Purchase price}}{\text{Par value}} \times \frac{360}{\text{Number of days to maturity}} \qquad (13\text{--}1)$$

For example, suppose you purchased a Treasury bill at auction for $97 on a $100 basis (par value) and the bill matured in 180 days. Then the discount rate on this bill would be:

$$DR = \frac{(100 - 97)}{100} \times \frac{360}{180} = 6\%$$

Because the rate of return on T bills is figured in a different way than the rate of return on most other debt instruments, the investor must convert bill yields to an investment (or coupon-equivalent) yield in order to make realistic comparisons with other securities. The investment yield or rate (IR) on Treasury bills is given by the following formula:

$$IR = \frac{365 \times DR}{360 - (DR \times \text{Days to maturity})} \qquad (13\text{--}2)$$

For example, the investment yield on the bill discussed above, which has a discount rate (DR) of 6 percent, would be calculated as follows:

$$IR = \frac{365 \times 0.06}{360 - (0.06 \times 180)} = 6.27\%$$

Because of the compounding of interest rates and the use of a 365-day year, the investment yield on a bill will always be higher than its discount rate.

Several other formulas have become popular among investors for calcu-

---

[4] While the income earned from investing in T bills is not exempt from federal taxes, it is exempt from state and local income taxes.

lating yields on Treasury bills when the bills are not held to maturity. Both Formulas 13–1 and 13–2 assume that the investor buys a T bill and ultimately redeems it with the Treasury on its due date. But what if the investor needs cash right away and sells bills to a dealer or other investor in advance of their maturity? In this instance we may use the following formulas:

Holding-period yield on bill
$$= \text{DR when purchased} \pm \text{Change in DR over the holding period} \quad \textbf{(13–3)}$$

where:

Change in DR over the investor's holding period
$$= \frac{(\text{Days to maturity when purchased} - \text{Days held})}{\text{Days held}} \quad \textbf{(13–4)}$$
$$\times \text{Difference in DR on date purchased and date sold}$$

For example, suppose the investor buys a new six-month (180-day) bill at a price which results in a discount rate (DR) of 6 percent. As is typical, the bill's price begins to rise (and DR to fall) as the bill approaches maturity. Thirty days after purchase, the investor needs immediate cash and is forced to sell at a price which results in a DR of 5.80 percent. What is the investor's holding-period yield? Using formula 13–4,

$$\text{Change in DR over holding period} = \frac{(180 - 30)}{30} \times (6.00\% - 5.80\%)$$

$$= \frac{150}{30} \times 0.20\% = 1.00\%$$

Then, using Formula 13–3,

$$\text{Holding-period yield on bill} = 6.00\% + 1.00\% = 7.00\%$$

Because this T bill rose in price, the investor experienced a gain which increased the bill's holding-period yield by 1 percent over the original discount rate of 6 percent.

Consider another problem which frequently confronts the T bill investor. Suppose a corporation has just purchased some bills to serve as a temporary reserve of liquidity, but it knows that sometime in the next few weeks it will need those funds to help finance a building project. However, the firm wants to hold the bills long enough to earn a specific *target yield.* How many days must the bills be held to hit the target yield? The correct formula is as follows:[5]

Number of days to hold bill for target yield

$$= \frac{\text{Days to maturity when purchased} \times \text{Difference in DR on date purchased and date sold}}{\text{Desired change in DR over holding period} + \text{Difference in DR on date purchased and date sold}} \quad (13\text{--}5)$$

To illustrate the use of this formula, we can draw upon the figures in the preceding example and assume the investor wants to achieve a 7 percent target yield. We have:

$$\frac{\text{Numbers of days to hold bills}}{\text{for 7 percent target yield}} = \frac{180 \times (0.20\%)}{1.00\% + 0.20\%} = \frac{36\%}{1.20\%} = 30 \text{ days}$$

Therefore, a 180-day bill purchased at a discount rate of 6 percent must be held for 30 days if the investor desires a 7 percent annual yield and expects the bill's discount rate to decline by 20 basis points.

Market Interest Rates on Treasury Bills

Due to the absence of default risk and because of the superior market-ability of T bills, the yields on these popular financial instruments are typically the lowest in the money market. And because of the tremendous size of the bill market, conditions there tend to set the tone in all other segments of the money market. A rise in T bill rates, for example, usually is quickly translated into increases in interest rates attached to bankers' acceptances, commercial paper, CDs, and other money market instruments. Easier conditions in the bill market that lead to lower T bill rates rapidly spread to other segments of the short-term market, and conditions there usually ease as well.

While the prices of Treasury bills, like those attached to all money market instruments, tend to be quite stable, yields on bills fluctuate widely in response to changes in economic conditions, government policy, the demand for credit, and a host of other factors. This can be seen quite

---

[5] Sometimes interest rates rise sharply after a Treasury bill auction, and the market price of bills falls below their original purchase price. An investor unloading bills in such a market will take a loss unless they can be held until prices rise again. Formula 13–5 can also be used to determine the number of days bills must be held to avoid a loss, provided the change in DR over the holding period is replaced by the DR on the date the bills were purchased.

EXHIBIT 13–3

Market Interest Rates on U.S. Treasury Bills, 3-, 6-, and 12-Month
Maturities (Annual percentage rates)

Year	3-Month	6-Month	12-Month	Year	3-Month	6-Month	12-Month
1971	4.33%	4.52%	4.60%	1978	7.19	7.58	7.74
1972	4.07	4.49	4.77	1979	10.07	10.06	9.75
1973	7.03	7.20	7.01	1980	11.43	11.37	10.89
1974	7.84	7.95	7.71	1981	14.03	13.80	13.14
1975	5.80	6.11	6.30	1982	10.61	11.07	11.07
1976	4.98	5.26	5.52	1983	8.61	8.73	8.80
1977	5.27	5.53	5.71	1984	9.52	9.76	9.92
				1985*	8.47	8.70	8.84

* Average for week ending March 1, 1985.
SOURCE: Board of Governors of the Federal Reserve System, *Federal Reserve Bulletin,* selected monthly issues.

clearly in Exhibit 13–3, which gives annual averages for the secondary market yields on 3-, 6-, and 12-month bills. T bill rates typically fall during periods of recession and sluggish economic activity as borrowing and spending sag. Note, for example, the decline in bill yields in 1971–72, 1975, and 1982–83, as shown in Exhibit 13–3. All of these years were periods in which the economy reached the peak of a boom period and then dropped into a recession. During periods of economic expansion, on the other hand, T bill rates frequently surge upward, as happened between 1976 and 1981 and again in 1984. Inflationary expectations also appear to have a potent impact on bill market yields, as evidenced by the sharp run-up in T bill rates during the late 1970s and early 1980s— both periods when price increases accelerated rapidly and, in the latter case, soared to double-digit levels.

It is interesting to examine the shape of the *yield curve* for bills. As Exhibit 13–3 suggests, that curve usually slopes *upward*, with 12-month bill maturities generally carrying the highest yields, 6-month next highest, and 3-month maturities the lowest yields. This is not always the case, however. During certain periods—1974 and 1979–81 are good examples—the bill yield curve seems to signal the onset of a recession by sloping downward. Occasionally, too, the yield curve for bills assumes a pronounced "humped" or inverted U shape, with middle maturities carrying the highest rates of return. This happened during the 1973–74 period, for example. It is difficult to assign any particular cause to this phenomenon. Sometimes the bend in the curve in the middle maturities appears to reflect heavy Treasury issues of new six-month bills or heavy commercial bank sales of T bills as bankers try to accommodate customer loan demand by converting their bills into loanable funds. It is noteworthy that the "humped" curve has generally appeared near the end of a boom period and shortly before the onset of a recession. During these periods investors in the financial marketplace are especially uncertain as to which way interest rates are headed.

Investors in Treasury Bills

Principal holders of Treasury bills include commercial banks, nonfinancial corporations, state and local governments, and the Federal Reserve banks. Commercial banks and private corporations hold large quantities of bills as a reserve of liquidity until cash is needed. The most attractive feature of bills for these institutions is their ready marketability and relatively stable price. The Federal Reserve banks conduct the bulk of their open-market operations in T bills because of the depth and volume of activity in this market. In fact, bills play a crucial role in the conduct of monetary policy by the Federal Reserve System. The Fed purchases and sells bills in an effort to influence other money market interest rates and thereby alter the volume and growth of bank credit and ultimately the total amount of investment spending and borrowing in the economy.[6]

DEALER LOANS AND REPURCHASE AGREEMENTS

The money market depends heavily upon the buying and selling activities of securities dealers to move funds from cash-rich units to those with cash shortages. About three dozen primary dealers in U.S. government securities trade today in both new and previously issued Treasury bills, bonds, and notes. Many of these dealers also buy and sell other money market instruments, such as commercial paper, CDs, and bankers' acceptances. They are the principal points of contact with the money market for thousands of individual and institutional investors and are essential to the efficient functioning of that market.

While the dealers supply a huge volume of securities daily to the financial marketplace, they also depend heavily on the money market for borrowed funds. Most dealer houses invest little of their own equity in the business. The bulk of dealer operating capital is obtained through borrowings from commercial banks, nonfinancial corporations, and other institutions. A major dealer firm carries hundreds of millions of dollars in securities in its trading portfolio, with 95 percent or more of that

---

[6] We will examine Federal Reserve open-market operations and the role of Treasury bills in those operations in Chapter 23.

portfolio supported by short-term loans, some carrying only 24-hour maturities.

The two most heavily used sources of dealer funds are demand loans from the nation's largest banks and repurchase agreements (RPs) with banks and other lenders. Every day, the major New York banks post rates at which they are willing to make short-term loans to dealers. Generally, one rate is quoted on new loans and a second (lower) rate is posted for renewals of existing loans. A *demand loan* may be called in at any time if the banks need cash in a hurry. Such loans are virtually riskless, however, because they usually are collateralized by U.S. government securities, which may be transferred temporarily to the lending bank or its agent.

Repurchase Agreements

An increasingly popular alternative to the demand loan is the repurchase agreement (RP). Under this arrangement, the dealer sells securities to a lender but makes a commitment to buy back the securities at a later date at a fixed price plus interest. Thus, *RPs are simply a temporary extension of credit collateralized by marketable securities.* Some RPs are for a set length of time (term), while others, known as *continuing contracts,* carry no explicit maturity date but may be terminated by either party on short notice. Larger commercial banks provide *both* demand loans and RPs to the dealers, while nonfinancial corporations have provided a growing volume of funds to dealers through RPs in recent years. Other lenders active in the RP market include state and local governments, insurance companies, and foreign financial institutions who find the market a convenient, relatively low-risk way to invest temporary cash surpluses that may be retrieved quickly and easily when the need arises. On some trading days the volume of RP loans is so huge that it approaches a trillion dollars or more.

The typical RP loan transaction can be described quite easily through the use of T accounts (i.e., an abbreviated balance sheet) for a security dealer and for the lender of funds. Exhibit 13–4 presents a typical example of such a loan. In this case we assume a manufacturing company has a temporary $1 million cash surplus. The manufacturer is eager to loan its temporary cash surplus right away to avoid losing even a single day's interest, while the dealer wishes to borrow at the low-cost RP loan rate in order to purchase interest-bearing securities. The borrowing dealer and the lending company agree on a $1 million RP loan collateralized by Treasury bills with the dealer agreeing to buy back the T bills within a few days plus pay the interest on the loan. Normally the securities that form the collateral for the RP loan are supposed to be placed in a

EXHIBIT 13–4

Examples of a Typical RP Loan Transaction

	Security Dealer		Manufacturing Company	
	Assets	Liabilities	Assets	Liabilities
a. Lender of funds—a manufacturing company—has a $1 million surplus in its cash account.			Deposit at bank +$1 million	
b. A security dealer and the manufacturing company settle on an RP with the dealer using the borrowed funds to buy securities.	Securities held +1 million	RP borrowing from manufacturer +$1 million	Deposit at bank −$1 million RP loan to security dealer +$1 million	
c. RP agreement is concluded and the funds returned (plus interest).	Deposit at bank −$1 million	RP borrowing from manufacturer −$1 million	Deposit at bank +$1 million RP loan to security dealer −$1 million	

custodial account at a bank.[7] When the loan is repaid, the dealer's RP liability is automatically canceled and the securities are returned to the dealer.

Until recently, RPs were principally overnight transactions or expired in a few days. Today, however, there is a substantial volume of one- to three-month agreements and some carry even longer maturities. Longer-term RPs are known as *term agreements*. The interest rate on RPs is the return that a dealer must pay a lender of short-term funds for the temporary use of money and is closely related to other money market interest rates.[8] To determine the lender's total interest income from an RP transaction, the agreed-upon rate is multiplied by the value of the

---

[7] There is evidence that this safety device of placing securities involved in an RP agreement in a separate bank-held custodial account is not always scrupulously followed. Moreover, because the majority of outstanding RP loans are simply recorded as book entries at the Federal Reserve banks, verification of what has been done with the pledged securities is very difficult. The result is that if a government securities dealer goes out of business, his or her customers may have difficulty recovering all the collateral behind some of the loans they have made to the dealer.

[8] The interest rate attached to an RP transaction is figured on the basis of a 360-day year like the yield on Treasury bills.

securities pledged as collateral behind the RP. Usually the securities pledged are valued at a discount from their current market prices, giving the lender added protection in case security prices fall. Periodically, RPs are "marked to market" and, if the price of the pledged securities has dropped, the borrower must return some money to the lender. Most RP transactions involve at least a million dollars in marketable securities.

In order to promote a smoothly functioning market, the Federal Reserve System through its trading desk at the New York Fed frequently participates with a Fed-approved list of 36 primary (recognized) government security dealers in RPs. In a *straight* RP transaction, the Federal Reserve buys securities from a dealer on a short-term basis and then sells the securities back at the end of the agreed-upon period. The Fed may also enter into a *reverse* RP transaction with one or more approved dealers. In this case the Federal Reserve Bank of New York will sell securities to a dealer with an agreement to buy them back after a short period of time, thus temporarily absorbing dealer funds and reducing the ability of the dealer's bank to make loans. Whereas the dealers use the RP to protect or increase their earnings from security trading, the Federal Reserve uses RPs to steady the money market and to promote national economic goals.[9]

Sources of Dealer Income

Securities dealers take on substantial risk in order to make a market for Treasury bills and other financial instruments. To be sure, the securities they deal in are among the highest-quality instruments available in the financial marketplace. However, the prices of even top-quality securities can experience rapid declines if interest rates rise. Moreover, established dealer houses cannot "run and hide" but are obliged to stand ready at all times to buy and sell on customer demand, regardless of the condition of the market. In contrast to securities brokers, who merely bring buyers and sellers together, dealers take a "position of risk," which means that they act as principals in the buying and selling of securities. Dealers add any securities purchased to their own portfolios.

Dealers stand ready to buy specified types of securities at an announced *bid* price and to sell them at an announced *asked* price. This is called "making a market" in a particular financial instrument. The dealer hopes to earn a profit from such market-making activities—in part from the positive *spread* between bid and asked prices for the same security. This spread varies with market activity and the outlook for interest rates but is very narrow on bills (often about 2 basis points or $50 per $1 million) and wider on more volatile notes and bonds (often $\frac{2}{32}$ or $\frac{4}{32}$ or $625 to

---

[9] We will discuss Federal Reserve RP transactions in more detail in Chapter 23.

$1,250 per $1 million). Spreads range higher on longer-term securities than on shorter-term securities, on small versus large transactions, and on securities not actively traded due to both greater risk and greater costs.[10] Dealers do not usually charge commissions on their trades.

As we have seen, the dealers' holdings of securities are financed by loans, so their portfolio positions are extremely sensitive to fluctuations in interest rates. For this reason dealers frequently will shift from long positions to short positions, depending on the outlook for interest rates. A *long position* means that dealers purchase securities outright, take title to them, and hold them in their portfolios as an investment or until a customer comes along. Long positions typically increase in a period of falling interest rates. A *short position,* on the other hand, means that dealers sell securities they do not presently own for future delivery to a customer. In so doing, they hope the prices of those securities will fall (and interest rates rise) before they must be delivered to the buyer. Obviously, as interest rates fall (and security prices rise), the dealer will experience capital gains on a long position but losses on a short position. On the other hand, if interest rates rise (resulting in a drop in security prices), the dealer's long position will experience capital losses while his short position will post a gain.

In periods when interest rates are expected to rise, dealers typically reduce their long positions and go short. Conversely, expectations of falling rates lead the dealers to increase their long positions and avoid short sales. By correctly anticipating rate movements, the dealer can earn sizable *position profits*. Dealers also receive *carry income,* which is the difference between interest earned on securities they hold and their cost of borrowing funds. Generally, dealers earn higher rates of return on the securities they hold than the interest rates they pay for loans, but this

---

[10] We recall from Chapter 8 that $\frac{1}{32}$ of a point is equal to $0.03125 for each $100. On a $1 million trade in Treasury bills, the dealer's spread would normally be $50 to $60. For shorter-term coupon issues the spread usually lies in the range of $312.50 to $1,250 for each million dollars in par value. However, dealer spreads are difficult to predict in advance because they vary with the nature and total size of each transaction and current demand and supply conditions in the marketplace.

Generally, dealers will deliver securities sold the next business day after a sale has been made (known as *regular delivery*), though smaller odd-lot transactions are usually completed within five business days—a method of delivery used for most Treasury bill trades. Large customers or dealers themselves may demand same-day settlement (known as *cash delivery*). In recent years an increasing number of dealer transactions have been *forward transactions* in which securities are purchased or sold for delivery after five business days from the date of the transaction if U.S. government securities are involved or after 30 days when mortgage-backed agency securities are the subject of the trade. Payment for all deliveries of securities is usually made in federal funds.

is not always so. Because most dealer borrowings are short term, securities dealers normally are better off if the yield curve is positively sloped.

Dealer Positions in Securities

As reflected in the first section of Exhibit 13–5, dealer holdings of U.S. government and other securities are both huge and subject to erratic fluctuations. For example, early in 1985 dealer positions in U.S. government securities rose sharply, following relatively modest government security holdings in 1983 and 1984. Why was there such a tremendous difference in the size of dealer portfolios during those years? Money market interest rates began falling late in 1984, creating opportunities for sizable dealer profits on short-term securities held in long positions as market prices rose. However, long-term interest rates did not fall and, in fact, rose, on balance, between November 1984 and February 1985, sending long-term government security prices lower. Thus, dealer holdings of long-term government securities in the 5–10 year range fell, while their holdings of Treasury bills and other U.S. government securities under 5 years to maturity as well as other short-term money market instruments (federal agency securities, certificates of deposit, acceptances, and commercial paper) rose substantially. In their futures and forward positions—contracts promising future delivery of securities—the dealers moved aggressively to protect themselves against fluctuating interest rates. The use of futures contracts and other interest-rate hedging devices became especially important in the period after October 1979 when the Federal Reserve System announced that it would allow interest rates and security prices to fluctuate more freely while it concentrated on controlling money-supply growth.[11]

Sources of Dealer Financing

Where do government security dealers derive most of their funds to purchase and carry securities? As the second section of Exhibit 13–5 shows, the dealers make heavy use of repurchase agreements, usually collateralized by securities held in their portfolios. Commercial banks are also a major source of dealer borrowed funds, year in and year out. Indeed, a dozen of the primary U.S. government security dealers are really dealer departments housed in some of the nation's largest banks and the remaining two dozen are nonbank dealers. However, nonfinancial business corporations are the most rapidly growing source of funds for major securities dealers. Many industrial corporations today find the

---

[11] See Chapter 17 for an explanation of financial futures contracts and Chapter 24 for a discussion of Federal Reserve money-supply control procedures.

EXHIBIT 13–5

Positions and Sources of Financing for U.S. Government Security Dealers
(Averages of daily figures expressed in $ millions at par)

Item	1981	1982	1983	1984	1985*
Net immediate positions:					
U.S. government securities	$ 9,033	$ 9,328	$ 6,263	$ 5,543	$13,585
Bills	6,485	4,837	4,282	5,504	12,441
Other securities within 1 year	−1,526	−199	−177	63	851
1–5-year issues	1,488	2,932	1,709	2,159	3,054
5–10-year issues	292	−341	−78	−1,119	−2,898
Over 10 years	2,294	2,001	528	−1,174	48
Federal agency securities	2,277	3,712	7,172	15,294	19,606
Certificates of deposit	3,435	5,531	5,839	7,369	9,487
Bankers' acceptances	1,746	2,832	3,332	3,874	4,725
Commercial paper	2,658	3,317	3,159	3,788	5,226
Futures Positions:					
Treasury bills	−8,934	−2,508	−4,125	−4,525	−2,549
Treasury coupons	−2,733	−2,361	−1,032	1,795	3,143
Federal agency securities	522	−224	170	233	−9
Forward positions:					
U.S. government securities	−603	−788	−1,935	−1,643	−1,742
Federal agency securities	−451	−1,190	−3,561	−9,204	−8,156
Sources of dealer financing:					
Reverse repurchase agreements:					
Overnight and continuing	14,568	26,754	29,009	44,078	59,989
term agreements	32,048	48,247	52,493	68,357	71,570
Repurchase agreements:					
Overnight and continuing	35,919	49,695	57,946	75,717	96,535
term agreements	29,449	43,410	44,410	57,047	62,327

* 1985 figures are averages for the month of February.
SOURCE: Board of Governors of the Federal Reserve System, *Federal Reserve Bulletin,* various monthly issues.

dealer loan market a convenient and safe way to dispose of temporarily idle monies. With wire transfer of funds between banks readily available, a company can lend a dealer millions of dollars in idle cash and recover those funds in a matter of hours if a cash emergency arises.

Dealer Transactions

Trading among securities dealers and between dealers and their customers amounts to billions of dollars a day. For example, average daily transactions in the U.S. government securities market were in the neighborhood of $60 billion in 1984. Indeed, so large is the government securities market that the volume of trading often exceeds several times over the total volume of trading on the major U.S. stock exchanges. About half the trades in this market involve Treasury bills. Government securities dealers trade heavily among themselves, usually through *brokers*. Government security brokers do not take investment positions themselves but try to match bids and offers placed with them by dealers and other investors. There are just four main brokers of Treasury securities today, each of which operates a closed-circuit TV network showing dealer prices and quantities available.

Dealerships are a cutthroat business in which each dealer firm is out to maximize its returns from trading, even if gains must be made at the expense of competing dealers. Indeed, market analysts housed within each dealer firm study the daily price quotations of their competitors. If one dealer firm temporarily underprices some securities (i.e., offers excessively generous yields), other dealers are likely to rush in for a "hit" before the offering firm has a chance to correct its mistake. It is a business with little room for the inexperienced or slow-moving trader and fraught with low margins, risk, and unstable earnings. For example, in 1982 two major firms—Drysdale Government Securities, Inc. and Lombard-Wall, Inc.—collapsed. These closings were followed by four more dealer failures: Lion Capital Group and RTD Securities in 1984, and E.S.M. Government Securities and Bevill, Bresler & Schulman Asset Management Corporation in 1985. Large losses in the hundreds of millions of dollars can be recorded in a few days or weeks and huge security positions are often amassed with little cash and heavy, unregulated borrowing. Dealers may buy large quantities of bonds that are not yet issued—"when-issued" securities—without any money down and payment not due until delivery a week or so later. Yet, as we have seen, the government securities dealers are essential to the smooth functioning of the financial markets and to the successful placement of billions of dollars in new securities issued each year by the U.S. Treasury.

CONCLUSIONS

In this chapter we have examined one of the most important of all securities markets—the market for Treasury bills and other U.S. government securities. This market has grown rapidly in recent years in response to huge Treasury borrowing needs and the needs of investors for highly liquid, readily marketable financial instruments. It is difficult to overestimate the importance of the government securities market in the functioning of the American financial system. This market sets the tone for the whole financial system in terms of interest rates, security prices, and the availability of credit. And it is in this market today that most government economic policy measures begin in the form of U.S. Treasury issues of new securities and Federal Reserve open-market operations. A thorough knowledge of the working of the market for government securities tells us much about the how and why of the American financial system.

STUDY QUESTIONS

1. Why has the volume of U.S. Treasury bills grown so rapidly in recent years? Explain why the T bill is so popular with money market investors.

2. List and define the various types of U.S. Treasury bills. Why are there so many different varieties?

3. Explain how a T bill auction works. Can you cite some advantages of this method of sale? Disadvantages?

4. How are the yields on U.S. Treasury bills calculated? How does this method differ from the method used to calculate bond yields? Why is this difference important?

5. What is the normal, or typical, slope of the yield curve for T bills? Why? What other slopes have been observed, and why do you think these occur?

6. Who are the principal investors in U.S. Treasury bills? What factors motivate these investors to buy bills?

7. Explain why dealers are essential to the smooth functioning of the securities markets. Where do most dealer funds come from?

8. What is a demand loan? An RP? Explain their role in dealer financing.

9. In what ways do dealers earn income and possibly make a profit? To what risk is each source of dealer income subject?

10. Are the majority of U.S. government security dealers' positions in short-term or long-term securities? What causes their positions to change?

11. Where do government securities dealers borrow most of the funds they need?

12. What types of securities dominate dealer trading? Why?

PROBLEMS

1. From the following sets of figures: (1) calculate the bank discount rate on each T bill; and (2) convert that rate to the appropriate investment (or coupon-equivalent) yield.
   a. A new three-month T bill sells for $98.25 on a $100 basis.
   b. The investor can buy a new 12-month T bill for $96 on a $100 basis.
   c. A 30-day bill is available from a U.S. government securities dealer at a price of $97.50 (per $100).

2. Calculate the holding-period yield for the following situations:
   a. The investor buys a new 12-month T bill at a discount rate of 7½ percent. Sixty days later the bill is sold at a price which results in a discount rate of 7 percent.
   b. A large manufacturing corporation acquires a T bill in the secondary market 30 days from its maturity but is forced to sell the bill 15 days later. At time of purchase the bill carried a discount rate of 8 percent, but it was sold at a discount rate of 7¾ percent.

SELECTED REFERENCES

Bowsher, Norman H. "Repurchase Agreements." *Review,* Federal Reserve Bank of St. Louis, September 1979, pp. 17–22.

Federal Reserve Bank of Dallas. *United States Treasury Securities—Basic Information,* August 1984.

Lucus, Charles M.; Marcus T. Jones; and Thom B. Thurston. "Federal Funds and Repurchase Agreements." *Quarterly Review,* Federal Reserve Bank of New York, Summer 1977, pp. 33–48.

Federal Reserve Bank of Philadelphia. *Buying Treasury Securities,* May 1984.

Federal Reserve Bank of Richmond. *Instruments of the Money Market.* 5th ed., 1981.

The First Boston Corporation. *Handbook of Securities of the United States Government and Federal Agencies.* 25th ed., 1972.

McCurdy, Christopher J. "The Dealer Market for United States Government Securities." *Quarterly Review,* Federal Reserve Bank of New York, Winter 1977–78, pp. 35–47.

Simpson, Thomas D. *The Market for Federal Funds and Repurchase Agreements.* Staff Study, Board of Governors of the Federal Reserve System, July 1979.

14

Federal Funds, Negotiable CDs, and Loans from the Discount Window

PURPOSE OF THIS CHAPTER

To describe the important role played by commercial banks, especially the largest money-center banks, in the nation's money market. The chapter illustrates the principal ways banks lend and borrow funds in the money market with special emphasis on their activities in the Federal funds and negotiable CD (certificate of deposit) markets.

KEY TERMS AND CONCEPTS IN THE CHAPTER

Asian dollar CDs	*federal funds*	*multitiered market*
bearer CDs	*Fed funds brokers*	*negotiable CDs*
contemporaneous	*Fed funds loans*	*registered CDs*
reserve accounting	*legal reserves*	*reserve requirements*
discount rate	*liability management*	*rollover CDs*
discount window	*LIBOR*	*variable-rate CDs*
Eurodollar CDs	*money market*	
excess reserves	*strategy*	

The single most important financial institution in the money market is the commercial bank. Large money-center banks, such as those headquartered in New York City, Chicago, San Francisco, Philadelphia, and a handful of other major cities, provide billions of dollars in funds daily through the money market to governments and corporations in need of cash. For example, as we saw in the previous chapter, bank loans and repurchase agreements are a principal source of financing for dealers in U.S. government securities, while banks also make large direct purchases of U.S. Treasury bills and other money market securities. Commercial banks support private corporations borrowing in the money market, both by purchasing their securities and by granting lines of credit to backstop their new security issue. Banks conduct acceptance financing to support the movement of goods in international trade, resulting in the creation of a high-grade money market instrument—the bankers' acceptance.[1] And both large and small banks today readily lend their cash reserves to other financial institutions and to industrial corporations overnight or for a few days to cover short-term liquidity needs.

In order for commercial banks to *lend* huge amounts of funds daily in the money market, they must also *borrow* heavily in that market. As we saw in Chapter 4, the owners (stockholders) supply only a minor portion of a commercial bank's total resources; *the bulk of bank funds must be borrowed.* While the majority of borrowed funds (at least 80 percent for most banks) comes from deposits, a growing portion of the industry's financing needs are supplied by the money market. However, bank managers today are more cautious in their use of money market borrowings than was true even a few years ago. Such funds are relatively expensive to use, and their interest cost is more volatile than for most kinds of deposits. Many large banks today follow the strategy of maintaining a roughly equal balance between their lending and borrowing activities in the money market. The volume of short-term bank debt is counterbalanced by a nearly equal volume of short-term bank assets.[2]

In this chapter we examine three of the most important money market sources of funds for banks and other deposit-type financial institutions—Federal funds, certificates of deposit (CDs), and loans from the Federal

---

[1] Bankers' acceptances are discussed in Chapter 16.

[2] The idea of maintaining a roughly *equal* balance between borrowing and lending in the money market follows one of the oldest concepts in the field of finance—the *hedging principle.* As discussed in Chapter 9, in a world of uncertainty, borrowers of funds can reduce risk by matching the maturity of their assets and liabilities. This approach reduces the risk of borrowing when funds are not needed and also lowers the risk of not having sufficient cash when interest payments and other bills come due.

Reserve's discount window. In Chapter 16 we discuss still another important source of funds for many of the nation's largest depository institutions—Eurodollars.

FEDERAL FUNDS

As we saw in the introductory chapter in the money market (see Chapter 12), Federal funds are among the most important of all money instruments for one key reason: *Fed funds are the principal means of making payments in the money market.* By definition, Federal funds are any monies available for immediate payment ("same-day money"). They are generally transferred from one depository institution to another by simple bookkeeping entries requested by wire or telephone after a purchase of securities is made or a loan is granted.

The Nature of Federal Funds

The name *Federal funds* came about because early in the development of the market the principal source of immediately available money was the reserve balance which each bank must keep at the Federal Reserve bank in its region of the country. If one bank needs to transfer funds to another, it need only contact the Federal Reserve bank in its district, and money is readily transferred into the appropriate reserve account—a transaction accomplished in minutes or seconds by computer.

Today, however, the Fed funds market is far broader in scope than just reserves on deposit with the Federal Reserve banks. For example, virtually all banks maintain deposits with large correspondent banks in the principal U.S. cities, and these deposits may be transferred readily by telephone and by wire from the account of one bank to that of another. They may also be borrowed by the institution that holds the correspondent deposit, simply by transferring funds from the correspondent deposit to an account titled "Federal funds purchased" and reversing the entries when the loan matures. Savings and loan associations, credit unions, and mutual savings banks maintain deposits with commercial banks that also are available for immediate transfer to a customer or to another financial institution.[3] Business corporations and state and local governments can lend Federal funds by executing repurchase agreements with securities

---

[3] As we saw in Chapters 4 and 5, nonbank thrift institutions that offer transactions accounts must also keep reserve balances at the Federal Reserve banks under the terms of the Depository Institutions Deregulation and Monetary Control Act of 1980. These reserve balances are available for borrowing and lending in the Federal funds market.

368 Part Four   The Money Market

dealers, banks, and other funds traders. Securities dealers who have received payment for securities sold can turn around and make their funds immediately available to borrowers through the Federal funds market. Borrowers of Federal funds include securities dealers, corporations, state and local governments, and nonbank financial intermediaries, such as savings and loan associations and insurance companies. Without question, however, the most important of all borrowers in the Fed funds market are commercial banks, who use this instrument as the principal way to adjust their legal reserve account at the Federal Reserve bank in their district.

Use of the Federal Funds Market to Meet Deposit Reserve Requirements

As we saw in Chapter 4, commercial banks and other depository institutions must hold liquid assets in a special reserve account, equal to a fraction of the funds deposited with them by the public. Only vault cash held on the premises and reserve balances kept with the Federal Reserve bank in the district count in meeting this legal reserve requirement. Frequently, commercial banks (especially small banks) hold more legal reserves than the law requires. Because these reserves earn little or no income, most bankers active in the money market try to dispose of any excess legal reserves in their possession, even if they can only lend the funds overnight.

Banks are aided greatly in this endeavor by the fact that their legal reserve requirement is calculated on a daily average basis over a two-week period, known as the *reserve computation period.* For example, the reserve computation period for *transaction deposits* (e.g., checking accounts and NOWs) stretches from a Tuesday to a Monday two weeks later. The Federal Reserve calculates the daily average level of transaction deposits held by each depository institution over this two-week period and then multiplies that average by the required reserve percentage (3 percent for smaller banks, for example) to determine the amount of legal reserves (i.e., vault cash and deposits with the Federal Reserve bank in the district) that must be held by each depository institution. These legal reserves must average the required amount over a two-week period known as the *reserve maintenance period.* For transaction deposits the reserve maintenance period starts on a Thursday—two days after the transaction-deposit reserve computation period begins—and ends on a Wednesday two weeks later. Thus, the reserve computation and reserve maintenance periods for transaction deposits overlap each other except for *two days.* This overlapping feature explains why this deposit reserve accounting system is often called *contemporaneous reserve accounting* (CRA).[4]

In theory at least, contemporaneous reserve accounting promotes a closer correspondence between the growth of deposits, which reflect bank lending, and the volume of legal reserves which can be controlled by the Federal Reserve System. Interestingly enough, however, the Federal Reserve allows depository institutions to calculate the legal reserves they must hold on *nonpersonal time deposits* (principally business CDs) and *other nontransaction liabilities* on the basis of the average level of these liabilities over a two-week period ending 16 days before the reserve maintenance period begins. Furthermore, each depository institution is allowed to count its average vault cash holdings over the same two-week computation period and then deduct that daily average vault cash figure from its required reserves.

Exhibit 14–1 illustrates the contemporaneous reserve accounting system now in use. As this exhibit illustrates, the manager of each *depository institution's money desk*—the department responsible for keeping track of the institution's legal reserve position—must adjust each deposit institution's reserve balance at the district Federal reserve bank to the right level over the two-week reserve maintenance period.[5] The *federal funds market is an indispensable tool for this kind of daily reserve management,* especially for the largest and most aggressive banks, which hold few reserves of their own. Indeed, many large U.S. banks today borrow virtually all of their entire reserve requirement on a more or less permanent basis from the federal funds market.

Mechanics of Federal Funds Trading

The mechanics of federal funds trading vary depending on the locations of the buying (borrowing) and selling (lending) institutions. For example, suppose two commercial banks involved in a federal funds transaction are located in the heart of the New York money market. These banks can simply exchange checks. The borrowing bank is given a check drawn on the lending bank's reserve account at the Federal Reserve Bank of New York or drawn on a correspondent balance held at some other bank

---

[4] The CRA system replaced the old lagged reserve accounting (LRA) system in February 1984. Under the old LRA system there was a two-week gap between the reserve computation and reserve maintenance periods.

[5] Actually, the money desk manager receives a little leeway under existing regulations because each depository institution is allowed to fall up to 2 percent below its required reserve level in a given reserve maintenance period, provided it runs a corresponding excess reserve position during the next maintenance period.

EXHIBIT 14–1

The Contemporaneous Reserve Accounting (CRA) System for Calculating
Deposit Reserve Requirements of Commercial Banks and Other U.S.
Depository Institutions

Week 1–Week 2	Week 3–Week 4	Week 5–Week 6
Reserve computation period for nonpersonal time deposits and other nontransaction liabilities	Skip over	Reserve computation period for transaction deposits
Tues. Mon. Mon. ↑_____↑		Tues. Mon. Mon. ↑_____↑
Calculate daily average levels of nonpersonal time deposits and other (nontransaction) liabilities and daily average holdings of vault cash over this two-week period		Reserve maintenance period for holding required daily average levels of legal reserves at the district Federal Reserve bank
		Thur. Thur. Wed. ↑_____↑

Example of Required Deposit Reserve Calculation

First National Bank holds a daily average of $10 million in nonpersonal time deposits and $100,000 in vault cash over weeks 1 and 2. Transaction deposits at First National Bank averaged $20 million daily during weeks 5 and 6 (Tuesday through Monday 14 days later). The reserve requirement percentage on nonpersonal time deposits and on transaction deposits as set by the Federal Reserve Board is 3 percent. Therefore, First National must hold $800,000 in its required daily average reserve balance over a two-week period (week 5–week 6, Thursday through Wednesday, 14 days hence). This required reserve figure was derived as follows:

Legal reserves required behind nonpersonal time deposits	= $10 million × 3% = $300,000
Legal reserves required behind transaction deposits	= $20 million × 3% = 600,000
Total legal reserve requirement	= $900,000
Less: Average vault cash holdings in weeks 1 and 2	= −100,000
Required daily average deposit to be held at the Federal Reserve bank during weeks 5 and 6	$800,000

in New York City. This check is payable immediately ("same-day money") and, therefore, Fed funds are transferred to the borrower's reserve account before the close of business that same day. The lender, on the other hand, receives a check drawn on the borrower. This last check is "one-day money" (i.e., payable the following day) because it must pass through the New York Clearing House for settlement. Thus, funds flow instantly to the borrowing bank's reserve account and are automatically returned to the lending bank's reserve account the next day or whenever the loan agreement terminates. Interest on the loan may be included when the funds are returned, paid by separate check, or settled by debiting and crediting correspondent balances.

If the transacting institutions are not both located within the New York Federal Reserve District, the loan transaction proceeds in much the same way except that two Federal Reserve banks are involved. Once borrower and lender agree on the terms of a Federal funds loan, the lending institution will directly, or indirectly through a major correspondent bank, contact the Federal Reserve bank in its district, requesting a wire transfer of funds. The Federal Reserve bank then merely transfers reserves through the Fed's wire network to the Federal Reserve bank serving the region of the country where the borrowing institution is located. Funds travel the reverse route when the loan is terminated.

Incidentally, how do Fed funds borrowers and lenders contact each other to find out who has surplus funds to lend and who is short funds? The telephone is the most common medium of communication with institutions in need of funds and those with surplus funds calling their regular Fed funds customers. In addition, there are a handful of Fed funds *brokers* active in the New York money market who work to bring buying and selling institutions together.

Volume of Borrowings in the Funds Market

Commercial banks borrow billions of dollars each day in the funds market. Total Federal funds borrowings by banks in all 50 states (including security resale agreements from nonbank institutions) stood at nearly $150 billion early in 1985. Borrowings between banks themselves can only be estimated, though figures released by the Federal Reserve Board indicate that the nation's largest money-center banks (the so-called weekly reporting banks) borrowed an average of between $30 and $40 billion daily from other commercial banks. Thus, the Federal funds market probably extends between $180 and $200 billion in credit *daily*. The large banks in New York City, by virtue of their strategic location at the heart of the money market, still account for a disproportionate share of Fed funds transactions. However, the market has broadened considerably in recent years to include banks in Atlanta, Chicago, Dallas, San Francisco, and other major U.S. cities, as well as thousands of smaller banks in outlying areas. Member banks of the Federal Reserve System, despite their smaller total numbers, are more important in this market than nonmember banks due to their greater average size and strategic locations.

Most Federal funds loans are either overnight (one-day) transactions or continuing contracts that have no specific maturity date and can be terminated without advance notice by either party. One-day loans carry a fixed rate of interest, but continuing contracts often do not. There is a growing volume of loans lasting beyond one day, often arising from security repurchase agreements. These longer maturity interbank loans are usually called *term* Federal funds and are being supplied increasingly by foreign banks and savings and loan associations as a safe, easy, and profitable way to warehouse funds until they are needed for long-term loan commitments.

Rates on Federal Funds

The Federal funds interest rate is highly volatile from day to day and week to week, though on an annual basis it tends to move roughly in line with other money market rates (see Exhibit 14–2). The short-run volatility of the rate arises from substantial variations in the volume of funds made available by lenders each day and the size of daily cash deficits experienced by banks and other money market participants. The funds rate tends to be most volatile toward the close of the reserve maintenance-period (especially on the last day), depending on whether larger

EXHIBIT 14–2

Effective Interest Rates on Federal Funds Transactions, 1971–1985
(percent per annum)*

Year	Average Daily Rate on Federal Funds	Year	Average Daily Rate on Federal Funds
1971	4.67%	1978	7.94%
1972	4.44	1979	11.20
1973	8.74	1980	13.36
1974	10.51	1981	16.38
1975	5.82	1982	12.26
1976	5.05	1983	9.09
1977	5.54	1984	10.23
		1985†	8.40

* Figures in the table are averages of daily effective rates for each week ended on Wednesday during the indicated year. The daily effective rate is an average of the interest rates on a given day weighted by the volume of transactions at these rates.
† Average for the week ended March 1, 1985.
SOURCE: Board of Governors of the Federal Reserve System, *Federal Reserve Bulletin*, selected monthly issues.

banks across the nation are flush with reserves or are short of reserves. There are also definite seasonal patterns, with the funds rate tending to rise around holiday periods when loan demand and deposit withdrawals are heavy.

Federal Funds and Government Policy

The Federal funds market is an easy and riskless way to invest excess reserves for short periods and still earn some interest income. It is essential to the daily management of bank reserves, because credit can be obtained in a matter of minutes to cover emergency situations. As we have seen, the Federal funds market is also critical to the whole money market because these funds serve as the principal means of payment for securities and loans. Moreover, the funds market transmits the effects of Federal Reserve monetary policy quickly throughout the banking system.

Prior to 1979 the Federal Reserve routinely set target levels for the Federal funds rate and raised or lowered those targets depending on whether the Fed wished to slow down borrowing and spending in the economy or speed it up. Using daily open-market operations—buying and selling securities—the Fed was able to push the funds rate in the desired direction on any given day. However, fearing accelerating inflation, the Fed announced in October 1979 that it would pay less attention to the daily Federal funds rates and try to control the nation's money supply. Since that time the Federal funds rate appears to have become much *more volatile* from day to day.

The Federal funds rate usually stays above the discount rate the Federal Reserve charges on loans of reserves to banks and other depository institutions. This is due to the fact that many banks prefer to borrow reserves directly from institutions in the private sector rather than deal with the government agency (the Federal Reserve System) that regulates them. Many bankers fear that heavy use of direct loans from the Fed rather than from the impersonal Federal funds market will subject them to closer scrutiny by the regulatory authorities.

NEGOTIABLE CERTIFICATES OF DEPOSIT

One of the largest of all money market instruments, measured by dollar volume, is the negotiable certificate of deposit (CD). A CD is an interest-bearing receipt for funds deposited in a bank or other depository institution for a set period of time.[6] While banks, savings and loan associa-

---

[6] The minimum maturity permitted for CDs under federal regulation is 14 days. There is no legal upper limit on maturities, however. CDs must be issued at par and trade on an interest-bearing basis, unlike Treasury bills. Payment is made in Federal funds on the day the CD matures.

tions, and other deposit-type institutions issue many types of CDs, the true money market CDs are negotiable instruments that may be sold any number of times before reaching maturity and carry minimum denominations of $100,000. The usual round-lot trading unit for CDs bought and sold in the money market is $1 million.

The interest rate on a large, negotiable CD is set by negotiation between the issuing institution and its customer and generally reflects prevailing market conditions. Therefore, like the rates on other money market securities, CD rates rise in periods of tight money when loanable funds are scarce and fall in periods of easy money when loanable funds are more abundant.

The negotiable CD is one of the youngest of all American money market instruments. It dates from 1961, when First National City Bank of New York began offering the instrument to its largest corporate customers. Simultaneously a small group of securities dealers agreed to make a secondary (resale) market for CDs of $100,000 or more. Other money-center banks soon entered the competition for corporate funds and began to offer their own CDs.

The decision to offer this new money market instrument was agonizing for the nation's major banks, because CDs have sharply raised the average cost of bank funds. However, commercial banks had little choice but to offer the new instrument or face the loss of billions of dollars in interest-sensitive deposits. The cash-management departments of major corporations have become increasingly aware of the many profitable ways available today to invest their short-term funds. Prior to the introduction of the negotiable CD, many bankers found that their biggest corporate customers were reducing their deposits (especially demand accounts) and buying U.S. Treasury bills, bankers' acceptances, RPs, and other money market instruments. The CD was developed to attract those lost deposits back into the banking system.

Growth of CDs

Negotiable CDs are a real success story for American banks. In February 1985 large ($100,000+) time deposits outstanding at banks operating in the U.S. totaled $325 billion. This compares with only about $100 billion in large CDs a decade earlier. Until the Penn Central crisis in 1970, large negotiable CDs were subject to legal interest-rate ceilings as specified in the Federal Reserve Board's Regulation Q. However, the bankruptcy of the huge Penn Central Transportation Company rocked the money market, and many large corporations could not sell their commercial notes to raise short-term funds. To ease this serious liquidity crunch, the Fed suspended interest-rate ceilings on large short-term (30–89 day) CDs in June 1970 and lifted the ceilings on longer-term CDs in May 1973. Freed from legal interest-rate ceilings, the volume of large CDs has soared, especially during periods of rapid economic growth.

Terms Attached to CDs

Negotiable CDs may be *registered* on the books of the issuing bank or other depository institution or issued in *bearer form* to the investor purchasing them. CDs issued in bearer form are more convenient for resale in the secondary market because they are in the hands of the investor who owns them. Denominations range from $25,000 to $10 million, though, as we noted previously, CDs traded in the money market carry minimum denominations of $100,000. Maturities range from 1 to about 18 months, depending on the customer's needs. However, most money market CDs have maturities of six months or less.

Interest rates in the CD market are computed as a yield to maturity but quoted on a 360-day basis (except in secondary market trading where the bank discount rate is used as a measure of CD yields). Therefore, to convert the yield on newly issued CDs to a coupon-equivalent basis, we must multiply their yield by the ratio 365:360. The yield on CDs normally is slightly above the U.S. Treasury bill rate, and sometimes lower than going rates on Federal funds and Eurodollars as alternative sources of bank funds. However, as Exhibit 14–3 shows, in 1984 and 1985 following severe problems at some of the nation's largest banks, risk premiums

EXHIBIT 14–3

Recent Interest Rates on Money Market CDs ($100,000 or More) versus Rates on Treasury Bills, Federal Funds, and Eurodollars

Instrument	Period (percent)				
	1981	1982	1983	1984	1985*
Certificates of deposit:					
Three-month	15.91%	12.27%	9.07%	10.37%	8.91%
Six-month	15.77	12.57	9.27	10.68	9.47
U.S. Treasury bills:					
Three-month	14.03	10.61	8.61	9.52	8.47
Six-month	13.80	11.07	8.73	9.76	8.70
Federal funds	16.38	12.26	9.09	10.23	8.40
Eurodollars, three-month	16.79	13.12	9.56	10.73	9.35

* Rates as of the week ended March 1, 1985.
Note: Based on five-day average rates for each week of the period as quoted by five dealers in CDs. All rates expressed in percent per annum. Bill yields in the secondary market are quoted on a bank discount basis from daily closing bid prices.
SOURCE: Board of Governors of the Federal Reserve System, *Federal Reserve Bulletin*, selected issues.

attached to large bank CDs rose, driving them well above the Federal funds rate and closer to Eurodollar deposit rates. The yield spread between CDs and other money market instruments varies over time, depending upon investor preferences, the supply of CDs and other money market instruments, and the changing financial condition of issuing banks.

One of the most interesting developments in recent years is the appearance of a *multitiered* (segmented) market for CDs. Investors have grouped issuing banks into different risk categories, and yields in the market are scaled accordingly. This development is a legacy of the collapse of such banking giants as United States National Bank of San Diego in October 1973 and Franklin National Bank of New York in October 1974, and Penn Square Bank in Oklahoma City in 1982. Faced with the specter of major-bank failures, those banks viewed as less stable by investors were forced to issue their CDs at significantly higher interest rates. CDs from the largest and most financially sound banks are rated *prime*, while smaller banks or those viewed as less stable issue *nonprime* CDs at higher interest rates. As is true for any depositor in a U.S. insured bank, the holder of a CD is covered against loss up to a maximum of $100,000 if the issuing bank fails. Unfortunately, this insurance protection is of limited value to a corporation holding a million dollar or larger CD.

Buyers of CDs

The principal buyers of large, negotiable CDs include nonfinancial corporations, state and local governments, foreign central banks and governments, wealthy individuals, and a wide variety of financial institutions. The latter include insurance companies, pension funds, investment companies, savings banks, and credit unions. Large CDs appeal to these investors because they are readily marketable at low risk, may be issued in any desired maturity, and carry a somewhat higher yield than on U.S. Treasury bills. However, the investor gives up some marketability in comparison with T bills because the resale market for CDs averages $3 to $4 billion a day—well below the average daily volume of trading in bills.

Most buyers hold CDs until they mature. However, prime-rated CDs issued by the nation's billion-dollar banks are actively traded in the secondary market, centered in New York City. The purpose of the secondary market is principally to accommodate corporations that need cash quickly or see profitable opportunities from the sale of their deposits. Also, buyers of CDs who desire shorter maturities or higher yields than are available on new issues will enter the secondary market. No bank is allowed to purchase its own CDs in the secondary market or redeem them in advance of maturity, except under special circumstances. Moreover, banks usually will not lend money using their own CDs as collateral because of the risk of borrower default.

CDs in Liability Management

Commercial banks and other depository institutions use the CD as a supplement to Federal funds when additional reserves are needed. A depository institution in need of funds simply raises the rate it is currently offering on CDs to attract new deposits. Financial institutions may also trade CDs (not their own) in the secondary market to raise funds, much as they might sell U.S. Treasury bills for cash. Today the negotiable CD plays a prominent role in the strategy of *liability management,* where banks control their funds sources as well as their funds uses to achieve both long- and short-range objectives.

New Types of CDs

Bankers are becoming increasingly innovative in packaging CDs to meet the needs of their customers. One notable innovation occurred in 1975 when the *variable-rate CD* was introduced. Variable-rate CDs issued by major banks today generally carry maturities of one year or less, with an interest rate that is adjusted every 30 to 90 days. The rate is usually based on a fixed premium over the average secondary market rate for major bank CDs. Variable-rate CDs give the investor a higher return than could be obtained by continually renewing shorter-term CDs and is a particularly popular investment for money market mutual funds.

Another interesting development occurred in 1976 when Morgan Guaranty Trust in New York City introduced the *rollover CD* (also known as the roly-poly CD). Because six-month CDs are the maximum maturity traded in the secondary market, Morgan offered its customers longer-term CDs with higher rates, but in packages composed of a series of six-month CDs extending over a period of at least two years. Thus, the roly-poly CD promised higher returns plus the ability to market some CDs in the package in advance of maturity to meet emergency cash needs. However, the bank's customer is still obligated to purchase the remaining certificates at each six-month anniversary date until the contract expires. Some roly-poly CDs are issued with fixed rates, while others carry floating rates that change every six months.

Another variation on the CD theme is the *Eurodollar CD,* developed in 1966. Eurodollar CDs are negotiable, dollar-denominated time deposits issued by the foreign branches of major U.S. banks and some foreign-owned banks. These instruments generally carry higher yields than comparable domestic CDs due to greater perceived risk. Most Eurodollar CDs carry fixed rates, but floating-rate instruments were introduced in

1977. These CDs carry maturities over one year with a rate adjusted every three to six months to match changes in the London Interbank Offer Rate (LIBOR). There is now an active secondary market for Eurodollar CDs centered in New York City and in London.

The 1970s ushered in still more CD innovations; for example, *Asian Dollar CDs, Jumbo CDs,* and *Yankee CDs.* Offered by U.S., Japanese, and other banks operating in Singapore, *Asian Dollar CDs* carry both fixed and floating interest rates based on the current level of the Singapore interbank offer rate, known as SIBOR. Payable in New York clearinghouse funds, Asian CDs normally trade in $1 million units like domestic CDs but at higher yields. *Jumbo CDs,* on the other hand, are large ($100,000+), negotiable CDs issued by nonbank thrift institutions such as savings and loans and mutual savings banks. *Yankee CDs* are large ($100,000+), negotiable CDs issued in the United States by foreign banks that usually have branch or agency offices in one or more major U.S. cities. Further innovations in CDs are likely in the future as banks face increasingly stiff competition for funds.

LOANS FROM THE FEDERAL RESERVE'S DISCOUNT WINDOW

A money market source of funds available to commercial banks and other depository institutions is the Federal Reserve's discount window. Each of the 12 Federal Reserve banks has a department where banks and other qualified borrowers can come to borrow reserves for short periods.[7] Most discount-window loans are short term (i.e., a maximum of 15 days), though longer-term credit can be arranged upon presentation of acceptable collateral and adequate reasons for the request. Today the Fed grants three types of loans: (1) adjustment credit, designed to cover short-term deficiencies in required legal reserves; (2) seasonal credit, designed to aid primarily small depository institutions experiencing seasonal fluctuations in loans and deposits; and (3) extended credit, aimed mainly at institutions facing serious financial problems of a long-term nature. Normally, adjustment credit to cover short-term reserve deficiencies accounts for the majority of loans granted by the Federal Reserve banks. However, the other forms of discount-window credit can be extremely

---

[7] Until 1980 only member banks could borrow from the Federal Reserve Banks except under special circumstances. However, with passage of the Monetary Control Act of 1980, nonmember commercial banks, mutual savings banks, savings and loan associations, and credit unions offering transaction accounts or nonpersonal time deposits were authorized to borrow from the Fed's discount window on the same basis as member banks.

important in emergency situations, such as the recent financial crisis experienced by Continental Illinois Bank in Chicago.

The mechanics of borrowing from the discount window are relatively simple. A depository institution granted a loan merely receives an increase in its reserve account at the Federal Reserve Bank in its district. When the loan comes due, the Fed merely removes the amount owed from the borrowing institution's reserve account.[8]

Causes and Effects of Borrowing from the Discount Window

Borrowing from the Fed increases the total volume of reserves available in the banking system until the loan is repaid. Many banks and other depository institutions come to the Federal Reserve near the end of their reserve settlement week when they find themselves short of legal reserves. Frequently, the funds available from the Federal Reserve carry a lower interest rate than prevails in the Federal funds market, on CDs, or on other money market sources of funds. This is especially true in periods of rapidly rising interest rates because the Fed changes its loan rate rather infrequently.[9] As the gap between open-market rates (especially on Federal funds) and the Fed's rate widens, demands on the discount window increase. In contrast, a period of falling rates usually brings about a decline in borrowings from the Fed.

This last point is illustrated by the figures shown in Exhibit 14–4. Money market interest rates rose to record levels in 1979 and 1980, spurred on by high rates of inflation. The Federal funds rate averaged just over 11 percent in 1979 and more than 13 percent in 1980, rising to a high of almost 20 percent in December 1980. Nevertheless, the Federal Reserve kept the rate on its loans around 10 percent until late 1979 and held it in the 10 to 12 percent range through most of 1980. With discount-window loans much cheaper than other money market sources of funds, borrowers predictably turned to the Federal Reserve banks for huge amounts of funds. Discount-window loans averaged more than $1.5 billion during the 1979–80 period and climbed to well over $2 billion in the fall of 1980. Much the same pattern developed in 1983 and 1984 when open-market interest rates in the money market climbed to double-digit levels, while the Fed kept its discount rate in the 8.5 to 9 percent range. The result was a sharp upsurge in borrowings from the Federal Reserve banks which reached a peak of more than $8 billion (on a daily average

---

[8] See Chapter 23 for a more complete discussion of the methods used by depository institutions to borrow from the Federal Reserve.

[9] For example, the discount rate was not changed at all in 1983 and once in 1984.

EXHIBIT 14–4

Volume of Borrowings from the Federal Reserve Banks, 1975–1985
($ millions at year-end)

Year	Discount-Window Loans to Depository Institutions	Year	Discount-Window Loans to Depository Institutions
1975	$ 211	1980	$1,617
1976	25	1981	642
1977	265	1982	697
1978	1,174	1983	774
1979	1,454	1984	3,186
		1985	1,289*

* As of February 1985.
SOURCE: Board of Governors of the Federal Reserve System, *Federal Reserve Bulletin,* selected issues.

basis) in August of 1984 before falling back as market interest rates eased down.

Collateral for Discount-Window Loans

Most loans granted through the Fed's discount window are secured by U.S. government securities. However, the Federal Reserve also will make loans against commercial or farm paper, bankers' acceptances, and bills of exchange. Discount-window loans may be for terms as long as 90 days if the collateral used consists of U.S. government securities or eligible paper, and up to four months on other forms of collateral. However, as we noted earlier, most loans from the discount window are for a maximum of 15 days. To make the borrowing process as simple as possible, many depository institutions keep U.S. government securities in the vaults of the Federal Reserve banks and sign loan authorization agreements with the Fed's discount department in advance so they can borrow over the telephone. Such requests must be confirmed in writing, however.

Restrictions on Federal Reserve Credit

Large money-center banks are the heaviest users of the discount window because they incur reserve deficits most frequently. However, less than 10 percent of all institutions eligible regularly borrow from the Federal Reserve System, despite the fact that it is often the cheapest source of reserves. In part, this is due to an uneasy feeling experienced by most bankers about being in debt to a government regulatory agency. The Fed's own regulations discourage heavy and frequent use of the window. For example, Federal Reserve officials stress that borrowing is a "privilege, not a right" and that no depository institution should come to rely on Federal Reserve credit. Borrowing institutions are required to alternate between the window and other money market sources, especially Federal funds.

The Federal Reserve's Discount Rate

The discount rate is the interest rate charged by the Fed on loans of reserves secured by U.S. government securities or other acceptable collateral. In reality, there are four different discount rates. The cheapest rate applies to loans (advances) for short-term liquidity adjustment or seasonal needs, secured by U.S. government securities of high-grade commercial ("eligible") paper. In the spring of 1985 this rate was set at 7½ percent. A slightly higher interest rate is levied against discount-window loans secured by collateral of lesser quality. In times of national emergency, the Fed may also extend credit to individuals, partnerships, and even nonfinancial corporations, but the interest rate is much higher on such loans.[10]

The individual Federal Reserve banks often recommend that the discount rate be changed; however, a change in that rate must be approved by the Federal Reserve Board in Washington, D.C. In recent years the Fed has levied a higher interest rate for emergency borrowings when a bank is in serious financial trouble. Large, continuous borrowings over a prolonged period of time may be approved at a rate of 1 to 2 percent above the regular Federal Reserve discount rate.

A CONCLUDING COMMENT ON BANK ACTIVITY IN THE MONEY MARKET

In this chapter we have focused our attention on the major money market sources of funds used by commercial banks and other depository institutions. As we have seen, banks operate on both sides of the money market, supplying billions of dollars in credit to governments, corporations, securities dealers, and financial intermediaries each day while also borrowing huge amounts daily from many of the same institutions.

The money market has not always been as important a source of funds for banks and other depository institutions as it is today. Prior to the 1960s even many of the largest money-center banks in the United States regarded short-term deposits and nondeposit borrowings from the money market as a secondary, supplementary source of funds. Bankers were

---

[10] See Chapter 23 for a schedule of rates charged on various types of discount-window loans.

aware that heavy dependence on money market borrowing would make their earnings more sensitive to fluctuations in interest rates. When interest rates rose rapidly, bank profit margins would be squeezed. However, the force of competition intervened in the 1960s and 1970s, and many banks were compelled to draw more heavily upon the money market simply to protect their share of credit and deposit markets.

The real catalyst for growing money market borrowing by U.S. banks and other depository institutions has been the growing financial sophistication of their largest customers. When major corporations began to seek alternative investments for their short-term funds, especially the purchase of commercial paper and U.S. Treasury bills, rather than holding most of their money in bank deposits, bankers were forced to turn to the money market for additional funds. As we have seen in this chapter, the banking community approached the problem in two ways. One was to offer a new financial instrument—the negotiable certificate of deposit—to compete directly for short-term corporate funds. The other approach to the problem was to draw more intensively upon existing sources of money market funds, especially the Federal funds market.

Prior to the 1960s and 1970s, the Federal funds market was confined principally to the nation's largest banks, who swapped reserves with each other. As bankers turned more and more to the funds market, however, it broadened tremendously. Thousands of small banks and other nonbank financial institutions in cities, towns, and rural areas across the United States began supplying their excess reserves to larger banks in the central cities, hoping to boost their earnings. In turn, the greater supply of Fed funds encouraged the nation's largest banks to rely even more heavily on the money market and less upon customer deposits as a source of reserves. The Federal funds market had become an accepted institution for both the smallest and the largest financial institutions in the nation.

As we will see in subsequent chapters, the rapid expansion of the CD and Federal funds markets was just the beginning of banking's *money market strategy*. When the Federal Reserve became concerned over the rapid growth of CDs and Federal funds, especially in periods of severe inflation, and clamped down with tight-money policies and a slower growth in available reserves, innovative financial managers were forced to find new sources of reserves or face a real cutback in their lending activities. Many turned to the Eurodollar market, borrowing deposits from abroad or organizing holding companies and issuing commercial paper through subsidiary corporations. Still others found innovative ways to use repurchase agreements backed by Treasury bills and other government securities to raise additional funds.

All of these clever maneuvers form part of what has been called the technique of *liability management*. For decades prior to the 1960s and 1970s bankers devoted most of their time and attention to the management of their assets—mainly loans and security investments—and assumed their deposits and other liabilities would take care of themselves. Many financial analysts argued that deposits were essentially beyond management's control, determined by such external factors as interest rates, economic conditions, and government policy. Heavier dependence on the money market for funds changed all that, however. Bankers very quickly came to realize that simply by varying the daily interest rates (yields) they were willing to offer on CDs, Federal funds, Eurodollars, commercial paper, and other funds sources, they could gain a measure of control over the volume of incoming funds. If more funds were needed on a given day to accommodate customer loan demand, for example, a bank active in the money market would simply offer a higher yield on the particular money market instrument it desired to use. If a smaller volume of funds were required at another time, the institution might simply lower its offer rate on money market borrowings.

What is especially fascinating about the growth of liability management strategies is that they have had precisely the effects many financial analysts predicted from the start. The earnings of banks and other financial institutions have become more sensitive to fluctuations in interest rates; and, in periods of rapidly escalating rates, profit margins have been squeezed. The use of liability-management strategies appears to have fundamentally altered the earnings-size relationship in banking. Until the 1970s the largest U.S. banks generally reported the highest earnings rates, but no more! Today the most profitable banks are generally those of only moderate size. The heavier use of expensive and often highly volatile money market borrowings has contributed in many instances to more rapid increases in bank expenses than in revenues.

Whether this adverse impact on the earnings of major banks will continue into the future remains to be seen. The great innovative abilities of these institutions freed in recent years by deregulation of the industry will do much to shape their earnings performance in the years ahead. But, whatever the future holds, bankers have transformed the money market into a far larger, more dynamic, and more vital institution than at any other time in history. The future rapid growth of money market transactions, with banks at the very center of trading activity, seems assured.

STUDY QUESTIONS

1. Define the term *Federal funds*. Why are Federal funds so important to the functioning of the money market?

2. Who are the principal borrowers in the Federal funds market? Principal lenders?

3. Describe the process of reserve position adjustment for commercial banks and other depository institutions. What role does the Federal funds market play in the management of depository institutions' money (reserve) position?

4. How does Federal funds trading take place?

5. Describe the different types of Federal funds loans. What factors explain why the daily rate on Federal funds is one of the most volatile interest rates in the U.S. financial system?

6. Why do you suppose the funds market is so important to the Federal Reserve in the conduct of monetary policy?

7. What is a large, negotiable CD? When and why were CDs first offered in the U.S. money market?

8. What factors appear to influence the interest rate offered on the CDs issued by any particular depository institution? Explain the meaning of the term *multitiered market.*

9. Who are the principal buyers of money market CDs? Why?

10. What role do large, negotiable CDs play in liability management?

11. What is a variable-rate CD? Roly-poly CD? Eurodollar CD? Many financial experts expect banks and other deposit institutions to continue to develop new and more innovative forms of CDs in the future. Can you explain why?

12. What is a discount-window loan? What types of loans do the Federal Reserve banks make? How are those loans made and repaid?

13. What role does the discount window play in managing the reserves of depository institutions?

PROBLEMS

1. Security State Bank has just verified by checking its legal reserve account on the computer of the Federal Reserve bank in its district that its daily average reserve balance for the current reserve maintenance period is $1.25 million. Today is the final day of the current reserve maintenance period and the bank's money market officer is concerned that Security might be running a large deficit in its legal reserve account. Checking the bank's own computer records the officer discovers that nontransaction deposits and other liabilities averaged $16 million and transaction deposits averaged $31 million over

the relevant two-week reserve computation period. Vault cash holdings over the same reserve computation period as that for nonpersonal time deposits averaged $250,000. Currently the Federal reserve imposes a 3 percent reserve requirement on the total of a depository institution's transaction deposits below $29 million and 12 percent for any amount of transaction deposits over $29 million. Nontransaction deposits are subject to a 3 percent required reserve. Does Security State have a reserve deficiency? If so, is it required to cover the reserve shortfall before this current reserve maintenance period ends today? Explain your answer. If Security State must borrow, what is the cheapest sources of legal reserves currently available?

SELECTED REFERENCES

Federal Reserve Bank of Boston. *Controlling Monetary Aggregates.* 1968.

Federal Reserve Bank of Richmond. *Instruments of the Money Market.* 5th ed., 1981.

Lucas, Charles M.; Marcos T. Jones; and Thom B. Thurston. "Federal Funds and Repurchase Agreements." *Quarterly Review,* Federal Reserve Bank of New York, Summer 1977, pp. 33–48.

Melton, William C. "The Market for Large Negotiable CDs." *Quarterly Review,* Federal Reserve Bank of New York, Winter 1977–78, pp. 22–24.

Poole, William. "The Making of Monetary Policy: Description and Analysis." *New England Economic Review,* Federal Reserve Bank of Boston, March–April 1974, pp. 21–30.

Simpson, Thomas D. *The Market for Federal Funds and Repurchase Agreements.* Staff Study, Board of Governors of the Federal Reserve System, July 1979.

Tarhan, Vefa. "Individual Bank Reserve Management." *Economic Perspectives,* Federal Reserve Bank of Chicago, May/June 1984, pp. 17–23.

15

Commercial Paper and Federal Agency Securities

PURPOSE OF THIS CHAPTER

To highlight the important role played by major corporations and various federal government agencies as large-scale borrowers in the money market. The chapter reviews the key characteristics of the financial instrument known as commercial paper—the oldest of all American money market instruments—and explains how this instrument reaches the financial marketplace. Federal credit agencies, such as Fannie Mae (FNMA) and the farm credit banks, are viewed as financial intermediaries, fulfilling the role of borrowers of funds in the money market while simultaneously lending funds to selected sectors of the economy, such as agriculture, housing, and small businesses.

KEY TERMS AND CONCEPTS IN THE CHAPTER

bank discount method
best efforts basis
certificates of
  participation (PC)
commercial paper
compensating balance
dealer paper
dealers

direct paper
disadvantaged sectors
federal agencies
federal agency
  securities
Federal Financing
  Bank

government-
  sponsored agencies
letters of credit
master note
paper ratings
solicitation method

In the previous chapter we discussed the vital role played by banks as major borrowers and lenders in the money market. However, banks have had to share the limelight in recent years with two other groups of money market borrowers—federal government agencies and large corporations. Indeed, the largest of all borrowers in the American money market is not a bank, but a unit of government—the U.S. Treasury Department. Moreover, in the 1960s and 70s, other units within the federal government's huge structure, known as federal agencies, came to be major demanders of money market funds. Many of these agencies, such as the Federal Land Banks, Small Business Administration, and Federal National Mortgage Association, have become familiar names to active investors, who are regularly offered a menu of attractive notes and bonds so that these agencies can carry out their mission of assisting the "disadvantaged" sectors of the economy.

The ranks of private money market participants have also grown rapidly in recent years due to the borrowing and lending activities of some of the nation's largest corporations. Each year companies like American Telephone & Telegraph, General Motors, and Philip Morris borrow billions of dollars in the money market through the sale of unsecured promissory notes, known as commercial paper. A 1982 study by the Federal Reserve Board found that, at that time, about 1,200 corporations were regularly selling their commercial notes to money market investors.[1] Commercial paper issued by large corporations and bought principally by other large corporations has become one of the most dynamic and rapidly growing segments of the American money market. In this chapter we take a close look at both commercial paper and federal agency securities and their important roles within the financial system.

COMMERCIAL PAPER

What Is Commercial Paper?

Commercial paper is one of the oldest of all money market instruments, dating back to the 18th century in the United States. By definition, commercial paper consists of short-term, unsecured promissory notes issued by well-known companies that are financially strong and carry high credit ratings.[2] The funds raised from a paper issue normally are used for current

---

[1] See Hurley (1982).

[2] As a further backstop to reduce investor risk, borrowers in the commercial paper market nearly always secure a line of credit at a commercial bank. However, because the line of credit cannot be used to directly guarantee payment if the company goes bankrupt, many commercial note issuers today also take out irrevocable letters of credit prepared by their banks. Such a letter makes the bank responsible for repayment if

transactions, that is, to purchase inventories, pay taxes, meet payrolls, and cover other short-term obligations. However, a growing number of paper issues today are used to provide "bridge financing" for such long-term projects as the building of pipelines, ships, office buildings, nuclear power plants, and manufacturing assembly lines. In these instances issuing companies usually plan to convert their short-term paper issues into long-term, more permanent financing when the capital market is more favorable.

Commercial paper is generally issued in multiples of $1,000 and in denominations designed to meet the needs of the buyer. It is traded mainly in the *primary* market. Opportunities for resale in the secondary market are limited, though some dealers will redeem the notes they sell in advance of maturity. Because of the limited resale possibilities, investors are usually quite careful to purchase those paper issues whose maturity matches their planned holding period.

Types of Commercial Paper

There are two major types of commercial paper—direct paper and dealer paper.

The main issuers of *direct paper* are large finance companies and bank holding companies, who deal directly with the investor rather than using a securities dealer as an intermediary and borrow continuously. These companies, which regularly extend installment credit to consumers and large working-capital loans and leases to business firms, announce the rates they are currently paying for various maturities. For example, on November 2, 1984, General Motors Acceptance Corporation (GMAC), the largest finance company borrower in this market, posted the following yields for interested investors:

Paper Maturity	Offered Yield
	(percent)
30 to 59 days	9.40%
60 to 89 days	9.30
90 to 119 days	9.25
120 to 209 days	9.05
210 to 270 days	9.50

Investors then select those maturities that most closely approximate their expected holding periods and buy the securities directly from the issuer.

Leading finance-company borrowers in the direct paper market in-

---

the corporation defaults on its commercial paper. In today's uncertain markets investors frequently need reassurance that a borrowing corporation can pay its bills either from current cash flow or by drawing upon an existing bank credit line.

clude GMAC, CIT Financial Corporation, Commercial Credit Corporation, and General Electric Credit Corporation. The leading bank holding companies which issue commercial paper are centered around the largest banks in New York, Chicago, San Francisco, and other major U.S. cities.[3] Today, about 80 financially oriented U.S. companies account for nearly all the directly placed paper, with finance companies issuing approximately three fourths of the total. All of these firms have an ongoing need for huge amounts of short-term money, possess top credit ratings, and have established working relationships with major institutional investors in order to rapidly place their new note issues.

Directly placed paper must be sold in large volume to cover the substantial costs of its distribution and marketing. On average, each direct issuer has between $600 and $700 million outstanding at any one time and will usually borrow at least $1 billion per month. While issuers of direct paper do not have to pay dealers' commissions and fees, these companies must operate a marketing division to maintain constant contact with active investors. Some times direct issuers must sell their paper even when they have no need for funds. This is the price of maintaining a good working relationship with active investor groups. These companies also cannot escape paying fees to banks for supporting lines of credit, to rating agencies who rate their paper issues, and to agents (usually banks) who dispense required payments and collect funds.

The other major variety of commercial paper is *dealer paper,* issued by security dealers on behalf of their corporate customers. Also known as industrial paper, dealer paper is issued mainly by nonfinancial companies as well as by smaller bank holding companies and finance companies. The issuing company may sell the paper directly to the dealer, who buys it less discount and commission and then attempts to sell it at the highest possible price in the market. Alternatively, the issuing company may carry all the risk, with the dealer agreeing only to sell the issue at the best price available less commission (often referred to as a best efforts basis). Finally, the open-rate method may be used in which the borrowing company receives some money in advance but the balance depends on how well the issue sells in the open market. Companies using dealers to place their paper are generally smaller and less frequent borrowers than issuers of direct paper.

---

[3] Bank holding companies issue both direct and dealer paper, with the largest companies going the direct placement route. Much of this so-called bank-related paper comes from finance-company subsidiaries of large bank holding companies. Frequently, a holding company will issue paper through a nonbank subsidiary and then funnel the proceeds to one or more of its subsidiary banks by purchasing some of the banks' assets. This gives the banks additional funds to lend and may be especially helpful when a bank is having difficulty attracting deposits through normal channels.

Recent Growth of Commercial Paper

As Exhibit 15–1 indicates, the volume of dealer-placed paper tripled between 1980 and 1985 and directly placed issues nearly doubled. By January 1985 more than 700 companies had nearly $250 billion in commercial notes outstanding. Slightly less than half the total was placed directly with investors by larger finance companies and bank holding companies, while the rest reached market through the efforts of security dealers.

What factors explain the rapid growth in commercial paper? One key factor is the relative cost of other sources of credit compared to interest rates prevailing on current commercial paper issues. For the largest, best-known corporations, commercial paper is often an efficient, cost-effective substitute for bank loans and other forms of borrowing. This is especially true for nonfinancial companies issuing notes through dealers. These firms usually come to the commercial paper market when it is significantly cheaper to borrow there rather than tap bank lines of credit. In recent years the paper market has also frequently been a cheaper alternative funds source than issuing long-term bonds and selling stock in a depressed market. Another reason for the market's rapid growth is the high quality of most commercial paper obligations. Many investors regard this instrument as a close substitute for Treasury bills, bank CDs, and other money market instruments. As a result, market yields on commercial notes tend to move in the same direction and by similar amounts as do the yields on other money market securities.

EXHIBIT 15–1

Volume of Commercial Paper Outstanding ($ billions, end of period)

Instrument	1980	1981	1982	1983	1984	1985*
All issuers	$124.4	$165.8	$166.7	$185.9	$239.1	$245.3
Finance companies:						
Dealer-placed paper						
Total	19.6	30.3	34.6	41.7	56.9	59.7
Bank-related	3.6	6.0	2.5	2.4	2.0	2.1
Directly placed paper						
Total	67.9	81.7	84.1	96.5	110.5	113.1
Bank-related	22.4	26.9	32.0	35.6	42.1	43.0
Nonfinancial companies	36.9	53.8	47.9	47.6	71.7	72.5

Note: Includes public utilities and firms engaged primarily in communications, construction, manufacturing, mining, wholesale and retail trade, transportation, and similar activities.
* Through January 1985.
SOURCE: Board of Governors of the Federal Reserve System, *Federal Reserve Bulletin,* selected issues.

This fact is shown clearly in Exhibit 15–2, which compares the market yields on three-month maturities of commercial paper, Treasury bills, negotiable CDs, and bankers' acceptances. Rates on these four money market instruments tend to stay within roughly a percentage point or two of each other. We note that commercial paper yields are always higher than market rates on comparable maturity U.S. Treasury bills, due to the greater risk and lower marketability of commercial notes.

Still another key factor in the market's recent growth is the expanding use of letters of credit and other payment guarantees. For example, a commercial bank or other lending institution may issue a certificate promising payment of principal and/or interest if the borrowing company fails to do so. The result is that such paper usually carries the higher credit rating of the guarantor rather than the lower credit rating of the issuing firm. Mortgage companies, utilities, and small manufacturers in large numbers have been attracted into a market otherwise closed to them, while still saving on interest costs even after paying the guarantor's backing fee. Other groups recently entering the market on the borrowing side include foreign industrial companies, international financial conglomerates, and state and local governments (which offer tax-exempt paper).

Maturities of Commercial Paper

Maturities of commercial paper range from three days ("weekend paper") to nine months. Most commercial notes carry an original maturity of 60 days or less, with an average maturity ranging from 20 to 45 days. Commercial paper is generally not issued for longer maturities than 270

EXHIBIT 15–2

Market Yields on Commercial Paper Compared to Yields on Other Money Market Instruments (Average yields on three-month maturities; percent per annum)

Instruments	1980	1981	1982	1983	1984	1985*
Commercial paper	12.66%	15.32%	11.89%	8.88%	10.10%	8.75%
U.S. Treasury bills	11.43	14.03	16.51	8.61	9.52	8.47
Certificates of deposit	13.07	15.91	12.27	9.07	10.37	8.91
Prime bankers' acceptances	12.78	15.32	11.89	8.90	10.14	8.80

Note: Commercial paper yields are unweighted averages of rates quoted by at least five dealers. Treasury bills are secondary-market yields computed from daily closing bid prices. CD rates are secondary-market yields quoted as five-day averages by five dealers. Bankers' acceptance rates are on 90-day maturities and are an average of the midpoint of the range of daily dealer closing rates offered for domestic issues. All yields except CDs are quoted on a bank discount basis.
* As of the week ending March 1, 1985.
SOURCE: Board of Governors of the Federal Reserve System, *Federal Reserve Bulletin,* selected issues.

days because, under the provisions of the Securities Act of 1933, any security sold in the open market for a longer term must be registered with the Securities and Exchange Commission.

Yields to the investor are calculated by the *bank discount method* as in the case of Treasury bills. Like T bills, most commercial paper is issued at a discount from par, and the investor's yield stems from the price appreciation of the security between purchase date and maturity date. However, coupon-bearing paper is also available. The minimum denomination is usually $25,000, and the notes typically are issued in bearer form. New issues generally average about $2 million each in total amount. Payment is made at maturity upon presentation to the particular bank listed as agent on the note. Settlement in federal funds is usually made the same day the note is presented for payment.

Changing Yields on Paper Issues

Because yields on commercial paper are open-market rates, they fluctuate daily with the ebb and flow of supply and demand forces in the marketplace. In the wide swings between easy and tight money, between depressed and resurgent economic activity that have characterized the 1980s, commercial paper rates have fluctuated between extreme highs and lows. For example, in 1983 and 1985—years of moderate credit demands and moderate inflation—paper rates averaged less than 9 percent (see Exhibit 15–2). In 1981, however, when intense credit demands and rapid inflation characterized the economic situation, paper rates ranged upward to nearly 18 percent and averaged about 15 percent for the year.[4] The commercial paper market is highly volatile and difficult to predict. This is why many corporations eligible to borrow there still maintain close working relationships with commercial banks and other institutional lenders.

Advantages of Issuing Commercial Paper

There are several financial advantages to a company able to tap the commercial paper market for funds. Generally, rates on paper are lower than on corporate loans extended by commercial banks. This is evident from the data shown in Exhibit 15–3. In late 1984 and early 1985, for example, the bank prime rate was consistently at least a full percentage point and often more than 2 percentage points higher than the rate on

---

[4] In most years, yields on longer-term paper issues are higher than on the shortest-term notes, resulting in an upward-sloping yield curve. However, near the peak of an economic boom, yield curves on commercial paper often slope downward.

EXHIBIT 15–3

Spread between the Average Prime Rate Quoted by Major U.S. Banks
and the Six-Month Commercial Paper Rate, Selected Months in 1984
and 1985

Month	Bank Prime Rate	Six-Month Commercial Paper Rate	Rate Spread
1984:			
November	11.77%	9.06%	+2.71%
December	11.06	8.55	+2.51
1985:			
January	10.61	8.15	+2.46
February	10.50	8.69	+1.81

* The prime rate is the average of rates posted by major U.S. banks. The commercial paper rate is an unweighted average of offering rates quoted by at least five dealers. Both rates are measured on a bank discount basis.
SOURCE: Board of Governors of the Federal Reserve System, *Federal Reserve Bulletin,* selected issues.

six-month dealer paper. This spread between the bank prime rate and the six-month paper rate at times has widened to 3 or 4 full percentage points, as occurred in 1980 and 1981.

Moreover, the effective rate on most commercial loans granted by banks is even higher than the quoted prime rate, due to the fact that corporate borrowers usually are required to keep a percentage of their loans in a bank deposit. This so-called *compensating balance requirement* is generally 15 to 20 percent of the amount of the loan. Suppose a corporation borrows $100,000 at a prime interest rate of 15 percent but must keep 20 percent of this amount on deposit with the bank granting the loan. Then the effective loan rate is 18.75 percent (or $15,000/$80,000).

Another advantage of borrowing in the commercial paper market is that interest rates there are more flexible than bank loan rates. Moreover, a company in need of funds can raise money quickly through either dealer or direct paper. Dealers maintain close contact with the market and generally know where cash may be found. Frequently, notes can be issued and funds raised the same day or within a day or two.

Generally, larger amounts of funds may be borrowed more conveniently through the paper market than from other sources, particularly bank loans. This situation arises due to federal and state regulations that limit the amount of money a bank can lend to any single borrower. For national banks, the maximum unsecured loan is 15 percent of the bank's capital and surplus account. Frequently, corporate credit needs exceed an individual bank's loan limit, and a group of banks (consortium) has to be assembled to make the loan. However, this takes time and requires lengthy and complicated negotiations. Using the paper market is generally much faster than trying to hammer out a loan agreement among several parties. Moreover, the ability to issue commercial paper gives a corporation considerable leverage when negotiating with banks. A banker who knows that the customer can draw upon the commercial paper market for funds is more likely to offer advantageous terms on a loan and be more receptive to future customer credit needs.

Possible Disadvantages of Issuing Commercial Paper

Despite the advantages, there are some risks for corporations that choose to borrow frequently in the commercial paper market. One of these is the risk of alienating banks whose loans might be needed when a real emergency develops. The paper market is highly volatile and sensitive to financial and economic problems. This fact was demonstrated quite convincingly in 1980 when Chrysler Financial, the finance-company subsidiary of Chrysler Corporation, was forced to drastically cut back its borrowings in the commercial paper market due to the widely publicized troubles of its parent company. At times, it is extremely difficult even for those companies in sound financial condition to raise funds in the paper market at reasonable rates of interest. It helps to have a loyal and friendly banker available to supply emergency credit when the market turns sour. Another problem lies in the fact that commercial paper cannot be paid off at the issuer's discretion but generally must remain outstanding until it reaches maturity. In contrast, many bank loans permit early retirement without penalty.

Principal Investors

The most important investors in the commercial paper market include nonfinancial corporations, money market mutual funds, bank trust departments, smaller commercial banks, pension funds, and insurance companies. In effect, this is a market in which corporations borrow from other corporations. These investor groups regard commercial paper as a low-risk outlet for their surplus funds.

A recent innovation in the direct paper market is the *master note*, most frequently issued to bank trust departments and other "permanent" money market investors by finance companies. Under a master note agreement, the investing company notifies the issuing company how much paper it will purchase each day for immediate payment. The investor agrees to take some paper each day up to an agreed-upon maximum amount. Interest owed is figured on the average daily volume of paper taken on by the investor during the current month. The prevailing interest rate on six-month commercial paper generally is used to determine the appropriate rate of return.

Commercial Paper Ratings

Commercial paper is generally rated as prime, desirable, or satisfactory, depending on the credit standing of the issuing company. Firms desiring to issue paper generally will seek a credit rating from one or more of five rating services—Moody's Investor Service, Standard & Poor's Corporation, Fitch Investor Service, Duff and Phelps, and McCarthy, Crisanti, and Maffei—with the first two especially prominent. Moody's assigns rating of Prime-1 (P-1) for the highest-quality paper, with lower-quality issues designated as Prime-2 (P-2) or Prime-3 (P-3), Standard & Poor's assigns ratings of A-1, A-2, or A-3, while Fitch uses F-1, F-2, or F-3. Any issue rated below P-2, A-2, or F-2 usually sells poorly.

It is extremely difficult in today's volatile conditions to market unrated commercial paper. Indeed, paper available is mainly from top-quality issuers; about three quarters of the firms currently selling notes carry A-1 or P-1 ratings. Generally, commercial notes bearing credit ratings from at least two rating agencies are preferred by both investors and dealers.

Dealers in Paper

The market is relatively concentrated among a handful of dealers who account for the bulk of all trading activity. The top commercial paper dealers today include Goldman Sachs & Co.; A. G. Becker, Inc.; the First Boston Corporation, Lehman Brothers; Kuhn Loeb, Inc.; Salomon Brothers; and Merrill Lynch, Pierce, Fenner & Smith, Inc. Dealer firms charge varying fees to borrowing companies depending on the size of an issue and how much paper the company has issued through the dealer recently (such as within the past year). Dealers maintain inventories of unsold new issues or repurchased paper, but they usually expect to turn over all their holdings within a week to 10 days. Like dealers in U.S. government securities, commercial paper dealers draw upon repurchase agreements (RPs) and demand loans from banks to help finance their inventory positions. They pay interest rates which usually are only a few basis points higher than on RPs collateralized by U.S. Treasury securities.

FEDERAL AGENCY SECURITIES

For at least the past 50 years, the federal government has attempted to aid certain sectors of the economy that appear to have an unusually difficult time raising funds in the nation's money and capital markets.

These so-called disadvantaged sectors include agriculture, housing, and small businesses. Dominated by smaller, less creditworthy borrowers, these sectors allegedly get "shoved aside" in the race for scarce funds by large corporate borrowers and governments, especially in periods of tight money. Beginning in the 1920s and 30s, the federal government created several agencies to make loans to or guarantee private loans for these disadvantaged borrowers. Today, the federal credit agencies are large enough and, with the government's blessing, financially sound enough to compete successfully for funds in the open market and channel those funds to areas of critical social need.

Types of Federal Credit Agencies

There are two types of federal credit agencies: government-sponsored agencies and the true federal agencies. *Government-sponsored agencies* are not officially a part of the federal government's structure, but are quasi-private institutions. They are federally chartered but privately owned; in fact, in some instances their stock is traded on a major securities exchange. The borrowing and lending activities of government-sponsored agencies are *not* reflected in the federal government's budget. This has aroused the ire of many fiscal conservatives who regard the credit-granting operations of government-sponsored agencies as a disguised form of federal government spending. Because these agencies are omitted from the federal government's books, annual federal budget deficits look considerably smaller and conceal the full extent of federal deficit financing.[5] True *federal agencies*, on the other hand, are legally a part

---

[5] Public concern over the growth of federal agency activities has increased in recent years, perhaps with some justification. To the extent that agency borrowing and lending activities increase the total amount of credit available in the economy and add to aggregate spending for goods and services, they may add to inflationary pressures. Agency borrowing is not limited by the debt ceiling or interest-rate restrictions that apply to direct obligations of the U.S. government.

Moreover, there is a tendency to create a new agency each time a new financial problem rears its head, increasing the cost burden of government activities. A prominent example is the Chrysler Corporation Loan Guarantee Board established by Congress in 1979. This board, whose voting members consisted of the Secretary of the Treasury, the chairman of the Federal Reserve Board, and the Comptroller General of the United States, was authorized to guarantee with the "full faith and credit of the United States" notes issued by financially troubled Chrysler Corporation and other eligible borrowers. The board's creation raised a number of significant issues concerning government involvement in the private sector of the economy. How many other firms should the federal government guarantee against failure in the future? Upon what basis are such guarantees to be made? What happens to the efficiency of the market system when some firms are not allowed to fail?

EXHIBIT 15–4

Principal Borrowers in the Federal Agency Market

Agencies Part of the Federal Government

Export-Import Bank (EXIM)

Farmers Home Administration (FmHA)

General Services Administration (GSA)

Government National Mortgage Association (GNMA, or Ginnie Mae)

Postal Service (PS)

Tennessee Valley Authority (TVA)

Government-Sponsored Agencies

Banks for Cooperatives (BC)

Federal Farm Credit Banks (FFCB)

Federal Home Loan Banks (FHLB)

Federal Home Loan Mortgage Corporation (FHLMC, or Freddie Mac)

Federal Intermediate Credit Banks (FICB)

Federal Land Banks (FLB)

Federal National Mortgage Association (FNMA, or Fannie Mae)

---

of the government structure, and their borrowing and lending activities are included in the federal budget. Exhibit 15–4 lists the principal federal and government-sponsored agencies that borrow in the money and capital markets.

In their borrowing and lending activities, federal and government-sponsored agencies act as true financial intermediaries. They issue attractively packaged certificates, notes, and bonds to capture funds from savers, and they direct the resulting flow of funds into loans and loan guarantees to farmers, ranchers, small-business owners, financial institutions, and mortgage borrowers. While the securities issued by these government agencies are usually *not* guaranteed by the federal government, most investors feel that the government is "only a step away" in the event any agency gets in trouble.[6]

Growth of the Agency Market

Armed with this implied government support, the agency market has grown rapidly, with the volume of outstanding securities climbing from about $2 billion during the 1950s to at least $260 billion today (see Exhibit

---

[6] The government-sponsored agencies are permitted to draw upon the U.S. Treasury for funds up to a specified limit with Treasury approval. However, neither the principal nor the interest on the debt of government-sponsored agencies is guaranteed by the federal government, though the issuing agency guarantees its own securities. In contrast, securities of those federal agencies operated by the federal government are fully guaranteed by the credit of the U.S. government.

EXHIBIT 15–5

Growth of Agency Market Debt ($ billions)

Year End	Total Agency Debt Outstanding
1961	$ 8.6
1966	22.7
1971	50.7
1976	103.8
1977	112.5
1978	137.1
1979	163.3
1980	193.2
1985*	260.8

* As of January 1985.
SOURCE: Board of Governors of the Federal Reserve System, *Federal Reserve Bulletin,* selected issues; and U.S. Treasury Department, *Treasury Bulletin,* selected issues.

15–5). Agency debt today equals about one fifth of the huge U.S. public debt and is roughly one third the amount of corporate bonds outstanding.

The agency market is dominated by the government-sponsored agencies, that have restricted access to federal government coffers and must rely mainly on the open market to raise money. The federal agencies, in contrast, are financed through the Federal Financing Bank (FFB), which borrows money from the Treasury. The FFB is closely supervised by the Treasury Department and, in fact, is staffed by Treasury employees. If present trends continue, all outstanding federal agency debt will be FFB securities issued to the Treasury, and only the government-sponsored agencies, which cannot borrow through the FFB, will directly tap the open market for funds.[7]

---

[7] Due to FFB activities, the Treasury has to add a certain amount to its regular borrowings each year in order to cover any FFB drawings. As of March 1984 the Federal Financing Bank had borrowed a total of $138 billion from the Treasury to fund the agencies.

The FFB was created by Congress in 1973. Up to that time, each federal agency did its own borrowing. As a result, the number of different federal agency issues was proliferating at a rapid rate, creating some confusion among investors as to the terms and characteristics of each issue. There were also fears expressed in Congress that agency borrowing was growing out of control. Centralization of borrowing in one agency, it was hoped, would increase efficiency in the fund-raising process, improve the marketability of agency securities, and give Congress a more adequate measure of the growth of agency activities. All FFB obligations are fully guaranteed by the U.S. government. The FFB, in turn, purchases only those securities fully guaranteed as to principal and interest by the issuing agency.

Terms on Agency Securities

Agency securities are generally short to medium term (out to 10 years), and about 40 percent have original maturities under 1 year. Longer-term agency securities are available in denominations as small as $1,000, while the shorter-term notes traded actively in the money market generally come in minimum denominations of $50,000 or more. They are subject to federal income taxes, but many are exempt from state and local income taxes. However, state and local government estate, gift, and inheritance taxes do apply to all agency obligations.

One of the most popular agency securities is the certificate of participation (PC) used by the Federal National Mortgage Association (FNMA or Fannie Mae). PCs represent an interest in a pool of securities which entitles the holder to receive a portion of any income earned by the pool. In addition, the agencies issue notes and debentures, some of these backed by security investments previously acquired by the issuing agency. The heaviest agency borrowers in recent years, as indicated in Exhibit 15–6, have been Fannie Mae, the Federal Home Loan Banks (FHLB), and the Farm Credit Banks. These three agencies accounted for about 80 percent of the outstanding debt issued by all federal and government-

EXHIBIT 15–6

Total Debt Outstanding of Federal and Government-Sponsored Agencies, January 1985 ($ billions)

Agency	Total Debt Outstanding
Federal agencies:	
Export-Import Bank	$ 15.9
Federal Housing Administration	0.1
Government National Mortgage Association	2.2
Postal Service	1.3
Tennessee Valley Authority	15.5
Other Agencies	0.2
Total federal agency debt	$ 35.2
Government-sponsored agencies:	
Federal Home Loan Banks	$ 64.7
Federal Home Loan Mortgage Corporation	NA
Federal National Mortgage Corporation	84.6
Farm Credit Banks*	70.6
Student Loan Marketing Association	5.6
Total government-sponsored agency debt	$225.5

* In January 1979 the Farm Credit Banks began issuing consolidated bonds to replace those securities previously issued by the Federal Land Banks, Federal Intermediate Credit Banks, and the Banks for Cooperatives.
SOURCE: Board of Governors of the Federal Reserve System, *Federal Reserve Bulletin,* May 1985.

sponsored agencies and an active secondary market exists for the short-term debt of these three agencies. Clearly, most agency borrowing goes to support the housing market and agriculture.

The securities of all government-sponsored agencies are regarded as highly similar to each other by investors, and therefore comparable maturities tend to have about the same yield regardless of the issuing agency. Each agency is able to borrow at interest rates below the average yield on its asset portfolio due to government support and control. Generally, the yield on agency securities is close to the yield on U.S. government securities of comparable maturity, but slightly higher. Most of this small difference in yield is due to the fact that agency securities are less marketable than Treasury IOUs. The Treasury issues a security homogeneous in quality and other financial characteristics, while the agency market is splintered into many small pieces due to differences among the agencies themselves. The yields on agency securities are lower than yields on private debt issues, however, due to their superior credit standing. Agency yields are calculated on a 360-day basis like Treasury bills with their prices quoted in 32ds of a point like corporate and U.S. government notes and bonds.

The Marketing of Agency Issues

Most agency issues are sold through the *solicitation method.* A fiscal agent in New York City assembles a group of banks, dealers, and brokers to bring each issue to market. This *solicitation group* conveys to potential investors information on the size, denomination, and maturity of a new issue and asks the investors on its list to make a firm commitment to buy a certain amount of agency securities. Investors are not told the price of the new securities, but are asked for their views on what the price should be and this pricing information is conveyed to the fiscal agent. The day after order books close the fiscal agent prices the new securities and delivery to committed investors then occurs normally a few days later. Thus, investors do *not* know the prices or yields on the securities they buy until after the sale, but must rely on the agent's knowledge and experience to correctly price each issue. A recent study by Puglisi and Vignola (1983) suggests that the fiscal agents generally are highly accurate in choosing competitive equilibrium yields on new issues of agency debt and when their price decisions are off the mark, they tend to err on the side of underpricing rather than overpricing a new security issue. The solicitation group of bank and nonbank dealers receives a commission from the fiscal agent for gathering investor orders and pricing information.

Among the most-active buyers of agency securities are commercial banks, mutual savings banks, state and local governments, savings and loan associations, U.S. government trust funds, and the Federal Reserve System. The Federal Reserve has been authorized to conduct open-market operations in agency IOUs since 1966. Fed buying and selling of these securities has helped to improve their marketability and stature among private investors. Major securities dealers who handle U.S. government securities also generally trade in agency issues.

SUMMARY AND CONCLUSIONS

In this chapter we have looked at two of the most rapidly growing securities markets of the past decade—commercial paper and agency securities. Major industrial corporations, faced with rapidly growing demands for their products and services, have turned increasingly to the market for short-term commercial notes to meet pressing cash needs. The commercial paper market, as we have seen, offers a flexible avenue for borrowing, often at lower interest rates than those available from commercial banks and other institutional lenders. At the same time, commercial banks and finance companies, faced with burgeoning demand for credit from households, business firms, and federal, state, and local governments, have found the commercial paper market an excellent avenue for raising large amounts of short-term funds quickly, at minimum cost and with minimum inconvenience. The pressure of demand from these large groups of industrial and financial firms caused the volume of commercial paper outstanding to increase fivefold during the 1960s and to nearly quadruple during the 1970s. Further rapid expansion of commercial paper issues has occurred in the decade of the 1980s.

Equally impressive has been the growth of debt securities issued by agencies created by the U.S. government. Their extensive borrowing and lending activities in the financial markets channel billions of dollars in funds to farmers, ranchers, commercial fishers, small businesses, mortgage borrowers, and mortgage-lending institutions on more generous terms than the open market often provides. Many of these agencies, especially those aiding agriculture and the mortgage market, have been operating since the 1920s and 30s, but their growth in recent years has been unprecedented. As we saw in this chapter, federal agency debt increased more than threefold during the 1970s and the rapid growth continued in the 1980s.

All federal agencies are creatures of Congress and may be destroyed, in theory at least, at the stroke of a pen. In reality, however, with continuing rapid growth in the number of new families formed in the United

States each year and the rising costs of housing, food, and fuel the role of the federal agencies in the nation's financial markets probably will continue to expand. Agency securities will continue to be an attractive investment for commercial banks, savings and loan associations, credit unions, industrial corporations, and other investors who seek competitive rates of return on their funds with minimal risk.

STUDY QUESTIONS

1. What is commercial paper? What features make it attractive to money market investors?
2. Distinguish between direct paper and dealer paper.
3. Describe the role that dealers play in the functioning of the commercial paper market.
4. What range of maturities is attached to newly issued commercial paper? Why?
5. How is the yield (or rate of return) on commercial paper calculated?
6. What are the principal advantages accruing to a company large enough to tap the commercial paper market for funds? Are there any disadvantages to issuing commercial paper?
7. Who are the principal investors in commercial paper? How and why is this paper rated?
8. What are "disadvantaged" sectors of the economy? Give some examples.
9. What is the difference between a government-sponsored agency and a federal agency? Give some examples of each.
10. Are federal or government-sponsored agencies really financial intermediaries? Why?
11. What are the principal investment characteristics of agency securities?
12. How are agency securities marketed? What is a *solicitation group?* What is unusual about the *pricing* of agency securities?

PROBLEMS

1. A new issue of 90-day commercial paper is available from a dealer in New York City at a price of $97.60 on a $100 basis. What is the bank discount yield on this note if held to maturity?

2. A note traded in the commercial paper market will mature in 15 days. The dealer will sell it to you at $98.35 on a $100 basis. What is the note's discount rate of return?

3. Commercial paper is purchased in the secondary market 30 days from maturity at a bank discount yield of 9 percent. Ten days later it was sold to a dealer at an 8 percent discount rate. What was the investor's holding-period yield?

SELECTED REFERENCES

Banks, Louis. "The Market for Agency Securities." *Quarterly Review*, Federal Reserve Bank of New York, Spring 1978.

Board of Governors of the Federal Reserve System. "Survey of Finance Companies, 1975." *Federal Reserve Bulletin*, March 1976.

Federal Reserve Bank of Richmond. *Instruments of the Money Market.* 5th ed., 1981.

Hurley, Evelyn M. "The Commercial Paper Market since the Mid-Seventies." *Federal Reserve Bulletin*, June 1982, pp. 327–34.

McCurdy, Christopher. "The Dealer Market for U.S. Government Securities." *Quarterly Review*, Federal Reserve Bank of New York, Winter 1977–78, pp. 35–47.

Puglisi, Donald J., and Anthony J. Vignola, Jr. "An Examination of Federal Agency Debt Pricing Practices." *The Journal of Financial Research*, 6, no. 2 (Summer 1983), pp. 83–92.

Resler, David, and Richard Lang. "Federal Agency Debt: Another Side of Federal Borrowing." *Review*, Federal Reserve Bank of St. Louis, November 1979, pp. 10–19.

16

International Money Market Instruments: Bankers' Acceptances and Eurodollars

PURPOSE OF THIS CHAPTER

To show how money market borrowing and lending of funds has reached worldwide to tie national financial markets together and make possible the global flow of capital. The chapter discusses two of the most important ways in which international trade and capital investment are financed—through the creation of bankers' acceptances and Eurodollars. Emphasis is placed on the process by which both acceptances and Eurodollars are created and destroyed.

KEY TERMS AND CONCEPTS IN THE CHAPTER

accepting bank	*discounting*	*LIBOR*
bankers' acceptances	*eligible acceptance*	*third-country bills*
correspondent bank	*Eurocurrency*	*time deposit*
deposit multiplier	*Eurodollars*	*time draft*

The money market today is not confined within the boundaries of a single nation. Money flows around the globe, seeking out those investments offering the highest expected returns for a given degree of risk. Moreover, world trade has expanded in recent years at a rapid pace, especially between the United States, Japan, Western Europe, and the Middle East. Further rapid increases in international trade and commerce are expected in the decade ahead, including a significant expansion of trade between East and West. China, the Soviet Union, and the Eastern European nations are developing close economic ties with several Western countries. The exporting of agricultural products and advanced technology by the United States, Japan, and Western Europe to Third World countries and, in some cases, to the Communist bloc constitutes one of the major avenues for international trade in the modern world.

And, of course, the growth and development of international commerce requires a concomitant expansion in both long- and short-term sources of financing. Long-term capital is needed to build new factories, transport systems, dams, deep-water ports, and energy-producing and refining facilities. Short-term capital from the money market is needed to finance the annual export and import of goods, the carrying of inventories, and the payment of tax obligations, and to provide other working-capital needs. In this chapter we focus upon two of the most widely used international money market instruments—bankers' acceptances and Eurodollars.

BANKERS' ACCEPTANCES

A banker's acceptance is a *time draft* drawn on a bank by an exporter or an importer to pay for merchandise or to buy foreign currencies.[1] If the bank honors the draft, it will stamp "accepted" on its face and endorse the instrument. By so doing, the issuing bank has unconditionally guaranteed to pay the face value of the acceptance at maturity. Acceptances carry maturities ranging from 30 to 180 days (with 90 days being the most common) and are considered prime-quality money market instruments. They are actively traded among bank and nonbank financial institutions, manufacturing and industrial corporations, and securities dealers as a high-quality investment and source of ready cash. An illustration of a typical banker's acceptance, prepared at the Federal Reserve Bank of New York, is shown in Exhibit 16–1.

---

[1] See Chapter 29 for a discussion and explanation of time drafts.

EXHIBIT 16–1

Illustration of a Banker's Acceptance

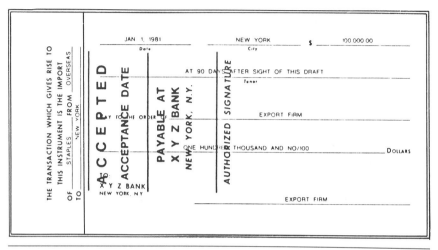

Why Acceptances Are Used in International Trade

Acceptances are used in the import and export trade because most exporters are uncertain of the credit standing of the importers to whom they ship goods. Exporters may also be concerned about business conditions or political developments in foreign countries. Nations experiencing terrorist violence or even civil war have serious problems in attracting financing for imports of goods and services because of the obvious risks carried by businesses extending credit to them. However, exporters usually are quite content to rely upon acceptance financing by a foreign bank. Thus, an acceptance is a financial instrument designed to shift the risk of international trade to a third party willing to take on that risk for a known cost. Banks are usually willing to take on such risk because they are specialists in granting credit, assessing credit risk, and spreading that risk over thousands of different loans.

How Acceptances Arise

Trade acceptances usually begin when an importer goes to a bank to secure a line of credit to pay for a shipment of goods from abroad. (See Figure 16–1 for a flowchart illustrating how acceptances can be created.) Once the line of credit is approved, the bank will issue an irrevocable letter of credit in favor of the foreign exporter. This document

FIGURE 16–1

The Creation of a Banker's Acceptance

Effect of an Acceptance: Reduces risk to seller from shipping goods on credit because the purchaser has received a bank's guarantee of future payment, thus transferring risk from the seller to the accepting bank and the seller can receive his or her funds right away by discounting the acceptance before it matures.
SOURCE: Adapted from William C. Melton and Jean M. Mahr, "Bankers' Acceptances," *Quarterly Review,* Federal Reserve Bank of New York, Summer 1981.

authorizes the exporter to draw a time draft for a specified amount against the issuing bank.

Because the letter of credit authorizes the drawing of a *time draft* and not a sight draft (which is payable immediately upon presentation), the exporter must wait until the draft matures (perhaps as long as six months) to be paid. However, such a delay is unacceptable for most export firms. They must meet payrolls, purchase inventories, pay taxes, and satisfy other near-term obligations. Moreover, the time draft will generally be redeemed in the home currency of the issuing bank, and this particular currency may not be needed by the exporter. A French exporter holding a time draft from a U.S. bank, for example, would be paid in dollars on its maturity date, even though the exporter probably needs francs to pay his or her employees and meet other expenses. Typically, then, the exporter will discount the time draft in advance of its maturity through his/her principal bank. The exporter then receives timely payment in local currency if he or she wishes and avoids the risk of trading in foreign currencies.

The foreign bank which has now acquired the time draft from the exporter will forward it (plus shipping documents if goods are being traded) to the bank issuing the original letter of credit. The issuing bank checks to see that the draft is correctly drawn and then stamps "accepted" on its face. Two things happen as a result of this action: (1) a banker's acceptance—a high-quality, negotiable money market instrument—has been created; and (2) the issuing bank has acknowledged an absolute liability which must be paid in full at maturity. Frequently, the issuing bank will discount the new acceptance for the foreign bank which sent it and credit that bank's correspondent account. The acceptance may then be held as an asset or sold to a dealer. Meanwhile, shipping documents for any goods that accompanied the acceptance are handed to the importer against a trust receipt, permitting the importer to pick up and distribute the goods. However, under the terms of the letter of credit, the importer must deposit the proceeds from selling those goods at the issuing bank in sufficient time to pay for the acceptance. When the time draft matures, the acceptance will be presented to the issuing bank for payment by its holder.

It should be clear that all three principal parties to the acceptance transaction—the exporter, importer, and issuing bank—benefit from this method of financing international trade. The exporter receives good funds with little or no delay. The importer, however, may delay payment for a time until the related bank line of credit expires. The issuing bank regards the acceptance as a readily marketable financial instrument which can be sold before maturity through an acceptance dealer in order to cover short-term cash needs. In fact, 85 to 90 percent of all acceptances created by U.S. banks are sold in the secondary market each year. However, there are costs associated with all of these benefits. A discount fee is charged off the face value of the acceptance whenever it is discounted in advance of maturity. And the accepting bank earns a commission (usually 50 to 100 basis points), which may be paid by either exporter or importer, in addition to the interest and fees associated with the original line of credit.

Recent Growth of Acceptance Financing

Reflecting the significant advantages of acceptance financing for exporters, importers, and banks, it is not surprising that the volume of bankers' acceptances outstanding has grown rapidly in recent years. As

EXHIBIT 16–2

The Growth of Bankers' Dollar Acceptances

Year-End	Volume Outstanding in Millions of Dollars at End of Period
1950	$ 394
1960	2,027
1970	7,058
1980	54,744
1985*	72,508

* Figures as of January 1985.
SOURCE: Board of Governors of the Federal Reserve System, *Federal Reserve Bulletin* and *Banking and Monetary Statistics*, selected issues.

Exhibit 16–2 shows, the volume of acceptances increased from less than $400 million in 1950 to just over $2 billion in 1960 and then tripled by 1970 to slightly more than $7 billion outstanding. However, even these rapid rates of growth look pale when compared with the virtual explosion of acceptance financing during the 1970s and early 1980s. By January 1985 the volume of bankers' acceptances outstanding exceeded $70 billion—a tenfold increase in about 15 years!

What factors account for this impressive growth in acceptances? Exhibit 16–3 helps us find the answer. The majority of acceptances created by U.S. banks arise from four types of financial transactions: (1) the financing of imports into the United States; (2) the financing of exports from the United States; (3) the acquisition of dollars to add to foreign exchange reserves; and (4) the financing of goods stored in or transported between other countries. Acceptances arising from the last source are called *third-country bills.* While these various types of acceptances have grown rapidly in recent years, it is the third-country bills which have dominated the growth in the volume of acceptance financing by U.S. bankers, led by dollar acceptance financing and trade with Japan, South Korea, and nations in the Middle East whose export and import trade have mushroomed during the past decade.

Despite their rapid growth abroad, however, acceptances are not widely used inside the United States for purely domestic trade. A small amount of domestic acceptance financing is carried out to support the storage of staple commodities, such as cotton, grain, rice, wood, or tobacco. However, if a company can borrow from a bank at or close to the prime

EXHIBIT 16–3

Uses of Acceptance Financing ($ millions)

Uses of Acceptance Financing	Year-End		
	1975	**1980**	**1985***
Imports into the United States	$ 3,726	$11,536	$16,757
Exports from the United States	4,001	11,339	15,477
All other uses	11,000	31,480	40,297

* As of January 1985.
SOURCE: Board of Governors of the Federal Reserve System, *Federal Reserve Bulletin,* selected issues.

interest rate, that is generally a cheaper source of funds than acceptance financing. Moreover, it is usually much easier for a domestic firm to assess the financial condition of its domestic customer than to evaluate the credit standing of a foreign firm thousands of miles distant. For this reason suppliers of goods in the domestic market usually extend short-term credit (accounts receivable) directly to their customers rather than insisting on time drafts against a bank (acceptances). Moreover, in domestic commerce no exchange of foreign currencies is necessary, eliminating one important type of business risk. However, financial experts have predicted greater use of acceptances in the financing of the domestic shipment of goods due to recent liberalization of banking regulations.

Acceptance Rates

Acceptances do not carry a fixed rate of interest but are sold at a discount in the open market like Treasury bills. The prime borrower under an acceptance contract is charged a commitment fee for this line of credit, which is usually 1½ percent (i.e., ⅛ of 1 percent per month) for top-quality customers. If the bank wishes to sell the acceptance in advance of its maturity, the rate of discount it must pay is determined by the current bid rate on acceptances of similar maturity in the open market. The yield on acceptances is usually only slightly higher than on U.S. Treasury bills because banks who issue them are among the nation's largest and have solid international reputations (see Exhibit 16–4). Adding to the stature and marketability of acceptances, depository institutions are permitted to borrow reserves from the Fed's discount

EXHIBIT 16–4

Interest Rates on Bankers' Acceptances and U.S. Treasury Bills* (average; percent per annum)

Instrument	1981	1982	1983	1984	1985†
Prime 90-day bankers' acceptances	15.32%	11.89%	8.90%	10.14%	8.80%
Three-month U.S. Treasury bills	14.03	10.61	8.61	9.52	8.47

* Both bankers' acceptances and Treasury bill yields are quoted on a bank discount basis. Acceptance yields are averages of the midpoint of the range of daily dealer closing rates offered for domestic issues. Bill rates are auction averages for the week in which bills were issued.
† Rates are for the week ending March 1, 1985.
SOURCE: Board of Governors of the Federal Reserve System, *Federal Reserve Bulletin,* selected issues.

window using eligible acceptances (90 days or less to maturity) as collateral.[2]

Investors in Acceptances

Commercial banks regard the acceptance as a high-grade negotiable instrument suitable for liquidity management purposes. In addition, the essential safety of acceptances is recognized by the U.S. Treasury, which permits banks to use acceptances as collateral to back the Treasury's tax and loan accounts held in a majority of the nation's commercial banks. As shown in Exhibit 16–5, U.S. bank holdings of acceptances amounted to about $10 billion (consisting mostly of their own drafts), which was about one fifth of the total amount of acceptances outstanding.

The majority of investors in this market, however, are foreign individuals and institutions. This is due to the fact that income earned on accep-

---

[2] The banker's acceptance is one of the safest of all financial instruments. It is an irrevocable primary debt of the bank stamping "accepted" on its face as well as a contingent liability of the drawing firm and of any other bank, firm, or individual who endorses the document. Moreover, domestic banks are limited in the volume of acceptances they can have outstanding relative to the size of their capital and surplus. At the same time the customer (usually an importer) who has requested the initiating letter of credit which gives rise to the acceptance has guaranteed payment by the maturity date. Then, too, any goods shipped under the letter of credit are nearly always insured and accompanied by trust and warehouse receipts and other documents specifying value and ownership. There is no record of a defaulted acceptance in the U.S. banking system, though, of course, the value of discounted acceptances does fluctuate with market conditions.

EXHIBIT 16–5

Holders of Bankers' Acceptances ($ millions)

| | Year-End | | | | |
Holders	1981	1982	1983	1984	1985*
Accepting banks:	$10,857	$10,910	$ 9,355	$10,256	$ 9,991
Own bills	8,743	9,491	8,125	9,065	8,818
Bills bought	1,115	1,439	1,230	1,191	1,713
Federal Reserve Banks:					
Own accounts	195	1,480	418	0	0
Foreign					
correspondents	1,442	949	729	671	679
Other holders	41,614	56,731	66,204	64,167	61,862

* As of January 1985.
SOURCE: Board of Governors of the Federal Reserve System, *Federal Reserve Bulletin,* selected issues.

tances by American investors is subject to federal income tax, but the same income usually is tax exempt to a foreign investor. Other important investors in the acceptance market include industrial corporations, savings banks, insurance companies, and individuals. To many investors, acceptances are a close substitute for U.S. Treasury bills, negotiable CDs, or commercial paper in terms of quality, though the acceptance market is far smaller in volume of trading.

Only a few dealers—today there are 15 major ones—regularly trade in acceptances, usually as an adjunct to their trading activities in Treasury bills and U.S. government notes and bonds. Trading is carried out purely on a negotiated basis, with most daily volume accounted for by swaps of holdings among accepting banks. Dealers' inventories of acceptances available for purchase are small, especially of acceptances created by the 10 largest U.S. banks which are prime rated. While a wide variety of denominations are available for both large and small investors, nonbank investors usually find the menu of fresh offerings very limited. Nevertheless, an investor who is willing to accept the odd-lot denominations in which acceptances are issued will generally find the investment quite rewarding in terms of a competitive rate of return, low risk, and brisk resale demand, especially from bank and foreign nonbank investors.

EURODOLLARS

Comparable to the domestic money market, a chain of international money markets trading in the world's most convertible currencies stretches around the globe. This so-called *Eurocurrency market* has arisen because of a tremendous need worldwide for funds denominated in dollars, marks, pounds, francs, yen, and other relatively stable currencies. For example, as American corporations have expanded their operations in Europe and the Middle East, they have needed huge amounts of U.S. dollars to purchase machinery and other goods in the United States to pay federal and state taxes. These same companies have also required huge amounts of other national currencies to carry out transactions in the countries where they are represented. To meet this kind of need, large international banks headquartered in the world's key financial centers—London, Paris, Zurich, Tokyo, New York, and other major cities— began in the 1950s to accept deposits denominated in currencies other than that of the host country and to make loans in those same foreign currencies. Thus, the Eurocurrency market was born.

What Is a Eurodollar?

Because the dollar is the chief international currency today, the market for Eurodollars dominates the Eurocurrency markets. What are Eurodollars? Eurodollars are deposits of U.S. dollars in banks located outside the United States. The banks in question record the deposits on their books in U.S. dollars, not in the home currency. While the large majority of Eurodollars (and other Eurocurrency) deposits are held in Europe, these deposits have spread worldwide and Europe's share of the total is actually declining.[3]

Frequently banks accepting Eurodollar deposits are foreign branches of American banks. For example, in the city of London—the center of the Eurocurrency market today—branches of American banks outnumber British banks and bid aggressively for deposits denominated in U.S. dollars.[4] Many of these funds will then be loaned to the home office in the states to meet reserve requirements and other liquidity needs. The remaining funds will be loaned to private corporations and governments abroad who have need of U.S. dollars.

No one knows exactly how large the Eurodollar market is. One reason is that the market is almost completely unregulated. Moreover, many international banks refuse to disclose publicly their deposit balances in various currencies. Another reason for the relative lack of information on market activity is that Eurocurrencies are merely bookkeeping entries

---

[3] Among the most important non-European centers for Eurocurrency trading are the Bahamas, Bahrain, Canada, the Caymen Islands, Hong Kong, Japan, Panama, and Singapore.

[4] U.S. banks are prohibited from accepting deposits or making loans in currencies other than U.S. dollars in the domestic market. However, banks in other countries and branches of U.S. banks abroad can accept foreign currency-denominated accounts.

on a bank's ledger and not really currencies at all. You cannot put Eurodollars in your pocket like bank notes. Moreover, Eurodollar deposits are continually on the move in the form of loans. They are employed to finance the import and export of goods, to supplement government tax revenues, to provide working capital for the foreign operations of U.S. multinational corporations, and, as we noted earlier, to provide liquid reserves to the largest banks headquartered in the United States.

One estimate for mid-1980 drawn from figures compiled by Morgan Guaranty Trust Company in New York gave the *gross* size of the entire Eurocurrency market at $1,470 billion. The term *gross* in this instance means the sum of all foreign currency-denominated liabilities outside the country of the currency's origin. The *net* size of the Eurocurrency market, netting out deposits owned by Eurocurrency banks, was estimated at close to $700 billion. Because Eurodollars represent about three quarters of all Eurocurrency liabilities, the gross size of the Eurodollar market would have been in the vicinity of $1,100 billion, while the net total was probably close to $500 billion.[5] Figures of this magnitude would make the Eurodollar market the largest of all money markets.

The Creation of Eurodollars

To illustrate how Eurodollars deposits arise, we trace through a simple, but quite typical example. While our discussion will be in terms of Eurodollars, the reader should be aware that the process being described really applies to any Eurocurrency.

Suppose a French exporter of fine wines ships cases of champagne to a New York importer, accompanied by a bill for $10,000. The importing firm pays for the champagne by issuing a check drawn on its local bank in the requested amount. Because the French exporter deals regularly in the United States, frequently buying American equipment and securities, it is happy to accept the importer's check denominated in dollars and deposits it right away in a U.S. bank—First American Bank—where the French firm maintains a commercial checking account. After this check clears, the results of the transaction are shown below.

French Exporter		**First American Bank**	
Assets	Liabilities	Assets	Liabilities
Demand +$10,000 deposit in U.S. bank			Demand +$10,000 deposit owed French exporter

----

[5] See Morgan Guaranty Trust Company of New York (1980).

Is the deposit shown above a Eurodollar deposit? *No,* because the deposit of dollars occurred in the United States, where the dollar is the official monetary unit. Suppose now, however, that the French exporter is offered an attractive rate of return on its dollar deposit by its own local bank in Paris and decides to move the money there. The Paris bank wants to loan these dollars to other customers who need them to pay bills or make purchases in the United States. After the wine exporter and its Paris bank exchange letters setting out the terms of the deposit, the French exporter will receive a receipt for a dollar-denominated time deposit in its Paris bank. That bank will now hold claim to the original dollar deposit in the United States. The Paris bank will have at least one U.S. correspondent bank and will ask to have the original dollar deposit transferred there. We show these transactions as follows:

French Exporter		
Assets		**Liabilities**
Demand −$10,000 deposit in U.S. bank		
Time +$10,000 deposit in Paris bank		

First American Bank		
Assets		**Liabilities**
Reserves −$10,000 trans- ferred to U.S. corre- spondent bank		Demand −$10,000 deposit owed French exporter

U.S. Correspondent Bank		
Assets		**Liabilities**
Reserves +$10,000 received from First American Bank		Demand +$10,000 deposit owed Paris bank

Paris Bank		
Assets		**Liabilities**
Deposit +$10,000 with U.S. corre- spondent bank		Time +$10,000 deposit owed French exporter

Do we now have a Eurodollar deposit? *Yes,* in the form of a $10,000 time deposit in a Paris bank. The wine exporter's deposit has been accepted and recorded on the Paris bank's books in U.S. dollars, even though the official monetary unit in France is the franc.[6]

Let us follow this Eurodollar deposit through one more step. Assume now that the Paris bank makes a loan of $10,000 to a small oil company based in Manchester, England. The British company needs dollars to pay for a shipment of petroleum drilling equipment from Houston, Texas.

---

[6] The $10,000 time deposit is used here for illustrative purposes only. The vast majority of Eurocurrency deposits are far larger. In fact, the normal trading unit in this market is 1 million currency units.

By securing a dollar credit from the Paris bank, the British oil firm, in effect, receives a claim against dollars deposited in U.S. banks. The appropriate accounting entries would be:

Paris Bank		**British Oil Company**	
Assets	Liabilities	Assets	Liabilities
Loan to +$10,000 British oil company		Demand +$10,000 deposit in U.S. correspondent bank	Loan +$10,000 owed to Paris bank
Deposit −$10,000 in U.S. correspondent bank			

U.S. Correspondent Bank	
Assets	Liabilities
	Deposit −$10,000 owed to Paris bank
	Deposit +$10,000 owed to British oil company

Note that we have assumed the British oil company held a deposit account in the same U.S. bank where the Paris bank held its correspondent deposits. This, of course, is often not the case, but it was done here to reduce the number of accounting entries. If another U.S. bank were involved, we would simply transfer deposits and reserves to it from the U.S. correspondent that held the account of the Paris bank. The end result would be exactly the same as in our example: *the total amount of dollar deposits and U.S. bank reserves remains unchanged.* These funds are merely passed from U.S. bank to U.S. bank as loans are extended and deposits made in the Eurodollar market. Thus, Eurodollar activity does not alter the total reserves of the U.S. banking system. In fact, the workings of the Eurodollar market remind us of a fundamental principle of international finance: *money itself usually does not leave the country where it originates; only the ownership of money is transferred across international boundaries.*

The chain of Eurodollar loans and deposits started in our example by the wine exporter's bank in Paris will go on unbroken as long as dollar loans are in demand and the funds are continually redeposited somewhere in the international banking system. Eurobanks, like domestic U.S. banks, can create a multiple volume of deposits and loans for each dollar of deposits they receive. Even though Eurobanks are not limited in their creation of deposits and loans by legal reserve requirements, most experts in the field believe there are more leakages of funds from the Eurocurrency system than there are from the U.S. banking system. Therefore, the size of the international deposit multiplier is probably smaller than the domestic deposit multiplier.[7]

Of course, just as Eurodollars are created by making loans, they are also destroyed as loans are repaid. In our example above, suppose the British oil company trades pounds for dollars with a foreign currency dealer and uses the dollars purchased to repay its loan from the Paris bank. At about the same time, the dollar time deposit held by the French exporter matures, and the exporter spends those dollars in the United States. As far as U.S. banks are concerned, total deposits and reserves remain unchanged. However, as a result of these transactions, all dollar deposits are now held in the United States and therefore have ceased to be Eurodollars.

Eurodollar Maturities and Risks

Most Eurodollar deposits are short term (ranging from overnight to call money loaned for a few days out to one year) and therefore are true money market instruments. However, a small percentage are long-term time deposits, extending in some instances out to about five years. However, most Eurodollar deposits carry one-month maturities to coincide with payments for shipments of goods. Other common maturities are 2, 3, 6, and 12 months.[8]

---

[7] See Chapters 4 and 23 for a discussion of the deposit multiplier. The granting of a Eurodollar loan to a borrower does *not* give the borrower "money" in a strict sense. Eurodollars are not generally acceptable as a medium of exchange to pay for goods and services. They are more like time deposits rather than checking accounts. The holder of a Eurodollar deposit must convert that deposit into some national currency unit before using it for spending. Thus, Eurodollars and other Eurocurrency deposits are not negotiable instruments. The Eurocurrency system can create credit, but not money. A lender of Eurocurrency who needs liquid funds before a deposit matures must go back into the market and negotiate a separate loan.

Interest usually is paid only at maturity unless the Eurodollar deposit has a term of more than one year. Most deposit interest rates are tied to the London Interbank Offer Rate (LIBOR) and are usually fixed for the life of the deposit, though floating rates tied to semiannual changes in LIBOR are not uncommon on longer-term deposits.

[8] Banks active in the Eurodollar market for liquidity-adjustment purposes use so-called *short date* deposits. Comparable to federal funds transactions in the domestic U.S. money market, short dates represent deposits available for as long as 14 days, though generally they are weekend or 2-day money, with some 7-day maturities as well. Short dates may carry fixed maturities or simply be payable on demand with minimal notice (such as 24 or 48 hours).

Even though Eurobanks do not issue demand deposits, funds move rapidly in the Eurocurrency market from bank to bank in response to demands for short-term liquidity from corporations, governments, and Eurobanks themselves. There is no central trading location in the market. Traders may be thousands of miles distant from each other, conduct negotiations by cable, telephone, or telex with written confirmation coming later. Funds normally are transferred on the second business day after an agreement is reached through correspondent banks.

Eurocurrency deposits are known to be volatile and highly sensitive to fluctuations in interest rates. A slight difference in interest rates or currency values between two countries can cause a massive flow of Eurocurrencies across national boundaries. One of the most famous examples of this phenomenon occurred in West Germany in 1971, when speculation that the German mark would be upvalued brought an inflow into Germany of billions in dollar deposits in a few days, forcing the West German government to cut the mark loose from its official exchange value and allow the currency to float.

As Goodfriend (1981) observes, Eurodollars are not without risk. There is *political risk* because governments may restrict or prohibit the movement or repatriation of funds across national borders as the United States did for a time during the Iranian crisis. There may also be disputes between nations over the legal jurisdiction and control of deposits. *Default risk* may also be a factor because banks in the Eurobanking system may fail and Eurocurrency deposits usually are not insured. This problem is compounded by the fact that it is more difficult to secure information on the financial condition of foreign banks than on domestic banks. However, on the positive side, Eurobanks are among the largest and most stable banking institutions in the world. Moreover, most foreign nations have tried to encourage the growth of the Eurocurrency markets through lenient regulation and taxation rather than restrict that growth.

The Supply of Eurodollars

Where do Eurodollars come from? A major factor in the market's growth has been the enormous balance-of-payments deficits which the United States has run since the late 1950's.[9] American firms building factories and purchasing goods and services abroad have transferred ownership of dollar deposits to foreign companies, banks, and governments. Domestic shortages of oil and natural gas have forced the United States to import from 30 to 40 percent of its petroleum needs, generating enormous outflows of dollars to oil-producing nations. The OPEC countries,

---

[9] See Chapter 27 for a discussion of the causes and effects of U.S. balance-of-payment deficits.

for example, accept dollars in payment for crude oil and use the dollar as a standard for valuing the oil they sell. American tourists visiting Europe, Japan, Singapore, and the Middle East frequently use dollar-denominated traveler's checks or take U.S. currency with them and convert it into local currency overseas. Dollar loans made by U.S. corporations and foreign-based firms have added to the vast Eurodollar pool. Many of these dollar deposits have gravitated to foreign central banks, such as the Bank of England and the Bundesbank in the Federal Republic of Germany, as these institutions have attempted to support the dollar and their own currencies in international markets.

Eurodollars in Domestic Bank Operations

Since the late 1960s American banks have drawn heavily upon Eurodollar deposits as a means of adjusting their domestic reserve positions. Thus, the manager of the money desk at a large U.S. bank, knowing the bank will need extra cash reserves in a few days, can contact foreign banks holding dollar deposits and arrange a loan. The manager can also contact other U.S. banks with branches abroad and borrow Eurodollars from them. Alternatively, if the money manager's own bank operates foreign branches accepting dollar deposits, these can be placed at the disposal of the home office.

Eurodollar borrowing of bank reserves has been especially heavy during periods of rapidly rising interest rates in the United States. For example, during the "credit crunches" of 1969–70 and 1979–80, when domestic money market rates rose to record levels, major U.S. banks tapped the

EXHIBIT 16–6

Eurodollar Borrowings by Commercial Banks Operating in the United States, Monthly Averages for December ($ billions)

Item	1980	1981	1982	1983	1984	1985*
Net balance due to foreign-related institutions	$ 8.2	$—18.1	$—47.7	$—42.7	$—32.0	$—33.1
Domestic chartered U.S. banks' net position with their own foreign branches	—14.7	—22.4	—39.6	—39.7	—31.4	—31.8
Gross due from balances	37.5	54.9	72.2	75.2	69.0	70.6
Gross due to balances	22.8	32.4	32.6	35.5	37.6	38.8

* Average for February 1985.
SOURCE: Board of Governors of the Federal Reserve System, *Federal Reserve Bulletin,* selected issues.

Eurodollar market for billions of dollars in short-term funds. In the midst of the 1969–70 credit crunch, U.S. bank dollar liabilities to their foreign branches reached $15 billion—a record not surpassed until 1979, when net Eurodollar borrowings by U.S. commercial banks totaled nearly $35 billion. Such borrowings are highly volatile, however, and extremely interest-rate sensitive. For example, when U.S. money market rates fell precipitously from all-time record highs in the spring of 1980 and domestic sources of reserves became much less expensive, American banks repaid their Eurodollar borrowings nearly as fast as they borrowed these international deposits months earlier. The volume of U.S. bank net Eurodollar borrowings from foreign-related institutions, which totaled $28 billion in December 1979, stood at only about $8 billion by the end of 1980 (see Exhibit 16–6).

Eurodollars usually carry *higher* reported interest rates than other sources of bank reserves, such as the federal funds market, or domestic deposits (see Exhibit 16–7). However, there are fewer legal and regulatory restrictions on the borrowing of Eurodollars. For example, Eurodollar deposits are not subject to interest-rate ceilings and, in most periods, have been free of reserve requirements. Moreover, U.S. banks must pay assessments to the Federal Deposit Insurance Corporation on domestic nonbank deposits to cover the costs of deposit insurance. Eurodollar deposits, however, are not insured.

EXHIBIT 16–7

Interest Rates on Eurodollar Deposits and Other Money Market
Instruments (percent)

Period	Eurodollar Deposits, Three-Month Maturities	U.S. Treasury Bills, Three-Month Maturities	Federal Funds Rate
1975	6.00%	5.84%	5.82%
1976	5.00	4.99	5.05
1977	7.25	5.27	5.54
1978	11.69	7.22	7.94
1979	14.94	10.04	11.20
1980	14.00	11.43	13.36
1981	16.79	14.03	16.38
1982	13.12	10.61	12.26
1983	9.56	8.61	9.09
1984	10.73	9.52	10.23
1985*	9.35	8.47	8.40

* Average for week ended March 1, 1985.
SOURCE: U.S. Department of Commerce, *Business Statistics*, selected editions; and Board of Governors of the Federal Reserve System, *Federal Reserve Bulletin*, selected monthly issues.

In addition to meeting their own reserve needs from the Eurodollar market, U.S. banks have actively aided their corporate customers in acquiring and transmitting Eurocurrency deposits. Direct loans in Eurodollars and other Eurocurrencies are made by U.S. banks, and these banks will readily swap Eurocurrencies at the customer's request. While most Eurocurrency loans to nonbank customers are short-term credits to provide working capital, a sizable percentage in recent years have consisted of medium-term (one-to-five-year) loans for equipment purchases, frequently set up under a revolving credit agreement. The total amount of Eurodollar and other Eurocurrency loans is unknown, though fairly reliable estimates are available concerning Eurodollar activity by branches of U.S. banks operating abroad. For example, foreign branches of U.S. banks reported holding dollar claims of more than $340 billion in 1985, of which $100 billion represented claims on foreign banks, $23 billion were claims on public borrowers, and another $100 billion were claims on other nonbank foreigners.

Eurodollar loan rates have two components: (1) the cost of acquiring Eurodollar deposits (usually measured by the London Interbank Offer Rate (LIBOR) on three- or six-month Eurodeposits); and (2) a profit margin ("spread") based on the riskiness of the loan and degree of competition. Profit margins generally are very low on Eurodollar loans (often ⅛ percentage point) because the market is highly competitive, the cost of lending operations is low, and the risk is normally low. Borrowers are generally well-known institutions with substantial net worth and solid credit standing. Market transactions are usually carried out in large, even denominations, ranging from about $500,000 to $5 million or more.

Benefits and Costs of the Eurodollar Market

For the most part, the development of Eurodollar trading has resulted in substantial benefits to the international community and especially to U.S. banks and multinational corporations. The market ensures a high degree of funds mobility between international capital markets and provides a true international market for bank and nonbank liquidity adjustments. It has provided a mechanism for absorbing huge amounts of U.S. dollars flowing overseas and generally lessened international pressure to forsake the dollar for gold and other currencies.

The market reduces the costs of international trade by providing an efficient method of economizing on transaction balances in the world's most heavily traded currency, the dollar.[10] Moreover, it acts as a check

---

[10] See Balbach and Resler (1980) on this point. In effect, the Eurodollar market lowers the cost of dollar-denominated financial intermediation.

on domestic monetary and fiscal policies, especially on the European continent, and encourages international cooperation in economic policies because interest-sensitive traders in the market will quickly spot interest rates that are out of line and move huge amounts of funds quickly to any point on the globe. Central banks, such as the Bank of England, the Bundesbank, and the Federal Reserve System, monitor the Eurodollar market continuously in order to moderate heavy inflows or outflows of funds which may damage their domestic economies.

The capacity of the Eurocurrency market to quickly mobilize massive amounts of funds has brought severe criticism of this market from central bankers in Europe and from certain government officials, economists, and financial analysts in the United States. They see the market as contributing to instability in currency values, particularly when Eurocurrency trading places severe downward pressure on the dollar and other key trading currencies. As noted above, the market can wreak havoc with monetary and fiscal policies designed to cure domestic economic problems. This is especially true if a nation is experiencing severe inflation and massive inflows of Eurocurrency occur at the same time. The net effect of Eurocurrency expansion, other things equal, is to push domestic interest rates down, stimulate credit expansion, and accelerate the rate of inflation. The ability of local authorities to deal with inflationary problems might be completely overwhelmed by a Eurocurrency glut. This danger is really the price of freedom, for an unregulated market will not always conform to the plans of government policymakers.[11]

It is not surprising that certain European central banks have for more than a decade called for controls on Eurocurrency trading. One of the most frequently heard proposals is to impose reserve requirements on Eurodollar deposits. For example, during the 1970s France levied a 9.5 percent reserve requirement on Eurodollar loans. But such controls have not really been effective because of lack of unanimity among foreign governments and central banks. Funds tend to flow away for areas employing controls and toward free and open markets. The key to the future of controls in this market probably rests with the Bank of England, because London is the heart of the Eurodollar market. And thus far, the Old Lady of Threadneedle Street, as that bank is often called, remains firmly against significant government restraints on Eurocurrency trading.

---

[11] There is little evidence that the rapid growth of the Eurodollar market has had any adverse effects on U.S. economic policies, however. For example, a recent study by Balbach and Resler (1980) concludes: "Eurodollar flows . . . have only minor effects on the U.S. money stock. This evidence warrants the conclusion that the Eurodollar market does not pose a serious threat to the ability of the Federal Reserve to control the money supply" (p. 11).

CONCLUSIONS

"The world is getting smaller all the time"—a familiar and trite phrase. It is also true. Travel time between distant cities and even across oceans is measured today in hours and minutes instead of days. Supersonic jet transports, such as the British Concorde, have cut in half jet travel time between London and New York and between the major European and American financial centers and their counterparts in Asia, the Middle East, and the Far East.

However, the great speed at which people can travel today is far outclassed by the velocity of funds and information transfers worldwide. Communications satellites, orbiting thousands of miles above the earth's surface, speed financial and other data to their destination in minutes, seconds, and microseconds. On the ground telex, telephone, and microwave transmissions link large and small financial centers and permit the carrying out of financial transactions between traders separated by thousands of miles, oceans, mountain ranges, and deserts almost as conveniently as among those traders who meet face-to-face on the floor of the New York Stock Exchange. The financial world is shrinking rapidly in size, and it is becoming intensely more competitive, better informed, and more sensitive to the receipt of relevant information.

It is within this environment of change, which emphasizes speed and the availability of relevant information, that the international money market instruments we have discussed in this chapter—bankers' acceptances and Eurodollars—have grown to a position of dominance. The vast improvements in information flow and speed have broadened markets for the products and services of all businesses and linked national economies into an interdependent network—a multinational economic and financial system. That system requires a fluid market for the flow of loanable funds from those businesses and governments with cash surpluses, and therefore a need to invest idle funds, to those business and governmental institutions with cash deficits and a need to borrow money as briefly as overnight or for periods covering months and years.

And, as in any money market, there is great concern for *risk* within the multinational financial and economic system. Will the borrower be able to repay a loan and make the interest payments on it? What is the borrower's true credit position? These burgeoning international needs—for financial and credit information, for credit to support trade and commerce, and for low-risk investment outlets—have led to the development and growth of both bankers' acceptances and Eurodollars. Both instruments provide large amounts of credit to businesses engaged in international trade and commerce and, at the same time, offer an attractive, high-quality investment. Moreover, both acceptances and Eurodollars are traded in large unregulated and efficient markets where interest rates are highly responsive to changing demand and supply forces and investor expectations. This is why thousands of American corporations, including the nation's largest commercial banks, have entered these international markets as both borrowers and lenders of funds. And, in the absence of government regulation and control, markets linking financial systems should continue to grow in size and relative importance, exerting an ever widening influence on the character of economic and political relationships in the international community.

There is one pressing need of today's money market investor that we have not fully addressed in this section of the book, however—the need to protect against future changes in interest rates and security prices. All the markets we have discussed to this point are *spot* markets, designed for the immediate delivery of credit and securities. However, today's financial markets are significantly more volatile—with wider swings in interest rates and security prices—than was true even a decade ago. This increased volatility and uncertainty have stimulated the development of a collection of financial markets where credit and securities are scheduled for future delivery with prices and rates set in advance. It is to these relatively new *futures markets* that we turn now in the next and final chapter on the money market.

STUDY QUESTIONS

1. What is a banker's acceptance? What does the word *accepted* mean?

2. Explain why acceptances are popular with exporters and importers of goods. Why are these instruments not as widely used within the United States as they are in financing international trade?

3. Evaluate bankers' acceptances as a security investment. What are their principal advantages and disadvantages from an investment point of view?

4. Who are the principal investors in the acceptance market? Why are they active in this market?

5. Describe the recent growth trend in acceptance financing. Which sector of the market has grown most rapidly? Why?

6. What is a Eurocurrency market? Why is it needed?

7. Define the term *Eurodollar*. Can a U.S. bank create Eurodollars? Why?

8. Describe the process by which Eurodollars are created. Explain what

happens to the total volume of U.S. bank reserves and deposits in the creation process.

9. Can Eurodollars be destroyed? How?

10. List the sources of Eurodollar deposits. List their principal uses.

11. What role do Eurodollar deposits play in the reserve management operations of major U.S. banks? What are the advantages of Eurodollar borrowings over other sources of bank reserves?

12. Evaluate the Eurocurrency markets from a social point of view. What are the major benefits and costs of this rapidly growing institution? Would you support closer regulation of the Eurocurrency markets? Why or why not?

PROBLEMS

1. A West German manufacturer of furniture sells a large order of home furnishings to a furniture outlet in Houston. The Houston firm pays for the shipment by wiring funds from its local bank through Fedwire to the West German firm's account at Chase Manhattan Bank in New York City. Subsequently, the West German manufacturer decides to invest half the funds received in a dollar deposit offered by a bank in London, Barclays Bank, where interest rates are particularly attractive. No sooner are the funds deposited in London when a Japanese auto company, shipping cars to the U.S. and to Western Europe, asks the London bank for a loan to purchase raw materials in the United States.

Later, when the loan falls due, the Japanese auto firm will go into the foreign currency market to purchase dollars to retire its Eurodollar loan at Barclays Bank, receiving a dollar deposit at a U.S. bank. When the loan is repaid, Barclays gains the dollar deposit in the United States and uses that deposit to pay off the West German firm when its time deposit matures. The West German firm chooses to deposit the funds received from Barclays in its demand deposit account at Chase Manhattan Bank in New York City because it now needs to buy goods and services in the United States.

Construct T accounts which reflect the foregoing transactions at each step. In particular, show the proper entries for: (1) payment by the Houston firm to the German furniture company; (2) deposit of the funds in London; (3) the loan to the Japanese automaker; (4) repayment of the loan; and (5) return of the funds to the United States. Indicate which deposit is a Eurodollar deposit and if any Eurodollars are destroyed at any particular stage.

2. A company known as Standard Quality Importing ships videocassette recorders made in Japan to retail dealers in the United States and Western Europe. It decides to place an order with its Japanese supplier for 10,000 Hi-Fi VCRs at $575 each after securing a line of credit from Guaranty Security Bank in Los Angeles. Guaranty issues a credit letter to the Japanese supplier promising payment in U.S. dollars 90 days hence. However, the Japanese firm needs the promised funds within seven days from receipt of the credit letter to make purchases of technical components from an electronics firm in Phoenix, Arizona. Carefully explain and illustrate with T accounts and diagrams how a banker's acceptance could arise from the foregoing transactions, how the Japanese supplier could receive the dollars he needs in timely fashion, and what would happen to the acceptance at the end of the 90-day period. Use T account entries to show the movement of funds from the importer to the Japanese supplier to the electronics firm and to money market investors.

SELECTED REFERENCES

Balbach, Anatol B., and David H. Resler. "Eurodollars and the U.S. Money Supply." *Review,* Federal Reserve Bank of St. Louis, June–July 1980, pp. 2–12.

Dufey, Gunter, and Ian H. Giddy. "Eurocurrency Deposit Risk." *Journal of Banking and Finance,* 8 (1984), pp. 567–89.

Einzig, Paul. *The Eurodollar System.* 5th ed. New York: St. Martin's Press, 1973.

Feder, Gershon, and Knud Ross. "Risk Assessments and Risk Premiums in the Eurodollar Market." *Journal of Finance,* June 1982, pp. 679–91.

Goodfriend, Marvin. "Eurodollars." *Economic Review,* Federal Reserve Bank of Richmond, May–June 1981, pp. 12–18.

Goodman, Laurie S. "The Pricing of Syndicated Eurocurrency Credits." *Quarterly Review,* Federal Reserve Bank of New York, Summer 1980, pp. 39–49.

Helfrich, Ralph T. "Trading in Bankers' Acceptances: A View from the Acceptance Desk of the Federal Reserve Bank of New York." *Monthly Review,* Federal Reserve Bank of New York, February 1976.

Hervey, Jack L. "Bankers' Acceptances Revisited." *Economic Perspectives,* Federal Reserve Bank of Chicago, May–June 1983, pp. 21–31.

Kreichen, Lawrence L. "Eurodollar Arbitrage." *Quarterly Review,* Federal Reserve Bank of New York, Summer 1982, pp. 10–22.

Lee, Boyden E. "The Eurodollar Multiplier." *Journal of Finance,* September 1973, pp. 867–74.

Makin, John H. "Identifying a Reserve Base for the Eurodollar System." *Journal of Finance*, June 1973, pp. 609–17.

Morgan Guaranty Trust Company of New York. *World Financial Markets*, December 1980.

Resler, David H. "Does Eurodollar Borrowing Improve the Dollar's Exchange Value?" *Review*, Federal Reserve Bank of St. Louis, August 1979, pp. 10–16.

17

The Financial Futures Market

PURPOSE OF THIS CHAPTER

To explain and illustrate how financial futures contracts can be used to offset the market risk associated with buying and selling securities and granting loans. The chapter introduces the concept of hedging and shows how hedging "works" to shift market risk to another investor by taking opposite positions in the futures and cash (spot) markets. Examples are provided of the three basic types of hedges: the long hedge, the short hedge, and the cross hedge.

KEY TERMS AND CONCEPTS IN THE CHAPTER

basis	financial institutions	market risk
clearinghouse	futures exchange	mark to market
closing a hedge	GNMA pass-throughs	opening a hedge
commodity pools	hedging	perfect hedge
cross hedge	long hedge	short hedge
financial futures	margin	

One of the most innovative markets to be developed in recent years and also one of the most rapidly growing is the market for financial futures. Futures trading is designed to protect the investor against *market risk.* In the financial futures market, the risk of future changes in the prices of securities is transferred to someone—an individual or an institution—willing to bear that risk. Financial futures are used in both the short-term money market and the long-term capital market to protect both borrowers and lenders of funds against changes in interest rates.

While relatively new in the field of finance, risk protection through futures trading is a very old concept in commodities trading. As far back as the Middle Ages, traders in farm commodities developed contracts calling for the future delivery of farm produce at a guaranteed price. Trading in rice futures began in Japan in 1697. In the United States, the Chicago Board of Trade established a futures market in grains in 1848. Later, the Board of Trade developed futures markets for metals and wood products; more recently, it has done so for selected kinds of financial instruments.[1]

THE NATURE OF FUTURES TRADING

In the futures market, buyers and sellers enter into contracts for the delivery of commodities, securities, or cash at a specific location and time and at a price that is set when the contract is made. The principal reason for the existence of a futures market is *hedging;* that is, the act of buying or selling a commodity or claim in order to protect against the risk of future price fluctuations. Adverse movements in prices can result in increased costs and lower profits and, in the case of financial instruments, reduced value and yield. Many business firms and investors today find that even modest changes in prices, interest rates, and other costs can lead to magnified changes in their net earnings. Some investors see the futures markets as a means to ensure that their profits depend more on planning and design than on the dictates of a treacherous and volatile market.

Hedging may be compared to *insurance.* Insurance protects an individual or business firm against risks to life and property. Hedging protects against the risk of fluctuations in market price. However, there is an

---

[1] The major commodities currently traded on various exchanges in the United States include: wheat, corn, soybean meal, soybean oil, cattle, hogs, pork bellies, barley, flaxseed, copper, platinum, oats, rye, eggs, iced broilers, lumber, plywood, sugar, coffee, orange juice, cotton, cocoa, potatoes, silver, gold, crude oil, distillate oil, and gasoline. As we will soon see, there is now an active futures market for U.S. Treasury bills, bonds, and notes; high-quality commercial paper; GNMA mortgage instruments; commercial bank certificates of deposit (CDs); and common stock indices.

important difference between insurance and hedging. Insurance rests on the principal of sharing or *distributing* risk over a large group of policyholders. Through an insurance policy the risk to any one individual or institution is reduced. Moreover, the risks covered by most insurance plans are highly predictable, especially the risk of death.

In contrast, hedging does *not* reduce risk. It is a relatively low-cost method of *transferring* the risk of unanticipated changes in interest rates from one investor or institution to another. Ultimately, some investor must bear the risk of fluctuations in the prices of commodities or securities. Moreover, that risk is generally less predictable than would be true of most insurance claims. The hedger who successfully transfers risk through a futures contract can protect an acceptable selling price for a commodity or a desired yield on a security weeks or months ahead of the sale or purchase of that item. In the financial futures market, the length of such contracts normally ranges from three months to two years.

GENERAL PRINCIPLES OF HEDGING

The basic principles of hedging may be described most easily through the use of a model. In this section we will examine the model of a *complete* or *perfect* hedge. Such a hedge contracts away *all* risk associated with fluctuations in the price of an asset. The hedger creates a situation in which *any* change in the market price of a commodity or security is exactly offset by a profit or loss on the futures contract. This enables the hedger to "lock in" the price or yield that he or she wishes to obtain.

Opening and Closing a Hedge

Suppose an agricultural firm produces a commodity such as wheat and is anticipating a decline in wheat prices. This unfavorable price movement can be hedged by *selling futures contracts* equal to the current value of the wheat. Sale of these contracts, which promise the future delivery of wheat days, weeks, or months from now, is called "opening a hedge."[2] When the firm does sell its wheat, it can buy back the same number of futures contracts as it sold originally and "close the hedge."

Of course, the firm could deliver the wheat as specified in the original futures contract. However, this is not usually done. If the price of wheat does decline as expected, then it costs the firm less to repurchase the futures contract than the price for which it originally sold that contract. Thus, the profit on the repurchase of wheat futures offsets the decrease in the price of wheat itself. The firm would have perfectly hedged itself

---

[2] Opening a hedge represents the forward sale of an asset.

FIGURE 17–1

Price Changes on Assets Can Be Offset by Profits or Losses on Futures
Contracts

A. When assets decline in price

B. When assets rise in price

against any adverse change in wheat prices over the life of the futures
contract.

What would happen if wheat *rose* in price instead of declined? A perfect hedge would result in a profit on the sale of the wheat itself, but a
loss on the futures contract. This happens because the firm must repurchase its futures contract at a higher price than its original cost due to
the higher price for wheat. Figure 17–1 summarizes how a profit (or
loss) on a futures contract can be used to *offset* a decrease (or increase)
in the market price of an asset, helping the hedger to achieve a desired
price level.

Why Hedging Can Be Effective

The hedging process can be effective in transferring risk because prices in the *spot* (or cash) market for commodities and securities are generally correlated with prices in the futures (or forward) market. Indeed, the price of a futures contract in today's market represents an estimate of what the spot (or cash) market price will be on the contract's delivery date (less any storage, insurance, and financing costs). Hedging essentially means adopting *equal* and *opposite* positions in the spot and futures markets for the same asset.

The relationship between the price of a commodity or security in the cash or spot market and its price in the forward or futures market is captured in the concept of *basis.* Specifically,

$$\text{Basis for a futures contract} = \begin{array}{l}\text{Spread between}\\ \text{the cash (spot) price of a}\\ \text{commodity or security and}\\ \text{the futures (forward) price}\\ \text{for that same commodity or}\\ \text{security at a point in time}\end{array}$$

For example, if long-term Treasury bonds are selling in today's cash market for immediate delivery at a price of $98 per bond (assuming a $100 par value), but are selling in the futures market today for forward delivery in three months at $88 per bond, the *basis* for this T-bond futures contract purchased today is $98 − $88 or $10. (This would be a $100 basis on a $1,000 par-value bond). We can also define *basis* in terms of interest rates; it is the difference between the interest rate attached to a security in the cash market and the interest rate on that same security in the financial futures market.

On the delivery day for a commodity or security the basis becomes *zero* (i.e., cash prices or rates and futures prices or rates should then be identical or nearly so except for any differences in transactions costs). Whether or not a futures trade ultimately turns out to be profitable depends on what happens to its basis between now and when the contract ends. *It is changes in the basis for futures contracts that create risk in the trading of commodity and financial futures contracts.*

Hedging through futures converts price or interest-rate risk to basis risk. The more stable the basis associated with a given futures trade, the greater the reduction of risk achieved by the futures trader. When cash and futures prices (or cash and futures interest rates) move in parallel, basis risk is *zero.* The futures markets "work" to reduce risk because the risk of changes in basis is generally *less* than the risk of changes in the price of a commodity or security. However, as we will soon see, there are both risks and costs to futures trading and losses can mount rapidly, especially for the unwary and uninformed investor.

Risk Selection through Hedging

In the wheat example discussed earlier we described a complete (perfect) hedge. In a perfect hedge the basis remains *constant* throughout the contract period. Profits (losses) in the cash market exactly offset losses (profits) in the futures market. Such a hedge is essentially a profitless hedging position and is rare; in most futures trades the basis fluctuates, introducing at least some degree of risk. Many speculators and investors, however, are willing to take on added risk by not fully closing a hedge, believing they can guess correctly which way prices are going. Through the futures markets, the investor can literally "dial" the degree of risk he or she wishes to accept. If the investor wishes to take on *all* the risk of price fluctuations in the hope of achieving the maximum return, no hedging will take place at all.[3]

FINANCIAL FUTURES

Beginning in October of 1975, the Chicago Board of Trade opened active trading in futures contracts for GNMA mortgage-backed certificates. In the ensuing months, futures contracts for U.S. Treasury securities, commercial paper, bank CDs, Eurodollar deposits, and even common stock appeared on the scene.

The development of futures markets for these securities was motivated by the extremely volatile interest-rate movements that have characterized the financial markets for the past two decades. Repeatedly, interest rates have risen to record levels under the pressure of tight money policies and inflation, shutting out important groups of borrowers from ready access to credit. These high and volatile rates have been a source of concern to regulatory authorities in the field of banking and financial institutions. Rising interest rates reduce the value of securities held by financial institutions, threatening them with a liquidity crisis and, in some cases, ultimate failure. Some members of the regulatory community have favored the growth of financial futures as a way to reduce the risks associated with security investments. However, as we will soon see, other regulatory authorities feel that the development of the futures markets may have encouraged speculation and increased the riskiness of those financial institutions participating in futures trading. These regulatory agencies

---

[3] Hedging in the futures market is not a costless exercise. There are brokerage commissions with each transaction. Moreover, a complete hedge denies the investor the benefits of any unanticipated, but favorable movements in the price of a security or commodity. Reducing the risk of losses also limits potential gains.

have placed tight restrictions on the use of the futures markets, especially by commercial banks.

The Purpose of Trading in Financial Futures

The basic principle behind trading in financial futures is the same as in the commodity markets. A securities dealer, commercial bank, or other investor may *sell* futures contracts on selected securities in order to protect against the risk of *falling* security prices (rising interest rates) and, therefore, a decline in the rate of return or yield from an investment. If the price of the security in question does fall, the investor can "lock in" the desired yield because a profit on the futures contract may fully offset the capital loss incurred when selling the security itself. On the other hand, a *rise* in the market price of a security (fall in interest rates) may be fully offset by a loss in the futures market. Either way, the investor or institution is able to maintain its desired holding-period yield. (These points are illustrated in Figure 17–2.) Many financial institutions prefer to use the futures market to hedge against interest-rate fluctuations rather than passing interest-rate risk on to their customers through floating-rate loans.

Financial futures may also be used by financial institutions and other investors to reduce the risk of interest-rate fluctuations when borrowing money. For example, suppose that a commercial bank is planning to raise funds by issuing certificates of deposit (CDs) and borrowing in the Eurodollar market one year from today. However, the bank's economics department forecasts that interest rates are likely to rise significantly by the time the borrowing takes place. The adverse impact of these expected higher borrowing costs on the bank's profit position could be reduced by a sale and then a purchase of financial futures contracts. For example, management could sell one-year Treasury bill futures contracts now and then "zero out" this sale by purchasing a like amount of T bill contracts when the delivery date arrives. Provided interest rates on Treasury bills, bank CDs, and Eurodollars increase by about the same magnitude, the added CD and Eurodollar borrowing costs would be offset by a profit on the futures position in T bills. The bank could "lock in" its desired borrowing cost.[4] A recent study of Western banks and savings and loans by Booth, Smith and Stotz (1984) finds that insuring against

---

[4] Note that even if interest rates fall, thereby *reducing* the bank's borrowing costs, the use of financial futures still stabilizes the bank's position. In this instance, losses would be incurred on the sale and purchase of financial futures but could be fully offset by reduced borrowing costs. However, if interest rates do fall, the bank would have been better off without its position in financial futures because its profits would have been greater. In addition, gains or losses on futures contracts are taxable, and there are brokerage commissions to consider.

FIGURE 17–2

Changes in the Yield on Securities Can Be Offset by Profits or Losses
on Futures Contracts

A. When interest rates rise and security prices fall

B. When interest rates fall and security prices rise

future increases in the cost of funds was the principal use of futures
trading by these financial institutions, followed by insuring against future
decreases in investment returns and the ability to offer fixed-rate loans
to customers safely.

Under a financial futures contract, the seller agrees to deliver a specific
security at a fixed price at a specific time in the future. Delivery under
the shortest contracts is usually in 3 months from today's date, while a
few contracts stretch out to 18 months or even 2 years. When the delivery
date arrives, the security's seller can do one of three things: (1) make

delivery of the security if he or she holds it; (2) buy the security in the spot (cash) market and deliver it as called for in the futures contract; or (3) purchase a futures contract for the same security with a delivery date exactly matching the first contract. This last option would result in a buy and a sell order maturing on the same day, which "zero out" and clear the market. In reality, settlement of contracts generally occurs exclusively in the futures market through offsetting buy and sell orders rather than by using spot (cash) transactions and making actual delivery of securities.

SECURITIES USED IN FINANCIAL FUTURES CONTRACTS

The number of futures markets and the types of securities and contracts traded in those markets have been expanding rapidly in recent years. In 1975 only one type of contract was traded at the Chicago Board of Trade. By the beginning of the 1980s, 25 different futures contracts were being traded on several different exchanges. However, most trading in financial futures today centers around six types of securities: (1) U.S. Treasury bills, (2) Treasury bonds and notes, (3) GNMA mortgage pass-through (or mortgage-backed) securities, (4) prime-quality commercial paper, (5) bank certificates of deposit (CDs), and (6) common stock. The Chicago Board of Trade first offered interest-rate futures contracts for GNMA mortgage instruments in October 1975. Soon, other commodity exchanges—the International Monetary Market of the Chicago Mercantile Exchange (IMM), the Amex Commodities Exchange, Inc. (ACE), and the Commodity Exchange, Inc. (Comex)—began offering futures trading in T bills and GNMA certificates. Then, in August 1980 the New York Stock Exchange opened its own futures floor. Known as the New York Futures Exchange, it has begun to capture a large share of the contract market, especially for trades in bank CDs.

Each of these exchanges completely controls which security contracts may be offered for sale, acceptable delivery dates, delivery methods, posting of prices, contract par values, and other essential terms of trade. Current terms of trade for eight securities now represented on the various exchanges are summarized below.[5]

---

[5] The contract exchanges carry a heavy burden of responsibility in preserving the integrity of futures trading and the orderliness of the markets. Each exchange stands behind the transactions conducted on its floor and imposes strict rules to minimize risk to the investor. For example, daily price fluctuations are not permitted to go beyond well-defined limits. Qualifications of floor traders and financial standards for member

U.S. Treasury Bonds and Notes

The futures market for U.S. Treasury bonds and notes is one of the most active markets for the forward delivery of an asset to be found anywhere in the world. As we will see in Chapter 25, Treasury bonds and notes are a popular investment medium for individuals and financial institutions because of their safety and liquidity. Nevertheless, there is substantial market risk involved with longer-term Treasury bonds and notes due to their lengthy maturities and relatively thin market. Because the market for Treasury bonds is thinner than for bills and their durations are longer, T-bond prices are more volatile, creating greater uncertainty for investors. Not surprisingly, then, Treasury bonds were among the first financial instruments for which a futures market was developed to hedge against the risk of price fluctuations.

Only those Treasury bonds that either have maturities of at least 15 years or cannot be called for at least 15 to 20 years from their date of delivery (depending on the exchange selected) are eligible for futures contracts. Moreover, all Treasury bonds delivered under a futures contract must come from the same issue. The basic trading unit is $100,000 (measured at par) with a coupon rate of 8 percent. Bonds with coupon rates above or below 8 percent are deliverable at a premium or discount from their par values. Delivery of Treasury bonds is accomplished by book entry and accrued interest is prorated. Price quotes in the market are expressed as a percentage of par value. The minimum price change that is recorded on published lists or in dealer quotations is $\frac{1}{32}$ of a point or $31.25 per futures contract.[6]

Contracts for U.S. Treasury notes and noncallable bonds with maturities of four to six years also are traded today. Like Treasury bond contracts, T note contracts are priced as a percentage of their par (or face) value, based on an 8 percent coupon rate. The basic trading unit is $100,000 in face value. Trading in Treasury note futures began at the Chicago Board of Trade in June 1979, while Treasury bonds contracts were first traded in August 1977.

U.S. Treasury Bills

In January 1976, U.S. Treasury bills were declared eligible for trading in the financial futures market. The International Monetary Market

---

firms are set and monitored on a continuing basis by management and the governing board. The federal government also regulates futures trading through the Commodity Futures Trading Commission.

[6] See Chapter 8 for a discussion of the meaning of 32ds and points and how security prices are measured.

(IMM), now a division of the Chicago Mercantile Exchange (CME), announced that contracts for future delivery would be written on T bills of 90-day and one-year maturities. Ninety-day T bill contracts are for $1 million each, while single contracts on one-year bills carry denominations of $250,000. T bill contracts mature once each quarter of the year in March, June, September, and December.

GNMA Mortgage Pass-Through or Mortgage-Backed Securities

During the 1970s the federal government became increasingly active in the secondary market for mortgages in order to expand the volume of funds available to the housing market. One of the most successful federal government programs in this area is carried out by the Government National Mortgage Association (GNMA or, more commonly, "Ginnie Mae"). Ginnie Mae both purchases residential mortgages and encourages private mortgage lenders such as mortgage bankers, to form *investment pools* with the residential mortgages they hold. All mortgages in the pool bear the same interest rate, carry similar maturities, and represent loans against similar types of residences. Then, Ginnie Mae guarantees the timely payment of principal and interest earned from the mortgage pool. Securities known as GNMA pass-throughs or mortgage-backed securities are issued against these mortgage pools which merely promise pass-through investors a claim against the principal and interest payments generated by the pool. The pass-throughs are standardized, readily marketable investments with yields generally above those on U.S. Treasury securities of comparable maturity.[7]

In October 1975 the Chicago Board of Trade opened trading activity in futures contracts for GNMA pass-through certificates. The basic trading unit was set at $100,000 for certificates with a stated interest rate of 8 percent (Ginnie Mae 8s). If the rate of interest on a Ginnie Mae issue is lower than 8 percent, then the basic trading unit will be greater than $100,000. On the other hand, if the interest rate is above 8 percent, the basic trading unit is scaled down below $100,000. (For example, $107,816.70 is the basic trading unit at a 7 percent interest rate, while $93,167.70 is the basic trading unit for an interest rate of 9 percent.) Prices on Ginnie Mae issues are quoted as a percent of par with minimum quotes in 32ds of a point. Delivery months on GNMA futures contracts

---

[7] For a more complete discussion of GNMA pass-throughs and their role in the nation's mortgage market, see Chapter 19.

are February, March, May, June, August, September, November, and December.[8]

Ninety-Day Commercial Paper

As noted in Chapter 15, one of the most important and rapidly growing money market instruments today is the short-term marketable debt obligation issued by major corporations, known as commercial paper. Commercial paper ranges in original maturity from nine months to as short as three or four days. However, the Chicago Board of Trade has ruled that commercial paper traded in the futures market must mature either 30 or 90 days from date of delivery. It must be of the highest quality, rated either A-1 by Standard & Poor's Corporation or P-1 by Moody's Investors Service,[9] and be approved by the Chicago Board of Trade. The basic trading unit for 90-day paper is a face value at maturity of $1 million, while contracts for 30-day paper are based on a $3 million face value. Prices are quoted on an annual discount basis, with minimum price fluctuations of one basis point or $25 per contract.

Futures trading in commercial paper is extremely light compared to the other securities represented on the major contract exchanges. For example, a survey by the Commodity Futures Trading Commission found that, on average, daily trading volume in 90-day commercial paper contracts was less than 5 percent of T bill contract trading volume. One major problem with paper futures is that contracts do not specify precisely what issue of commercial paper is to be delivered to fulfill each contract. Because paper issued by any number of firms may be used to satisfy the contractual agreement, investors face an unusual degree of uncertainty in this market. In addition, a substantial volume of commercial

---

[8] Two types of GNMA futures are traded today: (1) GNMA CDR (collateralized depositary receipt), and (2) GNMA CD (certificate delivery). The difference between these two contracts hinges on current market interest rates. As we noted above, GNMA certificates with an 8 percent coupon rate were chosen as the basis for GNMA futures contracts traded at the Chicago Board of Trade. The 8 percent figure was chosen because it was a common interest rate attached to GNMA certificates when trading first began. When interest rates rise above or fall below 8 percent, one of two types of adjustments are made in GNMA futures contracts. The dollar amount on the contract invoices can be adjusted with the principal balance unchanged—a GNMA CD. Alternatively, the amount of GNMA certificates actually delivered (known as the principal balance) can be altered to capture interest-rate changes with the dollar amount of the contract invoice remaining unchanged. This is known as a GNMA CDR contract. Also, a GNMA CD contract calls for delivery of the actual GNMA certificates, while a CDR contract requires the delivery of a receipt that evidences GNMA certificates held in safekeeping by an authorized depository.

[9] See Chapter 15 for a discussion of how commercial paper is rated.

paper is issued in original maturities of less than 90 days; so the supply of 90-day paper is often quite limited.

Bank Certificates of Deposit and Eurodollars

Futures trading in bank certificates of deposit (CDs) began in 1981. Three exchanges in the United States—the Chicago Board of Trade, the Chicago Mercantile Exchange, and the New York Futures Exchange—are most active in this market today. In addition, the London International Financial Futures Exchange was set up to begin trading in Eurodollar CDs in the spring of 1982. The CD futures market offers investors the opportunity to hedge against changing interest rates on commercial loans. CD futures contracts are obligations to deliver or receive a $1 million CD maturity in approximately 90 days. There is also a contract traded on the London International Financial Futures Exchange in million-dollar units (U.S. dollars) based on the three-month Eurodollar deposit, designed to hedge against changes in Eurodollar interest rates.

Stock Index Futures

In February 1982 futures contracts on the index value of those common stocks making up the Value Line Stock Index were first offered by the Kansas City Board of Trade. These contracts promised delivery of the *cash value* of a group of stocks at a set price on a specified future date. Two months later the Chicago Mercantile Exchange offered its own version of these so-called pin-stripe pork bellies by opening trading in a contract whose value was tied to daily fluctuations in the Standard & Poor's 500-Stock Index. And in May 1982, the New York Futures Exchange inaugurated trading in the NYSE's Composite Stock Price Index.

The advantage of these composite contracts is that they permit an investor to participate in the "action" of the stock market without buying individual stocks; the investor merely risks his or her cash on whether the stock index will rise or fall in value. This is accomplished by buying or selling a futures contract a few points above or below the current stock index value (multiplied by $500). If the stock index gains or loses a point, the associated futures contract will change by a greater amount, presenting the investor with gains or losses until he or she either cancels or makes delivery.[10] Buyers of stock index futures bet on rising stock prices causing the stock price index to rise, while sellers are forecasting declining stock prices and a falling stock index.

---

[10] Because of the inherent problems of trying to deliver the entire basket of stocks represented in any given index, a stock index contract is settled in cash if it hasn't been "zeroed out" before maturity.

TYPES OF HEDGING IN THE FINANCIAL FUTURES MARKET

There are basically three types of hedges used in the financial futures market today: the long hedge, the short hedge, and the cross hedge. Cross hedges, as ·we will see, may be either long or short. Each type of hedge meets the unique trading needs of a particular group of investors. All three types have become increasingly popular as interest rates and security prices have become more volatile in recent years.

The Long (or Buying) Hedge

A *long hedge* involves the *purchase* of futures contracts today, before the investor must buy the actual securities desired at a later date. The purpose of the long hedge is to guarantee ("lock in") a desired yield in case interest rates decline before securities are actually purchased in the cash market.

As an example of a typical long-hedge transaction, suppose that a commercial bank, life insurance company, pension fund, or other institutional investor anticipates receiving $1 million 90 days from today.[11] Assume that today is April 1 and the funds are expected on July 2. The *current* yield to maturity on securities the investor hopes to purchase in July is 12.26 percent. We might imagine that these securities are long-term U.S. Treasury bonds, which appeal to this investor because of their high liquidity and zero default risk. Suppose, however, that interest rates are expected to *decline* over the next three months due to a recession. If the investor waits until the $1 million in cash is available 90 days from now, the yield on Treasury bonds may well be lower than 12.26 percent. Is there a way to lock in the higher yield available *now* even though funds will not be available for another three months?

Yes, if a suitable long hedge can be negotiated with another trader. In this case the investor can purchase ("go long") 10 September Treasury bond futures contracts at their current market price. (Recall that Treasury bond futures are sold in $100,000 denominations.) Cash payment on these contracts will not be due until September. Suppose their price currently is 68–10, or $68,312.50 on a $100,000 face-value contract. Assume too that, as expected, bond prices rise and interest rates fall. At some later point the investor may be able to *sell* the bond futures contracts at a profit, because prices on these contracts tend to rise along with rising

---

[11] This example of the long hedge and the subsequent examples of short and cross hedges are drawn from examples developed by the Chicago Board of Trade in its instructional pamphlet, *An Introduction to Financial Futures,* February 1981, and are used with CBT's permission.

EXHIBIT 17–1

An Example of a Long Hedge Using U.S. Treasury Bonds

Spot (or Cash) Market Transactions	Futures (or Forward) Market Transactions
April 1: A portfolio manager for a financial institution wishes to "lock in" a yield of 12.26 percent on $1 million of 20-year, 8¼ percent U.S. Treasury bonds at 68–14.	**April 1:** The portfolio manager purchases 10 September Treasury bond futures contracts at 68–10.
July 2: The portfolio manager purchases $1 million of 20-year, 8¼ percent U.S. Treasury bonds at 82–13 for a yield of 10.14 percent	**July 2:** The portfolio manager sells 10 September Treasury bond futures contracts at 80–07.
Results: Opportunity loss of $139,687.50 due to lower Treasury bond yields and higher bond prices.	**Results:** Gain of $119,062.50 on futures trading.

Note: No commissions or exchange service fees are included in these transactions which would reduce the investor's gain from that shown here.
SOURCE: Based on an example developed by the Chicago Board of Trade in *An Introduction to Financial Futures,* February 1981. Reprinted by permission of the Chicago Board of Trade.

bond prices in the cash market. Selling the bond futures contracts at a profit will help this investor offset the lower yields on Treasury bonds that will prevail in the cash market once the $1 million actually becomes available on July 2.

The details of this long-hedge transaction are given in Exhibit 17–1. We note that on July 2 the investor goes into the spot market and buys $1 million in 8¼ percent, 20-year U.S. Treasury bonds at a price of 82–13. At the same time, the investor sells 10 September Treasury bond futures contracts at 80–07. Due to higher bond prices (lower yields) in July, the investor loses $139,687.50 because the market price of Treasury bonds has risen from 68–14 to 82–13. This represents an *opportunity loss* because the $1 million in investable funds was not available in April when interest rates were high and bond prices low. However, this loss is at least partially offset by a gain in the futures market of $119,062.50, because the 10 September bond futures purchased on April 1 were sold at a profit on July 2. Over this period, bond futures contracts rose in price from 68–10 to 80–07. In effect, this investor will pay only $705,000 for the Treasury bonds bought in the cash market on July 2. The market price of these bonds will be $824,062.50 (or 82–13) per bond, but the investor's *net* cost is lower by $119,062.50 due to a gain in the futures market.

The Short (or Selling) Hedge

A financial device of growing popularity is the *short hedge.* This hedge involves the immediate *sale* of financial futures contracts until the actual securities must be sold in the cash market at some later point. Short hedges are especially useful to investors who may hold a large portfolio of securities which they plan to sell in the future but, in the meantime, must be protected against the risk of declining security prices. We examine a typical situation where a securities dealer might employ the short hedge.

Suppose the dealer holds $1 million in U.S. Treasury bonds, carrying an 8¾ percent coupon and a maturity of 20 years. The current price of these bonds is 94–26 (or $948.125 per $1,000 par value), which amounts to a yield of 9.25 percent. However, the dealer is concerned because higher interest rates appear to be in the offing. Any upward climb in rates would bring about lower bond prices and therefore reduce the value of the dealer's portfolio. A possible remedy in this case is simply to sell bond futures contracts in order to counteract the anticipated decline in bond prices. For example, suppose the dealer decides to sell 10 Treasury bond futures contracts at 86–28, and 30 days later is able to sell $1 million of 20-year, 8¾ percent Treasury bonds at a price of 86–16 for a yield of 10.29 percent. At the same time the dealer goes into the futures market and buys 10 Treasury bond futures contracts at 79–26 to offset the previous forward sale of bond futures.

The financial consequences of these combined trades in the spot and

EXHIBIT 17–2

An Example of a Short Hedge Using U.S. Treasury Bonds

Spot (or Cash) Market Transactions	Futures (or Forward) Market Transactions
October 1: A securities dealer owns $1 million of 20-year, 8¾ percent U.S. Treasury bonds priced at 94–26 to yield 9.25%.	October 1: The dealer sells 10 Treasury bond futures contracts at 86–28.
October 31: The dealer sells $1 million of 20-year 8¾ percent U.S. Treasury bonds at 86–16 to yield 10.29%.	October 31: The dealer purchases 10 Treasury bond futures contracts at 79–26.
Results: Loss of $83,125 in spot market.	Results: Gain of $70,625 on futures trading.

Note: No commissions or exchange service fees are included in these transactions; their inclusion would reduce the dealer's gain from that shown here.
SOURCE: Based on an example developed by the Chicago Board of Trade in *An Introduction to Financial Futures,* February 1981. Reprinted by permission of the Chicago Board of Trade.

futures markets are offsetting, as shown in Exhibit 17–2. The dealer has lost $83,125 in the cash market due to the price decline in the bonds held. However, a gain of about $70,625 (less fees, commissions, and any tax liability) has resulted from the gain in the futures price. This dealer has helped to insulate the value of his or her security portfolio from the risk of price fluctuations through a short hedge.

Cross Hedging

Another approach to minimizing risk is the cross hedge—a combined transaction between the spot market and the futures market using different types of securities in each market. This device rests on the assumption that the prices of most financial instruments tend to move in the same direction and by roughly the same proportion. Because this is only approximately true in any real-world situation, cross hedging does not usually result in forming a perfect hedge. Profits or losses in the cash market will not exactly offset losses or profits in the futures market because basis risk is greater with a cross hedge. Nevertheless, if the investor's goal is to minimize risk, cross hedging is often preferable to a completely unhedged position.

EXHIBIT 17–3

An Example of a Short Cross Hedge Involving Corporate and U.S. Treasury Bonds

Spot (or Cash) Market Transactions	Futures (or Forward) Market Transactions
January 2: A commercial bank holds a diversified portfolio of $5 million in high-grade corporate bonds with an average maturity of 20 years and a current market value of 73–15 per bond. The market value of the total portfolio is, therefore, $3,673,437.50.	January 2: The bank's portfolio manager sells 50 U.S. Treasury bond futures contracts at 81–20.
March 14: The market price per bond falls to 64–13, for a total value of the portfolio of $3,220,312.50.	March 14: The portfolio manager purchases 50 U.S. Treasury bond futures contracts at 69–20.
Results: The total loss in value of the corporate bonds is $453,125.	Results: Gain of $600,000 on the Treasury bond futures contracts.

Note: No commissions or exchange service fees are included in these transactions; these costs would reduce the investor's gain from that shown here.
SOURCE: Based on an example developed by the Chicago Board of Trade in *An Introduction to Financial Futures,* February 1981. Reprinted by permission of the Chicago Board of Trade.

As an example, consider the case of a commercial bank that holds good-quality corporate bonds carrying a face value of $5 million with an average maturity of 20 years. The bank's portfolio manager anticipates a rise in interest rates, which will reduce the value of the corporate bonds. Unfortunately, there is no futures market for corporate bonds, and therefore the portfolio manager cannot construct a perfect hedge involving these securities. However, futures contracts can be negotiated in U.S. Treasury bonds or even in Ginnie Mae pass-throughs, providing either a long or a short hedge against the risk of a decline in the value of the corporate bonds.

To illustrate how such a cross-hedge transaction might take place, suppose that on January 2 the total market value of the bank's corporate bonds is $3,673,437.50. This means that each $1,000 par value bond currently carries a market price of $734.69 (or 73–15 on a $1,000 basis). The portfolio manager decides to sell 50 Treasury bond futures contracts at 81–20 (or $816.25 per $1,000 face value). About two and a half months later, on March 14, interest rates have risen significantly. The value of each corporate bond has fallen to 64–13 (or $644.06 per $1,000 bond). At this point the bank's portfolio manager decides to sell the bonds, receiving $3,220,312.50 from the buyer. This represents a loss on the bonds of $453,125. At the same time, however, the portfolio manager buys back 50 U.S. Treasury bond futures contracts at 69–20. The result is a gain from futures trading of $600,000. In this particular transaction the gain from futures trading more than offsets the loss in the cash market. (See Exhibit 17–3 for a summary of this transaction.)

Of course, this example of a cross hedge and the preceding examples of long and short hedges are simplified considerably to make the fundamental principle of futures trading easier to understand. In the real world the placing and removal of hedges is an exercise requiring detailed study of the futures market and, in most cases, a substantial amount of trading experience.

MECHANICS OF FUTURES TRADING

The mechanics of purchasing a futures contract are simple and straightforward. The investor chooses the commodity or security he or she wishes to trade and the preferred maturity date for a futures contract calling for delivery of that commodity or security. Then the investor contacts a futures broker or commission salesman, usually through a local brokerage house or service. The broker or salesman indicates today's available prices and denominations and the investor can then place an order. Such a request must be accompanied by the posting of a cash margin (often 5 percent or more of the contract value) with the broker which will be returned at the end of the trade less a fixed broker's commission.

The investor's order then will go from a brokerage firm to a floor trader working at the commodity exchange which handles that particular kind of futures contract. The floor trader will repeatedly call out the investor's offer to determine if there are any "takers" (i.e., a trader representing a buyer willing to take a contract at the seller's quantity and price or a trader with a seller client willing to dispose of his or her contracts at the buyer's proposed purchase price) on the exchange floor. When two floor traders agree on the proposed quantity and price, the contract is made and each writes on a card the price, quantity, and delivery month of the contract and passes the card to a clerk who will turn it in to the clearinghouse for recording at the close of the trading day. The floor traders will also notify observers situated around the trading "pit" of the terms of each new trade so that this information can be communicated to those outside the exchange interested in buying or selling contracts.

Once a contract is made, if you are the seller, you must deliver the commodity or security specified in the invoice on the date specified. Similarly, if you are the buyer, you must pay the commodity exchange's clearinghouse the invoice amount on the date spelled out in the futures contract. However, most contracts (well over 80 percent in financial futures trading) are "zeroed out" by going back through a broker and floor trader with an opposite order that offsets the first order on or before the first contract's due date.

What is the purpose of the cash margin that each investor must post? It protects customers, brokers, and traders against market risk. At the end of each trading day the clearinghouse is required to "mark to market" each contract outstanding based on its closing price. The cash margin covers the loss when a contract falls in price. If the price decline is more than a specified percentage of the margin, the investor may get a *margin call* to post additional cash or securities as protection.

TRADERS ACTIVE IN THE FUTURES MARKET

A wide variety of financial institutions and individuals are active in futures trading today. The principal traders in financial futures are individuals and commodity pools. Commodity pools are like mutual funds, offering shares to the individual investor who regularly purchases futures contracts. Commodity pools offer the advantage of diversifying risk by trading in many contracts with varied maturities; in addition, they are professionally managed. The majority of commodity pools try to limit the losses to the investor's original investment, liquidating investor holdings rather than issuing margin calls.

Firms and individual traders representing the futures industry run a close second to individual investors and commodity pools, as participants in daily futures trading. Many of these industry personnel speculate on interest-rate movements or arbitrage between spot and futures markets, purchasing one contract and selling another in the expectation that interest rates on purchased contracts will decline more than (or rise less than) rates on contracts sold. Alternatively, futures firms and industry traders will buy or sell futures contracts simultaneously with a sell or buy order in the spot market.

Financial institutions also play a prominent role in futures trading, led by securities dealers, commercial banks, mortgage bankers, and savings and loan associations. Securities dealers are interested both in risk reduction through hedging and in profitable trades arising from correctly guessing the future course of interest rates and contract prices. Savings and loan associations and mortgage bankers, not surprisingly, are most involved in futures trading of GNMA mortgage-backed instruments. Rapid increases in long-term mortgage rates and volatile swings in the demand for new housing over the past two decades have brought substantial risk to the mortgage-lending business, as we noted in Chapter 5. Under pressure from rising interest costs and deposit withdrawals, many savings and loan associations today have been forced to deeply discount and sell their old, low-yielding mortgage loans in the secondary market in order to raise funds. Losses incurred in the sale of old mortgages can be at least partially offset by gains made from trading in GNMA futures contracts. For their part, mortgage bankers frequently sell GNMA futures to hedge against interest-rate changes that may occur between the time mortgage loans are taken into their portfolios and the time they are sold in packages to other investors.

The participation of savings and loan associations in futures trading was given a substantial boost in July 1981. The Federal Home Loan Bank Board (FHLBB), the industry's chief regulator, loosened the old rules, which limited the total volume of futures contracts an S&L could have outstanding at any one time to no more than the association's net worth position (normally about 5 percent of total assets). These revised rules permit a savings and loan to hedge *all* of its assets if it so chooses. Trading may be carried out in any security that a savings association is legally entitled to hold. Many savings and loans sell GNMA futures to hedge the fixed-rate mortgages they hold on single-family homes. However, the new rules for futures trading set by the FHLBB allow savings associations to hedge on *both* the asset and liability sides of their balance sheets and especially to offset the rapidly rising cost of deposits and nondeposit borrowings. Recent usage of futures by S&Ls has tended to emphasize protection against the rising cost of borrowed funds.

Participation by commercial banks in futures trading has been quite limited to date. For example, a recent study by Booth, Smith, and Stotz (1984) found that only 17 percent of Western banks and savings and loans were using futures in 1983, 95 percent of which held over $100 million in assets. One major factor limiting commercial bank participation in the futures market is uncertainty over the attitude of the regulatory authorities, especially the Federal Reserve System and the Comptroller of the Currency. Another problem centers on the required accounting treatment of gains and losses from futures trading. Gains or losses on futures positions must be recorded daily even though these position changes are not realized until the contract is concluded or zeroed out. The result is volatile fluctuations in reported income for those banks active in futures trading. A further barrier to bank use of futures is a lack of qualified personnel and resistance from top management and boards of directors who do not see any material benefits. However, it is anticipated that bank participation in the futures market will expand significantly as the regulatory community becomes more comfortable with the hedging concept and bank management becomes more knowledgeable about futures trading.[12]

POTENTIAL BENEFITS TO FINANCIAL INSTITUTIONS FROM THE FUTURES MARKET

Trading in security futures opens up several potential advantages for financial institutions and for individual investors. The prospect of hedging against changes in security prices offers the potential for reducing risk and offsetting losses stemming from adverse movements in interest rates. Financial futures contracts can be especially beneficial for those financial institutions and individual investors heavily leveraged with debt, which makes their net earnings particularly sensitive to changes in interest rates. This is certainly true of major commercial banks, savings and loan associations, mutual savings banks, securities dealers, and mortgage banking institutions. These financial intermediaries experience marked fluctuations in net income with changes in the differential between interest rates on borrowed funds and returns on loans and other assets.[13]

---

[12] A recent simulation study by Koppenhaver (1983) suggests that commercial banks making fixed-rate loans could reduce the variability in their profits by as much as 80 percent through the use of appropriate futures hedging strategies.

[13] It is certainly not true that every financial institution would benefit from trading in financial futures. The critical determining factor is the overall interest-rate sensitivity of each institution's asset and liability portfolio. If *both* liabilities and assets carry floating interest rates, for example, hedging may be unnecessary, even in a period of rising interest rates. In fact, if an institution is already hedged, futures trading could increase the interest-sensitivity of a financial institution's earnings and do more harm than good.

Moreover, if the futures market does lead to a reduction of risk, this will enable many financial institutions to extend greater amounts of credit. The result could be a more efficient allocation of scarce funds within each financial institution and within the financial system. Moreover, the futures markets provide for a freer flow of information concerning alternative uses and outlets for funds, permitting each financial institution to rapidly adjust its risk position to changes in interest rates and other costs. As noted by Stevens (1976), the existence of a futures market may result in "increased market information, less search time, integration of markets and greater specialization of risk bearing."

SOCIAL CONSEQUENCES OF THE FUTURES MARKET

Not all observers agree that the futures market results in a net gain for society by helping financial institutions reduce risk and use scarce resources more efficiently. Some analysts believe that the futures markets are largely speculative and not really geared for the hedging of risks per se. They see these markets as aimed principally at providing wealthy investors with a speculative outlet for their funds, and resulting in unnecessary risks due to excessive speculation. Some have argued that futures markets increase the price volatility of those securities whose contracts are actively traded. If this is true, it would tend to make the impact of government economic policy, aimed at promoting high employment and low inflation, more difficult to predict. There is evidence from the commodities field that trading in futures tends to smooth out seasonal fluctuations, but only limited evidence exists to date as to the overall impact on the securities markets of contract trading.

Certainly the mere existence of the futures market and its continuing growth creates additional problems for regulatory authorities, especially those concerned with the regulation of financial institutions. Another market must be supervised and additional regulations prepared to cover new forms of risk and new fiduciary relationships. Some observers have expressed the fear that the futures markets substitute "gambling" with securities for "investing" in securities.[14] If this view is correct, it suggests a withdrawal of some risk-taking activity from the traditional securities markets and a redirection of this activity toward the futures market.

---

[14] See, in particular, Wallich (1979), p. 11. Regulations applying to use of financial futures by financial institutions require that futures trading cannot be used to increase the market risk of a regulated financial institution's portfolio, but must be a *bona fide* attempt to reduce each institution's net interest-rate exposure.

To the extent that risk taking by securities investors is curtailed, this limits the flow of funds into venture capital and decreases the aggregate volume of investment in the economy. Other things equal, the economy's rate of growth is reduced.

On balance, the financial futures market probably has resulted in a modest net benefit to the financial system and to the economy. Those who support the development of this market have certainly overdramatized its positive features, alleging, for example, that interest rates tend to be lower and less volatile with a well-functioning futures market. There is little evidence that this is, in fact, the case. Regardless, it seems clear that the futures market has separated the risk of changing security prices and interest rates from the lending of funds, at least for those institutions actively participating in this market. The risk of price and yield changes is transferred to investors quite willing to assume such risks. The futures market has helped to reduce search costs and expand the flow of information on market opportunities for those who seek risk reduction through hedging. In this sense, the market tends to promote greater efficiency in the use of scarce financial resources. Moreover, this developing institution has tended to unify many local markets into a national forward market, overcoming geographic and institutional rigidities that tend to separate one market from another.

It should not be forgotten that futures trading is not without its own special risks. While the risk of price and yield fluctuations is reduced through negotiating a futures contract, the investor faces the risk of changing interest rates and security prices *between* the futures and spot markets. It is rare that gains and losses from simultaneous trading in spot and futures markets will exactly offset each other, resulting in a perfect hedge. Moreover, there are substantial brokerage fees for executing futures contracts and required minimum deposits for margin accounts.[15] To the extent that the futures market encourages speculation, does not fully offset all price and interest-rate risk, and is characterized by substantial transactions costs, its net benefit to society will remain both limited and the subject of continuing controversy and close regulatory scrutiny.

---

[15] Brokerage commissions and margin requirements in futures trading are not inconsequential. For example, a so-called *round-trip*—buying and selling of contracts—in 90-day Treasury bill futures in the minimum denomination of $1 million will cost approximately $100. Margin accounts must be maintained above a specified minimum level. Each account is evaluated daily, and additional funds must be supplied when the account declines below the minimum level. Many traders pledge securities to their margin accounts to eliminate the necessity of repeatedly supplying new funds.

SUMMARY AND CONCLUSIONS

The increasingly volatile interest rates of recent years have increased the risk sensitivity of many investors. With increased uncertainty concerning the future course of interest rates, managers of security portfolios find that financial planning is a far more difficult task today than in years past. Financial institutions that both borrow and lend in the money and capital markets have found that both their earnings and their cost of funds have become less predictable and subject to wide swings. It is not surprising, therefore, that many individual and institutional investors have sought new and innovative ways to insulate their investments from fluctuations in interest rates and security prices. The financial futures market, inaugurated by the Chicago Board of Trade in 1975, has become an increasingly popular form of "insulation" against the risks of investing in debt securities.

Futures markets are based upon the notion of *hedging,* which is simply the act of contracting to buy or sell a security in the future but at a price agreed upon today. By setting the price and other terms of such a contract *now,* the investor is at least partially insulated against the risk of future changes in interest rates and security prices. Hedging, in effect, transfers risk for one investor to another willing to bear that risk in the hope of scoring a significant gain. The hedger contracts away all or a portion of the risk of security price fluctuations in order to "lock in" a targeted rate of return on an investment. This is accomplished by taking equal and opposite positions in the spot (or cash) market and in the forward (or futures) market. If interest rates are expected to fall and the investor desires to "lock in" a current high yield on a security, he or she should buy a contract calling for the future delivery of the security at a set price (i.e., take on a long hedge). Then, if interest rates do fall, the investor will earn a profit on the futures contract which will wholly or partially offset the lower yields available from buying the security in the spot (cash) market. An opposite set of buy-sell transactions in the futures market (i.e., a short hedge) would generally be used if interest rates were expected to rise.

Trading in financial futures is limited today to a list of high-quality financial instruments—U.S. Treasury bonds, notes, and bills; GNMA mortgage-backed securities; commercial paper; bank CDs; and common-stock price indexes. But the list is growing, and the volume of daily trading in these markets is rapidly expanding. Most observers expect continued growth in futures market activity due to volatile conditions in the financial markets and the increasing financial sophistication of investors.

STUDY QUESTIONS

1. What is the basic purpose of futures trading in commodities? In securities? Where is most futures trading carried out in the United States?
2. Explain the similarities and differences between hedging in the futures market and insurance.
3. What is a *perfect* or complete hedge? Define the terms *opening a hedge* and *closing a hedge.*
4. How do spot (cash) markets differ from futures (forward) markets?
5. What is *basis?* Explain how the basis for a futures contract relates to trading risk.
6. For what specific kinds of securities is there now an active futures market in the United States? Who issues these securities? Describe the restrictions imposed on trading in futures contracts involving securities.
7. Define and explain the use of the following:
   a. Long hedge.
   b. Short hedge.
   c. Cross hedge.
8. What are the principal benefits to financial institutions such as commercial banks, securities dealers, savings and loan associations, and mortgage bankers from the use of the futures market? Can you see any possible dangers?
9. What risks are inherent in futures trading? Costs? Evaluate the futures market from a social point of view.

PROBLEMS

1. An insurance company during the month of March committed itself to buy a block of home mortgages at a fixed price from a mortgage banker in September. The mortgages have a face value of $10 million. The insurer has recently prepared a forecast which indicates that mortgage interest rates will rise between now and September by a full percentage point. What kind of futures transaction would you recommend to protect the insurance company against a sizable loss on its mortgage commitment, particularly if it has to sell the mortgages shortly after they are taken into its portfolio? Indicate specifi-

cally what buy and sell transactions you would undertake in the futures market. Which futures contract would you most likely use? Why?

2. A large money-center bank plans to offer money market CDs in substantial volume (at least $100 million) in six months due to a projected upsurge in credit demands from some of its most valued corporate customers. Unfortunately, the bank's economist has just predicted that money market interest rates should rise over the next year with perhaps a full 1.5 percentage point gain within the next six months. Explain why the bank's management would be concerned about this development. Suppose management expects its corporate loan customers to resist any loan terms which would automatically result in loan rates being immediately adjusted upward to fully reflect any rate increases in the money market. What futures market transaction would you recommend? Please be specific and explain why.

SELECTED REFERENCES

Arak, Marcelle, and Christopher J. McCurdy. "Interest Rate Futures." *Quarterly Review,* Federal Reserve Bank of New York, Winter 1979–80, pp. 33–46.

Belongia, Michael T., and G. J. Santoni. "Hedging Interest Rate Risk with Financial Futures: Some Basic Principles." *Review,* Federal Reserve Bank of St. Louis, October 1984, pp. 15–25.

Board of Trade of the City of Chicago. *Hedging Interest Rate Risks.* 1st rev. ed. Chicago, 1977.

————. *An Introduction to Financial Futures.* Chicago, 1981.

————. *Introduction to Hedging.* Chicago, 1972.

Booth, James R.; Richard L. Smith; and W. Stotz. "Use of Interest Rate Futures by Financial Institutions." *Journal of Bank Research,* Spring 1984, pp. 15–20.

Chicago Mercantile Exchange. *Futures Trading in International Currencies. Chicago, 1977.*

Comptroller of the Currency, Federal Deposit Insurance Corporation, and Federal Reserve Board. "Regulators Adopt Revisions to Policy on Futures, Forward and Standby Contracts." *Joint News Release,* March 12, 1980.

Jaffe, Naomi L., and Ronald B. Hobson. *Survey of Interest-Rate Futures Markets.* Commodity Futures Trading Commission, 1979.

Kasriel, Paul L. "Hedging Interest Rate Fluctuations." *Business Conditions,* Federal Reserve Bank of Chicago, April 1976, pp. 3–10.

Kolb, Robert W., and Raymond Chiang. "Duration, Immunization, and Hedging with Interest Rate Futures." *The Journal of Financial Research,* 5, no. 2 (Summer 1982), pp. 161–70.

Koppenhaver, G. D. "A T-Bill Futures Hedging Strategy for Banks." *Economic Review*, Federal Reserve Bank of Dallas, March 1983, pp. 15–28.

————. "Bank Funding Risks, Risk Aversion, and the Choice of Futures Hedging Instrument." *The Journal of Finance*, 40, no. 1 (March 1985), pp. 241–55.

Menich, Judy Z. "Interest-Rate Futures." *Economic Commentary*, Federal Reserve Bank of Cleveland, June 16, 1980.

Polaris, Mark F., and David C. Fisher. "Banking on Interest Rate Futures." *The Magazine of Bank Administration*, August 1979, pp. 34–39.

Snider, Thomas E. "Using the Futures Market to Hedge." *Monthly Review*, Federal Reserve Bank of Richmond, August 1973, pp. 2–7.

Stevens, Neil A. "A Mortgage Futures Market: Its Development, Uses, Benefits, and Costs." *Review*, Federal Reserve Bank of St. Louis, April 1976, pp. 12–19.

U.S. Treasury Department and the Federal Reserve System. *Treasury Futures Markets: A Study by the Staffs of the U.S. Treasury and Federal Reserve System*, Washington, D.C.: 1979.

Wallich, Henry C., Member, Board of Governors of the Federal Reserve System. Speech before the Commodities and Financial Futures Conference, Federal Bar Association and Commerce Clearing House, Washington, D.C., November 1, 1979.

Part Five

The Consumer in the Financial Markets

18

Consumer Lending and Borrowing

PURPOSE OF THIS CHAPTER

To demonstrate the vital role played by consumers—individuals and families—in supplying loanable funds to the money and capital markets. In most years individuals and families are the principal *lender* of funds in the financial system, mainly by depositing funds with financial intermediaries that make direct loans to short- and long-term borrowers. But, the chapter also stresses the importance of the household sector as one of the chief *borrowers* of funds in the financial system, examining both the factors that influence the volume and timing of consumer borrowing and the characteristics of the principal consumer lending institutions—commercial banks, savings banks, credit unions, and finance companies.

KEY TERMS AND CONCEPTS IN THE CHAPTER

cash-management
  services
certificates of deposit
commercial banks
convenience users
credit cards
credit discrimination
credit unions
debit cards
discount brokerage

finance companies
financial assets
financial disclosure
households
installment credit
IRAs and Keoghs
MMDAs
noninstallment
  credit
NOWs

residential mortgage
  credit
savings and loans
share drafts
stage of life
time and savings
  deposits
truth in lending
universal life
  insurance

Among the most important of all financial markets are the markets providing savings instruments and credit to individuals and families. Many financial analysts have referred to the period since World War II as the "age of consumer finance" because individuals and families not only are the principal source of loanable funds flowing into the financial markets today but also are one of the largest borrowers groups in the entire financial system. Moreover, the market for consumer financial services is the one financial market which *everyone*, regardless of income or social status, will enter at one time or another during their lifetime. In this chapter we examine the major characteristics of the consumer market for financial services, the principal lenders active in this market, and some of the more important rules and regulations applying to consumer borrowing and lending today.

CONSUMERS AS LENDERS OF FUNDS

Each of us is a consumer of goods and services virtually every day of our lives. Scarcely a single day passes that we do not enter the marketplace to pur chase food, shelter, entertainment, books, newspapers, and thousands of other "essentials" of modern living. We are also well aware, perhaps from personal experience, that consumers often borrow heavily in the finan cial marketplace to achieve their desired standard of living. U.S. consumers borrowed about $200 billion in 1983, for example, and by the end of that year owed about $1.75 trillion to various lending institutions.

What is not nearly so well known or so often recognized, however, is the fact that consumers as a group are also the most important *lenders of funds* in the American economy. Loanable funds are supplied by consumers when they purchase financial assets from other units in the economy. In 1983 gross saving by U.S. households totaled nearly $520 billion, of which nearly $370 billion flowed into commercial bank deposits, savings deposits at nonbank financial institutions, bonds, stocks, and direct cash loans to others in the economy. By comparison, nonfinancial businesses recorded gross savings of only $365 billion, the federal government had negative savings (i.e., a budget deficit) of about $182 billion, and state and local governments racked up a paltry $51 billion in savings. Clearly, the consuming public is the chief source of the raw material—loanable funds—exchanged in the nation's financial markets.[1]

Financial Assets Purchased by Consumers

If consumers make loanable funds available to other units in the economy by purchasing financial assets, what kinds of *financial assets* do they

---

[1] The foregoing figures were taken from the Federal Reserve Board's Flow of Funds Accounts as discussed in Chapter 3. Portions of this chapter are drawn from Rose (1978, June 1979, and September 1979).

buy? And what are the principal sources of borrowed funds for consumers? The Federal Reserve Board's Flow of Funds Accounts provide us with a wealth of information on the borrowing and lending habits of American households. Exhibit 18–1 summarizes information contained in recent Flow of Funds reports on the kinds of financial assets acquired by households. One fact immediately evident is the wide diversity of financial assets purchased by individuals and families, ranging from those of very low risk and short maturity (such as bank deposits and U.S. government securities) to long-term, high-risk investments (such as mortgages and corporate stock).

The most important household financial asset today is time and savings deposits, held at commercial banks, savings and loan associations, credit unions, mutual savings banks, and other thrift institutions. These interest-bearing thrift accounts represented close to 30 percent of the total financial asset holdings of American consumers at year-end 1983. Moreover, as Exhibit 18–1 reveals, the importance of thrift deposits in consumer financial investments has generally *increased* as bank and nonbank thrift institutions have offered higher returns and greater convenience to savers.

While household investments in thrift deposits have been growing, purchases of corporate stock have declined drastically in relative terms. Exhibit 18–1 shows that individuals and families held as much as 40 percent of their financial investments in corporate stock in 1960 and nearly as much in 1970. However, the stock market's often volatile performance, coupled with attractive returns available elsewhere, have driven thousands of small investors out of the stock market. By year-end 1983 only one quarter of household financial investments remained committed to corporate stock. Other financial assets—U.S. government securities, state and local government bonds, life insurance policies, and cash itself—also have fallen in favor with the average consumer relative to bank and thrift deposits. Faced with volatile economic conditions and rapid inflation, households have come to emphasize safety, liquidity, and long-term financial security in choosing their financial assets. This is evidenced by the growing importance of consumer investments in time and savings deposits, shares in money market mutual funds, and pension plans in recent years.

The Growing Menu of Savings Instruments Available to Consumers Today

One of the most important of all trends affecting consumer savings and lending today is a veritable explosion of *new financial instruments*. Banks, brokerage houses, thrift institutions, and other financial institutions began in the 1970s to compete aggressively for consumer savings, not only by offering higher returns where the law allowed, but also by prolifer-

EXHIBIT 18–1

Principal Financial Assets Held by U.S. Households, Year-End 1960, 1970, 1980, and 1983 ($ billions)

Financial Assets Held	1960 Amount	1960 Percent	1970 Amount	1970 Percent	1980 Amount	1980 Percent	1983 Amount	1983 Percent
Demand deposits and currency	$ 70.2	7.3%	$ 126.5	6.5%	$ 268.0	6.0%	$ 338.7	5.6%
Time and savings accounts	165.3	17.1	422.4	21.7	1,294.4	28.8	1,673.7	27.7
At commercial banks	62.0	6.4	189.0	9.7	—	—	—	—
At nonbank thrift institutions	103.3	10.7	233.4	12.0	—	—	—	—
Shares in money market mutual funds	—	—	—	—	74.4	1.7	162.6	2.7
U.S. government securities	73.5	7.6	100.4	5.2	282.8	6.3	425.0	7.0
State and local government securities	30.8	3.2	47.4	2.4	74.2	1.7	160.0	2.6
Open-market paper	0.1	0.0	6.1	0.3	38.2	0.9	40.2	0.7
Corporate and foreign bonds	9.8	1.0	39.8	2.0	86.9	1.9	58.6	1.0
Mortgages	31.8	3.3	42.5	2.2	122.5	2.7	184.3	3.1
Corporate stock:	396.1	40.9	763.1	39.2	1,215.6	27.1	1,519.5	25.1
Investment companies	17.0	1.8	47.6	2.4	63.7	1.4	129.4	2.1
Other corporate shares	279.0	39.2	715.4	36.8	1,151.8	25.6	1,390.1	23.0
Life insurance reserves	85.2	8.8	130.3	6.7	222.5	5.0	262.6	4.3
Pension fund reserves	90.7	9.4	237.4	12.2	727.1	16.2	1,105.6	18.3
Security credit	1.1	0.1	2.2	0.1	12.6	0.3	19.3	0.3
Other assets	13.3	1.4	26.3	1.4	74.4	1.7	92.2	1.5
Total financial assets	$967.9	100.0%	$1,944.3	100.0%	$4,493.6	100.0%	$6,042.4	100.0%

Note: Columns may not add to to totals due to rounding.
SOURCE: Board of Governors of the Federal Reserve System, *Flow of Funds Accounts: Financial Assets and Liabilities Outstanding*, indicated years.

ating new financial services. Like a Baskin-Robbins' ice cream store, leading financial institutions began to offer their household customers 31 or more flavors of savings and transactions accounts as well as credit plans to meet a wide variety of personal financial needs. (For some examples, see Exhibit 18–2.)

EXHIBIT 18–2

Examples of Key Financial Services Offered to Consumers by U.S. Financial Institutions

Payments services:	
NOW accounts	Interest-bearing checking accounts offered by banks and thrift institutions. As of 1984 federal rate ceilings applied to these accounts were set at a maximum of 5¼ percent for deposits under $2,500.
Super NOW accounts	An interest-bearing checking account without restrictions on withdrawals, number of checks written, or on the interest rate that can be paid. Must have a minimum balance of $1,000 or the interest rate drops to regular NOW account rate.
Money market deposit accounts (MMDAs)	An interest-bearing checkbook deposit requiring a minimum average balance of $1,000 but with no federal interest-rate ceiling if the average balance does not fall below $1,000 (otherwise the regular NOW account rate applies). Up to six written preauthorized third-party transfers out of the account are permitted per month, only three of which may be by check. No legal restrictions are imposed, however, on withdrawals in person, by mail, or through a messenger or automated teller machine. A seven-day notice of withdrawal may be imposed by the offering financial institution.
Share drafts	Interest-bearing checking accounts offered by credit unions to members only with a maximum dividend rate set by federal regulation.
Share accounts	Shares in a money market mutual fund, representing an ownership interest in a pool of money market securities held by the fund; minimums are required to open an account and make deposits; checks may be written provided they are equal to or larger than some minimum amount (e.g., $500).
Automatic transfer service (ATS)	Allows the customer of a depository institution to transfer funds between checking and savings accounts, thus earning interest on unused balances until the funds are needed for expenditures.

EXHIBIT 18–2 *(concluded)*

Savings instruments:	
Passbook or regular savings accounts	Savings plan allowing withdrawals or deposits at any time; while technically a seven-day withdrawal notice may be required, this is usually not requested by the offering institution; the interest rate cannot exceed the federal legal ceiling which in 1985 was 5½ percent.
Regulated-rate certificate of deposit, 7 to 31 days to maturity	A time account with a $1,000 minimum carrying either a set maturity or with a required notice of withdrawal of 7 to 31 days; carries a penalty for premature withdrawal and cannot be used to secure a loan; interest rate is set by federal regulation.
Unregulated-rate certificate of deposit, 7 to 31 days to maturity	A time account requiring a $1,000 minimum deposit with set maturity or requiring minimum withdrawal notice as specified by the offering institution; a penalty is imposed for early withdrawal and the deposit cannot secure a loan, though automatic renewal is allowed and there is no federal rate ceiling unless the balance drops below $1,000.
Regular certificate of deposit, maturity greater than 31 days	A time deposit without a minimum balance and may be of any maturity over 31 days; no federal rate ceilings are imposed and the interest rate offered may be fixed or variable, depending upon the policies of the offering institution, though there is usually a penalty for premature withdrawal.
Universal life insurance plans	A combination risk-protection and savings instrument offering the customer money market interest rates on savings accumulated in a mutual fund plus the convenience of automatic withdrawals to cover premium payments on a life insurance policy.
IRAs and Keogh plans	Retirement funds which a wage earner (in the case of IRAs) or a self-employed person (in the case of Keoghs) can open up at local banks or nonbank thrifts, brokerage firms, insurance companies, or mutual funds and contribute limited amounts of annual income free of federal income taxes.
Combined brokerage (either full-service or discount) and cash-management services	A comprehensive financial management package offered primarily by brokerage companies and some banks and thrift institutions which may offer share accounts in money market funds and stock and bond funds, credit card and check-writing services, automatic funds transfers into and out of the customer's account, and low-cost execution of desired security trades along with option and margin accounts.

This trend toward financial service proliferation began with the introduction of the NOW account in New England in 1970. NOWs are checkbook deposits which, like any checking account, can be used to make payments for purchases of goods and services but also pay interest—something currently prohibited regular checking accounts by federal law. Initially confined to the six New England states NOWs were permitted nationwide beginning in 1981 as a result of passage of the Depository Institutions Deregulation and Monetary Control Act of 1980. This law, as we saw in Chapters 4 and 5, also called for the gradual phasing out of federal interest-rate ceilings on all bank and thrift institution deposits so that consumers could receive competitive, market-determined interest rates on their deposits.

The Depository Institutions Deregulation Act of 1980 (DIDMCA) also authorized two services which compete directly with NOWs. One of these—automatic transfers (ATS)—permits the consumer to preauthorize a bank to move funds from a savings account to a checking account in order to cover overdrafts. The net effect is to pay interest on transactions balances at the savings account rate. Credit unions are permitted to offer their own version of the NOW, known as the *share draft*. These interest-bearing checkbook plans give the consumer the advantage of a duplicate record system for any checks written, frequently offer extra float time, and potentially pay higher interest rates on liquid funds.

In 1973 money market mutual funds appeared, offering consumers *share accounts* with low denominations (most allowing accounts to be opened for as little as $1,000), but paying interest rates reflecting current rates in the money market. Like NOWs, share accounts at money funds were developed to skirt around federal deposit interest-rate ceilings and give smaller savers access to competitive rates of return on their funds. Later, several prominent brokerage houses began offering *consumer cash-management services* in which funds could be held in an interest-bearing money market fund until transfered into stocks, bonds, or other securities or accessed via check or credit card. Life insurance firms began offering a related service known as *universal life insurance* in which savings contributed by the policyholder are placed in a money market fund with the life insurer making periodic preauthorized withdrawals to pay the premiums on the life insurance policy. Thus, the consumer is offered both life insurance protection plus a higher return on savings. Finally, in 1981 with passage of the Economic Recovery Tax Act of 1981, wage earners and salaried individuals were granted the right to make limited contributions each year, tax free, to an individual retirement account (IRA) offered by local banks, savings institutions, brokerage firms, insurance companies, and mutual funds or by employers with qualified pension, profit-sharing, or savings plans. Similarly, Keogh plan retirement accounts have been open to self-employed persons since 1962 and may be offered by the same institutions that sell IRAs.

Beginning in the late 1970s flexible interest-rate savings plans became popular as many consumers fought to stay ahead of inflation through savings instruments whose rates of return were sensitive to changes in the cost of living. Money market certificates of deposit were authorized by federal regulation in 1978 with interest rates that changed as market yields on U.S. government securities fluctuated. Unfortunately, such accounts often carried high minimum deposits and stiff penalties for early withdrawal. Nevertheless, their popularity with consumers stirred Congress to act and, as we noted above, federal interest-rate ceilings were ordered gradually phased out beginning in 1981. In 1982 the Garn-St Germain Depository Institutions Act allowed banks and nonbank thrift institutions to offer deposits competitive with shares offered by money market mutual funds. The result was the appearance of money market deposit accounts (MMDAs) and Super NOWs, each offering flexible money market interest rates but accessible via check and preauthorized draft to pay for purchases of goods and services. The great success of the MMDAs is reflected in the fact that they exceeded $300 billion within six months of their inauguration.

These recent innovations in financial services have been designed largely to attract consumer savings and to bring individuals and families into the financial markets as more active lenders of funds. The newest financial services offer the consumer greater *financial flexibility*—easier access to liquid funds for transactions purposes and the ability to move funds more easily from one type of savings instrument to another. The newest savings instruments offer the potential for higher effective rates of return more closely tied to changing interest rates in the open market.

CONSUMERS AS BORROWERS OF FUNDS

We have noted that consumers provide most of the savings out of which loans are made and financial assets created in the money and capital markets. However, it is also true that consumers are among the most important *borrowers* in the financial system. For example, in 1983 households borrowed $167 billion in the nation's credit markets, while nonfinancial businesses raised just $126 billion and financial institutions raised only $90 billion in total credit funds. Equally impressive is the total amount of debt owed by households relative to other sectors of the economy. For example, total credit market debt owed by U.S. households approached $2 trillion by year-end 1983. This was just slightly less than the total indebtedness of all nonfinancial businesses in the U.S. economy, but exceeded the total amounts owed by the federal government and by all state and local governments.

Is Consumer Borrowing Excessive?

Are consumers too heavily in debt today? Have they jumped in over their heads? Certainly, the total volume of household debt outstanding is huge in both absolute terms and relative to most other sectors of the economy. However, to judge whether consumer borrowing is really excessive, that debt should be compared to the financial assets consumers hold. These assets, presumably, can be drawn upon to meet any interest and principal payments that come due on consumer borrowings. Exhibit 18–3 shows that, while the volume of consumer debt has increased rapidly in recent years, the volume of household financial assets also has grown rapidly. For example, in 1983 financial assets held by U.S. households exceeded their outstanding liabilities by $4.1 trillion. Moreover, the absolute dollar size of that financial asset "cushion" has increased dramatically over the past three decades.

When we measure the ratio of consumer liabilities to financial assets, however, the picture is not quite so optimistic. As shown in Exhibit 18–3, this liability-to-asset ratio has risen dramatically from less than 20 percent in 1950 to more than 30 percent in the most recent year. Indeed, in 1984 and 1985 consumer borrowing broke all-time records month after month. Whether the household liability-financial asset ratio has reached an "excessive" level depends, of course, on economic conditions and the educational level and degree of financial sophistication of individuals and families. If the average consumer today is better educated and more capable of managing a larger volume of debt, a higher ratio of liabilities to financial assets in household portfolios is probably not an alarming development. Moreover, the total wealth held by consumers includes not just their financial assets but also their real assets, such as homes, automobiles, and furniture. While we have no really reliable mea-

EXHIBIT 18–3

The Household Sector as a Net Lender of Funds

	Amounts Outstanding at Year-End ($ billions)				
Item	1950	1960	1970	1980	1983
Total financial assets held by households	$447.5	$967.9	$1,926.6	$4,493.6	$6,042.4
Total financial liabilities of households	77.4	226.2	502.0	1,493.5	1,923.0
Difference: financial assets—liabilities	$370.1	$741.7	$1,424.6	$3,000.1	$4,119.4
Ratio of household liabilities to financial assets	17.3%	23.4%	26.1%	33.2%	31.8%

SOURCE: Board of Governors of the Federal Reserve System, *Flow of Funds Accounts: Financial Assets and Liabilities Outstanding,* indicated years.

sure of the value of real assets held by consumers, it is obvious that the total wealth of individuals and families (including both real and financial assets) far exceeds their debt obligations.

Categories of Consumer Borrowing

The range of consumer borrowing needs is enormous. Loans to the household sector support a more diverse group of purchases of goods and services than is true of any other sector of the American economy. Consumers borrow *long term* to finance purchases of *durable goods,* such as single-family homes, automobiles, mobile homes, recreational vehicles, repair and modernization of existing homes, boats, and home appliances. They usually borrow *short term* to cover purchases of *nondurable goods and services,* such as medical care, vacations, fuel, and food and clothing. Financial analysts frequently divide the credit extended to consumers into three broad categories: (1) *residential mortgage credit* to support the purchase of new or existing single-family homes, duplexes, and other permanent dwellings; (2) *installment credit* used primarily for long-term nonresidential purposes; and (3) *noninstallment credit* for shorter-term cash needs.

Which of these forms of consumer borrowing is most important? Exhibit 18–4 provides a clear answer. Far and away the dominant form of consumer borrowing is aimed at providing shelter for individuals and families through *mortgage loans.* Home mortgage indebtedness by U.S. households reached nearly $1.2 trillion at year-end 1983, representing more than 60 percent of all household debt. Moreover, the volume of home mortgage credit flowing to households has grown rapidly in recent years with the increasing attractiveness of home ownership as a tax shelter. For example, residential mortgage loans taken on by households more than tripled during the 1970s. We will examine the huge residential mortgage market in much greater detail in Chapter 19.

Installment credit is the second major component of consumer debt in the United States. Installment debt consists of all consumer liabilities other than mortgages that are retired in two or more consecutive payments, usually made monthly or quarterly. Four major types of installment credit are extended by lenders in this field: automobile credit, revolving credit, mobile homes, and other consumer installment loans. An incredibly wide variety of consumer goods and services is financed by this kind of credit, including the purchase of furniture and appliances, payment of medical and dental expenses, vacations, the purchase of transportation and recreational vehicles, and the consolidation of outstanding debts. As shown in Exhibit 18–4, consumer installment debt totaled nearly $390 billion at year-end 1983, or more than triple the amount of such debt in 1970.

EXHIBIT 18–4

Principal Liabilities of U.S. Households Outstanding at Year-End 1960, 1970, 1980, and 1983 ($ billions)

Liabilities	1960		1970		1980		1983	
	Amount	Percent	Amount	Percent	Amount	Percent	Amount	Percent
Home mortgages	$136.8	60.5%	$273.1	56.5%	$ 940.4	63.0%	$1,199.5	62.4%
Other mortgages	9.2	4.1	20.5	4.2	30.9	2.1	38.9	2.4
Consumer installment credit	43.0	19.0	101.2	20.9	312.8	20.9	387.9	20.2
Other consumer credit	13.2	5.8	25.6	5.3	72.2	4.8	96.9	5.0
Bank loans n.e.c.*	7.2	3.2	21.9	4.5	28.8	1.9	32.3	1.7
Other loans	7.0	3.1	20.9	4.3	54.8	3.7	76.7	4.0
Security credit	5.4	2.4	10.0	2.1	23.7	1.6	47.8	2.5
Trade credit	2.1	0.9	5.3	1.1	16.9	1.1	26.5	1.4
Deferred and unpaid life insurance premiums	2.4	1.1	5.1	1.1	12.9	0.9	16.4	0.9
Total liabilities	$226.2	100.0%	$483.6	100.0%	$1,493.5	100.0%	$1,923.0	100.0%

Note: Columns may not add to totals due to rounding.
* Not elsewhere classified.
SOURCE: Board of Governors of the Federal Reserve System, *Flow of Funds Accounts: Financial Assets and Liabilities Outstanding*, indicated years.

For many years, the majority of installment loans extended to consumers in the United States were used to finance the purchase of automobiles. This is no longer the case, however, though auto paper still represents more than a third of all consumer installment debt outstanding. The largest installment debt category today is a miscellaneous group of loans that cover household expenses, debt consolidation, and purchases of durable goods other than automobiles. The high cost of energy and inflation have had a significant impact here. High-priced gasoline and new car prices have encouraged the substitution of smaller, less-expensive cars for the heavy gas-guzzlers. At the same time, faced with home heating and air-conditioning bills that frequently exceed their home mortgage payments, more consumers today are borrowing simply to cover home operating expenses, make home repairs, and consolidate outstanding debts.

The final major category of consumer debt is *noninstallment credit*, which is normally paid off in a lump sum. This form of consumer credit includes single-payment loans, charge accounts, and credit for services, such as medical care and utilities. The total amount of noninstallment loans outstanding is difficult to estimate because many such loans are made by one individual to another or by department stores, oil and gas companies, and professional service firms that do not report their lending activities. Commercial banks, however, make a substantial volume of noninstallment loans to consumers and are considered the leading lender in this field.

CREDIT AND DEBIT CARDS

One of the most popular forms of installment credit available to consumers today comes through the *credit card.* Through this encoded piece of plastic, the consumer has instant access to credit for any purchase up to a prespecified limit. More recently, another piece of plastic—the debit card—has made instant cash available and check cashing much easier. The growth of credit and debit cards has been truly phenomenal to date and the future looks equally promising. Current estimates suggest that there are nearly 1 trillion credit and debit cards in use worldwide.

In the future a wide array of new consumer financial services is likely to be offered through plastic credit and debit card programs. Such services may include consumer revolving credit lines and preauthorized borrowing, interest paid on surplus credit card balances, optional credit repayment plans, and the payment of other household bills. Many of these consumer-oriented financial services are already offered on a limited basis in selected markets across the United States. In the future customers will need to make fewer trips to their bank or other financial institution because transactions will be handled mainly over the telephone or through a conveniently located computer terminal, either in the home or in easily accessible public locations. The hometown financial institution will lose much of its convenience advantage for local customers. It will be nearly as convenient for the customer to maintain a checking, savings, or loan account in a city hundreds of miles away as to keep it in a local financial institution. In short, the ticket to many, perhaps most, consumer financial services will be a plastic credit or debit card, with electronic processing of consumer financial data across great distances.

Credit Cards

Credit cards are used for very different purposes today depending upon the social class, education, income, and lifestyle of the user. Customers who use their credit cards merely as a substitute for cash are referred to as *convenience users*. These people tend to be in the upper-middle or top income-earning brackets and do not necessarily seek out stores accepting their cards. Customers who purchase large items (such as furniture, appliances, and gifts) and generally maintain large outstanding credit card balances are referred to as *installment users* because they pay only a portion of their outstanding balances each month. These individuals frequently are in lower- and middle-income brackets and tend to be the most profitable credit card customers for card-issuing firms.

For both convenience and installment users, the principal advantage of credit cards is *convenience*. There is no minimum number of transactions for which the card must be used. Also, as two or three cards have become more widely accepted in thousands of stores, the number of different plastic cards needed by the consumer has been reduced. The installment feature of the credit card is a major attraction because it functions as a revolving line of credit. In addition, the card itself serves to identify the customer and makes pertinent information available when the privilege of using the card is exercised. Most cards are issued to customers today only after a careful analysis of their credit standing. That is why cardholders frequently are able to use thier cards as a credit reference to aid in the cashing of checks or to obtain other forms of credit. Most merchants know that charge cardholders tend to have higher incomes and better payment records than the general population.

Debit Cards

Until recently, commercial banks were the only major financial institution actively involved in the plastic card field. Other than banks, the other major issuers of cards have been retail department stores and oil companies. This situation changed rapidly during the 1970s and early 1980s, however, as nonbank financial institutions (principally credit

unions, mutual savings banks, and savings and loan associations) successfully invaded the plastic card market using debit cards.[2] While a credit
card permits the customer to buy now and pay later, *debit cards* are
merely a convenient way of paying *now.* A debit card enables its users
to make deposits and withdrawals from an automated teller ("money
machine") and also to pay for purchases by direct electronic transfer of
funds from their own account to the merchant's account. Debit cards
are also used for identification and check-clearing purposes and to access
remote computer terminals for information or for the transfer of funds.

An important feature of debit cards is their potential for the complete
elimination of checkbook float. Electronic funds transfer systems activated
with a debit card will take only seconds instead of days (as checks now
do) to move money from one account to another. Overall, the outlook
for debit cards is excellent. The fact that many credit card users do not
take advantage of the credit feature but merely use their card for convenience in shopping suggests that there is a market for debit card services.

Both the credit card and the debit card offer significant opportunities
to financial institutions to develop new services and open up new consumer markets. The overall cost of consumer lending can be reduced
by encouraging small borrowers to use a revolving charge card account
rather than negotiating separate loans each time funds are needed. Credit
and debit cards linked to money machines and point-of-sale terminals
can provide the means for moving funds in many different directions,
that is, for purchases of goods and services, for additions to savings, and
for investment in financial assets. Most, if not all, consumer financial services—credit, savings, and checking—may be offered through card programs, offering the consumer greater speed, convenience, and accuracy
in recordkeeping.

THE DETERMINANTS OF CONSUMER BORROWING

As we noted earlier, consumers represent one of the largest groups
of borrowers in the financial system. Yet individual consumers differ
widely in their use of credit and in their attitudes toward borrowing
money. What factors appear to influence the volume of borrowing carried
out by households?

Recent research points to a number of factors which bear on the con-

---

[2] With passage of DIDMCA in 1980, savings and loans and other federally regulated
thrifts were also authorized to extend credit through credit cards.

sumer's decision of when and how much to borrow.[3] Leading the list is the size of *individual or family income.* Families with larger incomes use greater amounts of debt both in absolute dollar amount and relative to income. In part, the debt-income relationship reflects the high correlation between income levels and *education.* Families whose principal breadwinners have made a significant investment in education are more often aware of the advantages (as well as the dangers) of using debt in order to supplement current income. Moreover, there is a high positive correlation between the level of education and the income-earning power of the principal breadwinners in a family. The result is a three-way interrelationship between income, education, and the use of household debt.

The *stage of life* in which adult income-earning members of a family find themselves is a major influence on household borrowing. The so-called life-cycle hypothesis contends that young families just starting out tend to be heavy users of debt.[4] The purchase of a new home, automobile, appliances, and furniture follow soon after a new family is formed. As children come along, living costs rise and a larger home may be necessary, resulting in additional borrowing. Research suggests families with children tend to borrow more heavily relative to their current income than either singles or childless couples. Moreover, the more volatile a family's income, the more debt it tends to use relative to current income. Similarly, a family that holds a low proportion of liquid assets (such as insurance policies, stocks, bonds, and deposits) tends to use more debt per dollar of income than a household with a high proportion of liquid assets.

Consumer borrowing is correlated with the *business cycle.* During periods of economic expansion the number of jobs increases, and many households become more optimistic about their future financial situation. New borrowings usually outstrip repayments of outstanding loans, and the net volume of household debt rises. When an economic expansion ends and a recession begins, however, unemployment increases and many households turn pessimistic about their future. Some, fearing a drop in income or even loss of their jobs, will attempt to build up their savings and cut back on borrowing. Loan repayments rise relative to new borrowings, and total household debt declines.

One factor which accentuates the cyclical behavior of consumer borrowing is fluctuations in the *demand for durable goods.*[5] When the econ-

---

[3] Two excellent discussions of the factors influencing household borrowing are the studies by Katona, Mandell, and Schiedeskamp (1971) and the National Commission on Consumer Finance (1972).

[4] See especially Ando and Modigliani (1963).

[5] For a discussion of the factors influencing purchases of consumer durables, see Dunkelberg and Stevenson (1972).

omy turns down into a recession, many households postpone replacement of worn-out furniture, home appliances, and automobiles. Repairing the old automobile, for example, is often viewed as a safer, less expensive alternative than incurring additional debt and committing uncertain future income to buy a new one. Therefore consumers are likely to cut back on purchases of durables and on the debt used to finance them when a recession hits. However, new furniture, appliances, and automobiles become more attractive in boom periods, and consumer debt used to buy these items usually increases during such periods.

In recent years *price expectations* have influenced consumer borrowing heavily; this has been especially the case since the late 1960s when the rate of inflation began to accelerate. Postponing the purchase of an automobile, a new home, furniture, or appliances usually means these goods will simply cost more in the future. If family incomes are not increasing at least as fast as consumer prices, it often pays to "buy now" through borrowing rather than postpone purchases of goods and services. This is especially true if funds can be borrowed either at fixed-interest rates or at interest rates that change more slowly than consumer prices.

Fluctuations in *interest rates* also play a role in shaping the volume and direction of consumer borrowing. Interest rates rise as the economy expands and gathers momentum. At first, the rising rates are not high enough to offset strong consumer optimism, and household borrowing continues to increase. As the period of economic expansion reaches a peak, however, the rise in interest rates and the accompanying increase in monthly payments on installment loans become so significant that consumer borrowing begins to decline. The drop in borrowing also leads to a decline in consumer spending, which may worsen the impending recession. We should note, however, that consumer loan rates tend to be "sticky" over the course of the business cycle and change slowly compared to the majority of other interest rates.[6]

CONSUMER LENDING INSTITUTIONS

Financial intermediaries—commercial banks, savings banks and savings and loan associations, credit unions, and finance companies—account for most of the loans made to consumers in the American economy. For example, of the $490 billion in nonmortgage installment loans owed by consumers in May 1985, financial intermediaries accounted for $450 billion, or about 90 percent. Intermediaries also dominate the market for noninstallment credit and make the bulk of home mortgage loans. While each type of financial institution prefers to specialize in one type

---

[6] See Chapter 11 for an explanation of the influence of the business cycle on both long- and short-term interest rates.

or a few selected areas of consumer lending, there has been a tendency in recent years for these institutions to diversify their lending operations. One important result of this diversification has been to bring all major consumer lenders into direct competition with each other.

Commercial Banks

The single most important consumer lending institution is the commercial bank. Commercial banks approach the consumer in three different ways—by direct lending, through purchases of installment paper from merchants, and by making loans to other consumer lending institutions. As Exhibit 18–5 shows, commercial banks held more than $440 billion in consumer mortgage and nonmortgage loans in 1985. Half of that total consisted of mortgages to support the purchase or construction of residential dwellings, while the rest consisted of installment and noninstallment credit to cover purchases of goods and services and debt retirement. In the mortgage field, commercial banks usually prefer to provide short-term construction financing rather than making long-term permanent loans for family housing.

Within the nonmortgage loan category, banks make a wider variety of consumer loans than any other lending institution and dominate most areas of consumer lending. Commercial banks grant about half of all auto loans extended by financial institutions to consumers each year. However, most bank credit in the auto field is indirect—installment paper purchased from auto dealers—rather than being made directly to the auto-buying consumer. Starting out behind, commercial banks also have

EXHIBIT 18–5

Consumer-Related Loans Held by Commercial Banks, March 1985
($ billions)

Type of Loan	Amount	Percent of Total*
Residential mortgage loans:		
One-to-four family	$200.0	45.2%
Multifamily	22.0	5.0
Nonmortgage consumer loans:		
Automobile	89.3	20.2
Revolving credit	63.7	14.4
Mobile homes	9.4	2.1
Other loans	57.6	13.0
Totals	$442.0	100.0%

* Column may not add to total due to rounding.
SOURCE: Board of Governors of the Federal Reserve System, *Federal Reserve Bulletin*, September 1985.

come to dominate lending to support the purchase of mobile homes. About 40 percent of all mobile home loans are held by banks, with finance companies and savings and loan associations accounting for the remainder. In other forms of consumer installment credit, however, the lead of commercial banks is narrower and the share of other consumer lending institutions is on the rise.

Finance Companies

Finance companies have a long history of active lending in the consumer installment field, providing funds directly to the consumer through thousands of small-loan offices and indirectly by purchasing installment paper from appliance dealers. These active household lenders provide auto loans, credit for home improvements and for the purchase of appliances and furniture, and revolving credit arrangements. (See Exhibit 18–6.)

As we noted in Chapter 6, there are actually two different kinds of finance companies serving the consumer. *Sales finance companies* purchase consumer installment contracts from retail merchants. These companies loan monies to retail dealers to acquire inventories of consumer goods—mainly home furniture, appliances, and automobiles. As the goods are sold, the dealer repays the loan. *Consumer finance companies* make cash loans directly to individuals and families. These companies borrow through bank lines of credit and frequently have large loan losses because they usually accept more risky loans than other consumer lenders. Consumer finance companies have legal limits on the interest rates they can charge for household loans and on the maximum size of such loans as set by state law. Loan rates usually cannot exceed 3 percent per month on a loan's unpaid balance, and single loans normally cannot exceed $5,000.

EXHIBIT 18–6

Consumer-Related Loans Held by Finance Companies, March 1985

Type of Loan	Amount	Percent of Total*
Automobile	$56.7	57.2%
Mobile home	9.0	9.1
Other installment loans	33.4	33.7
Totals	$99.1	100.0%

* Column may not add to total due to rounding.
SOURCE: Board of Governors of the Federal Reserve System, *Federal Reserve Bulletin*, May 1985.

Other Consumer Lending Institutions

The fastest-growing group of consumer installment lenders comprises credit unions, whose attractive interest rates on deposits and loans have swelled their membership greatly in recent years. Credit unions make a wide variety of loans for such diverse purposes as purchases of automobiles, vacations, medical expenses, home repair and modernization, and, more recently, mortgage credit for the purchase of new homes. In fact, as we saw in Chapter 5, loans to families and individuals make up about three quarters of the total assets of U.S. credit unions. Also making sizable inroads into the consumer loan field in recent years have been savings and loan associations and mutual savings banks. While these institutions have long been dominant in residential mortgage lending, they have aggressively expanded their portfolios of credit card, education, home improvement, furniture, appliance, and mobile home loans over the past decade. Savings and loans are likely to be an even greater factor in consumer credit markets in the years ahead due to passage of DIDMCA in 1980 and the Garn-St Germain Act in 1982. Both laws gave major concessions to savings and loans in granting consumer loans. The 1980 law granted credit card services to S&Ls, while the 1982 law allowed these associations to extend consumer loans up to 30 percent of their total assets (including loans to businesses to acquire inventories of consumer goods).

FACTORS CONSIDERED IN MAKING CONSUMER LOANS

Consumer loans are considered one of the most profitable uses of funds for most financial institutions. There is evidence, however, that such loans usually carry greater risk than most other kinds of loans, and they are more costly to make per dollar of loan.[7] On the other hand, the lender often can offset these costs by charging higher interest rates. Consumer credit markets in many communities are less competitive than the market for business loans or for marketable securities, giving the lender something of an advantage.

The making of consumer loans is one of the most challenging aspects of modern financial management. It requires not only a thorough knowledge of household financial statements but also an ability to assess the character of the borrower and the likelihood that he or she will honor financial commitments in the future. Over the years most loan officers

---

[7] Credit investigations and recordkeeping are the principal costs associated with consumer lending. See, for example, Federal Reserve Bank of Boston, *Analysis of High-Earning Banks,* Functional Cost Analysis Program, 1978.

have developed decision "rules of thumb" as an aid to processing and evaluating consumer loan applications. These decision rules often vary greatly with the financial institution doing the lending and the experience of each loan officer, but a few of the more common practices may be noted.

For example, many consumer loan officers insist that household debt (exclusive of housing costs) should not exceed a certain critical percentage of a family's monthly or annual gross income. A maximum of 15 to 20 percent of gross income is a common standard in this instance. For younger borrowers, without substantial assets to serve as collateral for a loan, a cosigner may be sought whose assets and financial standing represent more adequate security. The duration of employment of the borrower is often a critical factor, and many institutions will deny a loan request if the customer has been employed at his or her present job for less than a year.

The past payment record of a customer usually is the key indicator of *character* and the likelihood that the loan will be repaid in timely fashion. Many lenders refuse to make loans to those consumers who evidence "pyramiding of debt;" that is, borrowing from one financial institution to pay another. Evidence of sloppy money handling, such as unusually large balances carried on charge accounts or a heavy burden of installment payments, is regarded as a negative factor in a loan application. Loan officers are particularly alert to evidence of a lack of credit integrity as reflected in frequent late payments or actual default on past loans. The character of the borrower is the single, most important issue in the decision to grant or deny a consumer loan. Regardless of the strength of the borrower's financial position, if the customer lacks the willingness to repay his or her debt, then the lender has made a bad loan.

Most lenders feel that those who own valuable property, such as land, buildings, or marketable securities, are a better risk than those who do not own such property, especially if the property itself is pledged to secure the loan. For example, homeowners are usually considered to be better risks than those who rent. Moreover, a borrower's chance of getting a loan usually goes up if he or she does other business (such as maintain a deposit) with the lending institution. If more than one member of the family works, this is often reviewed as a more favorable factor than if the family depends on one breadwinner who may become ill, die, or simply lose his or her job. Having a telephone at home is another positive factor in evaluating a loan application because the telephone gives the lender an inexpensive way to contact the borrower. One way to lower the cost of a loan is for the consumer to pledge a bank deposit, marketable securities, or other liquid assets as security behind the loan. The disadvantage here is that such a promise "ties up" the asset pledged until the loan is repaid.

FINANCIAL DISCLOSURE AND CONSUMER CREDIT

A number of important new laws have appeared in recent years designed to protect the consumer in dealings with lending insitutions. One major area of emphasis in recent consumer legislation is *financial disclosure*—making all relevant information about the terms of a loan available to the borrower before a commitment is made. The basic assumption is that an informed borrower will be a wise user of credit. Moreover, if all important information is laid out "on the table" before a loan agreement is reached, this may encourage the consumer to shop around to find the cheapest and most convenient sources of credit available. However, there is considerable debate today on whether consumer-protection legislation has really accomplished its goals. Both lenders and borrowers are confronted with a confusing array of laws and regulations which encourage violations and may be of little net benefit to the consumer.[8]

Truth in Lending

In 1968 Congress passed a watershed piece of legislation in the consumer-credit field—the Consumer Credit Protection Act, more widely known as "Truth in Lending." However, the Consumer Credit Protection Act covered more than just truthful disclosure by lenders of the terms of a loan. It defined and prohibited extortionate credit practices, limited garnishment of wages, and created a National Commission on Consumer Finance to oversee enforcement of the law. Shortly after the act was passed, federal regulatory agencies prepared new rules to implement and enforce the principles of truth in lending. The most famous of these is the Federal Reserve Board's Regulation Z.

Truth in Lending simply requires banks and other lenders to provide sufficient information about a credit contract, in easily understood terms, so that the consumer can make an intelligent decision about purchasing credit. The law does not tell creditors how much to charge or to whom they may lend money. Rather, the lenders are required to tell the cus-

---

[8] Recent studies by Day and Brandt (1974), Mandell (1973, 1974), and Parker and Shay (1974) suggest that many of the goals sought by recent consumer-oriented financial legislation have not been achieved. Consumers rarely shop for credit and appear more concerned about the affordability of monthly payments on a loan than with how one lender's interest charge compares with that quoted by another. Survey evidence suggests that the majority of consumers are unaware of the rights and privileges granted them under recent federal financial legislation and see little practical benefit from these laws. See also Rose (June 1979).

tomer the true cost of a loan and any other terms of the loan that might have an impact on the consumer's financial well-being.

At the same time the consumers were granted certain rights. For example, they have the right to sue the lender for failure to conform to the Consumer Credit Protection Act and its supporting regulations. Consumers have the right to cancel or rescind a credit agreement within three business days if their home is included as part of the collateral for a loan. This so-called *right of rescission* usually applies to the repair or remodeling of a home or the taking out of a second mortgage on an existing home. It does not cover an application for a first mortgage to make the initial purchase of a home, however.

Commercial banks, credit unions, finance companies, savings and loan associations, life insurance companies, mortgage bankers, retailers extending credit, auto dealers, and real estate brokers all fall under the provisions of Truth in Lending. Still, some loans are exempted. The credit requested must be intended for personal, family, household, or agricultural purposes and result in a debt obligation repayable in more than four installments. Amounts in excess of $25,000 generally are not covered by the law unless real property is involved.

The most widely known provision of Truth in Lending is the requirement that a lender must tell the customer the annual percentage rate of interest (APR) charged on a loan. Lenders must disclose the total dollar cost associated with granting a loan—known as the finance charge—which is the sum of all charges the customer must pay as a condition for securing the loan. These charges may include credit investigation fees, insurance to protect the lender, and points on a mortgage loan. Once the finance charge is determined, it must then be converted into the APR by comparing it with the amount of the loan. The APR is really the ratio of the dollar finance charge to the declining unpaid balance of a loan, determined by the actuarial method.[9] Because all lenders must quote the APR, computed by the same method, this makes it easier (at least in theory) for the consumer to shop around and to purchase credit from the cheapest source available.

The concept of Truth in Lending has been extended in a number of directions in recent years. One important dimension concerns *advertising*. A lender who advertises one attractive feature of a credit package to consumers must also disclose other relevant credit terms. For example, if a car dealer advertises low down payments, he or she must also disclose other aspects of the loan, such as how many payments are required, what the amount of each payment is, and how many months or years are involved.

---

[9] See Chapter 8 for a discussion of how the APR can be figured and Rose (June 1979).

Fair Credit Billing Act

In 1974 Congress passed the Fair Credit Billing Act, which amended the original Truth in Lending law. The new amendment came in response to a torrent of consumer complaints about credit billing errors, especially on credit cards. Many individuals found that they were being billed for items never purchased or received, that some merchants would not respond when contacted about billing errors, and that finance charges were frequently assessed even though the consumer claimed no responsibility for charges listed on the billing statement.

The Fair Credit Billing Act requires a creditor to respond to a customer's billing inquiry within 30 days. In most cases, the dispute must be resolved within 90 days. The customer may withhold payment of any amounts in dispute, though he or she must pay any portions of a bill that are not in dispute. However, no creditor can report a customer as "delinquent" over amounts of a bill that are the subject of disagreement. A creditor who fails to respond to the customer's inquiry or makes no effort to settle the dispute may forfeit the disputed sum up to $50.

Fair Credit Reporting Act

A further extension of Truth in Lending occurred when the Fair Credit Reporting Act was passed by Congress in 1970. This law entitles consumers to have access to their credit files, which are kept by hundreds of credit bureaus active in the United States. These credit bureaus supply subscribing lenders with vital information on amounts owed and the payment records and credit ratings of individuals and families. (Current estimates suggest these bureaus contain detailed financial reports on as many as 140 million Americans.) They aid greatly in reducing the risks inherent in consumer lending. However, because the information credit bureaus supply has a substantial impact on the availability of credit to individuals and families, their activities and especially the accuracy of the information they provide have been brought under closer scrutiny in recent years by federal and state regulatory authorities.

Under the provisions of the Fair Credit Reporting Act, the consumer is entitled to review his or her other credit file at any time (after paying a required fee). Moreover, he or she may challenge any items that appear in the file and demand an investigation. The credit bureau must respond and, if inaccuracies exist, remove or modify the incorrect information. If the consumer determines that an item in the credit file is damaging and requires clarification, he or she may insert a statement of 100 words or less explaining the consumer's version of the matter. (At the very least this action indicates the consumer is concerned about and takes responsibility for his or her debts.) Data in the file may be shown only to properly identified individuals for approved purposes or upon direct written request from the consumer. No information may be disclosed to anyone after a period of seven years unless the consumer is seeking a loan of $50,000 or more, purchasing life insurance, applying for a job paying $20,000 or more per year, or has declared personal bankruptcy. The consumer may sue if damaged by incorrect information in his or her credit file. Many financial analysts today recommend that consumers check out their credit bureau report several months before applying for a major loan.

Consumer Leasing Act

In 1976 Congress passed the Consumer Leasing Act, which requires disclosure by leasing companies of the essential terms of any lease involving personal property. Short-term leases are excluded, but all those with terms over four months are covered by the law provided the property is leased for personal, family, or household use. The applicant (or lessee) is entitled to a written statement of all charges, specifying the number and amount of payments, any property maintenance costs, taxes, or other fees. The customer must be told about any insurance required, the terms under which the lease may be canceled, any penalties for late payment, and any express warranties that go with the property. The lease customer is entitled to sue for damages plus court costs if the requirements of the law are not met.

CREDIT DISCRIMINATION LAWS

The civil rights movement has had an impact on the granting of consumer loans. Among the most important civil rights laws involving consumer credit are the Equal Credit Opportunity Act of 1974 and its amendments in 1976, the Fair Housing Act of 1968, the Home Mortgage Disclosure Act of 1975, and the Community Reinvestment Act of 1977. The fundamental purpose of these laws is to outlaw discrimination in the granting of credit due to the age, color, marital status, national origin, race, religious affiliation, or sex of the borrower. Today, lenders must be able to justify in terms of fairness and objectivity, not only the loans that are made, but also those that are not made.

Community Reinvestment Act

One of the most important and controversial pieces of financial legislation in recent years is the Community Reinvestment Act, signed into law by President Carter on October 12, 1977. Under its terms financial institutions are required to make an "affirmative effort" to meet the credit needs of low- and middle-income customers, including households, small businesses, farms, and ranches. Each commercial and savings bank must define its own local "trade territory" and describe the services that it offers or is planning to offer in that local area. Once a year each institution must prepare an updated map which delineates the trade territory served, without deliberately excluding low- or moderate-income neighborhoods, and lists the principal types of credit offered in that territory. Customers are entitled to make written comments, which must be available for public inspection, concerning the lender's performance in meeting local credit needs. The basic purpose of the Community Reinvestment Act is to avoid "gerrymandering" out low-income neighborhoods and other areas that a lender may consider undesirable.

Equal Credit Opportunity Act

The Equal Credit Opportunity Act of 1974 forbids discrimination against credit applicants on the basis of age, sex, marital status, race, color, religion, national origin, receipt of public assistance, or good-faith exercise of rights under the federal consumer credit protection laws. Major beneficiaries of this law are women, who no longer can be denied credit solely on the basis of their sex, age, family plans, or the fact that they are or are not wage earners. Women may receive credit under their own signature, based on their own personal credit record and earnings, without having their husband's joint signature. Credit applicants must be notified of the approval or denial of their loan request within 30 days of filing a completed application. The reasons for denial of a loan application must be set forth in writing, and the lender may not request information on the borrower's race, color, religion, national origin, or sex, except in the case of residential mortgage loans.

Fair Housing and Home Mortgage Disclosure Act

Two other important antidiscrimination laws are the Fair Housing Act, which forbids discrimination in lending for the purchase or renovation of residential property, and the Home Mortgage Disclosure Act (HMDA). The latter requires financial institutions to disclose to the public the amount and location of their home mortgage and home improvement loans. HMDA was designed to eliminate "redlining" in which some lenders would mark out areas of a community as unsuitable for mortgage loans because of low income, high crime rates, or other negative factors. Not only was the law supposed to increase home mortgage loans to low- and moderate-income neighborhoods, but it was also intended to encourage the public to divert its funds away from those institutions practicing redlining.

Both HMDA and the Fair Housing Act require nondiscriminatory advertising by lenders. No longer can a consumer lending institution direct its advertisements solely to high-income neighborhoods to the exclusion of other potential customers. When loans to purchase, construct, improve, repair, or maintain a dwelling are advertised, the lender must state that such loans will be made without regard to race, color, religion, sex, or national origin. On written advertising the "Equal Housing" symbol must be attached. Clearly, then, in advertising the availability of credit, in accepting and evaluating loan applications, and in the actual granting of credit, the principles of civil rights and nondiscrimination apply. Lenders are free to choose who will receive credit, but that decision must be made within the framework of the nation's social goals.

CONSUMER BANKRUPTCY LAWS

Over the past decade the number of households filing for personal bankruptcy and relief from personal debts has soared. In 1984, for example, a record 60 out of every 100,000 U.S adults legally declared personal bankruptcy. One reason for this upsurge in household bankruptcies was certainly the rapid growth of consumer borrowing that we have reviewed in this chapter. Another reason lay in the deep back-to-back recessions in the early 1980s with protracted high levels of unemployment. However, the principal reason for these record bankruptcy filings appeared to be more lenient federal and state bankruptcy laws, especially the Bankruptcy Reform Act of 1978. This law allowed virtually any consumer to file a bankruptcy petition even if he or she could pay off outstanding debts from current income or savings or from future earnings. In addition, once bankruptcy was declared, the consumer could keep substantial personal assets (such as a home or personal clothing) that could not be sold or repossessed to repay outstanding debts. These and other lenient provisions in federal and state statutes reduced the cost of consumer bankruptcy and encouraged more households to attempt to make a "fresh start" in managing their financial affairs.

Responding to the record explosion of consumer bankruptcy filings, Congress passed the Bankruptcy Amendments and Federal Judgeship Act of 1984. This new law significantly increased bankruptcy costs and restricted the amount and types of household debt that could be discharged with the filing of a bankruptcy petition. For example, federal rules now exempt no more than $4,000 in household furniture and appliances, clothing, and other personal items from forced sale to pay debts. Moreover, the courts can now dismiss a consumer's request for debt relief if they feel the filing is an attempt to abuse the law. These and other recent revisions in applicable federal and state statutes have slowed consumer bankruptcy applications significantly. The new personal bankruptcy rules serve simply as a reminder to consumers to think carefully before borrowing money and to read closely the terms of any credit agreement before signing on the "dotted line."

SUMMARY AND CONCLUSIONS

One of the most remarkable developments in the financial system over the past century is the awakening of the consumer as a borrower and lender of funds. Better educated and more aware of their financial opportunities today, householders have become the principal source of loanable funds flowing into the financial markets and also one of the most important borrowers. Reflecting their key influence on the financial system and financial institutions, new consumer-oriented financial services have appeared in profusion in recent years in an effort to attract and hold consumer accounts. Examples include NOWs, money market deposits, share accounts in money market mutual funds, universal life insurance, and consumer cash-management services.

There is some concern today that households have become too deeply mired in debt. Those who see financial trouble ahead for the household sector point out, for example, that the ratio of household debt to financial assets has more than doubled over the past three decades. While consumer debt figures certainly bear close watching, especially in times of economic uncertainty, these fears must be gauged against the purposes for which consumers borrow today. Three fifths of all consumer debt consists of residential mortgages; for many families today their residence is their most important asset. In fact, ownership of residential property has been one of the most effective hedges against inflation open to individuals and families over the past generation.

The growing role of the consumer in the financial system has brought with it greater political influence. The 1960s and 1970s ushered in landmark pieces of federal legislation to aid the consumer in borrowing and lending funds. On the borrowing side, such laws as the Consumer Credit Protection Act of 1968 (Truth in Lending), the Fair Credit Billing Act (1974), the Consumer Leasing Act (1976), and the Fair Credit Reporting Act (1971) have supported the rights of consumers to know what they are being charged for credit and that their credit complaints are heard and acted upon. As a result of such laws as the Community Reinvestment Act (1977), the Equal Credit Opportunity Act (1974), the Fair Housing Act (1968), and the Home Mortgage Disclosure Act (1975), lenders must make an "affirmative effort" to make credit available to all segments of their local communities without regard to age, sex, marital status, race, color, religion, or national origin of the borrower. Consumers with the support of the federal government are asking today not only to be told more about the cost of credit but also why credit is denied to some and granted to others.

Until the 1980s consumers were largely neglected on the financial asset side of the ledger. Interest-rate ceilings (such as the Federal Reserve Board's Regulation Q) severely limited the yields banks and other deposit-type financial institutions could pay on consumer savings deposits. Federal banking laws have prohibited interest payments on checking accounts since the Great Depression. Consumers soon discovered that the returns they were earning on thrift deposits were so far below the rate of inflation that the purchasing power of their financial reserves was rapidly declining. Many switched their savings into gold, silver, precious stones, real estate, and other more speculative investments. Moreover, due to restrictive interest-rate ceilings (usury laws) imposed by the states on installment and mortgage loans, consumers found that the credit they needed to supplement their incomes was simply not available.

A rising chorus of consumer complaints led to passage of the Depository Institutions Deregulation and Monetary Control Act of 1980. This sweeping piece of consumer-oriented financial legislation legalized interest-bearing checking accounts (NOWs), authorized automatic transfers of funds from savings to checking accounts, set up regulatory machinery for a phaseout of deposit interest-rate ceilings, lifted ceiling rates on home mortgage loans and increased the amount of insurance behind the public's deposits held in commercial banks, savings banks, savings and loan associations, and credit unions. A follow-up bill in 1982—the Garn-St Germain Depository Institutions Act—expanded the number of borrowing alternatives open to consumers by granting broader consumer credit powers to savings and loans and other nonbank thrift institutions. At the same time the Garn bill allowed depository institutions to offer money market deposit accounts (MMDAs) that can be accessed by check but pay interest rates that change with short-term, open-market interest rates.

Unquestionably, there is more to come. Consumers have awakened financially to an awareness, not only of the critical role credit and savings play in determining their own well-being, but to their powerful collective influence on the whole financial system. The consumer now seems well aware that decisions made in the financial sector help to determine how many and what kinds of jobs are available, the rate of inflation and economic growth, and even the outcome of the great social issues of modern-day society—better housing, improved educational facilities, equality and justice under the law, and freedom of economic opportunity. For the most part, modern governments have shown a strong determination to ensure that the individual consumer is treated fairly in the financial marketplace and that the financial system contributes to, rather than impedes, the progress of peaceful social change. Unfortunately, we cannot yet determine whether the recent plethora of consumer-oriented financial laws have brought the laudable benefits hoped for by their authors, or simply threaten to mire our financial system in a debilitating swamp of bureaucracy and red tape. If the new rules reduce incentives in the financial community to compete, to offer new services, and to price existing financial services commensurate with the dictates of the marketplace, then both the consumer and society as a whole may have lost more then they have gained. On that important issue, we must await the impartial verdict afforded by time.

STUDY QUESTIONS

1. Which sector of the economy provides the largest amount of loanable funds for borrowers to draw upon? Does this sector make primarily direct loans or indirect loans to borrowers?

2. What is the most important financial asset held by households? What proportion of total household financial investments does this asset represent? What financial asset is in second place in household portfolios?

3. Summarize the main provisions of the Depository Institutions Deregulation and Monetary Control Act of 1980 and the Garn-St Germain Depository Institutions Act of 1982 affecting consumers.

4. Define the following terms:
   a. NOWs.
   b. ATS.
   c. Share drafts.
   d. Super NOWs.
   e. MMDAs.
   f. Universal life.
   g. Money market share accounts.
   In what ways do these financial services benefit the consumer? What kinds of problems might they create for financial institutions offering them?

5. How much money do U.S. households owe today? Do you believe American consumers are too heavily in debt? Why or why not?

6. Into what broad categories is consumer borrowing normally divided? Which is most important, and why?

7. Discuss the factors that influence the volume of borrowing by individuals and families. What role do you believe inflation plays in the borrowing and saving decisions of households today?

8. List the principal consumer lending institutions in the United States. What types of consumer loans does each institution prefer to grant?

9. What factors do consumer lending institutions usually look at when evaluating a loan application? Why?

10. What is Truth in Lending? Describe the law's major features and explain why it was enacted.

11. What protections are offered the consumer under the Fair Credit Billing Act? Consumer Leasing Act? Fair Credit Reporting Act? Why?

12. What are the principal purposes of the Community Reinvestment Act? Equal Credit Opportunity Act? Fair Housing Act? Home Mortgage Disclosure Act? Assess the benefits and costs of these pieces of social responsibility legislation.

SELECTED REFERENCES

Ando, Albert, and Franco Modigliani. "The 'Life Cycle' Hypothesis of Savings: Aggregate Implications and Tests." *American Economic Review*, March 1963, pp. 55–84.

Board of Governors of the Federal Reserve System. *Consumer Handbook to Credit Protection Laws.* Washington, D.C.: 1978.

Day, George S., and William K. Brandt. "Consumer Research and the Evaluation of Information Disclosure Requirements: The Case of Truth in Lending." *Journal of Consumer Research*, June 1974, pp. 21–32.

Dunkelberg, William C., and James Stevenson. *Durable Goods Ownership and the Rates of Return*, Washington, D.C.: National Commission on Consumer Finance, 1972.

Federal Reserve Bank of Boston. *Analysis of High-Earning Banks 1978*, Functional Cost Analysis Program.

Harris, Maury and Karen Bradley. "Are Households Financially Overextended?" *Quarterly Review*, Federal Reserve Bank of New York, Autumn 1977, pp. 22–26.

Katona, George; Lewis Mandell; and Joy Schiedeskamp. *1970 Survey of Consumer Finances.* Ann Arbor: University of Michigan Press, 1971.

Kowalewski, K. J. "Recent Changes in the Consumer Bankruptcy Laws." *Economic Commentary,* Federal Reserve Bank of Cleveland, February 1, 1985.

Mandell, Lewis. "Consumer Knowledge and Understanding of Consumer Credit." *Journal of Consumer Affairs,* Summer 1973, pp. 23–26.

———. "Consumer Perception of Incurred Interest Rates: An Empirical Test of the Efficiency of the Truth-in-Lending Law." *Journal of Finance,* March 1974, pp. 217–25.

National Commission on Consumer Finance. *Consumer Credit in the United States.* Washington, D.C., 1972.

Parker, George G. C., and Robert P. Shay. "Some Factors Affecting Awareness of Annual Percentage Rates in Consumer Installment Credit Transactions." *Journal of Finance,* March 1974, pp. 217–25.

Rose, Peter S. "Bank Cards: The Promise and The Peril." *The Canadian Banker and ICB Review,* December 1978, pp. 62–67.

———. "Social Responsibility in Banking: Pressures Intensify in the U.S." *The Canadian Banker and ICB Review,* June 1979, pp. 70–75.

———. "Credit Discrimination under Attack." *The Canadian Banker and ICB Review,* September 1979, pp. 70–75.

Smith, Randall. "Soaring Levels of Debt, National and Private, Cause Rising Worries." *The Wall Street Journal,* May 9, 1985, pp. 1 and 20.

19

The Residential Mortgage Market

PURPOSE OF THIS CHAPTER

To describe the workings of one of the most important of all financial markets to consumers—the market to finance the construction and purchase of residential dwellings, from single-family homes to apartments and condominiums. The chapter looks at recent trends in the residential mortgage market that have made home ownership more difficult for many individuals and families and the principal financial institutions lending money in this market. Government support of the the mortgage market is highlighted through a review of the lending, loan guarantee programs, and secondary market activities of such prominent federal agencies as Fannie Mae (FNMA), Ginnie Mae (GNMA), and Freddie Mac (FLHMC). The chapter concludes with a discussion of both old and new types of residential mortgage loans, including variable-rate mortgages and creative financing techniques.

KEY TERMS AND CONCEPTS IN THE CHAPTER

adjustable mortgage
  instruments
Canadian rollover
  mortgages
commercial banks
commercial mortgages
conventional
  mortgages
creative financing
Federal Home Loan
  Bank System
Federal Home Loan
  Mortgage Corporation

Federal National
  Mortgage Association
fixed-rate mortgages
government-
  guaranteed
  mortgages
Government National
  Mortgage Association
graduated-payment
  mortgages
life insurance
  companies

mortgage-backed
  securities
mortgage bankers
mutual savings banks
pass-throughs
renegotiated rate
  mortgages
residential mortgages
reverse-annuity
  mortgages
savings and loans
variable-rate
  mortgages

One of the most important goals for many American families is to own their own home. Besides the psychic benefits of privacy and a feeling of belonging to the local community, home ownership has conferred important financial and economic benefits upon those families and individuals both able and willing to make the investment. The market value of single-family residences has risen substantially faster than the rate of inflation over the long term, offering individuals and families of even modest means one of the few effective long-term hedges against inflation. Moreover, the interest cost on home mortgages is tax deductible, reducing significantly the *after-tax* interest rate levied on residential mortgage loans.

Unfortunately for those families seeking home ownership, the residential mortgage market has shifted in recent years from an accommodative posture to one of credit restraint and relatively high interest rates, limiting the affordability of home ownership to those with relatively high incomes or with outside financial support. And, as has been true historically, the residential mortgage market continues to experience wide swings in activity from "boom" to "bust," sending reverberations throughout the economy.

RECENT TRENDS IN NEW HOME PRICES AND THE TERMS OF MORTAGE LOANS

We can get a glimpse of the tremendous pressures buffeting the market for residential mortgages today by looking at recent trends in the prices

EXHIBIT 19–1

Prices and Yields of Conventional Home Mortgage Loans

Item	Terms and Yields						
	1974	1976	1978	1980	1982	1984	1985*
Primary market:							
Conventional mortgages on new homes:							
Purchase price ($000s)	$40.10	$48.40	$62.60	$83.50	$94.60	$96.80	$100.10
Amount of loan ($000s)	29.80	35.90	45.90	59.30	69.80	73.70	75.70
Loan/price ratio (percent)	74.30	74.20	75.30	73.30	76.60	78.70	77.80
Maturity (years)	26.30	27.20	28.00	28.20	27.60	27.80	28.40
Fees and charges (percent of loan)	1.30	1.44	1.39	2.10	2.95	2.64	2.62
Contract interest rate (percent)	8.71	8.76	9.30	12.25	14.47	11.87	11.70
Yield—FHLBB series	8.92	8.99	9.54	12.65	15.12	12.37	12.19
Yield—HUD series	9.22	8.99	9.68	13.95	15.79	13.80	13.06

* 1985 figures as of February of that year.
Source: Board of Governors of the Federal Reserve System, *Federal Reserve Bulletin*, May 1985.

of new homes and the cost of financing them. Exhibit 19–1 provides us with recent data on the average terms quoted nationwide on *conventional* mortgage loans. A conventional mortgage loan is *not* guaranteed by the government but is purely a private loan contract between the home buyer and the lending institution. In this case, the lender of funds bears the risk that the home buyer will default on principal or interest payments associated with a mortgage loan, forcing foreclosure and resale of the home, though today about 40 percent of conventional loans are insured by private insurance companies. In contrast, mortgage loans issued through the Federal Housing Administration (FHA) or Veterans Administration (VA) are partially guaranteed as to principal and interest by the federal government and are generally used to finance low-cost and moderately priced housing. Today about four fifths of all mortgage loans for residential structures are conventional, while about one fifth are FHA–VA insured.

As shown in Exhibit 19–1, the average purchase price of a conventional single-family residence in the United States more than doubled between 1974 and 1980, climbing above $83,000 in the latter year. Early in the 1980s, however, back-to-back recessions in 1980 and 1982 coupled with high interest rates and high energy prices significantly reduced the demand for new homes. The growth of new home prices slowed drastically and even declined briefly in 1983 and early 1984 before resuming a moderate upward trend. Lenders of funds compensated for the slowing demand for home mortgages by increasing the percentage of a new home's purchase price they were willing to lend in the 1980s, after doing exactly the opposite during the hectic home-buying spree of the 1970s.

Thus, home buyers were forced to come up with larger down payments both in total dollars and relative to the market value of a new home during the 1970s, but were able to get by with smaller down payments as builders and lenders tried to move homes in a sluggish market during the 1980s.

We note also from Exhibit 19–1 that mortgage lenders were willing to extend credit for longer periods as a partial offset to the higher cost of new homes. The average maturity of conventional home mortgage loans climbed from about 26 years in 1974 to more than 28 years in 1985. Extra fees and charges ("points") levied by lenders as a condition for making mortgage credit available also rose sharply in the surging housing market of the 1970s, and then eased back slightly in the 1980s to accommodate the softer demand. The average contract interest rate on conventional mortgages climbed from an 8.71 percent average in 1974 to a high of 14.47 percent in 1982 before declining to less than 12 percent in the most recent period.

The combination of higher home mortgage interest rates and higher market prices for new homes in recent years has greatly increased monthly mortgage payments and shut many families out of the housing market. For example, a family putting 10 percent down on a $40,000 home in 1974, when conventional home mortgage rates ranged from about 8½ to 9 percent, would have faced monthly payments (including taxes and insurance) in the $350 to $400 range. During 1985, however, the same house would have cost about $100,000 with mortgage rates in the 12 percent range, so that home mortgage payments would have averaged about $1,000 per month, depending on the specific terms of the loan.

Several factors account for this dramatic escalation in the cost of home ownership. Certainly, inflation has played a key role in driving up building costs, especially the prices of lumber and other building materials, and this increase has been passed onto the consumer. On the demand side, a substantial rise in the number of new family formations has occurred in recent years. Children born during the great postwar baby boom of the 1940s and 50s began to establish their own families in the 1970s and 1980s. An estimated 32 million Americans reached 30 years of age during the 1970s alone. Therefore, while the U.S. birthrate dropped to the lowest level in history, the sharp increase in new families and in numbers of children born into those new families dramatically increased the demand for housing, especially for low- and medium-priced homes. At the same time, the proportion of the U.S. population represented by Americans in their 40s and 50s began to decline. Yet, historically, this group has provided the bulk of savings out of which home mortgage lenders can make new loans. In fact, the ratio of savings to personal income in the United States fell to the lowest level since World War II during the late 1970s and early 1980s. This combination of increased demand for new family residences and a smaller savings flow has sharply raised the cost of housing and diminished the financial attractiveness of single-family homes. Financial analysts project that in future years as the population continues to age and new family formations slow, new housing demand will drop and increases in housing costs will moderate.[1]

THE STRUCTURE OF THE MORTGAGE MARKET

Volume of Mortgage Loans

Mortgages are among the most important securities in the financial system. The total of all mortgages outstanding in the United States exceeded $2 trillion in 1985. (See Exhibit 19–2.) This total represented just over half the nation's gross national product (GNP) and made the mortgage market the largest primary security market in the United States. In fact, the sum of mortgage loans outstanding exceeded the combined total of all money market instruments. Moreover, the mortgage market has grown rapidly in recent years under the combined pressures of inflation and economic growth. During the 1960s the volume of mortgages outstanding more than doubled and then tripled during the 1970s; growth in the 1980s has been somewhat more modest but still rapid. Thus, an enormously important market within the financial system became even more important as time progressed.

Residential versus Nonresidential Mortgage Loans

The mortgage market can be divided into two major segments: (1) *residential*, which encompasses all loans secured by single-family homes

EXHIBIT 19–2

Total Mortgage Debt Outstanding in the United States, Year-End ($ billions)

Year	Amount
1950	$ 72.8
1960	206.8
1970	451.7
1980	1,451.8
1985*	2,071.0

* Figures for first quarter of the year.
Sources: Board of Governors of the Federal Reserve System, *Annual Statistical Digest*, 1971–75 and *Federal Reserve Bulletin*, selected issues.

---

[1] See, for example, the discussion by Freund (1983).

EXHIBIT 19–3

Mortgage Loans Outstanding, First Quarter of 1985 ($ billions)

Type of Property	Amount	Percent
Residential properties (one to four family and multifamily structures)	$1,544.3	74.6%
Nonresidential properties (commercial and farm)	526.7	25.4
All properties	$2,071.0	100.0%

Source: Board of Governors of the Federal Reserve System, *Federal Reserve Bulletin*, September 1985.

and other dwelling units; and (2) *nonresidential*, which includes loans against business and farm properties. Which of these two sectors is the more important? As Exhibit 19–3 shows, loans to finance the building and purchase of homes, apartments, and other residential units dominate the American mortgage market. In 1985 residential mortgage loans on one-to-four-family properties and multifamily structures represented about three fourths of all mortgage loans outstanding. Mortgages on commercial and farm properties accounted for the remaining one fourth of all mortgages issued.

In recent years loans to support the construction of single-family homes and other small residential structures and commercial mortgages to fund

EXHIBIT 19–4

Recent Growth in Mortgage Loans

Property	1975	1980	1985*
In millions of dollars:			
One-to-four-family	$490,761	$ 960,422	$1,376,918
Multifamily	100,601	136,580	167,394
Commercial	159,289	258,338	415,408
Farm	50,877	96,500	111,262
Total	$801,528	$1,451,840	$2,070,982
Percent of total:			
One-to-four-family	61.2%	66.2%	66.5%
Multifamily	12.6	9.4	8.1
Commercial	19.9	17.8	20.0
Farm	6.3	6.6	5.4
Total	100.0%	100.0%	100.0%

* Figures are for first quarter of the year.
Source: Board of Governors of the Federal Reserve System, *Federal Reserve Bulletin*, selected issues.

EXHIBIT 19–5

Mortgage Debt Classified by Borrower

Borrower	1975	1980	1983
In millions of dollars:			
Households	$482.9	$ 967.5	$1,200.1
Nonprofit institutions	24.8	31.5	38.9
Nonfinancial corporations	65.9	80.0	79.7
Farms	50.9	92.0	109.6
Nonfarm noncorporate	173.2	289.0	391.7
Other	3.1	3.0	2.3
Totals	$800.8	$1,463.0	$1,822.3
Percent of total:			
Households	60.3%	66.1%	65.9%
Nonprofit institutions	3.1	2.2	2.1
Nonfinancial corporations	8.2	5.5	4.4
Farms	6.4	6.3	6.0
Nonfarm noncorporate	21.6	19.8	21.5
Other	0.4	0.2	0.1
Totals	100.0%	100.0%	100.0%

Source: Federal Reserve Board, *Flow of Funds Accounts: Assets and Liabilities Outstanding,* September 1984.

everything from shopping centers to office buildings, shipping ports, and factories have grown the most rapidly. (See Exhibit 19–4.) In contrast, farm mortgages have declined in relative terms as have multifamily project loans for condominiums and apartments. The proportion of one-to-four-family residential mortgage loans increased slightly in the 1980s to a secure two thirds of all U.S. mortgage loans outstanding. This category of mortgages is dominated by single-family home loans, which increased due to the rapid-growth of new family formations and the effects of inflation. And, because residential mortgages dominate the market, it should not be surprising that households are the leading mortgage borrower. As indicated in Exhibit 19–5, households account for about two thirds of outstanding mortgage debt. The next largest group of mortgage borrowers—unincorporated businesses—is a distant second.

MORTGAGE-LENDING INSTITUTIONS

In the years before World War II, mortgages were one of the most widely held securities in the financial system, comparable to stock in the great diversity of investors who chose to add these securities to their portfolios. Individuals were then the dominant mortgage investors, with financial institutions in second place. However, the rapid growth of commercial banks, savings and loan associations, mutual savings banks, and insurance companies as major mortgage lenders during the past three decades has forced individual investors into the background. As we will see later in this chapter, however, the 1980s have ushered in more creative types of mortgage financing, in which individuals are once again playing a larger role as lenders and investors in mortgages.

Exhibit 19–6 shows the total amounts of mortgage loans held by various investor groups in 1985. Clearly, savings and loan associations are the principal mortgage-lending institution in the United States, accounting for more than a quarter of all mortgage loans outstanding. Commercial banks rank second, holding about one sixth of all mortgage loans, followed by life insurance companies and mutual savings banks. In general, the relative share of the mortgage market accounted for by traditional private mortgage-lending institutions, such as savings and loans, savings banks, commercial banks, and insurance companies, has declined, while individuals, pension funds, and government agencies have accounted for a growing share of outstanding loans. Noteworthy in this regard has been the expanding role of mortgage pools, that is, continuing groups of high-quality residential mortgages insured or guaranteed by a government agency and in which investors hold shares entitling them to a portion of interest and principal payments generated by the pool. We will have more to say about mortgage pools later in this chapter when we discuss

EXHIBIT 19–6

Major Lenders in the U.S. Mortgage Market, First Quarter of 1985

Lender Group	Volume of Mortgage Loans Held ($ billions)	Percent of Total
Savings and loan associations	$ 559.3	27.0%
Commercial banks	383.2	18.5
Life insurance companies	158.2	7.6
Mutual savings banks	160.7	7.8
Mortgage pools or trusts	347.8	16.8
Federal and related government agencies	162.4	7.8
Individuals and others*	299.4	14.5
Totals	$2,071.0	100.0%

* Includes mortgage companies, REITs, state and local credit agencies, state and local government retirement funds, noninsured pension funds, credit unions, and U.S. government agencies for which amounts are small or separate data are not available.
Source: Board of Governors of the Federal Reserve System, *Federal Reserve Bulletin*, September 1985.

the expanding role of the federal government in the nation's mortgage market.

THE ROLES PLAYED BY FINANCIAL INSTITUTIONS IN THE MORTGAGE MARKET

Mortgage lenders tend to specialize in the types of loans they grant, and some are far more important to the residential market than in commercial mortgage lending. Moreover, even within the residential lending field, different institutional lenders will favor one type of mortgage (e.g., conventional versus government guaranteed) over another and also desire a certain range of maturities. Some lenders are organized to deal with home mortgage borrowers one at a time, while others may prefer to acquire large packages of mortgages associated with major residential building projects. In the sections that follow, the roles played by each of the principal residential mortgage-lending institutions are examined.

Savings and Loan Associations

Savings and loan associations are predominantly *local* lenders, making the majority of their mortgage loans in the communities where their offices are located. Moreover, S&Ls usually *service* the mortgage loans they make rather than turning that task over to a mortgage bank or trust company. Servicing a mortgage involves maintaining ownership and financial records on the mortgaged property, receiving installment payments from the borrower or an agent of the borrower, checking on the mortgaged property to ensure that its value is maintained, and, in the event of borrower default, foreclosing on the property to collect any unpaid balance on the loan. While, historically, S&Ls have preferred single-family home mortgages, they have diversified their portfolios in recent years to include many new kinds of assets, some mortgage related and some not. Prominent on that list are mobile home loans, mortgage credit for the purchase of duplexes and other multifamily housing units, apartment loans, and consumer installment loans for the purchase of automobiles, furniture, and home appliances, and short- and long-term commercial credit. Most financial analysts expect savings and loans to expand the proportion of their portfolios devoted to consumer and commercial nonmortgage loans in future years and decrease the proportion devoted to residential mortgage loans. This is due to the increased authority to make nonmortgage loans granted savings and loans with passage of the Garn-St Germain Depository Institutions Act of 1982 (discussed earlier in Chapter 5) and because of S&Ls' need for greater financial flexibility.

Commercial Banks

In recent years commercial banks have expanded their market share of nearly every type of mortgage loan and today are the second largest holder of mortgage debt. Overall, they rank second to savings and loans among all mortgage lenders, but hold more commercial mortgages than any other lender. Banks rank second among private lenders in farm mortgages (after life insurers), third in apartment loans (behind savings and loans and life insurers), and second in loans to finance the purchase of one-to-four-family residences (behind savings and loans). The bulk of bank mortgage credit, however, goes for shorter-term loans to finance the *construction* of new commercial and residential projects with other lenders taking on the long-term mortgage loans from these projects. By any measure, commercial banks are a powerful competitive force in the mortgage market, known for their flexibility and innovativeness in developing new credit programs.

Life Insurance Companies

Life insurance companies make substantial investments in commercial as well as residential mortgage properties. Commercial mortgages make up about 70 percent of the mortgage obligations held by life insurance companies, while residential mortgages account for 21 percent and farm mortgages, about 8 percent of the total mortgage loans held by life companies. These companies will search national and international markets for good mortgage investments instead of focusing on only one or a few local areas and often prefer to purchase residential mortgages in large blocks rather than one at a time.

In the past, life insurers strongly preferred government-guaranteed home mortgages. In recent years, however, the higher yields available on conventional mortgages have caused some shift of emphasis toward these more risky loans. Despite the greater flexibility of conventional single-family home mortgages, however, life insurance companies have been gradually reducing their holdings of single-family home mortgages and emphasizing commercial and apartment mortgages. Commercial and apartment loans often carry "equity kickers," which permit the lender to receive a portion of project earnings as well as a guaranteed interest rate.[2]

Mutual Savings Banks

Another lender of great importance in the residential mortgage market is the mutual savings bank, headquartered mainly in the New England

---

[2] See Chapter 20 for a discussion of equity kickers in commercial mortgage lending and Chapter 6 for an overview of the operations of the life insurance industry.

area and in the Middle Atlantic states of New York, New Jersey, and Pennsylvania.[3] These institutions invest in both government-guaranteed and conventional mortgage loans. While single-family homes constitute the bulk of savings bank mortgage loans, their loans supporting multi-family units (including large apartment projects) have grown rapidly in recent years. Like life insurance companies, mutuals often prefer to acquire residential mortgages in large blocks, such as a whole subdivision, rather than loan by loan.

Savings banks still provide most of their mortgage credit for the purchase of single-family homes and small multifamily dwellings. In 1985, about 70 percent of all mortgage obligations held by mutuals were secured by one-to-four-family residential properties. Commercial mortgages on shopping centers, office buildings, and factories represented about one sixth of all mortgage loans granted by this financial intermediary. Apartment loans accounted for about 13 percent of mutuals' mortgage investments. Among private mortgage lenders, mutuals rank fourth in total mortgages held, behind savings and loan associations, commercial banks, and life insurance companies. While the dollar total of mortgage loans held by mutuals has risen every year, their share of the market has declined over the past two decades. Mortgage lending by savings and loans, commercial banks, and federal government agencies has grown much faster.

Mortgage Bankers

Mortgage banking houses act as a channel through which builders or contractors in need of long-term funds can find permanent mortgage financing. In providing this service mortgage bankers take on portfolios of mortgages from property developers, using mainly bank credit to carry their inventories of mortgages. Then within a relatively short time span these mortgages are placed with long-term institutional investors. Mortgage bankers supply important services to *both* institutional investors and property developers. The developers receive a commitment for permanent financing, which allows them to proceed with planned real estate projects. Institutional investors, especially life insurance companies and mutual savings banks, receive mortgages appropriately packaged to match the timing of their cash flows and risk-return preferences.[4] The mortgage banker often secures servicing fees from institutional investors who purchase the mortgages he packages and sells.

---

[3] See Chapter 5 for a more complete discussion of the structure and characteristics of the mutual savings bank industry.

[4] See Chapter 6 for further discussion of the role played by mortgage bankers within the financial system.

Mortgage banking firms along with life insurance companies have been very active recently in developing so-called *private pass-throughs*—packaging groups of conventional or guaranteed mortgages and selling certificates of participation in the flow of interest and principal payments from the packaged mortgages to other investors. In 1983 the Reagan administration urged Congress to make changes in federal tax and securities laws allowing the formation of mortgage investment trusts (TIMs) to organize and manage mortgage security pools for investors. One of the benefits of private pass-throughs is to make more mortgages liquid, such as those on homes so high priced that they cannot receive federal loan guarantees. Also, these instruments may bring many new lenders, such as pension funds and mutual funds, into the home mortgage market at a time when the more traditional mortgage lenders, like savings and loans and mutual savings banks, are diverting more of their funds into nonmortgage areas.

GOVERNMENT ACTIVITY

Adequate housing for all U.S. citizens is a major goal of the federal government. One of the steps taken by Congress to achieve this goal was the establishment of the Federal Housing Administration (FHA) in 1934. FHA has sought to promote home ownership by reducing the risk to private lenders of residential mortgage contracts. At the same time efforts have been made to encourage the development of an active secondary market for existing mortgage lenders to raise cash to make new loans and to attract new investors into the mortgage business, such as pension funds, investment companies, individuals, and foreign buyers.

The combination of government guarantees (FHA–VA) and the development of a secondary market has led to greater participation in mortgage lending by so-called long-distance lenders—particularly insurance companies, pension funds, and savings banks. (Figure 19–1 provides an overall view of the role of private lenders and federal government agencies in the mortgage market.) Because of the predominantly localized nature of the housing industry and the wide variety of mortgage loans, the absence of an effective secondary market and government guarantees would make the home mortgage a long-term commitment of money with little flexibility for the lender.

The Impact of the Great Depression on Government Involvement in the Mortgage Market

Any attempt to understand how the mortgage market operates today must begin with the Great Depression and the enormous impact that

FIGURE 19–1

The Structure of the Mortgage Market

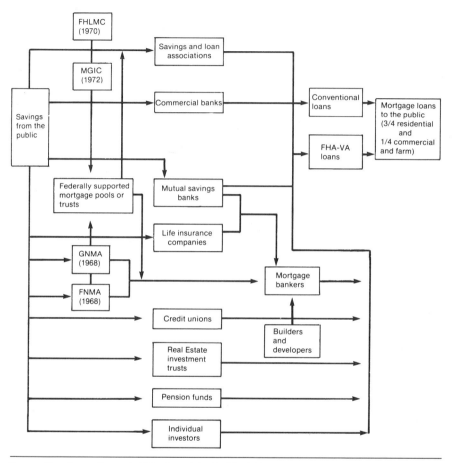

Source: Based on a diagram in "Structure of the Residential Mortgage Market," *Monthly Review,* Federal Reserve Bank of Richmond, September 1972, and modified by the author.

economic calamity had upon the market for property loans. The Great Depression generated massive, unprecedented unemployment; an estimated one quarter to one third of the civilian labor force was thrown out of work between 1929 and 1933. Moreover, the scarcity of jobs lasted not just a few months as in recent recessions, but for years. It was not until the United States began a military rearmament program in the late 1930s that the nation's employment picture really began to improve. Few new mortgage loans were made during this period, and thousands of existing mortgages were foreclosed. With so many forced sales, property values declined precipitously, endangering the financial solvency of thousands of mortgage lenders, particularly savings and loan associations and commercial banks. Indeed, scores of banks and S&Ls were forced either into bankruptcy or into mergers with larger institutions.

The federal government elected to tackle the mortgage market's problems by moving in several directions at once: (1) provided mortgage insurance through FHA for low- and medium-priced homes; (2) it insured the deposits of mortgage-lending institutions through such agencies as the Federal Deposit Insurance Corporation and the Federal Savings and Loan Insurance Corporation; (3) it placed more rigid controls on lending by banks, savings and loans, and other institutional lenders but also provided them with easier access to credit through direct government loans; and (4) it created several new federal agencies to buy and sell residential mortgages.

For example, in 1932 the Federal Home Loan Bank System (FHLB) was created to supervise the activities of savings and loan associations and make loans to those S&Ls in trouble. A year later the Home Owner's Loan Corporation was set up to refinance those mortgages on one-to-four-family dwellings which were due to be canceled or foreclosed. By the time this agency ceased operations in 1954, it had made a major contribution toward reshaping the nation's mortgage market by popularizing the long-term amortized mortgage, thereby fostering the growth of private home ownership in the United States.

In 1934, the National Housing Act was passed, setting up a system of federal insurance for qualified home mortgage loans. The Federal Housing Administration was authorized to guarantee repayment of up to 90 percent of acceptable home loans, encouraging private lenders to lend more of a home's market value, accept longer terms on home mortgages, and charge lower interest rates.

Shortly before the end of World War II, the Veterans Administration (VA) was created with passage of the Servicemen's Readjustment Act (1944). The VA was designed to aid military servicemen returning to civilian life in finding jobs and adequate housing. Like FHA, VA offered to insure residential mortgages. This program permitted mortgage lenders to commit their funds at low risk and reduced the required down payment on a new home.

The Creation of Fannie Mae (FNMA)

The FHA–VA insurance program was an almost instant success and home mortgage lending grew rapidly following its inception. Federal government efforts to create a resale (secondary) market for residential mortgages, however, were far less effective at first. An agency set up during the 1930s to purchase FHA–VA loans, the Reconstruction Finance

Corporation, was dissolved in 1948. However, one federal agency committed to improving the secondary mortgage market did survive the turmoil of the Great Depression and World War II. This was the Federal National Mortgage Association (FNMA), better known as Fannie Mae, created in 1938.

Fannie Mae was established for the purpose of buying and selling FHA-guaranteed mortgages in the secondary market. Later, in 1948, it was authorized to trade in VA-guaranteed mortgages as well. Adjusting to the changing character of the mortgage market, FNMA began to exert a potent impact on mortgage trading in the 1950s. One reason was the launching of its standby commitment program.

Standby Commitments.   Under the terms of a standby commitment, Fannie Mae agrees to purchase a specific mortgage within a stipulated period of time at a set price. The standby commitment aids builders and property developers because it provides a floor price for a mortgage and allows the holder to sell the instrument at a higher price if market conditions prove favorable. Such commitments usually are made for 4-month or 12-month periods and are sold at auction.

Following reorganization as a privately owned corporation in 1968, Fannie Mae announced that it would begin buying conventional home mortgages as well as FHA- and VA-guaranteed loans. In recent years close to half of its purchases have been conventional mortgage loans, acquired mainly from mortgage bankers. A major factor in supplying funds to the mortgage market, FNMA held about $86 billion in one-to-four-family home mortgages and $6 billion in multifamily (apartment) mortgages in 1985, covering literally millions of family dwellings. Fannie Mae raises funds for its mortgage purchases by selling short-term discount notes and medium-term debentures in the open market.

Purchase Options.   A second innovation developed by FNMA was the purchase option. The opposite of a standby commitment, a purchase option allows the seller of a mortgage to repurchase that mortgage from FNMA within nine months at the original price paid by the agency. FNMA conducts biweekly auctions where mortgage lenders indicate the interest rates at which they are willing to sell various amounts of mortgages. Based on its cost of funds and market conditions, FNMA will issue both standby commitments and purchase options to those institutions offering the best terms.

Mortgage-Backed Securities Program.   In 1981 FNMA began to issue and guarantee securities backed by conventional mortgage loans purchased from lenders. FNMA mortgage-backed securities are marketed either by the lenders that deal with FNMA or through security dealers, with many bought in recent years by pension funds.

The Mortgage Guarantee Insurance Corporation (MGIC)

Fannie Mae is the world's largest mortgage bank and, until recently, had a virtual monopoly in secondary market trading activities. Early in the 1970s, however, the Mortgage Guarantee Insurance Corporation (MGIC) was organized by a private group in Milwaukee, Wisconsin. Known as "Maggie Mae," this corporation insures conventional home mortgage loans carrying down payments as low as 5 percent. In contrast, Fannie Mae is permitted to acquire conventional mortgage loans with down payments only as low as 10 percent. Of course, Fannie Mae has a significant advantage over Maggie Mae and other more recently formed private mortgage insurance companies because it operates as a federally sponsored agency with a privileged borrowing status and normally can raise funds at lower cost. Today, mortgage insurance is usually required by lending institutions when the borrower makes a down payment of less than 20 percent of the purchase price of a home.

The Creation of Ginnie Mae (GNMA)

Efforts by Congress to make the federal government's budget "look better" resulted in the splitting of Fannie Mae into two agencies in 1968. Fannie Mae itself became a private, shareholder-owned corporation devoted to secondary market trading. At the same time, those loan programs requiring government subsidies or direct government credit were handed over to a new corporation set up within the Department of Housing and Urban Development, known as the Government National Mortgage Association (GNMA) or "Ginnie Mae." This federal agency pursues a two-part program to aid the nation's mortgage market. Under one portion of its program Ginnie Mae purchases mortgages to finance housing for low-income families at below-market interest rates. These "assistance mortgages" are eventually sold to FNMA or to private investors at current market prices.

Far more important for the secondary market, however, is GNMA's mortgage-backed securities program. Beginning in 1970, Ginnie Mae agreed to *guarantee* principal and interest payments on securities issued by private mortgage institutions if those securities were backed by pools of government-guaranteed mortgages. These so-called *pass-throughs* are popular with savings and loan associations, pension funds, commercial banks, and even individual investors as safe, readily marketable securities with attractive rates of return. They are issued mainly by mortgage bankers, though about a quarter of all pass-throughs issued each year come from savings and loan associations, mutual savings banks, and commercial banks. The issuing institutions raise cash to make new loans by selling the pass-throughs against mortgages they place in a pool and still continue to earn servicing income on the pooled mortgages. Today more than 90 percent of all newly originated FHA–VA mortgages on single-family dwellings are either in mortgage pools supporting pass-throughs or are sold to Fannie Mae.[5] GNMA-backed mortgage pools contained nearly $181 billion in one-to-four-family home mortgages in 1985—13 percent of all such loans outstanding in the United States—and another $5 billion in multifamily (apartment) credits.

The Federal Home Loan Mortgage Corporation (FHLMC)

Another federal agency created to aid the secondary mortgage market appeared in 1970. The Emergency Home Finance Act passed that year gave birth to the Federal Home Loan Mortgage Corporation (FHLMC), more popularly known as "Freddie Mac." FHLMC is a branch of the Federal Home Loan Bank System which, like Ginnie Mae, may combine the mortgages it buys (primarily from savings and loans) into pools and issue bonds against them. Securities issued by Freddie Mac are guaranteed by GNMA and are very popular with individual and institutional investors, particularly savings and loan associations and mutual savings banks.

The creation of Freddie Mac reflected a desire by the federal government to develop a stronger secondary market for conventional home mortgages. As we have seen, Fannie Mae and Ginnie Mae have made major contributions to the marketability of government-guaranteed (FHA–VA) mortgages, but four fifths of all home mortgages today are conventional, nonguaranteed loans. Freddie Mac buys *conventional* mortgages, about 80 percent of which come from savings and loan associations; the remainder are supplied by mortgage banking houses, commercial banks, and mutual savings banks.

To raise funds to support these purchases, Freddie Mac sells mortgage participation certificates (PCs) and guaranteed mortgage certificates (GMCs). PCs represent an ownership interest in a pool of conventional mortgages bought and held by Freddie Mac.[6] PCs are sold through Fred-

---

[5] See Sivesind (1979). All mortgages placed in a pool against which GNMA-guaranteed pass-throughs are issued must carry the same interest rate and have issue dates no older than one year. The coupon rate on pass-through securities must be one-half percentage point below the contract interest rate on the pooled mortgages with .06 of 1 percent (i.e., six basis points) paid to GNMA in return for its guarantee. Pass-throughs are registered securities with coupons, and pay interest and principal each month. As we saw in Chapter 17, GNMA-backed securities were one of the first securities for which a futures market was developed.

[6] As noted by Sivesind (1979), the pool underlying an average PC issue includes approximately 5,000 mortgages amounting to between $100 million and $300 million.

die Mac directly and through major security dealers, who also make an active resale market in these instruments. Freddie Mac guarantees the investor's monthly interest and principal payments passed through from the mortgage pool, but PCs are not guaranteed directly by the federal government. They are issued in minimum denominations of $100,000.

Guaranteed mortgage certificates (GMCs), like PCs, are claims against a pool of mortgages. They are similar to corporate bonds in that interest is paid semiannually to investors. Repayments of principal are made once a year. While not guaranteed by the federal government, GMCs are guaranteed as to principal and interest by Freddie Mac and are available in minimum denominations of $100,000. Freddie Mac agrees to repurchase any outstanding principal remaining after a period of 15 years.

Remaining Problems in Developing a Secondary Market for Mortgages

Though considerable progress has been made in the development of an active secondary mortgage market, there is still substantial room for improvement. Among the major obstacles are differences between one mortgage and another in the quality of property and borrower credit standing, which crucially affect each instrument's risk and market value. In addition, different lenders have their own particular preferences for certain kinds of mortgage instruments. For example, savings and loan associations tend to prefer conventional, single-family home mortgages of relatively long maturities, while life insurance companies and mutual savings banks have a preference for FHA–VA home mortgages and are actively expanding their lending in the multifamily and commercial mortgage fields. Differences in foreclosure laws among the states complicate the picture as do different state rules concerning the taxation of mortgage-lending institutions.

Other securities traded in the open market typically carry larger denominations than residential mortgages, are usually more uniform in quality, and are not amortized through installment payments. Moreover, on-site inspection of mortgaged property is often necessary to adequately judge the quality of the mortgage instrument. Government guarantee programs serve to lower mortgage risk but of course do not aid the purchaser of conventional mortgages unless a private firm guarantees these. The packaging of individual mortgages into pools by Freddie Mac, Ginnie Mae, and some private lenders is a positive development which tends to standardize the mortgage instrument and make it more attractive to investors. However, offsetting this positive factor is a negative one—the new adjustable-term mortgages developed in recent years have appeared in such profusion that further progress toward standardization of mortgage loans is now in doubt, thus inhibiting the continued growth of the secondary (resale) market. Overall, the secondary market for mortgages is still far less well developed than the markets for corporate, municipal, and U.S. government securities, though recent estimates suggest that two out of every three new home mortgages today wind up in the secondary market with the original lender selling out his or her interest to a new holder. However, substantially greater progress will be needed if we are to grapple effectively with the nation's enormous housing demands in the years ahead.

SENSITIVITY OF THE MORTGAGE MARKET TO MONETARY POLICY AND CREDIT CONDITIONS

The mortgage market is one of the most sensitive of all financial markets to changing interest rates and money and credit conditions. For example, as interest rates rise, the mortgage market is affected from two different directions. Lenders are forced to reduce their mortgage commitments in the face of rising interest rates due to *usury laws* in some states which impose maximum interest-rate ceilings on new loans. In addition, commercial banks, savings and loan associations, and mutual savings banks often lose deposits due to disintermediation as their more interest-sensitive depositors seek more attractive investment opportunities elsewhere.[7] With fewer deposits coming in, a smaller volume of funds is available for mortgage loans, and what funds *are* available usually carry higher rates. Finally, the total cost of a home goes up as interest rates rise, and this depresses the demand for housing. In many ways the mortgage market is a "boom-and-bust" affair, growing rapidly in easy-money periods when interest rates are relatively low and contracting sharply in high-rate, tight-money periods.

Fannie Mae, Ginnie Mae, Freddie Mac, and other government mortgage agencies have helped to stabilize the market to some extent by purchasing mortgages in tight-money periods and selling them in times of easy money and rapid credit expansion. One obvious problem, however, is that this approach frequently goes against Federal Reserve monetary policy designed to stabilize the economy and fight inflation. In tight-money periods, for example, the Federal Reserve System attempts to reduce the volume of borrowing and spending in the economy through high interest rates and slower growth of the nation's money supply. However, because these developments would tend to depress the mortgage

---

[7] See Chapter 2 for a discussion of the causes and effects of disintermediation. When the phaseout of federal deposit interest-rate ceilings (Regulation Q) is completed, disintermediation of deposits should become much less severe when interest rates rise in the future.

market and reduce the availability of mortgage funds, government mortgage agencies will respond by purchasing mortgages and making more loans to private mortgage-lending institutions.

Conversely, when the Federal Reserve attempts to pull the economy out of a recession by promoting low interest rates and more rapid money-supply growth, the government mortgage-lending agencies tend to sell mortgages in the secondary market and cut back on loans to the housing sector. Thus, the activities of the government mortgage agencies probably contribute to economic instability to an indeterminate extent. This is a clear example of a conflict in the nation's goals—stabilizing the economy versus supporting the housing industry.

INNOVATIONS IN MORTGAGE INSTRUMENTS

To this point in the chapter we have described a number of problems that have impaired the functioning of the mortgage market and limited the availability of funds for housing. The extreme sensitivity of the mortgage market to monetary policy and changing credit conditions and the struggle to develop a viable and active secondary mortgage market represent major difficulties that decades of work have only partially resolved. Still another problem with mortgages reared its head in the tumultuous economic and financial environment of the 1970s and early 1980s. This problem centers on the *inflexibility* of the conventional fixed-rate mortgage (FRM) in the face of inflation and rising interest rates.

Repeatedly in recent years interest rates have climbed to record levels, only to fall back during brief recessions and then to surge upward again. And each upward movement in interest rates forced mortgage lenders to cut back on the availability of funds for housing. In part, these cutbacks in mortgage funds were a response to the widespread use of fixed-rate mortgages (FRMs). Following the economic debacle of the 1930s, long-term home mortgages with 20- to 30-year maturities became popular and, until recently, the large majority of these carried fixed interest rates for the life of the loan. These FRMs, therefore, return to the lender the same annual interest income (cash flow) regardless of what is happening to inflation or to interest rates in the open market. When savings and loan associations, commercial banks, and other depository institutions are forced to pay higher rates on their deposits to attract funds, their profits tend to be squeezed because their revenues from FRMs remain unchanged. Of course, these lending institutions are able to charge higher rates on *new* mortgage loans, but new loans are always a small fraction of each institution's total loan portfolio. The bulk of that portfolio is in *old* mortgages granted during an era when interest rates usually were much lower.

In short, the FRM amplifies the normal up-and-down cycle of earnings for a mortgage-lending institution, leading to low or even negative earnings in periods of rising interest rates and positive earnings in periods of falling rates. FRMs require the *lender* to bear the risk of interest-rate fluctuations. An alternative to the FRM is needed that both guarantees lenders a satisfactory real rate of return on mortgage loans and makes funds available to home buyers on reasonable terms. Various new and old types of mortgage instruments are described in Exhibit 19–7.

Variable-Rate and Other Adjustable Mortgages

The problems created by fixed-rate mortgages led to the development of several new mortgage instruments. One of the most important is the *variable-rate mortgage* or VRM, which permits the lender to vary the contractual interest rate on a mortgage loan as market conditions change. Generally, the mortgage rate is linked to a reference interest rate *not* determined by the lender. For example, the yield on long-term U.S. Treasury bonds may be used as a reference rate so that, if Treasury bonds yields rise, the homeowner pays a higher contractual interest rate and makes a higher monthly payment on the mortgage. Alternatively, under a broader *adjustable mortgage instrument* (AMI), the maturity of the mortgage loan may be lengthened or a combination of rate increases and maturity changes may be made as interest rates rise.[8] In some cases the loan principal can be increased with interest-rate increases, reducing the growth of the homeowner's equity—a process known as "negative amortization." In effect, VRMs and other adjustable mortgage instruments shift the *risk* of interest-rate fluctuations, partially or wholly, from the lender to the borrower.

VRMs were first issued in California in 1975 and were authorized for other parts of the nation by the Federal Home Loan Bank Board in 1979. Many institutions offering VRMs have added "sweeteners" to induce borrowers to accept a variable rather than a fixed-rate mortgage contract. Examples of these special inducements include guaranteeing the borrower an open line of credit at the mortgage interest rate and no prepayment penalty if the borrower can pay off the mortgage early.

The broader *adjustable mortgage instruments* (AMIs) mentioned above are more flexible and have more lenient regulations than pure VRMs. Under most state and federal laws, changes in the interest rates attached to VRMs are limited as to frequency and amount. However, AMIs with their options of varying monthly payments, the maturity of a mortgage

---

[8] The loan rate on an AMI usually is tied either to U.S. government security rates, the national average mortgage contract rate, or some index of the lender's cost of funds, though the majority of such loans today impose a cap (ceiling) on how high rates or monthly payments can go.

EXHIBIT 19–7

Types of Mortgage Instruments

Fixed-Rate Mortgage (FRM).   The contract interest rate is set at the time a mortgage loan is made and does not change over the life of the loan. The maturity (term) and the size of the monthly payment called for by the mortgage usually is fixed as well.

Variable-Rate Mortgage (VRM).   The contract interest rate specified in the mortgage loan is tied to another interest rate which is sensitive to current supply and demand conditions in the open market. Higher interest rates usually result in higher monthly mortgage payments.

Adjustable Mortgage Instrument (AMI).   Changes in the interest rate attached to the mortgage loan can be passed along to the borrower by changing the loan principal, loan maturity, or monthly payment, or by varying some combination of these credit terms.

Graduated-Payment Mortgage (GPM).   Installment payments required under a mortgage contract are set lower than those required under a comparable fixed-rate mortgage but rise over time with inflation, borrower income, or some other index.

Canadian Rollover Mortgage (CRM).   This mortgage loan is of much shorter term than a conventional fixed-rate mortgage and usually requires the borrower to renegotiate and refinance the loan on the due date.

Renegotiated-Rate Mortgage (RRM).   With this long-term residential mortgage loan, the interest rate is set for a period shorter than the term of the mortgage and must be renegotiated between borrower and lender on a periodic basis.

Deferred-Interest Mortgage (DIM).   This mortgage loan has interest rates that are generally lower than on conventional fixed-rate mortgages, but at a later point the borrower must reimburse the lender for accumulated interest not paid earlier.

Flexible-Payment Mortgage (FPM).   The borrower pays only the interest on a mortgage loan for the first five years; subsequent payments must be high enough to fully amortize the loan, however.

Shared-Appreciation Mortgage (SAM).   The borrower agrees to give the lender a portion of the profits from the sale of mortgaged property in return for a lower contractual interest rate and lower monthly payments.

Reverse-Annuity Mortgage (RAM).   This is a device to raise money by borrowing against an existing home or other structure (usually a property whose original mortgage loan has been paid off), with the borrower receiving fixed annuity payments based on the value of the mortgaged property.

loan, or the loan principal as interest rates change face few legal restrictions on their terms and have grown rapidly in recent years. For example, in 1981 the Federal Home Loan Bank Board and the Comptroller of the Currency freed federally chartered savings and loan associations and commercial banks from any significant regulatory restrictions on the offering of adjustable mortgages. AMIs increase the affordability of homes to family borrowers and improve the flexibility of lender loan portfolios. By 1983–84 AMIs had replaced traditional fixed-rate mortgages (FRMs) as the dominant form of home mortgage loan in the United States. Part of the reason for the rapid growth of AMIs is their usual lower initial loan rate compared to FRMs with many mortgage lenders offering *teaser rates* to attract AMI customers.[9]

Canadian Rollover and Other Renegotiated Mortgage Loans

Recently, there has been considerable interest in the United States in *Canadian rollover mortgages* (CRMs). These instruments are usually issued for short to medium terms (e.g., 5- and 10-year maturities are common) at the end of which the note falls due. The borrower must then either pay off the note or negotiate a new loan. A related variety of loan is the *renegotiated rate mortgage* (RRM). Unlike the Canadian rollover mortgage, it carries a long maturity, but its interest rate must be renegotiated periodically—usually every three to five years.

Still another renegotiated-type property loan is the *deferred-interest mortgage* (DIM), in which the borrower pays a lower interest rate than with a conventional FRM and thus has lower mortgage payments. However, the borrower must reimburse the lender for any accumulated interest that is postponed during the life of the loan plus an additional fee. This reimbursement may occur through a refinancing of the loan at the end of a certain period or when the property is sold or transferred to another owner.[10]

---

[9] See Buynak (1985).

[10] A new type of mortgage related to CRMs, RRMs, and DIMs is the *flexible-payment mortgage* (FPM). This instrument requires the borrower to pay only the interest on the loan and no principal during the first five years. After the initial five-year period, however, the mortgage loan must be fully amortized as to both principal and interest. However, since the bulk of the early payments on conventional mortgage instruments go to pay interest anyway, with very little reduction of principal, the monthly savings from FPMs are usually small—typically under $50.

Another relatively new mortgage instrument developed in the western United States is the *shared-appreciation mortgage* (SAM). The borrower is offered substantially smaller monthly payments and a contractual interest rate well below rates prevailing on conven-

Reverse-Annuity Mortgages

A mortgage-financing device which may be of help to older families and retired individuals is the *reverse-annuity mortgage* (RAM). This financial instrument is designed to provide additional income to those who may have already paid off their home mortgage but intend to keep their present home. The lender determines the current value of the home and pays the borrower a fixed monthly annuity, amounting to a specified percentage of the property's value. The loan is secured by a gradually increasing mortgage on the borrower's home. Repayment of the loan occurs either when the annuity holder dies, with the loan being discharged against the deceased's estate, or when the home is sold.

Graduated-Payment Mortgages

A relatively new mortgage instrument developed in recent years to help lower-income families is the *graduated-payment mortgage* (GPM), which FHA began insuring in 1977. With the GPM initial monthly payments on a new home are lower at first, but then rise for a time before leveling off after several years. The idea is to tailor the debt service payments on a home mortgage to the financial needs and improving financial position of the borrower. GPMs have proven to be popular with young families who otherwise might be stymied by high mortgage payments until their earning power has increased.

Of course, the total amount of interest paid by the borrower will be much larger with a GPM than it would be under a conventional FRM. In part, this occurs because the low initial monthly payments do not cover the full amount of interest owed each month, forcing the lender to actually increase the amount of the mortgage loan in the early years. Moreover, due to the delayed receipt of income, lenders generally raise the interest rate on GPMs above rates prevailing on level-payment mortgages.

Epilogue on the Fixed-Rate Mortgage

It is interesting that, with all of the new mortgage instruments developed during the 1970s and early 1980s, fixed-rate mortgages (FRMs) continued to hold onto a substantial share of the residential loan market. This is true even though FRMs usually carry an interest rate at least 1 to 2 percentage points higher than an adjustable mortgage and often

---

tional mortgages in return for a commitment to turn over a fraction of any capital gain resulting from the sale of the mortgaged property. One popular SAM contract requires the borrower to pay one third of any profit earned on the sale of a home.

carry higher origination fees and prepayment penalties. One reason appears to be public mistrust of many of the new instruments coupled with fears of rising inflation which would push upward the interest rate on a variable-rate loan. Another factor is competition. Where FRMs and VRMs are offered in the same market, the fixed-rate loans tend to drive out the variable loans. It is likely, therefore, that both FRMs and VRMs will continue to exist side by side in the home mortgage market, each serving the special needs of individual mortgage lenders and new home-owners.

CREATIVE FINANCING TECHNIQUES

Soaring prices of new homes and high mortgage interest rates have frequently put a damper on the demand for single-family homes in recent years. Homeowners and real estate agents have sought out innovative financing techniques—"creative financing"—to make single-family homes more affordable for the average home buyer.

Second Mortgages

One of the most popular creative financing techniques is the second, or junior, mortgage. A second mortgage is a claim against real property which is subordinated to a first mortgage claim and usually payable in monthly installments. Its maturity typically is much shorter than that of a first-mortgage loan—5- to 10-year terms are common. Because the second-mortgage holder has a subordinated claim, the interest rate is often significantly higher than on a first-mortgage loan.

The shorter maturities and higher interest rates attached to second mortgages have made them attractive to many lenders, particularly savings and loan associations, commercial banks, and finance companies. Historically, second mortgages have been used by homeowners to draw upon the growing equity investment in their home in order to pay for improvements (such as adding an extra bedroom) or to raise cash to make other purchases or investments. More recently, second mortgages have been used as a form of seller financing to speed up home sales.

For example, a homeowner who has placed his or her house on the market with an $80,000 price tag may find few buyers due to high interest rates and many young families lacking the funds for a good down payment. A financial institution or the homeowner himself may be willing to take a second deed of trust in lieu of a portion of the required down payment. The home buyer benefits, even though the interest rate is usually higher on this second mortgage, by being able to more completely leverage the home purchase and gain a bigger tax deduction in the form of interest payments.

Home-Leasing Plans

In addition to second mortgages, *lease-purchase agreements* are now being used in certain markets. Under this arrangement the buyer leases a home while retaining the option to buy for a period of at least one year. The seller receives monthly lease payments plus option money, which the buyer may later apply toward a down payment on the home. The advantage of this financing technique is that is permits the buyer to move in right away and still have time to accumulate enough savings to make the required down payment. Meantime, the seller is receiving cash payments while still enjoying the tax advantages of owning and renting a home.

Land-Leasing Plans and Property Exchanges

A related lease-financing option is the *land lease*. In this case the buyer acquires title only to the house and any improvements on the land, and the seller retains title to the land on which the house stands. In return for monthly lease payments, the buyer will receive a long-term lease (sometimes stretching out to 100 years) on the land, frequently with an option to buy. This creative financing technique reduces monthly payments and results in a lower initial down payment.

A simpler but equally effective approach is a *property exchange* between buyer and seller. Any difference in value between the two houses exchanged can be handled by a promissory note issued by the owner of the cheaper property. Sometimes the difference in value will be made up by swapping personal property, such as savings deposits, stocks, bonds, jewelry, or automobiles.

Assumption of Old Mortgages and Wraparound Financing

One of the most popular of all creative financing techniques during the past three decades has been the assumption of existing, low-rate mortgages on homes by their purchasers. Assuming an older, low-rate home mortgage represents, in effect, the taking out of a new home loan at a submarket interest rate. Buyers, therefore, are usually willing to pay more for homes with low-rate assumable mortgages. As Esaki (1982–83) notes, the value of an assumable mortgage to a would-be home buyer equals the difference between the present discounted cost of the payment stream on the old assumable mortgage and the discounted cost of the payment stream on a new mortgage of the same amount bearing the current market interest rate. A low-rate assumable mortgage may add tens of thousands of dollars to the market value of a home. However, the home buyer does have to weigh the tax cost of such a deal because old mortgages usually involve less tax-deductible interest and larger repayments of principal than new mortgages. Moreover, a second (junior) mortgage may be needed to cover the large down payment often required to assume an old, low-rate mortgage.

In recent years some homeowners have used *wraparound financing* to lure buyers. With this technique the homeowner continues to make payments on the existing mortgage, but accepts a new high-rate mortgage from the buyer, pocketing the difference in interest earnings between the old and new mortgages. However, a portion of the homeowner's gain is passed on to the buyer who takes it in the form of a lower interest rate than other lenders would charge.

The use of assumable mortgages and wraparound financing will be hampered in future years because of passage of the Garn-St Germain Depository Institutions Act in 1982. This law grants many mortgage lenders the right to enforce *due-on-sale* clauses present in many conventional mortgage agreements. These clauses require immediate payment of the loan when the home is sold. The Garn bill overrode state and local laws which in many cases prevented due-on-sale clauses from being enforced. Certain of these laws are to remain in force until October 1985 and others may be extended further. Thus, the future of the assumable mortgage appears limited and highly uncertain.

The Message of Creative Financing Techniques

These and other creative financing techniques illustrate one favorable aspect of high interest rates and tight credit—such conditions frequently stimulate the invention of new financial instruments to better serve the public's needs and to more efficiently utilize scarce capital. Creative home-financing techniques also serve as a reminder to government agencies responsible for regulating the financial system: *Rules and regulations that ignore or try to suppress the basic forces of supply and demand in the financial marketplace soon will be outmoded by the ever changing technology of finance.*

SUMMARY AND CONCLUSIONS

In this chapter we have focused our attention on one of the most important and also one of the most troubled markets in the American financial system—the residential mortgage market. Huge by almost any standard, the total volume of mortgage debt outstanding in the United States exceeded $2 trillion in 1985, or more than half the size of the United States GNP and far larger than any other financial instrument. Mortgages on one-to-four-family dwellings and apartments totaled about $1.4 trillion, so that loans to support the building of residences for individuals and families accounted for about three quarters of all mortgage debt in the United States. The health and vitality of this market has a powerful impact on the nation's standard of living, social welfare, and public attitudes. It is inextricably intertwined with the political sphere and has been the object of government intervention, supervision, and regulation for decades.

Three major problems have affected the performance of the mortgage market in recent years. One concerns the relatively weak resale market for existing mortgages. When lenders have difficulty selling their old mortgages in order to make new loans, the availability of financial capital for the construction of new homes, apartments, shopping centers, office buildings, and other structures is curtailed. This is a particularly serious problem in view of the heavy demand for new housing expected in the 1980s and beyond. Between 1980 and 1990 an estimated 42 million Americans will reach age 30—considered a prime home-buying age. However, federal government efforts to deal with this problem through the creation of special agencies actively buying and selling mortgages in the open market have begun to bear fruit. An active and increasingly broad secondary market for both government-guaranteed and conventional mortgages has developed with many new buyers of old mortgages, including pension funds, banks, mutual funds, insurance companies, individuals, and foreign investors.

Government and private efforts to deal with a second major problem—the redesigning of the basic mortgage instrument itself—also appear to be making progress. Years of rapid inflation and record high interest rates have rendered the conventional fixed-rate mortgage inappropriate in today's financial environment. As a result, lenders have turned increasingly to new forms of mortgage credit whose cash flows vary with interest rates and general market conditions. Included in this list are graduated-payment mortgages, variable-rate mortgages, Canadian rollover mortgages, renegotiated-rate mortgages, deferred-interest mortgages, and reverse-annuity mortgages. Slow at first to authorize these newer and more flexible mortgage loans, Congress and the federal regulatory authorities have responded, initially allowing limited use of variable- and renegotiated-rate instruments. Further liberalization of mortgage-lending rules is expected in the future in response to the nation's growing demands for new and better housing.

The third major problem which marks mortgage-trading activity is the extreme volatility and sensitivity of this market. It tends to be a countercyclical market, expanding rapidly in periods when the economy is in a recession or experiencing a slow recovery and declining in expansion periods when the rest of the economy is buoyant. When the mortgage market is depressed, the building of new homes and other structures virtually grinds to a halt, and unemployment in the construction industry soars. In part, these difficulties are traceable to the nature of the conventional mortgage instrument itself, because its long maturity and in many cases its fixed-contract interest rate make the market value of this instrument highly sensitive to fluctuations in interest rates. Another problem is restrictive government regulations that either limit the terms mortgage lenders can pay savers in order to attract loanable funds or restrict the cash flows from mortgage loans already made. These regulations serve to accentuate the normal cyclical movements in the supply and demand for mortgage funds.

The federal government's response to these problems has been to create federal agencies with the power to borrow money and buy mortgages in the open market or to guarantee them against default. The buying and selling of mortgages has been carried out by such government agencies as the Federal National Mortgage Association (FNMA), the Government National Mortgage Association (GNMA), and the Federal Home Loan Mortgage Corporation (FHLMC). Government guarantees for residential mortgages are issued by the Federal Housing Administration (FHA) and the Veterans Administration (VA). Most recently, federal and state interest-rate ceilings which restrict both loan and deposit growth have been attacked. For example, passage of the Depository Institutions Deregulation and Monetary Control Act in 1980 marked the beginning of a planned six-year phaseout of interest-rate ceilings on deposits.

These serious problems in the mortgage market will not be solved overnight, as the record of the past several decades suggests. The best that can be said to date is that progress *is* being made. The residential mortgage market is slowly being released from the many artificial constraints which have limited the free interplay of demand and supply forces and prevented an optimal allocation of scarce resources. And none too soon, for the thousands of new families formed in the United States each year are placing unprecedented pressures on this huge and volatile market. Indeed, for many families seeking new homes the changes may be coming too late. Inflation, heavy tax burdens, and high interest rates have all but destroyed the dream of home ownership for families and individuals of modest means.

STUDY QUESTIONS

1. What has happened in recent years to the prices of new homes? To interest rates and other terms on conventional home mortgage loans? What are the causes of these trends?

2. Mortgages may be classified in several different ways. Describe the structure of the mortgage market as it relates to:
   a. Type of mortgage contract—conventional versus government guaranteed.
   b. Residential versus nonresidential mortgages.
   c. Type of mortgage borrower.

3. List the principal mortgage-lending institutions in the United States. Which is most important? In what mortgage-lending areas?

4. Compare and contrast the mortgage-lending activities of savings and loan associations, mutual savings banks, insurance companies, commercial banks, and mortgage banking houses. How are these institutions alike, and how do they differ in their mortgage-lending activities?

5. Why is it important to have a viable and active secondary market for mortgages? Discuss the efforts of the federal government to develop a secondary mortgage market.

6. Identify the following federal agencies and describe their function:
   a. FHA.
   b. VA.
   c. FHLB.
   d. FNMA.
   e. GNMA.
   f. FHLMC.

7. Why is the mortgage market particularly sensitive to monetary policy and changing credit conditions?

8. A number of new mortgage instruments have been developed in recent years to replace the conventional fixed-rate mortgage (FRM). These new financial instruments include:
   a. Graduated-payment mortgages (GPM).
   b. Variable-rate mortgages (VRM).
   c. Adjustable mortgage instruments (AMI).
   d. Canadian rollover mortgages (CRM).
   e. Renegotiated-rate mortgages (RRM).
   f. Flexible-payment mortgages (FPM).

    g. Shared-appreciation mortgages (SAM).

    h. Deferred-interest mortgages (DIM).

    i. Reverse-annuity mortgages (RAM).

Describe how each of these mortgage instruments work. Why have these alternatives to the fixed-rate mortgage been developed?

9. What is "creative financing"? What factors have given rise to its growth and development?

10. Explain what the following terms mean:

    a. Second mortgage.

    b. Lease-purchase agreement.

    c. Land lease.

    d. Property exchange.

SELECTED REFERENCES

Berkman, Neil G. "Mortgage Finance and the Housing Cycle." *New England Economic Review*, Federal Reserve Bank of Boston, September–October 1979, pp. 54–76.

Buynak, Thomas M. "Will Adjustable Rate Mortgages Survive?" *Economic Commentary*, Federal Reserve Bank of Cleveland, January 15, 1985.

Davidson, Philip H. "Structure of the Residential Mortgage Market." *Monthly Review*, Federal Reserve Bank of Richmond, Spetember 1972, pp. 2–6.

DeLeeuw, Frank, and Larry Ozanne. "The Impact of the Federal Income Tax on Investment in Housing." *Survey of Current Business*, December 1979, pp. 50–61.

Esaki, Howard. "Economic Effects of Enforcing Due-on-Sale Clauses." *Quarterly Review*, Federal Reserve Bank of New York, Winter 1982–83, pp. 33–36.

Estrella, Arturo, and Andrew Silver. "Collateralized Mortgage Obligations: Do They Reduce Uncertainty?" *Quarterly Review*, Federal Reserve Bank of New York, Summer 1984, pp. 58–60.

Freund, James L. "The Housing Market: Recent Developments and Underlying Trends." *Federal Reserve Bulletin*, February 1983, pp. 61–69.

Gillingham, Robert. "Estimating the User Cost of Owner-Occupied Housing." *Monthly Labor Review*, February 1980, pp. 31–35.

Melton, William C. "Graduated Payment Mortgages." *Quarterly Review*, Federal Reserve Bank of New York, Spring 1980, pp. 21–28.

Melton, William C., and Diane L. Heidt. "Variable Rate Mortgages." *Quarterly Review*, Federal Reserve Bank of New York, Summer 1979, pp. 23–31.

Sivesind, Charles M. "Mortgage-Backed Securities: The Revolution in Real Estate Finance." *Quarterly Review,* Federal Reserve Bank of New York, Autumn 1979, pp. 1–10.

United States League of Savings Associations. *Savings and Loan Fact Book '82.* Chicago, 1982.

Part Six

Businesses in the Financial Markets

20

Business Borrowing in the Money and Capital Markets

PURPOSE OF THIS CHAPTER

To show the many different methods and instruments used by business firms borrowing loanable funds from the money and capital markets. The chapter also stresses the powerful impact business borrowing has in causing interest rates and security prices to fluctuate from day to day in the financial markets and examines the factors that lead many businesses to raise external funds.

KEY TERMS AND CONCEPTS IN THE CHAPTER

base rate
call privileges
collateral trust bonds
commercial mortgages
convertible bonds
corporate bonds
corporate notes
coupon rate
debentures
equipment trust
 certificates

equity kicker
external fund-raising
income bonds
indenture
industrial
 development bonds
inflation-hedged
 bonds
investment banker
LIBOR
mortgage bonds

net proceeds
pollution control
 bonds
prime rate
private placements
public sale
restrictive convenants
serial bonds
syndicate
term bonds

Business firms draw upon a wide variety of sources of funds in order to finance their daily operations and to carry out long-term investment. In 1984, for example, nonfinancial business firms in the United States raised more than $600 billion in funds to carry out long-term investment, purchase inventories of goods and raw material, and acquire financial assets. Of this total, about $250 billion (40 percent) was supplied directly from the financial markets through issues of bonds, stocks, notes, and other financial instruments and through trade credit extended by suppliers. In this chapter we look at sources of borrowed (debt) funds used by businesses today. In the next chapter we will consider the advantages and disadvantages of stock (equity) as a source of business funds.

FACTORS AFFECTING BUSINESS ACTIVITY IN THE MONEY AND CAPITAL MARKETS

Many factors affect the extent to which business firms draw upon the money and capital markets for funds. One prominent factor is *the condition of the nation's economy and the demand for goods and services.* A booming economy will generate rapidly growing sales, encouraging businesspeople to borrow to expand inventories and to issue stocks and bonds in order to purchase new plant and equipment. In contrast, a sagging economy normally will be accompanied by declining sales and a reduction in both inventory purchases and long-term investment. Other factors held equal, the need for external fund-raising declines when the economy grows more slowly or heads down into a recession. In contrast, rising demand for business goods and services is usually translated into rising demand for short- and long-term capital supplied from the financial markets.

Credit availability and interest rates also have powerful effects on the level of business activity in the financial markets. Rising interest rates that typically accompany a period of economic prosperity or rapid inflation eventually choke off business borrowing and spending plans because of the increasing cost of carrying inventories, floating new securities, and renewing existing credit lines. Moreover, rising interest rates are usually accompanied by reduced credit availability to many business firms because commercial banks and other institutional lenders frequently lose funds ("disintermediation") during such periods. Falling interest rates, on the other hand, can stimulate business borrowing and spending, leading to a restocking of inventories and to an expansion of long-term business investment financed by bonds, stocks, and direct loans.

Because the financial markets are largely a *supplemental* funds source for business firms, drawn upon to backstop internal cash flows when credit availability, interest rates, and economic conditions are favorable, it should not surprise us to learn that business fund-raising activity in the financial system is highly volatile. Heavy business borrowings and new stock issues in one year often are followed by a dearth of new offerings and even significant paydowns of outstanding loans and securities in succeeding years. A good example is provided by the experience of the U.S. economy during the early 1980s.

In 1982, for example, with the U.S. economy in the midst of a deep recession, businesses sharply reduced their borrowings to expand inventories or to carry out long-term investment. Nonfinancial companies raised net only $79 billion in funds from the financial marketplace that year after $165 billion in borrowings and stock issues the previous year. During 1983, however, the economy was recovering. With interest rates at more moderate levels, business borrowing soared. Combined issues of corporate stocks, bonds, notes, and loans rose $160 billion in 1983 and $250 billion in 1984.

These marked fluctuations in business fund-raising activities in the financial markets result in wide swings in interest rates and security prices. Much of the volatility in stock and bond prices reported in the daily financial press may be attributed to the on-again-off-again character of financial market activity by the business sector. The key actors in this rapidly changing drama are, of course, the largest industrial and manufacturing corporations who have the reputation and financial stature to tap both the open market and negotiated-loan markets for debt and equity funds. Skillful security analysts often can read which way the wind is blowing as far as interest rates and security prices are concerned by watching what is happening to the current earnings and investment plans of the nation's major corporations.

CHARACTERISTICS OF CORPORATE NOTES AND BONDS

If a corporation decides to use long-term funds to finance its growth, the most popular form of long-term financing is the *corporate bond or note.* This is especially true for the largest corporations whose credit standing and reputation is so strong they can avoid dealing directly with an institutional lender such as a bank, finance company, or insurance company and sell their long-term IOUs in the open market. Smaller companies without the necessary "standing" in the eyes of security investors usually must confine their long-term financing operations to negotiated loans with an institutional lender, an occasional stock issue, and heavy use of internally generated cash.

Principal Features of Corporate Notes and Bonds

A distinction needs to be drawn here between notes and bonds. By convention, a *note* is a corporate debt contract whose original maturity is five years or less; a *bond* carries an original maturity of more than five years. Both securities promise the investor an amount equal to the security's par value at maturity plus interest payments at specified intervals until maturity is reached. Because both securities have similar characteristics other than maturity, we will use the term *bond* to refer to both notes and bonds in the discussion that follows.

Corporate bonds are generally issued in units of $1,000 and earn income that, in most cases, is fully taxable to the investor. Each bond is accompanied by an *indenture* which is a contract listing the rights, privileges, and obligations of the borrower and the investor. Indentures usually contain at least some *restrictive covenants* designed to protect bondholders against actions by a borrowing firm or its shareholders that might tend to weaken the value of the bonds. For example, typical restrictive covenants in an indenture may prohibit the raising of a borrowing corporation's dividend rate (which would reduce the growth of its net worth), limit additional borrowing, restrict merger agreements, or limit the sale of the borrower's assets. These and other terms in a bond indenture are enforced by a third party—the trustee (often a bank trust department)—who represents the entire group of investors holding the bonds.

Term Bonds versus Serial Bonds

The majority of corporate bonds issued today are *term bonds,* which means that all the bonds in a particular issue mature on a single date. In contrast, most bonds issued by state and local governments (municipals) and a few corporate bonds are *serial bonds,* carrying a range of maturity dates.[1]

Recent Trends in Original Maturities of Bonds

There is a trend today toward shorter and shorter original maturities for corporate bonds due to inflation, rapid changes in technology, and heavy borrowing demands from other sectors of the economy. During the 1950s and 60s corporations usually found a ready market for 20- to 30-year bonds. Such long-term debt contracts were extremely desirable from the borrowing company's standpoint because they locked in relatively low interest costs for many years and made financial planning much simpler. Today, with inflation and a volatile economy frequently sending

---

[1] See Chapter 26 for a discussion of the serial feature of municipal bonds.

market interest rates to record or near-record levels, bonds and notes
with 3- to 15-year maturities have become more common.

Call Privileges

Nearly all corporate bonds issued today carry *call privileges* allowing
early redemption of the bonds if market conditions prove favorable. The
call privilege represents a way to shorten the average maturity of corporate bonds in an era of rapid inflation and high borrowing costs. As we
saw in Chapter 10, the redemption (or "call") price decreases as a callable
bond approaches maturity. Depending on the call premium and market
conditions, investors generally prefer that the redemption of a bond be
deferred as long as possible to protect them against loss of income due
to lower interest rates. And most corporate bonds issued today defer
the call privilege for 5 to 10 years with utility company bonds usually
callable after 5 years and industrial bonds after 10 years. The call feature
gives the firm greater flexibility in financing its operations but can be
expensive to a company when interest rates are high and expected to
fall. Investors realize that the bond will likely be called if rates fall far
enough and, therefore, demand a higher yield as compensation for call
risk.

Sinking Fund and Refunding Provisions

Most corporate bonds issued in the United States are backed by *sinking
funds* designed to ensure that the issuing company will be able to pay
off the bonds when they come due. Periodic payments are made into
the sinking fund on a schedule which usually is related to the depreciation
of the assets supported by the bonds. The trustee is charged with the
responsibility of making sure that the user actually places the right amount
of money in the sinking fund each time a payment is due. Periodically,
a portion of the bonds outstanding may be retired from monies accumulated in the fund. The trustee will call in selected bonds at their par
value even though the market prices of those bonds may have risen
well above par due to falling interest rates.

As we noted in Chapter 10, the majority of bonds issued by corporations
today allow the borrowing company to "call" or "refund" its bonds in
advance of their maturity date. The refunding provisions in most bond
indentures specify that, after a designated period (usually after the first
5 to 10 years), the issuer may buy up the outstanding bonds at par value
plus a designated premium (often one year's worth of interest). The purpose of the refunding or call privilege is to give the borrowing firm greater
financial flexibility to rearrange its capital structure should interest rates
fall.

Yields and Costs of Corporate Bonds

Yields on corporate bonds tend to move in line with general business conditions and respond to swings in the credit market between tight and easy money. Yields on the highest-grade corporate issues tend to move closely with yields on U.S. government bonds. In contrast, yields carried by lower-grade corporate bonds are more closely tied to conditions in the nation's economy and to factors specifically affecting the risk position of each borrowing firm. Bonds issued by the largest U.S. industrial, manufacturing, and utility companies are, with few exceptions, listed and traded on the New York or American Stock exchanges, though the largest volume of bond trading passes through dealers operating off the exchanges.[2]

As noted in Chapter 8, there are several different ways to measure the rate of return to the investor or the cost to the firm of issuing a bond, note, or other debt security. From the point of view of the issuing company one widely quoted measure of the cost of a bond is its *coupon rate,* that is, the rate of interest the company promises to pay as printed on the face of the bond. However, the coupon rate may understate or overstate the true cost of a bond to the issuing company, depending on whether the bond was issued at a discount or at a premium from its par value. A better measure of the cost of issuing a bond is to compare the *net proceeds* available for the borrowing company's use from a bond sale to the present value of the stream of cash payments the firm must eventually make to the bondholders.

For example, suppose a corporation issues $1,000 par bonds, but flotation costs reduce the net proceeds to the company from each bond to $950.[3] If the bonds mature in 10 years and carry a 10 percent coupon rate, then the before-tax cost, k, to the issuing company is:

$$\text{Net proceeds per bond} = \frac{\text{Interest cost in year 1}}{(1+k)} + \frac{\text{Interest cost in year 2}}{(1+k)^2}$$

$$+ \cdots + \frac{\text{Interest cost in year 10}}{(1+k)^{10}}$$

$$+ \frac{\text{Principal payments in year 10}}{(1+k)^{10}}$$

---

[2] See Chapter 21 for a description of the workings of these major securities exchanges.

[3] The major elements of flotation cost for a new bond issue are the underwriting spread of the dealer selling the issue, registration fees, paper and printing charges, and legal fees.

In this example,

$$\$950 = \frac{\$100}{(1+k)^1} + \frac{\$100}{(1+k)^2} + \cdots + \frac{\$100}{(1+k)^{10}} + \frac{\$1,000}{(1+k)^{10}}$$

A check of the present value tables in Appendix B indicates that k is 10.85 percent.

However, interest charges on debt are *tax deductible*, making the after-tax cost considerably less than the before-tax cost, especially for the largest and most profitable firms. For corporations that earn over $100,000 per year, the marginal federal income tax rate is 46 percent.[4] Thus, a large company issuing the bond described above would incur an after-tax cost (k') of

$$k' = k(1 - t)$$

where k is the before-tax cost and t is the firm's marginal tax rate. In this example,

$$k' = 10.85\% \ (1 - 0.46) = 5.86\%$$

Of course, if the firm were in a lower tax bracket, the after-tax cost of its debt would be higher; and, in the case of an unprofitable company (whose effective tax rate is zero) the after-tax cost of debt would equal its before-tax cost.

The before- and after-tax cost of debt vary not only with each firm's tax rate, but also with conditions in the nation's financial markets. During periods of rapid economic expansion when the supply of credit is scarce relative to the demand for credit, the cost of borrowing debt capital will rise. Bonds and notes must be marketed at lower prices and higher yields. Conversely, in periods when the economy contracts and easier credit conditions prevail, the cost of borrowing debt capital tends to

---

[4] Since passage of the Revenue Act of 1978 and the Economic Recovery Tax Act of 1981, U.S. corporations have faced a five-step graduated income tax rate schedule. The tax rate schedule which took effect in 1984 was as follows:

If Corporate Taxable Income Is:	The Tax Rate Applying to Net Earnings Is:
$0–$25,000	15%
$25,001–$50,000	18%
$50,001–$75,000	30%
$75,001–$100,000	40%
Over $100,000	46%

decline. The prices of bonds and notes will rise and their yields will fall. It should not be surprising to learn that the volume of long-term corporate borrowings tends to increase markedly during business recessions as companies attempt to lock in the relatively low interest rates available at that time.

The Most Common Types of Corporate Bonds

Debentures.   There are many different types of corporate bonds issued every day in the nation's financial markets (see Exhibit 20–1). Among the most common is the *debenture*, which is not secured by any specific asset or assets owned by the issuing corporation. Instead, the holder of a debenture is a general creditor of the company and looks to the earning power and reputation of the borrower as the main source of the bond's value.

Subordinated Debentures.   A related form of bond is the subordinated debenture, frequently called a *junior security.* If a company goes out of business and its assets are liquidated, the holders of subordinated debentures will be paid only after all secured and unsecured senior creditors receive the monies to which they are entitled.

Mortgage Bonds.   Debt securities representing a claim against specific assets (normally plant and equipment) owned by a corporation are known as mortgage bonds. These bonds may be either *closed end* or *open end.* Closed-end mortgage bonds do not permit the issuance of any additional debt against the assets already pledged under the mortgage. Open-end bonds, on the other hand, do allow additional debt to be issued against pledged assets, and this may dilute the position of the current bondholders. For this reason, open-end mortgage bonds typically carry higher yields than closed-end bonds. Sometimes several different mortgage bonds with varying priorities of claim will be issued against the same assets. For example, the initial issue of bonds against a corporation's fixed assets may be designated first mortgage bonds, and later, second mortgage bonds may be issued against those same assets. If the company were liquidated and the pledged assets sold, holders of second mortgage bonds would receive only those funds left over after holders of the first mortgage bonds were paid off.

Collateral Trust Bonds.   A debt instrument secured by stocks, bonds, and notes issued by units of government or by other corporations is called a collateral trust bond. Such a bond is, therefore, really an interest

EXHIBIT 20–1

The Most Common Types of Corporate Notes and Bonds

Debentures.   Long-term debt instruments secured only by the earning power of the issuing corporation and not by any specific property.

Subordinated Debentures.   Unsecured bonds whose holders receive a claim on the issuing company's assets that ranks behind holders of senior debt securities but ahead of common and preferred stockholders.

Mortgage Bonds.   Long-term debt secured by a lien on specific assets (normally plant and equipment) held by the issuing corporation.

Equipment Trust Certificates.   A type of lease financing in which the title to certain assets (normally equipment or rolling stock) is held by a trustee and the company issuing the certificates makes lease payments to certificate holders through the trustee.

Collateral Trust Bonds.   Long-term debt representing an interest in a pool of securities held by the issuing corporation.

Industrial Development Bonds.   Debt securities issued by a local government agency to aid a private company in the construction of a plant and/or the purchase of equipment or land.

Convertible Bonds.   Long-term debt securities that can be exchanged for a specific number of shares of common stock at the option of the bondholder.

Income Bonds.   Debt instruments used mainly in corporate reorganizations that earn interest for the holder only when the issuing company has sufficient earnings.

Pollution Control Bonds.   Long-term debt securities issued by a local government agency (often on a tax-exempt basis) to assist a private company in purchasing pollution-control equipment or facilities.

in a pool of securities held by the bond issuer. The pledged securities are held in trust for the benefit of the bondholders, though the borrowing company usually receives any interest and dividend payments generated by the pledged securities and retains voting rights on any stock that is pledged.

Income Bonds.   Bonds often used in corporate reorganizations and in other situations when a company is in financial distress are known as income bonds. Interest on these bonds is paid only when enough income is actually earned, making an income bond similar to common stock. However, holders of income bonds do have a prior claim on earnings over both stockholders and holders of subordinated debentures. Moreover, some income bonds carry a cumulative feature under which unpaid interest accumulates and must be fully paid before the stockholders receive any dividends.

Equipment Trust Certificates. Resembling a lease in form, equipment trust certificates are used most frequently to acquire industrial equipment or rolling stock (such as trucks, railroad cars, or airplanes). Title to the assets acquired is vested in a trustee (often a bank trust department) who leases these assets to the company issuing the certificates. Periodic lease payments are made to the trustee who passes them along to certificate holders. Title to the assets passes to the borrowing company only after all lease payments are made.

Industrial Development Bonds. In recent years state and local governments have become much more active in aiding private corporations to meet their financial needs. One of the most controversial forms of government-aided, long-term business borrowing is the industrial development bond (IDB), developed originally in the southern states during the Great Depression of the 1930s and used today by local governments scattered throughout the nation. These bonds are issued by a local government borrowing authority in order to provide buildings, land, and/or equipment to a business firm. Because governmental units can borrow more cheaply than most private corporations the lower debt costs may be passed along to the firm as an added inducement to move to a new location, bringing new jobs to the local economy. The business firm normally guarantees both interest and principal payments on the IDBs by renting the buildings, land, and/or equipment at a rental fee high enough to cover debt-service costs.

Pollution Control Bonds. Related to industrial development bonds, pollution control bonds are used to aid private companies in financing the purchase of pollution control equipment. In this case local governments frequently will purchase pollution control equipment with the proceeds of a bond issue and lease that equipment to business firms in the area.[5]

---

[5] Another important type of corporate bond (discussed previously in Chapter 10) is the *convertible bond.* Convertibles may be exchanged for a specific number of shares of common stock at the option of the bondholder. These securities lie midway between stock and corporate debt in their financial characteristics. The value of converti-

Inflation-Hedged Securities—New Types of Corporate Bonds

Corporate bonds are traditionally called "fixed-income" securities because most bonds pay a fixed amount of interest each year, as determined by their coupon rate and par value. This creates a problem for bondholders when interest rates rise, inflation increases, or both because then the real market value of fixed-income securities falls. In recent years repeated bouts with inflation and high interest rates have spurred borrowers and investment bankers to develop new types of corporate bonds whose return to the investor is sensitive to changing inflation and changing bond values. Among the most popular of these innovative securities are discount bonds, stock-indexed bonds, floating-rate bonds, commodity-backed bonds, and warrant bonds.

Discount bonds, first used extensively in 1981, are sold at a price well below par and appreciate toward par as maturity approaches. Thus, the investor earns capital gains as well as interest, while the issuing corporation usually can issue discount bonds at a lower after-tax cost than on conventional bonds. Some discount bonds, known as zero-coupon bonds, pay no interest at all. First used by J. C. Penney in 1981 "zeros" pay a return based solely on their appreciation in market price as they approach maturity. However, the annual price increase in zeros is taxable as ordinary income, not as capital gains, under current IRS regulations. *Stock-indexed bonds* have an interest rate tied to stock market trends. For example, one $25 million issue sold in 1981 had its annual interest rate tied to the annual trading volume on the New York Stock Exchange. A rise in stock trading volume (on the theory that stocks are more eagerly sought by investors as a hedge when inflation increases) raises the bond's promised rate.

Floating-rate bonds, many issued by banking organizations, have their annual promised rate tied to changes in either long-term or short-term interest rates or both. Many investors regard floaters as realistic alternatives to buying money market securities. *Commodity-backed bonds* carry a face value tied to the market price of an internationally traded commodity, such as gold, silver, or oil, which presumably is sensitive to inflation. Finally, *warrant bonds* permit an investor to purchase additional bonds at the same yield as the original bonds or sell the detachable warrants to another investor. Warrant bonds are obviously most valuable when interest rates are expected to decline. While all of these new types of bonds do reasonably well in inflationary periods, when inflation falls, as it did in the mid-1980s, they often prove difficult to sell.

---

bles to the investor stems as much from the value of the issuing company's stock as it does from the value of the bonds themselves.

INVESTORS IN CORPORATE NOTES AND BONDS

Today, the investor market for corporate notes and bonds is dominated by insurance companies and pension funds (see Exhibit 20–2). The latter prefer buying corporate bonds in the open market, while insurance companies frequently purchase their corporate securities directly from the issuing company in an "off-the-market" transaction. The stability of cash flows experienced by pension funds and insurance companies permits them to pursue corporate debt obligations with long maturities and "lock in" their high market yields. Both federal and state laws, however, require these institutions to be "prudent" in their selection of notes and bonds, which generally means buying investment-grade issues in the top four rating categories established by Moody's and Standard & Poor's Corporation.[6]

Commercial banks are not prominent investors in corporate bonds.

EXHIBIT 20–2

Principal Investors in Corporate and Foreign Bonds, 1983
($ billions outstanding at year-end)

| | 1983 | |
Investor Group	Amount	Percent of Total
Households	$ 45.0	7.6%
Rest of the world	45.8	7.8
Commercial banks	13.1	2.2
Mutual savings banks	21.9	3.7
Life insurance companies	219.1	37.1
Property-casualty insurance companies	21.6	3.7
Private pension funds	92.3	15.6
Government pension funds	111.5	18.9
Mutual funds	13.0	2.2
Security brokers and dealers	6.7	1.1
Totals	$590.0	100.0%

Note: columns may not add to totals due to rounding.
SOURCE: Board of Governors of the Federal Reserve System, *Flow of Funds Accounts: Assets and Liabilities Outstanding, 1960–83.*

---

[6] See Chapter 9 for a discussion of bond-rating systems.

Generally, a banker would prefer to deal personally with his or her business customer and grant a loan specifically tailored to the borrower's needs rather than enter the highly impersonal bond market. Increasingly in recent years commerical banks have become direct competitors with the corporate note and bond markets through the granting of *term loans.* A term loan is any loan granted by a commercial bank for business purposes which has a maturity of more than one year. Responding to inflation and the soaring cost of business equipment and facilities, bankers have gradually extended the maturity of term loans with many now falling in the 5- to 10-year maturity range. Rates on such loans generally exceed the interest cost on corporate debt sold in the open market, however, especially when banks insist that the borrowing firm keep funds on deposit equal to a specified percentage of the loan.

THE SECONDARY MARKET FOR CORPORATE BONDS

The resale (secondary) market for corporate notes and bonds is relatively limited compared to the market for common stock, municipal bonds, and other long-term securities. Trading volume is thin, even for some bonds issued by the largest and best-known companies. Part of the reason is the small number of individuals active as investors in this market. Individuals generally have limited investment time horizons (holding periods) and tend to turn over their portfolios rapidly when attractive alternative investments appear. In the past secondary market trading in corporate bonds was also held back by the "buy and hold" strategy of major institutional investors, especially insurance companies and pension funds. Many of these firms purchased corporate bonds exclusively for their interest income and were content to purchase the longest-term issues and simply hold them to maturity. Today, however, under the pressure of volatile interest rates and inflation, many institutions buying corporate bonds have shifted into a new aggressive strategy often labeled *total performance.* Institutional portfolio managers are more sensitive today to changes in bond prices and look for near-term opportunities to trade bonds and score capital gains. In fact, a number of insurance companies, pension funds, and mutual bond funds operate their own trading departments and keep constant tab on developments in the corporate debt markets.

Unlike the stock market, there is no one central exchange for bond trading which dominates the market. While corporate bonds are traded on all major securities' exchanges, including the New York (NYSE) and American (AMEX) exchanges, most secondary market trading in bonds is conducted over the telephone through brokers and dealers. Bond brokers act as middlemen by arranging trades between dealers in return for a small commission. Dealers, on the other hand, commit themselves to take on large blocks of bonds either from other dealers or from pension funds, insurance companies, and other clients. While bond dealers used to carry large inventories of securities in anticipation of customer orders, most major dealer houses today have sharply reduced their inventory positions due to rapid and often unpredictable changes in interest rates. Many dealers now try to close out positions taken in individual corporate bond issues in just a few days, frequently act only as middlemen in trades between major institutional investors without committing their own capital, and often hedge against the risk of large trading losses by using the financial futures market.

THE MARKETING OF CORPORATE NOTES AND BONDS

New corporate bonds may be offered publicly in the open market to all interested buyers or sold privately to a limited number of investors. The first route, known as *public sale,* accounts for the largest proportion of corporate bond sales each year. Among smaller companies and those firms with unique financing requirements, however, the second route, known as *private* (or direct) *placement,* has become popular.

The Public Sale of Bonds

The sale of new corporate bonds and notes in the open market is handled principally by investment bankers. The term *investment banker* is somewhat misleading because these firms have little or nothing to do with banking as we know it. In fact, the Glass-Steagall Act of 1933 prohibits commercial banks from underwriting any corporate securities. This law was passed out of fear that commercial bank underwriting of corporate securities would lead either to bank failures or to control of nonfinancial businesses by the banking community.[7]

In contrast to commercial banks which accept deposits from the public,

---

[7] There is currently considerable agitation in the banking community to repeal the Glass-Steagall Act's prohibition against bank underwriting of new corporate securities. The principal reason is that investment banking houses increasingly are competing with commercial banks by offering brokerage accounts, which act as checking and savings deposits and lines of credit. Several investment banking houses, including Merrill Lynch, Bache Halsey, Stuart Shields, and others, have become "symbiotic" financial firms, offering businesses and consumers a wide array of financial services that compete effectively with depository institutions. Many bankers feel this is unfair competition because investment houses face fewer regulations than do commercial banks and other deposit-type financial institutions.

investment bankers underwrite new issues of corporate stocks and bonds and give advice to corporations on their financing requirements. Investment bankers are sometimes called "quick intermediaries" between the borrower and the ultimate investor in securities. An investment banking firm may singly take on a new issue of corporate securities or band together with other underwriters to form a *syndicate*. Either way, the investment banker's game plan is to acquire new corporate securities at the lowest possible price and sell them to other investors as quickly as possible in order to turn a profit. An investment banker may purchase the securities from the issuing company directly or merely guarantee the issuer a specific price for his securities. With either approach, it is the investment banker who carries the risk of substantial gains or significant losses when the securities are marked for sale in the open market.

The largest issues of corporate bonds and notes sold in the open market are usually bid on by several syndicates (i.e., groups of underwriters). Competition among syndicates to win a large underwriting contract is usually intense. Investment bankers hope to acquire a new issue at the lowest possible bid price and place the securities with investors at a significantly higher retail price, maximizing the banker's *spread* or return on invested capital. Unfortunately, each new bond issue is always somewhat different from those that have traded before and may involve hundreds of millions of dollars. Moreover, a decision on what price to bid for new securities must be made before the bonds are released for public trading; in the interim, the prices of bonds may change drastically. If the underwriter bids too high a price for the new issue, his firm may not be able to resell the securities at a price high enough to recover their cost and secure an adequate spread. To cite an example, in October 1979 IBM Corporation offered $1 billion in notes and debentures through a collection of Wall Street underwriters. Unfortunately, just as the IBM issue was coming to market, bond prices tumbled (due, in part, to an announcement made by the Federal Reserve implying that credit conditions would be tightened to deal with inflation) and the underwriters reportedly suffered a major loss (though actual losses apparently were less than could have occurred due to some timely hedging in the financial futures market).

Competition in the bidding process tends to narrow the underwriter's spread between bid price and retail (asked) price. If several investment banking houses band together in a syndicate, a consensus bid price must be hammered out among the participants. Disagreements frequently arise within a syndicate due to different perceptions on the probable future direction of interest rates and market conditions. Because more than a hundred underwriters may be included in a single syndicate, the task of reaching a compromise and placing a unified bid for a new security issue may prove impossible. The old syndicate will break apart with those bidders still interested in the issue hurriedly piecing together a new syndicate and a new bid.

A number of factors are considered in pricing a new corporate bond issue. Certainly the rating assigned by Moody's or Standard & Poor's Corporation is a key item because many investors rely on such agencies for assessing the degree of risk carried by a new security.[8] Another critical factor is the "forward calendar" of security offerings which lists new issues expected to come to market during the next few weeks. Obviously, if a heavy volume of new security offerings is anticipated in the near-term, prices will decline unless additional demand appears. Changes in government monetary and fiscal policy also must be anticipated because both can have profound effects on security prices and interest rates. Other factors considered by investment bankers include the overall size of the issue, how aggressive other bidders are likely to be, and the strength of the "book," which consists of indications of advance investor interest in the particular security being offered.

Once the securities are received from the issuing company, the underwriting syndicate will advertise their availability at the price agreed upon by all members of the syndicate. Exhibit 20–3 illustrates an announcement of a public offering of corporate bonds. *Delay* in selling new securities is one of the investment banker's worst enemies because additional financing must be obtained to carry his portfolio of unsold securities. Also there is the added risk of price declines as time stretches out. To speed the process of selling newly acquired bonds many investment banking firms today are affiliated with retail brokerage companies that maintain close working relationships with large bond buyers, such as insurance companies and pension funds.

What happens to the market prices of securities being sold by investment banking syndicates is, of course, the key determinant of the success or failure of the underwriting process. If the market price at which a new issue can be sold falls far enough, the syndicate will disband with individual underwriters scrambling to sell their allotments of securities at whatever price the market dictates. The spread between the selling (retail) price of corporate bonds and the proceeds paid to the issuing company (i.e., the flotation cost of a new issue) is usually less than a point.[9] Thus it obviously takes only a small decline in the retail price of a security before the underwriter's profit is eliminated. Moreover, unfavorable price movements can damage the reputation of the investment banker with both investors and the client companies who issue

---

[8] See Chapter 9 and Appendix A for a discussion of security ratings.

[9] See Chapter 8 for a discussion of *points* in the pricing of bonds.

EXHIBIT 20–3

An Announcement of a Public Offering of Corporate Bonds

This announcement is neither an offer to sell nor a solicitation of an offer to buy these securities. The offer is made only by the Prospectus.

$75,000,000

Leucadia National Corporation

14% Senior Subordinated Notes due May 15, 1993
(Interest payable May 15 and November 15)

Price 100%

Copies of the Prospectus are obtainable in any State from the undersigned and such other dealers as may lawfully offer these securities in such State.

Drexel Burnham Lambert
INCORPORATED

May 23, 1985

SOURCE: *The Wall Street Journal,* May 23, 1985, p. 38.

securities for public sale. The investment banking business is risky, subject to rapid changes with numerous uncertainties, and highly competitive.

Private Placements of Corporate Bonds.

In recent years private placements of bonds with one or a limited group of investors have declined relative to public sales, following a period of rapid growth during the 1970s. For example, in 1982, the latest year with complete data, private placements accounted for about one fifth of public market sales compared to 40 to 50 percent in the late 1970s. However, the ratio of private to public sales is sensitive to the changing composition of borrowing companies and to economic conditions. Usually periods of rising interest rates and reduced credit availability bring more borrowing companies into the public market, while falling rate periods often bring a rise in private placements. For the largest corporations public sales and private placements are *substitutes* for each other. When interest rates are high or credit is tight in one of these markets, the largest borrowers shift freely and easily to the other market.

Who buys privately placed bonds? Life insurance companies and pension funds are the principal investors in this market. These institutions hope to secure higher yields and protection against call privileges on bonds by engaging in *direct negotiation* with borrowing corporations. The avoidance of call privileges on corporate securities is of special concern to life insurance companies and pension funds because these institutions often prefer the stable income which comes from purchasing long-term bonds and holding them to maturity. In fact, institutional investors active in the private placement market frequently impose extra fees in a sales contract containing an allowance for early retirement or refunding of a security by the issuing corporation. Investors other than life insurance companies and pension funds tend to be shut out of the private market due to their lack of financial expertise, small portfolio size, and the absence of a resale market for privately placed securities.[10]

Most private placements are concentrated in the hands of the largest U.S. life insurance companies. Smaller insurance companies, having less technical support, tend to buy most of their securities in the open market or participate with larger companies in private placements. So dominant are life insurance companies in private placements that their financial condition at any particular point in time sets the tone of the whole private market. When these companies are highly liquid and the demand for funds from other sectors of the economy (especially the mortgage market) is weak, life insurers will bid aggressively for new private bonds, and business borrowing costs will drop. During such periods, many borrowers will switch from public to private bond sales to take advantage of the ready availability of relatively cheap credit.

The private market is selective by industry type. Corporations active as borrowers in private placements have generally fallen into three

---

[10] Most security offerings in the private placement market are less than $20 million. In contrast, new issues sold in the open market typically range from $20 million on up. Experience has shown the $20 million is just about the minimum amount necessary to develop a good secondary market and give a new security adequate liquidity. At the other extreme, a security issue can be too large for public sale with few investment bankers willing to accept the risks involved. For example, during the 1970s several utility bond and stock offerings exceeded $500 million and many of these were positioned through private sale to avoid market risks and large underwriting commissions. While there is much greater variation in security ratings in private as opposed to public sales, most private placements, like public sales, appear to involve *rated* securities.

groups: (1) public utilities; (2) real estate and financial firms; and (3) industrial companies. Public utilities usually prefer to offer their bonds in the open market; indeed, restrictions in their charters may require competitive bidding for new public utility issues. However, when credit conditions tighten, the private placement market may be a more hospitable place to fund the long-term capital needs of utilities. Real estate and financial firms generally have a preference for private placements over public sales, though they use both the public market and the private market extensively. Industrial firms frequently fluctuate between public and private markets in response to changes in relative interest rates.

There are several advantages to the borrower from a private placement. One is the lower cost of distribution because there are no legal registration fees or expenses associated with the issuance of a prospectus as there would be with a public sale. Generally, a more rapid placement of bonds takes place in the private market because only one or a few buyers are involved and the loan is confidential. Special concessions can often be secured through a private sale, such as a commitment for future borrowing. For example, a corporate borrower may negotiate a private sale of $15 million in bonds to an insurance company but also may be granted a line of credit in the amount of $2 million a year over the next five years. This kind of future commitment is simply not possible in the impersonal public market where most bonds are highly standardized. Moreover, lenders in the private market try to tailor the terms of a loan to match the specific cash-flow and maturity needs of borrowers. This may involve offering a conventional fixed-rate, single-sum credit contract at the prevailing interest rate, a floating-rate loan that can be retired early if cash flows permit, or even a participating loan in which the lender charges a lower interest rate in return for a share of net income from the project financed.[11]

One obvious disadvantage is that interest costs are higher in private sales—normally about 1 percentage point or more—than in public sales for bonds of comparable quality and maturity. However, private-sale bonds are less liquid and carry more risk.[12] One indication of this is that privately placed debt issues tend to have more restrictive convenants written into their accompanying indentures in order to protect lenders, as noted by Smith and Warner (1979). Still, the larger the size of a corporate issue, the smaller the cost differential between public and private placements.

---

[11] A participating loan in which the lender shares in a project's net earnings is often called an "equity kicker." Equity kickers are discussed later in this chapter.

[12] Privately placed securities generally carry maturities ranging from 3 years out to 20 years. There is, however, a trend toward shorter maturities, paralleling a similar trend in publicly traded issues.

THE VOLUME OF BORROWING IN THE CORPORATE BOND MARKET

The volume of borrowing through new issues of corporate note and bonds has grown rapidly in recent years (see Exhibit 20–4). For example, annual offerings of new corporate debt securities nearly quadrupled between 1960 and 1970 and then more than doubled between 1970 and 1985. Much of this growth in long-term corporate borrowing could be traced to inflation, which reduced the real cost of debt, and to increased use of financial leverage to boost returns to corporate stockholders. Faced with record-high interest rates and two back-to-back recessions in 1980 and 1982, however, long-term corporate borrowing leveled out in the early 1980s before surging ahead again in the mid-1980s with a stronger economy and lower interest rates. This track record reveals quite clearly that the corporate debt market is very sensitive to economic conditions (particularly fluctuations in corporate earnings, sales, and prices) and to changes in the cost of long-term credit.

Another factor that has spurred the private bond market's growth in the 1980s is a rash of corporate takeovers and merger proposals. Targets for these corporate raids have included such well-known companies as CBS, Hilton Hotels, Crown Zellerbach, and Uniroyal to name just a few.

EXHIBIT 20–4

Growth of Corporate Notes and Bonds Sold in the United States ($ millions)*

Year	New Issues of Corporate Bonds and Notes
1950	$ 4,920
1960	8,081
1970	30,321
1980	53,199
1981	45,092
1982	54,076
1983	68,495
1984	109,683
1985	85,628

* Figures are gross proceeds of issues maturing in more than one year, sold for cash in the United States. Excluded are issues of less than $100,000 and secondary offerings. Data for 1985 are for first quarter only at an annual rate.
SOURCE: U.S. Department of Commerce, *Business Statistics,* 1975 ed.; and Board of Governors of the Federal Reserve System, *Federal Reserve Bulletin,* selected issues.

Frequently, these proposed mergers include plans to offer millions or billions of dollars in so-called *junk bonds,* that is, high-yield, often unsecured debt obligations with low credit ratings (usually Ba/BB or lower). A substantial proportion of recent takeovers have been in the form of *leveraged buyouts* in which a single investor or small group of investors proposes to acquire a business firm by borrowing 80 to 90 percent or more of the purchase price from banks and the bond market. In this instance the takeover group is counting on faster growth and improved profitability of the targeted company to pay off the huge volume of acquisition debt. Because such expectations are fraught with risk, leading financial analysts have expressed concern over many of the proposed mergers and buyouts, fearing that they may undermine public confidence in the financial system and financial institutions.

Substantial changes have occurred in recent years in the types of firms issuing bonds and notes (see Exhibit 20–5). The manufacturing and commercial sectors have generally declined in relative importance as bond issuers with many of these firms turning instead to commercial banks and the commercial paper market to handle a growing portion of their credit needs. On the other hand, the rapid expansion of commercial banks, finance companies, mortgage banking houses, securities dealers, and real estate development corporations has resulted in significantly larger bond issues from these particular sectors of the economy.

EXHIBIT 20–5

Industry Source of Bonds and Notes Publicly Offered by U.S. Corporations in 1984 ($ millions)

	1984	
Issurers	**Amount**	**Percent of Total**
Totals	$109,683	100.0%
Industry group:		
Manufacturing	$ 24,607	22.5%
Commercial and miscellaneous	13,726	12.5
Transportation	4,694	4.3
Public utilities	10,679	9.8
Communications	2,997	2.7
Real estate and finance	52,980	48.4

Notes: Figures are gross proceeds of issues maturing in more than one year sold for cash in the United States. Offerings of less than $100,000 are excluded as are secondary market sales, intracorporate transactions, open-end investment companies, and employee stock plans.
SOURCE: Securities and Exchange Commission and Board of Governors of the Federal Reserve System.

BANK LOANS TO BUSINESS

Commercial banks are direct competitors with the corporate note and bond markets in making both long- and short-term loans to business. Early in 1985 total commercial and industrial loans extended by commercial banks operating in the United States exceeded $475 billion, or about one third of all commercial bank loans. Banks grant their loans to a wide variety of firms covering all major sectors of the business community.

In recent years the Federal Reserve Board has carried out surveys of business lending practices by banks across the United States. A summary of the findings from a recent business loan survey is shown in Exhibit 20–6. The Federal Reserve survey indicates that bank loans to business firms tend to be short- or medium-term in maturity. For example, short-term commercial and industrial loans averaged only about two months to maturity, while long-term business loans averaged just under four years. Moreover, the short-term loans, which are used principally to purchase inventories, pay wages and salaries, and meet other current expenses, average considerably larger at most banks than long-term business loans, which are taken out mainly to purchase equipment and to expand physical facilities.

EXHIBIT 20–6

Terms of Lending at U.S. Commercial Banks (Federal Reserve survey of loans made February 6–10, 1984)

Types of Loans and Terms	Average for Loans of All Sizes
Short-term commercial and industrial loans:	
Average loan size ($000s)	$223.7
Weighted-average maturity in months	1.1 months
Weighted-average interest rates	11.06%
Percentage carrying floating rate	32.6%
Long-term commercial and industrial loans:	
Average loan size ($000s)	$125.3
Weighted-average maturity in months	48.0 months
Weighted-average interest rates	11.92%
Percentage carrying floating rate	76.0%
Construction and land development loans:	
Average loan size ($000s)	$53.0
Weighted-average maturity in months	8.9 months
Weighted-average interest rates	13.34%
Percentage carrying floating rate	51.3%

SOURCE: Board of Governors of the Federal Reserve System, *Federal Reserve Bulletin,* June 1984.

The Federal Reserve survey suggests that longer-term business loans tend to carry *higher* average interest rates than short-term business loans. This is due, in part, to the greater risk associated with long-term credit. Moreover, yield curves have usually sloped upward in recent years, calling for higher average rates on long-term loans.[13] Especially interesting is the high proportion of business loans today that carry *floating* rather than fixed-interest rates. The larger and longer-term a business loan is, the more likely its rate will float with market conditions. For example, about one third of the short-term business loans included in the February 1984 Federal Reserve Survey of U.S. banks carried floating interest rates, while three quarters of the long-term business loans had floating rates. Clearly, banks became more determined to protect themselves against unexpected inflation and other adverse developments through floating interest rates as the maturity and the size of a business loan increase.

The Prime or Base Interest Rate

One of the best known and most widely followed interest rates in the financial system is the prime bank interest rate, sometimes called the *base rate* or *reference rate*.[14] The prime rate is the annual percentage

---

[13] See Chapter 9 for a discussion of recent patterns in yield curves and the factors which appear to cause them.

[14] *Base rate* is a more general term than prime, referring to that loan interest rate used as the basis for determining the current rate charged a business borrower. Most business loan rates are scaled upward from the base rate. Many commercial loans today, especially those made to the largest corporations, are tied to base rates other than prime, however. This is frequently the case for large multinational companies that have ready access to the Eurodollar market and other credit markets abroad. For example, the London interbank offering rate (LIBOR) on short-term Eurodollar deposits is often used as a base rate for large corporate loans. In some cases the commercial paper rate, the federal funds rate, or the secondary market rate on bank CDs is also used as a loan base rate. The use of alternative sources to fund prime-rate loans have led recently to unusual behavior in the prime rate. In particular, a majority of short-term business loans in the early and mid-1980s were made at below-prime rates; moreover, the prime tended to change more slowly than other money market rates, resulting in a widening spread relative to bank deposit rates, for example. Perhaps, as Arak, Englander, and Tong (1983) suggest, the smaller numbers of borrowers today who remain tied to the prime rate are less mobile customers with fewer alternatives than many of the largest corporations who not only maintain accounts with several different banks, but also have numerous alternative sources of funds and, therefore, can frequently demand credit at rates significantly less than prime. Such large loans are often made today at contract rates only fractions of a percentage point above a bank's actual cost of raising funds in the money market. In fact, a recent study by Brady (1985) for the Federal Reserve Board found that about 90 percent of business loans at 48 of the biggest U.S. banks carried contract loan rates *below* prime.

interest rate that banks quote on loans made to their most creditworthy customers. Most prime loans are unsecured, but the borrower usually is required to keep a deposit at the lending bank equal to a specified percentage of the loan. This so-called *compensating balance* normally is 15 to 20 percent of the amount loaned. Even for a prime borrower, therefore, the true cost of a bank loan is normally significantly higher than the prime rate itself.[15] Most prime loans are short term—one year or less—taken out to finance purchases of inventory and meet other working capital needs or to support construction projects. Only a small proportion of U.S. corporations—probably no more that 2,000 of the more than 3 million in existence—have the credit standing needed to qualify as prime-rate customers.

Each bank must set its own prime or base rate, following a vote by its board of directors. Beginning in the 1930s, however, a uniform nationwide prime rate began to appear with differences in rates from bank to bank quickly eliminated by competition. Improvements in communication, the broadening of markets, and the increasing propensity of corporate borrowers to shop around for cheap credit have created a national—even international—market for large corporate loans. Split primes do occur for brief periods, however, due to differences in the formulas used by individual banks to calculate their rates and differences in the availability of bank funds. Thus, a bank strapped for loanable funds may keep its prime temporarily above rates posted by other banks in order to ration the available supply of credit. Similarly, a bank with ample funds to lend may post a prime temporarily below market to encourage its best customers to borrow more frequently and in larger amounts.

Traditionally, the prime rate was set by one or more of the nation's leading banks and other banks played "follow the leader" in setting their own prime rate. Because changing the prime-rate incurs substantial risk for the bank making the change, shifts in prime prior to the 1970s were infrequent—averaging about once every six months—and usually very gradual (¼ to ½ percentage point) each time a change was made. How-

---

[15] For example, if a firm borrows $100,000 at a 15 percent prime rate and is required to keep 20 percent (or $20,000) in an interest-free demand deposit, then the effective rate charged by the bank is:

$$\text{Effective loan rate} = \frac{\$15,000}{(\$100,000 - 20,000)} = 18.75\%$$

Thus, the true loan rate in this case is 20 percent higher than the quoted prime rate of 15 percent.

There is a trend away from compensating balances today toward more explicit pricing of bank services. Instead of required deposit balances many banks, at the insistence of their largest corporate customers, are quoting explicit fees for each financial service used.

ever, a major innovation in the market for prime-rate loans occurred in October 1971 when First National City Bank of New York (Citibank) announced that it would *float* its prime. Citibank's basic lending rate was pegged on a weekly basis at ½ percentage point above the yield on 90-day commercial paper. Other major banks soon followed, pegging their prime rates to prevailing yields on U.S. Treasury bills, negotiable CDs, and other money market instruments.

Linking the prime to such active money market rates as those attached to negotiable CDs and commercial paper resulted in a more flexible, rapidly changing base lending rate, illustrated by the frequent prime rate changes shown in Exhibit 20–7. The prime has come to reflect somewhat more accurately the forces of shifting credit demands, fluctuations in government policy, and inflation. For example, as Exhibit 20–7 shows, market interest rates dropped sharply in 1982 and early 1983 and the prime followed, dropping more than 6 percentage points. The economy and interest rates leveled out in 1983 and 1984 and so did the prime rate, only to begin a modest decline late in 1984 and early 1985. A more flexible prime, while disconcerting to borrowers, has enabled banks to better protect their interest margins—the difference between the return on their loans and the cost of bank funds—and to make credit more readily available to those customers willing to pay the price.

EXHIBIT 20–7

The Prime Rate Charged by Banks on Short-Term Business Loans (percent per annum)

Effective Date	Announced Rate	Effective Date	Announced Rate
1981–Nov. 24	16.00%	1983–Jan. 11	11.00%
Dec. 1	15.75	Feb. 28	10.50
1982–Feb. 2	16.50	Aug. 8	11.00
Feb. 18	17.00		
Feb. 23	16.50	1984–Mar. 19	11.50
July 20	16.00	Apr. 5	12.00
July 9	15.50	May 8	12.50
Aug. 2	15.00	June 25	13.00
Aug. 16	14.50	Sept. 27	12.75
Aug. 18	14.00	Oct. 17	12.50
Aug. 23	13.50	Oct. 29	12.00
Oct. 7	13.00	Nov. 9	11.75
Oct. 14	12.00	Nov. 28	11.25
Nov. 22	11.50	Dec. 20	10.75
		1985–Jan. 15	10.50

SOURCE: Board of Governors of the Federal Reserve System, *Federal Reserve Bulletin,* May 1985.

Most business loans today are priced at *premiums* above the prime or other base rate because only the largest, most financially sound customers qualify for prime or below-prime loans. Nevertheless, commercial loan rates typically are tied to the base rate—prime or other reference rate—through a carefully worked out formula. One popular approach, known as *prime-plus,* adds on a rate premium for default risk and often an additional premium for longer maturities. Thus, the banker may quote his commercial customer "prime plus" with a 1 percent premium above the base rate for default risk and another 1 percent premium for term risk. Other banks use the *times-prime* method, which multiplies the base rate by a risk factor. For example, the business customer may be quoted a loan at 1.5 times prime. If the current prime is 10 percent, this customer will pay 15 percent initially. If the loan carries a floating rate then the interest rate in future periods can always be calculated by multiplying the base rate by 1.5.

Which of the above formulas the banker uses often depends on his forecast of interest rates. In a period of falling rates, interest charges on floating-rate loans figured on a times-prime basis decline faster than those based on prime-plus. And, when interest rates are on the rise, times-prime pricing results in more rapid increases in business loan rates. Therefore, times-prime financing is more sensitive to the changing cost of bank funds over the course of the business cycle.

COMMERCIAL MORTGAGES

The construction of office buildings, shopping centers, and other commercial structures is generally financed with an instrument known as the commercial mortgage. Short-term mortgage loans are used to finance the construction of commercial projects, while longer-term mortgages are employed to pay off short-term construction loans, purchase land, and cover property development costs. The majority of long-term commercial mortgage loans are made by life insurance companies, savings and loan associations, and pension funds, while commercial banks are the predominant short-term commercial mortgage lender. Banks support the construction of shopping centers, office buildings, and other commercial projects with loans secured by land and building materials. These short-term mortgage credits usually fall due when construction is completed with permanent mortgage financing of the project then passing to insurance companies, savings and loans, and other long-term lenders.

The growth of commercial mortgages has been rapid in recent years, as reflected in Exhibit 20–8. The dollar volume of such loans more than tripled during the 1970s, rising from about $80 billion to almost $260 billion. However, the market was buffeted by severe problems as the decade of the 80s began and the growth of commercial mortgages slowed

EXHIBIT 20–8

Recent Growth of Commercial Mortgage Loans (End-of-period figures)

Year	Volume of Commercial Mortgages Outstanding ($ billions)
1970	$ 82.3
1972	112.3
1974	146.4
1976	170.8
1978	212.7
1980	258.3
1982	301.4
1984	407.2
1985*	415.4

* First quarter only.
SOURCE: Board of Governors of the Federal Reserve System, *Federal Reserve Bulletin,* selected issues.

until the mid-1980s when lower interest rates stimulated a higher volume of commercial mortgage financing. Up to that point, most commercial real estate financing was provided through fixed-rate mortgages. Faced with rapid inflation, high interest rates and a more volatile economy, however, commercial mortgage lenders began searching for new financial instruments to protect their rates of return. Many mortgage lenders today combine both debt and equity financing in the same credit package. The best-known example is the *equity kicker,* where the lending institution grants a fixed-rate mortgage but also receives a share of any net earnings from the project. For example, a life insurance company may agree to provide $10 million to finance the construction of an office building. It agrees to accept a 15-year mortgage loan bearing a 12 percent annual interest rate against the property. However, as a hedge against inflation and higher interest rates, the insurance company may also insist on receiving 10 percent of any net earnings generated from office rentals over the 15-year period.

Another device used recently in commercial mortgage financing is *indexing.* In this case, the annual interest rate on a loan may be tied to the prevailing yields on high-quality U.S. government or public utility bonds of comparable maturity. Lender and borrower may agree to renegotiate the interest rate at certain intervals—every three to five years is common. There is also a trend toward shorter maturity commercial mortgage loans—many as short as five years—with the borrower either paying off the debt or refinancing the unpaid principal with the same or another lending institution.

SUMMARY AND CONCLUSIONS

The majority of funds drawn upon by business firms to meet their working capital and long-term investment needs come not from the financial markets, but from inside the individual firm. In most years well over half of business capital requirements are supplied by net earnings and noncash depreciation expenses—internal cash flow. However, a third to half of business investment needs in recent years have been met by selling debt and equity securities in the nation's financial markets. The financial system is a backstop for the operations of business firms for those periods when internally generated cash fails to increase fast enough to support the growth of sales and meet customer demands.

The financial markets provide both short-term working capital to purchase inventories and meet current expenses and long-term investment funds to support the purchase of buildings and equipment. The principal external sources of working capital include trade credit (accounts payable), bank loans and acceptances, short-term credits from nonbank financial institutions (such as finance companies and life insurance firms), and sales of commercial paper in the open market. For businesses in need of long-term funding the principal funds sources are the sale of bonds and notes to nonbank financial institutions and other investors, term loans from banks, and the issuance of common and preferred stock and commercial mortgages.

Corporate bonds have original maturities of more than five years, while notes carry maturities of five years or less. There is a trend today toward shorter maturities of corporate debt securities due to inflation, more rapid changes in technology, and huge federal government deficits that force corporations into intense competition for funds with the U.S. Treasury. Indexing of corporate bond rates to broader movements in the economy has also become more common. A wide variety of different bond and note issues have been developed to provide investors with varying degrees of security and risk protection, including debentures, mortgage bonds, equipment trust certificates, convertible bonds, and government-supported industrial development and pollution control bonds. Each type of bond is accompanied by an indenture spelling out in detail the rights and obligations of borrowers and investors. Corporate notes and bonds are purchased by a wide range of investors today, but the dominant buyers are life insurance companies and public and private pension funds.

New corporate bonds may be offered publicly in the open market where competitive bidding takes place or in a private sale to a limited group of investors. Public sales typically account for the largest portion of annual long-term borrowings, but the private market appeals to many smaller firms unable to tap the open market for funds and to companies with unique financing needs. Private sales offer the advantages of speed, lower distribution costs, and financing tailor-made to each company's special cash requirements. Public sales offer the advantage of competition as investment bankers, who underwrite new issues of stocks and bonds, bid against each other to win the right to market a new security issue. The process of competitive bidding tends to result in higher security prices and lower interest costs to corporations in need of funds.

The corporate bond market has faced aggressive competition in recent years from commercial banks making long-term business loans. These so-called term loans (about four years in average length) are generally used to purchase equipment. Most such loans carry floating, rather than fixed, interest rates tied to the prime lending rate—the interest rate levied on loans made to a bank's most creditworthy customers. Commercial banks also are the leading financial institution in extending mortgage loans to business. These loans support the construction of office buildings, shopping centers, and other commercial structures. Banks generally specialize in short-term mortgages that finance the construction of commercial facilities, while long-term commercial mortgage financing is provided mainly by insurance companies, savings banks, and pension funds.

Like all long-term debt markets, the trading of commercial mortgages has been profoundly affected by inflation and record-high interest rates in recent years. Traditionally the commercial mortgage, like the corporate bond, has carried a long maturity. Increasingly, however, institutional lenders are refusing to make long-term commitments of funds on such rigid terms in a volatile economic environment. Participation loans (equity kickers) in which lending institutions receive both interest income and a share of net earnings from business projects are becoming increasingly common. Interest rates on long-term loans frequently are tied to the bank prime rate, yields on high-quality U.S. government or public utility bonds of comparable maturity, or are subject to periodic renegotiation. And, loan maturities have shortened in recent years, placing more and more pressure on business borrowers to refinance their debt and plan more carefully for fluctuating interest rates and credit conditions.

STUDY QUESTIONS

1. Explain what is meant by the phrase, "the financial markets are a supplemental funds source for business." What factors appear to affect the volume of business fund-raising from the money and capital markets?

2. List the principal external sources of business working capital. Of long-term business investment funds. What factors influence which of these various funds sources a business firm will draw upon?

3. Carefully define each of the following terms:
   a. Indenture.
   b. Trustee.
   c. Term bond.
   d. Call privilege.
   e. Sinking fund.
   f. Refunding provision.
   g. Debenture.
   h. Subordinated debenture.
   i. Mortgage bond.
   j. Collateral trust bond.
   k. Income bond.
   l. Equipment trust certificate.
   m. Convertible bond.
   n. Industrial development bond.
   o. Pollution control bond.

4. Explain how the true cost of a corporate bond to the issuing company may be determined.

5. Who are the principal investors in corporate bonds and notes? Why?

6. Describe the role of investment bankers in the corporate bond market. What are the principal risks encountered by these firms? Discuss the factors that must be considered in pricing a new bond issue.

7. What is a *private placement?* Who buys privately placed bonds and why? What are the principal advantages to the borrower in a private placement of securities?

8. What is a leveraged buyout? Junk bonds? What are the dangers associated with these practices?

9. Provide a definition for each of the following terms:
   a. Term loan.
   b. Floating rate.
   c. Prime rate.
   d. Revolving credit.
   e. Standby arrangement.
   f. Compensating balance.

10. For what purposes are commercial mortgages issued? What changes have occurred recently in the terms on commercial mortgages? What is an *equity kicker?*

11. Carefully explain the term *indexing.* Why is this device necessary in today's economy?

PROBLEMS

1. A corporation sells $5,000 par value bonds at par in the open market, bearing an 8 percent coupon rate. Costs of marketing the issue, including dealer's commission, amounted to $200 per bond. If the bonds are due to mature in 15 years, what is their before-tax cost to the corporation? If the issuing company is in the 46 percent tax bracket, what is the bonds' after-tax cost to the firm?

2. A corporation borrows $5 million from a bank at a 12 percent prime rate. If the bank requires the company to hold 15 percent of the amount of the loan on deposit as a compensating balance, what is the effective rate of interest on the loan?

3. A bank quotes one of its corporate customers a loan at prime plus 4 percentage points when prime is 12 percent. Another bank, posting the same prime rate, quotes this same customer a loan at 1¼ times prime. Which loan would you recommend the corporation take?

   Suppose both loans quoted above carry floating rates. Prime increases to 16 percent. Which loan is the better deal? Which would be the better deal if prime rises to 18 percent? Explain what is happening here.

SELECTED REFERENCES

Arak, Marcell; A. Steven Englander; and Eric M. P. Tong. "Credit Cycles and the Pricing of the Prime Rate." *Quarterly Review*, Federal Reserve Bank of New York, Summer 1983, pp. 12–18.

Block, Earnest. "Pricing a Corporate Bond Issue: A Look behind the Scenes." *Monthly Review*, Federal Reserve Bank of New York, October 1961.

Brady, Thomas F. "Changes in Loan Pricing and Business Lending at Commercial Banks." *Federal Reserve Bulletin*, January 1985, pp. 1–13.

Brimmer, Andrew F. "Credit Conditions and Price Determination in the Corporate Bond Market." *Journal of Finance*, September 1960, pp. 364–70.

Budzeika, George. "Lending to Business by New York City Banks." *The Bulletin*, New York University, September 1971.

Crane, Dwight B., and William L. White. "Who Benefits from a Floating Prime Rate?" *Harvard Business Review*, January–February 1972, pp. 121–29.

Lanza, John W. "Criticism of the Prime Rate." *Journal of Commercial Bank Lending*, February 1973, pp. 48–58.

Mitchell, Karlyn. "Trends in Corporation Finance." *Economic Review,* Federal Reserve Bank of Kansas City, March 1983, pp. 3–15.

Moran, Michael. "Recent Financing Activity of Nonfinancial Corporations." *Federal Reserve Bulletin,* May 1984, pp. 401–10.

Rea, John D. "The Yield Spread between Newly Issued and Seasoned Corporation Bonds." *Monthly Review,* Federal Reserve Bank of Kansas City, June 1974, pp. 3–9.

Silver, Andrew. "Original Issue Deep Discount Bonds." *Quarterly Review,* Federal Reserve Bank of New York, Winter 1981–82, pp. 18–28.

Smith, Clifford W., and Jerold B. Warner. "On Financial Contracting: An Analysis of Bond Covenants." *Journal of Financial Economics,* 7 (1979), pp. 117–61.

Zwick, Burton. "The Market for Corporate Bonds." *Quarterly Review,* Federal Reserve Bank of New York, Autumn 1977, pp. 27–36.

21

Corporate Stock

PURPOSE OF THIS CHAPTER

To examine the characteristics of corporate stock and to explore the different parts of the stock market. Key investor groups and institutions that interact to make the stock market function are also discussed. Particular attention is directed at the role and operations of the organized exchanges and the less formal over-the-counter (OTC) market. The important concept of stock market efficiency is examined from both a theoretical and real-world point of view at the close of the chapter.

KEY TERMS AND CONCEPTS IN THE CHAPTER

calls	fourth market	principals
commission brokers	fundamental analysis	puts
common stock	listed stock	random walk
efficient markets	NASDAQ	specialists
equity	OTC market	stock options
exchanges	par value	technical analysis
floor brokers	preemptive right	third market
floor traders	preferred stock	unified market

In the preceding chapters we have focused exclusively on debt securities and the extension of credit. In this chapter we examine a unique security that is not debt, but equity. It is a certificate of *ownership* in a corporation—a residual claim against both the assets and the earnings of a business firm. Corporate stock grants the investor no promise of return as debt does but only the right to share in the firm's net assets and net earnings, if any.

Corporate stock is unique in one other important respect. All of the securities markets we have discussed to this point are intimately bound up with the process of moving funds from ultimate savers to ultimate borrowers in order to support investment and economic growth. In the stock market, however, the bulk of trading activity involves the buying and selling of securities already issued rather than the exchange of financial claims for new capital. Thus, trading in the stock market, for the most part, is *not* closely linked to the saving and investment process in the economy unless new stock is involved.

Nevertheless, a small portion of trading in corporate shares does involve the sale of new stock to support business investment. Moreover, the stock market has a significant impact on the *expectations* of businesspeople when planning future investment; and, therefore, stock trading indirectly affects employment, growth, and the general health of economy.[1] In this chapter we take a close look at the basic characteristics of corporate stock and the markets where that stock is traded.

CHARACTERISTICS OF CORPORATE STOCK

All corporate stock represents an ownership interest in a corporation, conferring on the holder a number of important rights and privileges

---

[1] One broad index of stock market prices—Standard & Poor's Composite Index—is considered to be a *leading indicator* of subsequent changes in economic conditions, especially of future developments in industrial production, employment, and total spending (GNP). Thus, the stock market often turns in its greatest gains in the deepest part of a recession and turns down before a boom is over. There appear to be several reasons for this. The stock market seems to provide a forecast of business capital spending plans, perhaps reflecting the fact that it captures the expectations of the business community. Stock prices anticipate future changes in corporate profits and, of course, these profits are a major source of capital spending which affects the nation's employment and economic growth. In addition, stock prices affect interest rates, which eventually influence business activity. In fact, there is a high *negative* correlation between interest rates (particularly short-term rates) and stock prices. As interest rates on bonds and other fixed-income securities decline, many investors rapidly switch their funds into the stock market.

as well as risks. In this section we examine the two types of corporate stock issued today—common and preferred shares.

Common Stock

The most important form of corporate stock is *common stock*. Like all forms of equity, common stock represents a *residual* claim against the assets of the issuing firm, entitling the owner to a share in the net earnings of the firm when it is profitable and to a share in the net market value (after all debts are paid) of the company's assets if it is liquidated. By owning common stock the investor is subject to the full risks of ownership, which means that the business may fail or its earnings may fall to unacceptable levels. However, the risks of equity ownership are limited because the stockholder is liable only for the amount of his or her investment of funds.

If a corporation with outstanding shares of common stock is liquidated, the debts of the firm must be paid first from any assets available. The preferred stockholders then receive their contractual share of any remaining funds. The residual, whatever is left, accrues to common stockholders on a pro rata basis. Unlike many debt securities, common stock is generally a registered instrument with the holder's name recorded on the issuing company's books.

The volume of stock that a corporation may issue is limited by the terms of its charter of incorporation. (See Exhibit 21–1 for an announcement of a new stock offering.) Additional shares beyond those authorized by the company's charter may be issued only by amending the charter with the approval of the current stockholders. Some companies have issued large numbers of corporate shares, reflecting not only their need for large amounts of equity capital, but also a desire to broaden their ownership base across millions of shareholders. For example, American Telephone and Telegraph (AT&T) has more than 700 million shares of common stock listed on the New York Stock Exchange.

The *par value* of common stock is an arbitrarily assigned value printed on each stock certificate. Par is usually set low relative to the stock's current market value. In fact, today some stock is issued without any par value. Originally, par was supposed to represent the owner's initial investment per share in the firm. The only real significance of par today is that the firm cannot pay any dividends to stockholders that would reduce the company's net worth per share below the par value of its stock. In addition, in the event of liquidation or bankruptcy, the common stockholders may be liable under some circumstances to creditors of the firm for the difference between par value and the subscription price of the stock.

EXHIBIT 21-1

Example of the Announcement of a New Stock Offering in *The Wall Street Journal*

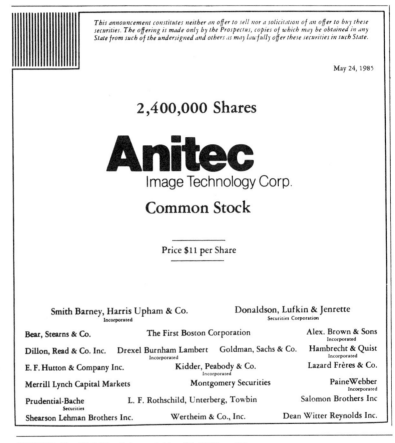

This announcement constitutes neither an offer to sell nor a solicitation of an offer to buy these securities. The offering is made only by the Prospectus, copies of which may be obtained in any State from such of the undersigned and others as may lawfully offer these securities in such State.

May 24, 1985

2,400,000 Shares

Anitec
Image Technology Corp.

Common Stock

Price $11 per Share

Smith Barney, Harris Upham & Co.
Incorporated

Donaldson, Lufkin & Jenrette
Securities Corporation

Bear, Stearns & Co.

The First Boston Corporation

Alex. Brown & Sons
Incorporated

Dillon, Read & Co. Inc.   Drexel Burnham Lambert   Goldman, Sachs & Co.   Hambrecht & Quist
Incorporated   Incorporated

E. F. Hutton & Company Inc.

Kidder, Peabody & Co.
Incorporated

Lazard Frères & Co.

Merrill Lynch Capital Markets

Montgomery Securities

PaineWebber
Incorporated

Prudential-Bache
Securities

L. F. Rothschild, Unterberg, Towbin

Salomon Brothers Inc

Shearson Lehman Brothers Inc.

Wertheim & Co., Inc.

Dean Witter Reynolds Inc.

SOURCE: *The Wall Street Journal,* May 24, 1985, p. 28.

Common stockholders are granted a number of rights when they buy a share of equity in a business corporation. Stock ownership permits them to elect the company's board of directors which, in turn, chooses the firm's officers responsible for day-to-day management of the company. Common shareholders have a *preemptive right* when stock is purchased (unless specifically denied by the firm's charter) which gives the individual shareholder the right to purchase any new voting stock, convertible bonds, or preferred stock issued by the firm in order to maintain his or her *pro rata* share of ownership. For example, if a stockholder holds 5

percent of all shares outstanding and 500 new shares are issued, this
stockholder has the right to subscribe to 25 new shares.[2]

While most common stock grants each stockholder one vote per share,
nonvoting common is also issued occasionally. Some companies issue Class
A common which has voting rights and Class B common which has a
prior claim on earnings but no voting power. The major stock exchanges
do not encourage publicly held firms to issue classified common stock,
but classified shares are used extensively by privately held firms.

A right granted to all common stockholders is the right of access to
the minutes of stockholder meetings and to lists of existing shareholders.
This gives the stockholders some power to reorganize the company if
existing management or the board of directors is performing poorly. Common stockholders may vote on all matters that affect the firm's property
as a whole, such as a merger, liquidation, or the issuance of additional
equity shares. This vote may be cast in person or by revocable proxy
(which is a temporary assignment of voting power and an instruction
on how to vote) granted to a trustee.

Preferred Stock

The other major form of stock issued today is *preferred stock*. Each
share of preferred stock carries a stated annual dividend expressed as a
percent of the stock's par value. For example, if preferred shares carry
a $100 par value with an 8 percent dividend rate, then each preferred
shareholder is entitled to dividends of $8 per year on each share owned,
provided the company declares a dividend. Common stockholders would
receive whatever dividends remain *after* the preferred shareholders receive their stated annual dividend.

Preferred stock occupies the middle ground between debt and equity
securities, including advantages and disadvantages of both forms of raising
long-term funds. Preferred stockholders have a prior claim over the firm's
assets and earnings relative to the claims of common stockholders. However, bondholders and other creditors of the firm must be paid before
either preferred or common stockholders receive anything. Unlike creditors of the firm, preferred stockholders cannot press for bankruptcy proceedings against a company that fails to pay them dividends. Nevertheless,
preferred stock is part of a firm's equity capital and strengthens a firm's
net worth account, allowing it to issue more debt in the future. It also
is a more flexible financing arrangement than debt because dividends

---

[2] Some common stock carries the right of *first refusal,* which means an investor
cannot sell his or her shares to someone other than the current stockholders without
offering those stockholders the shares first. The right of first refusal is generally used
to protect the owners of a small, closely held firm.

may be passed if earnings are inadequate or uncertain and there is no fixed maturity date when the securities must be retired.

Generally, preferred stockholders have no voice or vote in the selection of management unless the corporation "passes" dividends (i.e., fails to pay dividends at the agreed-upon time) for a stipulated period. A frequent provision in corporate charters gives preferred stockholders the right to elect some members of the board of directors if dividends are passed for a full year. Dividends on preferred stock, like those paid on common stock, are not a tax-deductible expense. This makes preferred shares nearly twice as expensive to issue as debt for companies in the top-income bracket. However, IRS regulations specify that 85 percent of the dividends on preferred stock received by a corporate investor are not taxable. This tax-exemption feature makes preferred stock especially attractive to companies seeking to acquire ownership shares in other firms and sometime allows preferred stock to be issued at a lower net interest cost than debt securities. In fact, corporations themselves are the principal buyers of preferred stock issues.

Most preferred stock is *cumulative,* which means that the passing of dividends results in an arrearage which must be paid in full before the common stockholders receive anything. A few preferred shares are *participating,* allowing the holder to share in the residual earnings normally accruing entirely to common stockholders. To illustrate how the participating feature might work, assume that an investor holds 8 percent participating preferred stock with a $100 par value. After the issuing company's board of directors votes to pay the preferred shareholders their stated annual dividend of $8 per share, the board also declares a $20-a-share common stock dividend. If the formula for dividend participation calls for common and preferred shareholders to share equally in any net earnings, then each preferred shareholder will earn an additional $12 to bring its total dividend to $20 per share as well. Not all participating formulas are this generous, however, and most preferred issues are nonparticipating because the participation feature is detrimental to the interests of common stockholders.

Most corporations plan to retire their preferred stock even though it carries no stated maturity. In fact, the bulk of preferred shares issued today have call provisions. When interest rates decline, the issuing company may exercise the call privilege at the price (which usually includes a premium over par) stated in the formal agreement between the firm and its shareholders. A few preferred issues are *convertible* into shares of common stock at the investor's option.[3] The company retires all converted preferred shares and may force conversion by simply exercising the stock's call privilege. New preferred issues today are often accompa-

---

[3] See Chapter 10 for a discussion of convertible preferred stock.

nied by a sinking fund provision whereby funds are gradually accumulated and set aside for eventual retirement of preferred shares. A trustee is appointed (usually a bank trust department) who collects sinking fund payments from the company and periodically calls in preferred shares or occasionally purchases them in the open market. While sinking fund provisions allow the issuing firm to sell preferred stock with lower dividend rates, payments into the fund drain earnings and reduce dividend payments flowing to common stockholders.

From the standpoint of the investor, preferred stock represents an intermediate investment between bonds and common stock. Preferred shares often provide more income than bonds but also carry greater risk. Preferred share prices fluctuate more widely than bond prices for the same change in interest rates. Compared to common stock, preferred shares generally provide less total income (considering both capital gains and dividend income) but are, in turn, less risky. They appeal to the investor who is looking for a favorable, but moderate rate of return. Among major corporations preferred stock experienced a resurgence of interest during the 1970s due to high debt financing costs, the greater flexibility of preferred stock financing over bonds, and pressure on many firms (especially public utilities) to rebuild their equity positions.

STOCK MARKET INVESTORS

Corporate stock is one of the most widely held financial assets in the United States. Only one other financial asset—U.S. government securities—is held by as large and as diverse a group of individuals and institutions as are common and preferred stock. One important source of information on stockholders in the United States is the Federal Reserve Board's Flow of Funds Accounts.[4] Exhibit 21–2 gives the names of major investor groups and their total holdings of common and preferred stock as of year-end 1970, 1980, and 1983. The exhibit makes clear that *households*—individuals and families—are the dominant holders of corporate stock in the United States. At year-end 1983, for example, households held just over two thirds of all corporate shares outstanding. Pension funds—both private and government—were a distant second, holding almost 15 percent of available shares. Foreign investors—principally foreign banks, brokers, trusts, and individuals—ranked third with close to 5 percent of the total. Life insurance companies, mutual funds, and property-casualty insurers each held about 2 to 3 percent of all corporate shares outstanding. The deposit-type financial intermediaries—commercial banks and savings banks—collectively held less than 1 percent of the

---

[4] See Chapter 3 for an explanation of the method of construction and types of information presented in the Flow of Funds Accounts.

EXHIBIT 21–2

Principal Investors in U.S. Corporate Stock ($ billions outstanding at year-end)*

Investor Group	1970 Amount	1970 Percent of Total	1980 Amount	1980 Percent of Total	1983 Amount	1983 Percent of Total
Households	$728.6	80.4%	$1,188.2	72.6%	$1,466.2	68.1%
Rest of the world	27.2	3.0	64.6	3.9	97.2	4.5
Commercial banks	0.1	—	0.1	—	0.1	—
Mutual savings banks	2.8	0.3	4.2	0.3	4.3	0.2
Life insurance companies	15.4	1.7	47.4	2.9	64.9	3.0
Property-casualty insurance companies	13.2	1.5	32.3	2.0	48.1	2.2
Private pension funds	67.1	7.4	209.5	12.8	306.2	14.2
Government pension funds	10.1	1.1	44.3	2.7	89.6	4.2
Mutual funds	39.7	4.4	42.2	2.6	73.5	3.4
Security brokers and dealers	2.0	0.2	2.9	0.2	1.4	0.1
Total market value of holdings	$906.2	100.0%	$1,635.6	100.0%	$2,151.5	100.0%

* Investor holdings valued at market.
SOURCE: Board of Governors of the Federal Reserve System, *Flow of Funds Accounts: Assets and Liabilities Outstanding,* 1960–83.

total. State laws severely limit savings bank investment in corporate stock, while both state and federal laws prohibit commercial banks from purchasing or underwriting corporate stock. Commercial banks do acquire stock pledged as collateral for loans when the borrower defaults, but such holdings usually must be worked out of the bank's portfolio at the earliest opportunity.

While individuals hold a majority of all equity shares outstanding, their interest in corporate stock has ebbed and flowed with market conditions. For example, as shown in Exhibit 21–3, households were *net sellers* of equity shares in every year between 1980 and 1984 except in 1983 when they purchased a modest amount. However, other investor groups took up the slack with large equity purchases. For example, private pension funds made heavy purchases of corporate shares until 1984 ushered in a year of lackluster stock market performance. State and local government pension funds and property-casualty insurers purchased net about $25 billion in equity issues during 1983 and more than $10 billion in 1984.

Fluctuations in the volume of stock purchases have been accompanied by marked changes in the number of shareholders. Periodically, the New York Stock Exchange conducts ownership surveys to determine the number and financial characteristics of stock market investors. Until recently,

EXHIBIT 21–3

Net Purchases of U.S. Corporate Stock by Investor Groups ($ billions at seasonably adjusted rates)

Investor Group	1980	1981	1982	1983	1984†
Households	$–8.0	$–30.6	$–7.8	$ 4.8	$–46.5
Rest of the world	5.4	5.8	3.9	5.4	–2.7
Commercial banks	*	–0.1	*	*	*
Mutual savings banks	–0.5	–0.6	–0.5	0.3	*
Life insurance companies	0.5	2.9	3.4	3.1	*
Private pension funds	17.7	5.4	20.1	15.3	–2.5
State and local government pension funds	5.3	8.3	10.1	22.2	8.4
Property-casualty insurance companies	3.1	2.0	3.0	3.2	2.0
Mutual funds	–1.8	–0.6	3.5	13.7	5.6
Security brokers and dealers	0.7	2.7	–0.5	–0.2	5.9

* Less than $50 million.
† Data for first quarter of the year at seasonally adjusted annual rates.
SOURCE: Board of Governors of the Federal Reserve System, *Flow of Funds Accounts,* February 1985.

the NYSE surveys reported a flight of individual shareowners declined from 30.8 million in 1970 to 25.3 million in 1975—the first reported decrease in individuals' stock ownership since the NYSE ownership surveys began in 1952. However, the number of individual shareholders rose in the late 1970s and early 1980s even as the total dollar volume of household stock investments fell. One reason for the increase in the number of equity investors was a rise in first-time stockholders, paralleling the rapid growth of new households in recent years. At the same time, the market posted strong rallies in 1983 and during the summer months of 1984 and the spring of 1985, though its upward momentum was frequently curtailed by fears of higher interest rates and a weakening economy. Other factors arousing recent investor interest in the stock market include a reduction in federal income, capital gains, and estate taxes and a perception on the part of many investors that common stocks are an effective long-run hedge against inflation.

Several financial institutions have increased their participation in the stock market in recent years. As Exhibit 21–2 shows, institutional shareholders held about 27 percent of all equity shares outstanding in 1983. This compares to only 23 percent in 1980 and 17 percent in 1970. Among the various financial institutions, private and public pension funds have expanded their share of the equities market the most with pension-held shares climbing from about 8 percent of the total value in 1970 to more than 18 percent in 1983. Over the same period, insurance companies increased their holdings from just 3 percent of all equity shares to more than 5 percent. The one financial institution whose share of all equities outstanding fell was mutual funds, traditionally heavy purchasers of common stock. As the stock market behaved erratically during the 1970s and 1980s, many mutual funds shifted their investment strategy, emphasizing bonds and money market securities more heavily in their investment programs. By year-end 1983, mutual funds held only about 3 percent of all equity shares available and ranked fifth in total stock holdings behind households, private pension funds, foreign investors, and government pension funds.

Just as financial institutions as a group have increased their share of total stock ownership, the proportion of daily trading volume in stocks represented by these institutions has also increased. Periodically since 1952, the New York Stock Exchange has conducted a study of the sources of trading volume executed by NYSE member firms in the over-the-counter market and on all U.S. stock exchanges. These periodic studies compare trading activity by dealers and specialists who are members of the NYSE with the volume of trading accounted for by individuals and financial institutions. An NYSE survey in 1976 shows that individuals accounted for 32 percent of the value and 33 percent of the total number of shares traded. Financial institutions, on the other hand, represented 55 percent of the value of all stock traded and slightly less than 45 percent of the total number of shares exchanged. On the New York Stock Exchange itself—the core of the public market—individuals represented 30 percent of the dollar volume of daily trades, while financial institutions represented 70 percent of the daily total.[5] As these figures suggest, professional traders working for financial institutions turn over their stock holdings much faster than individuals. In fact, in 1985 it was estimated that 60 percent of professionally managed stock portfolios turned over in a year's time. The increasing volatility of economic conditions coupled with the stock market's wildly fluctuating performance for most of the past decade has given a definite advantage to financial institutions with greater staying power and technical expertise than normally possessed by the small individual investor.

CHARACTERISTICS OF THE CORPORATE STOCK MARKET

There are two main branches of the market for trading corporate shares. One is the *organized exchanges* which in the United States include

---

[5] See New York Stock Exchange, *Fact Book 1980,* p. 51.

the New York (NYSE) and American (AMEX) exchanges plus regional exchanges, including the Pacific (PSE), Midwest (MSE), Philadelphia (PHLX), Boston (BSE), and Cincinnati (CSE) exchanges. The regional exchanges historically have served to promote trading mainly in securities of interest to investors in their particular region of the nation. Today, however, the regional exchanges have penetrated the national market and rely to a significant degree on transactions in securities listed on both AMEX and the NYSE. All the exchanges today use similar procedures for controlling membership, regulating trading, and recording purchases and sales of stock.

Trading on these exchanges is governed by regulations and formal procedures designed to ensure both competitive pricing of shares and an active market for the stock of the largest, financially stable companies. In contrast, the second branch of the equities market—the over-the-counter (OTC) market—involves trading of stock through brokers operating off the major exchanges. This "over the telephone" market is much more informal and fluid than exchange trading and includes the stocks and bonds of many small-and medium-sized companies and large numbers of banks, mutual funds, and other financial institutions.

The Major Organized Exchanges

Approximately three quarters of all trading in U.S. corporate shares occurs on the organized exchanges. By far the largest and best known of these is the Big Board—the New York Stock Exchange. In recent years the Big Board has accounted for four fifths or more of both the number of shares and total market value of all equities traded on U.S. exchanges. The second largest exchange—the American Stock Exchange (ASE or AMEX)—in most years accounts for about one 10th of all shares traded. The NYSE, AMEX, and the regional exchanges overlap each other in trading and function and therefore are competitive markets for the most actively traded U.S. stocks. For example, more than four fifths of the volume of trading on the regional exchanges is in stocks listed on the New York Stock Exchange. Moreover, in 1978 the Intermarket Trading System (ITS) was set up to electronically link the Big Board with five other exchanges and create additional intermarket competition. Stock brokers and specialists on one exchange thereafter could contact directly traders on the other exchanges in order to find the best prices for their customers.

Each exchange provides a physical location for trading, and trading by member firms must be carried on at that location. On the floor of the NYSE, for example, are 18 counters, each with several windows or *trading posts*. A handful of the more than 1,500 common stock listed and available for trading on the NYSE are traded from each post as prescribed by the Exchange's Board of Governors. The exchanges permit the enforcement of formal trading rules in order to achieve an efficient and speedy allocation of available equity shares.

In order to be eligible for trading on an organized exchange, the stock must be issued by a firm *listed* with the exchange. A substantial number of major U.S. corporations are listed simultaneously on several different exchanges. The listing qualifications demanded by the New York Stock Exchange are the most comprehensive and difficult to fulfill, which serves to limit NYSE trading to stocks issued by the largest and most financially stable companies. The most important listing requirements of the NYSE are summarized in Exhibit 21–4. The basic intent of these rules is to ensure that the listed company has a sufficient volume of shares available to create an active national market for its stock and discloses sufficient data so that interested investors can make informed decisions. Even if a company meets all of the formal listing requirements shown in Exhibit 21–4, its stock must still be approved for admission to the Exchange by the NYSE board of directors, which includes 10 members elected by

EXHIBIT 21–4

Requirements for Listing a Company on the New York Stock Exchange

Minimum Requirements for Initial Listing on the Exchange

A. Demonstrated earning power, with before-tax earnings of at least $2.5 million in the most recent year and at least $2 million during the previous two years.
B. Adequate size of company operations, with net tangible assets of at least $16 million.
C. Adequate minimum market value of publicly held shares, adjusted for market conditions.
D. A sufficient number (currently 1 million) of common shares held by the public.
E. Shares which are held enough to promote an active market—currently at least 2,000 shareholders with 100 or more shares each are required to qualify.

Requirements for Continued Listing

A. Periodic public disclosure of financial condition and earnings.
B. Maintenance of an adequate number of publicly traded shares outstanding. The Exchange would consider suspending or removing a company's security from the trading list if there are fewer than 1,200 round-lot investors, 600,000 or fewer shares in public hands, and the aggregate market value of publicly held shares falls below acceptable limits.

SOURCE: New York Stock Exchange.

firms with seats on the Exchange.[6] Corporations that are successful in listing their stock must make an annual disclosure of their financial condition, limit trading by insiders, publish quarterly earnings reports, and help maintain an active and deep public market for their shares. If trading interest in a particular firm's stock falls off significantly, the firm may be *delisted* from the Exchange. Under some circumstances a firm may be granted "unlisted trading privileges" if its stock has been listed previously on another exchange.

One of the most important advantages claimed for listing on an exchange is that it improves the *liquidity* of a corporation's stock. If a stock is liquid a relatively large volume of shares can be sold at any given time without significantly depressing its price. This feature is of special concern to large institutional investors (such as pension funds) that have come to dominate daily trading in the American equities market because these institutions typically trade in large blocks, rather than a few shares at one time. Allegedly, a corporation can improve the market for its stock by getting it listed on a national securities exchange. However, a recent study by Cooper, Groth, and Avera (1983) suggests that the price behavior of a stock during major up and down movements in the market is far more important in shaping its liquidity than whether or not the stock is listed on an exchange. Exchange listing appeared in their study to be of little benefit, at least from a liquidity standpoint, to corporations with actively traded stock.

Member firms of the exchange are the only ones who may trade in listed securities on the exchange floor, either for their own account or for their customers. Most members actually own "seats" on the exchange and hold claims against the exchange's net assets. The majority of seat owners are directors or partners of brokerage firms, and some of these firms own several seats. Member firms are allowed to sell or lease their seats with the approval of the exchange's governing board.

Member firms fulfill a variety of roles on an exchange. Some act as *floor traders* who buy and sell only for their own account. Floor traders

---

[6] Listing of a company which meets all of the NYSE requirements shown in Exhibit 21–4 is not automatic. The NYSE's board of directors also considers the degree of national interest in the company, whether it is in an expanding industry and is likely to at least retain its relative position, and the stability of the industry involved. Indeed, newly listed companies on the NYSE have been far and few between in recent years. Big Board listings, at 1,564 firms, have remained stable for several years now with many new companies opting to have their shares traded in the informal over-the-counter (OTC) market. Recently the NYSE began a review of its listing rules to see if they have become too restrictive, particularly the prohibitions against a listed company issuing different classes of common stock with different voting rights and the difficulties that newly formed companies (especially in high-tech industries) face in satisfying all listing requirements.

are really speculators whose portfolios turn over rapidly as they drift from post to post on the exchange floor looking for profitable trading opportunities. Other members serve as *commission brokers,* employed by member brokerage firms to represent the orders of their customers on the exchange floor, or *floor brokers,* who are usually individual entrepreneurs carrying out buy and sell orders from other brokers not present on the exchange floor.

A few traders holding exchange seats are *specialists* who trade in one or a limited number of stocks. The 56 specialist firms operating on the New York Stock Exchange act as *both* brokers and dealers, buying and selling for other brokers and for themselves when there is an imbalance between the supply and demand for the stocks in which they specialize. For example, when sell orders pile up for the stocks a specialist firm is responsible for, it will move in to buy some of the offered shares. Specialists help to create orderly and continuous markets and stabilize prices by agreeing to undertake immediate trading to cover unfilled customer orders.[7] However, in return for this service of immediate trading, specialists profit by purchasing stocks from public sellers at discounts from the market price and by selling stocks at a premium above the market price. Finally, a few *odd-lot traders,* typically representing large brokerage firms dealing with the public, also are active on the exchange floor. Odd lots are buy or sell orders involving less than 100 shares, that come primarily from small individual investors. The odd-lot trader typically will purchase 100 or more shares—a *round lot*—and retain any extra shares in his or her portfolio that are not needed by customers.

Stock exchanges are among the oldest American institutions. The New York Stock Exchange, for example, was set up following an agreement among 24 Wall Street brokers in May 1792, just three years after the U.S. Constitution was adopted. The exchanges provide a continuous market centered in an established location for buying and selling equity shares with rigid rules to ensure fairness in the trading process. By bringing together buyers and sellers, the exchanges, at one and the same time, make stock a liquid investment, promote efficient pricing of securities, and make possible the placement of huge amounts of financial capital.

The Informal Over-the-Counter Market

The large majority of securities bought and sold in the United States, especially debt securities, are traded over-the-counter (OTC) and not

---

[7] The specialist function entails considerable risk of failure in an adverse market and that risk has increased recently with the huge volume of market trading and wide price swings. Consequently, most exchanges impose minimum capital requirements on specialist firms and they may be subject to fines if they do not actively trade in the shares for which they are responsible.

on the organized exchanges. The customer places a buy or sell order with a bank, broker, or dealer which is then relayed via telephone, by wire, or by computer terminal to the particular dealer or broker with securities to sell or an order to buy. In this system of electronically linked market-makers each broker or dealer seeks the best possible price on behalf of himself or his customer, and the resulting competition to find the "best deal" brings together traders located hundreds or thousands of miles apart. The prices of actively traded securities respond almost instantly to the changing forces of demand and supply so that security prices constantly hover at or near competitive, market-determined levels.

All money market instruments are traded in the over-the-counter markets as are the large majority of government (federal, state, and local) bonds and corporate bonds. While most common stocks are traded on the exchanges, an estimated one quarter to one third of all stocks are traded OTC. The OTC market is generally preferred by financial institutions, especially commercial banks, bank holding companies, mutual funds, and insurance companies, because in many cases their shares are not actively traded and OTC trading and disclosure rules are less restrictive. The presence of financial institutions tends to give the OTC market a more conservative tone than the exchanges.

Many dealers in the OTC market act as *principals* instead of brokers as on the organized exchanges. That is, they take "positions of risk" by buying securities outright for their own portfolios as well as for retail customers. Several dealers will handle the same stock so that customers can shop around. All prices are determined by negotiation with dealers acquiring securities at *bid* prices and selling them at *asked* prices. The OTC market is regulated by a code of ethics established by the National Association of Security Dealers, a private organization that encourages ethical behavior among its members. Trading firms or their employees who break NASD's regulations may be fined, suspended, or thrown out of the organization.

One of the most important contributions of NASD has been the development of NASDAQ (the National Association of Security Dealers Automated Quotations system). Launched in 1971, NASDAQ displays bid and asked prices for nearly 4,000 OTC-traded securities on video screens connected electronically to a central computer system. All NASD-member firms trading in a particular stock report their bid-ask price quotations immediately to NASDAQ. This nationwide communications network allows dealers, brokers, and their customers to determine instantly the terms currently offered by major securities dealers.[8]

---

[8] NASDAQ is a quotation system designed to report completed transactions rather than a device to carry out actual transactions. To be listed on NASDAQ a minimum number of shares must be publicly held to ensure a relatively continuous market, and

THE THIRD MARKET: TRADING IN LISTED SECURITIES OFF THE EXCHANGE

The market for securities listed on a stock exchange but traded over the counter is known as the *third market*. Broker and dealer firms not members of an organized exchange are active in this market, which deals mainly in NYSE-listed stocks. The original purpose of the third market was to supply large blocks of shares to institutional investors, especially mutual funds, bank trust accounts, and pension funds. These investors engage mainly in *block trades,* defined as transactions involving 1,000 shares or more. Presumably, the largest block traders possess the technical know-how to make informed investment decisions and then carry out transactions without assistance from a stock exchange and the high brokerage commissions that may entail. By trading with third-market broker and dealer firms, who, in effect, compete directly with specialists on the exchanges, a large institutional investor frequently can lower transactions costs and trade securities faster. By offering few peripheral services and trading in large volume, the third-market broker or dealer has little overhead and low average costs per transaction.

It has been alleged in the past that the existence of the third market has had a number of undesirable effects. Prices may be more unstable on the organized exchanges due to the presence of third-market activity, creating more risk for the small investor who buys listed stock. The third market, however, provides additional competition for the organized exchanges, especially the New York Stock Exchange. Moreover, along with the other over-the-counter markets, the third market has been a catalyst in reducing brokerage fees and promoting trading efficiency. For example, the growth of the third market and other OTC trading during the 1970s encouraged the "unbundling" of commissions at many broker and dealer firms to more accurately reflect the true cost of each security trade. Many brokerage firms, especially those active in odd-lot trading, offer their customers an array of peripheral services, such as research on market trends and security credit accounting for purchases and sales, and often the customer pays for these services whether or not he uses them. The largest institutional investors have little need for such services,

---

there must be at least two registered market-makers for the security. In addition, the firm whose securities are included in the NASDAQ system must satisfy NASD's asset-size and equity capital standards. Today NASD maintains three stock lists: (1) a national market system list which reports last-sale price quotes and running volume on all national market-system stocks; (2) a national list; and (3) a supplemental list. The last two lists are generally reported in large-circulation daily newspapers in the form of closing bid and asked prices for their stocks.

however, and seek out brokers and dealers offering their services at minimum cost.

The flight of major stock investors into the third market and into other OTC markets brought about pricing policies in the industry geared more directly to actual services used. As a result, the third market itself declined in importance. While major stockbrokers and dealers used to quote set commissions, the practice of charging fixed brokerage commissions to stock investors ended on the New York Stock Exchange on May 1, 1975. The result was an upward surge in the volume of trading on the organized exchanges; in fact, stock trading on Wall Street multiplied fivefold between 1975 and 1985. In the latter year average daily trading on the New York Stock Exchange exceeded 100 million shares. More recently, numerous "discount" brokerage houses[9] have appeared, leading many institutional customers to abandon the third market and return to more traditional channels for executing their security orders as trading prices continue to decline. About 50 percent of all equity shares traded today on the New York Stock Exchange are part of large-block transactions of at least 10,000 shares apiece.[10]

THE FOURTH MARKET: DIRECT TRADING BETWEEN BUYERS AND SELLERS

Not all the institutions and individuals who buy and sell stock require the services of a broker or dealer. When buyer and seller trade *directly* with each other (usually by telephone or teletype), they become part of the "fourth market" for equity shares. Through a direct exchange of stock, individuals and institutions can escape large brokerage commissions, excess publicity, and security registration requirements. Generally, fourth-market transactions involve large blocks of securities exchanged with the aid of an individual or firm who arranges the terms of trade in return for a small commission or subscription fee. An automated communications system called INSTINET supplies quotations and automatic execution of trades for fourth-market traders. Subscribers to INSTINET

---

[9] *Discount brokerage firms* offer trading services at commission rates as much as 80 percent less than the rates quoted by so-called full-service brokerage firms. The more than 600 discount houses currently operating (many organized by banks) cut costs by not giving investment advice or offering personal account management to their customers. One of the most rapidly growing new financial institutions of the past decade, they represent about one fifth of all commission business today.

[10] Interestingly enough, while stock brokerage commissions charged institutional investors have generally declined in recent years, commissions charged individuals have risen since the end of fixed brokerage commissions in 1975.

can use the automated system to identify likely buyers or sellers of a security and then carry out negotiations over the telephone.

THE DEVELOPING MARKET FOR STOCK OPTIONS

Paralleling the exchange and over-the-counter markets for common and preferred stock is a market for *stock options.* An option is an agreement between two parties granting one party the right (but not the obligation) to purchase an asset from or sell an asset to the other party under specified conditions. The price of an option is known as the *option premium*—the cost to the option buyer of insuring against an adverse change in the price of a stock. In the stock market both *call* and *put* options are sold with the call option generally predominant. Both are designed as techniques to manage the risk of fluctuating security prices and interest rates.

Call Options

A *call* option on stock grants the buyer the right to purchase ("call away") a specified number of shares of a given stock at a specified price up to an expiration date. Call options become attractive when the investor expects the price of a given stock to rise above the price specified in the option contract (known as the "striking price" or "exercise price"). Thus, an option may be available to buy 500 shares of the common stock of Caledonia Manufacturing Company at $6 per share. If the stock rises to a price of $7.50 in the open market, the holder of the option can buy $3,750 worth of stock for only $3,000. Even if the option buyer does not wish to hold the stock, he or she can resell it in the open market and receive a nice short-term gain.

Another potential advantage of options is the amount of financial *leverage* they grant the investor. Less money is required to control a specified number of equity shares than would be necessary if the stock were purchased outright. However, the risk of loss is greater with options; even small changes in the price of a stock can lead to magnified changes in the value of an option. For example, it is not uncommon for an option to double or triple in price even though the price of the stock itself may increase by only 15 to 20 percent. And, of course, losses can double or triple as well. For this reason stock brokers usually prefer options customers who have greater net worth and market knowledge than the average stock market investor.

Trading in options gained widespread interest among U.S. investors early in the 1970s, and many corporations today offer stock options to their employees. In 1973, the Chicago Board Options Exchange initiated trading in options for selected stocks listed on the major exchanges. Today, *listed* or exchange-traded options are popular along with over-the-counter or negotiated options purchased through brokers and dealers. Listed options and their current holders are all recorded on computerized records maintained by the Options Clearing Corporation which also guarantees delivery of the stock in the event the seller defaults. Trading in stock options is by contract with each agreement normally covering 100 shares of stock.

Despite their popularity, call options are not without some serious disadvantages. One of these is the federal tax treatment of gains from trading in options. If the investor exercises his or her option, the difference between the option price and the market price of the stock at time of purchase is taxed as ordinary income, not capital gains, up to a maximum of 50 percent. For example, if an investor in the top-income bracket uses a call option to purchase 500 shares of Caledonia Manufacturing at $6, currently selling for $7.50 in the market, the $750 total paper gain will be subject to a maximum tax of $375 (i.e., 50 percent of the gain). However, if the stock continues to rise in price after it is purchased, any additional gain will be taxed at the more favorable capital gains rate, provided the stock is held for at least a year. Under IRS rules a call option can be valid for up to 10 years.

Puts

The opposite of a call option is known as a *put.* Puts grant the investor the right to *sell* a specified number of equity shares at a set price on or before the expiration date. Unlike a call, the investor in puts hopes the associated stock will *decline* in price so that he or she can sell at a price higher than is currently available in the market. In fact, the more market prices fall, the more money the holder of a put option expects to collect. In this sense, puts are similar to selling a stock *short* (i.e., the sale of borrowed stock) in the hope that its price will fall. However, puts require less capital and usually result in a lower total brokerage commission than short sales of stock. Also, the investor's potential loss is limited to the price of the put plus brokerage commission, regardless of what happens to the price of the underlying stock. Puts often become quite popular in bear markets or near the peak of a bull market when the long-run outlook is eventually for significant declines in stock values. Like calls, puts are traded both over-the-counter and on major organized exchanges.

Traditionally, puts, like call options, have been regarded as a speculative investment because they permit the use of considerable financial leverage. In reality, puts are similar to *insurance* because they enable the investor to place a "floor" under the price of a given stock. Puts may subject the investor to an adverse tax situation in some instances, however, because of their capacity to reduce risk. The IRS may rule in a given situation that the period during which a put was in effect cannot be counted toward establishing long-term capital gains when the associated stock is finally sold.

Straddles

Some investors will combine put and call options to establish a *straddle* on a given stock. A straddle is simply a combination trade in which the investor purchases a put and a call on the same stock, both carrying the same exercise price and maturing on the same date. For example, suppose the stock of Caledonia Manufacturing is selling for $7.50, but the market is so volatile the investor is highly uncertain as to its future direction. To protect against an unexpected move, the investor buys a call option with a strike price of $8 and an $8 put option, each costing $1. Profits will be made if either the call or the put increase in value by more than $2. A rise in the market value of Caledonia's stock will cause the call option to rise in value; a fall in the stock's price will cause the put's value to increase. Sometimes, if the market fluctuates violently, *both* the put and call options will turn out to be profitable, though usually one or the other will expire without being used. An option that expires without being exercised is worthless.

New Options Markets

Until 1982 only options for common stock were traded in organized markets such as the American Stock Exchange or the Chicago Board Options Exchange. However, beginning in 1982 new options markets appeared for *stock indexes* (such as the S&P 100, the Amex Market Value Index, the Value Line Composite Index, and the New York Stock Exchange Composite Index); for U.S. Treasury bills, notes, and bonds; foreign exchange (including Canadian dollars, German marks, Swiss francs, British sterling, and Japanese yen); gold; and for futures contracts for the S&P 500, NYSE Composite Stock Index, Treasury bonds, and gold. Stock index options are based on a basket (collection) of common stocks that are thought to be representative of the whole market. No securities are delivered to settle a stock-index option contract; instead, all transactions must be settled in cash on the one day each month that contracts normally expire. The purpose of a stock-index option is to permit speculative investors to bet on which way the stock market as a whole is likely to go, while simultaneously allowing risk-averse investors to protect against an adverse movement in the stock market as a whole. (See Exhibit 21–5.) Recently *subindex* options have appeared for small baskets of stocks,

EXHIBIT 21–5

Some of the Most Important New Options Markets

Instrument	Options on Physicals	Options on Futures Contracts
Stock indexes	**Chicago Board Options Exchange:** S&P 100 (formerly CBOE 100) S&P 500 S&P integrated international oil group S&P Computer and Business Equipment Index	**Chicago Mercantile Exchange:** S&P 500
	American Stock Exchange: Amex Major Market Index Amex Market Value Index Oil and Gas Index Computer Technology Index	**New York Futures Exchange:** NYSE Composite
	New York Stock Exchange: NYSE Composite Index	
U. S. Government debt	**American Stock Exchange:** Treasury bills Treasury notes	**Chicago Board of Trade:** Treasury bonds
	Chicago Board Options Exchange: Treasury bonds	
Foreign exchange	**Philadelphia Stock Exchange:** Various currencies*	
Precious metals		**The Commodity Exchange:** Gold
		Mid-American Exchange: Gold†

S&P = Standard & Poor's Corporation.
* Canadian dollars, German marks, Japanese yen, Swiss francs, and pound sterling.
† Approved, not traded.
SOURCE: Laurie S. Goodman, "New Options Markets," *Quarterly Review,* Federal Reserve Bank of New York, Autumn 1983, pp. 35–47.

such as the AMEX's computer-technology stock index. Options based on OTC stocks have also been proposed.

While options and futures contracts (the latter discussed in Chapter 17) can both serve as devices for hedging against security price or interest-rate risk, options have certain advantages over futures for hedging purposes, especially when an investor desires to hedge a transaction that may or may not actually occur in the future. The recent rapid growth of new options contracts and markets reflects a desire among many financial market participants to protect themselves against the wide swings in security prices and interest rates that have characterized the money and capital markets in recent years. Options allow a risk-averse investor to shift market risk to someone else willing to bear that risk and hoping to profit from risk-taking.

Options and Stock Prices

In the past two decades the finance theory on how options are priced has developed. The key contribution in the options pricing field was made in 1973 when Black and Scholes developed a model linking options prices to the risk-free interest rate. These researchers observed that an investor could achieve a riskless hedge combining options and stocks as long as the hedge could be modified at anytime to reflect changing market conditions. The price of a call option reaches equilibrium when a hedge's return approaches the risk-free or pure rate of interest. Later, the Black-Scholes model was extended to tracking stock prices. The value of equity shares issued by a corporation with outstanding debt was shown to be dependent on the market value of the company's assets, the variability of asset returns, the remaining term (maturity) of its debt obligations, and the amount of debt outstanding.

THE DEVELOPMENT OF A UNIFIED NATIONAL MARKET FOR STOCK

It is clear from the foregoing discussion that the stock market is fractured into several different parts, each with its own unique collection of brokers and dealers and, in some cases, its own unique collection of customers. However, one of the most significant developments during the 1970s was a movement spurred by government action and industry competition to weld all parts of the equities market together into a single national market. In 1975 Congress passed the Securities Acts Amendments—the most sweeping and potentially significant piece of securities legislation since the Great Depression of the 1930s. The Amendments instructed the Securities and Exchange Commission to "facilitate the establishment of a national market system for securities" in order to further the development of nationwide trading in equities and bring the fresh breath of open competition to stock trading rather than confining most such trading to the floor of an exchange.

While the 1975 Amendments did not specify what the proposed *national market system* would look like or what kinds of securities would be involved, the *intent* of Congress was to ensure that all investors, regardless of their location, would have ready access to information on security prices and could transact business at the best available price, wherever that might be. Moreover, with greater mobility of funds from one exchange to another or between the exchanges and the over-the-counter market, the resulting increase in competition in stock trading might reduce the cost to corporations of raising new equity capital. As the Securities Act Amendments state:

the linking of all markets for qualified securities through communication and data processing facilities will foster efficiency, enhance competition, increase the information available to brokers, dealers, and investors, facilitate the offsetting of investors' orders, and contribute to the best execution of such orders.[11]

Shortly after the Securities Act Amendments became law, the New York Stock Exchange announced that it would begin reporting daily trades of NYSE-listed stocks as they occurred on the principal exchanges. This meant that up-to-the-minute information on the latest stock trades would be reported on a *consolidated* or *composite tape,* available through the familiar stock ticker machines, regardless of which of the major American exchanges handled the transaction. The principal equities markets represented on the consolidated tape would include the NYSE, AMEX, Boston, Cincinnati, Midwest, Pacific, and Philadelphia exchanges. Data from the consolidated tape is used to compile the composite stock price averages that are reported on radio and television news programs and published in daily newspapers.

While the invention of the consolidated tape was an important step in developing a national market system, it only provided investors with an indication of current trends in the market. No information was provided on the best bid and asked prices available nationwide, even for the most actively traded stocks. The Securities and Exchange Commission responded to this need shortly after the Securities Act Amendments were passed by asking each stock exchange to make their quotations more readily available to brokers and dealers everywhere. The first major step in that direction occurred in April 1978 with the development of the Intermarket Trading System (ITS). Through this electronic medium, brokers and specialists could compare bid and ask prices on all the major exchanges for about 700 different stocks through a central computer system that stores and dispenses price information. If the Philadelphia Exchange, for example, is offering a better price for AT&T stock than prevails on the NYSE, a broker or market specialist could immediately place an order through the Philadelphia Exchange without any additional cost. In effect, ITS brought major equities markets into direct price competition with one another for trades in the most popular corporate stocks.

Paralleling the development of ITS, the Cincinnati Stock Exchange created the National Securities Trading System (NSTS). This system permitted automated purchases and sales from the offices of member brokerage firms as well as from the floor of the exchange. Also aiding the unified market's spread was a decision by the Securities and Exchange Commission, issued as Rule 19c-3. This rule stated that any stock not being traded on an organized exchange before April 26, 1979, could be traded off

---

[11] See Section 11a of the Securities Act Amendments of 1975.

the exchange by member firms. Previously, a broker or securities dealer with membership on a particular exchange could not trade listed stocks anywhere but on the floor of that exchange. Under Rule 19c-3, however, exchange members could trade *newly listed* stocks over the counter or on the exchange itself. This SEC decision brought the exchanges and OTC market into direct competition for the trading of *new* stock.

In 1979 and 1980 the National Association of Security Dealers (NASD) moved to promote a national market system by further automating price quotations on over-the-counter stock. Computer terminals with greatly expanded capacity were set up to include a wide array of information on bid and asked prices offered by traders who may be hundreds or thousands of miles distant. At the same time, NASD and representatives of the ITS moved to electronically link quotations and trading on the six major exchanges with OTC quotations and trading.

In February 1980, the Securities and Exchange Commission adopted new regulations aimed at improving the flow of stock-price information to both brokers and investors. Previously, the NASDAQ system for securities traded over the counter had carried only "representative" bid and asked prices. Effective in 1980, however, NASDAQ was required to display on its terminals the highest bid prices and the lowest asked price present in the market. The new rule aided investors in determining what price brokers were actually paying to execute a customer purchase order or what the true sales price is when the customer places his shares on the market. In theory, at least, the rule promoted competition among OTC brokers and made it easier for customers to negotiate low commission rates.

Another SEC rule, which took effect in October 1980, required that the consolidated tape carrying price quotations for stock listed on the major exchanges always include the best price available on *any* stock, regardless of which exchange is quoting that price. Previously, quotation display screens were linked to a system that made price quotations on the NYSE the easiest to retrieve, granting the Big Board a decided advantage over the regional exchanges. Moreover, under another recent SEC rule, price quotes on tape or display screens are considered firm and binding commitments to trade.

The trend toward deregulation of the financial sector began to exert its effects on stock purchases and sales in the 1980s. On March 5, 1982, the SEC put Rule 415—the Shelf Registration Rule—into operation. This allowed many large firms selling *new* corporate stocks and bonds to register an issue with the SEC and then sell securities from the issue at any time during the next two years. *Shelf registration* substantially reduced the cost of offering new stocks and bonds and gave offering companies greater flexibility in selecting when to enter the financial marketplace to sell new securities. There is also evidence that shelf registration increased competition among investment bankers in the underwriting of new security issues, further reducing the cost of preparing and marketing new stocks and bonds.[12]

It should be obvious from the foregoing discussion that substantial progress has been made toward a unified and less regulated equities' market, and a strong commitment on the part of Congress and the regulatory agencies (especially the Securities and Exchange Commission) should ensure further progress toward a true national stock market system. Rapid developments in the technology of information transfer are breaking down the barriers to free and open-stock trading posed by geography, traditional business practices, and outmoded regulations. One indication of this is the recent increase in American stock investors trading in foreign stock in Hong Kong, Singapore, Toronto, Tokyo, London and other world market centers. Satellites and new centralized computer systems coupled with cheaper electronic methods for information transfer and display permit the United States to preserve and integrate existing markets (including the major exchanges), instead of requiring the creation of an entirely new and untried market system. Thus, the new is merging with the old through the medium of electronics.

RANDOM WALK AND EFFICIENT MARKETS

Stock market behavior has figured prominently in the development of modern theories of what determines the market price or value of securities. One of the most popular of modern theories regarding the valuation of stocks and other securities is the *random-walk hypothesis.*

Random walk is a term used in mathematics and statistics to describe a process in which successive elements in a data series are independent of each other and therefore are essentially random and unpredictable. The theory of random walk applied to the valuation of stocks says that the future path of individual stock prices is no more predictable than is the path of a series of random numbers. Each share of stock is assumed to have an *intrinsic value* based on investor expectations of the discounted value of future cash flows generated by that stock. The market price per share is an unbiased estimator of a stock's intrinsic value and reflects the latest information available concerning the issuing company's condition and future prospects. Successive changes in the price of a stock are random fluctuations around that stock's intrinsic value, and these changes are independent of the sequence of price changes which occurred in the past. In effect, stock price changes act as though they were

---

[12] See, for example, the excellent study by Rogowski and Sorensen (1985). In most cases a corporation using shelf registration must have in excess of $150 million of equity shares outstanding.

independent random drawings from an infinite pool of possible prices. Therefore, it is impossible to predict this week's stock price from last week's stock price. Knowledge of the sequence of past price changes prior to the current time period is of little or no help in defining the probability distribution of price changes in any current or future period.[13]

The random-walk notion is not accepted by all stock market analysts. Many analysts still subscribe to chartist or *technical analysis* theories, which assume that the past behavior of a security's price is rich in information concerning the future behavior of that price. Patterns of past price behavior, technical analysts argue, will tend to reoccur in the future. For this reason, careful analysis of stock price averages and the prices of individual shares will reveal important data concerning future price movements.[14] Unfortunately, recent empirical evidence does not indicate any meaningful degree of dependence of future stock price movements on those occurring in the past. Important research studies by Fisher and Lorie (1964), Mandelbrot (1963), Fama (1965), Granger and Morgenstern (1970), and others show that recent changes in stock prices are not significantly related to past price changes. Stock price changes act as though they were independent random drawings.

Another test performed on the technical analysis theory has been to try various mechanical trading or "filter" rules to see if the investor is better off using these rules instead of a simple "buy and hold" strategy. Filter rules usually require the investor to buy if a security's price goes up at least Y percent and sell when the security's price declines by Y percent or more. Research studies by Alexander (1961), Fama and Blume (1966), Chang and Lewellen (1985) and others have found results that generally favor the simple "buy and hold" strategy, especially after brokerage commissions are considered. Average earnings generated by trading rules appear to be no better and often considerably worse than those achieved if the investor randomly selected a group of stocks representative of the market as a whole and held them for his full holding period.[15] Trading rules do not generate above-normal rates of return.

---

[13] Good explanations of the random-walk hypothesis are provided by Cootner (1962) and Fama (1965).

[14] See, for example, Edwards and Magee (1958) and Levy (1968). Technical analysts focus upon a study of the stock market itself and not upon external factors (such as economic conditions) which influence the market. External factors are presumed to be fully reflected in share prices and the volume of stock exchange trading. Thus, all the relevant information for analyzing and predicting stock price behavior is assumed to be provided by the market itself.

[15] Technical analysts are not the only group that argues that stock price behavior is inherently predictable. Another approach, *fundamental analysis,* attempts to forecast returns from holding certain types of securities or from securities of specific firms or

The random-walk notion has been supplemented in recent years by a much broader theory of stock price movements known as the *efficient markets hypothesis.* A market is "efficient" if scarce resources are allocated to their most productive uses. In each case those buyers willing and able to pay the highest prices for each resource must receive the resources they require. In a perfectly efficient securities market the prices of securities will fluctuate randomly around their intrinsic values and are always in equilibrium. Any temporary deviations from equilibrium prices are quickly (indeed, instantly) corrected. Information relevant to the valuation of securities is simultaneously available to all investors at virtually no cost, and existing security prices reflect fully the latest information available. Moreover, security market prices adjust instantaneously to *new* information, and a new set of intrinsic values results, leading some investors to adjust their portfolios. All of this happens almost instantaneously, however, so that market price always equals intrinsic value in a state of continuous equilibrium. As a result, it is impossible in a perfectly efficient market to make economic profits by trading on the information available because, as Davidson and Froyer (1982) observe, an efficient market is one that quickly processes all relevant information.

In recent years the efficient markets hypothesis has been tested on three different levels—each representing a different assumption about how efficient the securities markets really are. In its so-called *weak form,* the efficient markets hypothesis suggests that successive changes in stock prices are independent of each other. In other words, past stock price movements are *not* a reliable guide to future price movements. Technical trading rules which rely upon the past behavior of security prices to guide future security investments are unlikely to generate above-normal rates of return for the investor.

At a somewhat higher level of abstraction, the *semistrong form* of the efficient markets hypothesis declares that all relevant information concerning security prices that is available to the public is fully reflected in the prices actually observed in the marketplace. Thus, security prices hover around their intrinsic equilibrium values which reflect the latest publicly available information. The appearance of new relevant informa-

---

industries. Initially, forecasts are made of general economic conditions and then of supply and demand for the products of certain firms and industries. Complex econometric models may be used that consider such diverse factors as government monetary and fiscal policy, consumer spending and saving, inflation rates, and unemployment. The results provided by economic models are usually supplemented by a detailed analysis of individual firm financial statements and a comparison of key financial ratios for the firm with industrywide ratios. This permits the fundamental analyst to estimate future earnings and evaluate the riskiness of investor returns that are assumed to have a direct bearing on stock prices.

tion causes security prices to rapidly adjust to a new set of intrinsic values and a new equilibrium position.

Finally, the *strong form* of the efficient markets theory says that *all* forms of information—that which is publicly available and that which is available to securities analysts through their private inquiries—will be reflected fully in the existing set of security prices. This strong-form hypothesis suggests that such groups as stock specialists, security brokers and dealers, and corporate insiders who often have access to carefully concealed information cannot earn greater profits than those investors who do not have access to such information.

What does available research evidence have to say about these various levels of market efficiency? How efficient are U.S. securities markets? Research studies generally find that security prices respond promptly to new, publicly available information, including government policy actions.[16] Prices do appear to fluctuate around a base (or intrinsic) value in an essentially random and unbiased manner, as noted in excellent reviews by Fama (1970, 1976). Moreover, studies of the performance of mutual funds, such as the recent project by Chang and Lewellen (1985), and other professional portfolio management firms indicate that these firms do *not* consistently outperform randomly selected portfolios of securities bearing comparable risk. In general, the weak and semistrong forms of the efficient markets hypothesis are validated by recent research findings. However, there is disagreement with a few contrary findings [as noted by Jensen (1978)] and some evidence that traders possessed with inside information (including corporate executives, brokers, and stock specialists) have been able to score impressive gains beyond those available to the average investor. The strong form of the efficient markets hypothesis, therefore, is *not* consistent with *all* the facts for *all* time periods.

Nevertheless, on balance, the American securities markets must be regarded as highly efficient channels for directing the flow of savings into investment. Changes in security prices do appear to conform generally to a random-walk process in which daily price quotations cluster about a security's intrinsic value, reflecting the latest information available. Thus, above-normal profits from using publicly available information as a guide for security trades are most unlikely because that information is already impounded in current security prices.

A "buy and hold" strategy coupled with random selection of securities

---

[16] For example, a recent study by Davidson and Froyer (1982) finds that stock markets are efficient based on the response of stock prices to changes in the growth rate of the U.S. money supply. However, they find some evidence of market inefficiency when money market interest rates are considered. Rising money market rates generally resulted in falling stock prices.

from the entire market's portfolio will, in most cases, yield returns at least as good as those earned by professional traders who rapidly turn over their portfolios. Of course, financial analysts with extraordinary ability to uncover new information and act quickly on it are likely to achieve above-average rates of return, at least for short periods of time. Moreover, individual investors differ in their financial goals and circumstances, and professional advice is frequently required to meet these specialized needs. However, those who use technical analysis, looking for patterns and trends in historical security prices, are unlikely to earn above-average rates of return in a random-walk market.

SUMMARY AND CONCLUSIONS

The market for corporate stock is the best known to the general public and the most widely followed of all securities markets. U.S. corporations have outstanding well over a trillion dollars in equity shares with millions of shares changing hands each day. Prices of the most actively traded stocks are quoted daily in the financial press and watched avidly by millions of investors. Ownership surveys conducted by the New York Stock Exchange indicate there are more than 30 million stockholders in the United States.

Though one of the oldest of the American securities markets, the market for corporate shares even now is in a period of transition. Spurred by congressional legislation and competition within the securities industry, electronic links between the major exchanges and over-the-counter markets today help to ensure that investors, regardless of location, can transact business at competitive prices. Rapid developments in the technology of information transfer are breaking down the barriers to free and open trading posed by geography and outmoded practices and regulations. New centralized computer systems coupled with cheaper electronic methods of data transfer and display have paved the way for integrating existing markets into a new national system, retaining the benefits of experience while allowing ample room for innovation. A true national market for trading in common and preferred stock and stock options is emerging. And the benefits of stronger competition and a freer flow of information to all market participants are not likely to be confined to equities alone. Ultimately, all securities markets, all investors, and the financial system as a whole will benefit from the era of change and innovation through which the American stock market is now passing.

STUDY QUESTIONS

1. In what important ways does the stock market differ from the other securities markets we have dealt with up to this point?

2. What are the essential characteristics of *common stock?* What priority do common stockholders have in the event a corporation is liquidated? What limits the amount of shares a company may issue?

3. What are the principal *rights* of common stockholders?

4. Discuss the nature of *preferred stock.* In what ways are preferred shares similar to "debt" and in what ways are they "equity" securities?

5. Explain the meaning of the following terms associated with preferred stock:
   a. Cumulative.
   b. Participating.
   c. Convertible.
   d. Sinking fund.

6. What are the principal differences between trading in stocks OTC and trading on the organized exchanges? How would you rate these two markets in terms of their advantages for the small investor? The large investor?

7. What is the third market? The fourth market? Can you see any significant benefits from the existence of these two market channels?

8. Explain the possible linkages between economic conditions and the performance of the stock market. Why do stock price movements tend to *lead* changes in general economic conditions?

9. What is *shelf registration?* What benefits does it offer to security issuers and the financial markets?

10. What is the random-walk hypothesis? Does available research evidence tend to support or deny the validity of this hypothesis?

11. Explain the difference between fundamental security analysis and technical analysis. Which approach is likely to yield the best returns to the investor in today's markets, according to recent research findings?

12. What is an *efficient market?* What are the consequences of market efficiency for the behavior of security prices?

13. Recent research concerning the implications of the *efficient markets hypothesis* focuses on three different theories concerning the degree of market efficiency. These are known as the weak, semistrong, and

strong-form hypotheses. Explain the basic differences between these three hypotheses. Which of the three is supported by recent research?

SELECTED REFERENCES

Alexander, S. "Price Movements in Speculative Markets: Trends or Random Walks." *Industrial Management Review,* May 1961, pp. 7–26.

Black, Fischer, and Myron Scholes. "The Pricing of Options and Corporate Liabilities." *Journal of Political Economy,* 81 (1973), pp. 637–59.

Chang, Eric C., and Wilbur G. Lewellen. "An Arbitrage Pricing Approach to Evaluating Mutual Fund Performance." *The Journal of Financial Research,* 8, no. 1 (Spring 1985), pp. 15–30.

Cooper, Kerry; John C. Groth; and William E. Avera. *Liquidity, Exchange Listing, and Common Stock Performance,* Department of Finance, College of Business Administration, Texas A&M University, August 1983.

Cootner, Paul H. "Stock Prices: Random versus Systematic Changes." *Industrial Management Review,* Spring 1962, pp. 24–45.

Davidson, Lawrence S., and Richard T. Froyer. "Monetary Policy and Stock Returns: Are Stock Markets Efficient?" *Review,* Federal Reserve Bank of St. Louis, 64, no. 3 (March 1982), pp. 3–12.

Edwards, R. D., and John Magee, Jr. *Technical Analysis of Stock Trends.* 4th ed. Springfield, Mass.: Magee, 1958.

Fama, Eugene F. "The Behavior of Stock Market Prices." *Journal of Business,* January 1965, pp. 34–105.

———. "Efficient Capital Markets: A Review of Theory and Empirical Work." *Journal of Finance,* 25 (1970), pp. 383–417.

———. *Foundations of Finance.* New York: Basic Books, 1976.

Fama, E. F., and M. E. Blume. "Filter Rules and Stock Market Trading." *Journal of Business,* January 1966, pp. 226–41.

Fisher, L., and J. Lorie. "Rates of Return on Investments in Common Stock: The Year-by-Year Record, 1926–1965." *Journal of Business,* January 1964.

Goodman, Laurie S. "New Options Markets." *Quarterly Review,* Federal Reserve Bank of New York, Autumn 1983, pp. 35–47.

Granger, C. W., and D. Morgenstern. *Predictability of Stock Market Prices.* Lexington, Mass.: Lexington Books, 1970.

Jensen, Michael C. "Some Anomalous Evidence Regarding Market Efficiency." *Journal of Financial Economics,* 6 (1978), pp. 95–101.

Jensen, Michael C., and Clifford W. Smith, Jr. *The Theory of Corporate Finance: An Historical Overview.* Working Paper, University of Rochester, July 1983.

Levy, R. A. *The Relative Strength Concept of Common Stock Forecasting.* Larchmant, N.Y. Investors Intelligence, 1968.

Mandelbrot, Benoit. "The Variation of Certain Speculative Prices." *Journal of Business.* October 1963, pp. 394–419.

Mulhern, John J. "The National Stock Market: Taking Shape." *Business Review,* Federal Reserve Bank of Philadelphia, September–October 1980, pp. 3–11.

New York Stock Exchange. *Fact Book 1980.* New York, 1980.

Rogowski, Robert J., and Eric Sorensen. "Deregulation in Investment Banking: Shelf Registrations, Structure, and Performance." *Financial Management,* Spring 1985, pp. 5–15.

U.S. Securities and Exchange Commission, Directorate of Economic and Policy Research. *Staff Report on the Securities Industry in 1979,* July 1980.

Part Seven

Government in the Financial Markets

22

Central Banking and the Role of the Federal Reserve

PURPOSE OF THIS CHAPTER

To explain the roles and functions of central banks in the economy and financial system with particular focus on the U.S. central bank, the Federal Reserve System (the "Fed"). The chapter discusses the origins of the Fed—the problems in the American economy of the late 19th and early 20th centuries that led to congressional passage of the Federal Reserve Act. The organizational structure of the modern-day Fed is analyzed and its six major roles are discussed with emphasis on its most important role—carrying out monetary policy.

KEY TERMS AND CONCEPTS IN THE CHAPTER

Board of Governors
central bank
dual banking system
Federal Open Market
  Committee
Federal Reserve banks
Federal Reserve
  System
fiscal agent

full employment
Great Depression
lender of last resort
liquidity crisis
member banks
monetary policy
money supply or stock
National Banking Act
no par

payments mechanism
price stability
SOMA manager
stabilization
stable balance-of-
  payments position
sustained economic
  growth
trade-offs

One of the most important financial institutions in any modern economy is the *central bank*. Basically, a central bank is an agency of government which has important public policy functions in monitoring the operation of the nation's financial system and controlling the growth of its money supply. Central banks ordinarily do not deal directly with the public; rather they are "bankers' banks," communicating with commercial banks and securities dealers in carrying out their essential policymaking functions. The central bank of the United States is the *Federal Reserve System*, a creature of Congress charged with issuing currency, regulating the banking system, and taking measures to protect the value of the dollar and promote full employment. In this and the two succeeding chapters we examine in detail the nature and impact of central bank operations and the major problems of policymaking faced by Federal Reserve money managers today.

THE ROLE OF CENTRAL BANKS IN THE ECONOMY

Control of the Money Supply

Central banks, including the Federal Reserve System, perform several important functions in a modern economy. The first and most important of their functions is *control of the nation's money supply*.

What is money? Money is anything that serves as a *medium of exchange* in the purchase of goods and services. Money has another important function, however—serving as a *store of value,* for money is a financial asset that may be used to store purchasing power until it is needed by the owner.[1] If we define money exclusively as a medium of exchange, then the sum of all currency and coin held by the public plus the value of all publicly held checking accounts and other deposits against which drafts may be made (such as NOWs and money market accounts) would constitute the nation's money supply. If we define money as a store of value, on the other hand, then time and savings accounts at commercial banks and other nonbank financial intermediaries, such as credit unions and savings banks, would also be considered important components of the money supply. In Chapter 24 we will note that several different definitions of the money supply may be useful for the purpose of implementing and monitoring central bank policies.

However we define money, the power to regulate its quantity and value was delegated by Congress early in this century to the Federal Reserve System. The Fed has become not only the principal source of currency and coin (pocket money) used by the public, but also the princi-

---

[1] See Chapter 2 for a discussion of the functions performed by money in the economy.

pal government agency responsible for stabilizing the value of the dollar and protecting its integrity in the international financial markets. Why is control of the nation's money supply so important? One reason is that changes in the money supply are closely linked to changes in economic activity. A number of studies in recent years have found a statistically significant relationship between current and lagged changes in the money supply and movements in the nation's gross national product (GNP).[2] The essential implication of these studies is that, if the central bank carefully controls the rate of growth of money, then it can influence the growth rate of the economy as a whole. We will have more to say on this important issue in Chapter 24.

Another important reason for controlling the money supply is that, in the absence of effective controls, money in the form of paper notes or bank deposits could expand virtually without limit. The marginal cost of creating additional units of money is close to zero. Therefore, the banking system, the government, or both are capable of increasing the money supply well beyond the economy's capacity to produce goods and services. Because this action would bring on severe inflation, disrupt the nation's payments mechanism, and eventually bring business activity to a halt, it is not surprising that modern governments have come to rely so heavily on central banks as guardians of the quantity and value of their currencies. The Federal Reserve System enters the financial markets frequently in an attempt to control domestic price inflation in order to protect the purchasing power of the dollar at home, while occasionally intervening in foreign currency markets to protect the dollar abroad.

Stabilizing the Money and Capital Markets

A second vital function of central banking is *stabilization of the money and capital markets.* As we have seen, the financial system must transmit savings to those who require funds for investment so that the economy can grow. If the system of money and capital markets is to work efficiently, however, the public must have confidence in financial institutions and be willing to commit its savings to them. If the financial markets are unruly, with extremely volatile fluctuations in interest rates and security prices, or if financial institutions are prone to frequent collapse, the public's confidence in the financial system might well be lost. The flow of capital funds would dry up, resulting in a drastic slowing in the nation's rate of economic growth and a rise in unemployment. All central banks play a vital role in fostering the mature development of financial markets and in ensuring a stable flow of funds through those markets.

---

[2] See, for example, the studies by Burger (1971), Carlson (1980), Carlson and Hein (1980), and Poole and Lieberman (1972).

Pursuing this objective, the Federal Reserve System will, from time to time, provide funds to major securities dealers when they have difficulty financing their portfolios so that buyers and sellers may easily acquire or sell securities. When the money supply and interest rates rise or fall more rapidly than seems consistent with the nation's economic goals, the Fed will again intervene in the financial markets. The central bank may change the rates it charges banks on direct loans or engage in securities trading in an attempt to moderate changes occurring in the money and capital markets.

Lender of Last Resort

Another essential function of central banks is to serve as a *lender of last resort*. This means providing liquid funds to those financial institutions in need, especially when alternative sources of funds have dried up. For example, as discussed in Chapter 14, the Federal Reserve through its discount window will provide funds to selected deposit-type financial institutions, upon their request, to cover short-term cash deficiencies. As we will soon see, before the Fed was created, one of the weaknesses in the early financial system of the United States was the absence of a lender of last resort to aid financial institutions squeezed by severe liquidity pressures.

Maintaining and Improving the Payments Mechanism

Finally, central banks have a role to play in *maintaining and improving a nation's payments mechanism.* This involves the clearing of checks, providing an adequate supply of currency and coin, wiring funds, and preserving confidence in the value of the fundamental monetary unit. A smoothly functioning and efficient payments mechanism is vital for carrying on business and commerce. If checks cannot be cleared in timely fashion or if the public cannot get the currency and coin that it needs to carry out transactions, business activity will be severely curtailed. The result might well be large-scale unemployment and a decline in both capital investment and the nation's rate of economic growth.

THE GOALS AND CHANNELS OF CENTRAL BANKING

Central banking is *goal oriented.* Since World War II the United States and several other industrialized nations have accepted the premise that government is responsible to its citizens for maintaining high levels of employment, combating inflation, and supporting sustained growth in the economy. This is a relatively new idea since, in earlier periods, governments were assigned a much smaller role in the economic system and much less was expected of them by their citizens. It was felt that "automatic" mechanisms operated within the economy to provide stability and high employment in the long run. One of the bitter lessons of the Great Depression of the 1930s was that these mechanisms can break down and that innovative and skillfully managed government policies may be needed to restore the economy's stability and growth.

Central banking in the United States and in most other nations is directed toward four major goals:

1. Full employment of resources.
2. Reasonable stability in the general price level of all goods and services.
3. Sustained economic growth.
4. A stable balance of payments position for the nation vis-à-vis the rest of the world.

Through its influence over interest rates and the growth of the nation's money supply, the central bank is able to influence the economy's progress toward each of these goals. Achievement of all of these goals simultaneously has proven to be exceedingly difficult, however, as the recent track record of the economy demonstrates. One reason is that the goals often *conflict*. Pursuit of price stability and an improved balance-of-payments position, for example, may require higher interest rates and restricted credit availability—policies which tend to increase unemployment and slow investment spending and growth. Central bank policymaking is a matter of accepting *trade-offs* (compromises) among multiple goals. For example, the central bank can pursue policies leading to a lower rate of inflation and a stronger dollar in international markets but probably at the price of some additional unemployment and slower economic growth in the short run.

Central banking in most Western nations, including the United States, operates principally through the *marketplace*. Modern central banks operate as a balance wheel in promoting and stabilizing the flow of savings from surplus-spending units to deficit-spending units. They try to assure a smooth and orderly flow of funds through the money and capital markets so that adequate financing is available for worthwhile investment projects. This means, among other things, avoiding panic in the market due to sudden shortages of available credit or sharp declines in security prices. However, most of the actions taken by the central bank to promote a smooth flow of funds are carried out through the marketplace rather than by government order. For example, the central bank may encourage interest rates to rise in order to reduce borrowing and spending and combat inflation, but it does not usually allocate credit to particular borrowers. The private sector, working through supply and demand forces in the marketplace, is left to make its own decisions about how much borrowing and spending will take place at the current level of interest rates and who is to receive credit.

The Channels through Which Central Banks Work

Later on we will examine in some detail how the Federal Reserve System affects domestic and international economic conditions. It is useful at this point, however, to give a brief overview of the channels through which modern central banks influence conditions in the economy and financial system. Central bank policy affects the economy as a whole by making:

1. Changes in the cost and availability of credit to businesses, consumers, and governments.
2. Changes in the volume and rate of growth of the nation's money supply.
3. Changes in the wealth of investors as reflected in the market value of their security holdings. (See Figure 22–1.)

The central bank has a number of policy tools at its command that it can use to influence interest rates, the prices of securities, and the level and growth of reserves in the banking system. In the United States the principal policy tools used by the central bank are open-market operations, changes in required reserves held by depository institutions, and changes in the discount rate on central bank loans.[3] In turn, changes in interest rates, security prices, and bank reserves influence the cost and availability of credit. If borrowers find that credit is less available and more expensive to obtain, they are likely to restrain their borrowing and reduce spending for both capital and consumer goods. This results in a slowing in the economy's rate of growth and perhaps a reduction in inflationary pressures. Second, if the central bank can reduce the rate of growth of the nation's money supply, this policy will eventually slow the growth of income and production in the economy due to a reduction in the demand for goods and services. Finally, if the central bank raises interest rates and therefore lowers security prices, this will tend to reduce the market value of the public's holdings of stocks, bonds, and other securities. The result is a decline in the value of investors' wealth, altering

---

[3] Different central banks emphasize different policy tools. For example, the Bank of England relies principally on changes in its basic lending rate to influence economic and financial conditions, while the Bank of Canada uses changes in reserve requirements as its main policy tool. As we will see in Chapter 23, the Federal Reserve System relies mainly on open-market operations to pursue the goals of U.S. economic policy.

FIGURE 22–1

The Channels of Central Bank Policy

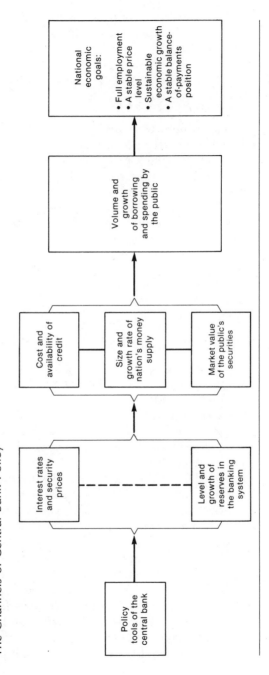

borrowing and spending plans and ultimately influencing employment, prices, and the economy's rate of growth. We will have more to say about these important channels of central bank policy in Chapters 23 and 24.

THE HISTORY OF THE FEDERAL RESERVE SYSTEM

The United States was one of the last major nations in the Western world to charter a central bank. The Bank of England was established in 1694; the Bank of France and the central banks of Switzerland and Italy were founded during the 18th century. Most major industrialized nations early in their history recognized the need for an institution which would provide a measure of stability and control over the growth of money and credit. Public officials in the United States were hesitant to charter a central bank, however, out of fear that it would possess great financial power, would restrict the availability of credit to a growing nation, and might be difficult to control. However, a series of economic and financial crises in the late 19th and early 20th centuries forced Congress to act.

Problems in the Early U.S. Banking System

To fully understand why the Federal Reserve System was created, we must understand the problems that plagued the U.S. financial system throughout much of the nation's early history. Many of these problems were born in the years prior to the Civil War when the states, not the federal government, regulated and controlled the nation's banking system. Unfortunately, with a few notable exceptions, the states did a poor job of regulating the banking industry. Charters for new banks were awarded by state legislatures and were therefore subject to political lobbying and influence peddling. If a new bank's organizers had the right political connections, a charter could be obtained by individuals with little banking experience and with minimal capital invested in the business.

Deposit banking was not as popular then as it is today. Most people preferred hard money (i.e., currency and coin) to deposits. As a result, banks made loans simply by printing and issuing their own paper notes, which circulated as currency. Because few controls existed, there was a tendency to overissue these notes well beyond the financial strength of the bank making the loan. Frequently charters were granted to "wildcat banks" that would issue a large quantity of notes and then disappear. Some banks, promising to redeem their notes in gold or silver coin, would set up "redemption centers" in locations nearly impossible for the public to reach, such as in the middle of a swamp. Needless to say, there was a high failure rate among these poorly capitalized, ill-managed institutions, resulting in substantial losses to their unlucky depositors.

Responding to these problems and also to the tremendous financial strain imposed by the Civil War, Congress passed the National Banking Act in 1863. This act and its subsequent amendments authorized the open establishment of federally licensed commercial banks, subject to regulations imposed by a newly created office, the Comptroller of the Currency—a part of the U.S. Treasury Department. Any group of businesspeople could organize a so-called *national bank*, provided they could show that the new bank would be profitable within a reasonable period of time (usually within three years), meet the minimum equity capital requirements imposed by the Comptroller's office, and not endanger the viability of banks already operating in the local area. Thus, under the provisions of the National Banking Act, the chartering of commercial banks was, in the main, removed from the political sphere and made subject to carefully spelled-out rules. At the same time, Congress attempted to drive state-chartered banks into the national banking system by imposing a 10 percent tax on state bank notes. It was argued that most bankers would prefer the more liberal state regulations and avoid seeking national bank charters unless they were forced to do so.

In order to help finance the Civil War, Congress authorized national banks to issue their own notes as circulating currency. However, these notes had to be collateralized by U.S. government securities. Under the terms of the National Banking Act federally chartered banks could issue notes up to 90 percent of the value of Treasury securities they deposited with the Comptroller of the Currency. The result was to create a money or cash medium under federal control and help pay for the Civil War by creating a demand from banks for U.S. government securities.

Even more important, the National Banking Act created a *dual banking system,* with both federal and state authorities having important regulatory powers over commercial banks. Unfortunately, these authorities were given overlapping powers, and in recent years competition between federal and state bank regulatory agencies has sometimes resulted in actions detrimental to the public interest. Moreover, one of the principal aims of the federal program—to drive out state-chartered banks—was not achieved. The state banks survived only because of the growing popularity of deposit banking which swept the nation in the years following the Civil War. Instead of issuing paper notes, commercial banks increasingly began to make loans by simply creating a deposit on their books in the borrower's name—the practice followed today. Acceptance by the public of deposits instead of notes led to the disappearance of state bank notes, making the federal government's tax on them ineffective. Although the number of state-chartered banks had dwindled to only about 500 out of an estimated bank population of 10,000, state banks made a dramatic comeback late in the 19th century and soon outnumbered national banks. As we saw earlier in Chapter 4, there are about twice as many state-chartered banks as national banks today, though the federally chartered institutions average much larger in size and include most of the nation's largest banking institutions.

Problems Leading to Creation of the Federal Reserve System

Several festering problems (including some traceable to the provisions of the National Banking Act) resulted in the creation of the Federal Reserve System. For one thing, the new national bank notes proved to be unresponsive to the nation's growing need for a money or cash medium. The need for money and credit grew rapidly as the United States became more heavily industrialized and the Midwest and Far West opened up to immigration. Farmers and ranchers in these newly developed areas of the nation demanded an "elastic" supply of money and credit—adequate to their needs at relatively low cost. As we will soon see, the new Federal Reserve System would attempt to deal with this problem by issuing a currency of its own and by closer control over the growth of the nation's supply of money and credit.

As deposit banking and the writing of checks became increasingly popular, another serious problem appeared that also limited the nation's growth. The process of clearing and collecting checks was slow and expensive. Then as now, most checks written by the public were local in character, moving funds from the account of one local customer to that of another. These checks normally are cleared routinely through the local clearinghouse, which is simply a location where representatives of local banks meet daily to exchange bundles of checks drawn on each other's banks. For checks sent outside the local area, however, the check-collection process is more complicated, with some checks passing through several banks before reaching their final destination.

Before the Federal Reserve System was created, many banks, especially smaller, outlying institutions, charged a fee (exchange charge) for the clearing and redemption of checks. This fee was usually calculated as a percentage of the par (or face) value of each check. Banks levying the fee were called *no-par* banks because they refused to honor checks at their full face value. To avoid exchange fees, bankers would route nonlocal checks they received only through banks accepting and redeeming them at par. Often this meant routing a check through scores of banks in distant cities until days or weeks had elapsed before the check was finally cleared. Such a delay was not just annoying but served as an impediment to commercial transactions and the speedy allocation of funds within the financial system. Exchange charges resulted in needless inefficiency and increased the true cost of business transactions far above their nominal cost. A new national check-clearing system was needed which honored checks at par and moved them swiftly between payee and payer. As we will soon see, this responsibility too was given to the Federal Reserve System which insisted that all checks cleared through its system be honored at full face (par) value without exchange charges.

A third problem with the banking and financial system of that time was recurring liquidity crises. Then as now, money and bank reserves tended to concentrate in the nation's leading financial centers, such as New York City, Chicago, Dallas, and San Francisco, where the greatest need for loanable funds existed. Bank reserves flowed into the major cities as smaller banks in outlying areas deposited their reserves with larger banking institutions to earn greater returns. However, when the pressures for agricultural credit increased in rural areas, many country banks were forced to draw upon their reserves in the cities, and the larger city banks, in turn, had to sell securities and call loans in order to come up with the necessary funds. When the reserve demands of country banks were larger than expected, security prices in the nation's major financial centers plummeted due to massive forced selling of bank-held securities. Panic selling by other investors soon followed, leading to chaos in the financial marketplace.

The nation's banking system clearly needed a lender of ready cash to provide liquidity to those banks with heavy cash drains and to protect the stability and smooth functioning of the financial system. A serious financial panic in 1907 finally led to the creation of the Federal Reserve System. In 1908 Congress created a National Monetary Commission to study the financial needs of the nation. The commission's recommendations were forwarded to Congress and ultimately resulted in passage of the Federal Reserve Act, signed into law by President Wilson in December 1913. The Federal Reserve banks opened for business as World War I began in Europe.

The Early Structure of the Federal Reserve System

In the beginning the Federal Reserve System was quite different from the Fed of today. The original Federal Reserve Act reflected a mix of diverse viewpoints—an effort to reconcile competing political and economic interests. There was, on the one hand, great fear that the Fed would have too much control over the nation's financial affairs and operate against the best interests of important segments of American society. For example, small businesses, consumer groups, farmers, and ranchers were concerned that the Fed might pursue restrictive credit policies leading to high interest rates. In addition, it was recognized that the Federal Reserve would become a major financial institution wherever it was located. Any city or state that housed a Federal Reserve bank was likely to become a major financial center.

Responding to these various needs and interest groups, Congress created a truly "decentralized" central bank. Not 1 but 12 Federal Reserve banks were chartered, stretching across the continental United States but located predominantly in the East, where the largest cities and banks were situated. Each Reserve bank was assigned its own district, over which it possessed important regulatory powers. In addition, 24 branch banks were created to better serve local areas and satisfy those not fortunate enough to have a full-fledged Federal Reserve bank in their area. A supervisory board of seven members was set up in Washington, D.C., in an effort to promote a common monetary policy for the nation. In fact, however, the regional Federal Reserve banks possessed the essential monetary tools and made the key policy decisions during the Fed's early history.

Goals and Policy Tools in the Early History of the Federal Reserve System

In order to deal with the economic and financial problems of that day the Federal Reserve Act permitted each regional Reserve bank to open up a discount window where eligible banks could borrow reserves for short periods of time. However, borrowing banks were required to present high-quality, short-term business loans (i.e., commercial paper) to the discount window to secure the loans they needed. The Fed's chief policy tool of the day was the *discount rate* charged on these loans, with each Reserve bank having the authority to set its own discount rate. By varying this rate, the Reserve banks could encourage or discourage commercial banks' propensity to discount commercial paper and borrow reserves from the Fed. In this way, central bankers could promote easy or tight credit conditions and indirectly influence the overall volume of bank loans.

The Federal Reserve banks were given authority to issue their own paper notes to serve as a circulating currency, but these notes had to be 100 percent backed by Fed holdings of commercial paper plus a 40 percent gold reserve. Almost as an afterthought, Congress authorized the Reserve banks to trade U.S. government securities in the open market, known as open-market operations—the Fed's principal policy tool today.

Reserve requirements were imposed on deposits held by member banks of the system, but the Fed could not change these requirements. In contrast to the provisions of the earlier National Banking Act, required reserves had to be held on deposit at the Federal Reserve banks instead of in correspondent balances (deposits) with other commercial banks.

Slowly but surely, economic, financial, and political forces combined to amend the original Federal Reserve Act and remake the character and methods of the central bank. The leading causes of change were war, economic recessions, and more recently, persistent inflation. For example, in order to combat economic recessions, fight wars, and pursue desired spending programs, the U.S. government issued billions of dollars in debt. As the debt began to grow, it seemed only "logical" to permit greater use of U.S. government securities in Federal Reserve operations. Banks were quickly authorized to use government securities as backing for loans from the Fed's discount window. The Fed itself was called upon to play a major role in smoothing and stabilizing the market for U.S. government securities so as to ensure that the Treasury would have little difficulty in refinancing its maturing debt. Government securities were made eligible as collateral for the issue of new Federal Reserve bank notes.

More than any other historical event, however, it was the Great Depression of the 1930s that changed the character of the Federal Reserve. Faced with the collapse of the banking system and unprecedented unemployment—some estimates suggest that a quarter of the nation's labor force was thrown out of work during the 1930s—Congress entrusted the Fed with sweeping monetary powers. Significant changes were made in the central bank's operating structure and lines of authority.

The seven-member Board of Governors in Washington, D.C., became the central administrative and policymaking group for the Fed. From 1933 on, any changes in discount rates charged by the Reserve banks have had to be approved in advance by the Board of Governors. The board was granted authority to set minimum reserve requirements on deposits and maximum interest rates that member banks could pay on those deposits. In order to control speculative buying of stocks, the Reserve Board was empowered to set margin requirements specifying what proportion of a security's market value the investor could borrow against to purchase the security. Recognizing that open-market operations in U.S. government securities were rapidly becoming the Fed's main policy tool, a powerful policymaking body—the Federal Open Market Committee—was created to oversee the conduct of open-market operations. And the majority of voting seats on this committee were given to the Federal Reserve Board. In summary, the Great Depression brought about a *concentration of power* within the Federal Reserve System so that the Fed could pursue a single unified policy and speak with one voice concerning the nation's monetary affairs.

HOW THE FED IS ORGANIZED

The Federal Reserve System today has an organizational structure that resembles a *pyramid*. As Figure 22–2 shows, the apex of that pyramid is the Board of Governors—the Federal Reserve's chief policymaking and administrative group. At the middle level of the pyramid are the Federal Reserve banks, which carry out system policy and provide essential services to banks and other depository financial institutions in their region, and the Federal Open Market Committee. The bottom of the pyramid contains the member banks of the system, which the Fed supervises and regulates, and the manager of the System Open Market Account, who is responsible for buying and selling securities to achieve the goals of Fed monetary policy.

Board of Governors of the Federal Reserve System

The key administrative body within the Federal Reserve System is the Board of Governors. The board consists of seven persons appointed

FIGURE 22–2

How the Federal Reserve System Is Organized

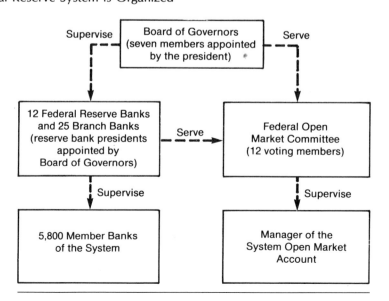

by the president of the United States and confirmed by the Senate for maximum 14-year terms. Terms of office are staggered, with one board member's appointment ending every two years. When a member of the Federal Reserve Board resigns or dies, the president may appoint a new person to complete the remainder of the unexpired term, and that member may be reappointed to a subsequent full term. However, no member who completes a full term can be reappointed to the Board of Governors. The president designates one member of the board as its chairman and another, as vice chairman, and both serve four-year terms in those appointed positions. In selecting new board members the president is required to seek a "fair representation of the financial, agricultural, industrial, and commercial interest and geographical divisions of the country" and may not choose more than one member from any one Federal Reserve district.

The powers of the Federal Reserve Board are extensive. The board sets reserve requirements on deposits held by member banks and other depository institutions subject to its rules,[4] reviews and determines the discount rate charged on loans to depository institutions, sets margin requirements on purchases of securities, and provides leadership in the conduct of open-market operations through the Federal Open Market Committee. Besides its monetary policy functions, the board supervises the activities of the 12 Reserve banks and has supervisory and regulatory control over member banks of the system. It regulates all bank holding companies, foreign banks entering the United States, and the overseas activities of U.S. banks.

In principle, the board is independent of both the Congress and the executive branch of the federal government. This independence is supported by terms of office much longer than the president's term and by the fact that the Fed does not depend on Congress for operating funds. The Federal Reserve supports itself from revenue generated by selling its services (such as clearing checks and shipping currency and coin), making loans through the discount window, and trading securities in the open market. These monies are not retained by the Fed, because it is operated in the public interest and not for profit. All net income left over after expenses, dividends, and minimal allocations to equity reserves is transferred to the U.S. Treasury. For example, in 1984 the Fed reported net earnings of just over $18 billion of which about $16

---

[4] Any depository institution—commercial bank, savings and loan association, mutual savings bank, or credit union—accepting transaction accounts (such as checking accounts, NOWs, or money market deposits) or nonpersonal time deposits (mainly business CDs) must hold legal reserves behind those accounts as specified by the Federal Reserve Board.

billion was paid to the U.S. Treasury, helping to reduce tax collections from the private sector.

The Federal Open Market Committee and Manager of the System Open Market Account

Aside from the Federal Reserve Board, the other key policymaking group within the system is the Federal Open Market Committee (FOMC). It has been called the most important committee of individuals in the United States because its decisions concerning the conduct of monetary policy and the cost and availability of credit affect the lives of millions of people. Membership on the FOMC consists of the seven members of the Federal Reserve Board and the presidents of the Reserve banks. Only members of the board and five of the Reserve bank presidents may vote when a final decision is reached on the future conduct of monetary policy, however. The president of the Federal Reserve Bank of New York is a permanent voting member of the FOMC, while the other 11 Reserve bank presidents rotate the four remaining voting seats among themselves. Each Reserve bank president serves a voting term of one year beginning on March 1.

By tradition, the chairman of the Federal Reserve Board and the president of the New York Federal Reserve bank serve as chairman and vice chairman of the FOMC. The law stipulates that the FOMC will meet in Washington, D.C., at least four times a year. In practice, however, the committee meets at least once every four to six weeks and more frequently if emergencies develop. Between regularly scheduled meetings, telephone conferences may occur, and the members of the FOMC may be asked to cast votes by telephone or telegram. FOMC meetings are *not* open to the public because confidential financial information frequently is discussed and also because the Fed wants to avoid sending "false signals" to the financial marketplace. Only Federal Reserve Board members, selected board staff, the Reserve bank presidents and their aids, and the manager and deputy manager of the System Open Market Account are permitted to attend FOMC meetings.

The name Federal Open Market Committee implies that this committee's sole concern is with the conduct of Federal Reserve open-market operations in securities, the most important policy tool of the system. In fact, the FOMC reviews current economic and financial conditions and considers all aspects and tools of monetary policy at each of its meetings. Once a consensus is reached concerning the appropriate future course for monetary policy, a policy directive is given orally and in writing to the manager of the System Open Market Account (SOMA), who is a vice president of the Federal Reserve Bank of New York. The SOMA manager is told in general terms how open-market operations should be conducted in the weeks ahead, and the FOMC's target growth rates for the nation's money supply.[5] Decisions made by the FOMC and actions of the SOMA manager at the securities trading desk in New York are binding on the entire Federal Reserve System.

The Federal Reserve Banks

When the Federal Reserve System was created in 1913, the nation was divided into 12 districts, with one Reserve bank in each district responsible for supervising and providing services to the other member banks there. Reserve banks were established in the cities of Atlanta, Boston, Chicago, Cleveland, Dallas, Kansas City, Minneapolis, New York, Philadelphia, Richmond, San Francisco, and St. Louis. In addition, 24 branches (later expanded to 25) were created to service particular regions within each of the 12 districts. (Figure 22–2 indicates the boundaries of each Federal Reserve District and the locations of the 12 Reserve banks and their branch offices.) The Reserve banks and their branches are an integral part of the Fed's efforts to supervise and regulate the banking system, ensure a smooth flow of payments, and control the growth of money and credit.

Using computers and high-speed sorting machines, the regional Reserve banks route checks and other cash items drawn on financial institutions in one city and deposited in another. While most checks are not cleared through the Fed, it still handles billions of checks and other paper information items each year. The Federal Reserve maintains a nationwide electronic network (known as Fed wire) to transfer funds and securities in minutes. Approximately 30 automated clearinghouses (ACHs) are operated by the Reserve banks and their branches to handle the direct deposit of payrolls, mortgage payments, and other funds transfer requests by electronic means instead of through pieces of paper. The Reserve banks ship currency and coin to banks and other depository institutions at those times when the public needs more pocket money and store excess currency and coin in their vaults when less pocket money is needed.

The Reserve banks serve as the federal government's *fiscal agent*. This involves keeping the operating financial account of the U.S. Treasury, delivering and redeeming U.S. government securities, and paying interest on securities issued by the Treasury and various federal agencies. The Reserve banks also accept deposits of federal income, excise, and unemployment taxes and honor checks drawn against the Treasury. In addition to serving as the federal government's fiscal agent, the Reserve banks closely supervise the activities of member banks within their districts.

---

[5] See Chapter 23 for an example of a recent FOMC policy directive.

They conduct field examinations of all state-chartered member banks and supervise bank holding companies headquartered in their region of the nation.

The Reserve banks play a significant role in the conduct of the nation's money and credit policy. Each reserve bank houses a research division to study regional economic and financial developments and convey this information to the Board of Governors and to the Federal Open Market Committee. While only 5 of the 12 Reserve bank presidents are voting members of the FOMC, all 12 Reserve bank presidents attend FOMC meetings to report on conditions and events in their region and give their views on the appropriate course for monetary policy. The Reserve banks also administer the discount windows where loans are made to financial institutions in their district, and they therefore have a direct impact on the growth of money and credit.

Each Federal Reserve bank is a corporation chartered by Congress. Officially, the Reserve banks are "owned" 100 percent by the member banks of their districts, who select a majority of each bank's board of directors. In fact, the regional Reserve banks are closely controlled by the Federal Reserve Board, which appoints three of their nine directors and approves appointments of all officers. While under the terms of the original Federal Reserve Act, the Reserve banks could set the discount rate on loans to depository institutions, these rate changes must now be approved by the board in Washington. The regional banks are required to participate in all open-market transactions on behalf of the system. These purchases and sales are centered in the FOMC, but the Reserve banks must provide the securities needed for open-market sales and also take their pro rata share of any purchases that the system makes.

The Member Banks of the Fed's System

The member banks of the Federal Reserve System consist of national banks, that are required to join the system, and state-chartered banks that agree to conform to the Fed's rules. Today, Federal Reserve member banks constitute a minority of all U.S. banks—about 40 percent of the total. As of year-end 1983 there were 4,752 national banks and 1,052 state-chartered banks registered as members of the Federal Reserve System, compared to approximately 9,000 nonmember banks.

Member banks must subscribe to the stock of the Reserve bank in their district in volume equal to 6 percent of their paid-in capital and surplus accounts. However, only half this amount must actually be paid, with the rest payable on call from the system. Member banks are bound by Federal Reserve rules regarding their capital structure, deposits, loans, branch operations, formation of holding companies, and policies regarding the conduct of officers and boards of directors. These banks are subject to supervision and examination by the Federal Reserve at any time, though most banks are examined only once a year. Moreover, member banks must hold reserves behind their deposits at levels specified by the Federal Reserve Board.

A number of important privileges are granted to member banks. Legally, they are "owners" of the Federal Reserve banks because they hold the stock of these institutions and may elect six of their nine directors. A 6 percent annual dividend is paid to member banks on their holdings of Federal Reserve bank stock. Member banks may borrow reserves through the discount window of the Reserve bank in their district, though the majority of these loans cover only a few days.[6]

Member banks may also use the nationwide check-clearing system of the Fed in order to process checks coming from distant cities. However, this is not a particularly distinctive privilege since nonmember financial institutions may also use the Fed's check-clearing facilities, provided they agree to maintain a clearing account with the Reserve bank in the region. An intangible benefit of membership is the prestige that comes from belonging to the Federal Reserve System. Many bankers feel that membership in the system attracts large business deposits and correspondent accounts from smaller banks that otherwise might go elsewhere.

MANY ROLES OF THE FEDERAL RESERVE SYSTEM TODAY

In the course of this chapter we have talked about the many roles that the Federal Reserve must play in the financial system of the United States and how those roles have changed over time. In this final section of the chapter we attempt to pull together all of the Fed's responsibilities and roles to give the reader a more complete view of how the central bank interfaces and interacts with the financial markets and the banking system.

The Clearing and Collection of Checks and Other Means of Payment

As we saw earlier in this chapter, one of the earliest tasks of the Federal Reserve System was to establish a nationwide system for clearing and collecting checks. When a depository institution receives a check drawn on another institution in a distant city, it can route this check directly

---

[6] As a result of the passage of the Monetary Control Act of 1980 any depository institution that holds transaction accounts or nonpersonal time deposits subject to mandatory reserve requirements may borrow from the Fed's discount window on the same terms as member banks.

through the Federal Reserve banks. The Fed credits an account called Deferred Availability Items on behalf of the institution sending in the check and routes that check toward the institution upon which it was drawn for eventual collection. At the end of a specified period, the depository institution sending in the check will receive credit in its legal reserve account for the amount of that check. Eventually, the check reaches the institution on which it was drawn and is deducted from that institution's reserve account.

Sometimes delays in the clearing system result in the creation of *float*. This occurs when a depository institution receives credit for a check deposited with the Federal Reserve before the institution on which the check was drawn actually loses reserves. When there are strikes or bad weather affecting surface or air transportation, the clearing of checks is delayed, and the volume of float rises. Because float is, in effect, an interest-free loan of reserves that banks can use to create credit, the Fed often has to take action through its open-market operations to offset fluctuations in the volume of float.

Issuing Currency and Coin and Providing Other Services

The Fed helps to promote an efficient payments mechanism, not just through the clearing of checks, but also by issuing its own currency in response to public need. Today nearly all the paper money in circulation consists of Federal Reserve notes, issued by all 12 of the Reserve banks and backed mainly by Federal Reserve holdings of government securities. These notes are liabilities of the Federal Reserve bank issuing them. In fact, Federal Reserve notes are a lien against the assets of the Fed, payable to the holder in the event the Reserve banks are ever liquidated. When the public demands more currency, financial institutions request a shipment of new currency and coin from the Federal Reserve bank in the region, which maintains an ample supply in its vault. Payment for the shipment is made simply by charging the legal reserve account of the institution requesting the shipment. In the opposite situation, when depository institutions receive deposits of currency and coin from the public beyond what they wish to hold in their vaults, the surplus is shipped back to the Reserve banks. Depository institutions receive credit for these return shipments through an increase in their legal reserve accounts at the Reserve bank.

Prior to 1981, most Federal Reserve services, including the clearing of checks and shipments of currency and coin, were provided free of charge. However, the Depository Institutions Deregulation Monetary Control Act (DIDMCA) of 1980 required the Fed to publish a set of pricing principles and to assess fees for such services as transportation of currency and coin, coin wrapping, check clearing and collection, wire transfer of funds, the use of Federal Reserve automated clearinghouse facilities, and book entry, safekeeping, and other services connected with the purchase and sale of government securities. All fees set by the Fed are to be reviewed annually and set at levels that, over the long run, simply recover the total costs of providing each service.

Why did Congress order the Fed to switch from free services to a fee basis? One reason was the rapid increase in the number of users of Federal Reserve services. DIDMCA of 1980, for the first time in U.S. history, provided for access by all nonmember depository institutions to the Fed's facilities and services. With so many new financial institutions eligible to receive Fed services, their total cost would soar. Second, Congress wanted to encourage as much competition as possible in the provision of these services so that the Fed would not be the only source of supply. Still another motivating factor was a feared loss of revenue to the Treasury. The Monetary Control Act of 1980, as we will see in the next chapter, gradually lowers deposit reserve requirements for member banks and requires the Federal Reserve to credit depository institutions with interest on their deposit balances held at the Reserve banks.[7] All of these developments together would have substantially reduced the Fed's annual net income, most of which flows to the Treasury, if the central bank had not begun charging for its services.

Maintaining a Sound Banking and Financial System

Another important function of the Federal Reserve System today is to maintain a sound banking and financial system. It contributes to this goal by serving as a lender of last resort, providing reserves to depository institutions through the discount window of each Reserve bank. The window represents a source of funds which can be drawn upon without taking reserves away from other banks, and it helps to avoid a liquidity squeeze brought about by sudden changes in economic and financial conditions. The Fed also promotes a sound banking system by regular examinations of member banks, reviewing the quality and quantity of their assets and capital and making sure that federal and state laws are adhered to.

---

[7] Under a set of procedures announced by the Board of Governors on February 27, 1981, depository institutions will receive "earnings credits" on their Fed balances based on the average federal funds rate each week. However, these credits may only be used to offset charges for Fed services. If the earnings credits exceed a financial institution's bill for Fed services in any given month, it can carry forward the unused credit to cover charges in subsequent months up to one year. All depository institutions must maintain at least a small clearing balance with a Federal Reserve bank in order to obtain these services.

Serving as the Federal Government's Fiscal Agent

The Fed serves as the government's chief *fiscal agent.* In this role, it holds the Treasury's checking account and clears any checks written against that account. The Fed supervises the thousands of Tax and Loan Accounts maintained in banks across the United States which hold the bulk of the Treasury's cash balances until the Treasury needs these monies for spending. The Federal Reserve banks receive bids when new Treasury securities are offered and provide securities to the purchasers. They redeem maturing U.S. government securities as well. In general, the Fed is responsible for maintaining reasonable stability in the government securities market so that any new Treasury security offerings sell quickly and the government raises the amount of money that it needs.

Carrying Out Monetary Policy

The most critical job of the Federal Reserve is to carry out monetary policy. Monetary policy may be defined as the use of various tools by the central bank to control the availability of loanable funds in an effort to achieve national economic goals, such as full employment and reasonable price stability. The policy tools reserved for the Federal Reserve include deposit reserve requirements, discount rates, open-market operations, and margin requirements on purchases of securities. We will examine the Fed's policy tools in detail in Chapter 23.

Providing Information to the Public

Another critical function which the Federal Reserve has performed particularly well in recent years is the provision of information to the public. Each Reserve bank has its own research staff, and the Board of Governors maintains a large staff of economists who follow current economic and financial developments and recommend changes in policy. The Fed makes available on a daily, weekly, and monthly basis an impressive volume of statistical releases, special reports, and studies concerning the financial markets, the nation's money supply, long- and short-term interest rates, the volume and composition of borrowing by the public, and national economic developments. In the international sector, the Federal Reserve supplies, on request, information dealing with developments in foreign currency markets, international loans and capital flows, and the U.S. foreign trade and balance-of-payments position. In addition, as we noted in Chapter 3, the Fed prepares the Flow of Funds Accounts each quarter of the year, providing extensive data on borrowing and lending activities among major sectors of the U.S. economy. This information function is often overlooked in discussions of the Federal Reserve's role within the nation's financial system, but it is one of the more important contributions of the central bank.

SUMMARY AND CONCLUSIONS

In this chapter we have examined the important role played by central banks and, in particular, the Federal Reserve System in the financial system and the economy. Central banks must function to control the nation's money supply, maintain stable conditions in the financial markets, serve as a lender of last resort to aid financial institutions in trouble, and maintain and improve the mechanism for making payments for goods and services. In most industrialized countries, including the United States, central banking is goal oriented, aimed principally at the major economic goals of full employment, reasonable price stability, sustainable economic growth, and a strong and stable balance-of-payments position with the rest of the world. In the Western world, central banks operate mainly through the marketplace, influencing credit conditions but leaving to private borrowers and lenders the basic decisions of whether to create credit, borrow, and spend.

While there is much disagreement today as to how central banks influence the economy through their actions, economists generally argue that these institutions affect the spending, saving, and borrowing decisions of millions of individuals and businesses through at least three interrelated channels. Central bank policies influence the cost and availability of credit, the volume and rate of growth of the money supply, and the market value of securities held by the public. Each of these policy channels ultimately affects the borrowing, consumption, and investment spending decisions of businesses, consumers, and governments.

Central banks around the world use a variety of tools to influence economic and financial decisions. The Bank of Canada, for example, relies heavily on changes in deposit reserve requirements, while the Bank of England uses its discount rate on loans as a major policy tool. In contrast, the Federal Reserve System depends principally on open-market operations—the buying and selling of securities—to achieve its policy objectives. As we will see in the next chapter, the Fed's heavy reliance on open-market operations reflects both the great flexibility of this policy tool and the great breadth and depth of security markets in the United States compared to the limited market systems which exist in the majority of other nations.

Just as the Federal Reserve System's heavy reliance on open-market operations is distinctive among the world's central banks, its organizational structure is also uniquely American. The main administrative body within the system is the Board of Governors, composed of seven persons appointed by the president of the United States and headquartered in Washington, D.C. The Federal Reserve Board appoints officers and staff of the system, sets budgets, and controls such important policy tools as deposit reserve requirements, margin requirements on stock, and changes in the discount rate on loans to banks and other deposit-type financial institutions. However, the board's authority over the future course of economic policy and the implementation of that policy is shared with other departments within the Federal Reserve System.

For example, the Federal Open Market Committee, composed of the seven members of the Federal Reserve Board and five presidents of the Federal Reserve banks, discusses all major policy initiatives by the Fed and closely controls the system's major policy tool—open-market operations. The 12 Federal Reserve banks, located in major financial centers across the United States, determine which banks and other depository financial institutions can borrow from the Fed and on what terms. These regional Reserve banks also supervise banks and bank holding company activities within their districts and provide important services, including the clearing and collection of checks, shipment of currency and coin, transfer of funds by wire, and the safekeeping of securities. Moreover, each of the Reserve banks serves as the federal government's fiscal agent, dispensing and collecting government funds, selling and redeeming government securities, and helping to maintain orderly market conditions so that the federal government can borrow new money and refinance its debt as smoothly as possible.

Each part of the Federal Reserve System, therefore, has a key role to play in the operation of the nation's financial system and the functioning of the economy. In the next two chapters we explore more fully what is generally considered the Federal Reserve's most important job, *monetary policy*—the regulation of money and credit conditions in order to achieve the nation's major economic goals.

STUDY QUESTIONS

1. What functions do central banks perform in a market-oriented economy? Explain why each is important to the efficient functioning of the financial and economic system.

2. What are the principal goals of the Federal Reserve System in its pursuit of monetary policy? To what extent are these goals consistent or inconsistent with each other?

3. What major problems in the late 19th and early 20th centuries led to the creation of the Federal Reserve System? What problems did the National Banking Act solve, and what problems did it create? How did the creation of the Fed help to solve these problems?

4. In what ways did the early Federal Reserve System differ from the Fed of today? Consider in your answer such factors as the goals pursued, structure, and policy tools used.

5. List the principal functions of the Federal Reserve System today and explain why each is important.

6. What are the principle responsibilities assigned to:
    a. The Board of Governors of the Federal Reserve System?
    b. The Federal Open Market Committee?
    c. The Federal Reserve Banks?
    d. The Manager of the System Open Market Account?

SELECTED REFERENCES

Board of Governors of the Federal Reserve System. *The Federal Reserve System—Purposes and Functions.* Washington, D.C., 1974.

Burger, Albert E. *The Money Supply Process.* Belmont, Calif.: Wadsworth, 1971, pp. 52–56.

Carlson, Keith M. "Money, Inflation, and Economic Growth: Some Updated Reduced-Form Results and Their Implications." *Review,* Federal Reserve Bank of St. Louis, April 1980.

Carlson, Keith M., and Scott E. Hein. "Monetary Aggregates as Monetary Indicators." *Review,* Federal Reserve Bank of St. Louis, November 1980.

Federal Reserve Bank of Chicago. "The Depository Institutions Deregulation and Monetary Control Act of 1980." *Economic Perspectives,* September–October 1980, pp. 3–23.

Poole, William, and Charles Lieberman. "Improving Monetary Control." In *Brookings Papers on Economic Activity,* 1972: 2, ed. Arthur M. Okun and George L. Perry. Washington, D.C.: The Brookings Institution, 1972.

23

The Tools of Monetary Policy

PURPOSE OF THIS CHAPTER

To explore the methods and procedures employed by the Federal Reserve System to control the supply of money and credit in the economy. The chapter begins by explaining the nature and importance of the legal reserves of the banking system and how these reserves are linked to the nation's supply of money and credit. An explanation then follows on how each of the Fed's policy tools affects the quantity and rate of growth of legal reserves available to banks for lending and investing. Six Federal Reserve policy tools are examined in the chapter—reserve requirements, the discount rate, open-market operations, moral suasion, deposit-rate ceilings, and margin requirements.

KEY TERMS AND CONCEPTS IN THE CHAPTER

announcement effect
conference call
defensive operations
deposit multiplier
DIDC
discount rate
dynamic operations
excess reserves
general credit controls
legal reserves

margin requirements
monetary base
money multiplier
moral suasion
open-market
 operations
outright transaction
policy directive
policy tools
Regulation Q

repurchase
 agreements
required reserves
reserve requirements
run off
selective credit
 controls
SOMA manager
substitution effect
transactions deposits

As we saw in the preceding chapter, the Federal Reserve System has been given the task of regulating the money and credit system in order to achieve the nation's economic goals. Prominent among these goals are the achievement of full employment, a stable price level, sustainable economic growth, and a strong balance-of-payments position with the rest of the world. As recent experience has demonstrated, these objectives are not easy to achieve and frequently conflict with one another. Still, the central bank has powerful policy tools at its disposal with which to pursue the nation's economic goals. Our purpose in this chapter is to examine the policy tools available to the Federal Reserve in carrying out its task of controlling the nation's supply of money and credit.

RESERVES AND MONEY—TARGETS OF FEDERAL RESERVE POLICY

The principal immediate target of Federal Reserve policy is the *reserves of the banking system,* consisting mainly of deposits held at the Federal Reserve banks plus currency and coin. These reserves are the "raw material" out of which banks and other depository institutions create credit and cause the money supply to grow. And because the growth of the nation's money supply is closely linked to changes in national income, production, prices, and employment, the Fed pays close attention on a daily basis to fluctuations in the quantity of reserves depository institutions have at their disposal. The total supply of reserves can be changed directly by Federal Reserve open-market operations and by making loans to depository institutions through the Fed's discount window. The Fed can also exert a powerful effect on the growth of money and credit by changing the legal reserve requirements applicable to deposits held by commercial banks and other depository institutions.

While the Fed's primary concern is the volume and rate of growth of reserves held by depository institutions, all of its policy tools have an impact on *interest rates* as well. Whenever the supply of reserves is reduced relative to the demand for reserves, interest rates tend to rise as funds are rationed among competing financial institutions. Conversely, an expansion in the supply of reserves usually leads to lower interest rates because of the increased availability of loanable funds. Why do these changes occur? What are the specific links between bank reserves and the money supply? Between reserves and interest rates?

THE COMPOSITION OF RESERVES

To answer these questions, we need to look closely at what makes up the supply of reserves at depository institutions. We recall from Chapter 4 that all depository institutions offering transaction accounts (principally demand deposits and NOWs) and nonpersonal time deposits are required to hold a small percentage of these deposits in an asset account known as *legal reserves.* Legal reserves consist of the amount of deposits each institution keeps with the Federal Reserve bank in its district plus the amount of currency and coin held in its vault.

We noted in Chapter 4 that legal reserves may be divided into two parts: required reserves and excess reserves. In particular,

$$\text{Total legal reserves} = \text{Required reserves} + \text{Excess reserves}$$
$$= \text{Deposits at the Federal Reserve banks}$$
$$+ \text{ Vault cash held on the premises of}$$
$$\text{depository institutions} \quad (23\text{--}1)$$

Required reserves are those holdings of cash and deposits at the Fed that a depository institution must hold in order to back the public's deposits or face a legal penalty. *Excess reserves* consist of cash and Fed deposits owned by depository institutions that are not needed to back the public's deposits and may be used to make loans, purchase securities, repay debts, or serve other purposes. Because legal reserve assets earn little or no income, most depository institutions try to keep their excess reserves close to zero. For example, the largest commercial banks today frequently run reserve deficits and must borrow additional legal reserves in the money market to avoid costly penalties.

The Deposit Multiplier

The distinction between excess and required reserves is important because it plays a key role in the growth of money and credit in the economy. As we observed in Chapter 4, depository institutions offering checkable deposits have the unique ability to create and destroy deposits—which are the bulk of the nation's money supply—at the stroke of a pen. While an individual depository institution cannot create more deposit money than the volume of excess reserves it holds, the banking system as a whole can *create* a multiple amount of deposit money from any given injection of reserves by using excess reserves to make loans and purchase securities.

How much deposit money can the banking system create if it has excess reserves available? The banking system's deposit-creating potential can be estimated using a concept known as the *deposit multiplier,* or coefficient of deposit expansion. The deposit multiplier indicates how many dollars of deposits (and loans) will result from any given injection of new excess reserves into the system. If we assume the existence of a very simple financial system in which the public makes all of its payments by check and does not convert any checkbook (demand deposit) money into thrift deposits, and where depository institutions do not wish to hold any excess reserve but rather loan out immediately all funds received, then:

The transaction deposit multiplier, or coefficient of expansion

$$= \frac{1}{\text{Reserve requirement on transaction deposits}} \qquad (23\text{--}2)$$

For example, if the Federal Reserve insists that depository institutions keep \$0.12 in required reserves for each new dollar of demand deposits and other transaction deposits they receive, then the deposit multiplier must be 1/0.12, or 8.33.

Then how much in new deposit money can the banking system create under these circumstances? If all depository institutions continually make loans with any excess reserves they receive, the maximum amount of new deposits (and loans) that can be created by the entire banking system may be found from the following equation:

Transaction deposit multiplier × Excess reserves

$$= \text{Maximum volume of new deposits and loans} \qquad (23\text{--}3)$$

If banks and other depository institutions receive additional excess reserves in the amount of \$1 million and the reserve requirement behind transaction deposits is 12 percent, we have:

$$1/0.12 \times \$1 \text{ million} = 8.33 \times \$1 \text{ million}$$
$$= \$8.33 \text{ million in new deposits and loans}$$

A *withdrawal* of reserves from depository institutions can work in the opposite direction, destroying deposits and loans. For example, a withdrawal of deposits by the public that causes depository institutions to have a \$1 million deficiency in their required reserves would eventually lead to an \$8.33 million *decline* in deposits, assuming a 12 percent reserve requirement.

Of course, the real world is quite different from the simple deposit expansion model outlined above. Leakages of funds from the banking system greatly reduce the size of the deposit multiplier, so that its actual value is probably somewhat less than two. Among the most important leakages are the public's desire to convert some portion of new checkbook money into pocket money (currency and coin) or into thrift deposits, and the presence of unutilized lending capacity. Banks and other depository institutions may choose to hold substantial excess reserves and not lend out all their excess funds, because they either cannot find enough qualified borrowers or wish to hold a protective "cushion" of reserves.

These various leakages of funds from transaction balances suggest the need for a slightly more complex model of the deposit and loan expansion process. In this model the deposit multiplier would be represented by the following expression:

Transaction deposit multiplier assuming drains of funds
into cash, time and savings deposits, and excess reserves   (23–4)

$$= \frac{1}{RR_D + CASH + EXR + (RR_T \times TIME)}$$

In this instance, RR_D represents the required legal reserve ratio for demand deposits and other transaction accounts, while RR_T is the required legal reserve ratio for time and savings deposits. CASH and TIME represent the amounts of additional currency and coin and time and savings deposits the public wishes to hold for each dollar of new transaction deposits they receive, while EXR stands for the quantity of excess reserves depository institutions desire to hold for precautionary purposes out of each dollar of new transaction deposits. The largest amount of transaction deposits and loans that the banking system can create, assuming all of the above drains of funds occur, would be given by this formula:

$$\frac{1}{RR_D + CASH + EXR + (RR_T \times TIME)} \times \text{Excess reserves}$$

$$= \text{Maximum volume of}$$
$$\text{new deposits and loans}$$

(23–5)

To illustrate the use of the above formula, assume depository institutions have just received an additional $1 million in excess reserves from some source outside the banking system. (One possible source, as we will soon see, is actions by the Federal Reserve lowering legal reserve requirements or buying securities from the public.) We further assume that, for each new dollar of transaction deposits received, the public will convert $0.25 into pocket money (i.e., CASH = 0.25), and $0.60 will be placed in time and savings deposits (i.e., TIME = 0.60). Further, suppose depository institutions elect to hold $0.05 of every new checkable deposit dollar received as excess reserves (i.e., EXR = 0.05) to protect against future contingencies. The reserve requirement on transaction deposits (RR_D) is assumed to be 12 percent and on time and savings deposits (RR_T), 3 percent. Then the maximum amount of new deposits and loans that depository institutions as a group can create with $1 million in excess reserves is calculated as follows:

$$\frac{1}{0.12 + 0.25 + 0.05 + (0.03 \times 0.60)} \times \$1 \text{ million} = \frac{1}{0.438} \times \$1 \text{ million}$$
$$= 2.28 \times \$1 \text{ million}$$
$$= \$2.28 \text{ million in new}$$
$$\text{deposits and loans}$$

Clearly, the deposit multiplier is far smaller when we allow for the conversion of checkable deposits into currency, coin, and thrift deposits and when banks and other depository institutions are unwilling to lend all of their excess reserves. This would appear to be "good news" for the central bank charged with controlling the rate of growth of the nation's money supply and deposits. A numerically small deposit multiplier implies that the banking system will not be able to significantly increase the size of the nation's deposit money supply unless the supply of excess reserves is also greatly increased. But the central bank has a potent influence on the quantity of excess reserves available to financial institutions.

Unfortunately the existence of cash drains, time and savings deposits, and other reserve-absorbing factors, while reducing the size of the deposit multiplier, also makes the forecasting of deposit flows much more difficult. The central bank must be constantly alert to shifts in the public's demand for currency and coin and time and savings deposits and also alert to the changing demands of depository institutions for excess reserves and other liquid assets. If the central bank cannot accurately forecast changes in the public's money and deposit preferences, control of the nation's money supply will be less precise and subject to erratic fluctuations, so that achievement of the nation's economic goals will be much more difficult.

The Money Multiplier

While the concept of the deposit multiplier is useful for some purposes, central bankers are more interested in a related concept known as the *money multiplier*, which defines the relationship between the size of the nation's money supply (including deposits, currency and coin, and other readily spendable funds) and the size of the total reserve base available to depository institutions. The money multiplier is defined as follows:

$$\text{Money multiplier} = \frac{1 + \text{CASH}}{\text{RR}_D + \text{CASH} + \text{EXR} + (\text{RR}_T \times \text{TIME})} \quad (23\text{--}6)$$

The terms CASH, EXR, RR_D, RR_T, and TIME are defined just as they were in the deposit-multiplier formula.

We note that the money multiplier differs from the deposit multiplier only in the addition of CASH— the proportion of new transaction deposits that the public desires to hold in the form of currency and coin—to the numerator of the multiplier ratio. This change is made because currency and coin held by the public also forms an important component of the nation's money supply and must be accounted for in measuring how fast the money supply grows over time. With the rapid spread of coin-operated machines, the amount of currency and coin outstanding actually has been growing faster than the volume of regular checking accounts.

Another important point to note about currency and coin is that fluctuations in the volume held by the public have a direct bearing on the reserves held by depository institutions. For example, when the public wishes to increase its holdings of pocket money—something that routinely occurs around holidays and over weekends—it will write checks against transaction deposits in depository institutions, drawing down both demand accounts and reserves. If the public desires to hold less pocket money, the excess currency and coin typically will be redeposited in transaction accounts, increasing both reserves and demand deposits. Recognizing this important link between currency and bank reserves, economists have developed the concept of the *monetary base*, which is simply the sum of legal reserves plus the amount of currency and coin held by the public.[1] Currency and coin represent almost 70 percent of the monetary base, and legal reserves account for about 30 percent.

Why is the monetary base important? It is one of the principal determinants of the nation's money supply. Specifically,

$$\text{Money multiplier} \times \text{Monetary base} = \text{Money supply} \qquad (23\text{–}7)$$

or,

$$\frac{1 + \text{CASH}}{RR_D + \text{CASH} + \text{EXR} + (RR_T \times \text{TIME})} \times \text{Monetary base} = \text{Money supply}$$

We may use this formula as a device to estimate the size of the money multiplier. For example, in February 1985 the monetary base was $202 billion, while the sum of transaction deposits (e.g., demand deposits,

---

[1] To be more precise, the Federal Reserve defines the monetary base as equal to total reserve balances plus currency and coin held outside the U.S. Treasury, Federal Reserve banks, and the vaults of commercial banks.

NOWs, Super NOWs, and travelers checks) and currency and coin stood at \$570 billion.[2] The money multiplier, therefore, was as follows:

$$\text{Money multiplier} = \frac{\$570 \text{ billion}}{\$202 \text{ billion}} = 2.82$$

On average, each \$1 increase in the monetary base resulted in a rise in the nation's money supply of about \$2.82. This is one reason the monetary base is frequently referred to as *high-powered money;* a change in the base, working through the money multiplier, produces a magnified change in the nation's money supply.

The monetary base-money multiplier relationship identifies for us the most important factors that explain changes in the nation's money supply, and it also helps us to understand how the Federal Reserve can influence the money-supply-creation process. The Fed is one of the principal determinants of the size of the monetary base along with the public and the U.S. Treasury. It can increase or decrease the total supply of reserves to change the size of the base. Alternatively, the Fed may choose merely to *offset* actions taken by the public or the Treasury in order to keep the size of the monetary base unchanged. Finally, the central bank can change the required reserve ratios behind transaction (RR_D) and time (RR_T) deposits, which will affect the magnitude of the money multiplier. Occasionally, when the central bank wishes to exert a potent impact on economic and financial conditions, it will make changes in *both* the monetary base and the money multiplier. In the next section we take a close look at the tools the Federal Reserve System uses to influence the size of the monetary base, the money multiplier, and, ultimately, the nation's money supply.

GENERAL VERSUS SELECTIVE CREDIT CONTROLS

In order to change the volume of reserves available to depository institutions for lending and investing and to influence interest rates in the economy, the Federal Reserve System uses a variety of policy tools. Some of these tools are *general credit controls,* which affect the entire banking and financial system. Included in this list are reserve requirements, the

---

[2] The definition of the money supply used in the formula above is the one labeled M-1 by the Federal Reserve System. Recently, the Fed developed four other money-supply definitions, which we will examine in Chapter 24. Each money-supply concept can be linked directly to the monetary base, provided the components of the money multiplier are altered to reflect the different kinds of deposits or financial assets available to the public under each money-supply definition.

discount rate, and open-market operations. A second set of policy tools may be labeled *selective credit controls* because they affect specific groups or sectors of the financial system. Moral suasion, legal interest-rate ceilings, and margin requirements on the purchase of listed securities are examples of selective credit controls. Of course, *all* the central bank's policy tools have as their ultimate goal the promotion of full employment, sustainable economic growth, price stability, and a stable balance-of-payments position for the United States. Our objective in this section is to look first at the Fed's general credit controls and then at its selective credit controls.

THE GENERAL CREDIT CONTROLS OF THE FED

Reserve Requirements

Since the 1930s the Federal Reserve Board has had the power to vary the amount of required legal reserves that member banks must hold behind deposits they receive from the public. With passage of DIDMCA in 1980, nonmember banks and all nonbank depository financial institutions (including credit unions, mutual savings banks, and savings and loan associations) were required to conform to the deposit reserve requirements set by the Fed. Early in the Fed's history it was felt that the primary purpose of reserve requirements was to safeguard the public's deposits. More recently we have come to realize that their principal use is to give the central bank a powerful tool that can be used in emergency situations. Indeed, reserve requirements are probably the most potent policy tool the Federal Reserve System has at its disposal today. However, changes in reserve requirements are a little-used tool, as we will soon see.

Effects of a Change in Deposit Reserve Requirements.   A change in deposit reserve requirements has at least *three* different effects on the financial system. First of all, it *changes the deposit multiplier* (or coefficient of expansion) which, as we saw earlier in this chapter, affects the amount of deposits and new loans the banking system can create for any given injection of new reserves. A change in reserve requirements also affects the size of the money multiplier, influencing the rate of increase in the nation's money supply. If the Fed increases reserve requirements, the deposit multiplier and the money multiplier are *reduced,* slowing the growth of money, deposits, and loans. On the other hand, a decrease in reserve requirements increases the size of both the

deposit and the money multiplier. In this instance each dollar of additional reserves available to the banking system will lead to accelerated growth in money, deposits, and loans.

A change in reserve requirements also affects the *mix* between excess and required legal reserves. Suppose all depository institutions are fully loaned up, and excess reserves are zero. If reserves requirements are *reduced,* a portion of what were required reserves now becomes excess reserves. Depository institutions will soon convert all or a portion of these newly created excess reserves into loans and investments, expanding the nation's money supply. Similarly, if all institutions are fully loaned up, with zero excess reserves, an *increase* in reserve requirements will mean that some depository institutions will be short required legal reserves. These institutions will be forced to sell securities, cut back on loans, and borrow reserves from other financial institutions in order to meet their reserve requirements. The money supply will grow more slowly and may even decline.

Interest rates also respond to a change in reserve requirements. A move by the Fed toward higher deposit reserve requirements soon leads to higher interest rates, particularly in the money market, as depository institutions scramble to cover any reserve deficiencies. Credit becomes less available and more costly. In contrast, a lowering of reserve requirements tends to bring interest rates down as well. Flush with excess reserves, depository institutions are willing to make more loans at lower interest rates, and fewer institutions will have to sell securities or borrow to meet their reserve requirements.

An illustration. Exhibit 23–1 illustrates the effects of changes in deposit reserve requirements. Suppose depository institutions are required to keep 12 percent of their deposits in legal reserves. Then, $120 of legal reserves will be needed to support each $1,000 in deposits. If there is sufficient demand for loanable funds, institutions will probably loan or invest the remaining $880. Suppose that the Federal Reserve *increases reserve requirements* from 12 to 15 percent. As a result, more legal reserves are necessary to support the same volume of deposits, and institutions have a $30 reserve deficit for each $1,000 of deposits. This deficit may be covered by selling loans or investment securities, borrowing funds, or reducing deposits.

On the other hand, suppose *required reserves are lowered* from 12 to 10 percent. There now are $20 in excess reserves for each $1,000 in deposits, and that excess can be loans or invested, creating new deposits. We should note that *total* legal reserves available to the banking system are *not* affected by changes in reserve requirements. A shift in deposit reserve requirements affects only the *mix* of legal reserves between required and excess, not the total amount of reserves.

EXHIBIT 23–1

Effects of Changes in Reserve Requirements on Deposits, Loans, and Investments

Commercial Bank

With a 12 percent reserve requirement $120 of reserves are needed to support each $1,000 of deposits.

Assets		Liabilities	
Loans and		Deposit	$1,000
investments	$ 880		
Legal reserves	120		
⌈Required	120⌉		
⌊Excess	0⌋		
	$1,000		$1,000

Increase in reserve requirements:

Commercial Bank

If required reserves are increased from 12 to 15 percent, more reserves are needed against the same volume of deposits. Any deficiencies (i.e., negative excess reserves) must be covered by liquidating loans and investments or by borrowing.

Assets		Liabilities	
Legal	$ 120	Deposits	$1,000
⌈Required	150⌉		
⌊Excess	−30⌋		
Loans and			
investments	880		
	$1,000		$1,000

Decrease in reserve requirements:

Commercial Bank

If required reserves are reduced from 12 to 10 percent, excess reserves are created which can be loaned to the public or invested in securities.

Assets		Liabilities	
Legal reserves	$ 120	Deposits	$1,000
⌈Required	100⌉		
⌊Excess	20⌋		
Loans and			
investments	880		
	$1,000		$1,000

Current Levels of Reserve Requirements.

Today deposit reserve requirements are imposed by the Federal Reserve Board on all depository institutions that are either federally insured or eligible to apply for federal insurance, including commercial banks, mutual savings banks, savings and loan associations, and credit unions. Under the terms of DIDMCA of 1980 three types of deposits are subject to legal reserve requirements:

1. *Transaction accounts,* which are those deposits used to make payments by negotiable or transferable instruments and include regular checking accounts, NOW accounts, and any account subject to automatic transfers of funds.

EXHIBIT 23–2

Reserve Requirements of Depository Institutions (percent of deposits)

Type of Deposit and Deposit Interval	Percentage Reserve Requirement	Permissible Statutory Range
Net transaction accounts:		
$0–$29.8 million	3%	3%
Over $29.8 million	12	8–14
Nonpersonal time deposits:		
Original maturity of:		
Less than 1½ years	3	0–9
1½ years or more	0	0–9
Eurocurrency liabilities:		
All types	3	None

Source: Board of Governors of the Federal Reserve System, *Federal Reserve Bulletin,* September 1985, Table 1.15.

2. *Nonpersonal time deposits,* which are interest-bearing time deposits [including savings deposits and money market accounts (MMDAs)] held by businesses and governmental units but not individuals.

3. *Eurocurrency liabilities,* which are borrowings of deposits from banks and branches located outside the United States.

As shown in Exhibit 23–2, the current reserve requirement on transaction accounts of $29.8 million or less is 3 percent, while the net amount of transaction deposits over $29.8 million is subject to a 12 percent reserve requirement.[3] Personal time and savings deposits carry no reserve requirement, but nonpersonal time deposits owned by businesses and units of government currently have a 3 percent required reserve. Average reserve requirements are higher on transaction accounts than on time and savings accounts because transaction balances are considered to be less stable deposits than time and savings deposits.

The largest depository institutions, holding more than $29.8 million

---

[3] The Federal Reserve Board is empowered under the Monetary Control Act to vary reserve requirements on transactions accounts over $29.8 million between 8 and 14 percent. The $29.8 million dividing line (known as the "tranche") is indexed and will change each calendar year by 80 percent of the percentage change in total transaction accounts of all depository institutions during the previous year ended June 30. In addition, the Garn-St Germain Depository Institutions Act of 1982 stipulated that $2 million of reservable liabilities (transaction accounts, nonpersonal time deposits, and Eurocurrency liabilities) of each depository institution be subject to a zero reserve requirement, adjusted each year by 80 percent of the percentage increase in total reservable liabilities.

in net transaction balances, carry the heaviest reserve requirements. This is due to the fact that larger financial institutions hold the deposits of thousands of smaller banks and other deposit-type intermediaries. Moreover, the failure of a large bank or other depository institution can send shock waves through the entire financial system and threaten the economic viability of many other institutions and individuals as well.[4]

Changes in reserve requirements, combined with other monetary policy measures, can be used to carry out major shifts in government economic policy. The reserve requirement tool is exceedingly powerful, however—even a small change affects hundreds of millions of dollars in legal reserves. Moreover, it is an *inflexible* tool. Required reserve ratios cannot be changed frequently because this would disrupt the nation's banking system. Not surprisingly, changes in reserve requirements do not occur very often, averaging about once every two years since World War II.

Changes in the Federal Reserve's Discount Rate

Any depository institution that accepts transaction accounts or nonpersonal time deposits may borrow reserves from the discount window of the Federal Reserve bank in its region. The Fed's Regulation A states, however, that these loans must be a *temporary* source of funds. In fact, Federal Reserve regulations require depository institutions to alternate their borrowings from the discount window with drawings from other sources, such as the federal funds market. Frequent borrowing is discouraged and may be penalized with a higher interest rate.[5]

The discount rate is the percentage interest charge levied against those institutions choosing to borrow from the Fed. The board of directors of each Federal Reserve bank votes to determine what the discount rate should be in its region of the country. However, the Federal Reserve Board in Washington, D.C., must approve the rate charged in each of the 12 Federal Reserve districts. As shown in Exhibit 23–3, the basic rate on short-term loans of reserves in May 1985 was 7½ percent. Depository institutions with marked seasonal movements in deposits could apply for extended credit at rates ranging from 9 to 11 percent, depending on how long funds were to be borrowed.

Borrowing and Repaying Discount-Window Loans.
Depository institutions that borrow regularly at the discount window keep a signed loan authorization form at the Federal Reserve bank in their district and also keep U.S. government securities or other acceptable collat-

---

[4] See, for example, Laurent (1979), Poole (1976), and Woodworth (1972).

[5] For a discussion of the use of the Federal Reserve's discount window as a reserve adjustment device for banks and other depository institutions, see Chapter 14.

EXHIBIT 23–3

The Discount Rates Charged by the Federal Reserve Banks on Loans to
Depository Institutions Effective May 1985 (percent per annum)

Type of Loan	Short-Term Adjustment Credit and Seasonal Credit	Extended Credit*		
		First 60 Days of Borrowing	Next 90 Days of Borrowing	After 150 Days of Borrowing
Discount Rates	7½%	7½%	8½%	9½%

* Credit may be extended for longer periods of time when a particular borrowing institution
needs support due to exceptional circumstances or unforeseen problems.
Source: Board of Governors of the Federal Reserve System, *Federal Reserve Bulletin*,
May 1985, Table 1.14.

eral on deposit there. Therefore, when a loan is needed, the officer responsible for managing the borrowing institution's legal reserve position will merely contact the district Federal Reserve bank and request that the necessary funds be deposited in that institution's reserve account.

In Exhibit 23–4 we illustrate the borrowing process by supposing that a bank has requested a loan of $1 million and the Fed has agreed to make the loan. The borrowing bank receives an increase in its account "Reserves Held at Federal Reserve Bank" of $1 million. At the same

EXHIBIT 23–4

Borrowing and Repaying Loans from the Fed's Discount Window

Borrowing from a Federal Reserve bank:

Federal Reserve Bank					Commercial Bank			
Assets		Liabilities			Assets		Liabilities	
Discounts and advances	$1 million	Bank Reserves	$1 million		Reserves held at Federal Reserve bank	$1 million	Bills payable	$1 million

Repayment of borrowings from the Fed:

Federal Reserve Bank					Commercial Bank			
Assets		Liabilities			Assets		Liabilities	
Discounts and advances	−$1 million	Bank Reserves	−$1 million		Reserves held at Federal Reserve bank	−$1 million	Bills payable	−$1 million

time, the bank's liability account, "Bills Payable," increases by $1 million. On the Federal Reserve bank's balance sheet, the loan shows up as an increase in "Bank Reserves" of $1 million—a liability of the Federal Reserve System—and also as an increase in a Fed asset account, "Discounts and Advances." When the loan is repaid, the transaction is completely reversed.

Quite clearly, borrowings from the Fed's discount window *increase* the total reserves available to the banking system. Repayments of those borrowings cause total reserves to fall.

Effects of a Discount Rate Change.

Effects of a Discount Rate Change.   Most observers today feel that at least three effects follow from a change in the Federal Reserve's discount rate. One is the *cost effect*. An increase in the discount rate means that it is more costly to borrow reserves from the Federal Reserve than to use some other source of funds. Other things equal, loans from the discount window and the total volume of borrowed reserves will decline. Conversely, a lower discount rate should result in an acceleration of borrowing from the Federal Reserve and more reserves flowing into the banking system.

Of course, the strength of the cost effect depends on the *spread* between the discount rate and other money market interest rates. If the Fed's rate remains well below other interest rates even after it is increased, then it would still be cheaper, relatively speaking, to draw upon the Fed for funds. There would be little reduction in loans from the discount window. This has happened frequently in recent years, with the discount rate usually lagging well behind other interest rates in the nation's money market.

A second consequence of changes in the discount rate is called the *substitution effect*. A change in the discount rate usually causes other interest rates to change as well. This is due to the fact that the Federal Reserve is one source of borrowed reserves, but certainly not the only source. An increase in the discount rate, for example, will make borrowing from the Fed less attractive, but borrowing from other sources such as the Federal funds and Eurodollar markets will become relatively more attractive. Banks and other borrowers will shift their attention to these other markets, causing interest rates there to rise as well.

A lowering of the discount rate, on the other hand, frequently causes a downward movement in money market rates and, ultimately, capital market rates. This happens because deposit-type financial institutions will begin borrowing more from the Federal Reserve, reducing the demand for credit in other segments of the financial marketplace.

The final effect of a discount rate change is called the *announcement effect*. The discount rate has a psychological impact on the financial markets because the Fed's rate is widely regarded as an indicator of monetary policy. If, for example, the Federal Reserve increases the discount rate, many observers regard this as a signal that the Fed is pushing for tighter credit conditions. Market participants may respond by reducing their borrowings and curtailing their spending plans.

Unfortunately, the psychological impact of the discount rate may work *against* the Fed as well as for it. It is quite likely, for example, that if the Federal Reserve increases the discount rate, borrowers will respond by accelerating their borrowings in an effort to secure the credit they need before interest rates move even higher. Such an action would thwart the Fed's objective of slowing down the growth of borrowing and spending. Because of the possibility of *negative psychological effects,* the discount rate is changed infrequently and often lags behind rates in the open market. Frequently, the Fed must make a technical adjustment in the rate just to bring it closer into line with other interest rates. Even so, market participants are likely to "read into" discount rate changes either a new policy position or more aggressive pursuit of existing policies by the Fed.

Open-Market Operations

The limitations of the discount-rate and reserve-requirement policy tools have led the Federal Reserve to rely more heavily in recent years upon open-market operations to accomplish its goals. By definition, open-market operations consist of the buying and selling of U.S. government and other securities by the Federal Reserve System to affect the quantity and growth of legal reserves and, ultimately, general credit conditions. Open-market operations are the most flexible policy tool available to the Fed and suitable for "fine tuning" of the financial markets when this is necessary.

Effects of Open-Market Operations on Interest Rates.   The open-market tool has two major effects upon the banking system and credit conditions. First of all, it has an *interest-rate effect* because the Fed usually buys or sells a large quantity (several hundred million dollars worth) of securities in the financial marketplace at any one time. If the Fed is *purchasing* securities, this adds additional demand for these securities in the market, which tends to increase their prices and lower their yields. Conversely, if the Federal Reserve is *selling* securities from its portfolio, this action increases the supply of securities available in the market, tending to depress their prices and raise their yields. The Fed has claimed for many years, however, that its principal objective is not to influence interest rates, but rather to alter the volume of *legal reserves* available to the banking system and, through reserves, the growth of money and credit. Nevertheless, interest-rate effects do follow from open-market operations.

Effects of Open-Market Operations on Reserves.   Most authorities agree, however, that the principal day-to-day effect of open-market operations is to change the level and growth of *legal reserves.* Generally, a Federal Reserve *purchase* of securities will increase the reserves of the banking system and expand its ability to make loans and create deposits, increasing the growth of money and credit. In contrast, a *sale* of securities by the Federal Reserve will decrease the level and growth of reserves and reduce the growth of money and credit. The impact of Federal Reserve open-market operations on the reserve position of banks and other deposit-type institutions is illustrated in Exhibit 23–5.

Fed purchases.   In the top portion of Exhibit 23–5 we assume that the Fed is making *purchases* of U.S. government securities in the open market from either deposit-type financial institutions, which keep their reserve accounts at the Federal Reserve banks, or from other institutions and individuals.[6] In the case of purchases from deposit-type institutions, the Federal Reserve records the acquisition of securities in the system's asset account—U.S. securities—and pays for the securities by increasing the reserve account of the selling institution. Thus, reserves of depository institutions at the Fed rise, while institutional holdings of securities fall by the same amount. Note that *both* total and excess reserves rise in the wake of a Fed purchase, assuming that depository institutions have no reserves deficiencies to begin with. With these extra reserves, additional loans can be made and deposits created that will have an expansionary impact on the availability of credit in the economy.

An expansionary effect also takes place when the Federal Reserve buys securities from an institution or individual other than a deposit-type financial institution. Legal reserves increase, but total deposits—a component of the nation's money supply—increase as well. Deposits rise because the Fed issues a check to pay for the securities it purchases, and that check will be deposited in some financial institution. Excess reserves rise, making possible an expansion of deposits and loans on the part of depository institutions. Note, however, that the rise in excess reserves is *less* in this case than would occur if the Fed bought securities only from institutions which maintain reserve accounts with the Federal Reserve banks. This is due to the fact some of the new legal reserves created by the Fed purchase must be pledged as required reserves behind the newly created deposits. Therefore, Federal Reserve open-market purchases of securities have less of an effect on total credit and deposit expan-

---

[6] In reality, all Fed security transactions are conducted with one or more of approximately three dozen primary dealers in U.S. government securities. However, as we will soon see, the effects of each transaction spread rapidly through the money market, affecting the financial position of many individuals and institutions.

EXHIBIT 23–5

Federal Reserve Open-Market Operations

The Fed Buys Securities

Open-market purchase from a bank or other deposit-type financial institution:

Depository Financial Institution

Assets		Liabilities
U.S. securities	−1,000	
Reserves at Fed	+1,000	

Federal Reserve Bank

Assets		Liabilities	
U.S. securities	+1,000	Reserves	+1,000

Effects: Total and excess legal reserves increase.

Open-market purchase not from a depository financial institution:

Depository Financial Institution

Assets		Liabilities	
Reserves at Fed	+1,000	Deposits	+1,000

Federal Reserve Bank

Assets		Liabilities	
U.S. securities	+1,000	Reserves	+1,000

Effects: Total and excess legal reserves increase. Deposits increase.

The Fed Sells Securities

Open-market sale to a bank or other deposit-type financial institution:

Depository Financial Institution

Assets		Liabilities
U.S. securities	+1,000	
Reserves at Fed	−1,000	

Federal Reserve Bank

Assets		Liabilities	
U.S. securities	−1,000	Reserves	−1,000

Effects: Total and excess legal reserves decrease.

Open-market sale not to a depository financial institution:

Depository Financial Institution

Assets		Liabilities	
Reserves at Fed	−1,000	Deposits	−1,000

Federal Reserve Bank

Assets		Liabilities	
U.S. securities	−1,000	Reserves	−1,000

Effects: Total and excess legal reserves decrease. Deposits decrease.

sion if the Fed's transaction involves only nondeposit financial institutions and individuals.

Fed sales.   Federal Reserve *sales* of securities reduce the growth of reserves, deposits, and loans. As shown in the bottom half of Exhibit 23–5, when the Fed sells U.S. government securities out of its portfolio to a depository financial institution, that institution must pay for those securities by letting the Fed deduct the amount of the purchase from its reserve account. Both total reserves and excess reserves fall. If deposit institutions were fully loaned up with no excess reserves available, the open-market sale would result in a reserve deficiency. Some institutions would be forced to sell loans and securities or borrow funds, reducing deposits and the availability of credit.

The Federal Reserve may also sell securities to an individual or a nondeposit institution. As Exhibit 23–5 reveals, in this instance *both* reserves and deposits fall. Credit becomes less available and usually more expensive.

How Open-Market Operations Are Conducted.   All trading in securities by the Federal Reserve is carried out through the system's Trading Desk, located at the Federal Reserve Bank of New York. The Trading Desk is supervised by the manager of the System Open Market Account (SOMA)—a vice president of the New York Fed. The SOMA manager's activities are, in turn, supervised and directed by the Federal Open Market Committee, which meets periodically in Washington, D.C. All Fed security purchases and sales are made through a select list of primary U.S. government securities dealers who agree to buy or sell in amounts called for by the Trading Desk at the time the Fed wishes to trade. About a dozen of these dealers are commercial banks that have securities departments. The rest—about two dozen—are exclusively dealers in U.S. government and selected private securities.

The policy directive.   How does the manager of SOMA decide whether or not to buy or sell securities in the open market on a given day? The manager is guided, first of all, by a policy directive issued to the Federal Reserve Bank of New York following the conclusion of each meeting of the Federal Open Market Committee (FOMC). The manager of SOMA attends each FOMC meeting and participates in its policy discussions. He or she listens to the views of each member of the Federal Reserve Board and the Reserve bank presidents, who describe economic conditions in their region of the country. The manager also receives the benefit of a presentation by staff economists of the Federal Reserve Board that analyzes current economic and financial developments.

An example of a recent Federal Reserve policy directive to the SOMA manager is shown in Exhibit 23–6. This directive summarizes the Federal Reserve's view of current economic developments, particularly those that

EXHIBIT 23–6

Domestic Policy Directive Issued to the Federal Reserve Bank of New
York Following the Federal Open Market Committee Meeting,
February 12–13, 1985

The information reviewed at this meeting suggests that real GNP expanded at a moderate
pace in the fourth quarter, reflecting some strengthening in late 1984 after several months of
considerably reduced growth, and there was evidence of continued moderate expansion in
early 1985. Total retail sales rose in January at about the same pace as the average for November
and December, while the decline in housing starts appears to have ended. Industrial production
and nonfarm payroll employment increased appreciably in the November–December period and
nonfarm payroll employment rose substantially further in January. The civilian unemployment
rate rose slightly in January to 7.4 percent. Information on business spending suggests less
rapid expansion in outlays for fixed investment, following exceptional growth earlier; businesses
also appear to have made substantial progress in adjusting their inventories. During 1984 broad
measures of prices generally increased at rates close to those recorded in 1983, and the index
of average hourly earnings rose somewhat more slowly.

The foreign exchange value of the dollar against a trade-weighted average of major foreign
currencies has continued to appreciate strongly since mid-December. After the announcement
on January 17 by the G-5 Ministers of Finance and Central Bank Governors regarding coordinated
intervention in exchange markets, and subsequent operations, the dollar's rise moderated
somewhat. The merchandise trade deficit declined sharply in December and for the fourth
quarter as a whole, primarily because of a large drop in imports from the high rate in the third
quarter. Nevertheless, the deficit for the full year 1984 was substantially higher than in 1983.

After growing little on balance since early summer, M1 expanded at a rapid pace in late
1984 and early 1985. The broader aggregates also expanded rapidly in recent months. For
the period from the fourth quarter of 1983 to the fourth quarter of 1984, M1 grew at a rate of
about 5¼ percent, somewhat below the midpoint of the Committee's range for the year, and
M2 increased at a rate of about 7¾ percent, a bit above the midpoint of its longer-run range.
Both M3 and total domestic nonfinancial debt expanded at rates above the Committee's ranges
for the year, reflecting very large government borrowing and strong private credit growth, boosted
in part by the unusual size of merger-related credit activity. Short-term interest rates have risen
somewhat on balance since the December meeting of the Committee, but long-term rates are
about unchanged to a little lower. On December 21, the Federal Reserve approved a reduction
in the discount rate from 8½ to 8 percent.

The Federal Open Market Committee seeks to foster monetary and financial conditions that
will help to reduce inflation further, promote growth in output on a sustainable basis, and
contribute to an improved pattern of international transactions. In furtherance of these objectives
the Committee agreed at this meeting to establish ranges for monetary growth of 4 to 7 percent
for M1, 6 to 9 percent for M2, and 6 to 9½ percent for M3 for the period from the fourth
quarter of 1984 to the fourth quarter of 1985. The associated range for total domestic nonfinancial
debt was set at 9 to 12 percent for the year 1985. The Committee agreed that growth in the
monetary aggregates in the upper part of their ranges for 1985 may be appropriate, depending
on developments with respect to velocity and provided that inflationary pressures remain
subdued.

The Committee understood that policy implementation would require continuing appraisal
of the relationships not only among the various measures of money and credit but also between

EXHIBIT 23–6 *(concluded)*

those aggregates and nominal GNP, including evaluation of conditions in domestic credit and foreign exchange markets.

In the implementation of policy for the immediate future, taking account of the progress against inflation, remaining uncertainties in the business outlook, and the strength of the dollar in the exchange markets, the Committee seeks to maintain reserve conditions characteristic of recent weeks. Should growth in M1 appear to be exceeding an annual rate of around 8 percent and M2 and M3 a rate of around 10 to 11 percent during the period from December to March, modest increases in reserve pressures would be sought, particularly if business activity is rising at a satisfactory rate and exchange market pressures diminish. Lesser restraint on reserve positions would be acceptable in the event of substantially slower growth in the monetary aggregates, particularly in the context of sluggish growth in economic activity and continued strength of the dollar in foreign exchange markets. The Chairman may call for Committee consultation if it appears to the Manager for Domestic Operations that pursuit of the monetary objectives and related reserve paths during the period before the next meeting is likely to be associated with a federal funds rate persistently outside a range of 6 to 10 percent.

Votes for short-run operational paragraph: Messrs. Volcker, Corrigan, Boehne, Boykin, Gramley, Mrs. Horn, Messrs. Martin, Partee, Rice, Ms. Seger, Messrs. Wallich and Balles. Votes against this action: None. (Mr. Balles voted as an alternate).

Source: Board of Governors of the Federal Reserve System, *Press Release,* March 29, 1985.

pertain to the growth of output in the economy and to movements in prices and employment. In line with the Fed's concern over international affairs and especially the value of the dollar in international markets, the directive also contains a synopsis of recent developments in the international money market.

Prominently mentioned in every directive are the *monetary aggregates*—M1, M2, and M3—all measures of the nation's money supply.[7] The FOMC sets target ranges for growth in the nation's money supply and asks the SOMA manager to use the open-market policy tool in an effort to achieve those targeted growth rates. In addition, a target range for a key money market interest rate—the average rate on federal funds loans—also is often specified. In the event that rates of growth in the money supply or the federal funds rate drifts outside these ranges, the SOMA manager is to notify the chairman of the Federal Reserve Board for further instructions.

We note that the directive issued to the SOMA manager is extremely *general* in nature, giving specific targets or target ranges but recognizing the need for flexibility as market conditions change. This is a reflection of the crude state of the art in trying to control money market conditions and the nation's money supply. Many factors other than Federal Reserve

---

[7] These and other money-supply measures are discussed in Chapter 24.

operations affect both interest rates and the money supply. While the Federal Reserve can have a significant impact on the *direction* of change, it has considerable difficulty in trying to hit specific targets, especially money-supply targets. The Federal Open Market Committee must be flexible and trust the SOMA manager's judgment in responding to daily conditions in the money market, which subsequently may be quite different from those anticipated when the FOMC held its last meeting.

The conference call.   As an added check on the decisions of the SOMA manager, a conference call between staff economists at the Federal Reserve Board, a member of the FOMC, and the SOMA manager is held each day before trading occurs. The SOMA manager will update those sitting in on the conference call concerning current conditions in the money market and then make a recommendation on the type and volume of securities to be bought or sold that day. At this point the conference call participants may make alternative recommendations for security purchases or sales. Usually, however, the SOMA manager's recommendation is taken, and trading proceeds.

Types of Open-Market Operations.

Types of Open-Market Operations.   There are three basic types of Federal Reserve open-market operations. The so-called *straight* or *outright transaction* refers to the sale or purchase of securities in which outright title passes to the buyer on a permanent basis. In this case, a *permanent* change occurs in the level of legal reserves, up or down. Thus, when the Federal Reserve wants to bring about a once-and-for-all change in reserves, it will tend to use the straight or outright type of transaction.

In contrast, when the Fed wishes to have a *temporary* effect on bank reserves it will employ a *repurchase agreement* with a securities dealer. Under a repurchase agreement (REPO or RP) the Fed will *buy* securities from dealers but agree to sell them back after a few days.[8] The result is a temporary increase in legal reserves which will be reversed when the Fed sells the securities back to the dealers. Such RPs frequently are used during holiday periods or when other temporary factors are at work that have resulted in a shortfall in reserves.

The Fed can also deal with a temporary excess quantity of reserves by using a matched-sale purchase transaction—commonly called a reverse RP or "reverse REPO." In this instance the Fed will agree to sell securities to dealers for a brief period and then to buy them back. Frequently, when mail deliveries are slowed by weather or strikes, the result is a sharp increase in the volume of uncollected checks ("float"), giving banks

---

[8] See Chapter 13 for an explanation of how these repurchase agreements are used as a source of funds for securities dealers.

and other depository institutions hundreds of millions of dollars in excess reserves until the checks are cleared. The Fed can absorb these excess reserves using reverse RPs until the situation returns to normal.

The final type of open-market operation is the *runoff*. The Federal Reserve may deal *directly* with the U.S. Treasury in purchasing and redeeming securities. Suppose the Fed has some U.S. Treasury securities that are about to mature. It may redeem these for new securities that are being offered by the Treasury in its latest public auction. The amount of securities that the Fed takes will not then be available to the public, thereby reducing the quantity of securities sold in the marketplace. Other things equal, this would tend to raise security prices and lower interest rates.

On the other hand, the Fed may decide *not* to acquire new securities from the Treasury to replace those that are maturing. This would mean the Treasury would be forced to sell an increased volume of securities in the open market in order to raise cash to pay off the Fed. Other things equal, security prices would fall and interest rates would rise. The banking system would, at least temporarily, lose additional reserves to the Treasury.

The Goals of Open-Market Operations: Defensive and Dynamic.

In the use of any of its policy tools, the Federal Reserve always has in mind the basic economic goals of full employment, a stable price level, sustainable economic growth, and a stable international balance of payments position for the United States. However, only a portion of the Federal Reserve's daily open-market activity is directed toward those particular goals. The Fed is also responsible on a day-to-day basis for stabilizing the money and capital markets and avoiding sharp changes in interest rates and credit conditions. A substantial portion of its operations are devoted to making fine adjustments in credit conditions and interest rates in order to keep the financial markets functioning smoothly. These technical adjustments in market conditions are often referred to as *defensive* open-market operations. Their basic purpose is to preserve the status quo and to keep the present pattern of interest rates and credit availability about where it is.

In contrast, when the Federal Reserve is more interested in the pursuit of broader economic goals, it will engage in *dynamic* open-market operations. These operations are designed to upset the status quo and to change money and credit conditions to a level the Fed believes is more consistent with the nation's economic goals.

The fact that open-market operations are carried out for a wide variety of purposes makes it difficult to follow the Fed's daily transactions in the marketplace and draw any firm conclusions about the direction of monetary policy. On any given day, the Fed may be buying or selling securities merely to stabilize market conditions without any longer-term objectives in mind. For example, even in periods when the Federal Reserve is pursuing a tight-money policy, it frequently is in the market *buying* securities because (in the Fed's judgment) other factors have been tightening the market too rapidly. The Fed will attempt to slow things down.

The central bank is really a "balance wheel" in the financial system, supplying or subtracting reserves as may be needed on any given day. While experienced Fed watchers find the daily pattern of open-market operations meaningful, many observers argue that, unless the investor possesses inside information on the motivation of Federal Reserve actions, it is exceedingly difficult to "read" daily open-market operations. A longer-run view usually is needed in order to see the direction in which the central bank is trying to move the financial system.

SELECTIVE CREDIT CONTROLS USED BY THE FED

The discount rate, reserve requirements, and open-market operations are often called *general credit controls* because each has an impact on the whole financial system. There is another set of policy tools available to the Federal Reserve, however, that is more *selective* in its impact, focusing on particular sectors of the economy. Nevertheless, use of these selective tools does contribute toward the overall objectives of the Fed to minimize unemployment, stabilize prices, sustain economic growth, and protect the nation's international payments position.

Moral Suasion by Federal Reserve Officials

A selective policy tool that has been used more frequently in recent years is moral suasion. This refers to the use of "arm twisting" or "jawboning" by Federal Reserve officials in order to encourage banks and other lending institutions to conform with the spirit of its policies. For example, if the Fed wishes to tighten credit controls and slow the growth of credit, Fed officials will issue letters and public statements urging financial institutions to use more restraint in granting loans. These public statements may be supplemented by personal phone calls from top Federal Reserve officials to individual lending institutions, stressing the need for more conservative policies. There is evidence that the Federal Reserve has made greater use of moral suasion in recent years, perhaps out of a feeling that its general policy tools have become less effective.[9]

---

[9] See especially Kane (1974).

Deposit Interest-Rate Ceilings

Another selective policy tool used frequently in the past consisted of manipulating legal interest-rate ceilings on deposits. These maximum legal deposit rates, usually called "Regulation Q Ceilings," after a set of deposit regulations once enforced exclusively by the Board of Governors of the Federal Reserve System, were begun during the Great Depression. The Banking Act of 1933 prohibited interest payments on regular checking accounts, for example. Later interest rates on time and savings deposits offered by any depository institution were restricted to a maximum (or ceiling) level as set by the regulatory agency responsible for each institution.

On March 31, 1980, the regulation of deposit interest-rate ceilings was turned over to the Depository Institutions Deregulation Committee (DIDC). Created by the Depository Institutions Deregulation Act of 1980, this committee includes the chairman of the Federal Reserve Board, the director of the Federal Deposit Insurance Corporation, the chairman of the Federal Home Loan Bank Board, and the chairman of the National Credit Union Administration. The Comptroller of the Currency is a nonvoting member of DIDC. The committee was asked to gradually phaseout these federal deposit rate ceilings no later than 1986 so that the public could earn a market rate of return on its savings. The phaseout process was to be gradual, however, in order to protect the safety and soundness of individual depository institutions. DIDC worked fairly rapidly, though, so that by 1985 only passbook savings accounts, regular NOW accounts, and short-term (7- to 31-day) time deposits under $1,000 still had federal rate ceilings. Regular checking accounts still were prohibited from paying any explicit interest. However, most authorities expect all remaining rate ceilings to disappear eventually.

Why were deposit rate ceilings set up in the first place? The original reason for limiting the interest rate financial institutions could pay on their deposits was to safeguard the public's funds and prevent failures among financial institutions. Thousands of banks and savings associations failed during the Great Depression, and many experts felt at the time that excessive competition for deposits had contributed to their collapse. Allegedly, smaller financial institutions, which are more prone to failure even today, are less able to compete for both checking and savings deposits than larger institutions. Thus, the legal rate ceilings were aimed at limiting competition to protect the most vulnerable depository intermediaries. Still another purpose was to ensure an adequate flow of funds to the housing industry by protecting the mortgage-lending activities of savings and loans and mutual savings banks.

Several times in the past the rate ceilings have been used as a tool of monetary policy. If interest rates on securities sold in the open market were rising rapidly but the ceilings were not adjusted upward, interest-sensitive savers would pull their funds out of time and savings deposits. Commercial banks, savings and loans, and mutual savings banks would experience a significant loss of funds, limiting their ability to make loans. Therefore, in theory, the rate ceilings could be used to regulate the flow of credit from depository financial institutions.

Unfortunately, it is not at all certain that the rate ceilings really could control the total volume of credit available in the economy. To be sure, when market interest rates rose above the legal ceilings, depository institutions were forced to reduce their loans to their principal customers— small businesses, households, and state and local governments; but, other borrowers who could readily tap the open market probably had little difficulty in raising funds. Thus, the ceiling rates, more than likely, resulted in credit discrimination rather than credit control.

To many observers legal interest-rate ceilings did far more harm than good. They tended to be inequitable to small savers, who are often forced to place their money in a time or savings deposit because they cannot afford or lack the knowledge to purchase higher-yielding securities in the open market. The ceilings undoubtedly discouraged savings when they were not adjusted fast enough to keep pace with market interest rates. They contributed to instability in the home mortgage market; when savers withdrew their funds from lower-yielding time and savings deposits at savings and loan associations and mutual savings banks, mortgage money tended to dry up. Widespread unemployment in the construction industry and high interest rates on home mortgage loans often followed. Fortunately, with the gradual phaseout of federal rate ceilings by the DIDC, as mandated by Congress, one hopes that their function as a policy tool has ended once and for all.

Margin Requirements

A selective credit control still under the exclusive control of the Federal Reserve Board is margin requirements on the purchase of stocks and convertible bonds and on short sales of those same securities. Margin requirements were enacted into law with passage of the Securities Exchange Act of 1934. This federal law limited the amount of credit that could be used to purchase and carry certain securities when those same securities were used as collateral for a loan. Regulations G, T, and U of the Federal Reserve Board prescribe a maximum loan value for marginable stocks, convertible bonds, and short sales. That maximum loan value is expressed as a specified percentage of the market value of the securities at the time they are used as loan collateral. The *margin requirement* on a regulated security, then, is simply the difference between its market value (100 percent) and the maximum loan value of that security.

EXHIBIT 23–7

Federal Reserve Margin Requirements on Stock, Convertible Bonds, and Short Sales (percent of market value and effective date)

Security	March 11, 1968	June 8, 1968	May 6, 1970	Dec. 6, 1971	Nov. 24, 1972	Jan. 3, 1974
Margin stocks	70%	80%	65%	55%	65%	50%
Convertible bonds	50	60	50	50	50	50
Short sales	70	80	65	55	65	50

Note: Regulations G, T, and U published by the Board of Governors of the Federal Reserve System, in accordance with the Securities Exchange Act of 1934, limit the amount of credit to purchase or carry margin stocks when the securities to be purchased are used as collateral. Margin requirements specify the maximum loan value of the securities expressed as a percentage of their market value at the time a loan is made. Margin requirements, therefore, are the difference between the market value of the securities and their maximum loan value.
Source: Board of Governors of the Federal Reserve System, *Federal Reserve Bulletin,* May 1985, Table 1.36.

For example, as shown in Exhibit 23–7, the current margin requirement on stock is 50 percent. This means that common and preferred stock can be purchased on credit with the stock itself used as collateral. However, the purchaser can only borrow up to a maximum of 50 percent of the stock's current market value. He or she must put up the remainder of the stock's purchase price in cash money.

As Exhibit 23–7 suggests, margin requirements are not changed very often. The current margin requirements on stocks, convertible bonds, and short sales of these securities have remained unchanged since January 1974. Most observers of the financial markets feel that the imposition of margin requirements was unnecessary. These requirements arose out of the turmoil of the Great Depression, when many felt that speculative buying and selling of stocks had contributed to the economy's sudden collapse. While this was probably not the case, margin requirements do ensure that a substantial amount of cash must be contributed by the buyer of securities and that borrowing against these securities is kept within reasonable limits. One serious limitation of this selective tool is that it does not cover purchases of all types of stocks and bonds. For this reason, its future use as a tool of Federal Reserve monetary policy is likely to remain very limited.

SUMMARY AND CONCLUSIONS

The policy tools used by the Federal Reserve System affect the quantity and rate of growth of legal reserves in the banking system which, in turn, impact on the capacity of financial institutions to make loans and investments. Central bank policy also influences the level of and direction of change in interest rates. For example, a policy of tight money and restricted growth in reserves usually results in higher interest rates and a diminished supply of credit available to borrowers. An easy money policy is usually accompanied by lower interest rates and an expanded supply of credit available. Working through both interest rates and legal reserves, the Federal Reserve has a direct impact on the size and rate of growth of the nation's money supply. Because changes in the money supply are highly correlated with changes in economic activity, the Fed ultimately influences *both* the level of economic activity and economic growth.

Over the years the Federal Reserve has developed a number of tools for carrying out the objectives of monetary policy. The Fed's primary policy tool is open-market operations—buying and selling of securities. Open-market operations are used not only to carry out major shifts in policy toward tighter or easier credit conditions (known as dynamic operations), but also to make technical adjustments in market conditions to preserve the status quo (known as defensive operations). Open-market operations are carried out by the Trading Desk of the New York Federal Reserve Bank on behalf of all 12 Federal Reserve banks. Policy guidelines for the conduct of open-market operations are set by the Federal Open Market Committee, which meets every few weeks in Washington, D.C.

When the Federal Reserve wishes to have a quick and powerful impact on the financial system, it may change the amount of legal reserves deposit-type financial institutions must hold behind their deposits. Changes in legal reserve requirements have a direct effect on the volume of funds available to financial institutions for lending and investing and therefore affect both the growth of the money supply and interest rates. However, the impact of reserve requirement changes is so potent that the Fed uses this tool infrequently. A third policy tool—changes in the discount rate charged by the Federal Reserve banks on loans made to depository institutions—is also used infrequently. While this tool affects interest rates in the short run, it has a psychological impact on credit uses that often works against the aims of the Fed. Nevertheless, loans to depository institutions provide an important safety valve for the Federal Reserve in the event its policies threaten the safety and soundness of individual financial institutions.

Other, minor tools of monetary policy have been used by the Federal Reserve from time to time to carry out its objectives. Through public speeches and testimony before Congress, private letters, and phone calls, the Fed frequently tries to persuade individuals and groups of the wisdom of its policies. Often called "jawboning" or moral suasion, this policy tool has seen increasing use in recent years to deal with the psychological aspects of the nation's major economic problems, especially inflation. Policy tools recently being phased out include deposit interest-rate ceilings and margin requirements on the purchase of selected stocks and convertible bonds. These infrequently used tools can affect the flow of credit available from selected financial institutions and discourage speculative borrowing. However, like many regulatory controls, these selective policy tools can lead to distortions in the allocation of scarce resources and discrimination in access to credit, especially for borrowers of limited means.

While it is useful to know what tools the Federal Reserve has at its disposal to deal with the nation's economic problems and what effects these policy tools are likely to have, the student of the financial system needs to know more. When is the Fed likely to use its policy tools? What factors indicate whether a change in monetary policy has occurred or perhaps soon will occur? How successful has the central bank been in helping to achieve the nation's economic goals? We address these critically important questions in the next and final chapter on the Federal Reserve System.

STUDY QUESTIONS

1. What is the principal target of Federal Reserve monetary policy? Why?

2. What are legal reserves? Required reserves? Excess reserves? Explain why these concepts are important.

3. Why are commercial banks and other deposit-type intermediaries able to create money? What factors increase the amount of deposits the banking system can create with any given injection of new reserves? What factors reduce the money-creating capabilities of the banking and financial system?

4. In what ways can the Federal Reserve influence the money-creation process? The public? The U.S. Treasury?

5. How does the reserve requirement tool affect the ability of deposit-type institutions to create money? What are the principal advantages and disadvantages of the reserve-requirement tool?

6. How and why does a depository institution borrow from the Federal Reserve? Explain what happens when the Fed changes the discount rate. What are the principal advantages and disadvantages of the discount mechanism as a policy tool?

7. Why are open-market operations the Fed's most popular and frequently used policy tool? What are the principal effects of open-market operations on the financial system?

8. Describe the relationship between the SOMA manager and the FOMC. What is a policy directive? What types of policy targets does the Fed use?

9. Explain the difference between an RP and a straight (or outright) open-market transaction. Why is each used? What is a "runoff"?

10. Explain the difference between defensive and dynamic open-market operations.

11. What is moral suasion? Do you believe this tool can be effective? Explain.

12. What is Regulation Q? How has it been used in recent years as a policy tool? Why is this tool being eliminated and who is responsible for its dismantling? What arguments would you advance in favor of and against interest-rate ceilings?

13. Explain how margin requirements affect the financial system. Why were these requirements instituted by Congress? Could they be effective in promoting the nation's economic goals?

PROBLEMS

1. Suppose the public wishes to hold $0.40 in pocket money (i.e., currency and coin) and $0.25 in time deposits (especially CDs), while depository institutions plan to keep $0.15 in excess reserves for each new dollar of transaction money received. If reserve requirements on transaction deposits and time and savings deposits are 3 percent, what is the size of the transaction deposit multiplier? The money multiplier? Suppose $5 million in new excess reserves appear in the banking system. How much will be created in the form of new deposits and loans?

2. Total legal reserves currently amount to $40 billion, while currency and coin in public hands total $160 billion. The nation's narrowly defined (transaction) money supply is $525 billion. How large is the money multiplier?

3. A bank holds $130 million in the form of transaction and time and savings deposits. Its reserve deposit at the Federal Reserve bank during the current reserve maintenance period contains a daily average balance of $4 million and its vault cash holdings have averaged daily $0.40 million for several weeks running. Calculate its required re-

serves and excess reserves if deposits are subject to a 5 percent legal reserve requirement. Now suppose the bank elects to buy $1 million in Treasury bills from the Fed. Do you see any problems with this? Explain.

SELECTED REFERENCES

Board of Governors of the Federal Reserve System. *The Federal Reserve System—Purposes and Functions.* Washington, D.C., 1974.

Cacy, J. A.; Bryon Higgins; and Gordon H. Sellon, Jr. "Should the Discount Rate Be a Penalty Rate?" *Economic Review,* Federal Reserve Bank of Kansas City, January 1981, pp. 3–10.

Federal Reserve Bank of Chicago. "The Depository Institutions Deregulation and Monetary Control Act of 1980." *Economic Perspectives,* September–October 1980, pp. 3–23.

Kane, Edward. "The Re-politicization of the Fed." *Journal of Financial and Quantitative Analysis,* Proceedings, November 1974, pp. 743–52.

Laurant, Robert. "Reserve Requirements: Are They Lagged in the Wrong Direction?" *Journal of Money, Credit, and Banking,* August 1979, pp. 171–76.

Lombra, R. E., and R. G. Torto. "Discount Rate Changes and Announcement Effects." *Quarterly Journal of Economics,* February 1977, pp. 171–76.

Poole, William. "A Proposal for Reforming Bank Reserve Requirements in the United States." *Journal of Money, Credit, and Banking,* May 1976, pp. 137–47.

Sellon, Gordon H., Jr. "The Role of the Discount Rate in Monetary Policy: A Theoretical Analysis." *Economic Review,* Federal Reserve Bank of Kansas City, June 1980, pp. 3–15.

Thorton, Daniel L. "An Early Look at the Volatility of Money and Interest Rates under CRR." *Review,* Federal Reserve Bank of St. Louis, October 1984, pp. 26–34.

Woodworth, G. Walter. *The Money Market and Monetary Management.* 2d ed. New York: Harper & Row, 1972.

24

Indicators and Goals of Monetary Policy

PURPOSE OF THIS CHAPTER

Two objectives are pursued in this chapter: (1) to explain the meaning and use of different methods of judging the magnitude and direction of Federal Reserve monetary policy; and (2) to explain how Federal Reserve monetary policy can be used to help achieve the nation's economic goals of controlling inflation and achieving full employment, sustained economic growth, and a stable balance-of-payments position. The chapter begins by considering several important *indicators* of the direction and magnitude of Fed policy actions, including the Federal Reserve Statement, measures of the nation's money supply or money stock, and such money market indicators as the Federal funds rate and free reserves. The basic method used by the Federal Reserve to control money-supply growth through open-market operations is also examined. Finally, the chapter focuses on different channels through which the Federal Reserve can influence market conditions to promote the nation's key economic objectives.

KEY TERMS AND CONCEPTS IN THE CHAPTER

balance-of-payments
equilibrium
borrowed reserves
credit availability
factors absorbing
reserves
factors supplying
reserves
full employment
inflation

legal reserves
limitations of
monetary policy
monetarism
money market
indicators
money-supply
measures
money-supply-reserve
aggregates approach

national economic
goals
nonborrowed reserves
policy goals
policy indicators
policy trade-offs
supply-side economics
sustainable economic
growth
total reserves

The Federal Reserve System exerts a powerful impact on the availability and cost of credit in the nation's financial markets. Because the Fed has a great deal to do with the broad changes that occur in interest rates, prices of securities, and the availability of credit, economists and financial analysts spend enormous amounts of time analyzing Federal Reserve actions in an attempt to predict the future course of monetary policy. Indeed, if the experts are able to guess correctly which way the Fed is going, they can make appropriate adjustments in security portfolios and in borrowing and spending plans in order to reduce costs and maximize earnings.

It should be noted, however, that understanding the Federal Reserve's intentions and predicting the direction of monetary policy are not easy tasks. Many factors influence interest rates, security prices, and the flow of loanable funds in the financial markets. For example, if we see interest rates on money market instruments rising, there is often a temptation to assume that this trend reflects government policy and, in particular, the actions of the Federal Reserve. In fact, interest rates are subject to all the forces of demand and supply operating in the financial marketplace. An upward surge in rates may reflect a sharp rise in borrowings by units of government and private investors, the impact of inflation, changes in the public's money-using habits, and a host of other factors. The Federal Reserve System is an extremely important influence on the financial system, to be sure, but only one of many influences.

FACTORS INFLUENCING THE RESERVES OF THE BANKING SYSTEM

To fully understand the role of the Federal Reserve in the complex environment of the financial marketplace, we need to focus on the principal target of Federal Reserve policy—*legal reserves.* We recall from the previous chapter that the reserves of the banking system consist of deposits kept at the Federal Reserve banks plus currency and coin held in the vaults of depository institutions. These reserves are the raw material out of which lenders create credit and cause the money supply to grow. This is why the total supply of reserves is the main target of Federal Reserve monetary policy. However, numerous factors affect the supply of reserves available to banks and other lenders. As shown in Exhibit 24–1, these factors fall into three groups: (1) actions of the public; (2) Federal Reserve operations; and (3) operations of the U.S. Treasury Department and foreign investors.

Actions of the Public Affecting Reserves

For example, suppose the public desires to increase its holdings of currency and coin (pocket money). It will do so by writing checks or drafts against deposits held in banks and thrift institutions, reducing the legal reserves of these lending institutions. If these institutions were already fully loaned up, with no excess reserves, then the withdrawal of currency and coin would force them to raise additional reserves by selling securities, calling loans, and borrowing. The stock of total reserves and the nation's money supply would begin to contract. On the other hand, if the public wishes to reduce its holdings of currency and coin, pocket money will be redeposited in banks and thrift institutions, increasing the total reserves of these institutions. The volume of bank lending and investing will rise, resulting in an increase in the nation's money supply, unless, of course, the Federal Reserve uses its policy tools to counteract the inflow of currency and coin.

Operations of the Treasury and Foreign Investors Affecting Reserves

Actions of the U.S. Treasury and foreign investors also affect the level and growth of legal reserves. The Treasury, foreign central banks, and international financial institutions keep large deposits with the Federal Reserve banks. Any increase in these deposits generally results in a decline in the reserves of deposit-type financial institutions. This is due to the fact that both the Treasury and foreign institutions frequently receive

EXHIBIT 24–1

Factors Affecting the Supply of Legal Reserves in the Banking System

Factors	Effect on Total Legal Reserves of the Banking System
Actions of the public:	
Increase in holdings of currency and coin	−
Decrease in holdings of currency and coin	+
Federal Reserve operations:	
Purchase of securities	+
Sale of securities	−
Loans to depository institutions	+
Repayment of loans made to depository institutions	−
Increase in Federal Reserve float	+
Decrease in Federal Reserve float	−
Increase in other assets of the Federal Reserve banks	+
Decrease in other assets of the Federal Reserve banks	−
Increase in other liabilities of the Federal Reserve banks	−
Decrease in other liabilities of the Federal Reserve banks	+
Increase in capital accounts of the Federal Reserve banks	−
Decrease in capital accounts of the Federal Resrve banks	+
U.S. Treasury and foreign operations:	
Increase in Treasury deposits at the Federal Reserve banks	−
Decrease in Treasury deposits at the Federal Reserve banks	+
Gold purchases	+
Gold sales	−
Increase in Treasury currency outstanding	+
Decrease in Treasury currency outstanding	−
Increase in Treasury cash holdings	−
Decrease in Treasury cash holdings	+
Increase in foreign and other deposits in Federal Reserve banks	−
Decrease in foreign and other deposits in Federal Reserve banks	+

payments from domestic businesses and households. These payments are nearly always made by check and drain reserves from private banks and thrift institutions as the checks are cleared at the Fed. Federal income tax payments by the public, which periodically flow out of private checkable deposits and into the Treasury's checking accounts at the Fed, are good examples of this process. Similarly, when the Treasury sells securities in the open market, investors write checks against their accounts that are eventually credited to the Treasury's deposits with the Federal Reserve banks. In both instances, the public's deposits and total reserves of the banking system fall. Conversely, whenever the Treasury or a foreign depositor write checks against their accounts, these are normally deposited somewhere in the banking system, causing total reserves to rise.

Occasionally, the Treasury buys and sells *gold* at the request of foreign governments or to hold in reserve. Payment for Treasury gold purchases is made by checks drawn on the Treasury's accounts at the Fed. Those individuals and institutions selling the gold will deposit the Treasury's checks somewhere in the banking system, leading to an increase in reserves and deposits. Conversely, if the Treasury sells gold, buyers write checks against their deposits, which forces a decline in both reserves and deposits of the banking system when those checks are collected. If the decline in reserves is too great, the Federal Reserve may have to offset the impact of Treasury gold transactions through open-market operations.

The Treasury's minting of new currency and coin also has an impact on reserves and deposits. Newly minted currency and coin are shipped to the vaults of the Federal Reserve banks in return for credit to the Treasury's checking accounts. When the Treasury spends these funds by issuing checks to the public, deposits and reserves in the banking system will rise. Similarly, when there is a decrease in Treasury currency outstanding as currency and coin are retired, total reserves must fall. This happens because the Treasury must pay for the redeemed currency and coin by writing checks against its deposits at the Fed. To cover those checks, it must draw down its deposits kept in private banks, which reduces total reserves available to the banking system.[1]

The Treasury does hold small amounts of currency and coin in its own vaults. When these vault deposits rise, the increase in Treasury cash holdings must have come from funds kept somewhere in the private banking system, leading to a decline in total reserves. Similarly, when Treasury cash holdings decline, the released currency and coin flow into the private banking system, and both deposits and total reserves rise.

Federal Reserve Operations Affecting Reserves

The Federal Reserve System can offset any of the foregoing actions by the public, foreign institutions, or the U.S. Treasury, keeping total reserves of the banking system at roughly the level it desires. As we observed in the preceding chapter, the Fed can increase total reserves by purchases of securities in the open market, or it can reduce total reserves by sales of securities. Loans made to depository institutions through the discount windows of the Reserve banks will increase reserves, while repayments of those loans will cause reserves to fall.

The Fed often increases reserves unintentionally when the volume

---

[1] As we noted in Chapter 13, the Treasury keeps deposits—known as Tax and Loan Accounts—in a majority of the nation's banks. The majority of Treasury receipts flow initially into these Tax and Loan Accounts before they are later transferred to the Federal Reserve banks.

of float from uncollected checks rises. Banks and other depository institutions that route their checks through the Federal Reserve banks for collection receive credit in their reserve accounts after a specified period (usually two or three days). However, many of those checks have not been collected at the time the Fed grants credit for them due to delays in processing, transportation, or other problems. Checkbook float is essentially an interest-free loan of reserves from the Fed and has the same effect on the total reserves of the banking system as a loan made through the Fed's discount window.

Finally, when the Federal Reserve banks acquire assets of any kind or issue checks to pay their debts or cover expenses, total reserves of the banking system will rise. In contrast, when the Fed receives payments from banks, securities dealers, and others, total reserves fall as checks written against financial institutions are sent to the Federal Reserve banks. Similarly, when a bank joins the Federal Reserve System, it must purchase Federal Reserve stock. This action increases the Fed's capital accounts and lowers the reserves available to private banks. Generally speaking, any Federal Reserve expenditure increases reserves, while any receipt of funds by the Fed reduces the reserves available to the banking system.

The Heart of the Monetary Policy Process— Controlling Reserves

The heart of the monetary policy process is to correctly anticipate changes in all of the foregoing factors that affect the legal reserves of the banking system. The Federal Reserve then tries to achieve a level and rate of growth in total reserves that is consistent with its targeted rate of growth in the nation's money supply and with the nation's economic goals.

THE FEDERAL RESERVE STATEMENT

One of the most widely followed indicators of what the Federal Reserve System is doing to influence conditions in the financial markets and the economy is known as the Federal Reserve Statement. It is published each week in the financial press and lists the factors that supply reserves to depository institutions and those that absorb reserves. The total amount of reserves held by depository institutions at any time equals the difference between the factors supplying reserves and the factors absorbing reserves. The Federal Reserve Statement shows levels of each reserve-supplying or reserve-absorbing factor for the current and previous month or week and any changes between the two time periods. It is the changes in each reserve factor that analysts concentrate on in attempting to understand what the Federal Reserve is trying to accomplish in the financial marketplace.

Factors Supplying Reserves

A Federal Reserve Statement for the months of March and April 1984 is shown in Exhibit 24–2. The first item listed on the statement is Reserve Bank Credit, including Federal Reserve purchases of securities, loans

EXHIBIT 24–2

Reserves of Depository Institutions ($ millions)

Item	March 1984	April 1984	Change
Factors supplying reserve funds:			
Reserve bank credit:			
U.S. government securities:			
Bought outright	$149,128	$152,859	+3,731
Held under repurchase agreement	418	1,367	+949
Federal agency securities:			
Bought outright	8,562	8,557	−6
Held under repurchase agreement	42	103	+61
Bankers acceptances acquired	14	87	+73
Loans from the discount window	905	1,285	+380
Float	1,002	837	−165
Other Federal Reserve assets	8,667	9,219	+552
Gold stock	11,115	11,110	−5
Special drawing rights (SDRs)	4,618	4,618	0
Treasury currency outstanding	15,863	15,915	+52
Total of factors supplying reserves	$200,334	$205,956	+5,622
Factors absorbing reserve funds:			
Currency in circulation	$168,317	$170,394	+2,077
Treasury cash holdings	488	522	+34
Deposits, other than member bank reserves, with Federal Reserve banks:			
Treasury	4,012	6,637	+2,625
Foreign	229	220	−9
Service-related balances and adjustments	1,940	1,215	−725
Other Federal Reserve liabilities and capital	5,705	6,098	+393
Total of factors absorbing reserves	$180,691	$184,986	+4,395
Reserve balances of all depository institutions	$ 19,066	$ 20,293	+1,227

Note: Figures in the table may not add exactly to column totals due to rounding error and other factors.
SOURCE: Board of Governors of the Federal Reserve System, *Federal Reserve Bulletin,* June 1984, Table 1.11.

from the discount windows of the Reserve banks, float, and other Federal Reserve assets. If each of these items increases, reserves available to depository institutions rise. Other factors held equal, the ability of financial institutions to make loans and investments and expand the nation's money supply also increases. A decrease in any component of Reserve bank credit results in a decline in the reserves of depository institutions.

Looking more closely at the statement, we note that the Federal Reserve held outright $152,859 million in U.S. government securities, $8,557 million in federal agency securities, and a small volume ($87 million) of bankers' acceptances in April 1984. In addition, $1,367 million in U.S. government securities and $103 million in federal agency securities were held under repurchase agreements with securities dealers. The column marked "Change" tells us that the Fed, on balance, *bought* securities between March and April 1984. Its total security holdings rose net $4,808 million (i.e., $3,731 + $949 + $61 + $73 − $6) over this one-month time span.

Because Federal Reserve purchases expand the supply of reserves, does this mean the Fed was moving toward an easier, less restrictive monetary policy in the spring of 1984? Perhaps, but we also know that much Federal Reserve activity is *defensive* in nature, that is, merely an effort to offset the effects of other factors on reserves and preserve the status quo in the financial markets.[2] Were other factors at work in this case, draining reserves from depository institutions and forcing the Fed to supply more reserves through security purchases just to keep total reserves reasonably stable? Exhibit 24–2 suggests the answer is *yes.* For example, checkbook float fell $165 million, costing the banking system that much in available reserves. In total, however, factors supplying reserves added a healthy $5,622 million to the total pool of reserves available for lending and investing by the banking system.

Factors Absorbing Reserves

There is more to the story, however, because most of these new reserves were absorbed by a second set of factors. As we can see in Exhibit 24–2, the second half of the Federal Reserve Statement looks at those factors that *reduce* reserves, including increases in currency in circulation, Treasury holdings of cash, miscellaneous deposits at the Fed, and the liability and capital accounts of the Federal Reserve banks. If these factors increase, reserve balances held by depository institutions *must* decline unless offset by reserve-supplying factors such as Federal Reserve Credit. However, a decrease in reserve-absorbing factors results in an increase in total reserves. Careful inspection of Exhibit 24–2 shows that a massive

---

[2] See Chapter 23 for a discussion of defensive open-market operations.

change occurred in the amount of currency and coin in circulation between March and April 1984. The public had greater need for pocket money and withdrew from banks and other depository institutions a net of $2,077 million in currency and coin. Without any offsetting action by the Fed, a sharp decrease in legal reserves and the nation's money supply would have occurred as depository institutions surrendered their vault cash reserves to meet the public's need for pocket money.

Another major factor draining reserves was a $2,625 million increase in Treasury deposits at the Federal Reserve banks. These funds were called in from commercial banks scattered across the country and these banks, therefore, surrendered reserves into the Treasury's account at the Federal Reserve. In total, reserve-draining factors absorbed a net $4,395 million in total legal reserves of the banking system—a massive reserve loss which the Fed normally will respond to with its credit-creating tools.

Interpreting the Federal Reserve Statement

If we compare the sum of changes in factors supplying reserves with changes in factors-absorbing reserves, the net change is about $1,200 million (plus or minus a small discrepancy due to rounding error and other influences). Because the factors-absorbing reserves increased, on balance, this would have deducted $4,395 million from the reserves of depository institutions. However, reserve-supplying factors added back $5,622 million. The net difference between these two amounts of approximately $1,200 million resulted in an increase in the total reserves of depository institutions from $19,066 in March to $20,293 in April 1984, as shown in the last line of Exhibit 24–2.

The Fed can use open-market operations to bring about any change in total reserves that it wishes. Why did it permit the reserves of the banking system to grow by about $1,200 million over the period shown in Exhibit 24–2? Probably because growth in the nation's money supply had declined in the spring of 1984, especially in April, as the reader can verify by looking at those months in Exhibit 24–4. The decrease in money growth brought this policy indicator close to the minimum acceptable money-growth target as planned by the Fed for 1984. Faced with these developments, the Fed allowed the reserves of depository institutions to rise temporarily as a stimulus to money growth.

MEASURES OF THE NATION'S MONEY SUPPLY

The Federal Reserve Statement is an important indicator of monetary policy but by no means the only one. Economists, business leaders, and investors look even more closely at weekly, monthly, quarterly, and annual changes in various measures of the nation's money supply. The money supply is the subject of widespread interest and attention for two reasons: (1) changes in money are highly correlated with changes in economic conditions; and (2) the Federal Reserve has a significant impact on money-supply growth through its control over the reserves of depository institutions.

Today, economists and other students of the financial system follow, not one definition of the money supply, but several, each reflecting a slightly different view of what money is. The public's money-using habits are changing rapidly, and many new financial instruments have recently appeared, complicating measurement of the nation's money supply. Examples of relatively new money-related financial instruments include automatic transfers of funds from savings to checking accounts (ATS), shares in money market mutual funds, interest-bearing negotiable-order-of-withdrawal (NOW) accounts, Super NOWs, and Money Market Deposit Accounts (MMDAs). Moreover, Eurodollar deposits and repurchase agreements, once the exclusive property of the largest banks, securities dealers, and corporations, now are available to individuals and smaller institutions for the rapid investment and transfer of funds. These innovations in money-related assets force the Federal Reserve Board occasionally to revise old definitions of the money supply and announce new ones.

Money-Supply Measures

The narrowest definition of the money supply in use today is known as M1—the sum of checking accounts and currency and coin held by the public. This definition views money exclusively as a *medium of exchange* and includes mostly noninterest-bearing assets. It excludes demand deposits owned by domestic banks (called "due from" or correspondent deposits), the U.S. government, and foreign banks and official institutions. Similarly, currency and coin held in the vaults of commercial banks, the U.S. Treasury, and the Federal Reserve banks are also excluded from M1. As shown in Exhibit 24–3, the narrow M1 definition of the money supply totaled nearly $600 billion in June 1985.

While all forms of the money serve as a medium of exchange, the newer forms of money today bear interest and therefore serve partly as a *store of value* or temporary repository of savings. Prominent examples include Super NOW accounts, money market deposit accounts (MMDAs), and shares in money market mutual funds held by the public that can be as accessible for making payments as conventional noninterest-bearing checking accounts. Other near-money accounts that are a temporary repository of savings but frequently accessible for spending include savings deposits and small time deposits (with denominations of less than $100,000) at all depository institutions, overnight RPs issued by commer-

EXHIBIT 24–3

Money-Supply Measures

Symbol	Definition	Amounts as of June 1985 ($ billions)
M1	Demand deposits at commercial banks (except those due other domestic banks, the U.S. government, and foreign banks and official institutions) less cash items in the process of collection and float + NOW accounts and automatic transfer service accounts at banks and thrift institutions + credit union share draft accounts + demand deposits at mutual savings banks + currency and coin held by the public outside bank and government vaults.	$ 591.2
M2	M1 + savings and small-denomination time deposits at all depository institutions + overnight and continuing contract repurchase agreements at commercial banks + overnight Eurodollars held by U.S. residents other than banks at Caribbean branches of member banks + money market mutual funds shares not held by institutions + MMDAs.	2,473.1
M3	M2 + large-denomination ($100,000+) time deposits at all depository institutions + term RPs at commercial banks and thrift Eurodollars held by U.S. residents + institutional money market funds.	3,103.7
L	M3 + nonbank holdings of bankers' acceptances, commercial paper, U.S. Treasury bills and other liquid Treasury securities.	3,626.3*
D	Debt of domestic nonfinancial sectors (U.S. government, state and local governments, and private nonfinancial units) as of the end of each month.	6,191.4*

* Figure as of April 1985.
SOURCE: Board of Governors of the Federal Reserve System, *Federal Reserve Bulletin,* September 1985, Table 1.21.

cial banks, overnight Eurodollars owned by U.S. nonbank residents issued by the Caribbean branches of member banks, and publicly held shares in money market mutual funds. These liquid funds plus everything in M1 make up the M2 definition of money.

An even broader measure of the money supply is M3, which includes all the components of M2 plus time deposits issued by depository institutions in denominations of $100,000 or more, term RPs offered by commercial banks and thrifts, Eurodollar deposits held by U.S. residents, and large-denomination deposits in money market funds. Financial institutions, governments, and corporations are the principal holders of these additional financial instruments, most of which are negotiable with an active resale market. Thus, M3 focuses on *liquid working balances.*

One of the broadest money-supply measures is L, which represents *total liquid assets.* The critical difference between L and other measures of the money supply is the addition of money market securities—bankers' acceptances, commercial paper, U.S. Treasury bills and other marketable Treasury obligations 18 months or less from maturity, and U.S. savings bonds. The fifth and last money-supply measure, D or debt, serves as an approximate measure of the nation's *total supply of credit* resulting from lending funds to federal, state, and local governments, corporations and other private businesses, and consumers.

Federal Reserve Control of Money-Supply Growth

The Federal Reserve attempts to regulate the growth of these measures of the nation's money supply, particularly M1 and M2. As we will soon see, changes in the money supply have been found to be closely correlated with changes in the economy's level of production (GNP) and, through production, both employment and prices. The problem is that the Fed is by no means the only factor determining the size and rate of growth of the nation's money supply. Changes in the public's money-using habits, income levels, and savings habits and the credit policies of financial institutions also play key roles in money growth.

How does the Fed attempt to control the growth of the nation's money supply? In October 1979 the Fed adopted new procedures for regulating money which have been called the *money-supply-reserve aggregates approach.*[3] These procedures focus on the legal reserves of the banking system whose level and rate of growth are regulated through open-market operations. Three steps are involved.

First, the Federal Open Market Committee (FOMC) *sets target growth rates for selected money-supply measures* (usually M1, M2, and M3) for the coming year and for shorter periods within the year.[4] These targets are stated in the form of annual percentage growth rate ranges. For example, in 1984 the Fed called for growth in M1 in the 4 to 8 percent range, while M2 and M3 were to grow between 6 and 9 percent during the year. As the year progressed and money growth fell above or below the annual target, shorter-run targets were set, covering calendar quarters or periods between FOMC meetings, in an effort to bring money's growth back into line with the annual target.

---

[3] See especially Cacy (1980).

[4] Under the terms of the Full-Employment and Balanced Growth Act of 1978 (known also as the Humphrey-Hawkins Act), the FOMC is required to establish calendar year growth ranges for money and credit aggregates by February of each year and review these at midyear. These ranges, which must be reported to Congress in February and July, are based on the period running from the fourth quarter of the previous year to the fourth quarter of the current year. The FOMC is at liberty to change the target growth ranges at any time, however, if it feels that new circumstances warrant a change.

The second step in money-supply control is to *set growth paths for the legal reserves of the banking system.* As we saw in Chapter 23, the total legal reserves of the banking system are linked to the nation's money supply through the money multiplier:

$$\text{Money supply} = \text{Money multiplier} \times \text{Monetary base} \qquad (24\text{-}1)$$

where the money multiplier tells us how many dollars of money result from each dollar increase in the monetary base; and, the monetary base includes both total legal reserves and currency and coin held by the public. The size of the money multiplier reflects the public's demand for currency and coin, shifts in deposits between transaction accounts and savings accounts, legal reserve requirements, and the credit-granting policies of financial institutions. The money-multiplier relationship suggests that the growth rate of the money supply will be approximately equal to the growth rate of the multiplier plus the rate of growth in the monetary base (including growth in bank reserves). Therefore, if the Fed is to control the money supply, it must control or influence the growth of the monetary base and project how the money multiplier will change over time. A staff paper released by the Board of Governors on January 31, 1980, sheds a little light on how the Fed makes its projections in order to control money growth:

> After the objective for money supply growth is set, reserve paths expected to achieve such growth are established for a family of reserve measures. These measures consist of total reserves, the monetary base (essentially total reserves of member banks plus currency in circulation), and nonborrowed reserves. Establishment of the paths involves projecting how much of the targeted money growth is likely to take the form of currency, of deposits at nonmember institutions, and of deposits at member institutions (taking account of differential reserve requirements by size of demand deposits and between the demand and time and savings deposit components of M2). Moreover, estimates are made of reserves likely to be absorbed by expansion in other bank liabilities consistent with money supply objectives and also takes account of tolerable changes in bank credit. . . . Estimates are also made of the amount of excess reserves banks are likely to hold.
>
> The projected mix of currency and demand deposits, given the reserve requirements for deposits and banks' excess reserves, yields an estimate of the increase in total reserves, and the monetary base consistent with FOMC monetary targets.[5]

Clearly, the Fed does not completely control either the monetary base or the size of the money multiplier. The public, by making decisions on how much currency and coin, demand deposits, and time and savings

---

[5] See Board of Governors of the Federal Reserve System (1980).

deposits it wishes to hold, and depository institutions, in deciding what excess reserves they choose to hold, exert a powerful influence on the growth of the monetary base and the money multiplier. The Federal Reserve must *estimate* what the public and depository institutions will do and try to *offset* those actions by manipulating the *total reserves* of the banking system—an important component of the monetary base. Unfortunately, the Fed does not fully control total reserves either. This is due to the fact that:

$$\text{Total reserves} = \text{Borrowed reserves} \\ + \text{Nonborrowed reserves} \qquad (24\text{–}2)$$

Borrowed reserves are supplied through the discount window of the Federal Reserve banks and depend on the demand for loans from depository institutions that hold their reserve accounts with the Fed as well as Fed regulations and policy decisions. The Fed has direct control only over the volume of *nonborrowed reserves,* which are influenced by open-market operations. The central bank must, therefore, make an initial assumption about the desired behavior of borrowed reserves—known as the borrowing path. Then the desired growth path of nonborrowed reserves needed to achieve the desired growth range for the nation's money supply will be estimated from the following relationship:

$$\begin{matrix} \text{Desired growth path} \\ \text{for nonborrowed} \\ \text{reserves} \end{matrix} = \begin{matrix} \text{Estimated growth path} \\ \text{for total reserves} \\ \underline{\quad} \text{ Desired growth path} \\ \text{for borrowed reserves} \end{matrix} \qquad (24\text{–}3)$$

Thus, the Federal Reserve targets *both* the growth path of nonborrowed reserves and the growth path of borrowing from the Federal Reserve banks.

The third step in the money-supply control process is to *undertake daily and weekly open-market operations through the Trading Desk of the Federal Reserve Bank of New York to achieve the desired growth path for nonborrowed reserves and for borrowed reserves.* The quantity of reserves is kept as close as possible to the desired growth path by either buying securities from the marketplace to add more reserves when reserve growth slows too much or by selling securities through the Trading Desk to reduce reserves when they are growing too fast.[6] The Federal Reserve's key focus in controlling the nation's money supply, then, is

---

[6] The specific procedures used by the Federal Reserve and the System Open Account Manager to control the growth of the money supply are described in more detail by Long (1980), Higgins (1980), and Sellon (1980), and Wallich (1984).

reserve availability. As described in the Fed's staff memorandum quoted below:

> because nonborrowed reserves are more closely under the control of the System Account manager for open market operations (though subject to a small range of error because of the behavior of noncontrolled factors affecting reserves, such as float), he would initially aim at a nonborrowed reserve target (seasonally unadjusted for operating purposes) established for the operating period between (FOMC) meetings.

Thus, if total reserves appear to be growing faster than is consistent with desired money-supply growth, the System Open Market Account (SOMA) manager will respond by lowering the desired nonborrowed reserve growth path. The SOMA manager will continue to add more nonborrowed reserves or take nonborrowed reserves away until both the money supply and total reserves move back toward their desired growth paths. The Federal Reserve banks, with the approval of the Board of Governors, may also decide to increase the discount rate or be more restrictive in granting loans in order to slow down bank borrowing from the discount window. These actions will also affect money market interest rates which will impact on the demand for reserves by depository institutions and on the public's demand for money.[7]

Achieving the Fed's Money-Supply Targets

How well has the Fed done in achieving its targeted growth rates for money? Overall, the Fed has held quite close to its target ranges on an *annual* basis. However, from month to month and quarter to quarter the Fed is frequently well outside its annual money-growth targets. A good example is presented in Exhibit 24–4 which shows selected actual monthly M1 and M2 growth rates in 1984 along with the Fed's targets for that year. Monthly and quarterly deviations from the targeted range are often very large. And, we don't know for sure how much damage is done to the achievement of the nation's economic goals from the deviations themselves and from the often hurried adjustments the Fed makes to get itself back on target.

The Fed does face a number of serious problems as it attempts to achieve its announced money-supply targets. Continuing changes in the

---

[7] In effect, Federal Reserve monetary policy focuses upon four groups of policy targets: (1) *operating targets,* represented by nonborrowed and borrowed reserves; (2) *instrumental targets,* including total reserves and interest rates in the money market; (3) *intermediate targets,* which include the nation's money supply and long-term interest rates which, presumably, have the greatest impact on investment spending in the economy; and (4) *final targets,* representing the ultimate goals of economic policy in the United States—high employment, noninflationary economic growth, and a stable international payments and trade position. See, for example, Wallich (1984).

EXHIBIT 24–4

U.S. Money Supply Growth (Annualized percentage changes), Actual and Planned, in 1984 (percent)

	M1	M2
January	8.0%	7.6%
February	6.5	8.3
March	7.2	6.8
April	4.3	6.7
May	7.6	7.8
June	11.1	7.8
July	–0.9	6.0
August	4.5	6.8
September	5.8	8.4
October	–6.5	5.5
November	12.7	15.0
December	10.9	14.0
Planned Target Range	4 to 8%	6 to 9%

SOURCE: Board of Governors of the Federal Reserve System and Federal Reserve Bank of St. Louis.

public's money-using habits, especially shifts from conventional time and savings deposits to NOWs, MMDAs, and other interest-bearing transaction accounts, distort the money-supply measures. Moreover, judging by the rapid pace of financial innovation over the past decade, many new types of savings and transaction instruments will be developed in the years ahead, forcing the Fed to frequently readjust its money-supply definitions, growth targets, and operating procedures. There is also some evidence that the Fed's greater emphasis today on controlling money growth rather than interest rates has resulted in more volatile interest rates that feed-back upon the public's money-using habits.[8] As we observed earlier, Fed-

---

[8] The volatility of interest rates appears to have moderated somewhat since the fall of 1982. Many Fed watchers believe that the smaller rate movements since that time reflect a change in Federal Reserve money-supply control procedures. During the fall of 1982 the Board of Governors announced that it would no longer simply make *automatic* corrections in the growth of reserves when money-supply growth deviated from the targeted path. Henceforth, *policy judgment* would be used, taking into account market conditions, before major adjustments in reserves were carried out. Thus, market forces were granted a larger role in affecting short-term Federal Reserve monetary policy actions. The key results of this policy shift appear to have been: (1) somewhat less variability in interest rates (especially in the key federal funds rate); (2) a greater role for money market interest rates in influencing Federal Reserve policy; and (3) somewhat greater variability in month-to-month growth in the nation's money supply. For a description of this policy shift and its effects see, for example, Wallich (1984).

eral Reserve policy is not the sole determinant of the money supply or of total reserves. Fluctuations in the public's demand for money can lead to enormous changes in the amount of credit creation and interest rates in the financial system. Moreover, many of these changes cannot be anticipated. The Fed frequently is forced to react after the fact, leading to sudden surges or sudden declines in the growth of the nation's money supply.

MONEY MARKET INDICATORS

While control of the money supply and reserves are now the principal focus of central bank policymaking in the United States, the Fed also keeps close watch on conditions in the nation's financial markets, especially *the cost and availability of credit in the money market.* Indeed, there is evidence that the Federal Open Market Committee also sets target levels or ranges for the interest rate on federal funds loans. One reason is that the Fed is charged with the responsibility for stabilizing conditions in the financial markets to assure a smooth flow of funds from savers to investors. In addition, it must ensure that the government securities market functions smoothly so that adequate supplies of credit are available to security dealers and the federal government can market its billions of dollars in debt securities without serious difficulty. This is a burdensome responsibility because the Treasury is in the market every week refunding and offering new bills, and both the Treasury and several federal agencies sell billions of dollars worth of notes and bonds each quarter of the year.

The Federal Funds Rate

We can often gather important clues about the magnitude and direction of Federal Reserve policy by carefully watching changes in the cost of credit in the money market. A key money market indicator for many financial analysts is the *daily average rate on federal funds transactions.* This interest rate is usually the first to feel the impact of Federal Reserve open-market operations because it reflects the "price" of reserves in the banking system. When the Fed sells securities, the supply of available legal reserves is reduced and, other things held equal, the Fed funds rate will tend to rise. On the other hand, a Federal Reserve purchase of securities will increase available reserves, which tends to push the Fed funds rate down. Because the Federal Reserve does not announce its interest-rate targets in advance, however, market watchers try to guess the Fed's target ranges for the Federal funds rate by following closely hourly and daily quotations of that interest rate.

Other Money Market Interest Rates

Other money market rates watched carefully by investors and financial analysts include yields on U.S. Treasury bills, rates charged securities dealers by major New York banks on short-term security loans, and the Federal Reserve's discount rate. When interest rates rise, this is often regarded as an indicator of tightening credit conditions resulting from the Fed's restricting the growth of credit. When rates on T bills and other money market securities fall, however, this may be regarded as a sign the Fed is easing up, with even lower interest rates soon to follow.

Dealer loans rates and the availability of credit for security dealers are especially sensitive to Federal Reserve policy. As we saw in Chapter 13, dealers in U.S. government securities require millions of dollars in financing each day in order to carry their extensive inventories. These dealers use relatively little of their own equity capital to finance their operations, relying heavily on borrowed funds from major banks and large nonfinancial corporations. Dealer loans rates, like the federal funds rate, are highly sensitive to market conditions and fluctuate daily as credit conditions change. Nevertheless, the Fed has a powerful influence on interest rates in the economy, especially money market rates. It is safe to say that interest rates are unlikely to move very far up or down unless the Federal Reserve sanctions the move.

Free Reserves

Another popular indicator of money market conditions is the free reserve position of the banking system. *Free reserves* are excess reserve balances of depository institutions held at the Federal Reserve banks minus borrowings from the discount window. (Recall that excess reserves are legal reserve balances kept at the Reserve banks plus vault cash less required reserves.) Both the level and direction of changes in free reserves are thought to have meaning.

The dynamic element in free reserves is borrowings by depository institutions from the discount windows of the Federal Reserve banks. When these borrowings increase, depository institutions feel more restricted in their lending and investing until they can repay their debt to the Fed. Credit becomes more difficult to obtain and more expensive. On the other hand, when discount-window borrowings fall relative to excess reserves, depository institutions feel less pressure against their reserves and may become more liberal in extending credit.

Free reserves can be either positive or negative, depending on whether excess reserves are larger or smaller than borrowings from the Reserve banks. When borrowings exceed excess reserves, a condition of *net borrowed reserves* prevails. On the other hand, if borrowings are less than excess reserves, the banking system has *net free reserves.* Movement from week to week toward deeper net borrowed reserves generally implies that tighter credit conditions are developing. In contrast, a change toward greater net free reserves is usually regarded as an indicator of easier credit conditions. One problem with the free-reserve indicator is that many forces affect free reserves other than just Federal Reserve policy. For example, individual depository institutions decide what volume of excess reserves they wish to hold and whether or not to borrow from the Federal Reserve banks. This indicator, then, is subject to much the same criticism as the other monetary policy indicators we have discussed—it is influenced by many factors other than just Federal Reserve policy.

Interpreting Money Market Indicators

The use of money market indicators to interpret the current course of monetary policy may be illustrated using the information given in Exhibit 24–5. Movements in the effective Federal funds rate, market yields on U.S. Treasury bills, the Federal Reserve Bank of New York's discount rate, and free reserves between February and May 1984 are shown in the exhibit. We note that money market interest rates *rose* over the period shown in the exhibit. At the same time, depository institu-

EXHIBIT 24–5

Money Market Indicators of Federal Reserve Policy

Money Market Indicator	1984			
	February	March	April	May
Effective federal funds rate	9.59%	9.91%	10.29%	10.32%
Interest rate on U.S. Treasury bills, secondary market:				
three-month	9.09	9.52	9.69	9.83
six-month	9.18	9.66	9.84	10.31
Federal Reserve Bank of New York discount rate	9.00	9.00	9.00	9.00
Net free (or net borrowed) reserves ($ millions)	375	(243)	(744)	NA

Notes: Figures for the Federal funds rate are averages of daily effective rates weighted by the volume of transactions at these rates. Treasury bill rates are computed on a bank discount basis from daily closing bid prices. Discount rates are averages supplied by the Federal Reserve Bank of New York. Free reserves are the difference between excess reserve balances with the Federal Reserve banks less total borrowings from the discount windows of the Reserve banks.
SOURCE: Board of Governors of the Federal Reserve System, *Federal Reserve Bulletin,* selected issues.

tions experienced a deepening net borrowed reserve position, with free reserves dropping from +$375 million to −$744 million. This was a signal to many money market analysts that the Federal Reserve was tightening credit conditions and so credit was becoming less available and more expensive. In part, the Fed appeared to be reacting against unusually heavy credit demands from the federal government, a sharp resurgence in consumer borrowing which was fueling something of a consumer "spending spree" following the last recession, and investors' fears that inflation might be rekindled.

THE FEDERAL RESERVE AND NATIONAL ECONOMIC GOALS

For many years now, the Federal Reserve System has played an active role in the stabilization of the economy and in the pursuit of the nation's economic goals. These goals include controlling inflation, promoting full employment and sustainable economic growth, and achieving a stable balance of international payments position for the United States. In recent years these goals have proved to be extremely difficult to achieve in practice and in fact have often required conflicting policies. Nevertheless, the Fed remains committed to them and sets its policies accordingly.

The Goal of Controlling Inflation

Inflation—a rise in the general price level for all goods and services produced in the economy—has been among the most serious economic problems in the United States in recent years. Indeed, inflation has been a worldwide problem with many nations experiencing far higher annual rates of inflation than those currently prevailing in the United States. Moreover, inflation is not new; price levels have been generally rising since the beginning of the Industrial Revolution in Europe nearly 300 years ago. There is also evidence of outbreaks of rampant inflation during the Middle Ages and in ancient times.

What is particularly alarming about inflation is its tendency to *accelerate* in the absence of strong efforts to control it. For example, between 1960 and 1965 the U.S. consumer price index (the CPI or cost-of-living index) rose an average of only 1.3 percent a year. Then between 1965 and 1970 in the midst of the Vietnam War, large federal budget deficits, and rapid expansion of the nation's money supply, the average annual growth rate of consumer prices more than tripled, to a 4.2 percent annual rate. From 1970 through 1975 the CPI's annual growth rate climbed to almost 7 percent and then soared to almost 9 percent through 1980.

EXHIBIT 24-6

Measures of the Rate of Inflation in the United States (Compound annual rates of change)

	Period					
Price Level Index	1960–65	1965–70	1970–75	1975–80	1980–84	1985
Consumer price index (CPI)	1.3%	4.2%	6.7%	8.9%	6.0%	3.5*
Producer price index, finished goods	0.4	2.9	8.6	8.6	4.2	0.7*
Implicit price deflator for gross national product	1.6	4.2	6.6	7.2	5.8	4.1**

* Rate of growth for 12 months ended February 1985.
** Rate of growth for first six months.
SOURCE: Federal Reserve Bank of St. Louis, *Annual U.S. Economic Data, Compound Rates of Change, 1960–79 and 1965–84;* U.S. Department of Commerce; and Board of Governors of the Federal Reserve System.

Finally, large-scale unemployment and two back-to-back recessions in 1980 and 1982 helped reverse the accelerating trend and significantly lowered the nation's inflation rate. (See Exhibit 24–6.)

What are the *causes* of inflation? During the 1960s and 70s war and government spending were certainly contributing factors. Soaring energy and food costs, higher home-mortgage rates, and rapid increases in unit labor and medical care costs also played key roles until the 1980s brought a turnaround. Another contributing factor until recently was the decline in the value of the U.S. dollar in international markets. The dollar's weakness relative to other major currencies (particularly the German mark and Swiss franc) raised the price of imports into the United States and lessened the impact for foreign competition on domestic producers. However, with a slackening in inflation in the early 1980s the dollar recovered strongly.

Still another causal factor is inflationary expectations—the anticipation of continued inflation by businesses and households. Once under way, inflation seems to develop a momentum of its own as consumers spend and borrow more freely to stay ahead of rising prices, sending prices still higher. Businesses and labor unions begin to build inflation into their price and wage decisions, passing higher costs along in the form of higher prices for goods and services. The result is a wage-price spiral where each plateau of increased costs is used as a basis for justifying still further price increases.

Inflation creates distortions in the allocation of the nation's scarce resources and definitely hurts certain groups. For example, it tends to discourage saving and encourages consumption at a faster rate to stay ahead of rising prices. Moreover, the decline in the savings rate tends to discourage capital investment. Unfortunately, this means that the economy's growth in productivity (i.e., output per worker-hour) tends to slow. The fall in productivity means that the supply of new goods and services cannot keep pace with rising demands, putting further upward pressure on prices. At the same time, workers usually seek cost-of-living adjustments in their wages and salaries, leading to a dramatic increase in unit labor costs. While some workers represented by strong unions or in growth industries manage to keep pace with inflation, other groups, including many savers, lenders of funds, retired persons, and government employees, whose income is fixed or rises slowly, often experience a decline in their real standard of living.

The Goal of Full Employment

The Employment Act of 1946 committed the federal government for the first time to minimizing unemployment as a major national goal. The Federal Reserve, as part of the government's structure, is therefore committed to this goal as well. In recent years, the U.S. unemployment rate as determined from monthly surveys conducted by the U.S. Department of Labor has hovered in the 6 to 10 percent range. In terms of numbers of people, between 6 and 11 million workers have been actively seeking jobs but have been unable to find them. The nation's output of goods and services and its real standard of living are reduced by unemployment which also breeds social unrest, increased crime, and higher tax burdens on those who are working.

In recent years the U.S. economy has experienced rising plateaus of unemployment. As the 1960s ended, unemployment affected less than 5 percent of the civilian labor force. However, a recession in 1970–71 led to substantial increases in the number of jobless workers, and there was little improvement until 1973, when the jobless rate fell below 5 percent. Following the Arab oil embargo and a deep recession in 1974–75, the nation's unemployment rate rose to a postwar record of almost 9 percent. The recovery of the economy between 1976 and 1979 brought the unemployment rate down to just under 6 percent midway in 1979. However, the double recessions of 1980 and 1982 sent it soaring again to 10 percent and above briefly and the jobless rate remained around 7 percent in the mid-1980s. (See Exhibit 24–7.)

Is it possible to have zero unemployment? What is full employment? In a market-oriented economy, where workers are free to change jobs and businesspeople are free to hire and fire, some unemployment is inevitable. There is a minimum level of unemployment, known as frictional unemployment, which arises from the temporary unemployment of persons who are changing jobs in response to higher wages or better working

EXHIBIT 24–7

U.S. Civilian Unemployment Rate (percent of civilian labor force)

1970	4.9%	1978	6.2%
1971	5.9	1979	5.8
1972	5.6	1980	7.1
1973	4.9	1981	7.6
1974	5.6	1982	9.7
1975	8.5	1983	9.6
1976	7.7	1984	7.5
1977	7.1	1985*	7.3

* As of June 1985.
SOURCE: Economic Report of the President, February 1984; and *Federal Reserve Bulletin*, May 1985.

conditions. Full employment, therefore, refers to a situation in which the only significant amount of unemployment is frictional in nature. In a fully employed economy, everyone actively seeking work will find it in a relatively short period. During the 1960s the President's Council of Economic Advisers defined full employment as a situation in which only 4 percent of the civilian labor force was unemployed.

In recent years, however, economists have raised their estimates of the amount of irreducible frictional unemployment. A key factor is the massive shifts which have occurred in the composition of the American labor force in recent years, especially the rapid increase in the number of adult women seeking jobs. Women 20 years of age and older, in fact, have accounted for more than half the net increase in the U.S. labor force in recent years. This upward surge in women's employment may be attributed to a decline in fertility rates, more varied jobs available to females, and the erosion of family incomes due to inflation. Teenage participation in the labor force also has expanded sharply since the late 1970s under the pressure of inflation, the rising cost of college training, and the spread of vocational schools. Historically, these two groups (women and teenagers) have reported higher average unemployment rates than those of most other workers. Both women and teenagers move in and out of the job market with much greater fluidity than do adult male workers, due to family needs and schooling opportunities, thus raising the average unemployment rate.

Other groups also increasing in importance who traditionally report high unemployment rates include nonwhite workers and unskilled labor. One of the most conspicuous shortcomings of U.S. economic policy has been its inability to significantly lower the unemployment rate among minority workers and the unskilled. Structural unemployment—jobless-ness due to a lack of necessary skills—has not been reduced to any appreciable extent in the U.S. economy since the mid-1960s.

The Goal of Sustainable Economic Growth

The Federal Reserve has declared that one of its most important long-run goals is to keep the economy growing at a relatively steady and stable rate—that is, high enough to absorb increases in the labor force and prevent the nation's unemployment rate from rising, but slow enough to avoid runaway inflation. Most economists believe this implies a rate of growth in the nation's GNP of close to 4 percent annually on a real (inflation-adjusted) basis. Periodically, however, the economy grows more slowly than this or turns down into a recession, resulting in rising unemployment.

While most U.S. recessions have been relatively brief and mild, they have averaged two each decade, or about once every three to four years. For example, during the 1970s the nation's real output of new goods and services declined in 1973–75 and again in 1980 (Exhibit 24–8). The 1980 recession was the shortest downturn ever recorded, lasting only six months, but was followed by a deep recession in 1982 when real GNP dropped about 2 percent. However, during the mid-1980s a strong economic recovery produced accelerated GNP growth in 1983 and 1984, only to be followed by a significant growth slowdown in 1985.

Forecasting the actual starting point of each recession and its duration has proven to be an exceedingly difficult problem for the Federal Reserve. Each downturn in the economy springs from somewhat different causes, though most recessions involve a sharp cutback in investment in invento-

EXHIBIT 24–8

Rates of Growth in Real U.S. GNP (Compounded annual rates of change)

Period	Annual Rate of Change in GNP (1972 dollars)	Period	Annual Rate of Change in GNP (1972 dollars)
1960–69	3.9%	1979–80	−0.3%
1970–79	3.5	1980–81	2.5
1980–84	2.7	1981–82	−2.1
1984–85*	1.9	1982–83	3.7
		1983–84	6.8

* Measured from the second quarter of 1984 through the second quarter of 1985.
SOURCE: Federal Reserve Bank of St. Louis, *National Economic Trends,* and *Annual U.S. Economic Data,* various issues.

ries as business decision makers come to anticipate lower sales volume. Fears of being caught with a large quantity of unsold goods lead to periodic cutbacks in new orders, throwing people out of work. At the same time, interest rates usually rise to peak levels shortly before a recession begins, gradually choking off private investment.

Traditional economic theory suggests that a decline in the nation's rate of economic growth should lead to a lower rate of inflation. This follows from the observation that recessions are marked by reduced demand for goods and services and falling incomes. Thus, in theory at least, a recession and slower economic growth are short-run cures for severe inflation, though for those without jobs they are certainly high-cost cures. Interestingly enough, however, recent recessions have been accompanied by substantial inflation. Many observers believe the bias in the U.S. economy toward inflation even during recessionary periods may be due to the rapid growth of service industries relative to the manufacturing sector, to welfare payments (especially unemployment compensation) that sustain money incomes, escalator clauses in wage contracts, and the expectation that government policy will always respond quickly to protect jobs whenever economic problems appear.

Equilibrium in the U.S. Balance of Payments and Protecting the Dollar

The Federal Reserve must be concerned, not only with domestic economic conditions, but also with developments in the international sector. In this area, the Fed pursues two interrelated goals: protecting the value of the dollar in foreign currency markets, and achieving an equilibrium position in the U.S. balance of payments.

When the United States buys more of the goods, services, and securities offered by other nations than those countries spend for what the United States sells, the difference must be made up by giving foreigners claims against U.S. reserves and resources. If the United States persists in purchasing or acquiring more abroad than foreigners purchase or acquire here, a disequilibrium position in the nation's balance of payments results. This means that the United States cannot continue to draw down its reserve assets (primarily gold, foreign currencies, and Special Drawing Rights at the International Monetary Fund) indefinitely, nor will it find foreigners willing to accept unlimited amounts of dollars.[9] At some point the federal government and the Federal Reserve must adopt policies that slow down the outflow of U.S. dollars and encourage foreigners

---

[9] See Chapter 27 for a discussion of reserve assets and disequilibrium problems in the U.S. balance of payments.

to buy more U.S. goods, services, and securities. Failing this, the value of the dollar in international markets begins to weaken.

In recent years the United States has experienced some deep deficits in its international balance-of-payments position. (See Exhibit 24–9.) One cause of these payments deficits, as we will see in Chapter 27, has been massive imports of increasingly expensive foreign oil. Petroleum imports now account for about one third of total U.S. merchandise imports each year. Other foreign imports into the United States experiencing considerable growth in recent years include European and Japanese autos, steel products, building materials, natural gas, and crude rubber.

While the U.S. international payments position and world trade balance has run into deep trouble in the past decade, the value of the dollar has held up surprisingly well in international markets. During the 1970s the U.S. dollar's trade value—purchasing power in foreign markets—declined due primarily to worsening inflation at home and soaring energy prices. However, as reflected in Exhibit 24–9, the dollar strengthened significantly in the early 1980s, gaining on virtually every other major international currency. Many American tourists, for example, happily discovered they could travel far more comfortably abroad because the dollar exchanged for more units of other currencies abroad, especially in Mexico and in Western Europe. The turnaround in the dollar's exchange value during the early and mid-1980s appears to be due to several major factors: (1) a slower rate of domestic inflation; (2) high American interest rates, offering foreign investors attractive returns from purchasing U.S. securities; (3) lower and more stable energy prices; and (4) a strengthening American economy.

EXHIBIT 24–9

World Trade Balance of the United States and the Value of the Dollar

	World Trade Balance of the United States (FOB Exports— CIF Imports)	Multilateral Trade- Weighted Value of the U.S. Dollar (March 1973 = 100)
1965	$4.3	—
1970	0.5	121.1
1975	2.2	98.5
1980	−36.2	87.4
1981	−39.7	102.9
1982	−42.6	116.6
1983	−69.7	125.3

SOURCE: *Economic Report of the President,* February 1984.

WHAT POLICIES SHOULD WE PURSUE TO ACHIEVE THE NATION'S ECONOMIC GOALS?

The four key economic goals we have discussed—avoidance of inflation, reducing unemployment, achieving healthy and sustainable economic growth, and achieving a strong international payments position—cannot be achieved by wishful thinking. They require carefully constructed and consistent national economic policies. Unfortunately, there is a long-standing controversy over what these policies should be. Three different views have emerged over the years on what public policy strategies contribute most to low inflation, high employment, strong growth, and stable international payments. These three competing viewpoints on public policy are known as:

1. The monetarist view.
2. The credit availability (Neo-Keynesian) view.
3. Supply-side economics.

In the sections that follow we look briefly at each one and how it proposes to solve the nation's economic problems.

The Monetarist View

An approach to economic policy growing rapidly in popularity in recent years is the *monetarist school.* Among the most important proponents of this particular approach to government policy are economists Milton Friedman, Karl Brunner, Alan Metzer, David Meiselman, Anna Schwartz, Christopher Sims, and others.[10] These economists argue that the nation's *money supply* is a dominant influence on prices, spending, production, and employment. Friedman and Schwartz, for example, after analyzing money and business cycles dating back to the Civil War, concluded that

> Appreciable changes in the rate of growth of the money stock are a necessary and sufficient condition for appreciable changes in the rate of growth of money income.[11]

Moreover, changes in the rate of money-supply growth appear to precede changes in economic activity and inflation, suggesting that money exerts an independent causal influence on economic conditions. They believe that the economy is inherently stable and tends toward full employment

---

[10] See especially Friedman and Schwartz (1963), Friedman and Meiselman (1963), Keran (1967), Anderson and Carlson (1970), and Sims (1972) in the list of references at the conclusion of this chapter.

[11] See Friedman and Schwartz (1963), p. 53.

and sustainable growth without inflation if left to its own devices. One of the ways in which government can aid the economy in achieving noninflationary growth and full employment is to avoid "fine tuning" the system. Allegedly, attempts at fine tuning do more harm than good, causing instability in the economy.

According to the monetarist view, Federal Reserve monetary policy affects the economy mainly through changes in the rate of monetary growth. For example, if the money supply grows too rapidly, exceeding the public's expectations, an excess stock of money results. Money demand for goods and services will rise rapidly and put upward pressure on prices.[12] In contrast, when the money supply grows too slowly relative to the demand for money, the public attempts to restore its desired money balances by cutting back on spending and purchases of financial assets. The result is a drop in income and demand in the economy and a rise in interest rates, so that employment and growth are slowed. The Federal Reserve can exert its most favorable effect on the economy simply by allowing the money supply to grow at a relatively constant rate (preferably about 4 to 6 percent a year), which approximates the rate of growth in the economy's capacity to produce goods and services.

The Credit Availability, or Neo–Keynesian, View

A more traditional approach to fighting inflation is known as the credit availability, or neo-Keynesian, view.[13] Adherents to this view believe that a wide range of factors—monetary and nonmonetary—influence employment, growth, and prices. They argue that the money supply is an important factor in generating business cycles but *not* necessarily *the* most important factor. Government spending and taxation (i.e., fiscal policy) as well as money and credit policy also play critical roles in creating or

---

[12] Monetarists base this conclusion on the assumption that each unit (individual or business) in the economy desires to hold a certain quantity of money. If the money supply grows so large that it exceeds desired levels, then the cost of holding additional money exceeds its benefits. Businesses and individuals will attempt to spend away their excess money balances by purchasing goods, services, and other assets. With the economy at or near full employment, prices must rise due to the added spending.

[13] The term *neo-Keynesian* is often used to describe economists who have adopted, amplified, and further refined many of the ideas of British economist John Maynard Keynes. While Keynes wrote several books and many articles covering the period from World War I through World War II, his views on the causes of unemployment, inflation, and other economic problems appear in his *The General Theory of Employment, Interest, and Money* (1936). Leading economists who have further refined and developed the original Keynesian theories include Patinkin (1976), Tobin (1965), Smith (1969), and Samuelson (1979).

reducing inflation, unemployment, and other problems because of their impact on investment spending.

We recall from Chapter 7 that investment spending includes household expenditures for housing, automobiles, and other durable goods and business expenditures for plant, equipment, and inventories. Investment spending is the most volatile component of the total demand for goods and services in the economy. When investment falls, a recession usually follows, while rising investment often precipitates an economic boom. Changes in investment expenditures have a multiplier effect on total income in the economy because new investment generates income, which leads to increased consumption and still more income. Thus, even small changes in the volume and mix of investment expenditures can lead to magnified changes in income, spending, employment, and prices.

How can government fiscal and monetary policy affect investment spending and ultimately exert an impact on inflation, employment, and growth? According to the neo-Keynesian view, the volume of investment spending is affected directly by the cost and availability of credit, monetary growth, and total wealth. The rate of interest is especially important here because it is a measure of the cost of financing new investment spending. A rise in interest rates, other things equal, will reduce the demand for investment funds, slowing not only investment spending but also the growth of employment, income, and prices. Higher rates will tend to increase unemployment but usually strengthen the dollar in international markets. In contrast, lower interest rates stimulate the demand for investment, which increases income and employment and may cause more inflation (if the economy is at or near full employment). The Federal Reserve can bring about changes in interest rates, up or down, by changing the real money supply (i.e., money adjusted for changes in the price level). For example, rising inflation can be countered by slower monetary growth. If the money supply grows more slowly than the public's demand for real money balances, interest rates will rise, leading to a decline in investment spending. Income and spending in the economy will grow more slowly, and inflationary pressures will be reduced.

We can illustrate these hypothesized effects of changes in the money supply on interest rates and the nation's income by using a familiar methodology in economics—IS-LM analysis. This well-known tool of economic analysis is based on two key relationships: (1) the effects of changing money supply and money demand on both interest rates and income; and (2) the effects of changing saving and investment decisions (including government borrowing) on both interest rates and income. IS-LM analysis assumes there are *two* equilibrium relationships between all of these factors, each represented in Figure 24–1 below. The *LM curve* is a locus (collection) of equilibrium interest rates for which money demand (L) equals money supply (M). For each level of national income specified along the horizontal axis in Figure 24–1, the point on the LM curve directly above that level of income gives the equilibrium interest rate at which L = M. Similarly, the *IS curve* is a locus (collection) of equilibrium levels of national income at which the volume of planned savings (S) equals the volume of planned investment (I), including government borrowing. For any given interest rate along the vertical axis of Figure 24–1, the IS curve will show that level of national income at which point the economy is in equilibrium (with S = I). At the exact point where the IS and LM curves cross *both* the economy and interest rates in the financial markets are in *equilibrium*.

But, suppose the Federal Reserve *increases the money supply.* In the short run, at least, the LM curve shifts outward and to the right to LM′, resulting in a *lower equilibrium interest rate* (i′). Moreover, because the lower equilibrium interest rate will stimulate new investment spending, there is a rise in economic activity to a new and *higher equilibrium level of income* (y′). Thus, a monetary policy action by the Fed affects *both* interest rates and the nation's income (production and spending). Suppose the Federal Reserve *decreases the money supply.* The LM curve contracts backward and to the left to LM″, resulting in a *higher equilibrium interest rate* (i″). Moreover, with higher interest rates some invest-

FIGURE 24–1

How Equilibrium Interest Rates and National Income Change with Shifts in the Nation's Money Supply

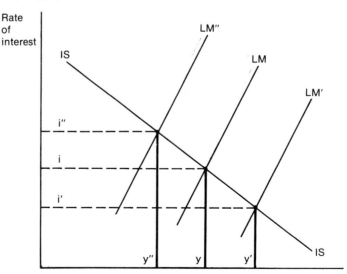

Level of nation's income (production and spending)

ment spending is discouraged, reducing the level of overall economic activity. A *lower equilibrium level of income* (y″) results.

Fiscal policy—government taxing and spending—also has a significant role to play in cooling inflation and promoting high employment and growth, according to the neo-Keynesian view. If total spending in the private sector of the economy grows too rapidly, generating inflation, government spending can be reduced, which will soon lead to less consumption spending and ultimately decrease private investment. In other words, government spending, like private investment spending, has a multiplier effect, up or down, on employment, income, and prices. Alternatively, private consumption and investment spending can be choked off by higher taxes. Through increased tax revenues, federal, state, and local governments can reduce budget deficits or even run budget surpluses so that the government sector actually withdraws funds from the private spending stream. Demand for goods and services will fall, leading to reduced inflationary pressures but also probably some increase in unemployment and slower economic growth.

Thus, the neo-Keynesian, or credit availability, view stresses the necessity of using *both* monetary and fiscal policy to achieve the nation's economic goals. Neo-Keynesians question whether merely maintaining a constant rate of growth in the money supply will, by itself, solve the problems of inflation and unemployment. The appropriate growth rate for money depends on economic conditions, the status of government fiscal policy, and especially the public's demand for money. Under some circumstances (especially if the demand for money were falling), a 4 percent rate of growth in the nation's money supply could be highly inflationary. Under other circumstances (such as following a rapid rise in money demand), 4 percent money growth could lead to severe recession and higher unemployment. In either case, suggest the neo-Keynesians, the key factors to watch in gauging the direction and impact of monetary policy are interest rates and the growth of the real money supply. To fight inflation reduce the growth rate of the real money supply and increase interest rates; to stimulate employment and economic growth speed up money growth and lower interest rates.

Supply-Side Economics

Shortly after President Ronald Reagan took office in January 1981, the administration announced a new approach to the nation's economic problems. It was labeled *supply-side* economics to differentiate this strategy from methods employed during most of the postwar period that attacked inflation and unemployment from the *demand* side of the marketplace. Just as logically, supply-siders claimed, we could solve inflation and unemployment problems from the *supply* side—by increasing the nation's output of goods and services. If the economy produces more relative to the public's demand, then there is less reason for prices to rise and more jobs open up.

How can this be done? Basically, by stimulating private investment and increasing savings to finance that investment. As Tatom notes, "supply-side economics is growth- and efficiency-oriented."[14] It argues that economic policy has a direct impact on the rate of growth in the supply of productive resources and upon technological innovation—factors that determine the economy's capacity to produce. The economy's productive capacity is lowered by government regulations which require the use of inefficient technologies or reduce incentives to save, invest, and use resources. The same is true of an excessive tax burden which transfers resources from the private to the public sector. In an effort to avoid high tax rates, resource owners will divert their resources to lower taxed but less efficient uses, such as by substituting labor for capital, retaining rather than replacing old equipment, and spending more on consumption instead of saving. Supply-siders in recent years have recommended:

1. A lower and more stable rate of monetary expansion.
2. Less govenment regulation of business in order to stimulate competition and technological innovation.
3. Reduced tax rates on individual incomes and business profits to stimulate saving.
4. Accelerated depreciation of business equipment to stimulate investment.
5. A reduction in the size of the government sector in order to divert more resources into the private sector and into free markets.

Can the supply-side approach really work to simultaneously subdue inflation, bring about stable long-term economic growth with low unemployment, and improve the U.S. international payments position? The jury is still out on this question. The U.S. inflation rate *has* dropped significantly since its record high levels in the late 1970s, but at the price of high unemployment. And the U.S. balance-of-payments situation, as we saw earlier, worsened in the early and mid-1980s. Much depends on the *psychological effects* of supply-side economics—its ability to persuade businesses to increase their investment in plant and equipment and to convince savers to spend less on current consumption and save more. Moreover, the lowering of tax rates in the 1980s contributed to higher federal budget deficits which, combined with other factors, kept interest rates at high levels and limited growth in capital investment.

---

[14] See Tatom (1981), p. 18.

Thus, it is not at all clear that supply-side economics, like monetarism or the Neo-Keynesian approach, can ensure progress toward *all* of the nation's economic goals.

THE TRADE–OFFS AMONG THE NATION'S ECONOMIC GOALS

As we have seen in this chapter, the United States faces some serious economic problems. Inflation is less severe today than in the turbulent 1970s, but unemployment and balance-of-payments problems present imposing difficulties. Does this mean the Federal Reserve System and other government policymaking agencies have simply failed to do their jobs?

Unfortunately, the problem is not that simple. For one thing, the nation's economic goals *conflict* with each other. For example, controlling inflation and stabilizing the U.S. international payments situation usually require the Fed to slow down the economy through restricted money growth and higher interest rates. However, this policy threatens to generate more unemployment and subdued economic growth. Evidence that national economic goals frequently conflict was provided by British economist A. W. Phillips and American economists Paul Samuelson and Robert Solow nearly three decades ago.[15] These economists uncovered an *inverse* relationship between price-level increases (inflation) and unemployment. For example, Samuelson and Solow, using data collected from the 1950s, found that stable prices could only be achieved if unemployment remained as high as 5 to 6 percent of the civilian labor force. And their estimate may prove to be conservative in today's economy. As we have seen, in the mid-1980s U.S. unemployment hovered in the 7 to 8 percent range, while prices continued to rise 3 to 4 percent a year. Such a policy trade-off may not be *inevitable* in the long run, but it is clear that the process of attaining economic stability is a difficult and painful one.

THE LIMITATIONS OF MONETARY POLICY

In addition to conflicts among the nation's economic goals, the Federal Reserve finds that it cannot completely control financial conditions or the money supply. Changes in the economy itself feedback upon the money supply. It becomes exceedingly difficult, especially on a weekly or monthly basis, to sort out the effects of monetary policy from the impact of broad economic forces.

Moreover, the Fed has received only limited cooperation from Congress in the pursuit of effective taxing and spending programs. Most econ-

---

[15] See, in particular, Phillips (1958) and Samuelson and Solow (1960).

omists agree that fiscal policy—the taxing and spending activities of the federal government—can have a potent impact on economic conditions. Unfortunately, changes in tax rates and federal spending programs require the cooperation of both the executive and legislative branches of the government. This kind of cooperation between Congress and the president has been difficult to achieve on a long-term basis. Frequently the Federal Reserve System has been forced to carry the burden of economic policy almost totally alone. Under these circumstances, we should not be too surprised that the Fed's past track record leaves much to be desired.

STUDY QUESTIONS

1. Why are indicators of Federal Reserve policy important to the Fed itself and to managers of financial institutions, corporate treasurers, and the public?

2. What is a *money market indicator?* Give examples and explain how these indicators reflect changes in credit conditions. What problems can you see in the use of money market indicators to gauge the direction of monetary policy?

3. List and define the various measures of the nation's money supply. Why do we need several different measures of money? Do you really think it matters which form of the money supply the Federal Reserve controls?

4. What are the principal items on the Federal Reserve Statement? Which of these items reflect Federal Reserve activities?

5. Define what is meant by *net free reserves* and *net borrowed reserves.* How would you interpret changes in these money market indicators?

6. Explain how the actions of the U.S. Treasury can influence the reserves of depository institutions.

7. What is *float?* Why is it of concern to Federal Reserve policymakers?

8. List the principal economic goals of Federal Reserve monetary policy and define each. Which of these goals have been reasonably well achieved in recent years, and which have not? Try to explain why.

9. Explain the basic similarities and differences between the monetarist

and neo-Keynesian approaches to monetary policy. How would each deal with inflation? With unemployment?

10. What is supply-side economics? Can you foresee any problems in trying to implement the supply-side approach?

11. Outline the steps that the Federal Reserve System goes through in trying to control the growth rate of the money supply and hit its money growth targets. What difficulties do you see in the Fed's approach?

12. What trade-offs appear to exist among the nation's key economic goals? Why do you think these trade-offs exist?

SELECTED REFERENCES

Anderson, Leonall C., and Keith Carlson. "A Monetarist Model for Economic Stabilization." *Review,* Federal Reserve Bank of St. Louis, April 1970.

Board of Governors of the Federal Reserve System. "The New Federal Reserve Technical Procedures for Controlling Money." *Staff Memorandum,* January 31, 1980.

Cacy, J. A. "Monetary Policy in 1980 and 1981." *Economic Review,* Federal Reserve Bank of Kansas City, December 1980, pp. 18–25.

Friedman, Milton, and David Meiselmen. "The Relative Stability of Monetary Velocity and the Investment Multiplier in the United States, 1897–1958." In *Stabilization Policies,* ed. Commission on Money and Credit. Englewood Cliffs, N.J.: Prentice-Hall, 1963.

Friedman, Milton, and Anna Jacobson Schwartz. "Money and Business Cycles." *Review of Economics and Statistics,* February 1963.

————. *A Monetary History of the United States, 1867–1960.* Princeton, N.J.: Princeton University Press, 1963.

Higgins, Bryan. "Free Reserves and Monetary Policy." *Economic Review,* Federal Reserve Bank of Kansas City, July–August 1980.

Keran, Michael. "Economic Theory and Forecasting." *Review,* Federal Reserve Bank of St. Louis, March 1967.

Keynes, John M. *The General Theory of Employment, Interest and Money,* London: Macmillan, 1936.

Long, Richard W. "The FOMC in 1979: Introducing Reserve Targeting." *Review,* Federal Reserve Bank of St. Louis, March 1980.

Patinkin, Don. *Keynes' Monetary Thought: A Study of Its Development.* Durham, N.C.: Duke University Press, 1976.

Phillips, A. W. "The Relation between Unemployment and the Rate of Change of Money Wage Rates in the United Kingdom, 1961–1957." *Economica,* November 1958.

Samuelson, Paul A. *Economics,* 7th ed. New York: McGraw-Hill, 1979.

Samuelson, Paul A., and Robert M. Solow. "The Problem of Achieving and Maintaining a Stable Price Level: Analytical Aspects of Anti-Inflation Policy." *American Economic Review,* May 1960.

Sellon, Gordon, Jr. "The Role of the Discount Rate in Monetary Policy: A Theoretical Analysis," *Economic Review,* Federal Reserve Bank of Kansas City, June 1980.

Sims, Christopher. "Money, Income, and Causality," *American Economic Review,* September 1972, pp. 540–52.

Smith, Warren L. "A Neo-Keynesian View of Monetary Policy." In *Controlling Monetary Aggregates,* ed. Federal Reserve Bank of Boston, 1969.

Tatom, John A. "We Are All Supply-Siders Now!" *Review,* Federal Reserve Bank of St. Louis, May 1981, pp. 18–30.

Thornton, Daniel L. "An Early Look at the Volatility of Money and Interest Rates under CRR." *Review,* Federal Reserve Bank of St. Louis, October 1984, pp. 26–32.

Tobin, James. "The Monetary Interpretation of History." *American Economic Review,* June 1965.

Wallich, Henry. Member of the Board of Governors of the Federal Reserve System. "Recent Techniques of Monetary Policy." Speech to the Midwest Finance Association, Chicago, April 5, 1984.

25

The Treasury in the Financial Markets

PURPOSE OF THIS CHAPTER

To explain and illustrate the impact that Treasury debt-management and fiscal policy operations have on the economy and the financial markets. The chapter discusses the principal sources and uses of federal government funds and reviews recent tax and expenditure legislation passed by Congress. T accounts are then used to illustrate the effects of government borrowing and debt retirement on the economy and financial system. The concluding sections of the chapter examine the composition of the federal (public) debt, the techniques the Treasury uses to sell new securities, and strategies used to minimize the impact of Treasury operations on the financial system and the economy.

KEY TERMS AND CONCEPTS IN THE CHAPTER

auction method
bearer securities
book entry
borrowing from depository institutions
borrowing from the Federal Reserve banks
borrowing from the nonbank public
budget deficit

budget surplus
cash offering
debt-management policy
debt maturity
Economic Recovery Act
exchange offering
fiscal policy
floating debt
housekeeping goals

interest-bearing public debt
IS-LM
marketable public debt
noninterest-bearing public debt
nonmarketable public debt
retiring government debt
stabilization goals

One of the most important financial institutions in any nation's economy is the government treasury. In the United States the Treasury Department exerts a powerful impact on the financial system because of two activities that it pursues on a continuing basis. One of these is *fiscal policy*, which refers to the taxing and spending programs of the federal government designed to promote high employment, reasonable price stability, economic growth, and other worthwhile economic goals. A second area in which the Treasury exerts a potent effect on financial conditions is *debt-management policy*, which involves the refunding or refinancing of the federal government's huge debt. These Treasury policymaking activities influence interest rates, the prices of securities traded in the open market, and the availability of credit to both private and public sectors of the economy. In general, the Treasury pursues policies designed to achieve major economic goals but not to severely disturb the functioning of the nation's financial markets. It must be especially careful not to pursue policies that conflict with the operations of the Federal Reserve System, because both institutions have a profound effect on the cost and availability of loanable funds within the financial system.

THE FISCAL POLICY ACTIVITIES OF THE U.S. TREASURY

Congress dictates the amount of funds which the federal government will spend each year for a variety of federal programs ranging from welfare to national defense, education, the preservation of environmental quality, and the construction of highways, buildings, and other public facilities. Congress also determines the sources of tax revenue and the tax rates that must be paid by individuals, families, and businesses. Frequently, the Congress will vote for a greater amount of spending than can be supported by tax revenues and other governmental receipts. Alternatively, due to a slowdown in the economy, tax revenues may fall short of projections and not be sufficient to cover planned government expenditures. Either way, the result is a *budget deficit*, requiring the U.S. Treasury to borrow additional funds in the financial markets. On the other hand, government revenues may exceed expenditures, resulting in a *budget surplus*, which the Treasury may use to build up its cash balances or to retire debt previously issued.

As shown in Exhibit 25–1, U.S. Treasury budget surpluses have been very rare in recent years. In fact, the federal budget has been in surplus in only three fiscal years since 1931. The last federal budget surplus occurred during the 1969 fiscal year, when revenues exceeded expenditures

EXHIBIT 25–1

Federal Government Revenues, Expenditures, and Net Budget Surplus
or Deficit, Fiscal Years 1960–1986 ($ millions)

Fiscal Year	Total Revenues	Total Expenditures	Net Budget Surplus or Deficit (−)
1960	$ 92,492	$ 92,223	$ 269
1961	94,389	97,795	−3,406
1962	99,676	106,813	−7,137
1963	106,560	111,311	−4,751
1964	112,662	118,584	−5,992
1965	116,833	118,430	−1,597
1966	130,856	134,652	−3,796
1967	149,552	158,254	−8,702
1968	153,671	178,833	−25,162
1969	187,784	184,548	3,236
1970	193,743	196,588	−2,845
1971	188,392	211,425	−23,033
1972	208,649	232,021	−23,372
1973	232,225	247,074	−14,849
1974	264,932	269,620	−4,688
1975	280,997	326,151	−45,154
1976	300,000	366,418	−66,418
1977	357,762	402,710	−44,948
1978	401,997	450,804	−48,807
1979	465,940	493,635	−27,695
1980	517,112	576,675	−59,563.
1981	599,272	657,204	−57,932
1982	617,766	728,375	−110,609
1983	600,562	795,969	−195,407
1984	670,071	853,760	−183,689
1985	745,127	925,492	−180,365
1986*	793,700	973,700	−180,000

* Estimated by Office of Management and Budget and U.S. Department of Commerce.
Notes: Figures based on the unified budget for fiscal years. Prior to 1977 fiscal years ran from July 1 through June 30. Thereafter, the federal budget year runs from October 1 through September 30.
SOURCES: U.S. Department of Commerce; *Business Statistics,* 1977 ed.; *Survey of Current Business,* September 1979; Board of Governors of the Federal Reserve System, *Banking and Monetary Statistics, 1941–1970;* and Council of Economic Advisors, *Economic Report of the President, February 1984.*

by about $3 billion. Since that time, the federal budget has been continually in deficit. It seems safe to assume at this point that federal budget deficits will continue to be frequent occurrences in the future, forcing the Treasury to borrow huge amounts of funds annually in the nation's financial markets.

Sources of Federal Government Funds

It is interesting to analyze what sources of revenue the federal government draws upon to fund its activities. Exhibit 25–2 presents information on the principal sources of federal revenue and major spending programs. On the revenue side, the bulk of incoming funds is derived from taxes levied against individual and family incomes. In fiscal 1985, for example, individuals paid an estimated $328 billion in income taxes, representing

EXHIBIT 25–2

Federal Government Revenues, Expenditures, and Net Budget Surplus or Deficit, 1985 (Estimate; $ millions)

Budget Item	Amounts	Percent of Total
Budget revenues by source:		
Individual income taxes	$328,410	44.07%
Corporation income taxes	76,540	10.27
Social insurance taxes and contributions	270,683	36.33
Excise taxes	38,443	5.16
Estate and gift taxes	5,645	0.76
Customs duties	9,370	1.26
Miscellaneous receipts	16,037	2.15
Total budget revenue	$745,127	100.00%
Budget expenditures by function:		
National defense	$272,040	29.39%
International affairs	17,492	1.89
General science, space and technology	8,818	0.95
Energy	3,144	0.34
Natural resources and environment	11,346	1.23
Agriculture	14,319	1.55
Commerce and housing credit	1,127	0.12
Transportation	27,061	2.92
Community and regional development	7,586	0.82
Education, training, employment, and social services	27,893	3.01
Health	32,916	3.56
Income security: Social security and medicare	260,321	28.13
Other income security programs	114,360	12.56
Veterans benefits and services	26,723	2.89
Administration of justice	6,140	0.66
General government	5,744	0.62
General-purpose fiscal assistance	6,658	0.72
Interest on federal debt	116,138	12.55
Allowances	938	.10
Undistributed offsetting receipts	−35,273	−3,81
Total budget expenditures	$925,492	100.02%

Note: Columns may not add to totals due to rounding.
SOURCES: Executive Office of the President and Office of Management and the Budget.

about 45 percent of all federal revenues that year. Social security taxes supplied $270 billion—roughly a third of total federal income. Corporate income taxes were a distant third at 10 percent, while other taxes and fees for government services provided a little less than 10 percent of all federal revenues.

During the 1970s and early 1980s the share of federal revenues produced by corporate and personal income taxes declined. This was due to efforts by Congress to reduce withholding taxes and increase personal deductions against individual income taxes. At the same time, however, payroll taxes for social insurance rose sharply as Congress attempted to rescue the Social Security System from ever deepening deficits. These recent changes in tax rates suggest that the federal government has attempted in recent years to make the federal tax structure somewhat more responsive to the nation's economic problems. When the economy headed down into a recession, or inflation pushed individuals into higher tax brackets, Congress generally responded with income tax reductions.[1] Unfortunately, scheduled increases in social security taxes and the rapid growth of corporate and individual income taxes associated with inflation have usually outpaced tax reductions in recent years.

Federal Government Expenditures

Reflecting the effects of rising taxes and inflation, the federal government collects today an enormous volume of revenue from its citizens. For example, federal revenues exceeded $500 billion in 1980 and are expected to approach $800 billion in 1986 or 1987. Where does the federal government spend this money? What programs account for the bulk of federal expenditures?

Exhibit 25–2 indicates that more than half of all federal spending goes for national defense and various income security programs, including social security, medicare, and unemployment compensation. The latter programs are designed to sustain the spending power and standard of living of individuals retired, disabled, or temporarily unemployed. For example, outlays for federal income security programs and federal grants to states and localities arising out of the federal revenue-sharing programs

---

[1] One of the most serious limitations of fiscal policy in the past has been the long *lag* between the recognition of a need for new fiscal policies and the passage of new legislation. For example, it may take several months before tax cuts or budgetary changes are made. By that time, the underlying economic problems might have changed so that the wrong kind of policy is being pursued. For example, a tax cut proposed to stimulate an economy mired in the depths of a recession may be passed several months later when a strong economic recovery is under way, adding fuel to inflation. There is some evidence, however, that fiscal policy lags have shortened in recent years and Congress has become somewhat more flexible.

climbed from about 9 percent of the nation's GNP in 1970 to about 13 percent in the 1980s. Federal benefit payments under the social security program more than tripled during the 1970s alone, while outlays under the federal food stamp program increased almost 10 times over the same period. However, the growth of income security programs leveled off significantly in the 1980s, while a major national defense buildup occurred. Expenditures for defense climbed from just under 24 percent of federal outlays in 1980 to nearly 30 percent in 1985.

Viewing the federal government's budget as a whole, the share of the nation's economic activity accounted for by federal programs has been on a long-term uptrend. Federal expenditures accounted for about 24 percent of the nation's GNP in 1980, up from less than 20 percent in 1970. This growth relative to other sectors of the American economy represents both an expansion of existing programs, particularly national defense since 1980, and the birth of several new programs designed to deal with pressing social, economic, and environmental needs.

Recent Tax and Expenditure Legislation

Confronted with serious inflation and deepening federal deficits Congress and the president responded in the 1980s with a number of major pieces of fiscal legislation—legislation that continues to affect the financial markets today. For example, in August 1981 Congress passed and President Ronald Reagan signed the Economic Recovery Tax Act which brought about the most significant cuts in individual income tax rates in recent U.S. history. In addition, new accelerated depreciation allowances, investment tax credits, and tax incentives from business research and development expenditures were included in the Recovery Act in an attempt to increase investment spending and create jobs. The 1981 tax law grew out of a comprehensive package of reductions in federal expenditures and tax rates proposed by the Reagan administration to step up production of goods and services and thereby reduce inflation. The Economic Recovery Act reduced individual income tax rates, lowering the maximum individual income tax rate from 70 percent of 50 percent.[2] Income tax brackets, standard deductions, and personal exemptions were adjusted for the effects of inflation as measured by the consumer price index (CPI). This last provision, known as "indexing," is designed to eliminate "bracket creep," that is, the tendency for inflation to push individual incomes into higher and higher tax brackets.

The ultimate purpose of the foregoing changes is to stimulate added

---

[2] As noted in Chapter 10, this new top-bracket tax rate reduces the maximum effective tax rate on net long-term capital gains to 20 percent.

saving by individuals and families, providing additional funds for business investment. To further encourage household saving, individual taxpayers are allowed to exclude from federal income taxes 15 percent of their net interest income (less interest deductions) up to a maximum of $3,000 (or $6,000 on a joint return). Employees who participate in a qualified retirement plan may deduct from taxable income any contributions to individual retirement accounts (IRAs) or voluntary contributions to their qualified retirement plans up to $2,000 or 100 percent of total compensation, whichever is less. The maximum unified estate and gift tax rate was gradually reduced between 1982 and 1985 from 70 percent to 50 percent.

In order to stimulate additional business capital outlays, the Economic Recovery Act instituted an Accelerated Cost Recovery System (ACRS), which permits asset costs to be recovered over a predetermined period less than their estimated useful life. Under the 1981 law most business assets will be depreciated over a 3-, 5-, 10-, or 15-year time period, provided they were acquired after December 31, 1980. Additional research and experimentation outlays made by businesses are eligible for a 25 percent tax credit. Corporations earning less than $50,000 a year were permitted to retain more funds for investment through lower tax rates. Corporate tax rates were reduced to 15 percent on the first $25,000 of taxable corporate income and 18 percent on taxable income in excess of $25,000 but less than $50,000. These and other provisions of the Economic Recovery Tax Act were designed not only to lighten current tax burdens carried by businesses and households, but also to dampen expectations of continuing inflation.

While the Economic Recovery Act appeared to make a significant contribution toward reducing inflation, it probably contributed as well to deepening federal budget deficits. As Exhibit 25–1 shows, the federal budget deficit more than tripled between 1981 and 1983, forcing the U.S. Treasury to borrow unprecedented amounts in the nation's financial markets and confronting private borrowers with both higher interest rates and more limited availability of credit funds. Repeatedly Congress and the president attempted to reach agreement on a package of tax increases and spending reductions to reduce the deficit. One bill, the Deficit Reduction Act of 1984, made a partial contribution to the problem by calling for about $50 billion in combined spending reductions and tax increases. And, in 1985 Congress and the administration agreed on a new budget that called for a slowing in the rate of growth in defense spending and selected cuts in domestic programs, resulting in some planned moderation of the deficit. However, it is clear that additional policy measures by the president, the Congress, the Federal Reserve, or all three will be needed to significantly reduce federal budget deficits.

Tax Reform

A strong drive for federal income tax reform was launched in the mid-1980s. Proponents of basic changes in federal tax laws and IRS regulations cited numerous abuses of the existing tax system, such as pseudo-business ventures begun exclusively to shelter income from taxation and many wealthy individuals and corporations paying no taxes at all. Under a proposed reform program unveiled by the Reagan administration, both corporations and individuals would be subject to lower maximum income tax rates, but a proposed minimum tax of about 20 percent would mean that fewer taxpayers would be able to escape paying at least some taxes. Investment tax credits were targeted for reduction or elimination and the whole tax code would be simplified. The president also proposed increasing the personal exemption that may be deducted from an individual's gross income before taxes are calculated, thereby benefiting larger size families. However, other allowable deductions, such as for charitable gifts, state and local taxes, and interest on loans, were proposed targets for elimination or reduction in future tax-reform proposals.

Most of the proposed reforms appear to be aimed at making the federal tax code "neutral" in its effects on economic and financial decisions by businesses and individuals. Presumably, revisions in the federal tax code would result in a fairer tax system with the burden of financing federal government services shared more equitably by all taxpayers. However, thoroughgoing tax reform is an ideal that is most difficult to achieve in the real world because of its potent impact on thousands of individuals and institutions.

Effects of Federal Borrowing and Budget Deficits on the Financial System and the Economy

What are the effects of government borrowing on the economy and the financial markets? If the federal government runs a *small* budget deficit, it is possible for the Treasury to cover the shortfall in revenues by drawing upon its accumulated cash balances held at the Federal Reserve banks or even by issuing new currency. In recent years, however, federal deficits have been so large that substantial amounts of new debt securities have been issued in the money and capital markets. The impact of these massive borrowings on the money and capital markets and the economy depends on the *source* of borrowed funds. Exhibit 25–3 summarizes the probable effects of government borrowing designed to cover a budget deficit.

Borrowing from the Nonbank Public.

For example, suppose the Treasury needs to borrow $20 billion, which it raises by selling govern-

EXHIBIT 25–3

Effects of Government Borrowing on the Financial Markets and the Economy

Borrowing from the Nonbank Public

	Federal Reserve Banks		Depository Financial Institutions	
	Assets	Liabilities	Assets	Liabilities
Sale of securities		Legal reserves −20 of depository institutions Government +20 deposits	Legal reserves −20	Deposits of −20 the public
Spending of borrowed funds		Government −20 deposits Legal reserves +20 of depository institutions	Legal reserves +20	Deposits of +20 the public

EFFECTS: No change in the money supply or total reserves; total spending in the economy and interest rates rise.

Borrowing from Depository Institutions

	Federal Reserve Banks		Depository Financial Institutions	
	Assets	Liabilities	Assets	Liabilities
Sale of securities		Legal reserves −20 of depository institutions Government +20 deposits	Government +20 securities Legal reserves −20	
Spending of borrowed funds		Legal reserves +20 of depository institutions Government −20 deposits	Legal reserves +20	Deposits of +20 the public

EFFECTS: The money supply increases; total reserves are unchanged, but excess reserves fall due to increases in deposits; total spending and interest rates rise.

Borrowing from the Federal Reserve Banks

	Federal Reserve Banks		Depository Financial Institutions	
	Assets	Liabilities	Assets	Liabilities
Sale of securities	Government +20 securities	Government +20 deposits		
Spending of borrowed funds		Government −20 deposits Legal reserves +20 of depository institutions	Legal reserves +20	Deposits of +20 the public

EFFECTS: The money supply and total reserves increase, while total spending in the economy rises and interest rates tend to fall.

ment bonds to the nonbank public. As the public pays for these securities, it writes checks against its deposits held with depository institutions, initially reducing the size of the nation's money supply. As the checks are cleared and deposited in the Treasury's accounts at the Federal Reserve banks, legal reserves held by depository institutions decline by $20 billion.

To gauge the full effects of government borrowing, however, we must consider the fact that the government plans to *spend* its borrowed funds. In our example the Treasury will write checks totaling $20 billion against its Federal Reserve accounts and distribute these checks to the public. Deposits of the public rise by $20 billion, also increasing the legal reserves held by depository institutions.

On balance, after all transactions are completed, there is *no change* in the nation's money supply or in the total amount of reserves held by the banking system. However, there is likely to be an *increase* in total spending and income in the economy due to the fact that funds are transferred from those who purchase securities to members of the public receiving government checks. We are assuming that recipients of government checks have a higher propensity to spend new income than security investors who presumably have a higher marginal propensity to save any new income received. Aggregate consumption spending will probably increase, and, if the economy is at or near full employment, prices may rise. Initially, the increased sale of Treasury securities should put upward pressure on interest rates. Over a longer-run period, however, it is quite possible that interest rates will fall due to the higher levels of income and increased saving out of that income.

Borrowing from Depository Institutions.

The effects of government borrowing are somewhat different if the borrowing takes place entirely from depository institutions. If we assume, once again, that the Treasury borrows $20 billion, deposit-type institutions will pay for the securities they purchase by drafts against their legal reserve accounts held at the Federal Reserve banks. Reserves of depository institutions drop by $20 billion, as shown in Exhibit 25–3, and the Treasury's deposits, of course, rise by a like amount. Once again, however, the Treasury spends these borrowed funds, resulting in an increase in deposits held by the public and in legal reserves. The money supply rises because the public's deposit holdings increase.

On balance, after all transactions are completed, total legal reserves remain unchanged, but excess reserves fall because of the increase in deposits. There is also likely to be an increase in total spending and income in the economy as the public gains additional funds. Prices may rise if unemployment is low. Interest rates will increase in the short run with the increased quantity of government securities available. However, the gain in total spending should lead eventually to a decline in interest rates.

Borrowing from the Federal Reserve Banks.
Still a third route for government borrowing would be to secure credit directly from the central bank. In the United States this could be done by having the Treasury issue securities directly to the Federal Reserve banks. However, borrowing directly from the Federal Reserve is a highly *inflationary* way for the federal government to raise money. Financially speaking, it is the equivalent of printing money. Therefore, borrowing from the Fed is restricted by law. Nevertheless, in a severe national emergency such as a serious depression, it would probably be called upon to support a sagging economy.

How would borrowing from the central bank work and what would its effects be? The Federal Reserve banks acquire securities and increase the Treasury's deposits by the same amount. Initially, there is no withdrawal of reserves from the banking system, nor does the public lose deposits. Instead, both legal reserves and the public's deposits rise by the amount of any borrowed funds actually spent by the Treasury. In the example shown in Exhibit 25–3, the Treasury sells $20 billion in securities to the Federal Reserve banks, and its deposit accounts at the Fed rise by a like amount. As the Treasury spends the $20 billion, public deposits and reserves rise, causing increases in the nation's money supply, total spending, and income. Interest rates tend to fall due to the increase in income, which generates added savings.

Effects of the Retirement of Government Debt from a Budget Surplus on the Financial System and the Economy

Occasionally, the federal government collects more in revenue than it spends, running a budget *surplus.* By definition, a budget surplus implies that the government withdraws a greater amount of funds from the economy in the form of tax collections than it puts back into the economy through government expenditures. The Treasury could save these surplus funds to cover deficits in later years. However, this is usually unpopular from a political standpoint. It is more likely that a government budget surplus would be used to retire debt previously issued. But the impact of government debt retirement on the economy and the financial system depends on who happens to hold the debt securities the government plans to retire.

Retiring Government Debt Held by the Nonbank Public.
Suppose the securities scheduled for retirement are held by individuals

and institutions not a part of the banking system. In this case, there will be little or no change in the nation's money supply or in the reserves held by depository institutions.

This is illustrated in Exhibit 25–4, where the act of retiring government debt is separated into two steps. In the first step we assume the U.S. Treasury collects a surplus of $20 billion in tax revenues. This might arise, for example, if the federal government spent $100 billion but collected $120 billion in taxes from the public. Clearly, the public's deposits will drop a *net* $20 billion. Moreover, as members of the public write checks against their transaction deposits to pay taxes, legal reserves of depository institutions will also fall a net $20 billion. The Treasury's deposits at the Federal Reserve banks will rise by a like amount.

Assume now that the Treasury uses its surplus funds to retire securities held by the nonbank public. Security holders receive government checks totaling $20 billion, which are deposited in bank and nonbank thrift institutions. Legal reserves of these institutions rise by $20 billion. Of course, the Treasury now loses the same amount of money from its deposits at the Federal Reserve as the government's checks are cleared. The public's deposits and therefore its money supply first decline and then rise by $20 billion, with reserves following the same path. Is there no effect, then, from retiring securities held by the nonbank public? Not likely, because the government has transferred money from the general public (taxpayers), with a high propensity to spend, to security investors who, as a group, tend to be heavy savers. The net effect is probably to *reduce* total spending in the economy. Prices of goods and services may fall and unemployment may rise. It is likely, too, that interest rates will decline because the total supply of securities is being reduced.

Retiring Government Debt Held by Depository Institutions.

What happens if the government uses its budget surplus to retire securities held by banks and other depository institutions? Initially, the effects are much the same. Funds are withdrawn from taxpayer deposit accounts and transferred to the U.S. Treasury's deposits at the Federal Reserve. Legal reserves of depository institutions fall by the amount of the tax surplus (in Exhibit 25–4 by $20 billion). Now, however, the surplus funds are paid to depository institutions, who turn their securities in to the Treasury. Legal reserves rise as the government spends down its $20 billion deposit.

In the short run, the money supply is reduced due to the drain on taxpayer funds. Total legal reserves are unchanged, first falling and then rising. Note, however, that excess reserves must increase because total legal reserves are unchanged when deposits fall. In the long run the nation's money supply expands due to the gain in excess reserves. With fewer taxpayer funds, however, spending in the economy should decline,

EXHIBIT 25–4

Effects of Retiring Government Debt on the Financial Markets and the Economy

Retiring Government Securities Held by the Nonbank Public

	Federal Reserve Banks			Depository Financial Institutions		
	Assets	Liabilities		Assets	Liabilities	
Collection of tax surplus		Legal reserves of depository institutions Government deposits	−20 +20	Legal reserves −20	Deposits of taxpayers	−20
Retiring government securities		Government deposits Legal reserves of depository institutions	−20 +20	Legal reserves +20	Deposits of security holders	+20

EFFECTS: No change in money supply or in bank reserves; but total spending tends to fall, because funds move from active to passive spenders; interest rates decline.

Retiring Government Securities Held by Depository Institutions

	Federal Reserve Banks			Depository Financial Institutions		
	Assets	Liabilities		Assets	Liabilities	
Collection of tax surplus		Legal reserves of depository institutions Government deposits	−20 +20	Legal reserves −20	Deposits of taxpayers	−20
Retiring government securities		Legal reserves of depository institutions Government deposits	+20 −20	Government securities −20 Legal reserves +20		

EFFECTS: Money supply falls in short run, while total bank reserves are unchanged. Excess reserves increase due to a fall in deposits. Total spending and interest rates decline.

Retiring Securities Held by the Federal Reserve Banks

	Federal Reserve Banks			Depository Financial Institutions		
	Assets	Liabilities		Assets	Liabilities	
Collection of tax surplus		Legal reserves of depository institutions Government deposits	−20 +20	Legal reserves −20	Deposits of taxpayers	−20
Retiring government securities	Government securities −20	Government deposits	−20			

EFFECTS: Money supply and total reserves decrease by the amount of the budget surplus; total spending and interest rates decline.

which may increase unemployment. Interest rates, too, will probably decline because fewer securities are now available to investors.

It should be clear from the example above that budget surpluses and the retirement of government debt tend to slow down economic activity and, therefore, could be used as a vehicle to combat inflation. If the federal government wanted to have a maximum deflationary impact on the economy, whose government securities should it retire? The banking system's? No! The Treasury could have the greatest anti-inflationary impact by retiring government securities held by the Federal Reserve banks. This approach would be the equivalent of destroying money.

Retiring Government Debt Held by the Federal Reserve Banks. As the bottom panel of Exhibit 25–4 shows, retiring government securities held by the Federal Reserve drains funds from taxpayers. However, those funds are not returned to the private spending stream. Instead, the government uses its increased deposits to pay off the Federal Reserve banks and retrieve the securities they hold. Legal reserves of the banking system and the nation's money supply decline by the full amount of the budget surplus. Spending, interest rates, and the prices of goods and services are likely to fall as well.

Overall Impact of Government Borrowing and Spending

We may summarize all of these various impacts of government borrowing and spending with an IS-LM diagram. We recall our earlier discussion of IS-LM analysis in Chapter 24 (see Figure 24–1), which links determination of equilibrium interest rates with equilibrium national income (spending). In this analysis the LM curve represents a collection of *equilibrium interest rates* [where money demand (L) = money supply (M)] for various levels of national income (Y). We can also draw an IS curve, representing a collection of points at different levels of interest rates at which the *nation's income is in equilibrium;* that is, the volume of planned saving (S) by the public exactly equals the volume of planned investment plus government borrowing (I). As shown in Figure 25–1 below, the point where the IS and LM curves intersect yields *both* an equilibrium interest rate and an equilibrium level of income and spending in the economy.

What happens, then, when the government runs a deficit and increases its borrowing to finance it? As Figure 25–1 suggests, the added government borrowing adds to planned investment spending and, with the nation's money supply and money demand unchanged, equilibrium interest rates *rise* and the nation's income, production, and spending also *rise.* Of course the higher interest rates discourage some additional private borrowing and spending—the so-called *crowding out* effect—even as government borrowing and spending increases. If there is substantial unem-

FIGURE 25–1

Effects of Additional Government Borrowing and Deficit Spending on
the Nation's Income and Interest Rates

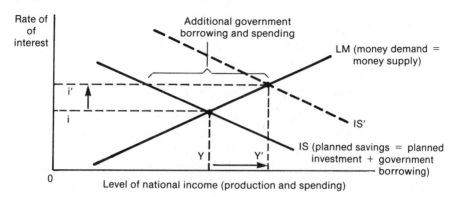

ployment, more jobs probably will be made available and the nation's
unemployment rate will fall. If the economy is already close to full employment, the added income and spending may drive the prices of goods.
and services higher, generating inflation.

This conventional view of government deficits and borrowing adding
to the nation's income and possibly driving up interest rates and inflation
has been challenged from several different directions in recent years.
One line of counterargument is that interest rates and security prices
in an *efficient* market simply may not respond to increased government
borrowing, either because an equal amount of *private* borrowing and
spending are "crowded out" of the marketplace due to fears of rising
interest rates and other factors, or because the added government borrowing is already anticipated by the market and has been discounted by
investors. Thus, there may be little *net* gain in terms of economic activity
or change in interest rates from government deficit spending.

Several recent studies tend to support these arguments. For example,
Plosser (1982), Roley (1981), and Sheehan (1985) find that security prices
and interest rates do *not* respond significantly to the presence or absence
of government deficits or to the sheer size of those deficits. While interest
rates may tend to rise as government borrowing increases, the demand
for money tends to fall at the same time which reduces the pressure of
total credit demands on the financial markets. Canto and Rapp (1982)
found that information on *past* budget deficits did *not* improve forecasts
of current interest rates, nor was the current budget deficit significantly
correlated with *future* changes in rates. And, finally, Dwyer (1982) finds
that government budget deficits did *not* appear to *cause* the rising U.S.

inflation rate over the 1952–81 period. Rather, Dwyer suggests that current budget deficits appear to be more influenced by past inflation, with nominal government deficits increasing *following* a rise in inflation rather than the other way around. Thus, there is considerable controversy today about the true effects of government deficits and borrowing on the financial markets and the economy. More research on this important issue clearly is needed.

MANAGEMENT OF THE FEDERAL DEBT

As we noted at the beginning of this chapter, one of the most important activities of the Treasury today is managing the huge public debt of the United States. The U.S. public debt is the largest single collection of securities available in the financial system today. Securities issued directly by the Treasury, which make up the bulk of the public debt, are regarded by investors as having zero *default risk* because the federal government possesses both taxing power and the power to create money. The government, unless it is overthrown by war or revolution, can always pay its bills.

Government securities do carry *market risk*, however, because their prices fluctuate with changes in demand and supply. In fact, the longer the term to maturity of a government security, the more market risk it possesses. Treasury bills, the shortest-term government IOUs, have relatively stable prices compared to long-term government bonds and notes.

The principal role of government securities in the financial system is to provide *liquidity*. Corporations, commercial banks, insurance companies, and other major institutional investors rely heavily on government securities as a readily marketable reserve to be drawn upon when cash is needed quickly. While private debt securities do carry higher explicit yields than government debt of comparable maturity, the greater liquidity and marketability of government securities represents an added return to the investor.

The Size and Growth of the Public Debt

How much money does the federal government owe? As shown in Exhibit 25–5, the gross public debt of the United States totaled over $1.7 trillion in 1985. On a per capita basis the public debt amounts to about $6,000 for every man, woman, and child living in the United States.

How did the federal debt become so huge? Wars, recessions, inflation, and the rapid expansion of military expenditures and social programs have been the principal causes. The federal government's debt was insignificant until the Great Depression of the 1930s, when the administration

EXHIBIT 25–5

The Public Debt of the United States, 1985 ($ billions)*

Types of Securities		Amount
Interest-bearing public debt		$1,695.2
Marketable debt	$1,271.7	
Bills	379.5	
Notes	713.8	
Bonds	178.4	
Nonmarketable debt	$ 423.6	
State and local government series	47.7	
Foreign issues	9.1	
Savings bonds and notes	74.4	
Government account series	292.2	
Noninterest-bearing debt		15.5
Total gross public debt		$1,710.7

Note: Columns may not add to totals due to rounding.
* First quarter of the year.
SOURCE: Board of Governors of the Federal Reserve System, *Federal Reserve Bulletin*, September 1985.

of President Franklin Roosevelt chose to borrow heavily to fund government programs and provide jobs. Even so, the public debt amounted to scarcely more than $50 billion at the beginning of World War II. The public debt multiplied five times over during the war years, however, approaching $260 billion by the end of World War II. Embroiled in the most destructive and costly war in history, the U.S. government borrowed and taxed away resources from the private sector to build tanks, planes, ships, and other war materials in enormous quantities.

For a brief period following World War II, it appeared that much of the public debt might be repaid. However, the Korean War intervened in the early 1950s, followed by a series of deep recessions when government tax revenues declined. Early in the 1960s the public debt reached $300 billion (see Exhibit 25–6). The advent of the Vietnam War and rapid inflation during the late 1960s and 1970s sent the debt soaring above its earlier levels. During the 70s rising inflation was combined with a sharp expansion in federal programs to provide aid to the elderly, support research, and supply funding for social welfare programs. Between 1970 and 1980 the public debt of the United States more than doubled, rising from just under $400 billion to over $900 billion and then rose more than 50 percent to climb over $1.7 trillion during 1985. This latest surge could be traced to the combined effects of business recessions that lowered tax collections, inflationary increases in government costs, a strong national defense buildup, and federal tax cuts. The rapid rise in the government's debt has prompted a grass-roots effort

EXHIBIT 25–6

The Public Debt of the U.S. Government, 1946–1985 ($ billions)

Year	Total Gross Public Debt	Year	Total Gross Public Debt
1946	$259.1	1966	$ 325.6
1947	255.6	1967	341.8
1948	251.7	1968	356.2
1949	256.1	1969	367.4
1950	255.4	1970	388.3
1951	258.1	1971	424.1
1952	266.1	1972	449.3
1953	273.8	1973	469.9
1954	277.2	1974	492.7
1955	279.1	1975	576.6
1956	275.5	1976	653.5
1957	274.2	1977	718.9
1958	282.2	1978	789.2
1959	288.7	1979	845.1
1960	287.7	1980	930.2
1961	293.6	1981	1,028.7
1962	300.2	1982	1,197.1
1963	306.0	1983	1,410.7
1964	314.3	1984	1,663.0
1965	317.2	1985*	1,710.7

* First quarter only.
SOURCE: Board of Governors of the Federal Reserve System, *Banking and Monetary Statistics, 1941–70;* and *Federal Reserve Bulletin,* various monthly issues.

to force Congress to adhere to a balanced budget. Petitions from more than 30 states have urged the passage of a constitutional amendment mandating a balanced budget.

Is this much debt simply too much? Have we as a society borrowed beyond our means? Or was Alexander Hamilton, the first Treasury secretary, accurate when he wrote: "a national debt, if it is not excessive, will be to us a national blessing"? The answer depends, in part, on the standard (or base) used to gauge the size of the public debt. Measured against the national income (i.e., the earnings of individuals and businesses which can be taxed to repay the debt), the public debt is lower now than it was a generation ago. For example, in 1985 the gross public debt amounted to about 45 percent of the U.S. GNP, compared to well over 100 percent at the end of World War II. Moreover, other forms of debt in the U.S. economy totaled as much or more than the public debt. For example, total mortgage debt outstanding in 1985 was about $2.1 trillion.

It should be remembered that U.S. government securities are at one and the same time debt obligations and also readily marketable, liquid assets to the millions of investors who hold them.

Another problem to keep in mind about today's huge federal debt and its possible burden on the economy and financial markets is the difficulties we face in trying to accurately *measure* the true size of the debt. It turns out that the answer to the question—How big is the federal debt?—is not all that easy. For example, *inflation* tends to increase the size of the debt because it tends to increase government budget deficits. Thus, in an inflationary period the government typically must borrow more, but this does not necessarily mean that the *burden* of the debt has increased; that is, government may not be exerting a greater impact on the economy or commanding a greater volume of real resources. An interesting study by Eisner and Pieper (1984), for example, concludes that the real size of the U.S. federal debt (adjusted for inflation) actually *fell* between 1946 and 1980. Moreover, the size of the public debt is typically measured in terms of the *par value* of government securities outstanding. But, when interest rates rise, the *market value* of government debt falls. Thus, a significant rise in interest rates will cause the value of that portion of the government's debt held by private investors to decline and may result in increased saving in the private sector.

Accurate measurement of the burden imposed by government debt probably also means that we must consider the value of the *assets* held by government. For example, most national governments hold a reserve of gold, foreign currencies, and securities. We might also add to these financial assets the estimated value of government buildings, office equipment, vehicles, military hardware, highways, port facilities, and airports. Thus, we may distinguish between the *gross liabilities* of the federal government—the total amount of its debt outstanding—and its *net liabilities*—government debt minus government assets. Including all of the government's assets at their fair market value would yield substantially smaller net government liabilities than gross liabilities. Of course, to be fair we probably would also have to consider the amount of total indebtedness of off-budget federal agencies (such as the farm credit agencies or federal mortgage agencies) which now amounts to about one fifth of the gross public debt. And, there are *contingent liabilities* that might well be added to the government's debt total, such as deposit insurance funds like that maintained by the FDIC to guarantee bank deposits or the social security fund which must eventually pay promised retirement benefits out of its accumulated reserves to millions of citizens. Clearly, measuring the *true* size of the government's debt is an extremely difficult assignment. For this reason we must be careful before jumping to any hasty conclusions about how large or significant the debt is or what its impact on the economy or financial markets might be.

The Composition of the Public Debt

The public debt as it is traditionally measured consists of a wide variety of government IOUs with differing maturities, interest rates, and other features. A small amount—less than 1 percent—carries no interest rate at all. This *noninterest-bearing public debt* consists of paper currency and coins issued by the U.S. Treasury Department, including silver certificates, greenbacks, and national bank notes, that are gradually being retired as they are turned in by the public. Virtually all paper money in circulation today is Federal Reserve notes, which are not officially a part of the public debt but obligations of the Federal Reserve banks.

More than 99 percent of all federal debt securities are *interest bearing* and may be divided into two broad groups—marketable securities and nonmarketable securities. By definition, *marketable* securities may be traded any number of times before they reach maturity. In contrast, *nonmarketable* securities must be held by the original purchaser until they mature or are redeemed by the Treasury. It is the marketable debt over which the Treasury exercises the greatest measure of control and which has the greatest impact on the cost and availability of credit in the nation's financial markets.

Marketable Public Debt

The marketable public debt totaled almost $1.3 trillion in 1985, representing three quarters of all interest-bearing U.S. government obligations. As Exhibit 25–5 reveals, the marketable public debt today is composed of just three types of securities—Treasury bills, notes, and bonds. By law, a U.S. Treasury bill must mature in one year or less. In contrast, U.S. Treasury notes range in original maturity from 1 year to 10 years, while Treasury bonds may carry any maturity, though generally they have a maturity at issue of more than 10 years.[3]

Under federal law, Treasury bonds can carry a maximum interest rate of 4¼ percent, unless special exemption from this legal interest-rate ceiling is granted by Congress. Because only limited exemptions have been granted and interest rates have been far higher than 4¼ percent in

---

[3] Both Treasury notes and bonds bear interest at a fixed rate payable semiannually, while bills do not carry a fixed rate. Bonds can carry a call option, allowing the Treasury to redeem them before maturity with four months' notice. Notes and bonds are issued in denominations of $1,000, $5,000, $10,000, $100,000, and $1 million, while bills are available in denominations of $10,000, $15,000, $50,000, $100,000, $500,000, and $1 million. Payment for purchases of Treasury securities generally must be made in cash, immediately available funds, the exchange of eligible securities (accepted at par value), or by check to the Federal Reserve banks or to the Treasury, provided the check is issued early enough to clear by the required payment date.

EXHIBIT 25–7

Volume of Marketable U.S. Government Debt by Type of Security, Year-End ($ billions)

Year	Total	Bills	Certificates	Notes	Bonds
1960	$ 189.0	$ 32.4	$18.4	$ 51.3	$ 79.8
1965	214.6	53.7	—	50.2	104.2
1970	247.7	80.6	—	101.2	58.6
1975	363.2	157.5	—	167.1	38.6
1980	623.2	216.1	—	321.6	85.4
1981	720.3	245.0	—	375.3	99.9
1982	281.5	311.8	—	465.0	104.6
1983	1,050.9	343.8	—	573.4	133.7
1984	1,247.4	374.4	—	705.1	167.9
1985*	1,271.7	379.5	—	713.8	187.9

* First quarter only.
SOURCE: Board of Governors of the Federal Reserve System, *Banking and Monetary Statistics,* 1941–70; and *Federal Reserve Bulletin,* various issues.

recent years, the proportion of long-term bonds making up the Treasury's marketable debt has declined significantly. In contrast, Treasury bills and notes carry no legal interest-rate ceiling. Moreover with their greater liquidity and marketability, bills and notes have been especially attractive to investors in recent years. As shown in Exhibit 25–7, bills and notes represented about 40 percent of all marketable government obligations in 1960; by 1985, however, these securities accounted for about 85 percent of the marketable public debt.

Nonmarketable Public Debt

The nonmarketable public debt consists mainly of Government Account series securities issued by the Treasury to various government agencies and trust funds (see Exhibit 25–5). These agencies and trust funds include the Social Security Administration, the Rural Electrification Administration, the Tennessee Valley Authority, and several smaller government agencies. As these governmental units accumulate funds, they turn them over to the Treasury in exchange for special, nonmarketable IOUs, thus reducing the federal government's borrowing activity in the open market.

Another significant component of the nonmarketable debt is U.S. Savings Bonds and Notes, sold to the general public in small denominations. The volume of Savings Bonds increased during the 1960s and 70s, reaching a high of almost $81 billion in 1978. Then, soaring interest rates encouraged even small savers to invest their funds elsewhere, particularly in money market mutual funds. By 1985 the amount of Savings Bonds outstanding sagged to about $74 billion, or less than 5 percent of the public debt.

As we will discuss later in Chapter 27, holdings of U.S. dollars by foreign governments and foreign investors have expanded enormously in recent years due to oil imports and the flow of American capital to Europe, Asia, the Middle East, and the Far East. Because large foreign holdings of dollars and dollar deposits represent a constant threat to the value of the U.S. dollar in international markets, the Treasury periodically issues small amounts of nonmarketable dollar-denominated securities to attract these overseas funds. In order to increase U.S. government holdings of foreign currencies that can be used to settle international claims, the Treasury also occasionally issues foreign currency-denominated securities to investors abroad. These dollar-denominated and foreign currency-denominated issues totaled about $9 billion in 1985, representing about 2 percent of the nonmarketable portion of the public debt.

The Treasury also issues special securities to state and local governments. These securities provide a temporary investment outlet for the funds raised by local governments when they borrow in the open market. Special issues to state and local governments totaled almost $48 billion in 1985, about 10 percent of all Treasury nonmarketable securities.

Investors in U.S. Government Securities

Who *holds* the public debt of the United States? Each month the Treasury makes estimates of the distribution of its securities among various groups of investors, drawing upon data supplied by the Federal Reserve banks, U.S. government agencies and trust funds, banking associations, trade organizations, and government security dealers. The results from a recent Treasury ownership survey are shown in Exhibit 25–8.

It is evident from the survey that most Treasury debt—almost three quarters—is held by private individuals and institutions in the domestic economy and abroad. Rather surprising to many observers, however, is the large proportion of the public debt—almost 30 percent—held by the federal government itself. For example, in 1985, U.S. government agencies and trust funds, including the Social Security Trust Fund, Tennessee Valley Authority, and other federal departments, held about one fifth of the total debt. The Federal Reserve banks hold about 10 percent of all public debt securities outstanding.

While the ratio of government to private holdings of federal securities has declined over the past decade, the sheer size of the government's holdings of its own debt is viewed with alarm by some analysts. A large volume of government debt held out of circulation in federal vaults tends to "thin out" the market for government securities, reducing the volume of trading. Other factors held constant, interest rates and security prices

EXHIBIT 25–8

Principal Investors in U.S. Treasury Debt, 1985 ($ billions, end of period)

Investor Group	Amount Held in First Quarter, 1985		Percent Total Holdings
Federal government:			
U.S. government agencies and			
trust funds		$ 295.5	18.9%
Federal Reserve banks		161.0	10.3
Private investors:			
Commercial banks	$195.0		12.5
Money market funds	26.6		1.7
Insurance companies	84.0		5.4
Other companies	51.9		3.3
State and local governments	155.1*		9.9
Individuals:			
Savings Bonds	75.4		4.8
Other securities	69.9		4.5
Total private investors		657.9	42.2
Foreign and international	186.3		11.9
Other investors†	259.8*		16.6
Total for all investor groups		$1,560.5	100.0%

* Figures for 1983 because 1984–85 are not available.
† Includes savings and loan associations, nonprofit institutions, corporate pension trust funds, dealers and brokers, certain government deposit accounts, and government-sponsored agencies.
SOURCE: Board of Governors of the Federal Reserve System, *Federal Reserve Bulletin,* September 1985.

become more volatile and unpredictable, discouraging investment. This can be critical because the market for U.S. government securities is the anchor of the whole financial system.

Among private holders of the public debt, commercial banks and individuals are at or near the top of the list. At year-end 1985, for example, individual investors held more than $145 billion in public securities or around 10 percent of the total—the majority in U.S. Savings Bonds. Commercial banks held an even larger government portfolio with almost $200 billion in government issues. Other financial institutions with significant holdings of U.S. government securities included insurance companies, pension funds, mutual savings banks, savings and loan associations, and nonfinancial corporations that hold these securities as a ready reserve of liquid funds.

The proportion of the public U.S. debt held by foreign and international investors, including foreign central banks, foreign governments, and other international investors has increased in recent years and totaled close to $190 billion in 1985. Foreign holdings of government securities result from a rise in U.S. imports of goods and services, especially oil imports, that has led foreign investors to build up substantial dollar deposits in banks abroad. These investors have converted many of their dollars into purchases of Treasury securities in the New York money market and into foreign currency-denominated securities purchased directly from the U.S. Treasury. In addition, the interest returns and high liquidity of Treasuries has attracted foreign savers and institutional investors into the U.S. government securities market.

A Trend toward Shorter Maturities

One of the most serious problems the Treasury faces today in the debt-management field is a long-term trend toward shorter and shorter maturities. As shown in Exhibit 25–9, the percentage of marketable federal securities over five years to maturity held by private investors was a full 40 percent in 1950. By 1984, however, this long-term component of the public debt was scarcely more than a fifth of all marketable issues. The average maturity of the entire marketable public debt in 1984 at four years, seven months was about half what it was at the end of World War II. Today, nearly half (about 42 percent) of the debt comes due each year, though it should be noted the debt has lengthened somewhat in recent years.

This is a potentially serious problem because it requires the Treasury to come to market more frequently to retire or refund debt as securities

EXHIBIT 25–9

Distribution of the U.S. Marketable Public Debt Held by Private Investors by Maturity

	Percent of Total Maturing within:				
Year	1 Year	1–5 Years	5–10 Years	Over 10 Years	Total
1946	31.1%	22.4%	15.5%	31.0%	100%
1950	38.1	21.9	11.4	28.6	100
1955	37.1	23.5	19.2	20.2	100
1960	39.0	38.3	9.9	12.8	100
1965	43.5	28.2	16.3	11.9	100
1970	49.8	32.2	9.1	7.8	100
1975	55.0	30.9	7.3	6.8	100
1980	47.7	31.7	8.7	12.0	100
1984	42.1	33.8	12.9	11.4	100

SOURCE: U.S. Treasury Department, *Treasury Bulletin;* and Board of Governors of the Federal Reserve System, *Federal Reserve Bulletin,* various issues.

pile up in shorter maturities. Moreover, in recent years the Federal Reserve has been especially cautious about making significant changes in the posture of monetary policy at a time when the Treasury is actively in the market selling notes and bonds. If the Treasury must refund and issue debt more frequently, this reduces the period of time over which the Federal Reserve can make significant changes in monetary policy. Suppose, for example, that the Fed wanted to increase interest rates and reduce the availability of credit at precisely the time the Treasury was coming to market with a new issue of bonds. Clearly, the government would have some difficulty in selling its bonds in an environment of rising interest rates and falling bond prices. If maturing securities were coming due and had to be paid off, the Treasury might not be able to raise enough cash to meet its obligations. Conditions in the financial marketplace might border on panic. Therefore, a public debt of short maturity tends to reduce the flexibility of monetary policy. It limits the options open to the Federal Reserve.

Many analysts believe as well that a substantial buildup of short-term government debt contributes to inflation. Of special concern is the proportion of government securities maturing within one year—the so-called *floating debt.* These short-term issues are the most liquid and readily marketable of all securities in the American financial system. Most are held by commercial banks and other lenders of funds, who use them as an extra source of funds when reserves are scarce and credit demand is high. If the Federal Reserve wishes to reduce the growth of money and credit, it must wrestle with the problem that banks and other financial institutions can sell off their floating-debt issues and generate still more credit. It is perhaps more than just coincidence that both inflation and the short-term federal debt have grown rapidly in recent years.

Methods of Offering Treasury Securities

Management of the public debt is a complicated task. Treasury debt managers are called upon continually to make decisions about raising new money and refunding maturing securities. They must decide what kinds of securities to issue, which maturities would appeal to investors, and the form in which an offering of securities should be made.

Cash Offerings and Exchange Offerings.
For example, the Treasury can make a *cash offering*, in which buyers simply pay cash for any securities they receive. On the other hand, if some existing securities must be refunded (rolled over), the Treasury can offer new securities just to holders of the maturing issues. This is called an *exchange offering.* In this type of sale, investors who want to acquire a portion of the new issue must purchase securities from those who hold the maturing issue.

The maturing securities are known as "rights" to the new debt being offered.

The choice between a cash offering and an exchange offering can be a difficult one because of changing market conditions. For example, if interest rates rise, holders of maturing securities may not wish to acquire any new Treasury securities offered in exchange; instead, they will seek the higher yields available on other securities sold in the open market. Those investors electing not to exchange with the Treasury will demand cash payment instead. The Treasury may find itself with a substantial amount of unsold securities and in the embarrassing position of not having sufficient cash to pay off holders of maturing issues. A cash offering usually solves this attrition problem. However, cash offerings have a far more powerful impact on interest rates and security prices than exchange offerings do because they represent a net withdrawal of funds from the financial system. Nevertheless, since 1973 the Treasury has elected to use *cash offerings* rather than exchange offerings, due primarily to the enormous volume of new securities it has needed to sell.

The Auction Method.   Today the *auction* method is the principal means of selling Treasury notes, bonds, and bills. While there are several different auction methods in use, all such techniques have a number of features in common. Both competitive and noncompetitive tenders are accepted from the public.[4] All noncompetitive bidders receive an allotment of securities from the auction up to a maximum amount determined by the Treasury. As we have seen, federal government agencies and trust funds and the Federal Reserve banks purchase and hold large amounts of Treasury issues. These agencies participate in virtually every auction but pay the price charged noncompetitive bidders. They receive a special allotment of securities in exchange for their maturing issues after the regular auction is concluded.

Types of Treasury Auctions.   The Treasury has used three different auction methods in recent years:

1. Price auctions.
2. Dutch auctions.
3. Yield auctions.

---

[4] Those investors tendering an offer in a Treasury auction must submit a deposit of 5 percent of the amount bid, unless they represent an institution specifically exempt from the required deposit. Institutions that can submit tender offers without deposit include commercial banks, state and local governments, public pension funds, federally insured savings and loan associations, major government securities dealers, Federal Reserve banks, U.S. government agencies and trust funds, foreign central banks and governments, and selected international organizations.

The *price auction* is used regularly for sales of Treasury bills and occasionally for note and bond sales. Under this method, the Treasury sets the coupon rate and minimum price it is willing to accept on notes and bonds and announces the amount of securities available for public sale.[5] Competitive bids are accepted with prices above or below par, accurate to two decimal places (assuming a par value of $100), though bills must be priced accurate to three decimal places. Securities are allotted first to the highest bidder and then to those investors submitting successively lower bids until the amount available (less any noncompetitive tenders) has been exhausted. Noncompetitive bidders pay the average price established by competitive bidders.

On a few occasions, the Treasury has employed the *uniform price,* or *Dutch auction,* method to sell long-term bonds. After all competitive bids are in, the Treasury proceeds to award the available securities (once noncompetitive orders are filled) beginning with the highest bidder on down until all securities are allocated. However, the price actually paid by all bidders is that tendered by the *lowest* accepted competitive bid. Therefore, all investors receiving securities in a Dutch auction pay the *same* price.

The auction method used most often for Treasury notes and bonds is known as a *yield auction.* Neither the price nor the coupon rate on the new securities is set in advance by the Treasury. Instead, it merely announces the amount of securities available and calls for yield bids. Investors submitting competitive bids must express their offers on an annual percentage yield basis, accurate to two decimal places. For example, we might place a yield bid of 11.75 percent in the current auction. When the auction closes, noncompetitive bidders will first receive their securities; then those bidding the lowest annual percentage yield (i.e., the highest price) will be awarded their securities. Awards will continue to be made at successively higher yields (lower prices) until the issue is exhausted.

Marketing Techniques.   Unlike borrowers in the corporate and municipal bond markets, the Treasury does *not* use dealers to underwrite its new debt issues (though dealers play a key role, as discussed in Chapter 13, in purchasing new Treasury securities in the auctions and reselling a portion of their holdings to other investors). The Treasury places new securities *directly* with the investing public. New Treasury bills, notes, and bonds can be bought directly from the Treasury Department or from the Treasury's agents—the Federal Reserve banks and their

---

[5] See Chapter 13 for a more detailed discussion of the weekly price auctions for U.S. Treasury bills. Unlike notes and bonds, the Treasury does *not* set minimum prices in bill auctions, nor do bills carry coupon rates.

branches. Bids or tender offers are accepted from private and government investors at the Federal Reserve banks until 1:30 P.M., Eastern Standard Time, the day the new securities are sold. Individuals may also file bids for new Treasury securities with the Bureau of the Public Debt in Washington, D.C. Many investors place orders for new Treasury issues through a security broker or dealer, commercial bank, or nonbank financial institution that offers such a service.

Before issuing new notes and bonds, the Treasury will consult with Federal Reserve officials and government securities dealers as to the appropriate terms to be offered. It also frequently is necessary to tailor the terms of a new issue to appeal to investor groups who have the necessary funds to spend.

Book Entry.   The marketable public debt is generally issued today in *book-entry form*. This means that the investor does not receive an engraved certificate representing the Treasury's debt obligation. Instead, the investor's name and amount of securities held are recorded on the books of a bank or at the Treasury Department. Member banks of the Federal Reserve System are permitted to hold security safekeeping accounts at the Federal Reserve banks where their own security holdings and those of their customers are recorded. As interest is received or securities are sold or purchased, banks will credit or debit their own or their customers' accounts accordingly.

The Treasury also accepts book-entry accounts from the public, subject to a number of restrictions. While there is no charge for the Treasury's bookkeeping services, securities held there cannot be sold until they are transferred to a bank book-entry account held at the Federal Reserve. Moreover, such transfers are not allowed less than 30 days before a security matures and no sooner than 10 days after issue. When a security matures, the Treasury will mail the investor of record a check in the amount of its par value plus any interest due, unless notified at least 10 days prior to the maturity date that these monies should be reinvested in new securities.

Book entry is the safest form in which to hold any security because this method significantly reduces the risk of theft. Some investors still prefer the much riskier *bearer* securities, however, in which the engraved certificates are actually kept in the investor's possession. The ownership of such securities is not recorded on the books of a bank or the Treasury Department nor is there any notice to the Treasury of a change of ownership when such securities are traded in the open market.

Bearer notes and bonds with interest coupons attached are known as *coupon securities*. In order for the holder to receive interest, the coupons must be detached and presented to the Treasury Department or to a Federal Reserve bank. Similarly, when bearer securities are redeemed or rolled over at maturity in exchange for new securities, they must be presented to the Treasury or to the Federal Reserve banks for these purposes.

Registered Securities.

A safer way to hold Treasury securities is in *registered* form. A Treasury issue is registered when the securities are engraved with the owner's name, which is also recorded on the Treasury's books. While the owner physically holds registered securities, the Treasury automatically pays (without notice or receipt of coupon) any interest due on these securities to the owner of record.

If Treasury securities held by an investor are lost, stolen, destroyed, or mutilated, the investor *may* be able to recover his or her funds. Each year the Treasury honors a few such claims after careful screening, but usually only after the investor deposits an indemnity bond.

Other Services Offered Investors.

In order to encourage greater participation in the government securities market and stimulate demand for new Treasury issues, both the Federal Reserve and the Treasury offer a number of other services to investors. For example, securities held in book-entry accounts at the Federal Reserve banks may be transferred by wire almost anywhere using the Fed's electronic wire transfer network. This device makes it easy to sell Treasury securities before maturity on a same-day basis. Moreover, in 1985 the Treasury announced a STRIPS program in which the principal and interest payments on Treasury securities can be separately owned and traded. However, in order to be eligible for "stripping" the investor must keep his or her securities in a book-entry account at a Federal Reserve bank.

The Goals of Federal Debt Management

Over the years the Treasury has pursued several different goals in the management of the public debt. These goals may be divided into two broad groups: (1) *housekeeping goals,* that pertain to the cost and composition of the public debt; and (2) *stabilization goals,* that have to do with the impact of the debt on the economy and the financial markets.

Minimize Interest Costs.

The most important housekeeping goal is to keep the interest burden of the public debt as low as possible. The Treasury has not always been successful in the pursuit of this goal, however. Today, the interest burden on the public debt is the third-largest category of federal expenditures, after welfare payments and national defense. As Exhibit 25–2 reveals, net interest on the debt reached more than $116 billion, or more than 12 percent of total federal government spending, in fiscal 1985. This interest burden on the American taxpayer has been rising rapidly in the wake of inflation and record-high interest rates.

Reduce the Frequency of Refundings.

The Treasury also tries to minimize the number of "trips" it must make to the market to refund old securities or issue new ones. As we have seen, this housekeeping goal is particularly important to the Federal Reserve's conduct of monetary policy.

For several decades now the Fed has followed a loosely defined policy known as "even keel" when the Treasury is in the market offering a substantial volume of notes or bonds. Even-keel policy calls for the Fed to exert a *steadying* influence on the financial markets, making sure that security trading is orderly and that changes in interest rates are moderate. In principle, "even keel" protects the Treasury's financing operations from catastrophic failure, as might occur if interest rates rose sharply and security prices plunged at the time of a Treasury refunding. Unfortunately, the Fed may be compelled to "even keel" the markets at a time when it should be pursuing a policy of tight money and higher interest rates to fight inflation.

Economic Stabilization.

A much broader goal of debt management is to stabilize the economy—promoting high employment and sustainable growth while avoiding rampant inflation. In strict terms this would involve issuing long-term Treasury securities in a period of economic expansion and issuing short-term securities in a period of recession. The long-term securities would tend to increase long-term interest rates and therefore act as a brake on private investment spending, slowing the economy down. On the other hand, issuing short-term securities during a recession keeps pressure off long-term interest rates and avoids discouraging investment spending that is needed to provide jobs.

Unfortunately, the goal of economic stabilization often conflicts with other debt-management goals, particularly the goal of minimizing the interest burden of the public debt. If the Treasury sells short-term securities in a period of expansion when interest rates are high and then rolls over those short-term securities into long-term bonds during a recession when rates are low, this strategy will tend to minimize the debt's average interest cost. The Treasury will be able to lock in cheap long-term rates. From a stabilization point of view, however, this is exactly the wrong thing to do. The short-term debt will fuel inflation during an economic expansion, while long-term debt issued during a recession will drive up interest rates and reduce private investment. Like Federal Reserve officials, Treasury debt managers are confronted with tough choices among conflicting goals.

The Impact of Federal Debt Management on the Financial Markets and the Economy

What effect do Treasury debt-management activities have on the financial markets and the economy? This is a subject of heated debate among economists and financial analysts. Most experts agree that in the short run the financial markets become more agitated and interest rates tend to rise when the Treasury is borrowing, especially when new money is involved. A mere exchange of new for old securities usually has minimal effects, however, unless the offering is very large.

The longer-run impact of Treasury debt-management operations is less clear. Certainly the *liquidity* of the public's portfolio of securities changes, though we are uncertain by how much or what the exact impact might be. For example, suppose $10 billion in Treasury bonds are maturing next month. Treasury debt managers decide to offer investors $10 billion in 10-year notes in exchange for the maturing bonds. The bonds, regardless of what their original maturity might have been, are now short-term securities (with one-month maturities). If investors accept the new 10-year notes in exchange for the one-month bonds, the average maturity of the public's security holdings obviously has lengthened, all else equal. Longer-term securities, as a rule, are less liquid than shorter-term securities.

Will this reduction in public liquidity affect spending habits and interest rates? The research evidence on this question is conflicting, with many studies finding little or no effect from debt-management activities.[6] However, there is some evidence that *lengthening debt maturities* in investor portfolios increases the public's demand for money and *raises interest rates.* In contrast, if the Treasury offers shorter-term securities, this tends to make the public's portfolio of securities more liquid and may reduce the demand for money. The result would be an increase in total spending for goods and services and, for a time, *lower* interest rates.

Still another possible debt-management impact is on the *shape of the yield curve. Lengthening* the average maturity of the debt tends to increase long-term interest rates relative to short rates. The yield curve assumes a *steeper positive slope,* favoring short-term investment over long-term investment. On the other hand, *shortening* the debt's maturity would tend to reduce longer-term interest rates and raise short-term rates. The yield curve would tend to *flatten out,* if positively sloped, or even turn down, favoring long-term investment over short-term investment. The net impact on total investment spending would depend on whether private investment is more responsive to short-term interest

---

[6] See especially the studies by Lang and Rasche (1977), Pierson (1970), Roley (1978), and Smith (1960).

rates or to long-term interest rates. We believe that long-term rates are more critical than short-term rates for most business investment decisions.

On balance, most authorities are convinced that the debt-management activities of the Treasury do *not* have a major impact on economic conditions. The effects of debt-management operations appear to be secondary compared to the powerful impact of monetary and fiscal policy on the economy and financial markets. The optimal debt-management policy is probably one that makes Treasury refunding operations as *unobtrusive* as possible, especially where these operations might interfere with the activities of the Federal Reserve System. Nevertheless, debt management represents yet another policy tool that can be used by the federal government in the face of serious economic problems.

SUMMARY AND CONCLUSIONS

In this chapter we have examined the many roles played by the Treasury Department in financing federal expenditures and managing the huge public debt of the United States. We have noted that the federal government affects the nation's financial system through its taxing and spending activities (fiscal policy) and through refunding or refinancing the government's debt (debt-management policy). Both tasks involve enormous amounts of money today. The public debt of the United States now is well over $1 trillion, while annual federal expenditures approached the trillion dollar mark in the mid-1980s. It should certainly come as no surprise that spending and borrowing of such magnitude can have powerful effects on interest rates, security prices, the availability of credit to all borrowers, and the pursuit of the nation's economic goals.

We have observed in this chapter that government borrowing tends to raise interest rates, increase the money supply, and add to total spending and demand in the economy. In general, the economy will grow faster, with reduced unemployment, when the government borrows and spends additional funds, but often at the price of more rapid inflation and threats to the dollar abroad. Government budget surpluses, especially where these surpluses are used to retire government debt, often lead to lower interest rates, a decline in the nation's money supply, and reduced spending. A move toward more conservative fiscal policy and toward budget surpluses tends to dampen inflation and strengthen the dollar abroad, but increases the risk of high unemployment and slower economic growth.

Management of the public debt can also be used to alter economic conditions, reduce unemployment, and counter inflation. We have noted in this chapter that, if the Treasury refunds maturing short-term securities with longer-term debt, it can reduce the liquidity of the public's security holdings. Interest rates tend to rise, credit becomes more difficult to obtain, and spending and employment tend to fall. Long-term Treasury borrowing, therefore, tends to slow the economy's rate of growth and reduces inflationary pressures. In contrast, a debt-management policy that emphasizes short-term government borrowing often leads to more rapid economic expansion and reduced unemployment, but these are sometimes purchased at the price of higher inflation.

As we saw in the preceding chapter on the Federal Reserve System, government policymakers face few happy choices. The nation's goals of full employment, reasonable stability in prices, sustainable economic growth, and a stable balance of payments position are elusive targets. Successful fiscal, monetary, and debt-management policies require careful coordination among all branches of government, a farsighted view of national goals, and a firm determination to achieve those goals despite the political pressures of the moment.

STUDY QUESTIONS

1. What exactly is fiscal policy? Debt-management policy?

2. Explain how fiscal policy and debt-management policy might be used to fight inflation. How about unemployment?

3. How frequently have budget surpluses occurred during the past three decades? Can you explain why?

4. List from largest to smallest the principal sources of federal government revenue. What are the principal federal spending programs?

5. Describe the effects of government borrowing on the financial system and the economy. If the federal government wished to increase total spending in the economy the most, from whom should it borrow funds?

6. Describe the effects of retiring government securities on the financial system and the economy. Whose securities should be paid off if the federal government wants to have the maximum contractionary impact on the economy?

7. What is the crowding-out theory? What does recent research say about the linkages between government deficits, interest rates, and inflation?

8. What are the principal reasons investors purchase and hold U.S. government securities?

9. Describe the principal types of securities that make up the public debt of the United States. What portions of the debt can the Treasury most closely control?

10. What problems exist in trying to measure the size of the public debt?

11. List the principal holders of the public debt. What are the most important trends in the ownership of federal securities?

12. What is happening to the average maturity of the public debt? Why is this trend important? What measures has the U.S. Treasury employed in the past to deal with the problem?

13. Define the following methods of selling U.S. Treasury securities and explain under what circumstances each might be used:
    a. Cash offering.
    b. Exchange offering.
    c. Price auction.
    d. Dutch auction.
    e. Yield auction.

14. What factors must Treasury officials consider when coming to market with a new security issue?

15. List the *goals* of Treasury debt management. What is the essential difference between the so-called housekeeping goals and the stabilization goals? To what extent do these goals conflict?

16. Explain how changes in the maturity structure of the public debt can affect interest rates, the yield curve, and spending for goods and services in the economy.

PROBLEMS

1. Due to an unexpected decline in federal income tax collections the Treasury will be compelled to borrow an extra $40 billion to cover planned expenditures in the current government budget. Using T accounts and IS-LM analysis discussed in this chapter trace through the likely effects of this additional borrowing on the financial markets and on the economy. Assume that 50 percent of the securities to be issued will be absorbed by nonbank institutions and private individuals and 50 percent by depository institutions. How would your analysis change if the economy were at full employment?

2. Due to drastic cuts in federal spending and strong economic growth it now appears that the federal government will experience a $10 billion budget surplus during the current fiscal year. If the Treasury plans to retain $2 billion of this surplus in its cash account at the Federal Reserve and to use the balance to retire $5 billion in government securities held by depository institutions and $3 billion held by the general public, use T accounts to show the effects of this debt-retirement operation. Using IS-LM analysis and the results from your T account analysis, what effects do you predict for interest rates, security prices, total spending, and employment?

SELECTED REFERENCES

Aaron, Henry J., and A. Joseph Pechman, eds. *How Taxes Affect Economic Behavior.* Washington, D.C.: The Brookings Institution, 1981.

Barro, Robert. "Are Government Bonds Net Wealth?" *Journal of Political Economy,* November/December 1984.

Canto, Victor A., and Donald Rapp. "The 'Crowding Out' Controversy: Arguments and Evidence." *Economic Review,* Federal Reserve Bank of Atlanta, August 1982.

Dwyer, Gerald P., Jr. "Is Inflation a Consequence of Government Deficits?" *Economic Review,* Federal Reserve Bank of Atlanta, August 1982.

Eisner, Robert, and Paul J. Pieper. "A New View of the Federal Debt and Budget Deficits." *The American Economic Review,* March 1984, pp. 11–29.

Feldstein, Martin. "Government Deficits and Aggregate Demand." *Journal of Monetary Economics,* 9 (1982), pp. 1–20.

Kochin, L. "Are Future Taxes Anticipated by Consumers?" *Journal of Money, Credit and Banking,* 6 (1974), pp. 385–94.

Lang, Richard W., and Robert H. Rasche. "Debt Management Policy and the Own-Price Elasticity of Demand for U.S. Government Notes and Bonds." *Review,* Federal Reserve Bank of St. Louis, September 1977, pp. 8–22.

Pierson, Gail. "Effect of Economic Policy on the Term Structure of Interest Rates." *Review of Economics and Statistics,* February 1970, pp. 1–11.

Plosser, Charles I. "Government Financing Decisions and Asset Returns." *Journal of Monetary Economics,* 9 (1982), pp. 325–52.

Roley, V. Vance. "A Theory of Federal Debt Management." *Research Working Paper,* Federal Reserve Bank of Kansas City, March 1978.

_____. "The Financing of Federal Deficits: An Analysis of Crowding Out." *Economic Review,* Federal Reserve Bank of Kansas City, July/August 1981, pp. 16–29.

Sheehan, Richard G. "The Federal Reserve Reaction Function." *Review,* Federal Reserve Bank of St. Louis, March 1985, pp. 24–33.

Smith, Warren L. "Debt Management in the United States." In *Study of Employment, Growth, and Price Levels,* ed. Joint Economic Committee. Washington, D.C.: U.S. Government Printing Office, 1960.

Tanner, J. R. "Fiscal Policy and Consumer Behavior." *Review of Economics and Statistics,* August 1979.

Tatom, John A. "The 1981 Personal Income Tax Cuts: A Retrospective Look at Their Effects on the Federal Tax Burden." *Review,* Federal Reserve Bank of St. Louis, December 1984, pp. 5–17.

26

State and Local Governments in the Financial Markets

PURPOSE OF THIS CHAPTER

To examine the methods and instruments used by state, county, city, and other local units of government to raise funds. The chapter explores the reasons behind the recent rapid growth of state and local government borrowing and the composition of local government revenues and expenditures. The major types and features of short- and long-term securities offered by local units of government are discussed along with an explanation of recent innovations and an exploration of the unique characteristics of the whole state and local debt market. The municipal marketing process and recent problems in this growing market are explored in the chapter's two concluding sections.

KEY TERMS AND CONCEPTS IN THE CHAPTER

BANs	*market volatility*	*RANs*
credit ratings	*mortgage revenue*	*revenue bonds*
floaters	*bonds*	*Section 8 bonds*
GOs	*municipals*	*serialization*
hospital revenue	*NIC*	*SLROs*
bonds	*option bonds*	*syndicates*
IDBs	*PHAs*	*TANs*
interest subsidy	*Proposition 13*	*tax exemption*
life-care bonds		

The borrowing and spending activities of state and local governments have been one of the most dynamic, rapidly growing segments of the U.S. financial system in recent years. Pressured by rising population and inflated costs, states, counties, school districts, and other local units of government have been forced to borrow in growing numbers in order to meet increased demands for their services. As we will see later in this chapter, the volume of state and local government debt has nearly tripled since 1970, totaling more than $480 billion in 1983.

Despite the rapid growth in borrowing by state and local governments, many investors consider state and local debt obligations a highly desirable investment medium due to their high quality, ready marketability, and tax-exemption feature. The interest income generated by state and local securities is exempt from federal income taxes, and most states exempt their own securities from state income taxes. As a result, these high-quality debt obligations (known as "municipals") appeal to such heavily taxed investors as commercial banks, top-income-bracket individuals, property-casualty insurance companies, and large nonfinancial corporations. In addition, an active secondary market permits the early resale of many state and local government bonds.

GROWTH OF STATE AND LOCAL GOVERNMENT BORROWING

The rapid growth of state and local government borrowing is reflected in Exhibit 26–1, which shows the total volume of municipal securities outstanding between the years 1940 and 1983. State and local government indebtedness grew slowly until the 1950s, when it nearly tripled. The volume of municipal debt doubled again during the 1960s and more than doubled during the 1970s. In 1983 state and local debt outstand-

EXHIBIT 26–1

Total Debt Issued by State and Local Governments in the United States, 1940–1983 ($ billions)

Year	Debt Outstanding at Year-end
1940	$ 20.3
1950	24.1
1960	70.8
1970	144.4
1980	351.9
1983	484.6

SOURCES: U.S. Department of Commerce, Bureau of the Census, *1977 Census of Governments;* and Board of Governors of the Federal Reserve System, *Flow of Funds: Assets and Liabilities Outstanding,* 1960–83.

ing had climbed to nearly $485 billion, almost a third of the size of the federal government's debt.

What factors account for this strong record of growth in municipal borrowing? *Rapid population and income growth* are two of the most important causes. The U.S. population, spurred by a postwar baby boom, rose from less than 132 million in 1940 to an estimated 230 million in the early 1980s, a gain of nearly 100 million people in four decades. Rapid population growth implies that many local government services, such as schools, highways, public libraries, and lighting and sewer systems, must also expand rapidly. Tax revenues cannot provide all the moneys needed to fund these facilities and services. Indeed, during the 1948–71 period, for example, the combined operating and capital account of state and local governments was in deficit (measured on an NIA basis) every year,[1] encouraging many local governments to enter the money and capital markets for supplemental funding.

Another factor pushing state and local borrowings higher is the *uneven distribution of population growth across the nation.* Beginning in the 1950s a massive shift of the U.S. population began to take place out of the central cities into suburban areas. This demographic change was augmented during the 1970s by a movement of population and industry into small towns and rural areas to escape the social, political, and environmental problems of urban living. Smaller outlaying communities were rapidly transformed into moderate-sized cities with a corresponding need

---

[1] See Rubin (1984), p. 792.

for new streets and schools, sewer and lighting facilities, utilities, expanded police and fire protection, and new airports and freeways to commute back to the central cities for work, recreation, and shopping. The result was an upsurge in borrowing by existing local units of government and the creation of thousands of new borrowing units in the form of sewer and lighting districts, power and water authorities, airport and toll-road boards, and public housing authorities. There are nearly 80,000 state, county, municipal, and other units of local government in the United States. And, the majority of these governmental units have the authority to issue debt securities.

Accompanying the growth and shifting of the U.S. population has come *an upgrading of citizens' expectations concerning the quality of government services.* We expect much more from government today than even 10 years ago, due in part to higher levels of income and education and greater public concern for the quality as well as the quantity of government services. Particularly noticeable is an increased demand for government services that directly affect the quality of life, such as more modern and better designed schools, parks, swimming pools, tennis courts, auditoriums, and football stadiums. Instead of gravel roads and narrow highways, local citizens demand paved and guttered streets and all-weather, controlled-access highways. Many municipal governments are active in providing cultural facilities, such as libraries, museums, and convention centers, and are expected to play leading roles in the control of environmental pollution.

All of these public demands have had to be financed in an era of rapid inflation in construction and labor costs, exacerbating the money burdens of local governments. The rapid growth of local government borrowing is expected to continue in future years, with the federal government making smaller contributions to local funding. Adding to local financial needs will be a continuing expansion of suburban and rural communities, especially in the southern and western regions of the United States.

SOURCES OF REVENUE FOR STATE AND LOCAL GOVERNMENTS

Borrowing by state and local governments supplements their tax revenues and income from fees charged users of government services. When tax and fee revenues decline or fail to grow as fast as public demands, municipal borrowings rise. Moreover, when long-term capital projects are undertaken, long-term borrowing rather than taxation is the preferred method of governmental finance.

As we study state and local government borrowing in the financial markets, it is useful to have in mind the principal sources and uses of state and local funds. Where do the majority of state and local government revenues come from? And where does most of the money go? Exhibits 26–2 and 26–3, drawn from a recent census of state and local units of government, provide some answers to these questions.

As expected, most state and local government *revenues* are derived from *local* sources of funds, that is, from the citizens these govenmental units serve. For example, more than 70 percent of state government revenues and nearly 60 percent of local government revenues were derived from local sources, according to a 1982 Department of Commerce census. However, intergovernmental transfer of funds, including the federal revenue-sharing program and state aid to local schools, also provides a significant share of total revenues. For example, local governments received more than 40 percent of their revenues and state governments about 25 percent from other governmental units in 1982. Most outside aid for state governments comes from federal sources, though federal

EXHIBIT 26–2

Sources of Revenue for State and Local Governments, 1981–1982
(percent of total general revenues)

Source	State and Local Governments	State Governments	Local Governments
General revenue from own sources	80.9%	74.9%	58.5%
Taxes	58.4	59.1	37.1
Property	18.0	1.1	28.2
Sales and gross receipts	20.5	28.6	5.3
General sales and gross receipts	13.3	18.3	3.7
Selective sales and gross receipts	7.2	10.3	1.6
Motor fuel	2.3	3.8	0.1
Alcoholic beverages	0.6	1.0	0.1
Tobacco products	0.9	1.4	—
Public utility	1.7	1.8	1.0
Other	1.7	2.3	—
Income	14.4	21.7	2.2
Individual	11.1	16.6	1.8
Corporate	3.3	5.1	0.4
Motor vehicle license	1.4	2.2	0.1
Death and gift	0.5	0.9	—
All other taxes	3.5	4.6	1.2
Current charges	12.3	7.6	12.5
Miscellaneous general revenue	10.3	8.1	8.8
Intergovernmental revenue	19.1	25.1	41.5
General revenue, total	100.0%	100.0%	100.0%

Note: Blank items are either zero or round to zero.
Columns may not add to totals due to rounding.
SOURCE: U.S. Department of Commerce, Bureau of the Census, *1982 Census of Governments.*

EXHIBIT 26–3

Annual Expenditure by State and Local Governments, 1981–1982 (percent of total general expenditures)

Function	State Governments	Local Governments
Education and library services	24.9%	45.4%
Social services and income maintenance:		
Public welfare	24.3	5.6
Hospitals	8.1	6.0
Health	3.2	2.0
Social insurance administration	1.3	*
Veterans' service	*	—
Transportation:		
Highway	11.8	5.5
Air transportation	0.2	0.9
Other	0.3	0.5
Public safety:		
Police protection	1.4	5.4
Fire protection	—	2.6
Correction and other	4.4	1.5
Environmental and housing:		
Sewerage	0.2	4.0
Natural resources	3.0	0.5
Housing and urban renewal	0.8	2.9
Parks and recreation	—	2.3
Other	—	1.6
Governmental administration:		
Financial administration	2.1	1.7
General control	2.2	2.7
General public buildings	0.5	0.9
Interest on general debt	5.3	4.2
Other and unallowable	5.6	5.9
Direct general expenditures, total	100.0%	100.0%

Note: Columns may not add to totals due to rounding.
* Indicates that the percentage figure is less than half the unit of measurement shown.
SOURCE: U.S. Department of Commerce, Bureau of the Census, *1982 Census of Governments.*

grants began declining in the 1980s, while state governments provide the bulk of external assistance for their own local governments, especially school districts.

Not surprisingly, *taxes* are the largest single revenue source for state and local governments. Property taxes are the mainstay of local government support, providing about 30 percent of general revenues. State governments, in contrast, rely principally on sales and income taxes. During the 1981–82 fiscal years, tax levies against sales and gross business receipts provided nearly a third of state government revenues but only about 5 percent of local government funds. Selective sales taxes on alcoholic beverages, entertainment, gasoline, tobacco, and other specialized products and services are levied almost entirely at the state level and provide about 10 percent of state government funds. Income taxes are imposed almost exclusively at the state level and are levied mainly against individuals rather than corporations. Income taxes contributed about 20 percent of state government revenues but only about 2 percent of local government revenues during the 1981–82 fiscal year.

A taxpayer revolt in the late 1970s and early 1980s significantly altered state and local revenue flows in terms of both size and source. As Rubin (1984) notes, for example, 38 states raised at least one tax in 1983 alone, but these concessions from taxpayers were won only when they simultaneously agreed to put a cap on government spending. During 1983 alone 41 states refused to give their employees higher average wages or limited wage increases to 5 percent or less. And, 40 states either reduced the number of people on their payrolls or froze hiring. Among the taxes raised in the early 1980s were personal income taxes (increased by 16 states), business and corporate taxes, alcoholic beverage levies, cigarette and fuel taxes, and general sales taxes. These higher taxes coupled with a stronger-than-expected economic recovery materially strengthened the budget positions of state and local governments in the early and mid-1980s and led to record budget surpluses in the state and local sector.

State and Local Government Expenditures

Where do state and local governments spend most of their funds? As Exhibit 26–3 suggests, *education* is the number one item on the budgets of local governmental units and ranks number two on state budgets. The U.S. Department of Commerce reported that during the 1981–82 fiscal year, nearly 45 percent of local government funds and about one quarter of state revenues flowed into education and library services. *Social services,* including public welfare and medical care, occupied a distant second place in local government spending, representing about one eighth of total outlays, but ranked first in state budgets at about 40 percent of total spending. *Transportation services,* especially highway construction and maintenance, ranked third in the volume of state spending and fourth for local governments.

It is interesting that some of the most important local government services account for only a minor share of annual public budgets. For example, the cost of insuring public safety—principally police and fire protection—accounted for less than 10 percent of local government expenditures. Sewer services, protection of the environment and natural resources, and housing programs to aid the poor and the disadvantaged represented only about 11 percent of local government costs and less

EXHIBIT 26–4

State and Local Government Receipts and Expenditures, NIA Accounts,
($ billions)

Year	Total Receipts	Total Expenditures	Surplus or Deficit (−)
1946	$ 13.0	$ 11.1	$ 1.9
1950	21.3	22.5	− 1.2
1955	31.7	32.9	− 1.3
1960	49.9	49.8	0.1
1965	75.1	75.1	− 0.0
1970	135.4	133.5	1.9
1975	237.7	232.2	5.5
1980	386.1	355.5	30.6
1984	523.2	471.1	52.1

SOURCE: U.S. Department of Commerce, Bureau of Economic Analysis.

than 6 percent of state government spending. Moreover, despite the tremendous expansion of municipal debt in recent years, interest on that debt represented only about 5 percent of annual state and local government expenditures in the most recent governmental census report.

State and local government expenditures have grown rapidly in recent years. During 1984, expenditures by state and local units totaled about $470 billion, as shown in Exhibit 26–4. This figure was more than three times larger than the level of state and local government spending in 1970.[2] In fact, state and local outlays have more than doubled in each decade since World War II. Local tax revenues have simply been inadequate to handle this kind of growth in current (short-term) and capital (long-term) expenditures. Moreover, while state and local governments racked up substantial budget surpluses in the 1970s and early 1980s, a growing perception across the nation has been that many municipal facili-

---

[2] It is interesting to compare the size of state and local government expenditures with federal government outlays. Which is larger? Federal expenditures are significantly larger in total. For example, in 1984, federal outlays amounted to $880 billion, while state and local expenditures totaled $471 billion. In recent years state and local spending has fluctuated between 60 and 70 percent of total federal outlays.

One interesting difference between federal and local government budgets is the frequency of budget deficits. For the most part, state and local governments operate with small budget surpluses each year, while, as we saw in Chapter 25, the federal budget has been in deficit in the majority of recent years. Statistics provided by the U.S. Department of Commerce indicate that during the years 1946–84 the state and local government sector as a whole reported budget surpluses in 27 years and deficits during the remaining 12 years.

ties, especially highways, ports, electrical and service systems, need up-grading and modernizing. Accordingly, borrowing in the money and capital markets against future revenues surged upward in the early and mid-1980s to accommodate local needs for renovation and modernization and for expansion of facilities.

MOTIVATIONS FOR STATE AND LOCAL GOVERNMENT BORROWING

There are several reasons why state and local governments borrow money. The first is *to satisfy short-run cash needs,* that is, to meet payrolls, make repairs, purchase supplies and equipment, cover fuel costs, and maintain adequate levels of working capital. Most state and local governments will use tax-anticipation notes and other forms of short-term borrowing from local sources as a supplement to tax revenues to meet these immediate cash needs. Frequently, the construction phase of a building project will be financed out of short-term funds and then permanent financing will be obtained by selling long-term bonds.

The second major reason for state and local government borrowing is *to finance long-term capital investment,* that is, the building of schools, water, gas and electric systems, highways, public buildings, and similar permanent facilities. Long-term projects of this sort account for the bulk of all municipal securities issued each year. Some governmental units try to anticipate future financial needs, borrowing when interest rates are low even though project construction will not begin for a substantial period of time. Funds raised through anticipatory borrowing will then be "warehoused" in various investments (such as U.S. Treasury bills) until actual construction begins.

In recent years local governments have occasionally employed *advance refunding* of securities. Advance refundings often occur when a governmental unit has been granted a higher credit rating on its bonds by a rating agency, such as Moody's Investors Service or Standard & Poor's Corporation.[3] Bonds issued previously with lower credit ratings (i.e., higher interest rates) will be called in, and new securities issued at lower cost. Any significant decline in market interest rates usually gives rise to increased advance refunding activity by state and local governments.

USES OF BORROWED FUNDS

Where does the money raised from state and local borrowings go? There have been wide fluctuations in the purposes of municipal borrowing in recent years, but the principal uses of borrowed state and local funds

---

[3] See Appendix A for a discussion of municipal and other security ratings.

historically have been to provide support for social welfare programs, public utilities, energy conservation, education, and transportation systems. In most recent years, social welfare programs (including housing) have accounted for 25 to 30 percent of state and local borrowing—the largest single category. Utilities and energy-conservation programs have ranked a close second, accounting for 15 to 20 percent of total tax-exempt borrowings. Public education represents a declining (for example, the U.S. grade school population peaked in 1967), but still important percentage (20 to 25 percent) of state and local borrowing each year. Borrowing for transportation purposes, including airports, bridges, roads, tunnels, and the like, now represents about 10 percent of all state and local borrowing. The remaining proportion of local borrowed funds is distributed among a wide variety of projects, including support for local industry, debt refunding, fire protection, street lighting, and sewer services. There is a trend under way toward increased borrowing for utilities, social welfare programs, and transportation with welfare funding becoming a high-priority item during the 1970s. Rising energy costs have accelerated the need for mass transit systems and for the conversion of electric-generating plants from gas and other petroleum-based fuels to coal and lignite.

TYPES OF SECURITIES ISSUED BY STATE AND LOCAL GOVERNMENTS

There are many different types of securities issued by state and local governments today and, as we will soon see, the variety of municipal securities available to investors is expanding rapidly. One useful distinction is between short-term securities, which are generally issued to provide working capital and support construction, and long-term securities, used to fund capital projects.

Short-Term Securities

The two most popular short-term securities issued by state and local governments are tax-anticipation notes and bond-anticipation notes.

Tax-Anticipation and Revenue-Anticipation Notes. These notes, also called TANs and RANs, are used to attract funds in lieu of tax receipts or other sources of revenue expected to be received in the near future. Governments, like businesses and households, have a daily need for cash to meet payrolls, purchase supplies, make repairs, and so on. However, funds raised through taxes usually flow in only at certain times of the year. In order to satisfy their continuing need for cash between tax dates, state and local governments will issue short-term notes with maturities ranging from a few days to a few months. Most of these short-term issues are acquired by local banks. When tax funds are received, the issuing government simply pays off note holders and retires any outstanding securities.

Bond-Anticipation Notes. These short-term IOUs, also called BANs, are used to provide temporary financing of a long-term project until the time is right to sell long-term bonds. A school district, for example, may need to get construction started on new school facilities due to pressure from rising student enrollments. If interest rates currently are too high to permit the issue of bonds, then construction will be started out of funds raised with bond-anticipation notes. Once the project is under way and interest rates decline to more modest levels, the school district will then sell its long-term bonds and retire the bond-anticipation notes. The majority of short-term notes issued by state and local governments are backed by the "full faith and credit" of the issuing governmental unit. They sell at interest rates competitive with current money market yields and reflect the credit rating of the issuer. (As shown in Appendix A, Moody's Investor Service rates investment-grade municipal notes 1, 2, 3, or 4.) Like municipal bonds, interest on short-term local government notes is exempt from federal income taxes. These notes range in original maturity from one month to the more common six-month and one-year maturities. The volume of municipal notes has been quite large in recent years, reflecting the rising cost of state and local government services. These short-term IOUs are usually sold through underwriting syndicates who file competitive bids for the securities. Short-term tax-exempt notes are issued in marketable bearer form, with denominations ranging typically from $5,000 to $1 million. Both principal and interest are paid at maturity.[4]

Long-Term Securities

The most common type of municipal borrowing is through long-term bonds. There are two major types of municipal bonds issued today—general obligation and revenue bonds—and both are used principally to finance public construction.

General Obligation Bonds. These bonds, known as GOs, are the safest and most secure form of municipal borrowing from the standpoint of the investor because they are backed by the "full faith and credit" of the issuing government and may be paid from *any* revenue

---

[4] Tax-exempt notes with maturities longer than a year generally bear coupons. For most tax-exempt notes, interest is computed on the basis of a 30-day month or a 360-day year, like the interest on Treasury bills and bank CDs.

source. State, county, and city governments along with school districts have the power to tax their citizens in order to meet principal and interest payments on any debt issued. GOs are fully backed by this taxing power and usually must be approved by public referendum before issue.[5] The quality or level of risk of GOs depends, therefore, on the economic base (i.e., income and property values) of local communities and the total amount of debt issued.

Revenue Bonds.   In constrast, revenue bonds are payable only from a specified source of revenue, such as a toll road or toll bridge or user fees from a water, sewer, electrification, or other revenue-gathering project, and usually do not require a public referendum before they can be issued. These securities are not guaranteed or backed by the taxing power of the local unit of government. Instead, revenue bonds depend for their value on the revenue-generating capacity of the particular project they support.[6]

The total amount of general obligation bonds outstanding today exceeds the total supply of revenue bonds. However, as shown in Exhibit 26–5, revenue issues have been increasing much faster in recent years. For example, during 1984, nearly $80 billion in revenue bonds reached market, while only $26 billion in GOs were issued. There has been a virtual explosion of different types of revenue bonds within the past decade. Much of the growth in amount and variety of revenue issues is due to welfare programs of the federal government designed to provide housing for low-income groups, improved medical-care facilities, and student loans. In addition, the passage of Proposition 13 in California during the summer of 1978 and the enactment of similar laws by other states in subsequent years has encouraged many local authorities to substitute

---

[5] In some cases the issuing government's taxing power is limited by state law to a specified maximum tax rate. In this instance the GOs would be classified as *limited tax bonds.*

[6] Some municipal bonds display characteristics of both GO and revenue securities. For example, a *special tax bond* is payable from the revenues generated by a special tax, such as on gasoline. Many special tax bonds are backed by the full faith, credit, and taxing power of the issuing governmental unit, giving them the character of GOs. *Special assessment bonds* are payable only from assessments against property constructed or purchased from the proceeds of the bonds issued and arise from water and sewer projects, street construction, and similar projects. As in the case of special tax bonds, however, special assessment issues may take on the character of GOs when backed by the taxing power of the issuer. *Authority bonds* are issued by special governmental units set up by states, cities, or counties to construct and manage certain facilities, such as airports or water and sewer projects. Sometimes these special governmental units are set up to avoid legal debt limits in state constitutions, and most have taxing power. Authority bonds may be either GOs or revenue issues.

EXHIBIT 26–5

New Security Issues of State and Local Governments ($ billions)

Type of Issue, Issuer or Use of Funds	Years			
	1981	1982	1983	1984
All issues	$47.7	$79.0	$86.4	$105.0
Type of issue:				
General obligation	12.4	21.1	21.6	26.4
Revenue	35.3	58.0	64.9	78.6
U.S. government loans	0.1	0.7	0.3	NA
Type of issuer:				
State	5.3	8.4	7.1	9.1
Special district and statutory authority	27.5	45.1	51.3	62.4
Municipalities, counties, townships, and				
school districts	14.9	25.6	28.0	33.1
Uses of funds raised from issues for new capital:				
Education	4.5	6.5	8.1	7.5
Transportation	3.4	6.3	4.4	7.4
Utilities and conservation	10.0	14.3	13.6	16.6
Social welfare	12.7	26.6	26.9	29.4
Industrial aid	7.7	8.3	7.8	15.9
Other purposes	8.1	12.8	11.6	15.7

Notes: Figures include all state and local government security issues to raise new capital and to refund outstanding debt. Securities are valued at par based on date of sale.
SOURCE: Board of Governors of the Federal Reserve System, *Federal Reserve Bulletin,* various issues.

revenue bonds for GOs. Many of the newer revenue bonds are not well known to the majority of investors and may, in some cases, provide a higher rate of return to the well-informed buyer.

Types of Revenue Bonds

One of the most popular newer revenue issues is *student-loan bonds* (SLROs) which are issued by state government agencies that lend money to college students. The federal government guarantees 100 percent of the principal and interest of an SLRO, provided the issuing agency's loan-default ratio is less than 5 percent. If a higher percentage of students default on their loans, federal guarantees are limited to only a certain portion (usually 80 to 90 percent) of principal and interest payments on the bonds. SLROs are issued in minimum denominations of $1,000.

In the housing field several new forms of guaranteed and nonguaranteed state and local revenue bonds have appeared in recent years. For example, *life-care bonds,* also known as retirement community bonds, are issued by state and local development agencies to provide housing for the elderly. The housing is not government subsidized but supported by rental fees paid by the tenants. Frequently, nonprofit agencies organized by religious groups administer the property. Investor funds are secured by lease rentals and mortgages against the property. Life-care bonds are issued in minimum denominations of $5,000.

A related security is the *Section 8 bonds* issued under the terms of the Federal Housing Act. These bonds finance low- and middle-income rental housing, usually designed for elderly citizens. Section 8s are not federally guaranteed, but the U.S. Department of Housing and Urban Development (HUD) must accumulate a cash reserve for each project that protects against the failure of project residents to pay their rent. Security for Section 8s is provided by rent subsidies and a mortgage on the housing project. Section 8 bonds carry a minimum denomination of $5,000.

Joint federal and state support for low-income housing is frequently provided through *public housing authority notes* (PHAs). These securities are used to finance the construction of public housing projects for low-income families, many of whom live on welfare. PHAs are attractive to many investors because they are guaranteed by the federal government as well as being tax exempt.

Construction of hospital facilities is frequently supported by *hospital revenue bonds.* These bonds are not guaranteed but are issued by state authorities to build hospitals for lease to public or private operating agencies. Issued in minimum denominations of $1,000, hospital revenue bonds have their principal and interest secured by lease rentals and a mortgage against hospital property.

The late 1970s ushered in widespread use of *mortgage revenue bonds.* Proceeds of these bonds are loaned to low- and moderate-income home buyers who, in turn, eventually pay off the bonds by making monthly mortgage payments. Mortgage revenue bonds typically are issued by cities or counties and carry the tax-exempt privilege, thereby permitting eligible home buyers to borrow at rates below those on conventional residential mortgages. Such issues have aroused a storm of controversy because they represent the use of public funds for private benefit and divert substantial revenues away from the U.S. Treasury. Nevertheless, in the Deficit Reduction Act of 1984 Congress extended the authority of municipal governments to issue tax-exempt, single-family mortgage revenue bonds until the end of 1987.

An unusual type of municipal security which serves both public and private interests is the *industrial development bond* (IDB). These securities originally were used to finance plant construction and the purchase of land which is then leased to a private company. More recently, IDBs have financed the construction of industrial plants, electric-generating plants, commuter systems, rental properties, and pollution control equipment. The purpose is to attract industry into the local area and increase both the number of jobs available and local tax revenues. IDBs were first issued by the state of Mississippi during the Great Depression. Soon the concept of using government credit to promote local industry became common practice across the nation, especially in those areas experiencing declining population or the exodus of large firms. However, the use of public funds raised through the tax-exempt borrowing privilege for private purposes disturbed many members of Congress. Following extensive hearings, Congress in 1968 enacted a law limiting each issue of tax-exempt IDBs to a maximum of $1 million. Then in 1982 Congress passed the Tax Equity and Fiscal Responsibility Act (TEFRA) which further restricted the use of IDBs, reducing depreciation allowances on newly constructed equipment and facilities, eliminating some business activities from the tax-exempt category, and prohibiting small-issue (usually $1 million or less) IDBs after 1986. Finally, the Deficit Reduction Act of 1984 widened the list of prohibited uses of IDB money, placed a ceiling of $40 million on small IDBs from a single issuer, and restricted the total amount that could be issued from each state based on statewide population.

Innovations in Municipal Securities

The vast majority of state and local securities promise the investor a *fixed* rate of return. Unfortunately, this reduces the attractiveness of GOs and revenue bonds in periods of rising interest rates and inflation. During the 1970s and early 1980s a few new municipal instruments were developed to deal with this "inflexibility" problem. For example, several tax-exempt housing-revenue and pollution-control bonds have recently been issued as *floaters*. In one case, U.S. Steel issued $48 million in government-sponsored pollution-control bonds with a flexible (floating) interest rate to protect investors against future rate changes. Buyers were so attracted by this novel idea that an additional $500 million in floating-rate housing bonds soon came to market. These bonds promised a yield tied to changes in the weekly rates on 13-week Treasury bills and 30-year Treasury bonds.

Still another recent innovation is the *option bond.* Option bonds bear a fixed rate of interest but can be sold back to the issuer or his agent at par after a specified period. One example was a $43 million issue of 9 percent, single-family mortgage bonds offered by Denton County, Texas, in December 1980. While these bonds do not come due until the year 2013, a trustee with the backing of First National City Bank of New York guaranteed to buy back eligible bonds beginning December

1, 1985. More recently, several municipal borrowers have reduced the maturities of their bonds from 30 years into the 10- to 15-year range to improve their flexibility to the investor.

These innovations in state and local government borrowing are not without their risks. Other things equal, they will require more frequent borrowing by municipal governments and, more than likely, increase the average cost of government funds, further burdening the taxpayer. In effect, floaters, option bonds, and shorter-maturity financial instruments shift risk from investors to borrowers and, ultimately, to taxpayers. Financial planning becomes more difficult for those local governments electing to use these new financial instruments. Perhaps fortunately for municipal planners, investor interest in flexible-return municipal securities dampened significantly when the rate of inflation declined in the mid-1980s.

Types of Securities Issued by Different Governmental Units

Whether a state or local unit of government issues general obligation or revenue bonds depends upon the type of governmental unit involved. For example, school districts issue only general obligation (GO) bonds. In contrast, special districts which provide such services as water, sanitation, bridges and toll roads, street lighting, and electricity tend to use revenue bonds. City and state governments are about evenly split between GO and revenue issues, while counties generally borrow using revenue bonds.

KEY FEATURES OF MUNICIPAL DEBT

Tax Exemption

Certainly the outstanding and unique feature of municipal securities is the tax-exemption privilege. The interest income from municipal securities is exempt from federal income taxes; in addition, state law usually exempts municipals from income taxes levied by the state of issuance. This exemption feature was created so that federal, state, and local governments would not interfere with each other in raising funds and providing securities to their citizens. Capital gains on municipal securities are not tax exempt, however, unless the security is issued at a discount from par. In that special case any increase in price up to par value is considered part of the security's interest return and is tax exempt. However, if the security continues to rise in price, that portion of the gain above par is subject to taxation once the investor realizes the gain.

EXHIBIT 26–6

The Impact of the Tax-Exemption Feature on the After-Tax Yields of Long-Term Corporate and Municipal Bonds

Investor Group	Before-Tax Yield on Seasoned Aaa Corporate Bonds	Appropriate Federal Income Tax Bracket for Investor Group	After-Tax Yield on Seasoned Aaa Corporate Bonds	Before-Tax and After-Tax Yield on Aaa Municipal Bonds
Individuals in the highest income tax bracket	13%	50%	6.5%	9%
Large corporate investors:				
Manufacturing and industrial corporations	13	46	7.0	9
Property-casualty insurance companies	13	46	7.0	9
Commercial banks	13	46	7.0	9
Individuals in middle-income tax brackets	13	30–45	9.1–7.2	9
Individuals and institutions in the lowest-income tax brackets	13	20–28	10.4–9.4	9
Tax-exempt investors:				
Governments, pension funds, charities, foundations, and credit unions	13	0	13	9

An Interest Subsidy to High-Income Investors.   The tax-exempt feature has been a controversial issue for many years. Clearly, it is a government subsidy to high-tax-bracket investors. This is true because the value of the exemption privilege increases with the investor's marginal income tax rate. Exhibit 26–6 illustrates the impact of the investor's marginal tax rate (or tax bracket) on the relative attractiveness of municipals compared to taxable securities. This exhibit compares the approximate after-tax yield on high-grade corporate bonds, which are fully taxable, with the yield on comparable-quality municipal bonds, assuming that Aaa-rated corporate bonds are trading currently at a 13 percent before-tax yield and Aaa municipal bonds are trading at 9 percent. Because the 13 percent corporate bond yield is a before-tax rate of return, we must adjust it using the investor's marginal income tax rate to derive the after-tax rate of return. The before-tax corporate yield is multiplied by $(1 - t)$ where t is the investor's applicable federal tax rate.[7] Exhibit

---

[7] See Chapter 10 for further discussion of the impact of tax exemption on security yields.

26–6 illustrates the effect of this calculation for investors with marginal tax rates ranging from 0 to 50 percent.[8] For an individual investor in the top 50 percent tax bracket, the after-tax return on Aaa corporate bonds was 13 percent $\times$ (1 − 0.50), or 6.5 percent. Clearly, an investor in this high-income group would prefer to purchase municipal bonds yielding 9 percent rather than corporate bonds returning less than 7 percent after taxes, other factors held equal. The same conclusion holds true for large manufacturing and industrial corporations, property-casualty insurance companies, and commercial banks confronted with the top, 46 percent corporate federal tax rate.[9]

Of course, the foregoing analysis focuses exclusively on after-tax rates of return, ignoring differences in liquidity and other features of taxable and tax-exempt securities. A corporation that needs to hold securities for liquidity purposes, for example, might well hold taxable issues, such as U.S. government securities, which can usually be converted into cash quickly with little risk of loss, even though their after-tax yields may be lower than the yields on municipal bonds.

For income tax brackets below the top rung, corporate bonds and other taxable securities compare more favorably with municipals. For example, life insurance companies, savings banks, and many small private investors whose applicable income tax rate is in the 20 to 30 percent range usually find taxable securities more lucrative and purchase few municipals. In effect, the tax-exempt feature limits the demand for state and local government securities to high-income individuals, commercial banks, property-casualty insurers, and large nonfinancial corporations. This limitation may represent a serious problem in future years when local governments in some areas of the nation must raise an enormous volume of new funds to accommodate rapidly expanding populations.

The tax-exemption feature is an advantage to municipal governments because it keeps their interest costs low relative to interest rates paid by other borrowers. These savings can be passed on to local citizens in

---

[8] The maximum federal income tax rate for individuals was 70 percent until passage of the Economic Recovery Act of 1981, when the maximum rate was reduced to 50 percent. See Chapter 25 for a discussion of recent changes in federal income tax laws.

[9] Two recent federal tax laws have reduced the attractiveness of municipal securities to commercial banks. The Tax Equity and Fiscal Responsibility Act of 1982 ruled that banks borrowing funds (such as through issuing deposits) to buy municipals could only deduct 85 percent of the interest cost on any borrowed funds that were invested in municipals. Then, the Deficit Reduction Act of 1984 stipulated that just 80 percent of borrowing costs could be deducted from taxable bank income when those borrowings were placed in tax-exempt municipal securities.

the form of lower local tax rates. Of course, the U.S. Treasury is able to collect less revenue from high-tax-bracket investors as a result of the exemption privilege and must tax lower-bracket taxpayers more heavily to make up the difference. Therefore, the *total* tax bill from all levels of government is probably little affected by the tax-exempt feature of municipals.

Exemption Contributes to Market Volatility.

Because the market for municipal bonds is limited by the tax-exempt privilege to top-tax-bracket investors, prices and interest rates on municipal bonds tend to be highly volatile and unpredictable. Prices of tax-exempt bonds tend to rise during those periods when corporate and individual incomes are rising, because top-bracket investors have greater need to shelter their earnings from taxation at those times. However, a fall in individual or corporate earnings, especially the earnings of banks and property-casualty insurance companies, often leads to sharp reductions in the demand for municipal bonds. Prices of tax-exempt issues may plummet, and interest costs confronting borrowing governments may rise dramatically during those periods when corporate profits are squeezed. This makes financial planning in the state and local government sector an extremely difficult task.

A Market of "Fair-Weather" Investors.

Another problem that exacerbates the volatility of municipal bond prices is the limited investment horizon of many tax-exempt bond buyers. For the most part, investors active in the tax-exempt market are "fair-weather" friends. Commercial banks, for example, build up their state and local bond holdings when customer loan demand is weak, only to sell off substantial quantities of municipals when loan demand revives. Another major group of tax-exempt investors (high-income individuals) have finite life spans and, therefore, their bonds are often sold after only a short holding period. The net result is to create an active secondary market and relatively high turnover rate for the larger, better-known municipal issues.

Credit Ratings

A feature of municipal securities that makes them especially attractive to investors is their high credit rating. About 10 percent of all municipal securities are AAA-rated by Moody's Investors Service and Standard & Poor's Corporation, while close to 60 percent are AA or A rated. Only about 10 percent of all state and local government securities are rated BA or lower or carry no published rating. This means that the large majority of municipal issues are considered to be of investment quality rather than speculative buys.[10]

Factors behind Setting Credit Ratings.

In assigning credit ratings to municipals, Moody's and other investor-rating services consider the past repayment record of the borrowing unit of government, the quality and size of its tax base, the volume of debt outstanding, local economic conditions, and future prospects for growth in the local economy. The fact that many municipal issues are backed by taxing authority or may draw upon several different sources of revenue for repayment of principal and interest helps to keep the investment quality of most tax-exempt issues high. This is particularly important for the largest buyer of new municipal bonds and notes—commercial banks. Federal regulations applying to national banks, and most state banking regulations as well, prohibit commercial banks from acquiring debt securities rated below BAA (so-called speculative issues). These restrictive rules encourage state and local governments to keep their credit ratings high in order to encourage active participation by banks in bidding for new municipal bonds.

Recent Credit Quality Problems.

Until recently, state and local governments possessed virtually unblemished credit records. No major defaults on municipal securities had occurred since the Depression. However, the turbulent economic and financial environment of the 1970s and 1980s caused many investors to reassess the credit standing of municipals, especially the bonds and notes issued by some of the largest cities in the nation and those associated with special local government projects, such as nuclear power production.

This problem first surfaced dramatically in the financial crisis experienced by New York City in the mid-1970s. Soaring costs for municipal services, excessive reliance on short-term debt, and high unemployment combined to threaten that city with record-high interest costs and financial default. And in the wake of New York City's fiscal crisis, other northeastern cities—Boston, Buffalo, Cleveland, Detroit, Philadelphia, and Newark—also found their credit costs rising to unprecedented levels. In 1975 at the peak of New York City's financial crisis, the yield spread between the highest-quality (Aaa-rated) and lowest-quality investment-grade (Baa) municipal bonds climbed from about half a percentage point

---

[10] See Chapter 10 and Appendix A for a discussion of published credit ratings for corporate and municipal bonds. Moody's Investors Service rates municipals according to the following scale from high to low quality: Aaa, Aa, A, Baa, Ba, B, and C. Standard & Poor's Corporation uses the following rating symbols: AAA, AA, A, BBB, BB, B, CCC, CC, C, DDD, and D.

to nearly 2 full percentage points. Even though there have been few actual defaults on municipal bonds in recent years and the investors involved nearly always have been paid off eventually, risk premiums demanded by investors purchasing lower-grade municipal bonds have, at times, exceeded risk premiums on comparable-quality corporate bonds, setting in motion a periodic "flight to quality" by high-tax bracket investors.

This fundamental concern about the investment quality of municipal issues was heightened in December 1978, when Cleveland became the first major U.S. city to default on its debt since the Depression. However, Cleveland was able to work out an acceptable agreement with local banks to belatedly pay off approximately $15 million in short-term notes. This favorable outcome in the Cleveland case unfortunately did not carry over to the case of Washington Public Power Supply System (WPPSS), a nuclear power consortium. This company was caught in an environmental squabble coupled with serious project delays and cost overruns on nuclear power facilities under construction. The result in the summer of 1983 was the largest default on a local government bond issue in American history. Since that time utility companies with large nuclear power plants in the construction phase have frequently seen their bond interest rates rise sharply (as high as 3 or 4 percentage points) as market investors came to fear greater risk of default.

Serialization

Most municipal bonds are *serial* securities. Serialization refers to the splitting up of a single bond issue into several different maturities. Thus, an issue of $20 million in bonds to build a municipal auditorium might include the following securities:

Amount	Due in
$1 million	1 year
$1 million	2 years
$1 million	3 years
⋮	⋮
$1 million	20 years

Splitting a single issue of municipals into multiple maturities contrasts with the practice employed by most corporate borrowers and the federal government. Corporations, for example, generally issue *term* bonds in which all securities in the same issue come due on the same date. In effect, serialization of municipal bonds is a way of *amortizing* state and local debt.

Why has serialization become so popular in the municipal field? Before serial bonds were widely adopted, state and local bonds were generally term securities. A sinking fund was usually created at the time of issue, and annual contributions were made to the fund until sufficient monies were accumulated to pay off the bond issue at maturity. However, sinking funds proved irresistible to unscrupulous politicians and to governments facing financial emergencies. Accumulated funds often disappeared, leaving virtually nothing to retire municipal debt when it came due. The serial feature seemed to offer an ideal solution to this problem.

Unfortunately, serialization has created as many problems as it has solved. For one thing, splitting a security issue into a number of different maturities reduces the liquidity and marketability of municipal securities. The average-sized municipal issue sold publicly contains about $20 to $30 million in securities. Therefore, when such an issue is split into multiple maturities, there is only a small amount outstanding in any one maturity class. The potential volume of trading for particular maturities is therefore extremely limited. Serialization also complicates the offering of new securities because a number of different investor groups must be attracted into the bidding. For example, commercial banks generally prefer the shorter-term (1- to 10-year) securities, while insurance companies, individuals, and other investors often want only the longest-term bonds.

HOW MUNICIPAL BONDS ARE MARKETED

The selling of municipals is usually carried out through a syndicate of commercial banks, investment banks, and securities dealers. These institutions underwrite municipals by purchasing them from issuing units of government and reselling the securities in the open market, hopefully at a higher price. Commercial banks dominate the underwriting of general obligation bonds, while investment banks (dealers) handle most of the revenue issues.[11] Prices paid by the underwriting firms may be determined either by competitive bidding among several syndicates or by negotiation with a single securities dealer or syndicate. Competitive bidding normally is employed in the marketing of general obligation bonds, while revenue bonds more frequently are placed through negotiation.

In competitive bidding, syndicates (which may contain from 2 to upwards of 50 underwriters) interested in a particular bond issue will estimate its potential reoffer price in the open market and what their desired

---

[11] Commercial banks are permitted to underwrite for resale only GOs and revenue bonds used to finance university, dormitory, or housing projects or those revenue bonds collateralized at least indirectly by the "full faith and credit" of a state or local unit of government. Investment banks, however, legally can underwrite any form of municipal bond or note.

underwriting commission must be. Each syndicate wants to bid a price high enough to win the bid, but low enough so that the securities later can be sold in the open market at a price sufficient to protect the group's commission. That is,

Bid price + Underwriting commission = Market reoffer price

The winning bid carries the lowest *net interest cost* (NIC) to the issuing unit of government. The NIC is simply the sum of all interest payments that will be owed on the new issue divided by its principal amount.

Bidding for new issues of municipal bonds is a treacherous business. Prices, interest rates, and market demand for municipals all change rapidly, often without warning. In fact, the tax-exempt securities market is one of the most volatile of all financial markets. This is due in part to the dominant role of commercial banks, whose demand for municipals fluctuates with their net earnings and loan demand. Legal interest-rate ceilings, which prohibit some local governments from borrowing when market interest rates climb above those celings, also play a significant role in the volatility of municipal trading. These combined factors render the tax-exempt market highly sensitive to the business cycle, monetary policy, inflation, and a host of other economic and financial factors. The specter of high interest rates often forces the postponement of hundreds of millions of dollars of new issues, while the onset of lower rates may unleash a flood of new security offerings. There is a trend today away from competitive bidding and toward negotiated sales of new state and local bonds, due partly to the treacherous character of the tax-exempt market. This trend has aroused some concern among financial analysts because competitive bidding should result in the lowest net interest cost, reducing the burden on local taxpayers. On the other side of the coin, underwriting firms argue that they provide extra services to borrowing governments during the negotiation process—services not generally available through competitive bidding. These include preparing legal offering statements, scheduling the sale of new securities, helping to secure desirable credit ratings, and contacting potential buyers.

PROBLEMS IN THE MUNICIPAL MARKET

Problems and Proposals Regarding Tax Exemption

The municipal market has been plagued by a number of problems over the years, some of these related to its unique tax-exempt character. Many observers question the social benefit of the tax-exemption privilege. As we noted earlier, while state and local governments can borrow more cheaply as a result of tax exemption, the federal government must tax nonexempt groups more heavily to make up the lost revenue. As we have also noted, tax exemption contributes to the cyclical sensitivity of the municipal market, principally because demand for state and local securities comes mainly from commercial banks and individuals, neither of which are permanent investors. Fluctuations in economic conditions frequently lead to large net sales of municipals in the open market and soaring interest rates. Many important investor groups, such as pension funds, life insurance companies, and mutual funds, display very little interest in municipal bonds because they have little need for this type of tax shelter.

A number of proposals have been advanced over the years for improving the depth and stability of the municipal market and eliminating the tax-exempt feature. One interesting idea calls for reimbursing state and local governments for loss of the tax-exempt privilege through federal interest subsidies. Local governments would be offered the option of selling their debt in either the taxable or tax-exempt security markets. Those choosing taxable securities would be eligible for federal subsidies. This step would open the municipal market to life insurance companies, pension funds, and other active capital market investors. A related idea calls for paying a subsidy directly to investors who choose to buy municipal securities. An *Urbank* has also been proposed which, under federal sponsorship, would issue its own bonds, and direct the proceeds of bonds sales to municipal governments. One criticism of this approach is the danger of increased federal controls over state and local governments.

California's Proposition 13

The municipal market was rocked to its foundations in 1978 when California voters approved Proposition 13. This law set maximum real property tax rates in California at 1 percent of the full cash value of taxable property, except for those bonds which had already been approved by the voters. An effective ceiling on tax rates equal to $4 per $100 of assessed value was established—a figure well below the average of $8 to $16 per $100 valuation that prevailed in the state at that time. Proposition 13 also required state officials to roll back their valuation of real property to 1975–76 levels and limited property-value adjustments to only 2 percent a year (except for new construction projects or when property changed hands). The net effect was to reduce funds available to schools and other units of local government by about $7 billion a year.

The state of California was prohibited from enacting a statewide property tax or property transfer tax, and any increase in state taxes required a two-thirds vote of the legislature. In effect, Proposition 13 called for a 60 percent decline in real-property tax collections without making provision for other sources of funds to take up the slack. Finally, the new law permitted local governments to impose special taxes, provided two thirds of the voters gave their approval. However, ad valorem sales and transfer taxes on real property were disallowed.

The success of Proposition 13 in California resulted in the creation of taxpayer lobby groups in other states intent on enacting similar legislation. A taxpayer revolt that has continued into the 1980s resulted subsequently in more than 30 states passing legislation to limit the growth of local government or directly reduce taxes. Budget balancing was required in 49 of the 50 states. Many financial analysts predicted dire consequences for the municipal market stemming from such laws. General obligation bonds were expected to fade away if other states joined California in a move to limit state and local taxing authority. While the new law certainly did not prohibit the issue of municipal bonds, it did prevent increases in taxes to finance many new bonds issues. This fact suggested to many observers that revenue bonds rather than GOs would be more heavily used in the future, especially for utilities, lighting districts, and other revenue-generating services—a trend that has, in fact, occurred.

Laws like Proposition 13 might well encourage the shifting of the local tax base from real property to personal property. Moreover, Proposition 13 appeared to shift a substantial measure of fiscal authority away from state governments toward local governments. Beyond this, there was great concern in California about layoffs of public employees, reduced school hours, and severe limitations on the availability of essential services due to the lack of available funds. One estimate suggested that up to 45,000 people would lose their jobs in California as a result of the passage of Proposition 13. However, few of these "calamities" materialized. Indeed, the prospect of lower taxes appears to have stimulated additional private investment. The added jobs and tax revenues springing from expanded private investment activity appear to have filled in much of the gap left by Proposition 13's fiscal restrictions.

The Growing Burden of Local Taxes and Debt

California's passage of Proposition 13 and strong voter interest in similar laws in other states reflects the tremendous growth in state and local taxes and debt in recent years. The tax burden faced by the average taxpayer today has been worsened by inflation, which pushes individuals into higher and higher tax brackets at both federal and state levels. Moreover, rising property values subject taxpayers to increased tax payments against their homes and other forms of real and personal property.

Local property taxes are particularly onerous to the average citizen because they are so *visible*. Each year, the homeowner is confronted with a large lump-sum property assessment to cover the cost of local schools, street improvements, and other essential services. The fact is that income and sales taxes have increased more rapidly than property taxes, but they are less visible to the taxpayer and therefore often ignored. An added problem is that many citizens do not see a direct correlation between the size of their tax burdens and the quantity and quality of government services available to them. Moreover, the public has come to question the wisdom of both higher taxes and increased borrowing in the face of a favorable trend in state and local government revenues in recent years. Spurred by larger federal grants and increased tax collections, state and local governmental units experienced rising budget surpluses that ultimately reached close to $10 billion as the 1970s drew to a close. Recessions and a cutback in federal grants (particularly for job training) led to diminishing surpluses and some deficit positions in the early 1980s, but economic recovery in the mid-1980s drove the aggregate of state and local budgets back into the black. Taxpayers responded with pressure on legislative bodies and boards to freeze wages and hiring and cut back construction.

In short, with rising taxes and growing investor concern over the credit quality of many municipal issues it seems clear that the market for state and local government debt has an "image problem" to deal with in the years ahead. The need for more local government services is not likely to fade, but the continued willingness of taxpayers to authorize new construction and new borrowing and the continued willingness of large numbers of investors to fund those needs in a volatile and uncertain economic environment are the key issues in municipal finance for the period ahead.

STUDY QUESTIONS

1. The market for state and local government bonds has been one of the most rapidly growing financial markets in the United States since World War II. Why has this been the case? Can you foresee any serious problems on the horizon for the continued growth of the municipal market?

2. What are the principal sources of revenue for state and local governments today? Where do they spend the bulk of their incoming funds?

3. For what reasons do state and local governments borrow short- and long-term funds?

4. Give a concise definition of each of the following state and local government securities, and explain how each is used.
    a. Tax-anticipation notes.
    b. Revenue-anticipation notes.
    c. Bond-anticipation notes.
    d. General obligation (GO) bonds.
    e. Revenue bonds.
    f. Special tax bonds.
    g. Special assessment bonds.
    h. Authority bonds.

5. Revenue bonds issued by local governments and public agencies have grown more rapidly than any other type of municipal security in recent years. Moreover, many new kinds of revenue bonds have been developed to deal with specialized public needs. Several different kinds of revenue bonds are listed below. Please explain the principal purpose or function of each of these securities.
    a. SLROs.
    b. Life-care bonds.
    c. Section 8 bonds.
    d. PHAs.
    e. Hospital revenue bonds.
    f. Mortgage revenue bonds.
    g. IDBs.

6. What are the principal features of municipal bonds that have made them attractive to many groups of investors? What factors or features often limit the demand for these bonds?

7. Describe how municipal bonds are marketed. What risks do syndicates face? What advantages do you see for competitive bidding versus negotiated sales?

8. What recommendations would you make to improve the functioning of the municipal bond market? Carefully explain the purpose and probable effects of each of your recommendations.

9. Why do you think Proposition 13 was enacted into law in the state of California? What impact might such laws have on local economies and the municipal market? Would you favor a similar law for your state if it does not already have one? Please explain your answers.

10. In what ways is the municipal bond market dealing with the problem of "inflexibility"? What is a "floater"? An option bond? How might these devices assist the marketability of municipals in future years?

SELECTED REFERENCES

Advisory Commission on Intergovernmental Relations. *State and Local Finances in Recession and Inflation: An Economic Analysis.* Washington, D.C.: U.S. Government Printing Office, 1979.

Beek, David C. "Rethinking Tax-Exempt Financing for State and Local Governments." *Quarterly Review,* Federal Reserve Bank of New York, Autumn 1982, pp. 30–40.

Bradbury, Katherine L. "Structural Fiscal Distress in Cities—Causes and Consequences." *New England Economic Review,* Federal Reserve Bank of Boston, February 1983, pp. 32–43.

Browne, Lynn E., and Richard F. Syron. "Big City Bonds after New York." *New England Economic Review,* Federal Reserve Bank of Boston, July–August 1977.

_____. "The Municipal Market since the New York City Crisis." *New England Economic Review.* Federal Reserve Bank of Boston, July–August 1979, pp. 11–26.

_____. "How Much Government Is Too Much?" *New England Economic Review,* Federal Reserve Bank of Boston, March–April 1981, pp. 21–34.

Fortune, Peter. "Tax-Exemption of State and Local Interest Payments: An Economic Analysis of the Issues and an Alternative." *New England Economic Review.* Federal Reserve Bank of Boston, March–April 1978, pp. 21–31.

Kaufman, George G. "Municipal Bond Underwriting: Market Structure." *Journal of Bank Research,* Spring 1981, pp. 24–31.

National Governors' Association. *Understanding the Fiscal Condition of the States.* Washington, D.C., 1978.

Rubin, Lamar S. "Recent Developments in the State and Local Government Sector," *Federal Reserve Bulletin,* November 1984, pp. 791–801.

U.S. House of Representatives. *Tax-Exempt Bonds for Single-Family Housing.* A Study Prepared by the Congressional Budget Office for the Subcommittee on the City of the Committee on Banking, Finance and Urban Affairs, 96th Cong., 1st Sess. Washington, D.C.: U.S. Government Printing Office, 1979.

Part Eight

The International Financial System

27

The Balance of Payments and International Transactions

PURPOSE OF THIS CHAPTER

To explore the functions and the character of international financial markets. The chapter examines the manner in which transactions between nations are accounted for through the balance-of-payments accounts. The chapter concludes with a discussion of the problems created by the wide variety of monetary units (standards of value) used by different nations and how these problems have been dealt with through a succession of international agreements.

KEY TERMS AND CONCEPTS IN THE CHAPTER

balance of payments
balance of trade
basic balance
Bretton Woods
capital account
capital flows
comparative
 advantage
current account
disequilibrium

European Monetary
 System
gold exchange
 standard
gold standard
international
 financial markets
managed floating
 currency standard

modified exchange
 standard
monetary unit
official reserve
 transactions
pegging
service balance
special drawing rights
unilateral
 transactions

In many ways the world we live in is rapidly shrinking in size. Jet planes such as the British Concorde can cross the Atlantic between New York and London in less than four hours, about the same time it takes a Boeing 747 jetliner to travel across the United States. Teletype, telex, and transoceanic cable can move financial information and instructions from one spot on the globe to another in minutes. Orbiting satellites can bring news of major international significance to home television sets the same day an event takes place and make possible video as well as voice communication between those involved in international business transactions.

Accompanying these dramatic improvements in communication and transportation is an enormous growth in world trade and international investment. For example, in 1965 total exports of goods and services worldwide reached $190 billion. Eighteen years later, in 1984, the estimated dollar value of world trade had multiplied 10-fold to $2 trillion, or almost as large as the U.S. GNP. Moreover, the United States itself has become increasingly dependent upon world trade; for example, imports into the United States represented just 4.6 percent of GNP in 1960, but had jumped to 10 percent of GNP by 1984, while U.S. exports climbed from 6 percent to nearly 12 percent of GNP over the same period. Thus, about one fifth of the value of income and production in the U.S. economy stems directly from foreign trade. The international financial markets have had to grow enormously in recent years just to keep up with the burgeoning in world trade and finance. Many new financial institutions and innovations have appeared in an international environment of dynamic growth and change.

Actually, the international financial markets perform the same basic function as do the domestic financial markets. They bring international lenders of funds (savers) into contact with borrowers, thereby permitting an increased flow of scarce funds toward their most productive uses. The volume of capital investment worldwide is made larger because of the workings of the global financial system. And, with increased capital investment, the productivity of individual firms and nations is increased and economic growth in the international sector accelerates. The international financial markets also facilitate the flow of consumer goods and services across national boundaries, making possible an optimal allocation of resources in response to consumer demand on a global scale. With increased efficiency in resource use, the output of consumer goods and services in the international sector is increased and costs of production are minimized.[1]

---

[1] These benefits from international trade and finance are most likely to occur if each nation involved follows the principle of *comparative advantage*. This principle argues that each country will have a higher real standard of living if it specializes in the production of those goods and services in which it has a comparative advantage

Just as the domestic financial markets have given rise to a unique collection of financial institutions and methods for transferring funds, so the international financial system has spawned institutions and practices unique to that system. As we will see later in this chapter and in the two chapters to follow, the global financial markets are dominated by huge multinational corporations, central banks, government agencies, the largest commercial banks and financial conglomerates, investment banking houses, security and foreign exchange dealers, and major brokerage houses. Our purpose in this section of the book is to examine the unique roles played by each of these institutions within a rapidly expanding international financial system.

THE BALANCE OF PAYMENTS

One of the most widely used sources of information concerning flows of funds, goods, and services between nations is each country's *balance-of-payments (BOP) accounts.* This annual statistical report summarizes all the economic and financial transactions between residents of one nation and the rest of the world during a specific period of time. It is a report capturing flows (rather than stocks) of payments between nations. Thus, the BOP accounts reflect *changes* in the assets and liabilities of units, such as businesses, individuals, and governments, involved in international transactions, rather than the levels of their assets and liabilities.[2] The major transactions captured in the BOP accounts include exports and imports of goods and services; tourist expenditures; income from debt and equity investments made abroad; government loans, grants, and military expenditures overseas; and net private capital flows between nations.

In a statistical sense, a nation's BOP accounts always "balance" because a system of double-entry bookkeeping is used. For example, every payment made for goods and services imported from abroad simultaneously creates a claim on the home country's resources or extinguishes an existing liability. Similarly, every time a domestic business firm receives payment from overseas, either it acquires a claim against resources in a foreign

---

in resource costs, while importing those goods and services where it is at a comparative resource-cost disadvantage. In simplest terms, a country should acquire goods and services from those sources—foreign or domestic—which result in the lowest cost in terms of its own resources. The principle of comparative advantage works best, of course, in an environment of free international trade which permits nations to specialize in their most efficient productive activities.

[2] In this sense the balance-of-payments accounts are analogous to the Flow of Funds Accounts discussed in Chapter 3. The BOP accounts are really sources and uses of funds statements for a whole nation vis-à-vis the rest of the world.

country, or a claim the firm held against a foreign individual or institution is erased. In practice, however, imbalances frequently show up in the BOP accounts due to unreported transactions or inconsistencies in reporting. These errors and omissions are handled through a Statistical Discrepancy account.

The U.S. Balance of International Payments

The U.S. BOP accounts are prepared and published quarterly by the Department of Commerce. The quarterly figures usuallly are *annualized* to permit comparisons across years. The full set of U.S. international accounts is quite complex because several different groups of international transactions (balances) are calculated to meet the varying needs of policymakers and financial analysts. However, the transactions recorded in the U.S. balance of payments (and those for other countries as well) fall into three broad groups:

1. *Transactions on current account,* which include imports and exports of goods and services and unilateral transfers (gifts).
2. *Transactions on capital account,* which include both long- and short-term investment at home and abroad and usually involve the transfer of financial assets (acceptances, bonds, deposits, stock, etc.).
3. *Official reserve transactions,* which are used by monetary authorities (the Treasury, central bank, exchange stabilization fund, etc.) to settle BOP deficits, usually through transferring the ownership of official reserve assets (including government foreign currency holdings, gold, special drawing rights at the International Monetary Fund, and government-held securities) to countries with BOP surpluses.

Transactions that bring about an inflow of foreign currency into the home country are recorded as *credits* (+). Transactions resulting in an outflow of foreign currency from the home country are listed as *debits* (−).[3] Thus, credit (+) items in the BOP represent sources of funds—an increase in a nation's external buying power or ability to command goods and services from abroad or to invest abroad. Debit (−) items represent uses of funds, which decrease a nation's buying power abroad. If a country sells goods and services or borrows abroad, these transactions are credit items because they increase a nation's external buying power. On the

---

[3] Therefore, any economic transaction that involves only domestic residents and is conducted only in the home currency would not be reflected in the home country's BOP accounts.

EXHIBIT 27–1

Principal Credit and Debt Items Recorded in a Nation's Balance of Payments (BOP)

Credit Entries (inflows of funds, +)	Debit Entries (outflows of funds, −)
Exports of merchandise	Imports of merchandise
Services provided to foreign countries	Services provided to domestic citizens by foreign countries
Interest and dividends due domestic citizens from business firms abroad	Gifts of money sent abroad by domestic citizens
Remittances received from domestic citizens employed in foreign countries	Capital invested abroad by domestic citizens
Foreign purchases of securities issued by domestic firms and units of government	Dividend and interest payments to foreign countries on investments made in the domestic economy
Repayments by foreigners of funds borrowed from domestic lending institutions	

other hand, a purchase of goods and services abroad or a paydown of a nation's international liabilities is a debit item because that country is surrendering part of its external buying power. A summary of the major credit and debit items making up the BOP accounts is shown in Exhibit 27–1.

The actual U.S. BOP accounts for the years 1982 and 1983 as reported by the Department of Commerce are shown in Exhibit 27–2. We have subdivided these international accounts into the three major categories discussed above—the current account, capital account, and official reserve transactions account—to more fully understand how the BOP bookkeeping system operates.

The Current Account

One of the most highly publicized components of the U.S. BOP is the *current account*, which contains three elements:

1. The *merchandise trade balance*, comparing the volume of goods exported to those imported.
2. The *service balance*, comparing exports and imports of services.
3. *Unilateral transfers*, reflecting the amount of gifts made to foreigners by domestic citizens.

The Merchandise Trade Balance.   Prior to the 1970s the United States reported a positive merchandise trade balance, with exports exceeding imports in most years due to substantial demand for American

EXHIBIT 27–2

The Balance of Payments of the United States, 1982 and 1983 ($ billions)

Credit (+) and Debit (−) Items	1982	1983
The current account:*		
Exports of merchandise†	$211.2	$200.2
Imports of merchandise	−247.6	−260.8
Balance on merchandise trade	−36.4	−60.6
Exports of services‡	$137.1	$134.0
Imports of services‡	−103.9	−105.7
Service balance	+33.2	+28.3
Balance on goods and services	−3.2	−32.3
Unilateral transfers (excluding military grants), net	−8.0	−8.6
Balance on current account	−11.2	−40.8
The capital account:		
Private capital flows:		
U.S. bank-reported capital, net (outflow,−)	−45.1	+26.3
U.S. net purchase (−) of foreign securities	−8.0	−7.5
Foreign net purchases (+) of U.S. Treasury securities	+7.0	+8.6
Foreign net purchases (−) of other U.S. securities	+6.1	+8.6
U.S. direct investment abroad	+3.0	−7.6
Foreign direct investment in the United States	10.4	9.5
Other private capital flows, net	−3.9	−4.2
Total private capital flows, net	−22.7	+33.7
Official reserve transactions:		
Change in foreign official assets in the United States (increase,+)	+3.1	+6.1
Change in U.S. government		
Official assets, net (increase,−)	−5.0	−1.2
Reserve position in IMF	−3.6	−4.4
Holdings of convertible currencies	−1.0	+3.3
Special drawing rights (SDRs)	−1.4	−0.1
Gold stock	0	0
Statistical discrepancy (errors and omissions)	41.4	7.1

Note: Details may not add to column totals due to rounding.
* The current account is seasonally adjusted, but the other components are not seasonally adjusted.
† These export and import figures exclude military purchases.
‡ The service balances include transfers under U.S. military agency sales contracts in the case of exports and direct defense expenditures in the case of imports.
SOURCES: Federal Reserve Bank of St. Louis, *International Economic Conditions*, June 1984 and Board of Governors of the Federal Reserve System, *Federal Reserve Bulletin*, June 1984.

agricultural products, machinery, and equipment overseas. However, uncertainty over the value of the U.S. dollar, rapid inflation, and a dramatic increase in crude oil prices turned U.S. trade surpluses into substantial deficits. In general, U.S. *sources* of external buying power have generally been less than its *uses* of external buying power. Moreover, American merchandise trade deficits generally have deepened over time. For example, in 1970, the U.S. merchandise trade balance was +$2.6 billion; in

1980, −$25.5 billion; and in 1984 − $107 billion. These huge trade deficits continued to grow even as U.S. oil imports dropped to their lowest levels since the Middle East Oil Embargo of the early 1970s.

The Service Balance.   Because Americans have purchased more goods from abroad in recent years than they have sold to other countries, how has this deficit (debit balance) in the merchandise trade account been paid for? Funds must be acquired from some other source to finance the excess of merchandise imports over exports. Part of the needed funds have come from the service balance—exports of services minus service imports—which has been in surplus (credit balance) for many years. Services counted in the BOP accounts include insurance policies covering foreign shipments of goods, shipping of ocean freight and other transportation services, hotel accommodations for foreigners visiting the United States, and property management services, entertainment, and medical care for foreign residents. Also included in the service balance are receipts of income from U.S. direct investments abroad (usually in the form of interest and dividends).[4] These income flows are created when U.S. residents purchase foreign securities and acquire equity interests in foreign businesses. When exports of services exceed service imports, the result is a credit (+) balance in the services account. The balance in the service accounts is sometimes called the *balance in invisibles* because services are intangible items. In 1983 the U.S. service balance, or balance in invisibles, was in surplus by $28.3 billion, helping to offset about half the U.S. merchandise trade deficit, though the positive service balance has been falling recently.

Balance on Goods and Services.   If we combine the merchandise trade balance with the service balance, the resulting figure is labeled the balance on goods and services. In 1983 the U.S. reported a merchandise trade deficit of $60.6 billion and a credit balance in services of $28.3 billion, resulting in a debit balance on goods and services of −$32.3 billion during 1983 and an even deeper −$91 billion in 1984.

Unilateral Transfers.   The third category of transactions recorded in the current account, labeled unilateral transfers, consists of gifts of goods and money from U.S. residents to foreigners. Gifts of food, clothing, furniture, appliances, money, and other items are referred to as unilateral

---

[4] In effect, interest and dividend payments received by domestic residents from international investments reflect services that the nation's capital is providing overseas. The interest and dividend payments increase a nation's external buying power.

transfers because they represent a *one-way flow* of resources to the recipient; nothing is expected in return. Of course, foreigners send gifts to U.S. residents as well, but American gift-giving abroad far exceeds the return flow. For example, gifts to foreigners from Americans (due principally to a sharp rise in transfers to Israel) were almost $9 billion larger than foreign gifts flowing into the United States in 1983 (see Exhibit 27–2) and more than $11 billion in 1984. Each gift sent overseas represents a *use* of the nation's external buying power and therefore is recorded as a *debit* (−) item.

The Balance on Current Account.   When we put the three components—balance on merchandise trade, balance on services, and net unilateral transfers together—we derive the balance on current account. As Exhibit 27–2 reveals, the U.S. balance on current account in 1983 was a debit balance of $40.8 billion—then the largest current account deficit in American history until the 1984 BOP reports showed a current account deficit of almost $102 billion. The United States experienced such a huge debit balance primarily because of a rising value of the U.S. dollar in international markets that discouraged sales of U.S. goods abroad, inflation, and a lagging economic recovery abroad even while the U.S. economy was growing rapidly.

The Capital Account

Flows of funds destined for investment abroad are recorded in the *capital account*. Investments abroad may be long term, as in the case of an American automobile company building an assembly plant in West Germany, or short term, such as the purchase of six-month British Treasury bills by U.S. citizens. Of course, capital investment flows both ways across national boundaries. For example, in 1983 U.S. citizens and private organizations invested more than $44 billion overseas, but foreign individuals and private institutions, attracted by high interest rates here, invested about $78 billion in U.S. assets. The result was a *net private capital inflow* into the United States of almost $34 billion in 1983; and 1984 brought an even larger net U.S. capital inflow of more than $77 billion.

Interestingly enough, investments by foreigners in the United States are growing faster today than U.S. investments overseas. The relative prosperity experienced by the American economy over the past decade and the strength of the dollar in international markets coupled with political upheavals abroad have brought forth an increasing volume of foreign investment within the continental United States. American banks, hotels, chemical manufacturers, insurance companies, wholesale traders in motor vehicles, metals, and farm products, energy companies, and numerous other businesses have all been acquisition targets for foreign investors.[5] In effect, these huge foreign-capital inflows (especially short-term funds from overseas and unrecorded capital flows) have financed a substantial portion of the U.S. trade deficit.

Components of the Capital Account.

The capital account in the balance of payments includes three different types of international investment: (1) short-term capital flows, (2) direct investments, and (3) portfolio investments. The latter two—direct and portfolio investments— represent a long-term commitment of funds, involving the purchase of stocks, bonds, and other financial assets having a maturity of more than one year. Short-term capital flows, on the other hand, reflect purchases of financial assets with maturities of less than one year. These short-term financial assets are mainly government notes and bills, bank deposits, bills of exchange, and foreign currencies.

What is the essential difference between direct investment and portfolio investment? The key factor is *control.* Portfolio investment merely involves purchasing securities to hold in order to receive interest, dividends, or capital gains. Direct investment, on the other hand, refers to the purchase of land or the acquisition of ownership shares in an attempt to control a foreign business firm.[6]

Claims against Foreigners.

In addition to direct investment and purchases of foreign securities, the capital account also records claims against foreigners reported by domestic banks and nonbanking concerns. The bulk of these claims comprises loans extended by domestic banks to firms and governments abroad.

In 1983 U.S. bank claims on foreigners rose $25 billion and increased another $7 billion in 1984. Most of the gain was due to loans made by U.S. banks to their Caribbean branches, which then turned around and made loans in the global Eurocurrency markets.[7] However, U.S. banks also borrowed heavily abroad to sustain their domestic and international

---

[5] The leading foreign nations with ownership interests in U.S.-based firms are the United Kingdom, Canada, the Netherlands, West Germany, and Japan. These five nations have accounted for about three quarters of the total assets of all U.S. affiliates of foreign firms, according to Department of Commerce estimates. Most of the remaining foreign-controlled U.S. assets were held by Latin American companies.

[6] The U.S. Department of Commerce defines direct investment as ownership of 10 percent or more of the voting stock or the exercise of other means of control over a foreign business enterprise by an individual or corporation. Ownership of less than 10 percent of a foreign firm's stock is referred to as portfolio investment.

[7] See Chapter 16 for a discussion of borrowing and lending activity in the Eurodollar and other Eurocurrency markets.

lending operations, giving foreign investors substantial claims against American banks. For example, short- and long-term liabilities to foreigners reported by U.S. banking concerns rose $51.3 billion in 1983 and another $28 billion in 1984. If we combine U.S. bank loans abroad of $25 billion [a capital outflow or debit (−) item] with U.S. bank borrowings abroad of $51.3 billion [a capital inflow or credit (+) item] the result is a net U.S. bank-reported capital inflow of $26.3 billion in 1983, the figure shown in Exhibt 27–2.

Interestingly enough, U.S. bank loans abroad declined sharply in 1983 and 1984 from what they had been in earlier years. For example, new U.S. bank loans overseas reached an all-time record high of $109 billion in 1982, following previous record increases of $84 billion in 1981 and $47 billion in 1980. What reversed the trend? Several foreign countries, most notably in Central and South America and in Eastern Europe, have been unable to service their huge loans from American banks and many international energy loans nose-dived in value due to continuing weakness in the oil market. As a result, many U.S. banks began to sell off their nonperforming foreign credits and to sharply reduce their foreign lending activities. Investment abroad by U.S. lenders has also been discouraged in recent years by sluggish economic activity and excess industrial capacity overseas. Then, too, many U.S. corporations have brought the earnings of their foreign affiliates home (known as *repatriation* of funds) to take advantage of relatively high domestic interest rates.

The Basic Balance

If the current account balance is added to the long-term investment balance in the nation's international accounts, the net figure is known as the *basic balance.* We can calculate this for the United States in 1983 as follows:

		$ Billions
U.S. balance on current account		−40.8
Long-term capital flows:		
Net direct investment abroad[8]	−1.9	
Net portflio investment[8]	−9.2	
Net long-term capital outflow		−11.1
Basic balance		−51.9

---

[8] The net figure is derived by subtracting foreign investments in the United States from investments by U.S. residents abroad. The basic balance is designed to capture only basic, long-term trends in a nation's balance of payments. Short-term capital flows, excluded from the basic balance, are assumed to result from temporary factors (such as the financing of current transactions) which will "net out" in the long run.

Therefore, when merchandise trade, services, gifts, and long-term capital flows are taken into consideration, the United States had a $51.9 billion deficit in its basic balance account. This deficit has to be covered either by giving up U.S. reserves of gold, foreign currency, and other assets or by giving foreigners larger claims (in the form of securities, bank deposits, etc.) against U.S. resources.

Cumulative Balance in International Accounts and Short-Term Capital Flows

Actually, the total or cumulative U.S. balance-of-payments deficit may be larger or smaller than the basic balance. The principal reason is that the basic balance fails to consider short-term capital flows. For example, in 1983 private investors in the United States invested about $44 billion in assets abroad, while foreign private investors acquired about $78 billion in U.S. assets—a difference of approximately $34 billion, representing a net *inflow* to the United States of both short- and long-term private capital. However, we must also consider the possibility of a statistical discrepancy in the reported figures due to thousands of unreported transactions that occur across national borders each day.

As noted earlier, because the balance of payments is based on a double-entry system of bookkeeping, it should always balance out except for errors in recording and reporting transactions and the omission of many unrecorded items. Errors and omissions are captured in an account called Statistical Discrepancy, which is the difference between the reported current account and capital account balances. Many authorities believe that the Statistical Discrepancy reflects primarily unreported current earnings and unrecorded short-term capital flows. This account often increases in size when large amounts of short-term capital are known to be in motion from one country to another in response to differences in interest rates or currency values. The 1983 Statistical Discrepancy was a credit (+) balance of $7.1 billion, suggesting that U.S. security issuers were able to attract relatively large amounts of foreign funds.[9] After adjusting for foreign capital flowing into the United States, therefore,

---

[9] The Statistical Discrepancy account has generally increased in size in recent years. For example, in 1983 it was about $7 billion and in 1984 $30 billion. Several factors have contributed to the account's growth, including political unrest abroad, secret and illegal transactions, errors on the part of clerks filling out or processing government report forms, and concealment by governments of their true international reserve positions. The major problem is probably unreported investment funds flowing in from abroad in search of safety from political upheavals. Many of these funds are secretly invested or are tagged with names not reflecting their true ownership. Increased trading in foreign currencies also has been a factor here.

the *net* amount of funds which flowed out of the country in 1983 was probably much less than the basic balance deficit we have just calculated.

Official Reserve Transactions

When a nation has a deficit in its international payments accounts, it must settle up by surrendering assets or claims to foreign individuals and institutions. Official reserve transactions, involving transfer of the ownership of gold, convertible foreign currencies, deposits in the International Monetary Fund and special drawing rights (SDRs[10]), are usually the vehicle for settling net differences in international claims between nations.

Official reserve accounts are immediately available assets for making international payments. When these assets *increase,* this represents a *use* of external buying power by the nation experiencing the increase. On the other hand, a *decrease* in the official reserve accounts represents a *source* of external buying power. If a nation has a surplus (credit balance) in its current and capital accounts, the balance in its official reserve accounts generally rises, indicating an excess of sales abroad over foreign purchases. Conversely, a country experiencing a deficit (debit balance) in its current and capital accounts usually will find that the balance in its official reserve accounts is falling. Such a decline can be temporarily offset, however, by official borrowing by the federal government, the central bank, or by some other designated government agency.

In 1983 offsetting movements occurred in U.S. and foreign holdings of official reserve assets. Foreign governments and central banks increased their holdings of gold, currencies, and other official assets in the United States by $6.1 billion, net. Also, reflecting its huge BOP deficit the U.S. government lost official reserve assets in the net amount of $1.2 billion in 1983 and more than twice that amount in 1984. However, as we noted earlier, most of the American BOP deficits in recent years have not been financed through changes in official reserve assets, but through capital inflows from abroad.

Disequilibrium in the Balance of Payments

The deficit in the U.S. basic balance reported in 1983 and in more recent years is not an isolated phenomenon, as we noted earlier. For several years running now, the United States has displayed a disequilibrium position in its balance of international payments. This means that the nation has relied on foreign credit, foreign capital inflows into the United States, and the U.S. stock of gold, foreign currencies, and other

---

[10] SDRs are discussed later in this chapter.

reserve assets to settle continuing BOP deficits. However, the amount of these financing devices is *limited—no nation can go on indefinitely accumulating BOP deficits, borrowing abroad, and using up its exchange reserves.* Moreover, relying on foreign capital inflows is dangerous because the perceptions of foreign investors regarding the desirability of placing funds in the United States may change quite abruptly.

To this point foreign central banks and foreign investors have regarded American securities and interest-bearing, dollar-denominated deposits (Eurodollars) as good investments and have been willing to extend an increasing volume of international credit to the United States. At some point, however, foreign governments, central banks, and private investors may become satiated with dollars and dollar claims; at this point the value of the U.S. dollar must begin to decline in international markets. American purchases of goods and services abroad would also decline because of the dollar's reduced purchasing power. All else equal, the nation's standard of living would begin to fall until equilibrium in its balance-of-payments position was restored.

Trends in the U.S. Balance of Payments

Is this long-term disequilibrium position in U.S. international payments likely to continue? What components of the American balance of payments have contributed the most to recent payments deficits?

As Exhibit 27–3 reveals, one of the most persistent problems has been in the U.S. merchandise trade account. Following a series of annual trade surpluses during the 1960s, the 1970s ushered in a period when merchandise imports substantially exceeded exports. These U.S. trade deficits have had many causes—sharply higher prices for imported oil, declining industrial productivity, the success of several foreign nations (especially Japan) in marketing their goods in U.S. markets, burgeoning demand for imported automobiles, domestic inflation, and most recently, the rise in the value of the dollar relative to many other national currencies, making U.S. goods more expensive in foreign markets. At the same time, imports into the United States (particularly from less developed countries) accelerated as foreign businesses realized that the dollar's rise was making imported goods in the United States relatively less expensive. The net effect of all these developments, of course, was to create and then deepen the U.S. *merchandise trade deficit.* Among recent U.S. efforts to deal with this trade deficit one of the most important advances was passage of the Trade and Tariff Act of 1984 (also known as the Omnibus Trade bill) that will make it easier for the United States to negotiate free trade agreements and tariff reductions with other nations and to further reduce barriers to international investment.

A positive factor in the U.S. international payments position is the

EXHIBIT 27–3

Annual Series, U.S. International Transactions ($ millions)*

Year	Trade Flows					Capital Flows								
	Merchandise Exports	Merchandise Imports	Service Exports	Service Imports	Current Account Balance	Direct Investment Abroad	Direct Investment in U.S.	Security Purchases Abroad	Security Purchases in U.S.	Bank Claims on Foreigners	Bank Liabilities to Foreigners	U.S. Government Assets Abroad	Foreign Official Assets in U.S.	Monetary Base Effect†
1960	19,650	14,758	9,211	8,971	2,824	2,940	315	603	82	1,148	678	−1,045	1,473	−2,128
1961	20,108	14,537	9,829	9,054	3,822	2,653	311	762	475	1,261	928	303	765	−1,061
1962	20,781	16,260	11,022	9,518	3,387	2,851	346	969	68	450	336	−450	1,270	−1,012
1963	22,272	17,046	11,942	9,999	4,414	3,483	231	1,105	138	1,556	898	1,284	1,986	−539
1964	25,501	18,700	13,325	10,522	6,823	3,760	322	677	−231	2,505	1,818	1,509	1,660	−114
1965	26,461	21,510	14,626	11,291	5,432	5,011	415	759	−489	−93	503	380	134	−1,378
1966	29,310	25,493	15,252	13,106	3,031	5,418	425	720	550	−233	2,882	973	−672	−879
1967	30,666	26,866	16,648	14,740	2,583	4,805	698	1,308	881	495	1,765	2,370	3,451	1,748
1968	33,626	32,991	18,737	15,809	611	5,295	807	1,569	4,550	−233	3,871	3,144	−774	−1,540
1969	36,414	35,807	21,108	18,322	339	5,890	1,263	1,459	3,062	570	8,886	3,379	−1,301	−72
1970	42,469	39,866	23,205	20,184	2,331	7,590	1,464	1,076	2,270	967	−6,298	−892	6,908	−355
1971	43,319	45,579	25,519	20,990	−1,433	7,618	367	1,113	2,265	2,980	−6,911	−465	26,879	−922
1972	49,381	55,797	28,114	23,638	−5,795	7,747	949	618	4,468	3,506	4,754	1,572	10,475	−39
1973	71,410	70,499	38,831	28,720	7,140	11,353	2,800	671	3,825	5,980	4,702	2,486	6,026	−328
1974	98,306	103,811	48,360	33,708	1,962	9,052	4,760	1,854	1,075	19,516	16,017	1,101	10,546	−34
1975	107,088	98,185	48,641	34,795	18,136	14,244	2,603	6,247	5,093	13,532	628	4,323	7,027	469
1976	114,745	124,228	56,885	38,197	4,207	11,949	4,347	8,885	4,067	21,368	10,990	6,772	17,693	759
1977	120,816	151,907	63,460	42,263	−14,511	11,890	3,728	5,460	2,971	11,427	6,719	4,068	36,816	−414
1978	142,054	176,020	77,940	54,315	−15,446	16,056	7,897	3,626	4,432	33,667	16,141	3,928	33,678	693
1979	184,473	212,028	102,328	70,082	−964	25,222	11,877	4,726	6,311	26,213	32,607	4,876	−13,665	2,039
1980	224,237	249,781	117,836	84,815	421	19,222	13,666	3,524	8,102	46,838	10,743	13,295	15,566	2,947
1981	237,019	265,086	137,602	98,012	4,592	9,680	21,998	5,636	10,153	83,851	42,154	10,253	5,430	1,907
1982	211,217	247,606	137,107	103,896	−11,211	−3,008	10,390	7,986	13,145	109,346	64,263	10,697	3,172	1,246
1983	200,203p	260,753p	134,030p	105,657p	−40,776p	7,608p	9,514p	7,484p	17,186p	24,966p	51,295p	6,093p	6,083p	−1,556

p = preliminary.
* The signs in this table do *not* indicate whether a particular transaction is an inflow or an outflow. In this table a negative sign indicates a reduction in the stock of a particular class of assets during a particular time period.
† Beginning in 1979, official U.S. holdings of assets denominated in foreign currencies are revalued monthly at market exchange rates. As of July 1980 the monetary base effect includes the addition of official U.S. holdings of Swiss franc-denominated assets. Consequently, this series after July 1980 is not directly comparable to that reported for previous periods.

SOURCE: Federal Reserve Bank of St. Louis.

long-term surplus in the services account. As we noted earlier, exports of services exceeded service imports by $28 billion in 1983. In fact, the United States has had a service account surplus each year for more than two decades, as Exhibit 27–3 reveals, and that surplus has been growing over time. As American shipping lines and airline companies, hotels, travel agencies, insurance companies, and banks continue to expand their service offerings abroad, the U.S. service account should continue to display substantial surplus (credit) balances in the future.

Another positive factor for the American BOP lies in the *capital account* where growing investment by foreigners in the United States has offset outflows of capital funds from U.S. investors. Capital inflows into the United States have grown faster in recent years than U.S. investments abroad. The most rapid gains in foreign investment inside the United States have been centered in service-oriented industries—banking and finance, insurance, and trade. However, investments in U.S. trade industries and petroleum affiliates have also continued to grow rapidly. A major factor accelerating foreign direct investment in the United States is the desire to avoid American import restrictions by developing production facilities inside the United States. Even more significant are relatively high U.S. interest rates and domestic political stability offering an attractive haven for international investors. If this capital inflow continues in the future, it will do much to alleviate the serious international payments problems of the United States.[11]

THE PROBLEM OF DIFFERENT MONETARY UNITS IN INTERNATIONAL TRADE AND FINANCE

Businesses and individuals trading goods and services in international markets encounter a problem not experienced by those who buy and sell only in domestic markets. This is the problem of different monetary units used as the standard of value from country to country. Americans, of course, use the dollar as a medium of exchange and standard of value in domestic markets. British citizens employ pounds sterling for domestic exchange, while the Swiss and the French rely on the franc as their basic monetary unit. There are more than 100 different monetary units around the world (see Exhibit 27–4). As a result, whenever goods and

---

[11] It is worth noting here that U.S. BOP deficits are more easily dealt with (and perhaps less consequential for the nation's economic health) than is true for most other countries. The reason is the U.S. dollar's pivotal role as the principal medium of exchange and reserve asset in the international financial system. Other nations usually are willing to add more U.S. dollars to their official exchange reserves in order to hedge against their own future exchange-rate or BOP problems.

EXHIBIT 27–4

Principal Monetary Units Used in International Trade and Finance

Country	Monetary Unit	Country	Monetary Unit
Argentina	Peso	Japan	Yen
Australia	Dollar	Malaysia	Ringgit
Austria	Schilling	Mexico	Peso
Belgium	Franc	Netherlands	Guilder
Canada	Dollar	New Zealand	Dollar
Denmark	Krone	Norway	Krone
Finland	Markka	Portugal	Escudo
France	Franc	Saudi Arabia	Riyal
Germany	Deutsche mark	South Africa	Rand
Honduras	Lempira	Spain	Peseta
India	Rupee	Sri Lanka	Rupee
Iran	Rial	Sweden	Krona
Ireland	Pound	Switzerland	Franc
Italy	Lira	United Kingdom	Pound sterling
		United States	Dollar

services are sold or capital flows across national boundaries, it is usually necessary to sell one currency and buy another.

Unfortunately, the act of trading currencies entails substantial *risk*. [12] Exporters and importers may be forced to purchase a foreign currency when its value is rising while, at the same time, the home country's currency is falling in value. Any profits earned on the sale of goods and services abroad may be outweighed by losses suffered in currency exchange. Moreover, the very existence of different monetary units encourages speculation over future currency values, which in turn increases the instability of exchange rates and adds to the costs of international trade. Differing monetary units also complicate government monetary policy aimed at curbing inflation and ensuring adequate economic growth. Repeatedly in recent years massive flows of funds surged through foreign and domestic markets from speculative buying and selling of dollars, francs, pounds, and other major currencies. These speculative currency flows greatly increased the problems of economic recovery, the control of inflation, and adjustments to fluctuations in energy prices.

The Gold Standard

The problem of trading in different monetary units whose prices change frequently is one of the world's oldest financial problems. It has

---

[12] See Chapter 28 for a discussion of the risks involved in currency trading.

been dealt with in a wide variety of ways over the centuries. One of the most successful solutions prior to the modern era centered on *gold* as an international standard of value. During the 17th and 18th centuries, a period that gave birth to the Industrial Revolution and the rapid expansion of world trade, major trading nations in Western Europe made their currencies freely convertible into gold. Gold bullion and gold coins could be exported and imported from one country to another without significant restriction, and each unit of currency was defined in terms of so many grains of fine gold. Nations adopting the gold standard agreed to exchange paper money or gold coins for gold bullion in unlimited amounts at fixed, predetermined prices.

One advantage of the gold standard was that it imposed a common standard of value on all national currencies. This brought a measure of security to international trade and investment, dampened exchange-rate fluctuations, and stimulated the expansion of commerce and long-term investment abroad. A second advantage of the gold standard was economic discipline. Tying national currencies to gold regulated the growth and stability of national economies. A nation experiencing severe inflation or excessively rapid growth in consumption of imported goods and services soon found itself losing gold reserves. Exports declined, unemployment rose, and domestic prices soon began to fall. As a result, the volume of imports was curtailed, and the outflow of gold reduced. Eventually, export industries would recover and the country would begin to rebuild its gold reserves, providing a basis for further expansion of its international trade.[13]

These advantages of security and economic discipline were offset by a number of limitations inherent in the gold standard. For one thing, maintenance of that standard depended crucially on free trade. Nations desiring to protect their industry and jobs from foreign competition through export or import restrictions could not do so. Moreover, the growth of a nation's money supply was limited by the size of its gold stock. Problems of rising unemployment or lagging economic growth might call for a stimulative monetary policy, leading to lower interest rates and rapid expansion of the domestic money supply. However, such a policy required a suspension of gold convertibility, taking the nation off the gold standard. Thus, the gold standard often conflicted with na-

---

[13] The role of gold in promoting monetary discipline may be more important than many financial analysts and policymakers assume. In 1971 the U.S. government severed the link between gold and foreign official holdings of dollars by suspending the convertibility of these holdings into bullion. Following that official break, the volume of Eurodollar deposits in the world monetary system increased by a factor of 10 times during the 1970s, while interest rates and the prices of gold, silver, crude oil, and other commodities soared.

tional economic goals and drastically limited the policy alternatives open to governmental authorities.

The Gold Exchange Standard

While government policymakers are mainly concerned about the effects of the gold standard on domestic economies, investors and commercial traders found that gold bullion was not a particularly convenient medium of exchange. Gold is bulky, expensive to transport, and risky to handle. Moreover, the world's gold supply was limited relative to the rapidly expanding volume of international trade. These problems gave rise in the 19th century to the *gold exchange standard.* Central banks, governments, major commercial banks, and other institutions actively engaged in international commerce began to hold stocks of convertible currencies. Each currency was freely convertible into gold at a fixed rate but also was freely convertible into other currencies at relatively stable prices. In practice, virtually all transactions took place in convertible currencies, while gold faded into the background as an international medium of exchange.

Without question, the gold exchange standard provided greater convenience for international traders and investors. However, this monetary standard possessed the same inherent limitations as the original gold standard. National currencies were still tied to gold, and growth in world trade depended crucially upon growth of the international gold stock. The gold exchange standard collapsed during the economic chaos of the Depression.

Despite the problems inherent in the gold and gold exchange standards, there continues to be considerable interest in the United States in returning to some type of gold standard. For example, Congress created a 17-member Gold Commission in 1980 to "study and make recommendations concerning the role of gold in the domestic and international monetary systems." Chaired by the Secretary of the Treasury, the Gold Commission was charged with the responsibility of reviewing systems for linking the dollar's value to gold as a way of controlling monetary growth and stabilizing or eliminating inflation. But, at least two problems appear to stand in the way of a return to even a modified gold standard. First, while a dollar-gold link may stabilize prices in the long run, a gold standard is likely to produce substantial short-run swings in prices and domestic employment, some of which would be politically unacceptable. Moreover, setting the price for the conversion of various currencies into gold is a most difficult problem in today's volatile financial marketplace. Finally, world production of gold is expected to be essentially flat or possibly even turn downward over the next two decades. The result, in all probability, would be a sharply inflated gold price and significant instability in the international payments system.

The Modified Exchange Standard

Dissatisfaction with international monetary systems tied exclusively to gold resulted in a search for a new payments system following World War II. Major Western countries convened an international monetary conference in Bretton Woods, New Hampshire, in 1944 to devise a more stable money and payments system. The conference created a new mechanism for settling international payments, a new system of currency values (known as the Bretton Woods System), and an agency for monitoring the exchange-rate practices of member nations (known as the International Monetary Fund, or IMF, with headquarters in Washington, D.C.).[14]

The centerpiece of the Bretton Woods System was the linking of foreign currency prices to the U.S. dollar and to gold. The United States committed itself to buy and sell gold at $35 per ounce upon request from foreign monetary authorities. Other IMF member nations pledged to keep their currency's price within 1 percent of its par value in terms of gold or the dollar. Central banks would use their foreign exchange reserves to buy or sell their own currency in the foreign exchange market. In practice, this usually meant that, if a foreign currency fell in value *below* par (the lower intervention point), a central bank would sell its holding of dollars and put that currency in the market, driving its price

---

[14] The IMF, which is headed by a Board of Governors with a representative from each member nation, establishes rules for settling international accounts between nations and grants short-term loans to member nations who lack sufficient international reserve assets to settle their BOP deficits. IMF balance-of-payments loans usually are accompanied by strict requirements that a member nation receiving credit must adopt stern economic measures to curtail the growth of its imports and expand sales of goods and services abroad. The IMF's credit guarantee often encourages banks and other nations to grant loans and aid to a member nation in trouble. Most IMF loans are for 4 to 8 years, occasionally stretching out to 10 years, and are designed to give a borrowing country time to restructure its economy to promote greater efficiency and reduced consumption of imports. The funds loaned by the IMF come mainly from *quotas* which each member nation must contribute in dollars or other reserve assets and in its own home currency. The size of the quota for each of the IMF's nearly 150-member nations determines that nation's voting power in any IMF decisions with each member of the fund's Board of Governors casting the number of votes to which his or her nation is entitled. The quota sizes also limit how much each member country may borrow from the IMF.

A companion organization to the IMF is the World Bank, also created under the Bretton Woods Agreement. The World Bank makes long-term loans to speed the economic development of IMF member nations.

up toward par. If the price of a nation's currency rose more than 1 percent *above* par (the upper intervention point), the central bank involved would sell its own currency and buy dollars, driving the currency's price down toward par. If a currency fell too far in value or rose too high, resulting in market disruption and threatening a massive loss of foreign exchange reserves, the country involved would simply revalue its currency, establishing a new par value.[15]

Fundamentally, the success of the Bretton Woods System depended on the ability of the United States to maintain confidence in the dollar and to protect its value. One of the weaknesses of the new system was that the U.S. dollar was in short supply early in the postwar period, as gold had been in short supply during the 18th and 19th centuries. Initially, there was a substantial excess demand for dollars abroad; however, the system worked well at first because the dollar was by far the most stable money medium around. Moreover, the United States held a strong BOP position until the late 1950s. Later, however, the United States began to export large amounts of capital to Western Europe and Asia (principally Japan). The result was sizeable U.S. trade deficits, that were dealt with by drains on the American gold stock and by a buildup of dollar holdings abroad. In one sense, this was a favorable development because it increased the supply of dollars in foreign hands and alleviated the shortage of dollars needed to finance international trade. In another sense, however, it was an indication of fundamental problems developing in the U.S. economy.

The 1960s and 70s ushered in a massive outflow of U.S. dollars as American investors were attracted by higher interest rates abroad. At the same time the favorable merchandise trade surplus that the United States had enjoyed for many years began to erode in the 1960s and turned negative in the 70s, contributing to deepening American BOP deficits. Presidents Kennedy and Johnson attempted to deal with the problem of capital outflows by creating an Interest Equalization Tax in 1963 and a Voluntary Credit Restraint Program in 1965, respectively. Unfortunately, an accelerating rate of inflation in the late 1960s and 70s undermined government efforts to improve the American payments position. Rising prices for domestically produced goods relative to foreign products

---

[15] A key advantage of the Bretton Woods System over the gold standard was a severing of the old link between the supply of gold and a nation's money supply. There was no commitment to redeem paper currency with gold in unlimited amounts to anyone filing a claim for gold. Only dollars held by foreign governments could be exchanged for gold (at a fixed price of $35 per ounce). Each nation was expected to create an exchange stabilization fund, which held a reserve of gold and currency and stood ready to buy or sell dollars and other currencies to maintain exchange rates within 1 percent of their agreed-upon par values.

increased the volume of U.S. imports and restrained the growth of American exports. Foreign governments and both foreign and domestic investors began to lose confidence in the ability of U.S. policymakers to control the American economy and subdue inflation.

Abandonment of the Bretton Woods System

Continuing inflation and other economic weaknesses forced the abandonment of the Bretton Woods System early in the 1970s. The first and most important step in the dismantling of the old system was taken by the Nixon administration in August 1971, when the dollar was devalued and the convertibility of foreign official holdings of dollars into gold suspended. Gold ceased to be an international monetary medium; it is traded today only as a commodity.

A second step toward a new monetary system was taken in March 1973, when IMF member nations agreed to allow their currencies to float over a wider range, intervening only when currency-exchange rates varied from their par values by more than 2.25 percent. However, volatile economic conditions continued to generate massive speculative flows of capital across national boundaries. Using improved communications and funds-transfer techniques, speculators anticipating changes in official currency exchange rates could now move huge amounts of funds from one nation to another both cheaply and quickly. Central banks, including the Federal Reserve System, soon found themselves compelled to intervene in the currency markets almost daily and to use up huge amounts of foreign exchange reserves.[16] Soon, the largest IMF member countries were allowing their currencies to float in value, responding more actively to demand and supply forces in the marketplace.

The Managed Floating Currency Standard

In 1978 a new international payments system—often called a managed floating currency standard—was formally adopted by member nations of the IMF. Known as the Second Amendment to the International Monetary Fund's Articles of Agreement, the official rules under which today's international money system is supposed to operate allow each nation to choose its own exchange-rate policy, consistent with the structure of its economy and its economic goals. There are, however, three principles that each member country must follow in establishing its exchange-rate policy:

---

[16] See Chapter 28 for a discussion of government intervention in the foreign exchange markets.

1. When a nation intervenes in the foreign exchange markets to protect its own currency, it must take into account the interests and welfare of other IMF member countries.

2. Government intervention in the foreign exchange markets should be carried out to correct disorderly conditions in those markets that are essentially short term in nature.

3. No member nation should intervene in the exchange markets in order to gain an unfair competitive advantage over other IMF members or to prevent effective adjustments in a nation's BOP position.

DETERMINING CURRENCY VALUES IN THE MODERN WORLD

With nations now free to choose their own exchange-rate policies, many different approaches to establishing the value of national currencies have been adopted around the world. Basically, two types of exchange-rate policies are followed today—*pegging* and *floating*.

Pegging Exchange Rates

Nations that attempt to keep the exchange value of their currencies within a fixed range around the value of some other currency or basket of currencies are known as *peggers*. The majority of pegging nations are developing countries that have strong commercial and financial links with one or more industrialized trading partners. Examples include the Bahamas, Ecuador, El Salvador, Egypt, Guatemala, Iraq, Korea, Panama, and Venezuela, all of which peg the exchange rate on their currency to the U.S. dollar. Madagascar and several other African republics have tied their currencies to the French franc, while Gambia's monetary unit is pegged to the value of the British pound sterling.

Frequently, when a small, developing country has strong trade relations with more than one industrialized nation, it will use a basket (group) of major currencies to set the value of its own monetary unit in order to "average out" fluctuations in the value of its exports and imports. The currency basket will reflect the current exchange rates for each major trading partner, weighted by the proportion of trade carried on with each partner. A good example is Sweden, which pegs its krona to a basket of 15 currencies, each representing a trading partner. Other nations relying on baskets of trading-partner currencies to set the value of their own currencies include Algeria, Austria, Norway, Singapore, Thailand, and Finland.

Special Drawing Rights

Several nations peg their currency's exchange rate to a basket of currencies assembled by the International Monetary Fund, known as the special drawing right (SDR). The SDR is an official international monetary reserve unit designed to settle international claims arising from transactions between the IMF, governments of member nations, central banks, and various international agencies. SDRs are really "book entries" on the ledgers of the IMF and are sometimes referred to as "paper gold." Periodically, that organization will issue new SDRs and credit them to the international reserve accounts of member nations based on each nation's IMF quota (i.e., contributions of currency and reserve assets to the fund). To spend its SDRs, a nation simply requests the IMF to transfer some amount of SDRs from its own reserve account to the reserve account of another nation, usually one whose currency is widely accepted in the international markets. In return, the country asking for the transfer gets deposit balances denominated in the currency of the nation receiving the SDRs. These deposit balances may then be used to make international payments.

The value of SDRs today is based on a basket of currencies representing the five IMF member nations with the largest volume of exports. These five countries currently are the United States, the Federal Republic of Germany, France, Japan, and the United Kingdom. In determining the current value of SDRs the currency of each of these five nations is weighted according to the value of their exports and currency holdings valued at current exchange rates. Countries that peg their currency's value to the value of the SDR basket include Burma, Guinea, Kenya, Jordan, Vietnam, and Zambia.

Floating Currency Values

Most of the developed nations *float,* rather than peg, their currencies. This means that the value of any particular currency is determined by demand and supply forces operating in the marketplace. Usually a *managed float* is used, in which governments will intervene on occasion, either by buying or selling one or more currencies, to stabilize the value of their home currency. As Carlozzi (1980) notes:

> Some nations follow a policy of leaning against the wind—intervening in order to reduce daily fluctuations in their exchange rates without attempting to adhere to any target rate. Others choose target exchange rates and intervene in order to support them. Even nations that do target exchange rates usually do not reveal their targets. Thus, they discourage speculation against these targets and retain greater flexibility to adjust them.

Three nations—Brazil, Colombia, and Portugal—employ economic indicators, such as inflation rates in various countries, to set targets for their exchange rates. Others set currency-value targets based upon the level of growth of their reserve assets or BOP position. The United States has officially adopted a managed-float policy but in practice often follows a "free" floating exchange-rate policy, in which the open market determines the value of the dollar, with U.S. monetary authorities intervening only in emergency situations.[17]

In theory at least, a system of floating currency values should help the United States and other nations who are experiencing severe BOP deficits today. The theory of BOP adjustments suggests that, with floating currency values, the international marketplace will set supply and demand forces in motion to reduce and eventually eradicate any nation's balance-of-payments deficit. For example, if Americans are importing more goods from abroad then they are able to sell to overseas customers, an excess supply of U.S. dollars should build up abroad. The result should be an eventual decline in the dollar's market value vis-à-vis other world currencies, making U.S. exports cheaper and foreign goods sold in the United States relatively more expensive. Ultimately, American exports and imports should become more evenly balanced. Only time will tell whether these theoretically expected effects will work out in practice. Much will depend upon the future course of interest rates in the United States.

The European Monetary System

A compromise currency-valuation system, including elements of both the peg and the float, has appeared recently among the eight European nations that comprise the European Monetary System (EMS).[18] Known as a "joint float," the EMS arrangement calls for member countries to peg their exchange rates with each other, maintaining EMS currencies within 2¼ percent of their pegged exchange values. However, exchange rates with currencies outside the EMS group are subject to a managed float. EMS member countries intervene in the market as a group to maintain the purchasing power of their group's currencies vis-à-vis those of outside nations. The EMS is viewed as a further step toward economic integration (and, perhaps, eventual political integration) in Western Europe.

---

[17] See Chapter 28 for a discussion of recent U.S. policies in the management of the dollar's international value.

[18] The eight countries are Belgium, Denmark, West Germany, France, Ireland, Italy, Luxembourg, and the Netherlands.

Freedom and a Flexible Exchange-Rate System

It should be clear from the foregoing discussion of pegs and floats that wide diversity exists today in the manner in which national monetary units are valued. More than 90 countries currently peg their currency exchange rates (nearly half of these tied to the U.S. dollar), while 45 nations allow their currencies to float (usually with some form of limited government intervention). There is a strong trend today toward greater flexibility and diversity in the management of the international monetary system. And that trend is reinforced by the International Monetary Fund's current rules, which allow each member nation to adjust its exchange policies in line with changing economic and financial conditions.

We must note, however, that in the international field as elsewhere, greater freedom carries greater risk. Trading nations have sought greater freedom in settling their exchange-rate policies in the hope of gaining an increased measure of control over their domestic economies. However, there is now for the first time in history a true international financial system, in which the economic destinies of trading nations are inextricably linked to each other. For the most part capital flows freely across international boundaries today in response to differences in interest rates, currency values, and economic conditions. These relatively unrestricted capital flows have increased the risk that domestic policies designed to fight inflation, counter unemployment, and speed economic growth and development will be thwarted by shifting currents in a largely unregulated international marketplace. Today, successful economic policy at home requires the cooperation and coordinated action of major trading nations.

There are signs that international cooperation on global financial and economic matters *is* increasing. The emergence of the European Monetary System, the recently negotiated Second Amendment to the IMF's Articles of Agreement, recent economic summits between leaders of major Western governments, and the coordinated energy policy agreements of the Western oil-importing nations are all indications of a new spirit in international financial affairs. And that spirit will give rise to new institutions designed to deal with conflicts between the desire for national autonomy and independence and the urgent need for international economic and monetary cooperation. The International Monetary Fund— the international agency charged with the responsibility to monitor the international currency and payments policies of member nations—is likely to play an even larger role in the international financial system of the future. SDRs, the reserve asset created by the IMF to settle international claims between nations, will be more widely used to facilitate global payments. Closer government scrutiny and possibly outright regulation of international capital flows, international banking, and the vast Eurocurrency markets will be key issues of global economics and global politics for years to come.

STUDY QUESTIONS

1. What is meant by the term balance of payments? Describe the principal components of the balance-of-payments accounts.

2. Please supply a brief definition of each of the following terms associated with the balance of payments:
    a. Current account.
    b. Merchandise trade balance.
    c. Service transactions.
    d. Capital account.
    e. Official reserve assets.
    f. Special drawing rights.
    g. Direct investment.
    h. Errors and omissions.

3. Describe and discuss the principal trends which have occurred in the following components of the U.S. balance-of-payments accounts in recent years:
    a. Merchandise trade balance.
    b. Investment in assets abroad by U.S. residents.
    c. Investment in U.S. assets by foreign residents.

4. What is currency risk? Explain how it affects exporters, importers, and securities investors active in the international markets.

5. Why was the gold standard developed? What problems did it solve, and what problems did it create? What is the difference between the gold standard and the gold exchange standard?

6. When and where was the Modified Exchange Standard created? Explain how this system worked to stabilize the value of foreign currencies. Why was the modified exchange standard abandoned in the 1970s?

7. The international monetary system of today has been called a "managed floating currency standard." Briefly and concisely explain what this term means. Why, in your opinion, have we adopted this system today? Can you foresee any problems with this approach?

8. Explain the difference between pegging and floating currency values. What are the advantages of each? What is a basket of currencies?

9. What are SDRs? Describe their function in settling international payments and in determining certain exchange rates.

10. What is a managed float? A joint float? What advantages can you see from each? Any disadvantages?

SELECTED REFERENCES

Abrams, Richard K., and Donald V. Kimball. "U.S. Investment in Foreign Equity Markets." *Economic Review,* Federal Reserve Bank of Kansas City, April 1981, pp. 17–31.

Carlozzi, Nicholas. "Pegs and Floats: The Changing Face of the Foreign Exchange Market." *Business Review,* Federal Reserve Bank of Philadelphia, May–June 1980, pp. 13–23.

Clarke, Stephen V. O. "Perspective on the United States External Position since World War II." *Quarterly Review,* Federal Reserve Bank of New York, Summer 1980, pp. 21–38.

Kubarych, Roger M. "Financing the U.S. Current Account Deficit." *Quarterly Review,* Federal Reserve Bank of New York, Summer 1984, pp. 24–31.

Kuwayama, Patrick H. "Measuring the United States Balance of Payments." *Monthly Review,* Federal Reserve Bank of New York, August 1975, pp. 183–94.

Lees, Francis A. *International Banking and Finance.* New York: John Wiley & Sons, 1973.

Morgan Guaranty Trust Company of New York. *World Financial Markets,* various issues.

Williamson, John. *The Failure of Monetary Reform,* 1971–1974. New York: New York University Press, 1977.

28

The Markets for Foreign Exchange

PURPOSE OF THIS CHAPTER

To explain how the various national currencies are priced and traded in the foreign exchange market. The chapter opens with a discussion of how fluctuating currency values affect international trading in goods and services and international investment. The roles played by multinational banks and foreign exchange brokers in trading and speculating in various currencies are then examined, followed by a review of the key financial instruments used in the international currency markets. The chapter then explores the features and methods of the spot, forward, and futures currency markets along with a discussion of how foreign exchange rates are calculated. Key factors determining the level of foreign exchange rates are reviewed, concluding with a discussion of how government policy and intervention influence currency prices.

KEY TERMS AND CONCEPTS IN THE CHAPTER

balance-of-payments
  position
bills of exchange
buying and selling
  hedges
central bank
  intervention
commercial covering
covered interest
  arbitrage
currency futures

emergency
  intervention
exchange rates
exchange-rate
  quotations
foreign currency
  futures
foreign exchange
  market
forward contracts
forward market

hedging
interest-rate parity
market structure
money-center banks
option contracts
speculation
spot contracts
spot market
three-tiered market
transfers
vehicle currency

As we saw in the preceding chapter, the markets where the world's major currencies, including the U.S. dollar, are traded have changed dramatically in recent years. Major international economic and political developments (i.e., inflation, wide swings in the price of oil, political revolutions, and a growing spirit of nationalism and independence in the less developed countries), all have had profound effects on the relative value of the U.S. dollar, the German deutsche mark, the British pound, the Japanese yen, and most of the world's other actively traded currencies. So unsettling have been these changes that, during the 1970s, the U.S. government and its major trading partners were no longer able to preserve the official exchange rates among the world's major currencies. Since the early 1970s major international currencies, including the dollar, have floated with relative freedom, their values dependent essentially upon demand and supply forces in the marketplace.

With this newfound freedom for currency prices and the rapid expansion of world commerce, the volume of currency trading and the number of financial institutions actively participating in that trading have virtually exploded. This is especially evident in the New York money market, where brokers have opened up their business to bring in currency trading orders from financial institutions worldwide. U.S. banks today no longer purchase foreign currencies exclusively from domestic sources but deal with foreign exchange brokers in the world's leading financial centers. Trading in foreign currency futures, begun in the United States at the International Money Market in Chicago, now takes place in major financial centers around the globe. Deregulation of financial institutions has brought scores of nonbank financial companies (such as insurance companies, security brokerage houses, and commodity traders) into the currency markets to wrest away a portion of what has always been a commercial bank-dominated activity.

This phenomenal explosion of activity and interest in foreign currency trading and prices reflects, in large measure, a desire for self-preservation by businesses, governments, and individuals. As the international financial system has moved increasingly toward freely floating exchange rates, currency prices have become significantly more volatile and uncertain. The risks of buying and selling dollars, francs, deutsche marks, pounds, and other currencies have increased markedly in recent years. Moreover, fluctuations in the prices of foreign currencies affect domestic economic conditions, international investment, and the success or failure of government economic policies. Governments, businesses, and individuals involved in international affairs find that it is more important today than ever before to understand how foreign currencies are traded and what affects their relative values. A few examples serve to illustrate the importance of the topic.

Consider the problems faced by a corporation headquartered in the

United States and selling machinery overseas. This firm frequently negotiates sales contracts with a foreign importer months before the machines are shipped and payment is made. In the meantime, the value of the foreign currency that the American company expects to receive in payment for sales of its products may have declined precipitously, canceling out any expected profits. Similarly, an American importer bringing fine wines, precious gems, petroleum products, or any number of other goods into our domestic markets frequently must pay for incoming shipments in the particular currency demanded by a foreign exporter. The American importer's profits could be significantly reduced if the value of the dollar declined relative to the values of foreign currencies used by the importer to pay for goods purchased abroad. Both exporters and importers, then, require practical knowledge of how the foreign exchange markets operate and how to use those currency markets to their advantage.

The same problems confront investors in foreign securities who find that attractive interest rates frequently available overseas must be protected from an erosion in currency values through suitable purchases and sales of foreign currencies. Knowledge of the foreign exchange markets is the *first step* toward successful international business, foreign travel, and economic policy. In subsequent sections of this chapter we examine the structure, instruments, and price-determining forces of the world's major currency markets.

THE STRUCTURE OF THE FOREIGN EXCHANGE MARKET[1]

The purpose of the foreign exchange markets is to bring buyers and sellers of currencies together. It is essentially an *over-the-counter market,* with no central trading location and no set hours of trading. Prices and other terms of trade are determined by negotiation over the telephone or via telex. The foreign exchange market is *informal* in its operations; there are no special requirements for market participants, and trading conforms to an unwritten code of rules among active traders.

The Role of Banks in the Foreign Exchange Market

The central institution in modern foreign exchange markets is the *commercial bank.* Most transactions in foreign currency of any size repre-

---

[1] This section draws heavily upon the booklets *The New York Foreign Exchange Market* by Alan R. Holmes, first published in 1959 and revised in 1965 by Holmes and Francis H. Schott; and *Foreign Exchange Markets in the United States,* prepared by Roger M. Kubarych for the Federal Reserve Bank of New York in 1978.

sent merely an exchange of the deposits of one bank for the deposits of another bank. That is, if an individual or business firm needs foreign currency, it will contact a bank, which in turn will secure a deposit denominated in foreign money or actually take delivery of foreign currency if the customer requires it. If the bank is a large money-center institution, it may hold inventories of foreign currency just to accommodate its customers. Smaller banks typically do not hold stocks of foreign currency or foreign currency-denominated deposits. Rather, they will contact larger correspondent banks, who in turn will contact bank and nonbank foreign exchange brokers or dealers.

The largest money-center banks headquartered in New York, London, Zurich, Tokyo, Frankfurt, and other financial capitals of the world not only maintain large inventories of key foreign currencies but trade currencies with each other simply through an exchange of deposits. For example, if a major U.S. bank needs to acquire pounds sterling, it can contact its correspondent bank in London and ask that bank to transfer an additional amount of sterling to the U.S. banks' correspondent account. In turn, the U.S. bank will increase the dollar deposit held with it by the London bank. In this way money never really leaves the country of its origin; only its ownership does, as deposits denominated in various currencies are moved from one holder to the next.

The heart of the foreign exchange market in the United States is New York City. Approximately one dozen banks in that city plus a dozen banks headquartered in other U.S. cities keep active positions in 12 to 15 principal currencies, with smaller holdings of less traded currencies. Most large foreign exchange transactions take place between the biggest U.S. banks and major banks headquartered abroad. The largest American banks hold dollar and foreign currency-denominated deposits in banks overseas in order to make foreign exchange trading possible. At the same time, more than 100 foreign banks maintain offices in the United States to handle the exchange accounts of foreign investors, commercial traders, and government agencies.

Foreign exchange trading takes place in a *three-tiered market.* Banks trade with their commercial customers who need large amounts of foreign exchange for purchases of imported goods or to convert funds received from abroad into domestic currency. A second tier consists of trading mainly between domestic banks in order to make a market for foreign exchange. This tier includes exchange trading among domestic banks, foreign central banks represented in the United States, and the Federal Reserve System. The market's third tier consists of trading between U.S. banks and foreign banking institutions.

As we noted above, the largest U.S. banks with foreign exchange departments routinely keep working balances of foreign currencies with major banks abroad. These working balances rise when a bank buys currency for itself or its customers, sells dollars to foreign banks, or purchases financial documents (such as bills of exchange, traveler's checks, and bond coupons) that are denominated in foreign currencies. Transactions affecting a bank's working currency balance are carried out by specialized traders with the aid of telephones, video screens, and teletype equipment to keep them in constant touch with other exchange brokers and dealers. The foreign exchange trader must also keep in close contact with the bank's money desk and senior management because foreign exchange trading can have a profound effect on the bank's overall financial position.

This last point was brought home dramatically in 1974 when Franklin National Bank of New York, then the nation's 14th-largest commercial bank, was forced into bankruptcy. While numerous factors led to Franklin's demise, massive losses from foreign exchange trading were one of the primary factors in that bank's ultimate collapse. In an era of freely floating exchange rates, trading in foreign currencies can be exceedingly risky, requiring considerable skill and experience.

Foreign Exchange Brokers

Frequently, currency-trading banks do not deal directly with each other, but rely on foreign exchange brokers. Less than a dozen in number, these brokerage firms are in constant communication with the exchange trading rooms of the world's major banks. Their principal function is simply to bring buyers and sellers of foreign exchange together.

For example, a bank wishing to sell foreign currency simply contacts a broker on its active list by telephone, indicating the amount and type of currency for sale. The broker then contacts buyers on his or her active customer list, ascertaining the preferred price and quantity of each potential buyer. Once a deal is struck, the selling bank is notified to initiate a transfer of funds, and the broker receives a commission for his or her efforts. The foreign exchange broker's essential contribution is to reduce the search costs associated with finding buyers of foreign exchange. By providing convenience and an essential flow of trading information, the broker makes the foreign exchange market more efficient. The broker ensures that prices for the world's major currencies accurately reflect the forces of supply and demand in the marketplace.

Nonbank Financial Institutions

As we noted in the introduction to this chapter, security brokerage firms, commodity traders, insurance companies, and scores of other nonbank companies have come to play a growing role in the foreign exchange markets of the 1980s. These institutions have entered in the wake of greater deregulation of the financial marketplace and the lifting of some foreign controls on international investment, especially by Japan and the United Kingdom. Nonbank currency traders now offer a wide range of services to international security investors, borrowers, and export-import firms, including assistance with foreign mergers, currency swaps and options, hedging foreign security offerings against exchange-rate fluctuations, and providing currencies needed for routine purchases abroad and for speculation.

INSTRUMENTS OF THE FOREIGN EXCHANGE MARKET

Cable Transfers

There are several financial instruments that are used to facilitate foreign exchange trading by bank and nonbank institutions and individuals. One of the most important is the *cable transfer,* that is, an execute order sent by cable to a foreign bank holding a currency seller's account. The seller directs the bank to debit the seller's account and credit the account of a buyer or someone the buyer designates (such as a commercial bank).

For example, suppose a U.S. export firm has just received payment from one of its overseas customers in francs. The U.S. firm is paid in the form of a deposit denominated in francs residing currently in a bank in Paris. The U.S. exporter cables the Paris bank to transfer the francs to the account of a New York bank, receiving a dollar deposit from the New York bank at the current dollar-franc exchange rate. The export firm now has dollars that can be spent in the United States for raw materials, to meet payrolls, pay taxes, and so on, while its New York bank now owns a deposit in francs that can be loaned out or used for other purposes.

The essential advantage of the cable transfer is speed because the transaction can be carried out the same day or within one or two business days. Business firms selling their goods in international markets can avoid tying up substantial sums of money in foreign exchange by using cable transfers.

Mail Transfers

When speed is not a critical factor, a mail transfer of foreign exchange may be used. Such transfers are simply written orders from a holder of a foreign exchange deposit to a bank to pay a designated individual, firm, or institution upon presentation of a draft. A mail transfer may, of course, require days to execute, depending on the speed of mail deliveries.

Bills of Exchange

One of the oldest and most important of all international financial instruments is the bill of exchange.[2] Frequently today the word *draft* is used instead of *bill*. Either way, a draft or bill of exchange is a written order requiring a person, business firm, or bank to pay a specified sum of money to the bearer of the bill.

We may distinguish *sight bills,* which are payable on demand (presentation), from *time bills,* which mature at a future date and are payable only at that time. There are also *documentary bills,* which typically accompany the international shipment of goods. A documentary bill must be accompanied by shipping papers (such as bills of lading), allowing importers of goods to pick up their merchandise. In contrast, a *clean bill* has no accompanying documents and is simply an order to a bank to pay a certain sum of money. The most common example arises when an importer requests its bank to send a letter of credit to an exporter in another country. The letter authorizes the exporter to draw bills for payment, either against the importer's bank or against one of its correspondent banks. Most bills of exchange drawn in connection with U.S. imports and exports are payable in U.S. dollars.

Foreign Currency and Coin

Foreign currency and coin itself (as opposed to bank deposits) is an important instrument for payment in the foreign exchange markets. This is especially true for tourists who require pocket money to pay for lodging, meals, transportation, and so on. Usually this money winds up in the hands of merchants accepting it in payment for purchases and is deposited in domestic banks. For example, many U.S. banks operating along the Canadian and Mexican borders receive a substantial volume of Canadian dollars and Mexican pesos each day. These funds normally are routed through the banking system back to banks in the country of issue, and the U.S. banks receive credit in the form of a deposit denominated in a foreign currency. This deposit may then be loaned to a customer or to another bank that needs foreign currency. Some dealers in the New York money market buy and sell foreign bank notes and coins.

Other Foreign Exchange Instruments

There are a wide variety of other financial instruments denominated in various foreign currencies, most of these small in amount. For example,

---

[2] A negotiable form of time bill, known as a bankers' acceptance, is discussed at length in Chapter 16.

traveler's checks denominated in pounds, francs, dollars, and other convertible currencies may be spent directly or converted into the currency of the country where purchases are being made. International investors frequently receive interest coupons or dividend warrants denominated in various foreign currencies. These documents normally are sold to a domestic bank at the current foreign exchange rate.

FOREIGN EXCHANGE RATES

Exchange Rate Quotations

The prices of foreign currencies expressed in terms of other currencies are called *foreign exchange rates.* There are today three markets for foreign exchange: (1) the *spot market,* which deals in currency for immediate delivery; (2) the *forward market,* which involves the future delivery of foreign currency; and (3) the *currency futures* market, which deals in contracts to hedge against future changes in foreign exchange rates. Immediate delivery is defined as one or two business days for most transactions. Future delivery typically means one, three, or six months from today.

Exhibit 28–1 cites some recent foreign exchange rates between the U.S. dollar and the world's other major currencies. The exhibit shows, for example, that an American importer or investor could obtain pounds sterling (£) that could be used to buy British bonds or other British goods and services at a cost of about $1.0931 per pound (i.e., $1.0931/£) in February 1985. Conversely, a British investor or importer seeking to make purchases in the United States would have to pay 0.9147 pounds (i.e., $1/1.0931 or 0.915/$) for each dollar needed. Clearly, the exchange rate between dollars and pounds is the *reciprocal* of the exchange rate between pounds and dollars, which is also true for any other pair of currencies. In truth, currencies are merely commodities, the prices of which are expressed in terms of one currency per unit of another. Exhibit 28–2 illustrates the commonly accepted procedures for calculating foreign exchange rates.[3]

Dealers and brokers in foreign exchange actually post not one, but

---

[3] We note that in each quotation of a foreign exchange rate, one currency always serves as a unit of account (i.e., the unit of value) and the other currency functions as the unit for which a price is stated. For example, a quote of $0.40/DM tell us that one deutsche mark costs $0.40. In this instance the dollar serves as the unit of account, and the currency whose price is quoted is the mark. It is customary to place the symbol for the currency serving as the unit of account (in this case, $) before the stated number and the symbol of the currency whose price is being quoted (in this case, DM) following the number.

EXHIBIT 28–1

Foreign Exchange Rates (Currency units per dollar)

Country/currency	1981	1982	1983	1984	1985*
1 Australia/dollar†	114.95	101.65	90.14	87.937	73.74
2 Austria/schilling	15.948	17.060	17.968	20.005	23.190
3 Belgium/franc	37.194	45.780	51.121	57.749	66.310
4 Brazil/cruzeiro	92.374	179.22	573.27	1841.50	3768.17
5 Canada/dollar	1.1990	1.2344	1.2325	1.2953	1.3547
6 China, P.R./yuan	1.7031	1.8978	1.9809	2.3308	2.8347
7 Denmark/krone	7.1350	8.3443	9.1483	10.354	11.807
8 Finland/markka	4.3128	4.8086	5.5636	6.0007	6.8616
9 France/franc	5.4396	6.5793	7.6203	8.7355	10.093
10 Germany/deutsche mark	2.2631	2.428	2.5539	2.8454	3.3025
11 Greece/drachma	n.a.	66.872	87.895	112.73	134.73
12 Hong Kong/dollar	5.5678	6.0697	7.2569	7.8188	7.8017
13 India/rupee	8.6807	9.4846	10.1040	11.348	12.922
14 Ireland/pound†	161.32	142.05	124.81	108.64	94.23
15 Israel/shekel	n.a.	24.407	55.865	n.a.	n.a.
16 Italy/lira	1138.60	1354.00	1519.30	1756.10	2042.00
17 Japan/yen	220.63	249.06	237.55	237.45	260.48
18 Malaysia/ringgit	2.3048	2.3395	2.3204	2.3448	2.5513
19 Mexico/peso	24.547	72.990	155.01	192.31	236.06
20 Netherlands/guilder	2.4998	2.6719	2.8543	3.2083	3.7387
21 New Zealand/dollar†	86.848	75.101	66.790	57.837	45.223
22 Norway/krone	5.7430	6.4567	7.3012	8.1596	9.4695
23 Philippines/peso	7.8113	8.5324	11.0940	n.a.	n.a.
24 Portugal/escudo	61.739	80.101	111.610	147.70	183.24
25 Singapore/dollar	2.1053	2.1406	2.1136	2.1325	2.2557
26 South Africa/rand	114.77	92.297	89.85	69.534	50.57
27 South Korea/won	n.a.	731.93	776.04	807.91	839.16
28 Spain/peseta	92.396	110.09	143.500	160.78	182.35
29 Sri Lanka/rupee	18.967	20.756	23.510	25.428	26.605
30 Sweden/krona	5.0659	6.2838	7.6717	8.2706	9.3364
31 Switzerland/franc	1.9674	2.0327	2.1006	2.3500	2.8045
32 Taiwan/dollar	n.a.	n.a.	n.a.	39.633	39.228
33 Thailand/baht	21.731	23.014	22.991	23.582	27.961
34 United Kingdom/pound†	202.43	174.80	151.59	133.66	109.31
35 Venezuela/bolivar	4.2781	4.2981	10.6840	n.a.	n.a.
MEMO					
United States/dollar‡	102.94	116.57	125.34	138.19	158.43

* Average for the month of February 1985.
† Value in U.S. cents.
‡ Index of weighted-average exchange value of U.S. dollar against currencies of other G–10 countries plus Switzerland. March 1973 = 100. Weights are 1972–76 global trade of each of the 10 countries.
SOURCE: Board of Governors of the Federal Reserve System, *Federal Reserve Bulletin*, various issues.

two exchange rates for each pair of currencies. That is, each trader sets a *bid* (buy) price and an *asked* (sell) price at which currencies will be exchanged. For example, the dealer department in a large New York bank might be posting a bid price for pounds sterling of £ = $1.0930US (or $1.0930/£) and an asked price of £ = $1.0932US (or $1.0932/£). This means the dealer is willing to buy sterling at $1.0930 per pound

EXHIBIT 28-2

Methods for Calculating Foreign Exchange Rates

Exchange Rate Conversion

Suppose the exchange rate between German deutsche marks (DM) and the U.S. dollar ($) is DM/$ = 2.500, or DM 2.50/$.
   What is the $/DM exchange rate?
   Answer: 1 ÷ 2.500 = $0.40/DM.

Exchange Rate Appreciation

Suppose the exchange rate between German marks and the U.S. dollar rises from DM/$ = 2.000, or DM 2.00/$, to DM 2.50/$.
   How much has the dollar appreciated, in percent?
   Answer: 2.500 ÷ 2.000 = 1.25, or 25%.
   Suppose the mark-dollar exchange rate is DM/$ = 2.5000, or DM 2.50/$. If the dollar has appreciated by 3 percent, what is the new mark-dollar exchange rate?
   Answer: 2.500 × 1.03 = 2.5750, or DM 2.575/$.

Exchange Rate Depreciation

Suppose the exchange rate between marks and U.S. dollars rises from DM/$ = 2.000 to DM/$ = 2.5000.
   How much has the mark depreciated, in percent?
   Answer: Note that the $/DM exchange rate has changed from 1 ÷ 2.000 = $0.50/DM to 1 ÷ 2.500 = $0.40/DM. The ratio of these two exchange rates is 0.4000 ÷ 0.5000, or 0.8000. Then, 1 − 0.8000 = 0.2000, or an exchange-rate depreciation of 20%.
   Suppose the mark-dollar exchange rate is DM/$ = 2.50 or DM 2.50/$. If the mark has depreciated 5 percent, what is the new mark-dollar exchange rate?
   Answer: Because 0.4000 × 0.95 = 0.3800, the new exchange rate is 1 ÷ 0.3800 = 2.6316, or DM 2.6316/$.
   Suppose, once again, the mark-dollar exchange rate is DM/$ = 2.5000. If the U.S. dollar has depreciated 5 percent, what is the new mark-dollar exchange rate?
   Answer: 2.5000 × 0.95 = 2.3750, or DM 2.375/$.

Cross Exchange Rates

Suppose the mark-dollar exchange rate is DM/$ = 2.5000, or DM 2.50/$, and the Swiss franc-dollar exchange rate is 2.000, or SF2.00/$. What is the SF/DM exchange rate?
   Answer: 2.000 ÷ 2.500 = 0.8000, or SF 0.80/DM.
   Suppose the mark-dollar exchange rate is DM/$ = 2.500, or DM 2.50/$ and the dollar-Swiss franc exchange rate is $/SF = 0.5000 or 0.50/SF. What, then, is the DM/SF exchange rate?
   Answer: 2.5000 ÷ (1 ÷ 0.5000) = 2.5000 ÷ 2.000 = 1.25, or DM 1.25/SF.

SOURCE: Public Information Center, Federal Reserve Bank of Chicago.

and sell it at $1.0932. (These two exchange rates are sometimes referred to as "double-barreled" quotations.) The dealer makes a profit on the *spread* between the bid and asked price, though that spread is normally very small.[4]

Traders in the market continually watch exchange rate quotations in order to take advantage of any arbitrage opportunities. Arbitrage refers to the purchase of one currency in a certain market and the sale of that currency in another market in response to differences in price between the two markets. The force of arbitrage generally keeps foreign exchange rates from getting too far out of line in different markets. Thus, if pounds are selling for $1.0932US in New York and $1.0936US in London, professional traders will quickly eliminate this discrepancy by purchasing sterling in the New York market and selling it in London.

Factors Affecting Foreign Exchange Rates

The exchange rate for any foreign currency depends on a multitude of factors reflecting economic and financial conditions in the country issuing the currency. One of the most important factors is the status of a nation's *balance-of-payments position.* When a country experiences a deficit in its balance of payments, it becomes a net demander of foreign currencies and may be forced to sell substantial amounts of its own currency to pay for imports of goods and services. Therefore, balance-of-payments deficits often lead to price depreciation of a nation's currency relative to the prices of other currencies. During the 1970s, when the United States was experiencing deep balance-of-payments deficits and owed substantial amounts abroad for imported oil, the value of the dollar sagged dramatically. Both the Federal Reserve System and the Treasury entered the foreign exchange markets with heavy purchases of dollars and offerings of dollar-denominated government securities to create a demand for dollars and prop up the dollar's exchange value. However, as events in the early and mid-1980s demonstrated, when the U.S. dollar gained dramatically in price against other major currencies despite record U.S. balance-of-payments deficits, a nation's balance-of-payments position is by no means the sole determinant of the exchange value of its currency.

---

[4] Dealers will usually quote the bid price first and the asked price second and, as a rule, only the last digits will be quoted to the buyer or seller. Thus, the spot bid and asked rates on pounds might be quoted by a foreign exchange dealer as 30/32. It is assumed the customer is aware of current foreign exchange rates and knows, therefore, that the bid price being quoted is $1.0930/£ and the asked price is $1.0932/£.

Speculation.   Exchange rates also are profoundly affected by speculation over *future* currency values. Brokers, dealers, and investors in foreign exchange monitor the currency markets daily, looking for profitable trading opportunities. A currency viewed as temporarily undervalued will quickly bring forth numerous buy orders, driving its price higher vis-à-vis other currencies. A currency considered to be overvalued will soon be greeted by a rash of sell orders, depressing its price. Today the international financial system is so efficient and finely tuned that billions of dollars can flow across national boundaries in a matter of hours in response to speculative fever. As we saw earlier in our review of the Eurodollar market,[5] these massive unregulated flows can wreak havoc with the plans of economic policymakers because currency trading affects interest rates and the money supply.

Domestic Economic and Political Conditions.   The market for a national currency is, of course, influenced by domestic conditions. Wars, revolutions, the death of a major political leader, inflation, recession, and labor strikes have all been observed to have adverse effects on the currency of a nation experiencing these problems. On the other hand, signs of rapid economic growth, industrial development, improving government finances, rising stock and bond prices, and successful economic policies to control inflation and unemployment usually lead to a stronger national currency in the exchange markets.

Central Bank Intervention.   Overhanging the currency markets today is the ever present possibility that central banks will become active participants. Major central banks around the world, including the Federal Reserve System, the Bundesbank in West Germany, and the Bank of England, may decide on a given day that their national currency is declining too rapidly in value relative to one or more other key currencies. Thus, if the dollar falls precipitously against the mark, support operations by the Federal Reserve System in the form of heavy sales of marks and corresponding purchases of dollars in cooperation with the Bundesbank may be employed to stabilize the currency markets. Usually, central bank intervention is temporary, designed to promote a smooth adjustment in currency values toward a new equilibrium level rather than to permanently "prop up" a weak currency. We will have more to say about central bank intervention in the currency markets later in this chapter.

---

[5] See Chapter 16 for a discussion of recent problems in attempting to regulate the Eurodollar market.

Supply and Demand for Foreign Exchange

The factors influencing a currency's rate of exchange with other currencies may be expressed in terms of the market forces of demand and supply. Figure 28–1, for example, illustrates a demand curve and a supply curve for dollars in terms of British pounds (£). Note that the demand curve for dollars is also labeled the supply curve for pounds. This is due to the fact that an individual or institution holding pounds and demanding dollars would be supplying pounds to the foreign exchange market. Similarly, the supply curve for dollars is identical to the demand curve for pounds because someone holding dollars and demanding pounds must supply dollars to the foreign currency markets in order to purchase pounds. We recall, too, that the price of dollars in terms of pounds is the reciprocal of the price of pounds in terms of dollars.

To illustrate how demand and supply forces operate in the foreign exchange markets, suppose the current exchange rate between dollars and pounds is £ = \$1.0930. To purchase dollars, we would have to pay 0.915 pounds per dollar, while to purchase pounds would cost us \$1.0937 per pound. This exchange rate between dollars and pounds is set in the foreign exchange markets by the interaction of the supply and demand

FIGURE 28–1

Demand and Supply of U.S. Dollars in Terms of British Pounds

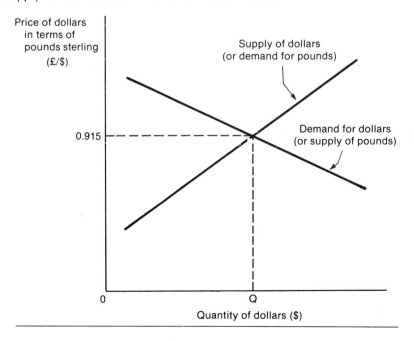

for each currency. Figure 28–1 indicates that, at an exchange rate of 0.915 pounds, the quantity of dollars supplied is exactly equal to the quantity of dollars demanded.

If the price of dollars in terms of pounds were to fall temporarily *below* this exchange rate, more dollars would be demanded than supplied. Some buyers needing dollars would bid up the exchange rate toward the point where the demand for and supply of dollars were perfectly in balance. On the other hand, if the price of dollars were temporarily *above* 0.915 pounds, more dollars would be supplied to the foreign exchange markets. The price of dollars in terms of pounds would fall as suppliers of dollars willingly accepted a lower exchange rate to dispose of their excess dollar holdings. Only at that point where the exchange rate stood at 0.915 pounds per dollar would quantity supplied equal quantity of dollars demanded. Only at that point would there be no reason for future changes in the exchange rate between the dollar and the pound unless and until changes occurred in the demand or supply of either currency.

Effects of Changes in the Relative Supply and Demand for Currencies

As we noted earlier, a number of factors affect the exchange rates between national currencies, including the export and import of goods, services, and capital as reflected in a nation's balance-of-payments position, currency speculation, domestic political and economic developments, and central bank intervention. Each of these factors leads to a shift in either the demand for or supply of one currency vis-à-vis another, which brings about a change in their relative rates of exchange.

To illustrate the impact of shifts in currency demand and supply, suppose that consumers in Great Britain increase their demand for U.S. goods and services. As Figure 28–2 indicates, the demand curve for dollars would increase from D_1 to D_2. This is equivalent, as noted earlier, to an increase in the supply of pounds seeking dollars. The cost of dollars in terms of pounds, therefore, will rise from E_1 to E_2. British importers will be forced to surrender a greater quantity of pounds per dollar in order to satisfy the demands of British consumers for American goods and services. Other things equal, the prices of imported goods from the United States will tend to rise.

The opposite effects would tend to occur if American consumers demanded a larger quantity of British goods and services. In this case the supply-of-dollars (demand-for-pounds) curve slides downward and to the right from S_1 to S_2, as shown in Figure 28–3. Reflecting the increased demand for pounds and associated sales of dollars for pounds by American importers, the dollar's price in pounds sterling falls from E_1 to E_2. At

FIGURE 28–2

Effects on the Exchange Rate for Dollars of an Increase in Foreign Demand for U.S. Goods and Services

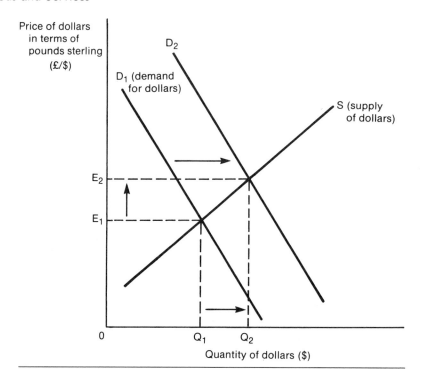

the same time, the market prices of British goods and services imported into the United States will tend to rise.

What happens if a central bank, such as the Bank of England, intervenes to stabilize the dollar-pound exchange rate at some arbitrary level? The answer depends, among other things, on which side of the market the central bank intervenes, which currency is used as the vehicle for central bank intervention, and the particular exchange-rate target chosen.

For example, suppose that increased British demand for American goods and services had driven the dollar-pound exchange rate up to E_1, as shown in Figure 28–4. However, this surge in the dollar's value had sharply reduced the purchasing power of the pound for dollar-denominated goods and services and threatened to have damaging effects on British foreign trade and industrial output. Speculators had begun to sell pounds in anticipation of even lower exchange rates. The Bank of England might intervene to force the dollar-pound exchange rate down

FIGURE 28–3

Effects on the Exchange Rate for Dollars of an Increase in U.S. Demand
for Foreign Goods and Services

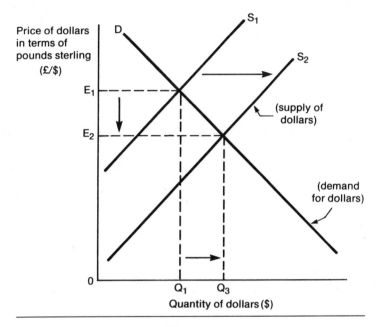

to E_2 by selling dollars out of its currency reserve and demanding pounds
in the foreign exchange market. In effect, the supply-of-dollars curve
would be "kinked" at the stabilization price, E_2. In order to peg the
dollar-pound exchange rate at E_2, the central bank would have to spend
$Q'-Q$ of its dollar reserves. Otherwise, the price of dollars would once
again rise toward E_1—the level dictated by private demand and supply
forces in the foreign exchange markets. Conversely, if the dollar were
falling to unacceptably low levels against the pound, the Bank of England
or the Federal Reserve System might enter on the opposite side of the
market, purchasing dollars with pounds and driving the dollar's price
higher.[6]

---

[6] In the United States the Treasury Department is the designated agency to pursue
intervention measures to protect the dollar and stabilize currency values. While the
Treasury must decide what to do, however, it is the Federal Reserve System that must
do the buying and selling of currencies on the Treasury's behalf. Mechanically, purchases
are paid for by check or other form of draft with the buying institution generally receiving,
not currency "in the hand," but rather deposit balances held in various banks overseas.
A central bank, like the Federal Reserve, can then spend these deposit balances to
purchase foreign currency-denominated securities, pay off its obligations to other institu-

FIGURE 28–4

Effects of Central Bank Intervention to Stabilize the Dollar-Pound Exchange Rate

THE FORWARD MARKET FOR CURRENCIES

Knowledge of how the foreign exchange markets work and the ways in which currency risk can be reduced is indispensable for business managers today. Changes in the relative values of various currencies can wreak havoc with planning by firms engaged in the export or import business. Of course, the problem of fluctuating currency values is not so serious if payment for goods, services, or securities must be made right away. Spot-market prices of foreign currencies normally change

---

tions, purchase deposit balances elsewhere in the world, or otherwise add to its foreign exchange reserves.

It is important to note that central bank intervention not only affects relative currency values but the reserves held by the private banking system and the money supply of the nations where intervention has occurred. For example, if the Federal Reserve purchases bank deposits, it will add to the reserves of those banks which will ultimately result in an expansion of bank loans and investments, similar to the impact of open-market operations as described in Chapter 23. Thus, a decision by a central bank to intervene in the foreign currency markets will have both currency market and money-supply effects.

very little from day to day. However, if payment must be made weeks or months in the future, there is considerable uncertainty as to what the spot rate will be for any given currency on any given future date. When substantial sums of money are involved, the rational investor or commercial trader will try to *guarantee* the future price at which currency can be purchased. This is the function of the *forward exchange market*—to reduce the risk associated with the future purchase and delivery of foreign currency by agreeing upon a price in advance.

The need for hedging against the risk of fluctuating currency-exchange rates was recognized as early as the 14th century, when forward-market trading first appeared. However, the market developed slowly due to numerous political upheavals, wars, and a poorly developed communications network. Following a burst of forward exchange trading during the 1920s, the forward market almost disappeared during the Great Depression years and World War II. It revived during the 1950s, however, and grew dramatically during the 1970s as currency prices became extremely volatile. Thousands of corporations, foreign governments, and central banks have entered the market during the past decade, responding to problems created by the wide ranges over which national currencies float today.

Spot, Forward, and Option Contracts

Earlier in this chapter we distinguished between the spot market, or market for immediate delivery of a currency, and the forward market, where contracts are made for future currency delivery. Trading in the spot market results in spot contracts, which are agreements to deliver a specified amount of foreign currency at an agreed-upon price, usually within one or two business days and sometimes on the same day. In contrast, a *forward contract* is an agreement to deliver a specified amount of foreign currency at a set price on some future date (usually within 30, 90, or 120 days).

In the forward market, therefore, the currency is purchased or sold now at a price agreed upon today, but delivery and payment are made in the future. The actual delivery date is referred to by traders as the *value date.* In the event customers do not know when they will receive or will need foreign currency, then an *option forward contract* frequently is used.[7]

---

[7] Another type of foreign exchange agreement used frequently is the *swap contract.* Swaps involve the sale (or purchase) of a currency for delivery at a particular date matched by a purchase (sale) of an equivalent amount of the same currency for delivery usually within one week. The majority of foreign exchange transactions involve spot contracts. For example, a survey by the Federal Reserve Bank of New York of transactions

Methods of Quoting Forward Exchange Rates

There are several different ways of measuring and quoting forward exchange rates. Suppose the spot exchange rate on German marks today is $0.40US (or 0.40/DM) and that dealers in foreign exchange are selling forward contracts for delivery of marks in six months at $0.3846US. (This means that the spot exchange rate for converting marks into dollars is DM/$ = 2.500 and the six-month forward rate is DM/$ = 2.600.) We may express the forward exchange rate for marks simply as $0.3846US, or $0.3846/DM,—known as the *outright rate*.

Another popular method is to express the forward rate as a premium or discount from the spot rate, known as the swap rate.[8] In this case, marks are selling at a 1.54 cent *discount* in the forward market. Traders in the forward market may be signaling an expectation that the mark will fall in value over the next few weeks.

We may also express forward exchange rates in terms of an annualized percentage rate above or below the current spot price. To use the example above, $/DM spot = 0.4000 and $/DM forward = 0.3846.[9] Then, the discount on forward DM for delivery in six months is:

$$\frac{\text{Forward rate} - \text{Spot rate}}{\text{Spot rate}} \times \frac{12}{\text{Number of months forward}} \times 100$$

$$= \frac{0.3846 - 0.4000}{0.4000} \times \frac{12}{6} \times 100$$

$$= -0.0385 \times 2 \times 100$$

$$= -7.7\%$$

Marks are selling at a 7.7 percent *discount* from spot in the forward market. Because marks are selling at a discount from their spot price, forward dollars must be selling at a *premium* over spot.

Suppose we know the current spot exchange rate between two currencies and the forward premium or discount. We want to know the actual forward exchange rate. What formula should be used? The following will suffice:

---

in U.S. foreign exchange markets found that 64 percent were spot contracts, 30 percent were swap contracts, and 6 percent were forward contracts. The German mark was the most actively traded foreign currency in U.S. markets, followed by the British pound, Canadian dollars, Japanese yen, and Swiss francs.

[8] Quite obviously, the current outright rate is the current spot exchange rate adjusted by the current swap rate.

[9] This example is based on one developed by the Public Information Center, Federal Reserve Bank of Chicago in their *Exchange Rate Calculation Guide*.

$$\text{Spot rate} + \frac{\begin{array}{c}\text{Spot rate} \times [\text{Premium }(+)\text{ or Discount }(-)\\ \text{expressed as an annual rate}] \times \text{Number of months forward}\end{array}}{100 \times \text{Number of months in a year}}$$

Suppose that \$/DM spot $= 0.4000$ and forward marks for delivery in three months are selling at a 4 percent premium over spot. Using the formula above, we have

$$0.4000 + \frac{0.4000 \times 4.0 \times 3}{1{,}200} = 0.4040\$/\text{DM forward}$$

This means DM/\$ forward is 2.4752, or DM 2.4752/\$.

FUNCTIONS OF THE FORWARD EXCHANGE MARKET

Contracts calling for the future delivery of currency are employed to cover a number or risks faced by investors and commercial traders. Some analysts group the functions or uses of forward contracts into four categories: commercial covering, hedging an investment position, speculation, and covered interest arbitrage. These four uses of the forward market are discussed below.[10]

Commercial Covering

The export or import of goods and service usually requires someone to deliver payment in a foreign currency or to receive payment in a foreign currency. Either the payor or payee, then, is subject to currency risk because no one knows for sure what the spot price will be for a currency at the time payment must be made. The forward exchange market can be used as a buffer against currency risk associated with the export or import of goods and services.

To illustrate, suppose an American importer of cameras has agreed to pay 5,000 marks to a West German manufacturer upon receipt of a new shipment. The cameras are expected to arrive dockside in 30 days. The importer has no idea at this point what 5,000 marks will cost in U.S. dollars 30 days from now. To reduce the risk that the price of marks in terms of dollars may rise significantly, the importer negotiates a forward contract with his or her bank for delivery of 5,000 marks at 0.30/DM in 30 days. When payment is due, the importer simply takes delivery

---

[10] The discussion which follows is indebted to the excellent article by Anderson (1972).

of the marks (usually by acquiring ownership of a deposit denominated in marks) at the agreed-upon price and pays the West German manufacturer. Because the price is fixed in advance, the risk associated with fluctuations in foreign exchange rates has been eliminated. Today, export and import firms routinely cover their large purchases overseas with forward currency contracts.

Hedging an Investment Position

As we saw in the preceding chapter, thousands of American corporations have invested in long-term capital projects overseas, building manufacturing plants, warehouse and dock facilities, retail stores, shopping centers, and office buildings. In recent years a large return flow of long-term investments by foreign firms in the United States also has occurred. Of course, the market value of these foreign investments may change drastically as the price of a foreign currency changes over time. For example, a drop in the exchange value of the British pound against the dollar may turn an otherwise profitable commercial project launched by a U.S. firm in Britain into a loss, particularly if the firm involved plans to sell the property while currency values are depressed.

To illustrate, suppose an American commercial bank constructed an office building in downtown London. When completed, the office facility had an estimated market value of £ 2 million. The current spot rate on pounds is, let us say, $1.40/£. The bank values the new building on its consolidated financial statement, therefore, at $2.8 million. However, suppose the pound has declined rapidly in value in recent months due to persistent balance-of-payments problems and rapid inflation in the British economy. Some market analysts expect pounds to be selling at $1.20/£ in a few months. In the absence of a hedged position, the bank would take a loss of $400,000 on its building. This is due to the fact that, at an exchange rate of $1.20/£, the office building will have a value of only $2.4 million.

Can this kind of loss be avoided or at least reduced? Yes, provided the bank can negotiate a sale of pounds forward at a higher price. For example, the bank may be able to arrange with a dealer for the sale of £2 million for future delivery at $1.30US (i.e., $1.30/£). When this forward contract matures, if the spot price has fallen to $1.20/£, the bank can buy pounds at this rate and deliver them to the dealer at $1.30US as agreed. The result is a profit on the foreign exchange transaction of $200,000, partially offsetting the financial loss on the building due to declining currency values.[11]

---

[11] The problem of the exposure of corporate balance sheets, especially fixed investments, to currency risk was ameliorated somewhat in the early 1980s by a ruling of

Speculation on Future Currency Prices

A third use of the forward exchange market is speculative investment based on expectations concerning future movements in currency prices. Speculators will *buy* currency for future delivery if they believe the future spot rate will be higher on the delivery date than the current forward rate. They will *sell* currency under a forward contract if the future spot rate appears likely to be below the forward rate on the day of delivery. Such speculative purchases and sales carry the advantage of requiring little or no capital and no borrowing costs in advance of the delivery date. A speculator whose forecast of future spot rates turns out to be correct makes a profit on the spread between the purchase price and sale price.

Covered Interest Arbitrage

One of the most common transactions in the international financial system arises when an investor discovers a higher interest rate available on foreign securities and invests funds abroad. When the currency risk associated with the purchase of foreign securities is reduced by using a forward contract, this transaction is often referred to as "covered interest arbitrage."

To illustrate the interest arbitrage process, let us suppose that a British auto company is selling high-grade bonds with a promised annual yield of 12 percent. Comparable bonds in the United States offer a 10 percent annual return. While the bonds are of good quality and there is probably little default risk, there is currency risk in this transaction. The U.S. investor must purchase pounds in order to buy the British bonds. When the bonds earn interest or reach maturity, the issuing auto company will pay foreign and domestic investors in pounds sterling. Then the pounds must be converted into dollars to allow the U.S. investor to spend the earnings in the United States. If the spot price of sterling falls, the U.S. investor's net yield from the bonds will be reduced.

Indeed, if the market value of pounds declines far enough, any profit from the bond purchase may be eliminated. Specifically, while the investor expects an interest spread of 2 percent a year over U.S. interest rates

---

the Financial Accounting Standards Board (FASB). Under a rule known as FASB 52, gains or losses on corporate balance sheets due to currency fluctuations are supposed to be reported in a specially designated item in the capital (net worth) accounts rather than as a charge against current earnings. The result has been to reduce the use of options and futures contracts to hedge against potential losses due to currency risk and to place greater emphasis upon the *economic fundamentals* of foreign investment, rather than on *translation gains or losses* (i.e., the impact of changing from one currency to another as a standard for valuing one's assets).

by purchasing British bonds, if the spot rate on pounds declines by 2 percent (on an annual basis), the interest gain will be exactly offset by the loss on trading pounds. Clearly, a series of forward contracts is needed to sell pounds at a guaranteed price as the bonds generate a stream of cash payments. In this case the investor will probably purchase sterling spot in order to buy the bonds and sell sterling forward to protect his expected income.

The Principle of Interest-Rate Parity

The foregoing example suggests an important rule regarding international capital flows and foreign exchange rates: *The rate of return to the investor from any foreign investment is equal to the interest earned plus or minus the premium or discount on the price of the foreign currency involved in the transaction.* The theory of forward exchange states that, under normal conditions, the forward discount or premium on one currency relative to another is directly related to the difference in interest rates between the two countries involved. More specifically, the currency of the nation experiencing higher interest rates normally will sell at a forward *discount* in terms of the currency issued by the nation with lower interest rates. And the currency of the nation with relatively low interest rates normally will sell at a *premium* forward relative to that of the high-rate country. A condition known as *interest-rate parity* exists when the interest-rate differential between two nations is exactly equal to the forward discount or premium on their two currencies. When parity exists, the currency markets are in equilibrium, and capital funds will not flow from one country to another. This is due to the fact that the gain from investing abroad at higher interest rates is fully offset by the cost of covering currency risk in the forward exchange market.

To illustrate the principle of interest-rate parity, suppose interest rates in a foreign country are 3 percent above those in the United States. Then, the currency of that foreign nation will, in equilibrium, sell at a 3 percent discount in the forward exchange market. Similarly, if interest rates are 1 percent lower abroad than in the United States, in equilibrium the foreign currency of the nations involved should sell at a 1 percent premium against the dollar. When such an equilibrium position is reached movements of funds between nations, even with currency risk covered, do not generate excess returns relative to domestic investments of comparable risk. Capital funds tend to stay in the domestic market rather than flowing abroad.

It is when interest parity does not exist that capital tends to flow across national boundaries in response to differences in domestic and foreign interest rates. For example, suppose interest rates in a foreign nation are 3 percent above U.S. interest rates on securities of comparable quality and the foreign currency involved is selling at a 1 percent discount against the dollar in the forward exchange market. In this case, investing abroad with exchange risks covered will yield the investor a net return of 2 percent per year. Clearly, there is a positive incentive to invest overseas. In the absence of exchange controls, capital will flow abroad.

Is this situation likely to persist for a long period of time? No, because the movement of funds into a country offering higher interest rates tends to increase the forward discount on its currency and lowers the net interest return to the investor. Other factors held constant, the flow of funds abroad eventually will subside, and capital funds will tend to stay at home until further changes in currency prices and interest rates take place.

TRADING CENTERS FOR FORWARD EXCHANGE CONTRACTS

Wherever there are major spot-currency markets operating, forward exchange contracts are usually traded as well. Leading currency markets today are situated in Amsterdam, Brussels, Frankfurt, London, Montreal, New York City, Paris, Toronto, and Zurich. London continues to be the predominant location for spot and forward currency trading, offering forward contracts for Canadian and U.S. dollars, deutsche marks, guilders, and both French and Swiss francs. The New York market specializes in forward trading of Canadian dollars, marks, Swiss francs, and the pound. In 1972 the Chicago Mercantile Exchange (CME) inaugurated trading in forward contracts for Canadian dollars, sterling, Swiss francs, marks, yen, lira, and pesos. As in the spot markets, most trading in forward currency contracts occurs between dealer departments of major banks and foreign exchange brokers.

THE MARKET FOR FOREIGN CURRENCY FUTURES

Forward contracts, as we have seen, call for the delivery of a specific currency on a specified date in the future at a set price. Thus, the intent of buyer and seller in a forward contract is to actually *deliver* the currency mentioned in the contract. In recent years, an important variation of the forward currency contract has developed—*foreign currency futures.* These too are contracts calling for the future delivery of a specific currency at a price agreed upon today, *but there is usually no intent to actually deliver the currencies mentioned in the contracts.* Rather, *currency futures are traded in the majority of cases to reduce the risk associated with fluctuating currency prices.* Today, currency futures contracts are traded in the United States and in a number of other world financial centers for U.S. dollars, Canadian dollars, Mexican pesos, French francs, Swiss francs, British pounds, Dutch guilders, German marks, and Japanese yen.

Foreign currency futures trading developed rapidly following the collapse in 1971 of the fixed-exchange rate system that had been established (as we saw in Chapter 27) after World War II. With the world's major currencies no longer tied to gold, the value of major currencies began to freely float in international markets, buffeted by the changing demands of world trade and commerce, by political developments, and by the activities of currency speculators. The result, of course, was to introduce a new and important element of currency risk in international transactions—an element that was simply too great to be ignored by both commercial traders and foreign investors.

In response to this new need for risk protection, commodity and security exchanges in the United States and in a few other world-trade centers set up a mechanism for trading currency futures. The movement was led by the Chicago Mercantile Exchange which established the International Monetary Market (IMM), designed primarily to appeal to businesses, individuals, and financial firms that found the traditional forward currency contracts inadequate for their specific needs. The IMM offered futures contracts in eight major currencies with the heaviest trading now concentrated in contracts for German marks, Swiss francs, British pounds, Japanese yen, and Canadian dollars. The operating rules and procedures of the CME and its IMM division parallel those of other commodity and financial futures exchanges around the world and are explained in detail in Chapter 17 of this book. Currency futures contract terms, sizes, and allowable price changes are set by each exchange and generally call for delivery of the currency specified in the contract on the third Wednesday of March, June, September, and December at a price quoted in U.S. dollars per unit of the foreign currency involved.

As in all futures trading, currency futures are attractive to two groups: foreign exchange hedgers and foreign exchange speculators. The *hedgers,* who typically are dealer and broker houses, commercial banks, individuals, trading companies, and multinational corporations, seek to avoid damage to their profits from normal business transactions caused by unexpected changes in currency exchange rates. Usually a hedging individual or institution will seek out, through traders or an exchange, a currency *speculator* who hopes to profit from changes in relative currency rates by taking on the risk the hedger seeks to avoid or minimize. Two basic types of transactions take place on currency futures exchanges: the buying hedge and the selling hedge.

Importers of goods typically use the *buying hedge.* In this case a domestic importer who is committed to pay in a foreign currency, such as British pounds, when goods are received from abroad fears that currency may rise in price. He therefore *purchases* a futures contract, agreeing to take delivery of pounds at a set price as near as possible to the date on which the goods must be paid for. Because the price of this contract is fixed, the importer, in effect, has "locked in" the value of the imported goods, thus helping to protect his potential profit on the business transaction. As a final step on or close to the date the goods are paid for, the importer will "zero out" his or her futures contract purchase by *selling* a comparable currency futures contract through a broker trading on the exchange floor. The exchange's clearinghouse, which records each transaction taking place on the exchange, will automatically cancel out the importer's obligation to either take delivery of or to deliver foreign currency. The only moneys the importer must come up with is paying the broker's commission.

How has the importer protected himself against loss due to currency fluctuations? If the pound or other currency rises in value during the life of a futures contract, the importer will experience reduced profits or increased losses on the imported goods themselves because the pound has risen in value relative to his/her home currency. However, the market value of a currency futures contract also rises when the market value of the underlying currency increases. Therefore, the importer will be able to sell currency futures contracts at a higher price than he originally purchased them for. The resulting profit in currency futures wholly or at least partially offsets the reduced gains or losses on purchase of the imported goods. On the other hand, if currency values fall, potential profits on the imported goods will increase because they can be bought more cheaply, but an offsetting loss will be recorded in futures trading because contracts must be sold at a lower price than they were purchased for. Cash-market gains (losses) offset futures market losses (gains).

The opposite kind of hedge in currency futures is known as the *selling hedge*. This transaction is often employed by investors who purchase foreign securities and want to protect their interest or dividend earnings from those securities from a drop in currency values. In this instance the investors could hedge their expected earnings by *selling* futures contracts in the currency involved at the time the securities are acquired in the cash (spot) market. If contracts are sold in an amount that covers both principal and interest or dividends, then the investors have, in effect, "locked in" their investment return regardless of which way exchange rates go by the time they must convert foreign-denominated investment earnings into home currency. If the foreign currency involved has declined in price relative to the home currency when the security pays interest or dividends, matures, or must be sold, a loss will be incurred in cash received but the investors will earn an offsetting futures-market profit by *buying* futures contracts in an amount equivalent to those sold earlier. Conversely, if the foreign currency appreciates relative to the home currency, cash-market revenues from the security will rise when the foreign currency is converted to home money, offsetting a futures-market loss from buying back contracts that now cost more.

In summary, the development of the currency futures market in recent years has opened up a new way for commercial traders and investors in foreign securities to hedge against volatile foreign exchange rates, stimulating both international trade and international investment. Futures markets broaden the availability of currency hedging tools to a wider range of individuals and institutions exposed to foreign exchange risk.[12] The result in the long run is an increase in the flow of goods and services across international boundaries, adding to each nation's standard of living.

GOVERNMENT INTERVENTION IN THE FOREIGN EXCHANGE MARKETS

The value of a nation's currency in the international markets has long been a source of concern to governments around the world. National pride plays a significant role in this case because a strong currency, avidly sought by traders and investors in the international marketplace, implies the existence of a strong, vigorous, and well-managed economy at home. A strong and stable currency encourages investment in the home country, stimulating its economic growth and development. Moreover, as we observed in Chapter 27, changes in currency values affect a nation's balance-of-payments position. A weak and declining currency makes foreign imports more expensive, lowering the standard of living at home. And a nation whose currency is not well regarded in the international marketplace will have difficulty selling its goods and services abroad, giving rise to unemployment and economic recession at home.

The United States has pursued an active policy of supporting the dollar *in international markets for many years.* In part, this policy has been motivated by concern over the condition of the U.S. economy, particularly the effects of inflation. Another factor, however, is the key role played

---

[12] In 1982 a new hedging instrument, known as the *currency option,* appeared which is really a combination of both forward and futures contracts. A currency option gives a buyer the right, though not the obligation, to either deliver or to take delivery of a designated currency at a set price any time before the option expires. Thus, unlike the forward market, actual delivery may not occur, but unlike futures trading no follow-up purchases or sales are needed to stop currency delivery. The advantage of the currency option is that it limits downside risk, but not upside profits. However, the new instrument is available only from a limited number of banks or from a few exchanges and exposes offering banks to additional risk which may limit the market's future growth.

by the U.S. dollar in the international financial system. The dollar is a *vehicle currency* that facilitates trade and investment between many nations in addition to the United States. For example, international shipments of crude oil, regardless of their origin or destination, are usually valued in dollars. As noted in Chapter 16, the market for dollar deposits held in banks abroad—Eurodollars—is the world's largest international money market, financing commercial projects and even providing operating funds for many foreign governments around the world. For all of the foregoing reasons, then, the United States as well as foreign governments and central banks have repeatedly intervened in the foreign exchange markets to stabilize currency values and insulate domestic economic conditions from adverse financial developments abroad.

As we observed in the preceding chapter, during the years immediately following World War II, the United States agreed to maintain a fixed-exchange ratio between the dollar and gold. The Treasury Department stood ready to buy gold from or sell gold to foreign central banks and other monetary authorities at a fixed price of $35 per ounce. The secretary of the Treasury was also responsible for maintaining the U.S. Exchange Stabilization Fund, to be drawn upon when necessary to intervene in foreign currency markets and protect the dollar. While the United States committed itself to intervene in the currency markets to preserve the desired ratio of dollars to gold, other nations agreed to keep the exchange ratios between their currencies and the dollar centered about a fixed rate. Whenever a currency's exchange rate against the dollar deviated significantly from the agreed-upon rate, central banks and government agencies would intervene (either on the demand side or the supply side of the exchange market) to restore the proper dollar-currency ratio.

U.S. Intervention in the Currency Markets during the 1960s

This relatively passive U.S. foreign exchange policy, which relied mainly upon other nations to stabilize the international financial system, was modified during the 1960s because of serious economic problems. Massive outflows of capital from the United States into Western Europe, Japan, Latin America, and the Middle East weakened the dollar in foreign markets. High unemployment rates in the United States during the early 60s coupled with significant inflation in later years further eroded the pivotal role of the dollar in the international financial system. Beginning in 1961, the U.S. Treasury, acting in cooperation with the monetary authorities of other Western nations, began to intervene in the currency markets to counter speculative attacks against the dollar.

Later, the Federal Reserve System joined in the cooperative effort to support the dollar and stabilize the currency system. The Fed established a network of swap agreements with foreign central banks. These agreements created lines of credit through which a participating central bank could obtain foreign currencies in order to sell them in the exchange markets and protect its home currency. Typically, any drawings against these currency credit lines were repaid within a few weeks or months. The Federal Reserve pledged to absorb excess dollars that had been accumulated by foreign central banks in their attempt to keep the dollar's value at its officially established level. The Fed would borrow foreign currencies against its swap lines and use these currencies to purchase unwanted dollars held by the Bank of England and other major central banks on a temporary basis. When the exchange markets calmed and the dollar recovered, the Fed would simply repay its swap drawings by purchasing foreign currency from private dealers.

U.S. Foreign Exchange Policy during the 1970s

Federal Reserve swap operations and Treasury intervention in the exchange markets came to an abrupt halt in August 1971, when the Nixon administration snapped the official link between the dollar and gold. Because the dollar was no longer convertible into gold at a government-guaranteed rate, there seemed little reason to interfere with supply and demand forces in the exchange marketplace. The dollar began to "float." However, concern over the stability of all exchange rates and the possible threats to world trade from unbridled speculation in foreign currencies brought another reversal of U.S. intervention policy in the summer of 1972. The Federal Reserve began actively drawing on its swap lines again to stabilize the currency markets and protect the dollar.

When the Carter administration took office in 1977, it announced a policy of nonintervention, but it abandoned this policy in favor of active intervention only a year later. The Treasury and the Fed publicly committed themselves in 1978 to stop speculative attacks against the dollar and bring stability to the currency markets. The Federal Reserve increased its currency swap lines with other central banks, while the Treasury drew on the International Monetary Fund for credit, floated foreign currency-denominated securities to gain additional exchange reserves, and increased its sales of gold. Moreover, rising foreign interest rates, higher OPEC oil prices, and rapid inflation at home forced even more strenuous efforts by U.S. monetary authorities to protect the dollar from erosion.

The year 1980 brought a complete 180-degree change of direction for U.S. foreign exchange policies. The dollar began to rise rapidly in value due to record-high interest rates in the United States, which attracted huge amounts of foreign capital. U.S. government securities and American corporate stocks and bonds were among the hottest selling items in the international financial markets as the 1980s began. U.S. and foreign authorities suddenly had to switch from a timeworn policy of supporting the dollar through heavy dollar purchases in the exchange markets to one of selling dollars and purchasing other beleaguered currencies in order to moderate the greenback's rapidly rising value. As a result, the Federal Reserve and the Treasury began to accumulate large stocks of foreign currencies. For example, between July 1980 and January 1981 the Fed and the Treasury purchased over $12 billion in overseas currencies to slow down the dollar's rapid appreciation. The Fed used its share of this vast currency pool to repay its past drawings from the swap network and accumulate funds that eventually could be employed to redeem foreign currency-denominated securities issued by the Treasury in earlier years.[13] The U.S. government's pool of reserve assets was also expanded to deal with any future problems that might arise in the currency markets.

A Limited Intervention Policy for the 1980s

The inauguration of President Reagan in January 1981 ushered in another new foreign exchange policy for the United States. For want of a more convenient label, this latest official foreign exchange market approach might be called "Emergency Intervention Only." In May 1981 the Reagan administration announced that U.S. monetary authorities would intervene in the foreign exchange markets only if an emergency developed that threatened to disrupt the smooth functioning of the currency markets. The new policy received its first test almost immediately after its inception when the president was shot in an assassination attempt outside a Washington hotel. The Fed and the Treasury immediately began dollar-support operations to calm the exchange markets amidst worldwide concern over the stability and continuity of U.S. government policies and programs.

Once this emergency had passed, the Federal Reserve and the Treasury were confronted with a long-term and very dramatic rise in the dollar's market price vis-à-vis virtually all other major foreign currencies. A number of factors accounted for the dollar's unprecedented increase in value—the cooling off of domestic inflation, the rapid economic recovery of the United States after deep recessions in the early 1980s while European recovery lagged, and continuing political and social turmoil in the Middle East and Africa. Whatever the causes of the dollar's market appreciation, the benefits and costs of that rise left few individuals and institutions untouched. Many foreign exporters rejoiced because it meant that their goods could be sold more cheaply in the United States; however,

---

[13] See Chapter 25 for a discussion of the issue of foreign currency-denominated securities by the U.S. Treasury Department.

American farmers and other U.S.-based exporting industries were badly damaged because the dollar's rise made U.S. exports more expensive overseas, drastically reducing their salability in foreign markets. Unemployment and business failures in U.S. export industries increased significantly; some American firms began to move their production operations overseas. The U.S. balance-of-payments accounts reflected record payments deficits. Moreover, a shortage of international financial capital began to develop as foreign investors diverted more and more of their investments into the United States.

The Treasury and the Federal Reserve were finally goaded into action by the dollar's persistent gains. The Reagan administration announced in September 1985 a cooperative program with central bankers in Britain, France, Japan, and West Germany to force the dollar's exchange value down against other major national currencies. This new interventionist policy was an effort to avert international trade wars and the erection of import restrictions by the U.S. and other countries. It also reflected concern over the loss of jobs in U.S. export industries and a dramatic rise in farm bankruptcies.

Many authorities have serious doubts that a policy of nonintervention can last for long in today's currency markets. Certainly, new and possibly severe tests await the dollar in the future. Another oil embargo comparable to that of 1973–74 would undoubtedly send the dollar, the yen, the mark, and most other Western currencies into a sharp downward spiral, demanding massive central-bank intervention, possibly for a considerable period. Faced with unhappy outcomes of that sort, it seems clear that the U.S. government would not hesitate to intervene as often as necessary to ensure that the foreign exchange markets function smoothly and efficiently.

STUDY QUESTIONS

1. Describe the important role played by commercial banks in the operation of the foreign exchange market. Why do you think banks are so dominant in this market?

2. The foreign exchange market consists of three tiers. What are these three divisions of the market?

3. What role do foreign exchange brokers play in currency trading? Why are broker operations important to the smooth functioning of the foreign exchange market?

4. Please supply a definition of the following terms:
    a. Cable transfers.
    b. Mail transfers.
    c. Bills of exchange.
    d. Sight bills.
    e. Time bills.
    f. Documentary bills.
    g. Clean bills.

5. What are the principal factors affecting the value of any particular currency in the international exchange markets? What role does a nation's balance-of-payments position play in affecting the value of its currency?

6. Define "double-barreled" quotations. Arbitrage.

7. Distinguish between the spot and forward markets for foreign exchange. Why is it necessary to have two markets rather than one?

8. How are forward exchange rates measured? Where is the forward market located?

9. Describe the principal uses of forward exchange contracts today. Give an example of each use.

10. What is interest-rate parity? How does it influence the flow of capital funds abroad?

11. In recent years central banks (including the Federal Reserve System) have intervened in the foreign exchange markets from time to time to support one currency or another. Why do you think central bank intervention in the market might be necessary? What impact are central-bank operations likely to have? Would you expect this impact to be temporary or long lasting?

12. What is the latest U.S. government policy regarding intervention in the foreign exchange markets? Why, in your opinion, was this policy adopted?

PROBLEMS

1. Suppose the exchange rate between British pounds (£) and U.S. dollars ($) is $1.35 per pound. What is the correct way to write this pound-dollar exchange rate? The dollar-pound exchange rate?

2. Suppose the pound-dollar exchange rate is now 1.3500. Then the U.S. dollar increases in value by 5 percent. What is the new pound-

dollar exchange rate? What is the new exchange rate if the U.S. dollar appreciates by 10 percent?

3. If the pound-dollar exchange rate increases from £/$ = 1.3500 to 1.4000, by what percentage amount has the pound depreciated?

4. If the pound-dollar exchange rate is 1.4000 and the pound declines 10 percent in value, what is the new pound-dollar exchange rate?

5. Suppose the pound-dollar exchange rate is 1.4000 and the yen-dollar exchange rate is 2.3000. What is the yen-pound exchange rate?

SELECTED REFERENCES

Anderson, Gerald H. "The Nature and Use of Forward Exchange." *Economic Review*, Federal Reserve Bank of Cleveland, April–May 1972, pp. 7–15.

Andrews, Michael D. "Recent Trends in the U.S. Foreign Exchange Market." *Quarterly Review*, Federal Reserve Bank of New York, Summer 1984, pp. 38–47.

Balback, Anatol B. "The Mechanics of Intervention in Exchange Markets." *Monthly Review*, Federal Reserve Bank of St. Louis, February 1978, pp. 2–7.

Chalupa, Karel V. "Foreign Currency Futures: Reducing Foreign Exchange Risk." *Economic Perspectives*, Federal Reserve Bank of Chicago, Winter 1982, pp. 3–11.

Chicago Mercantile Exchange. *Understanding Futures in Foreign Exchange*, Chicago, 1977.

Chrystal, K. Alec. "A Guide to Foreign Exchange Markets." *Review*, Federal Reserve Bank of St. Louis, March 1984, pp. 5–18.

Hakkio, Craigs. "Exchange Rate Volatility and Federal Reserve Policy." *Economic Review*, Federal Reserve Bank of Kansas City, July/August 1984, pp. 18–31.

Holmes, Alan R., and Francis H. Schott. *The New York Foreign Exchange Market.* rev. ed. New York: Federal Reserve Bank of New York, 1965.

Kubarych, Roger M. *Foreign Exchange Markets in the United States.* New York: Federal Reserve Bank of New York, 1978.

Westerfield, Janice M. "How U.S. Multinationals Manage Currency Risk." *Business Review*, Federal Reserve Bank of Philadelphia, March–April 1980, pp. 19–27.

29

International Banking

PURPOSE OF THIS CHAPTER

To explore the functions and roles played by the major multinational banks that serve both domestic and international markets around the globe. The different types of overseas facilities maintained by these banks are discussed and the recent growth of international banking is traced and explained. Services offered by multinational banking corporations are listed and defined. The impact of foreign banks on U.S. domestic markets is then examined along with recent federal legislation and regulation bearing on the activities of foreign banks. The chapter concludes with a discussion of the difficulties of regulating international banking and the risks involved in overseas lending.

KEY TERMS AND CONCEPTS IN THE CHAPTER

bankers' acceptances
capital positions
currency risk
Edge Acts
Eurobonds
Eurocurrencies
FOREX
IBFs

international banking
International Banking
 Act
international banking
 departments
international loans
letters of credit

multinational
 corporations
mutual
 nondiscrimination
political risk
representative offices
shell branches

No review of the international financial system would be complete without a discussion of the role of international banking institutions. Through these large and vitally important financial institutions flow the majority of commercial and financial transactions that cross international borders. Along with British and Canadian banks, American commercial banking institutions have led in the development of international banking facilities to meet the far-flung financial needs of foreign governments, agencies, and multinational corporations. Until recently, the international activities of U.S. banks were concentrated principally in foreign offices, due mainly to federal government controls over foreign lending. However, the relaxation of government controls in 1974 and the rapid growth of international trade and commerce in the ensuing years brought a veritable explosion of international banking services provided from domestic offices and institutions. More recently, though, international banking has retreated somewhat from its earlier gains due to problems with foreign loans and a recent slowing in the growth of world trade.

The continuing development of multinational banking over the past half century has resulted in several benefits for international trade. One obvious benefit to the public is greater competition in international financial markets, reducing profit margins and prices on loans. The long-term development of multinational banking also has tied together more effectively the various national money markets into a unified international financial system, permitting a more optimal allocation of scarce resources. Funds flow quite freely today across national boundaries in response to differences in relative interest rates and currency values. While these developments undoubtedly have benefited both borrowers and investors, they also have created problems for governments trying to control the volume of credit, interest rates, and inflation.

THE SCOPE OF INTERNATIONAL BANKING ACTIVITIES

Multinational Banking Corporations

The term *multinational corporation* usually is reserved for large nonfinancial corporations with manufacturing or trading operations in several different countries. However, this term is equally applicable to the world's major commercial banks, most of whom have their home offices in Canada, the United States, and Great Britain, but have established offices worldwide. In terms of sheer numbers, however, it is the largest U.S. banks that have accounted for most of the growth in multinational banking over the past three decades.

Types of Facilities Operated by U.S. Banks Abroad

U.S. banks and other major banks around the world have used several vehicles to expand their international operations. All major banks have international departments, and many operate full-service branches in foreign markets as well. U.S. banks also operate Edge Act and Agreement Corporations, shell branches, and representative offices in targeted overseas markets. In addition, most multinational banks make direct investments in the stock of foreign companies, either alone or as part of a consortium with other banks.

International Banking Departments. A major bank's international department generally has 20 to 30 officers and staff and maintains close personal contact with customers and correspondent banks overseas. The larger international banking departments buy and sell foreign currencies for immediate or future delivery, issue letters of credit, and engage in acceptance financing.

Shell Branches. Booking offices of major banks, also known as shell branches, are located today mainly in the Bahamas and Grand Cayman Islands. These branches have been set up to attract Eurodollars and other Eurocurrency deposits from abroad, making these deposits available to domestic banks.

Representative Offices. These offices house staff whose job is to find new loan customers and help meet the service needs of existing bank customers. However, a representative office cannot accept deposits, but must refer them to the home office.

Edge Act and Agreement Corporations. These corporations are special subsidiaries of U.S. banks authorized to offer international banking services. Federal legislation passed at the end of World War I permitted American banks to seek charters through the Federal Reserve Board for Edge Act and Agreement Corporations. These subsidiaries could be set up in any location in the United States, provided the bank organizing them could come up with the required capital. Edge Acts can engage in activities such as equity financing that normally are prohibited to commercial banks themselves, but the majority of their accounts must be directly related to international transactions.

International Banking Facilities (IBFs). Authorized by the Federal Reserve Board in December 1981, IBFs are a set of computerized accounts showing flows of funds through the credit and deposit accounts of foreign residents and foreign banks. However, the IBF must be located in the United States, reflecting an effort by federal regulatory authorities to bring a substantial share of U.S. foreign bank operations back home. Unlike domestic deposits received by a U.S. bank, deposits in an IBF are not subject to reserve requirements nor can they be insured. By the end of 1983 nearly 500 domestic and foreign banks had established IBFs with assets approaching $175 billion.

Which organizational form is adopted by a multinational bank to serve its customers depends upon government regulations and the bank's size, goals, and location. Most banks begin with international departments or Edge Acts and then, if business warrants, open shell branches, representative offices, and ultimately full-service branches and subsidiaries. A recent trend toward legal liberalization of foreign trade and international lending has stimulated the growth of *home-based offices* that send officers to call on customers overseas or serve clients by wire. However, many multinational banks argue that successful international operations require an institution to have a stable presence overseas in the form of agencies, branches, or representative offices.

Growth of U.S. International Banking Activities

U.S. international banking really began on a major scale in the early 1960s when the domestic economy was soft and loan demand for credit was strong, particularly from Japanese firms. Moreover, interest-rate differentials in the international money market generally favored the United States as a source of loanable funds. By the late 1960s restrictive interest-rate ceilings on domestic deposits encouraged the largest U.S. banks to draw more heavily on the international Eurodollar market as a source of reserves. When the administration of President Lyndon Johnson imposed restrictions on overseas lending from domestic offices through a Voluntary Foreign Credit Restraint Program in 1965, U.S. banks saw offshore facilities as a vital link to foreign deposits and loans.

The number of foreign offices operated by American banking organizations rose dramatically during the 1960s and 70s. In 1960 only 7 U.S. banks operated a total of 132 foreign branches and offices. By 1974, 125 American banks controlled 732 foreign branch offices. A much slower growth in the internationalization of U.S. banking then set in as global economic conditions softened due to inflation, high interest rates, and higher energy prices. By year-end 1979, 130 U.S. banks were represented by close to 800 overseas branch offices. Foreign assets held by U.S. banking organizations had climbed to $495 billion in 1981, up from only $9 billion in 1965 and $150 billion in 1974.[1]

---

[1] See especially Abrams (1980), Board of Governors of the Federal Reserve System (1979), and Houpt and Martinson (1982).

As shown in Exhibit 29–1, the majority of assets and liabilities held by U.S. bank branches abroad are concentrated in Western Europe (particularly the United Kingdom), Latin America, and the Caribbean. Assets held by U.S. bank branches in the United Kingdom—most of these headquartered in London, the center of the worldwide Eurodollar market—accounted for close to one third of the assets of all U.S. bank branches abroad. Other nations where U.S. bank branches hold substantial assets include Japan, France, Belgium-Luxembourg, West Germany, Brazil, the Bahamas, Mexico, and the Cayman Islands.

EXHIBIT 29–1

Geographical Distribution of Assets and Liabilities of Major Foreign Branches of U.S. Banks* As of June 30, 1984 ($ millions)

Country of Customer	Assets	Liabilities	Country of Customer	Assets	Liabilities
Europe	110,171	72,010	Latin America and		
Austria	1,490	527	Caribbean—cont'd.		
Belgium-Luxembourg	7,752	4,683	Bolivia	115	80
Bulgaria	79	29	Brazil	9,195	2,180
Czechoslovakia	68	64	Cayman Islands	4,423	2,000
Denmark	2,096	316	Chile	1,963	473
Finland	1,286	190	Colombia	452	219
France	10,180	5,113	Costa Rica	118	81
Germany (East)	174	95	Ecuador	423	279
Germany (West)	10,546	2,696	Jamaica	94	12
Hungary	124	179	Mexico	8,615	2,561
Ireland	1,043	745	Netherlands Antilles	2,344	1,829
Italy	6,553	3,579	Nicaragua	260	20
Netherlands	2,617	3,061	Panama	4,783	2,366
Norway	2,538	469	Peru	349	470
Poland	637	22	Venezuela	2,861	1,295
Portugal	540	123	Others	740	1,272
Romania	198	26	Asia	67,338	52,485
Spain	4,333	2,936	China (PRC)	73	139
Sweden	1,469	237	Taiwan	4,032	5,832
Switzerland	3,462	13,059	Hong Kong	10,351	10,315
Turkey	932	155	India	681	668
U.S.S.R.	104	12	Indonesia	3,193	3,157
United Kingdom	48,254	29,173	Israel	456	909
Yugoslavia	975	88	Japan	20,072	8,911
Others (including BIS)	2,721	4,433	Korea (South)	4,660	610
			Malaysia	2,156	1,382
Canada	4,228	3,413	Philippines	4,354	1,839
			Singapore	9,341	4,701
Latin America and			Thailand	1,244	894
Caribbean	45,098	23,464	Middle East oil-exporting		
Argentina	2,939	1,391	countries†	5,960	10,708
Bahamas	4,942	5,049	Others	765	2,420
Bermuda	482	1,887			

EXHIBIT 29–1 *(concluded)*

Country of Customer	Assets	Liabilities	Country of Customer	Assets	Liabilities
Africa	9,017	3,189	Unallocated§	13,041	53,314‖
Egypt	887	1,179	Total excluding the United		
Liberia	2,599	509	States, Puerto Rico, and		
South Africa	2,143	382	U.S. dependencies	253,096	207,983
Morocco	345	8	United States	124,808	167,038
Zaire	84	9	Puerto Rico and U.S.		
African oil-exporting			dependencies	5,850	5,808
countries‡	1,787	602	Grand total	383,754	380,829
Others	1,172	500			
Oceania	4,203	108			
Australia	3,650	76			
New Zealand	458	10			
Others	95	22			

* Beginning with data for June 1984, total reported assets and liabilities have been reduced by an increase in the reporting threshold for "shell" branches from $50 million to $150 million equivalent in total assets. Coverage thus differs from that for earlier dates described in previous releases.
† Bahrain, Iran, Iraq, Kuwait, Oman, Qatar, Saudi Arabia, and the United Arab Emirates.
‡ Algeria, Gabon, Libya, and Nigeria.
§ Including international organizations.
‖ Beginning with data for June 1984, negotiable CDs issued by the branches are included in the "unallocated" line.
SOURCE: Federal Reserve Bank of Chicago.

In terms of total offices, Latin America leads the list with more than 200 branches and other office facilities operated by U.S. banks. Shell branches in the Bahamas and Grand Cayman Islands ranked second in total numbers, and the Far East and continental Europe were not far behind with well over 100 branches, representative offices, and other facilities of American banks stationed there. Significant numbers of U.S. banking offices may also be found today in Africa, the Middle East, and U.S. possessions and trust territories.

Laws and regulations play a major role in determining where multinational banking offices are located around the globe. For example, Australia, India, and Saudi Arabia prohibit or severely restrict the operation of branches by foreign banks. In other areas of the world fears of political upheaval or outright expropriation of foreign-owned facilities have severely limited the entry of multinational banks.

For several of the largest U.S. banks, international operations yield from one third to as much as one half of their income, and a few receive more than half their earnings from international activities. Particularly noteworthy has been U.S.-bank penetration of foreign consumer banking markets, such as the "money shops" operated by New York's Citibank in Great Britain. Much as U.S. banks did in the 19th and early 20th centuries, many foreign banks today neglect the needs of consumers. American banks entered the consumer lending field in the 1920s, and they have developed considerable expertise in that field. Personal loans and other personal financial services often represent extremely attractive opportunities in foreign markets, and U.S. banks hold a significant share of consumer loan and deposit markets abroad, especially in Great Britain and Western Europe.

SERVICES OFFERED BY INTERNATIONAL BANKS

Multinational banks today offer a wide variety of international financial services to their customers. These services, described briefly below, include issuing letters of credit, buying and selling foreign exchange, issuing bankers' acceptances, accepting Eurocurrency deposits, making Eurocurrency loans, and assisting in the marketing of Eurobonds. Of course, the particular services offered by each bank depend heavily on its size, location, and the types of facilities it maintains overseas.

Issuing Letters of Credit (LC)

Most banks enter the international sector to finance trade. In trading across national borders rarely are goods and services paid for in advance. Nearly always financing is needed to bridge the gap between cash expenditures and cash receipts and to reduce the risks associated with long-distance trading. In these situations a *letter of credit* is often the ideal financing instrument. A letter of credit is simply an international bank's future promise to pay for goods stored overseas or goods shipped between two countries. Such letters may be issued to finance exports and imports or to provide standby credit, such as a guarantee of payment behind commercial paper issued by a corporate customer. Through a letter of credit, which is usually irrevocable, the bank merely substitutes its own future promise to pay for the promise to pay of one of its customers. However, the bank's promise to pay is more readily accepted by a seller of goods than is a buyer's promise of payment. By substituting its promise, the bank acts as a guarantor of payment and thereby reduces the seller's risk, facilitating the flow of goods and services through international markets. Occasionally, the seller becomes concerned about the soundness of the *bank* issuing the letter of credit; he may then ask his own bank to issue a *confirmation* letter in which his bank guarantees against foreign bank default.

Buying and Selling Foreign Exchange (FOREX)

Major multinational banks, as we saw in the preceding chapter, have dealer departments that specialize in trading foreign currencies. The largest multinationals hold inventories of selected currencies for themselves and for the convenience of their customers. Major international banks will buy and sell foreign currencies on a 24-hour basis around the globe to support the import and export of goods and services, the making of investments, the distribution of earnings from foreign business ventures, the giving of gifts, and the financing of tourism. They also negotiate forward contracts for the future delivery of foreign exchange and some speculate on future currency price movements in hopes of turning a profit. Smaller banks usually hold very small currency inventories, purchasing whatever currency is needed for immediate or future delivery to a customer from larger international banks that maintain active currency positions.

Issuing Bankers' Acceptances

Bankers' acceptances are time drafts used mainly to finance the shipment of goods or commodities.[2] With a banker's acceptance the bank agrees to pay a seller of goods when the time draft expires. For example, an exporter and importer may agree upon "60-day sight" terms on the shipment of certain items. This tells us that the exporter will receive payment from a bank 60 days following the date when the issuing bank affirms that the draft and certain documents associated with the transaction are in good order. Once this is affirmed, the issuing bank will stamp "Accepted" across the face of the draft. The bank's stamp is a guarantee of payment (in our example, in 60 days from date of the draft), and it makes the acceptance a negotiable instrument. The exporter may sell (discount) the acceptance to a bank or other investor and thereby receive payment before the draft's due date.

Accepting Eurocurrency Deposits and Making Eurocurrency Loans

As we saw in Chapter 16, international banks accept deposits denominated in currencies other than that of their home country. Thus, London banks will accept deposits denominated in dollars, francs, and other major convertible currencies. Eurocurrency deposits are used to pay for goods shipped between countries, as investment vehicles because they pay a competitive rate of return, and as a source of loanable funds for banks.

Eurocurrency deposits may be loaned in the interbank market, usually on an unsecured basis, to corporations, governments, and other large

---

[2] See Chapter 16 for a detailed discussion of the creation and uses of bankers' acceptances.

wholesale borrowers. The majority of Eurocurrency loans carry floating interest rates based, in most cases, on the London Interbank Offer Rate (LIBOR) for three-month and six-month Eurocurrency deposits. Eurocurrency credit normally goes to borrowers with impeccable credit ratings. Often, several multinational banks will spread the risk of international lending by forming a syndicate and jointly participating in a single currency loan. One important innovation in this field in recent years is the *syndicated Eurocurrency credit* in which one or more large multinational banks will put together a loan package accompanied by an information memorandum. Smaller banks can then participate in the loan without direct communication with the borrower. Syndicated credits are a fast method of raising loanable funds and spreading risk.

Assisting in the Marketing of Eurocurrency Bonds

In recent years multinational banks have become active as agents, underwriters, and, in some instances, investors in the rapidly growing market for Eurobonds. A *Eurobond* is a debt security denominated in a currency other than that of the country or countries where most or all of the security is sold. For example, an American automobile company may desire to float an issue of long-term bonds to raise capital for one of its subsidiaries operating in Greece. The company might issue bonds denominated in British pounds to be sold in several countries in Western Europe through an underwriting syndicate made up of banks, securities dealers, and other firms.

Most Eurobonds are denominated in dollars, though substantial amounts are also denominated today in deutsche marks, guilders, pounds, and francs. Eurobonds normally are straight debt offerings with maturities ranging out to about 15 years, though warrants and conversion features occasionally are attached to improve the marketability of a particular issue. The majority are callable bearer bonds with coupons attached.

Large multinational banks assist the Eurobond market in several ways. Major banks such as Morgan Guaranty Trust Company of New York have established international clearing systems to expedite the delivery of Eurobonds. Banks and security brokers are the principal intermediaries through which both old and new Eurobonds find their way to the long-term investor. The borrower (a government or large corporation) usually contacts a major international bank and asks it to organize a syndicate to place a new issue. At this point a *consortium* will be formed, embracing at least four or five American, British, Belgian, French, or German banks and a bank located in the borrowing country. The consortium typically agrees to subscribe to the Eurobond issue at issue price minus a commission (usually in the 2 to 3 percent range) and then organizes a large group of banks and securities dealers as underwriters. Sometimes more than 100 banks are included in the underwriting syndicate. Once formed, the underwriting group gives the borrower a firm offer for its bonds and proceeds to place the issue with a large, geographically diverse group of investors representing many different countries.

Other Services Provided by International Banks

In addition to the foregoing services, international banks offer extensive *advisory services* to their customers. These include analyses of foreign market conditions, evaluation of sales prospects and plant location sites, and advice on foreign laws and regulations affecting commerce. International banks often prepare credit reports on overseas buyers for exporters of goods and services, and assist domestic firms interested in entering foreign markets.

International banks offer cash-management services and lease capital assets for their corporate customers. They frequently engage in interest-rate swaps to aid multinational corporations in dealing with the risk of fluctuating market interest rates. And, in recent years, many international banks have added sales of insurance, credit cards, mortgage brokering services, consumer installment loans, and factoring to their traditional service lines.

SMALLER BANKS ENTER THE INTERNATIONAL FIELD

One of the unique features of international banking in recent years is the opening of offshore offices by smaller, essentially regional banks. Regional banks are usually defined as those large banks with a billion dollars or more in assets located in a U.S. city other than New York, Chicago, or San Francisco. Large downtown banks in Atlanta, Boston, Dallas, Houston, Miami, Los Angeles, Seattle, Portland, and New Orleans are examples of regional banks. A study by Thompson (1979) concludes that more than half the regional banks among the top 300 American commercial banks operate international departments. Other smaller banks without formal departments still provide such international services as letters of credit and bankers' acceptances.

Expansion offshore has given some of the smaller banks an opportunity to diversify out of slowly growing domestic markets and to open up entirely new markets. Only the largest regionals actually open foreign branches or set up Edge Act Corporations, and only a handful have purchased majority interests in foreign financial organizations. However, many regional banks have opened shell branches, mainly in the Caribbean area. These shells provide a convenient source of loanable funds when domestic reserves are scarce. Moreover, shell operations are low cost compared to most other forms of international banking. Most of the regional banks rely heavily on loan participations with better established multinational lenders. Some of the smaller banks have become quite successful in international lending by centering their activities on selected industries and developing expertise in only one area or a few areas, such as ship financing and petroleum exploration.

FOREIGN BANKS IN THE UNITED STATES[3]

Banks owned by foreign individuals and companies have entered the United States in great numbers in recent years, especially since 1970. The reasons behind the expansion of foreign banking activities in the United States reflect both the growth in international trade and investments and the opportunity for profit in the huge U.S. common market. Originally, foreign-based banks penetrated U.S. markets for essentially the same reason U.S. banks established facilities overseas—to follow their customers who had established operations in other countries. Once in the United States, however, foreign banks found the possibility of attracting deposits and loans from major American corporations irresistible. Moreover, the U.S. economy has been more stable and prosperous than many other national economies where foreign banks are headquartered or represented.

Recent Growth of Foreign Banks in the United States

The size of foreign bank operations in the United States is impressive. By year-end 1981, there were more than 440 foreign bank offices in the United States, including 195 agency offices, 194 branches, and 52 subsidiary firms. (See Exhibit 29–2.) Japanese banking offices led all others by a wide margin, followed by Canada and the United Kingdom. Data released by the Federal Reserve Board indicates those foreign-based institutions held assets of nearly $230 billion at year-end 1983, compared to less than $40 billion just 10 years earlier. In relative terms U.S. offices of foreign banks held about 14 percent of total assets of all banks in the United States in 1983. The growth rate of foreign bank assets held at their U.S. offices has averaged more than double the growth rate of domestic bank assets. Such rapid growth has made foreign banks a significant factor in U.S. financial markets, especially in the market for business loans, where their commercial credits now average about one sixth of the volume of all such loans made by American banks.[4]

---

[3] This section is based, in part, on an earlier article by Rose (1976) in *The Canadian Banker and ICB Review.*

[4] See, for example, Board of Governors of the Federal Reserve System (1979) and Segala (1979).

EXHIBIT 29–2

Offices of Foreign Banks in the United States, Year-end 1981

Location of Parent Bank	Number of Physical Offices in the United States by Category:				Total Assets ($ billions)
	Agencies	Branches	Subsidiaries	Total	
Japan	27	31	12	70	$ 88.9
Canada	20	18	10	48	23.4
United Kingdom	12	19	7	38	46.2
France	7	14	1	22	16.1
Israel	6	13	3	22	4.2
Brazil	14	6	0	20	4.0
Germany	6	14	0	20	7.3
Spain	8	6	6	20	4.0
Korea	11	5	1	17	1.9
Hong Kong	8	6	1	15	12.4
Italy	5	9	1	15	10.9
Netherlands	4	7	1	12	4.8
Mexico	10	0	1	11	3.1
Switzerland	5	6	0	11	11.1
Other Asia	23	19	2	44	1.7
Other Latin America	13	4	3	20	7.9
Australia and New Zealand	6	7	0	13	1.3
Other Europe	3	7	2	12	5.7
Middle East and Africa	7	3	1	11	0.7
Total	195	194	52	441	$255.7

Note: Columns may not add to totals due to rounding.
SOURCE: Betsy Buttrill White, "Foreign Banking in the United States: A Regulatory Supervision Perspective," *Quarterly Review,* Federal Reserve Bank of New York, Summer 1982, p. 50.

Types of Organizations Operated by Foreign Banks in the United States

Foreign banks use a variety of institutional arrangements to market their services in the United States. Of course, the particular vehicles used by foreign banks to enter U.S. markets depends on the financial services they offer, their expected volume of foreign business, and the nature of their domestic operations.

British banks generally have set up full-service banking facilities on the American continent by establishing branches and acquiring domestically chartered banks, principally in California and New York. Canadian banks were the first to enter the United States, establishing agency offices during the last century. The large Canadian-chartered banks then and now rely on the American money market as a source of liquidity. Canadian banks make loans to U.S. security brokers and dealers and hold substantial deposits with U.S. money-center banks. Canadian banks in the main have used four devices to carry on their operations in the United States: (1) trust companies in New York to provide for the safekeeping of valuables and the transfer and processing of bank payments; (2) New York and San Francisco agencies; (3) wholesale-retail affiliates, principally in California; and (4) representative offices. Banks in Switzerland and Germany have used branch offices and securities affiliates. Japanese banks have established wholesale banking affiliates in New York, retail banking offices in California, and agency offices in New York that service loans and finance trade.

It is important to maintain some perspective on the relative importance of foreign bank activities in the United States versus the foreign activities of U.S. banks. U.S. banking activities abroad are enormous in scope—a major factor in foreign credit markets. For example, in the London money market American banks outnumber British institutions and dominate the market for Eurodollars. It has been estimated that the London branches of U.S. banks hold about 10 percent of all bank loans in pounds sterling made to British residents. The foreign branches of American banks hold roughly three times the total assets of all foreign bank agencies, branches, and affiliates operating in the United States. This figure does not take into account the equity holdings of U.S. banks in various financial institutions abroad (including commercial banks, finance companies, leasing firms, factors, and merchant banks) which are substantial. Clearly, U.S. commercial banks play a much larger and more significant role in foreign banking markets than do their counterparts that have entered the United States. Moreover, foreign banks bring more capital annually into the United States than they remove. Certainly, the volume of foreign trade financed in the United States is much larger as a result of foreign bank activity.

Federal Regulation of Foreign Bank Activity

Until recently, there were no federal laws which regulated foreign bank activity within U.S. borders. However, Congress has been monitoring foreign bank operations since 1966 when IntraBank, a Lebanese institution, collapsed and several U.S. banks suffered severe losses. Passage of the Bank Holding Company Act Amendments of 1970 marked an initial step toward federal regulation of foreign banking. Under the terms of these amendments, any corporation controlling one or more domestic banks became subject to regulation and supervision by the Federal Reserve Board. An additional step was taken in 1972, when the Federal

Reserve began monitoring foreign bank activities by gathering monthly balance sheet reports from these banks.

However, with foreign bank operations in the United States growing more rapidly than domestic banks, the pressure on Congress for regulation of foreign banks intensified. Proponents of restrictive legislation argued that the presence of foreign banks reduced the effectiveness of domestic monetary policy, especially control over the nation's money supply. Moreover, the lack of specific regulations applying to foreign banks seemed unfair to domestic financial institutions, which must conform to an elaborate system of regulations. Perhaps more important, foreign banks could branch across state lines—a privilege denied American banks since passage of the McFadden Act in 1927.

There was also a disparity between foreign and domestic banks in the financial services each group of institutions was permitted to offer. American banks are prohibited from offering services in domestic markets not *closely related* to traditional banking services, for example, the extension of credit and the taking of deposits. Prior to the 1930s many of the nation's largest banks combined investment banking services with their traditional commercial banking functions. However, passage of the Glass-Steagall Act in 1933 prohibited American banks from investment underwriting of either corporate bonds or stock. Such a prohibition does not apply to foreign-owned banks and several foreign banking organizations moved in to take advantage of this loophole. For example, a number of West German and Swiss banks established U.S. affiliates to trade equity securities.

Foreign Banks and the International Banking Act of 1978

Responding to these various arguments, Congress passed the International Banking Act (IBA) which became law on September 17, 1978 (see Exhibit 29–3). However, it was not until November 13, 1980 that Federal Reserve regulations governing the interstate operations of U.S. branches, agencies, commercial lending companies, and subsidiaries of foreign banks became effective.

Under the terms of the IBA and subsequent regulations, branches and agencies of foreign banks with worldwide consolidated assets of $1 billion or more are subject to legal reserve requirements and federal interest-rate ceilings on their deposits. Foreign banks that maintain U.S. offices other than branches or agencies are required to register with the Secretary of the Treasury upon establishment of such an office. Each foreign bank with an office accepting deposits from the public must select a "home state." If it does not do so, the Federal Reserve Board will designate the home state for the bank and no foreign bank may directly or indirectly establish and operate a federal- or state-chartered branch outside its home

EXHIBIT 29–3

Purposes and Provisions of the International Banking Act (IBA) of 1978

Purpose: To promote competitive equality between domestic and foreign banking institutions operating in the United States.

Provisions: Limited the interstate branching of foreign banks.

Provided for federal licensing of branches and agencies of foreign banks.

Authorized the Federal Reserve Board to impose reserve requirements on branches and agencies of foreign banks.

Provided for foreign bank access to Federal Reserve services such as the discount window.

Provided for federal deposit insurance for branches of foreign banks.

Granted broader powers to Edge Act corporations of U.S. banks so they can compete more effectively with branches and agencies of foreign banks.

Subjected foreign banks operating branches and agencies to the prohibitions against nonbank business ventures of the U.S. Bank Holding Company Act.

SOURCE: Federal Reserve Bank of Chicago, *International Letter,* May 22, 1981.

state. This provision of the law limits a foreign bank's ability to accept deposits across state lines, especially retail (consumer-type) deposits.

The IBA proved to be a more lenient piece of legislation than many analysts had expected. It did not attempt to punish or discriminate against foreign banks relative to their U.S. counterparts. In fact, the act set down in law the principle of *mutual nondiscrimination,* used widely abroad as a regulatory standard. This principle permits foreign-owned banks to operate under the same conditions and to possess the same powers as domestic banks. It is a policy that avoids establishing two sets of banking regulations—one for domestic institutions and the other for foreign-owned banks. Foreign banks can even acquire majority control of U.S. Edge Acts under the terms of the IBA.

Federal regulation of foreign banks was extended a step further in 1980 when the Depository Institutions Deregulation and Monetary Control Act (DIDMCA) was passed. All foreign banking organizations offering services to U.S. residents became eligible for deposit insurance from the Federal Deposit Insurance Corporation and all such organizations, regardless of size, were required to conform to deposit reserve requirements set by the Federal Reserve Board. Moreover, when a foreign bank opens an agency, branch, or loan production office in the United States it must register as a bank holding company and conform with all holding company laws and regulations as administered by the Federal Reserve System. These new legal requirements even more firmly reflected Congress's intention to place all banks (foreign and domestic) on the same regulatory footing and on the same field of competition.

REGULATION OF THE INTERNATIONAL BANKING ACTIVITIES OF U.S. BANKS

A far more significant problem than regulating foreign banking activities in the United States is the regulation, supervision, and control of U.S. banks offering their services overseas. As we have seen, U.S. bank involvement abroad is far more extensive than foreign bank penetration of U.S. domestic markets. What limits should be placed on U.S. banks operating overseas? Who should enforce those limits?

The first of these questions is not yet fully resolved, but the second has a ready answer. The Federal Reserve Board has been designated as the chief regulatory agency for international banking activities, especially where Fed member banks are involved. A member bank choosing to expand its activities abroad through the creation of foreign branches or through investments in foreign firms must secure the approval of the Federal Reserve Board. In contrast, state laws govern the foreign operations of state-chartered banks. However, with the exception of a handful of states (notably New York), state governments have exerted only nominal control over foreign banking activities.

Of prime concern to the Federal Reserve is the protection of domestic deposits and the stability of the domestic banking system. The Fed has argued that it is difficult, if not impossible, to separate a bank's foreign operations from its domestic activities. If a foreign subsidiary gets into trouble, the danger exists that public confidence in the soundness of the domestic bank will be undermined. For this reason, the Fed, in passing upon applications of American banks to expand abroad, examines closely the condition of their domestic offices to determine if their home-based operations are adequately capitalized and if the bank possesses sufficient management skill to support both foreign and domestic operations.

The regulatory authorities would like to develop ways to "insulate" the foreign activities of U.S. banks from their domestic operations. Such insulation would grant wider latitude to banking activities abroad and, at the same time, shield domestic banks from the hazards associated with foreign operations. This problem is similar to that of trying to insulate domestic banks from the other business activities of their holding companies. Legally, one subsidiary is not liable for the debts of another. However, in practice, a domestic bank might feel compelled to aid at least its wholly owned affiliates operating in foreign markets. The practical, if not legal, links between foreign and domestic subsidiaries of multinational banks force regulators to keep close tabs on the foreign operations of all commercial banks.

One central problem the Federal Reserve Board faces in regulating multinational banking activities is the wider latitude given most foreign commercial banks by the regulatory authorities of other countries. For example, banks outside the United States frequently are permitted to make equity investments in nonfinancial corporations but domestic U.S. banks are not. The board, therefore, typically allows U.S. banks to offer a greater variety of services in foreign markets than at home, including investment banking services and noncontrolling equity investments in nonfinancial corporations. While American banks do not play an important direct role in our own capital markets, the broader powers available to them for international operations have brought them into the long-term Eurobond market, as we saw earlier in this chapter. The Fed argues that banking regulations in the United States reflect this nation's views on how much competition there should be in the financial system. However, competition in foreign markets depends on the policies of other nations, and Federal Reserve officials have preferred to leave such questions to the host country. Thus, the Fed tries to balance freedom against risk in deciding on the proper scope of multinational banking activities.

PROBLEMS AND THE FUTURE OF INTERNATIONAL BANKING

Early in 1974 the Nixon administration announced the lifting of controls on loans extended by domestic financial institutions for offshore projects. Many experts interpreted the move as encouraging the growth of U.S.-based international finance, especially from banks headquartered in New York City, which would become even more of a world financial center. In the long run the development of a more efficient, responsive, and viable system of international banking seems likely now that the controls are gone. Since the lifting of controls, however, other developments have raised serious questions about the future stability of multinational banking.

The Risks of International Lending

For one thing, lending funds in the international arena is risky—probably more risky, on average, than domestic lending. *Political risk*—the risk that government laws and regulations will change to the detriment of business interests—is particularly significant in international operations. Governments are frequently overthrown and confiscation of private property is a common occurrence in many parts of the world.[5] There is also *currency risk*, that is, the risk associated with changing relative prices of foreign currencies. The value of property pledged behind an international loan will fall if the currency of the home country is devalued, thus eroding the lender's collateral. Geography, too, works against the international lender of funds. The larger distances that frequently separate lender and borrower make it more difficult for the bank loan officer to see that the terms of a loan are being adhered to.

Beginning in the late 1970s the Federal Reserve Board, the Comptroller of the Currency, and the Federal Deposit Insurance Corporation inaugurated semiannual surveys of foreign lending by 140 U.S. banking organizations. The principal concern of these regulatory agencies was that U.S. multinational banks were overly committed to loans in certain countries where political and economic risks were unusually high. If this were the case, it might threaten the confidence of the public in the stability and soundness of this nation's largest banks. By December 1983, the federal banking agencies discovered, foreign loans held by major U.S. banks approached $360 billion. In the mid-1980s many of these loans had to have their payments rescheduled and many international banks felt compelled to tighten their credit standards. This impact of these changing standards for foreign lending was felt in the United States as the American balance-of-payments position deteriorated.

As shown in Exhibit 29–4, most loans extended by U.S. multinational banks were made to industrially developed nations and to Central and South America. About 40 percent of the loans extended by these U.S.-based banks flowed to residents of Switzerland and to other developed nations in the Group of Ten (G–10).[6] However, close to a third of all the foreign loans were made to lesser developed countries—a number of which were in serious financial difficulty. Examples included Argentina, Brazil, and Mexico. Fortunately, about two thirds of the loans to distant nations were short term (maturity of one year or less) and a slight majority

---

[5] Many financial analysts often lump political and other risks in international lending under the general term, *country risk*. This is the possibility that governments borrowing money from multinational banks may be unable or unwilling to repay and that private borrowers may, because of law and regulation, be unable to pay on their loans. For example, private borrowers may be prevented from paying due to *transfer risk*—a component of country risk in which a nation prohibits outflows of capital, dividends, or interest payments due to an internal shortage of foreign exchange. The other component of country risk—*political risk*—arises when loans cannot be repaid due to war, revolution, or changes in regulatory philosophy that adversely affect the ability of a borrower to fulfill a debt obligation.

[6] The Group of Ten countries include Belgium-Luxembourg, Canada, France, West Germany, Italy, Japan, the Netherlands, Sweden, Switzerland, and the United Kingdom.

were to banks themselves. It seems clear that, on the whole, multinational banks are relatively conservative lenders, directing their credits mainly to large bank, corporate, and governmental borrowers situated mainly in Western Europe. Moreover, the bulk of such loans (close to 60 percent) are concentrated in the nine largest U.S. banks, as Exhibit 29–4 suggests. This is a potentially troublesome situation, however, because hundreds of smaller banks keep sizable deposits with those leading multinationals and would be themselves threatened if any of the top banks became insolvent.

Public Confidence and Bank Failures

The key problem in the international banking field today is the preservation of public confidence in the banking system. Essentially, this means protecting the major multinationals against ultimate failure. This problem charged into the headlines in 1974 when both Franklin National Bank in New York, then the 20th largest U.S. bank, and Bankhaus Herstatt of West Germany were forced into bankruptcy. More recently Continental Illinois Bank of Chicago had to be bailed out by a $4 billion-plus loan from the Federal Deposit Insurance Corporation. In the wake of these major bank problems, public confidence in virtually all of the world's multinational banks was shaken. International lending, particularly in the Eurodollar market, was often limited to the largest, prime-quality borrowers, and smaller banks were forced to pay substantially higher rates in order to attract funds. Many loan syndicates disbanded and business investment slowed.

In order to avert future failures and serious financial difficulties among the world's largest banks, regulatory authorities in the United States and elsewhere today look closely at the *capital positions* of multinational banks. Regulators have urged a slower, more considered expansion of international loans, avoiding excessive credit exposure in loans to any one country, especially to nonoil-producing nations of the Third World. This is coupled today with an insistence on adequate levels of equity capital, adjusted for differences in loan risk among major banks. For example, in June 1983 the Federal Reserve and the Comptroller of the Currency issued minimum capital guidelines for major U.S. multinational banks. Unfortunately, determining what is an adequate capital position to support foreign banking activities is a complicated problem. Fluctuations in foreign exchange rates, barriers to the flow of information, and foreign political developments add to the unique risks inherent in international banking.

To further ensure that U.S. multinational banks adhere to more stringent regulatory standards in making foreign loans, Congress passed the

EXHIBIT 29–4

Foreign loans by major U.S. banks (end of December 1983)

Gross Outstanding Claims ($ million)

Country	Total	By Type of Borrower			By Remaining Maturity			By Size of U.S. Bank		
		Banks	Public Borrowers	Private Nonbank Borrowers	One-Year and under	Over One Year–Five Years	Over Five Years	Largest 9 Banks	Next 15 Banks	All Others
G–10 and Switzerland:										
Belgium-Luxembourg	10,982	8,912	1,297	772	9,541	1,251	190	6,151	2,486	2,345
Canada	11,877	7,403	606	3,868	8,878	1,498	1,500	6,030	2,146	3,701
France	13,757	10,443	1,821	1,493	10,785	1,837	1,134	8,501	2,739	2,517
Germany, Federal Republic of	6,051	1,820	637	3,593	4,820	1,004	227	4,911	585	555
Italy	9,983	5,979	2,354	1,651	6,835	2,421	727	5,340	2,555	2,088
Japan	21,308	13,834	112	7,361	17,052	3,900	356	13,065	3,661	4,582
Netherlands	3,371	2,034	115	1,222	2,639	428	305	1,925	668	778
Sweden	5,465	3,035	1,608	822	3,662	1,517	286	2,062	1,372	2,030
Switzerland	3,673	1,877	164	1,633	3,260	332	81	2,408	440	824
United Kingdom	50,299	39,295	968	10,036	44,631	3,603	2,065	21,800	9,478	19,021
Subtotal	136,767	94,632	9,682	32,452	112,104	17,791	6,872	72,194	26,131	38,442
Non G–10 developed countries:										
Australia	5,735	872	526	4,338	2,681	1,536	1,518	3,919	1,065	752
Denmark	3,682	1,049	1,208	1,425	1,560	1,604	518	2,230	611	841
Greece	3,426	289	820	2,317	1,339	1,350	738	3,034	255	137
Norway	3,423	815	95	2,513	1,458	1,306	659	2,654	339	430
South Africa	4,637	2,936	487	1,213	3,881	700	56	3,158	838	641
Spain	6,434	2,638	1,563	2,233	3,455	1,912	1,067	3,994	1,322	1,118
Other	10,247	4,278	3,970	2,000	5,744	2,905	1,598	6,062	2,373	1,811
Subtotal	37,584	12,877	8,669	16,039	20,118	11,313	6,154	25,051	6,803	5,730
Eastern Europe:										
Poland	1,067	449	610	7	379	526	161	682	184	200
Yugoslavia	2,432	1,400	656	376	887	1,210	335	1,557	456	420
Other	2,038	543	1,460	35	1,042	904	92	1,361	280	396
Subtotal	5,537	2,392	2,726	418	2,308	2,640	588	3,600	920	1,016

OPEC members:									
Ecuador	2,086	420	1,238	428	1,297	596	193	1,229	364	493
Indonesia	3,559	370	1,085	2,104	1,986	945	627	3,026	371	163
Nigeria	2,066	349	1,553	164	754	1,090	222	1,532	361	174
Saudi Arabia	2,192	589	23	1,579	1,763	281	147	1,853	234	105
Venezuela	11,257	2,526	5,346	3,385	8,278	2,554	426	7,636	2,136	1,486
Other	4,974	2,688	1,408	879	3,793	901	280	3,626	904	441
Subtotal	26,134	6,942	10,653	8,539	17,871	6,367	1,895	18,902	4,370	2,862
Non-OPEC LDCs/Latin America and Caribbean:									
Argentina	8,504	2,292	3,596	2,616	6,058	1,888	558	5,354	1,969	1,181
Brazil	20,653	8,207	8,250	4,196	8,163	7,355	5,134	13,298	4,290	3,065
Chile	6,200	3,136	1,754	1,311	2,800	2,512	888	3,438	1,294	1,468
Colombia	3,316	1,408	1,051	857	2,140	662	515	2,240	563	513
Mexico	26,338	4,474	12,008	9,856	13,301	7,516	5,520	14,127	5,324	6,887
Peru	2,495	516	1,610	370	1,537	707	251	1,353	730	413
Other	4,162	567	2,892	701	2,009	1,576	579	2,766	691	704
Subtotal	71,668	20,600	31,161	19,907	36,008	22,216	13,445	42,576	14,861	14,231
Non-OPEC LDCs/Asia:									
China, Taiwan	3,746	1,008	1,295	1,444	1,973	1,182	591	2,524	690	533
Israel	2,093	1,638	300	155	1,693	340	59	1,213	283	597
Korea, South	11,482	6,355	2,282	2,844	8,260	2,264	957	6,650	2,712	2,120
Philippines	6,062	1,285	2,795	1,982	3,774	1,496	792	3,931	1,251	880
Thailand	2,102	1,060	403	638	1,656	358	89	1,374	518	210
Other	4,751	1,164	2,180	1,408	2,516	1,178	1,059	3,754	670	326
Subtotal	30,236	12,510	9,255	8,471	19,872	6,818	3,547	19,446	6,124	4,666
Non-OPEC LDCs/Africa	4,850	1,808	2,204	839	3,329	1,113	408	3,800	594	456
Total Non-OPEC LDCs	106,754	34,918	42,620	29,217	59,209	30,147	17,400	65,822	21,579	19,353
Offshore banking centers	43,530	31,886	947	10,696	37,470	4,167	1,894	21,083	8,016	14,430
International and regional organizations	1,042	—	1,042	—	467	382	193	445	44	553
Grand total	357,348	183,648	76,340	97,360	249,544	72,807	34,997	207,097	67,865	82,386

Note: The total capital of the reporting banks, including equity, subordinated notes and debentures, and provisions for loan loss in all reporting banks is $79.3 billion; nine largest banks $31.5 billion; fifteen other large banks $14.9 billion; and all other reporting banks $33.0 billion. The total assets of the reporting banks are: all reporting banks, $1,336 billion; nine largest banks, $582 billion; fifteen other large banks, $262 billion; and all reporting banks $493 billion.
SOURCE: Federal Financial Institutions Examination Council, *Country Exposure Lending Survey*, Washington, D.C., December 1983.

International Lending Supervision Act in 1983. This law ordered federal bank regulatory agencies to prepare new rules requiring U.S. banks to:

1. Maintain special reserves against foreign loans in those instances where the quality of a bank's assets has been impaired by protracted borrower inability to pay out loans.
2. Limit loan rescheduling fees that may be charged troubled foreign borrowers.
3. Disclose a bank's exposure to foreign borrowers.
4. Hold minimum levels of capital as protection for an international bank's depositors.
5. Conduct feasibility studies of large foreign projects involving mining, metal, or mineral primary processing operations before approving a loan.

Many members of Congress saw this law as an essential precondition before the United States approved any additional contributions to the International Monetary Fund to support further growth in world trade and finance.

PROSPECTS AND ISSUES IN THE 1980s

These recent trends suggest a much different future for international banking than seemed likely in the 1960s and 70s. Growth—limited by capital and the availability of experienced management—should be more gradual and loan quality more of a factor in future extensions of credit to businesses and governments abroad. Continuing rapid expansion of foreign banking activities in the United States may be anticipated. It is significant, perhaps, that the absorption of New York's failed Franklin National Bank was carried out by a foreign-owned banking consortium, European-American Bank and Trust Company. And more recently, Harris Trust, one of the top 10 U.S. banks, was the acquisition target of a leading Canadian bank.

Certainly a number of critical questions lie ahead for international banking. For example, to what extent can and will the regulatory authorities of different nations cooperate to control foreign banking activities? How can we reconcile different banking rules from one country to the next so as to promote competition and innovation, but also public safety? What is an appropriate capital position for banks engaged in foreign lending, and how does this relate to their domestic capital needs? Where must regulation end and the free play of market forces be allowed to operate in international banking? Should multinational banks be subject to the same rigid controls as domestic banks? What impact are developments in multinational banking, especially in the Eurocurrency market, likely to have on domestic financial markets, and how can domestic monetary policy best deal with that impact?

These are perplexing issues that have few clear answers. However, the importance of international banking and the penetration of domestic markets all over the globe by foreign banking institutions demand that effective answers be found that strengthen the system and provide a basis for future growth and development.

STUDY QUESTIONS

1. What are the essential differences between the following types of banking organizations?
    a. International banking departments.
    b. Edge Act corporations.
    c. Agreement corporations.
    d. Shell branches.
    e. Representative offices.
    f. Full-service branches.
    g. Consortiums.

2. In what parts of the world are most U.S. banking offices located? Can you explain why?

3. Explain why many smaller U.S. regional banks have entered the international banking field in recent years. What specific problems is management likely to encounter in trying to establish banking facilities and offer financial services abroad?

4. What are the principal powers and functions of Edge Act Corporations? How did the International Banking Act of 1978 affect Edges?

5. What role have Edge Acts played in the U.S. branch banking controversy? What are LPOs, and why are they important in both domestic and international banking markets?

6. Explain why foreign banks have entered the United States in such large numbers in recent years. What types of organizations do these banks operate in the United States?

7. What federal regulations apply to foreign banks operating in the United States today? What factors motivated Congress to pass the International Banking Act of 1978?

8. What federal agency is the chief regulator of international banking in the United States? What are its principal powers?

9. What is the principle of mutual nondiscrimination? Do you agree with this principle? What problems could it create for regulators?

10. What major problems have been encountered by the international banking community in recent years? How have these problems been dealt with?

SELECTED REFERENCES

Abrams, Richard K. "Regional Banks and International Banking." *Economic Review,* Federal Reserve Bank of Kansas City, November 1980, pp. 3–14.

Board of Governors of the Federal Reserve System. "Implementation of the International Banking Act." *Federal Reserve Bulletin,* October 1979, pp. 785–96.

Chrystal, K. A. "International Banking Facilities." *Review,* Federal Reserve Bank of St. Louis, April 1984, pp. 5–11.

Edwards, Franklin R. *Regulation of Foreign Banking in the United States: International Reciprocity and Federal-State Conflicts.* New York: Columbia University, Graduate School of Business, 1974.

Houpt, James V., and Michael G. Martinson. *Foreign Subsidiaries of U.S. Banking Organizations.* Staff Economic Study, Board of Governors of the Federal Reserve System, 1982.

Klopstock, Fred H. "Foreign Banks in the United States: Scope and Growth of Operations." *Monthly Review,* Federal Reserve Bank of New York, June 1973, pp. 140–54.

Lees, Francis A. *International Banking and Finance.* New York: John Wiley & Sons, 1973.

Pardee, Scott E. "Prospects for LDC Debt and the Dollar." *Economic Review,* Federal Reserve Bank of Kansas City, January 1984, pp. 3–8.

Rose, Peter S. "Foreign Banking in the United States." *The Canadian Banker and ICB Review,* 1976, pp. 58–61.

Rose, Peter S., and Habib G. Bassoul, "Edge Acts: Outside-In," *The Canadian Banker and ICB Review,* 1980, pp. 52–56.

Segala, John P. "A Summary of the International Banking Act of 1978." *Economic Review,* Federal Reserve Bank of Richmond, January–February 1979, pp. 16–21.

Teeters, Nancy H. "The Role of Banks in the International Financial System." *Federal Reserve Bulletin,* September 1983, pp. 663–71.

Thompson, I. B. "The International Banking Activities of Regional Banks." *American Banker,* March 23, 1979, pp. 14, 36, and 38.

The Canadian Bankers' Association. *Importing and Exporting: How Canadian Banks Can Help.* Montreal, Can., 1984.

White, Betsy Butrill. "Foreign Banking in the United States: A Regulatory and Supervisory Perspective." *Quarterly Review,* Federal Reserve Bank of New York, Summer 1982, pp. 48–58.

Appendix A: Security Credit Ratings

SECURITY CREDIT RATINGS

What Are Credit Ratings?

As discussed in Chapter 10, corporate and municipal debt securities sold in the financial markets today generally must carry a credit rating assigned by one or more rating agencies. The two most widely respected credit-rating agencies in the United States are Moody's Investor Service and Standard & Poor's Corporation, both headquartered in New York City. The ratings assigned by these private companies are generally regarded in the investment community as an objective evaluation of the probability that a borrower will *default* on a given security issue.

Default occurs whenever a security issuer is late in making one or more payments that it is legally obligated to make. In the case of a bond, when any interest or principal payment falls due and is not made on time, the bond is legally in default. While many defaulted bonds ultimately resume the payment of principal and interest, others never do, and the issuing company winds up in bankruptcy proceedings. In most instances, holders of bonds issued by a bankrupt company receive only pennies on each dollar invested, once the company's assets are sold at auction. Thus, the investor who holds title to bankrupt bonds typically loses both principal and interest. It is no wonder, then, that security ratings are so closely followed by investors. In fact, many investors accept the ratings assigned by credit agencies as a substitute for their own investigation of a security's investment quality.

Factors Affecting Assigned Ratings

Each rating assigned to a security issue is a reflection of at least three factors: (1) the character and terms of the particular security being issued;

(2) the probability that the issuer will default on the security and the ability and willingness of the issuer to make timely payments as specified in the indenture (contract) accompanying the security; and (3) the degree of protection afforded investors if the security issuer is liquidated, reorganized, and/or declares bankruptcy. As a matter of practice, the investment agencies focus principally upon: (1) the past and probable future cash flows of the security issuer as an indication of the institution's ability to service its debt; (2) the volume and composition of outstanding debt; and (3) the stability of the issuer's cash flows over time. Other factors influencing quality ratings are the value of assets pledged as collateral for a security and the security's priority of claim against the issuing firm's assets. Quality analysts also place heavy emphasis upon interest-coverage ratios and liquidity of the issuing firm.

The rating agencies stress that their evaluations of individual security issues are not recommendations to buy or sell or an indication of the suitability of any particular security for the investor. The agencies do not act as financial advisers to the businesses or units of government whose securities they rate, which helps to promote objectivity in assigning quality ratings.[1] Both domestic and foreign securities are rated using the same criteria.

Standard & Poor's Corporate and Municipal Bond Ratings

The credit ratings assigned to corporate and municipal bonds by Standard & Poor's Corporation are listed below along with the definitions used by S&P for each rating category:[2]

1. AAA—Bonds rated AAA have the highest rating assigned by Standard & Poor's to a debt obligation. Capacity to pay interest and repay principal is extremely strong.

2. AA—Bonds rated AA have a very strong capacity to pay interest and repay principal and differ from the highest-rated issues only in small degree.

3. A—Bonds rated A have a strong capacity to pay interest and repay principal, although they are somewhat more susceptible to the adverse effects of changes in circumstances and economic conditions than bonds in higher-rated categories.

---

[1] Fees are assessed for ratings according to the time and effort expended in gathering sufficient information to determine an appropriate rating. These fees are usually paid either by the security issuer or by the firm or syndicate underwriting the security issue.

[2] See Standard & Poor's Corporation, *Bond Guide,* October 1980, p. 6.

4. BBB—Bonds rated BBB are regarded as having an adequate capacity to pay interest and repay principal. Whereas they normally exhibit adequate protection parameters, adverse economic conditions or changing circumstances are more likely to lead to a weakened capacity to pay interest and repay principal for bonds in this category than for bonds in higher-rated categories.

5. BB, B, CCC, CC—Bonds rated BB, B, CCC, and CC are regarded, on balance, as predominantly speculative with respect to capacity to pay interest and repay principal in accordance with the terms of the obligation. BB indicates the lowest degree of speculation and CC the highest degree of speculation. While such bonds will likely have some quality and protective characteristics, these are outweighed by large uncertainties or major risk exposures to adverse conditions.

6. C—The rating C is reserved for income bonds on which no interest is being paid.

7. D—Bonds rated D are in default, and payment of interest and/or repayment of principal is in arrears.

The ratings from AA to B may be modified by the addition of a plus· (+) or minus (−) sign to show relative standing within the major rating categories. A plus (+) sign indicates a bond of better-than-average quality in the particular rating category chosen, while a minus (−) sign denotes a bond that is worse than average in that category. Provisional ratings may also be assigned, as indicated by the letter *P*. According to Standard & Poor's, this may be interpreted as follows:

> A provisional rating assumes the successful completion of the project being financed by the bonds being rated and indicates that payment of debt service requirements is largely or entirely dependent upon the successful and timely completion of the project. This rating, however, while addressing credit quality subsequent to completion of the project, makes no comment on the likelihood of, or the risk of default upon failure of, such completion. The investor should exercise his own judgment with respect to such likelihood and risk. When no rating is requested for a security or the agency feels that insufficient information exists to assign a rating, it will designate the security as NR.[3]

S&P publishes a *Bond Guide* each month that contains data revised through the last business day of the preceding month. The S&P *Bond Guide* gives a brief description of each security issue, including its yield, listing status, eligibility for certain institutional investors, form (coupon or registered), redemption provisions, and earnings coverage.

---

[3] Standard & Poor's Corporation, *Bond Guide,* October 1980, p. 6.

Moody's Investors Service

Beginning in 1909, John Moody developed and published a simple system of letter grades which indicated the relative investment quality of corporate bonds. Today, Moody's Investors Service rates thousands of issues of corporate and municipal bonds, commercial paper, short-term municipal notes, and preferred stock. These security ratings are reported in *Moody's Bond Record,* which is published monthly. In addition to assigning issue ratings, Moody's also notes for its subscribers the essential terms on each security issue; dates when interest, principal, or dividend payments are due; call provisions (if any); registration status; bid and asked price quotations; yield to maturity; tax status; coverage; and amount of securities outstanding.

Moody's Corporate and Municipal Bond Ratings

The credit ratings assigned by Moody's to corporate and state and local government (municipal) bonds are listed below with the definitions of each rating category:[4]

Aaa

Bonds which are rated Aaa are judged to be of the best quality. They carry the smallest degree of investment risk and are generally referred to as "gilt edge." Interest payments are protected by a large or by an exceptionally stable margin and principal is secure. While the various protective elements are likely to change, such changes as can be visualized are most unlikely to impair the fundamentally strong position of such issues.

Aa

Bonds which are rated Aa are judged to be of high quality by all standards. Together with the Aaa group they comprise what are generally known as high-grade bonds. They are rated lower than the best bonds because margins of protection may not be as large as in Aaa securities or fluctuation of protective elements may be of greater amplitude or there may be other elements present which make the long-term risks appear somewhat larger than in Aaa securities.

A

Bonds which are rated A possess many favorable investment attributes and are to be considered as upper medium-grade obligations. Factors giving security to principal and interest are considered adequate but elements may be present which suggest a susceptibility to impairment sometime in the future.

Baa

Bonds which are rated Baa are considered as medium-grade obligations, i.e., they are neither highly protected nor poorly secured. Interest payments

---

[4] See *Moody's Bond Record,* October 1979.

and principal security appear adequate for the present but certain protective elements may be lacking or may be characteristically unreliable over any great length of time. Such bonds lack outstanding investment characteristics and, in fact, have speculative characteristics as well.

Ba

Bonds which are rated Ba are judged to have speculative elements; their future cannot be considered as well assured. Often the protection of interest and principal payments may be very moderate and thereby not well safeguarded during both good and bad times over the future. Uncertainty of position characterizes bonds in this class.

B

Bonds which are rated B generally lack characteristics of a desirable investment. Assurance of interest and principal payments or of maintenance of other terms of the contract over any long period of time may be small.

Caa

Bonds which are rated Caa are of poor standing. Such issues may be in default and there may be present elements of danger with respect to principal or interest.

Ca

Bonds which are rated Ca represent obligations which are speculative in some degree. Such issues are often in default or have other marked shortcomings.

C

Bonds which are rated C are the lowest rated class of bonds and issues so rated are to be regarded as having extremely poor prospects of ever attaining any real investment standing.

Con. (—)

Bonds for which the security depends on the completion of some act or the fulfillment of some condition are rated conditionally. These are bonds secured by (a) earnings of projects under construction, (b) earnings of projects unseasoned in operation experience, (c) rentals which begin when facilities are completed, or (d) payments to which some other limiting condition attaches. Parenthetical rating denotes probable credit stature upon completion of construction or elimination of basis of condition.

Like Standard & Poor's Corporation, Moody's Investors Service will sometimes affix an additional symbol to its bond ratings to denote finer gradations of quality. For example, an A-rated municipal bond that appears to be superior to other bonds in this category may be designated as A1. Similarly, a better-than-average Baa obligation may be labeled Baa1.

Moody's Commercial Paper Ratings

Promissory notes sold in the open market by large corporations and having an original maturity of nine months or less are known as commercial paper. Moody's assigns those commercial notes it is willing to rate to one of three quality categories.[5]

Prime-1 (or P-1)—Highest quality

Prime-2 (or P-2)—Higher quality

Prime-3 (or P-3)—High quality

Moody's Ratings of Short-Term Municipal Notes

Short-term securities issued by states, cities, counties, and other local governments are also rated by Moody's as to their investment quality. For these short-term issues Moody's uses the rating symbol MIG, meaning Moody's Investment Grade. As shown below, only four rating categories are used and speculative issues or those for which adequate information is not available are not rated. The rating categories are as follows:[6]

MIG 1

Loans bearing this designation are of the best quality, enjoying strong protection from established cash flows of funds for their servicing or from established and broad-based access to the market for refinancing, or both.

MIG 2

Loans bearing this designation are of high quality, with margins of protection ample though not so large as in the preceding group.

MIG 3

Loans bearing this designation are of favorable quality, with all security elements accounted for but lacking the undeniable strength of the preceding grades. Market access for refinancing, in particular, is likely to be less well established.

MIG 4

Loans bearing this designation are of adequate quality, carrying specific risk but having protection commonly regarded as required of an investment security and not distinctly or predominantly speculative.

Moody's Preferred Stock Ratings

Beginning in 1973 Moody's extended its rating system to include preferred stock issues. As discussed in Chapter 21, preferred shares occupy middle ground between common stock and corporate bonds in terms of protection afforded the investor. Preferred dividend payments are not required as are interest payments on bonds and, in the event of liquidation, preferred stockholders can recover their funds only after

---

[5] See *Moody's Bond Record,* October 1979.

[6] See *Moody's Bond Record,* October 1979.

bondholders and other creditors are paid. However, preferred shareholders have priority in claims against both current earnings and assets ahead of common stockholders. Because preferred stock does have a different status than bonds, Moody's stresses that preferred stock ratings should not be compared in absolute terms with bond ratings.

The preferred stock ratings currently assigned by Moody's are as follows:[7]

aaa

An issue which is rated "aaa" is considered to be a top-quality preferred stock. This rating indicates good asset protection and the least risk of dividend impairment within the universe of preferred stocks.

aa

An issue which is rated "aa" is considered a high-grade preferred stock. This rating indicates that there is reasonable assurance that earnings and asset protection will remain relatively well maintained in the foreseeable future.

a

An issue which is rated "a" is considered to be an upper-medium-grade preferred stock. While risks are judged to be somewhat greater than in the "aaa" and "aa" classifications, earnings and asset protection are, nevertheless, expected to be maintained at adequate levels.

baa

An issue which is rated "baa" is considered to be medium grade, neither highly protected nor poorly secured. Earnings and asset protection appear adequate at present but may be questionable over any great length of time.

ba

An issue which is rated "ba" is considered to have speculative elements and its future cannot be considered well assured. Earnings and asset protection may be very moderate and not well safeguarded during adverse periods. Uncertainty of position characterizes preferred stocks in this class.

b

An issue which is rated "b" generally lacks the characteristics of a desirable investment. Assurance of dividend payments and maintenance of other terms of the issue over any long period of time may be small.

caa

An issue which is rated "caa" is likely to be in arrears on dividend payments. This rating designation does not purport to indicate the future status of payments.

---

[7] See *Moody's Bond Record,* October 1979.

Appendix B: Present Value, Annuity, and Compound Interest Tables

Present Value Table

Present Value of $1

Years Hence	1%	2%	4%	6%	8%	10%	12%	14%	15%	16%	18%	20%	22%	24%	25%	26%	28%	30%	35%	40%	45%	50%
1	0.990	0.980	0.962	0.943	0.926	0.909	0.893	0.877	0.870	0.862	0.847	0.833	0.820	0.806	0.800	0.794	0.781	0.769	0.741	0.714	0.690	0.667
2	0.980	0.961	0.925	0.890	0.857	0.826	0.797	0.769	0.756	0.743	0.718	0.694	0.672	0.650	0.640	0.630	0.610	0.592	0.549	0.510	0.476	0.444
3	0.971	0.942	0.889	0.840	0.794	0.751	0.712	0.675	0.658	0.641	0.609	0.579	0.551	0.524	0.512	0.500	0.477	0.455	0.406	0.364	0.328	0.296
4	0.961	0.924	0.855	0.792	0.735	0.683	0.636	0.592	0.572	0.552	0.516	0.482	0.451	0.423	0.410	0.397	0.373	0.350	0.301	0.260	0.226	0.198
5	0.951	0.906	0.822	0.747	0.681	0.621	0.567	0.519	0.497	0.476	0.437	0.402	0.370	0.341	0.328	0.315	0.291	0.269	0.223	0.186	0.156	0.132
6	0.942	0.888	0.790	0.705	0.630	0.564	0.507	0.456	0.432	0.410	0.370	0.335	0.303	0.275	0.262	0.250	0.227	0.207	0.165	0.133	0.108	0.088
7	0.933	0.871	0.760	0.665	0.583	0.513	0.452	0.400	0.376	0.354	0.314	0.279	0.249	0.222	0.210	0.198	0.178	0.159	0.122	0.095	0.074	0.059
8	0.923	0.853	0.731	0.627	0.540	0.467	0.404	0.351	0.327	0.305	0.266	0.233	0.204	0.179	0.168	0.157	0.139	0.123	0.091	0.068	0.051	0.039
9	0.914	0.837	0.703	0.592	0.500	0.424	0.361	0.308	0.284	0.263	0.225	0.194	0.167	0.144	0.134	0.125	0.108	0.094	0.067	0.048	0.035	0.026
10	0.905	0.820	0.676	0.558	0.463	0.386	0.322	0.270	0.247	0.227	0.191	0.162	0.137	0.116	0.107	0.099	0.085	0.073	0.050	0.035	0.024	0.017
11	0.896	0.804	0.650	0.527	0.429	0.350	0.287	0.237	0.215	0.195	0.162	0.135	0.112	0.094	0.086	0.079	0.066	0.056	0.037	0.025	0.017	0.012
12	0.887	0.788	0.625	0.497	0.397	0.319	0.257	0.208	0.187	0.168	0.137	0.112	0.092	0.076	0.069	0.062	0.052	0.043	0.027	0.018	0.012	0.008
13	0.879	0.773	0.601	0.469	0.368	0.290	0.229	0.182	0.163	0.145	0.116	0.093	0.075	0.061	0.055	0.050	0.040	0.033	0.020	0.013	0.008	0.005
14	0.870	0.758	0.577	0.442	0.340	0.263	0.205	0.160	0.141	0.125	0.099	0.078	0.062	0.049	0.044	0.039	0.032	0.025	0.015	0.009	0.006	0.003
15	0.861	0.743	0.555	0.417	0.315	0.239	0.183	0.140	0.123	0.108	0.084	0.065	0.051	0.040	0.035	0.031	0.025	0.020	0.011	0.006	0.004	0.002
16	0.853	0.728	0.534	0.394	0.292	0.218	0.163	0.123	0.107	0.093	0.071	0.054	0.042	0.032	0.028	0.025	0.019	0.015	0.008	0.005	0.003	0.002
17	0.844	0.714	0.513	0.371	0.270	0.198	0.146	0.108	0.093	0.080	0.060	0.045	0.034	0.026	0.023	0.020	0.015	0.012	0.006	0.003	0.002	0.001
18	0.836	0.700	0.494	0.350	0.250	0.180	0.130	0.095	0.081	0.069	0.051	0.038	0.028	0.021	0.018	0.016	0.012	0.009	0.005	0.002	0.001	0.001
19	0.828	0.686	0.475	0.331	0.232	0.164	0.116	0.083	0.070	0.060	0.043	0.031	0.023	0.017	0.014	0.012	0.009	0.007	0.003	0.002	0.001	
20	0.820	0.673	0.456	0.312	0.215	0.149	0.104	0.073	0.061	0.051	0.037	0.026	0.019	0.014	0.012	0.010	0.007	0.005	0.002	0.001	0.001	
21	0.811	0.660	0.439	0.294	0.199	0.135	0.093	0.064	0.053	0.044	0.031	0.022	0.015	0.011	0.009	0.008	0.006	0.004	0.002	0.001		
22	0.803	0.647	0.422	0.278	0.184	0.123	0.083	0.056	0.046	0.038	0.026	0.018	0.013	0.009	0.007	0.006	0.004	0.003	0.001	0.001		
23	0.795	0.634	0.406	0.262	0.170	0.112	0.074	0.049	0.040	0.033	0.022	0.015	0.010	0.007	0.006	0.005	0.003	0.002	0.001			
24	0.788	0.622	0.390	0.247	0.158	0.102	0.066	0.043	0.035	0.028	0.019	0.013	0.008	0.006	0.005	0.004	0.003	0.002	0.001			
25	0.780	0.610	0.375	0.233	0.146	0.092	0.059	0.038	0.030	0.024	0.016	0.010	0.007	0.005	0.004	0.003	0.002	0.001	0.001			
26	0.772	0.598	0.361	0.220	0.135	0.084	0.053	0.033	0.026	0.021	0.014	0.009	0.006	0.004	0.003	0.002	0.002	0.001				
27	0.764	0.586	0.347	0.207	0.125	0.076	0.047	0.029	0.023	0.018	0.011	0.007	0.005	0.003	0.002	0.002	0.001	0.001				
28	0.757	0.574	0.333	0.196	0.116	0.069	0.042	0.026	0.020	0.016	0.010	0.006	0.004	0.002	0.002	0.002	0.001	0.001				
29	0.749	0.563	0.321	0.185	0.107	0.063	0.037	0.022	0.017	0.014	0.008	0.005	0.003	0.002	0.002	0.001	0.001	0.001				
30	0.742	0.552	0.308	0.174	0.099	0.057	0.033	0.020	0.015	0.012	0.007	0.004	0.003	0.002	0.001	0.001	0.001					
40	0.672	0.453	0.208	0.097	0.046	0.022	0.011	0.005	0.004	0.003	0.001	0.001										
50	0.608	0.372	0.141	0.054	0.021	0.009	0.003	0.001	0.001	0.001												

SOURCE: Robert N. Anthony and James S. Reece, Accounting Principles, 4th ed. (Homewood, Ill.: Richard D. Irwin, 1979).

Annuity Table

Present Value of $1 Received Annually for N Years

Years (N)	1%	2%	4%	6%	8%	10%	12%	14%	15%	16%	18%	20%	22%	24%	25%	26%	28%	30%	35%	40%	45%	50%
1	0.990	0.980	0.962	0.943	0.926	0.909	0.893	0.877	0.870	0.862	0.847	0.833	0.820	0.806	0.800	0.794	0.781	0.769	0.741	0.714	0.690	0.667
2	1.970	1.942	1.886	1.833	1.783	1.736	1.690	1.647	1.626	1.605	1.566	1.528	1.492	1.457	1.440	1.424	1.392	1.361	1.289	1.224	1.165	1.111
3	2.941	2.884	2.775	2.673	2.577	2.487	2.402	2.322	2.283	2.246	2.174	2.106	2.042	1.981	1.952	1.923	1.868	1.816	1.696	1.589	1.493	1.407
4	3.902	3.808	3.630	3.465	3.312	3.170	3.037	2.914	2.855	2.798	2.690	2.589	2.494	2.404	2.362	2.320	2.241	2.166	1.997	1.849	1.720	1.605
5	4.853	4.713	4.452	4.212	3.993	3.791	3.605	3.433	3.352	3.274	3.127	2.991	2.864	2.745	2.689	2.635	2.532	2.436	2.220	2.035	1.876	1.737
6	5.795	5.601	5.242	4.917	4.623	4.355	4.111	3.889	3.784	3.685	3.498	3.326	3.167	3.020	2.951	2.885	2.759	2.643	2.385	2.168	1.983	1.824
7	6.728	6.472	6.002	5.582	5.206	4.868	4.564	4.288	4.160	4.039	3.812	3.605	3.416	3.242	3.161	3.083	2.937	2.802	2.508	2.263	2.057	1.883
8	7.652	7.325	6.733	6.210	5.747	5.335	4.968	4.639	4.487	4.344	4.078	3.837	3.619	3.421	3.329	3.241	3.076	2.925	2.598	2.331	2.108	1.922
9	8.566	8.162	7.435	6.802	6.247	5.759	5.328	4.946	4.772	4.607	4.303	4.031	3.786	3.566	3.463	3.366	3.184	3.019	2.665	2.379	2.144	1.948
10	9.471	8.983	8.111	7.360	6.710	6.145	5.650	5.216	5.019	4.833	4.494	4.192	3.923	3.682	3.571	3.465	3.269	3.092	2.715	2.414	2.168	1.965
11	10.368	9.787	8.760	7.887	7.139	6.495	5.937	5.453	5.234	5.029	4.656	4.327	4.035	3.776	3.656	3.544	3.335	3.147	2.757	2.438	2.185	1.977
12	11.255	10.575	9.385	8.384	7.536	6.814	6.194	5.660	5.421	5.197	4.793	4.439	4.127	3.851	3.725	3.606	3.387	3.190	2.779	2.456	2.196	1.985
13	12.134	11.343	9.986	8.853	7.904	7.103	6.424	5.842	5.583	5.342	4.910	4.533	4.203	3.912	3.780	3.656	3.427	3.223	2.799	2.468	2.204	1.990
14	13.004	12.106	10.563	9.295	8.244	7.367	6.628	6.002	5.724	5.468	5.008	4.611	4.265	3.962	3.824	3.695	3.459	3.249	2.814	2.477	2.210	1.993
15	13.865	12.849	11.118	9.712	8.559	7.606	6.811	6.142	5.847	5.575	5.092	4.675	4.315	4.001	3.859	3.726	3.483	3.268	2.825	2.484	2.214	1.995
16	14.718	13.578	11.652	10.106	8.851	7.824	6.974	6.265	5.954	5.669	5.162	4.730	4.357	4.033	3.887	3.751	3.503	3.283	2.834	2.489	2.216	1.997
17	15.562	14.292	12.166	10.477	9.122	8.022	7.120	6.373	6.047	5.749	5.222	4.775	4.391	4.059	3.910	3.771	3.518	3.295	2.840	2.492	2.218	1.998
18	16.398	14.992	12.659	10.828	9.372	8.201	7.250	6.467	6.128	5.818	5.273	4.812	4.419	4.080	3.928	3.786	3.529	3.304	2.844	2.494	2.219	1.999
19	17.226	15.678	13.134	11.158	9.604	8.365	7.366	6.550	6.198	5.877	5.316	4.844	4.442	4.097	3.942	3.799	3.539	3.311	2.848	2.496	2.220	1.999
20	18.046	16.351	13.590	11.470	9.818	8.514	7.469	6.623	6.259	5.929	5.353	4.870	4.460	4.110	3.954	3.808	3.546	3.316	2.850	2.497	2.221	1.999
21	18.857	17.011	14.029	11.764	10.017	8.649	7.562	6.687	6.312	5.973	5.384	4.891	4.476	4.121	3.963	3.816	3.551	3.320	2.852	2.498	2.221	2.000
22	19.660	17.658	14.451	12.042	10.201	8.772	7.645	6.743	6.359	6.011	5.410	4.909	4.488	4.130	3.970	3.822	3.556	3.323	2.853	2.498	2.222	2.000
23	20.456	18.292	14.857	12.303	10.371	8.883	7.718	6.792	6.399	6.044	5.432	4.925	4.499	4.137	3.976	3.827	3.559	3.325	2.854	2.499	2.222	2.000
24	21.243	18.914	15.247	12.550	10.529	8.985	7.784	6.835	6.434	6.073	5.451	4.937	4.507	4.143	3.981	3.831	3.562	3.327	2.855	2.499	2.222	2.000
25	22.023	19.523	15.622	12.783	10.675	9.077	7.843	6.873	6.464	6.097	5.467	4.948	4.514	4.147	3.985	3.834	3.564	3.329	2.856	2.499	2.222	2.000
26	22.795	20.121	15.983	13.003	10.810	9.161	7.896	6.906	6.491	6.118	5.480	4.956	4.520	4.151	3.988	3.837	3.566	3.330	2.856	2.500	2.222	2.000
27	23.560	20.707	16.330	13.211	10.935	9.237	7.943	6.935	6.514	6.136	5.492	4.964	4.524	4.154	3.990	3.839	3.567	3.331	2.856	2.500	2.222	2.000
28	24.316	21.281	16.663	13.406	11.051	9.307	7.984	6.961	6.534	6.152	5.502	4.970	4.528	4.157	3.992	3.840	3.568	3.331	2.857	2.500	2.222	2.000
29	25.066	21.844	16.984	13.591	11.158	9.370	8.022	6.983	6.551	6.166	5.510	4.975	4.531	4.159	3.994	3.841	3.569	3.332	2.857	2.500	2.222	2.000
30	25.808	22.396	17.292	13.765	11.258	9.427	8.055	7.003	6.566	6.177	5.517	4.979	4.534	4.160	3.995	3.842	3.569	3.332	2.857	2.500	2.222	2.000
40	32.835	27.355	19.793	15.046	11.925	9.779	8.244	7.105	6.642	6.234	5.548	4.997	4.544	4.166	3.999	3.846	3.571	3.333	2.857	2.500	2.222	2.000
50	39.196	31.424	21.482	15.762	12.234	9.915	8.304	7.133	6.661	6.246	5.554	4.999	4.545	4.167	4.000	3.846	3.571	3.333	2.857	2.500	2.222	2.000

SOURCE: Robert N. Anthony and James S. Reece, *Accounting Principles*, 4th ed. (Homewood, Ill.: Richard D. Irwin, 1979).

Compound Interest Rate Table

Annual Percentage Rate

Number of Periods	1.00%	1.50%	2.00%	2.50%	3.00%	3.50%	4.00%	4.50%	5.00%	6.00%	7.00%	8.00%	9.00%	10.00%	12.00%	14.00%	16.00%	18.00%
							(Future Value of $1—Principal Plus Accumulated Interest)											
1	1.010	1.015	1.020	1.025	1.030	1.035	1.040	1.045	1.050	1.060	1.070	1.080	1.090	1.100	1.120	1.140	1.160	1.180
2	1.020	1.030	1.040	1.051	1.061	1.071	1.082	1.092	1.103	1.124	1.145	1.166	1.188	1.210	1.254	1.300	1.346	1.392
3	1.030	1.046	1.061	1.077	1.093	1.109	1.125	1.141	1.158	1.191	1.225	1.260	1.295	1.331	1.405	1.482	1.561	1.643
4	1.041	1.061	1.082	1.104	1.126	1.148	1.170	1.193	1.216	1.262	1.311	1.360	1.412	1.464	1.574	1.689	1.811	1.939
5	1.051	1.077	1.104	1.131	1.159	1.188	1.217	1.246	1.276	1.338	1.403	1.469	1.539	1.611	1.762	1.925	2.100	2.288
6	1.062	1.093	1.126	1.160	1.194	1.229	1.265	1.302	1.340	1.419	1.501	1.587	1.677	1.772	1.974	2.195	2.436	2.700
7	1.072	1.110	1.149	1.189	1.230	1.272	1.316	1.361	1.407	1.504	1.606	1.714	1.828	1.949	2.211	2.502	2.826	3.185
8	1.083	1.126	1.172	1.218	1.267	1.317	1.369	1.422	1.477	1.594	1.718	1.851	1.993	2.144	2.476	2.853	3.278	3.759
9	1.094	1.143	1.195	1.249	1.305	1.363	1.423	1.486	1.551	1.689	1.838	1.999	2.172	2.358	2.773	3.252	3.803	4.435
10	1.105	1.161	1.219	1.280	1.344	1.411	1.480	1.553	1.629	1.791	1.967	2.159	2.367	2.594	3.106	3.707	4.411	5.234
11	1.116	1.178	1.243	1.312	1.384	1.460	1.539	1.623	1.710	1.898	2.105	2.332	2.580	2.853	3.479	4.226	5.117	6.176
12	1.127	1.196	1.268	1.345	1.426	1.511	1.601	1.696	1.796	2.012	2.252	2.518	2.813	3.138	3.896	4.818	5.936	7.288
14	1.149	1.232	1.319	1.413	1.513	1.619	1.732	1.852	1.980	2.261	2.579	2.937	3.342	3.797	4.887	6.261	7.988	10.147
16	1.173	1.269	1.373	1.485	1.605	1.734	1.873	2.022	2.183	2.540	2.952	3.426	3.970	4.595	6.130	8.137	10.748	14.129
18	1.196	1.307	1.428	1.560	1.702	1.857	2.026	2.208	2.407	2.854	3.380	3.996	4.717	5.560	7.690	10.575	14.463	19.673

20	1.220	1.347	1.486	1.639	1.806	1.990	2.191	2.412	2.653	3.207	3.870	4.661	5.604	6.727	9.646	13.743	19.461	27.393
22	1.245	1.388	1.546	1.722	1.916	2.132	2.370	2.634	2.925	3.604	4.430	5.437	6.659	8.140	12.100	17.861	26.186	38.142
24	1.270	1.430	1.608	1.809	2.033	2.283	2.563	2.876	3.225	4.049	5.072	6.341	7.911	9.850	15.179	23.212	35.236	53.109
26	1.295	1.473	1.673	1.900	2.157	2.446	2.772	3.141	3.556	4.549	5.807	7.396	9.399	11.918	19.040	30.167	47.414	73.949
28	1.321	1.517	1.741	1.996	2.288	2.620	2.999	3.430	3.920	5.112	6.649	8.627	11.167	14.421	23.884	39.204	63.800	102.967
30	1.348	1.563	1.811	2.098	2.427	2.807	3.243	3.745	4.322	5.743	7.612	10.063	13.268	17.449	29.960	50.950	85.850	143.371
32	1.375	1.610	1.884	2.204	2.575	3.007	3.508	4.090	4.765	6.453	8.715	11.737	15.763	21.114	37.582	66.215	115.520	199.629
34	1.403	1.659	1.961	2.315	2.732	3.221	3.794	4.466	5.253	7.251	9.978	13.690	18.728	25.548	47.143	86.053	155.443	277.964
36	1.431	1.709	2.040	2.433	2.898	3.450	4.104	4.877	5.792	8.147	11.424	15.968	22.251	30.913	59.136	111.834	209.164	387.037
38	1.460	1.761	2.122	2.556	3.075	3.696	4.439	5.326	6.385	9.154	13.079	18.625	26.437	37.404	74.180	145.340	281.452	538.910
40	1.489	1.814	2.208	2.685	3.262	3.959	4.801	5.816	7.040	10.286	14.974	21.725	31.409	45.259	93.051	188.884	378.721	750.378
42	1.519	1.869	2.297	2.821	3.461	4.241	5.193	6.352	7.762	11.557	17.144	25.339	37.318	54.764	116.723	245.473	509.607	1044.827
44	1.549	1.925	2.390	2.964	3.671	4.543	5.617	6.936	8.557	12.985	19.628	29.556	44.337	66.264	146.418	319.017	685.727	1454.817
46	1.580	1.984	2.487	3.114	3.895	4.867	6.075	7.574	9.434	14.590	22.473	34.474	52.677	80.180	183.666	414.594	922.715	2025.687
48	1.612	2.043	2.587	3.271	4.132	5.214	6.571	8.271	10.401	16.394	25.729	40.211	62.585	97.017	230.391	538.807	1241.605	2820.567
50	1.645	2.105	2.692	3.437	4.384	5.585	7.107	9.033	11.467	18.420	29.457	46.902	74.357	117.391	289.002	700.233	1670.704	3927.357
52	1.678	2.169	2.800	3.611	4.651	5.983	7.687	9.864	12.643	20.697	33.725	54.706	88.344	142.043	362.524	910.023	2248.099	5468.452
54	1.711	2.234	2.913	3.794	4.934	6.409	8.314	10.771	13.939	23.255	38.612	63.809	104.962	171.872	454.751	1182.666	3025.042	7614.272
56	1.746	2.302	3.031	3.986	5.235	6.865	8.992	11.763	15.367	26.129	44.207	74.427	124.705	207.965	570.439	1536.992	4070.497	10602.113
58	1.781	2.372	3.154	4.188	5.553	7.354	9.726	12.845	16.943	29.359	50.613	86.812	148.162	251.638	715.559	1997.475	5477.260	14762.381
60	1.817	2.443	3.281	4.400	5.892	7.878	10.520	14.027	18.679	32.988	57.946	101.257	176.031	304.482	897.597	2595.919	7370.201	20555.140

SOURCE: Federal Reserve Bank of New York, *The Arithmetic of Interest Rates*, pp. 26–27.

INDEX

*This book has been set VideoComp in 10 and
9 point Gael, leaded 2 points. Part numbers and
chapter numbers are 42 and 48 point Roma. Part
titles are 36 point Roma Italic and chapter titles
are 30 point Roma. The size of the type area is
32 by 47 picas.*